5 STARRED REVIEWS

★ "In creatively telling a complicated story with the kind of feeling words alone rarely relay, *The Best We Could Do* does the very best that comics can do. This is a necessary, ever-timely story to share far and wide."

> **—BOOKLIST**, starred review

★ "Be prepared to take your heart on an emotional roller-coaster journey with this thought-provoking account that completely satisfies as the story comes full circle. Highly recommended for teens and adults; an excellent choice for book clubs."

> **—LIBRARY JOURNAL**, starred review

★ "Bui transmutes the base metal of war and struggle into gold . . . In this mélange of comedy and tragedy, family love and brokenness, she finds beauty."

> **—PUBLISHERS WEEKLY**, starred review

★ "A compelling narrative and breathtakingly elegant artwork with subtle colors and expressive and finely drawn characters make this title a standout."

> **—SCHOOL LIBRARY JOURNAL**, starred review

★ "A moving, visually stimulating account of the author's personal story and an insightful look at the refugee experience, juxtaposed against Vietnam's turbulent history."

> **—SHELF AWARENESS**

"With great mastery of writing and drawing, Thi Bui shows the consequences of war lasting from generation to generation. *The Best We Could Do* honors Vietnam the way Marjane Satrapi's *Persepolis* honors Iran."

> **—MAXINE HONG KINGSTON**, author of *The Fifth Book of Peace* and *I Love a Broad Margin to My Life*

"Thi Bui's book took my breath away. In a time of continuing refugee crisis, its message is necessary."

> **—CRAIG THOMPSON**, author and illustrator of *Blankets* and *Habibi*

"Devastating and luminous."

> **—TOM HART**, author and illustrator of the #1 *New York Times* bestseller *Rosalie Lightning: A Graphic Memoir*

"At once intimate and sweeping in its portrayal of human experience, *The Best We Could Do* made me weep."

> **—LEELA CORMAN**, author and illustrator of *Unterzakhn*

"Infused with Vietnam's tumultuous history, Bui's memoir reflects her family's experience against the larger context of war, poverty, and dislocation, and then pulls back, showing how these heavy matters affect life at home in the quieter days that follow."

> —**CECILY WONG**, author of *Diamond Head: A Novel*

"Thi Bui paints the portrait of a single family across three generations, as many continents, and thousands of panels without one false stroke of the brush. Comics don't get much better than *The Best We Could Do*."

> —**JAKE WYATT**, author and illustrator of *Necropolis* and *Ms. Marvel*

"Thi's exploration of becoming a mother in the shadow of her own parents' history is Thi drawing her past to write her future. It's a story that I—as a child turned parent myself—found emotional, introspective, and a cautionary tale of what we pass to our next generation."

> —**GB TRAN**, author and illustrator of *Vietnamerica: A Family's Journey*

"*The Best We Could Do* teaches us how to say no to fear and yes to truth."

> —**FAE MYENNE NG**, author of *Bone*, a PEN/Faulkner Award finalist, and *Steer Toward Rock*, winner of the American Book Award

"*The Best We Could Do* burns back the dead skin of public war memory. Underneath is the raw flesh of another kind of war story—of mothers and fathers, sons and daughters, brutally intimate and intimately brutal. This book is a must-read."

> —**LAWRENCE-MINH BÙI DAVIS**, editor in chief of *The Asian American Literary Review* and curator of the Smithsonian Asian Pacific American Center

---

"This book is beautiful. It is personally meditative while also deeply informative, telling the history that lives in one family's bones while spanning multiple nations, borders, and generations."

> —**BOING BOING**

"Bui's minimalist approach ensures readers can't gloss over the harsh realities of her family's immigrant experience, but it also forces us to recognize the universal struggles and triumphs that all families experience. Fans of Marjane Satrapi's *Persepolis* will not want to miss this incredibly relevant work."

> —**BOOKPAGE**

"Bui worked on the book for years, but its arrival feels urgent amid today's travel bans and growing refugee crisis."

> —*BOSTON GLOBE*

"*The Best We Could Do* is a moving memoir and corrective to Trump-era xenophobia."

—COMICS BULLETIN

"Thematically rich and complex, melding together grief and hope, the personal and the political, the familial and the national, *The Best We Could Do* is an important, wise, and loving book."

—COMICS JOURNAL

"Timely and poignant."

—ENTERTAINMENT WEEKLY

"A powerful and intimate look at the modern immigrant experience in America."

—ICV2

"If you want to better understand the history and scope of the Vietnam War, if you want to understand what immigrants have endured, and continue to endure, you can start with no better book."

—MINNEAPOLIS STAR TRIBUNE

"Bui artfully weaves personal sagas with historical and political stories . . . By tracing the threads of fear and sorrow and hope from one generation to the next, Bui gives powerful context to the lives of refugees everywhere."

—NEW YORK TIMES BOOK REVIEW

"It's a deeply personal tale, but universal in so many ways, filled with familiar struggles and joys that so many of us will relate to. You need to read this book."

—PEN AMERICA

"Like Art Spiegelman's masterpiece, *Maus*, Bui's memoir elicits complex emotions from understated pen-and-ink drawings."

—SAN FRANCISCO CHRONICLE

"Gorgeously illustrated."

—TEEN VOGUE

"When Bui began work on *The Best We Could Do* in 2005, she couldn't have predicted the significance it would hold when it was released in 2017, but now that it's here, it feels like one of the first great works of socially relevant comics art of the Trump era . . . Bui presents that saga in a way that is narratively intricate, intellectually fastidious, and visually stunning."

—VULTURE

THE
BEST
WE
COULD
DO

AN ILLUSTRATED MEMOIR
THI BUI

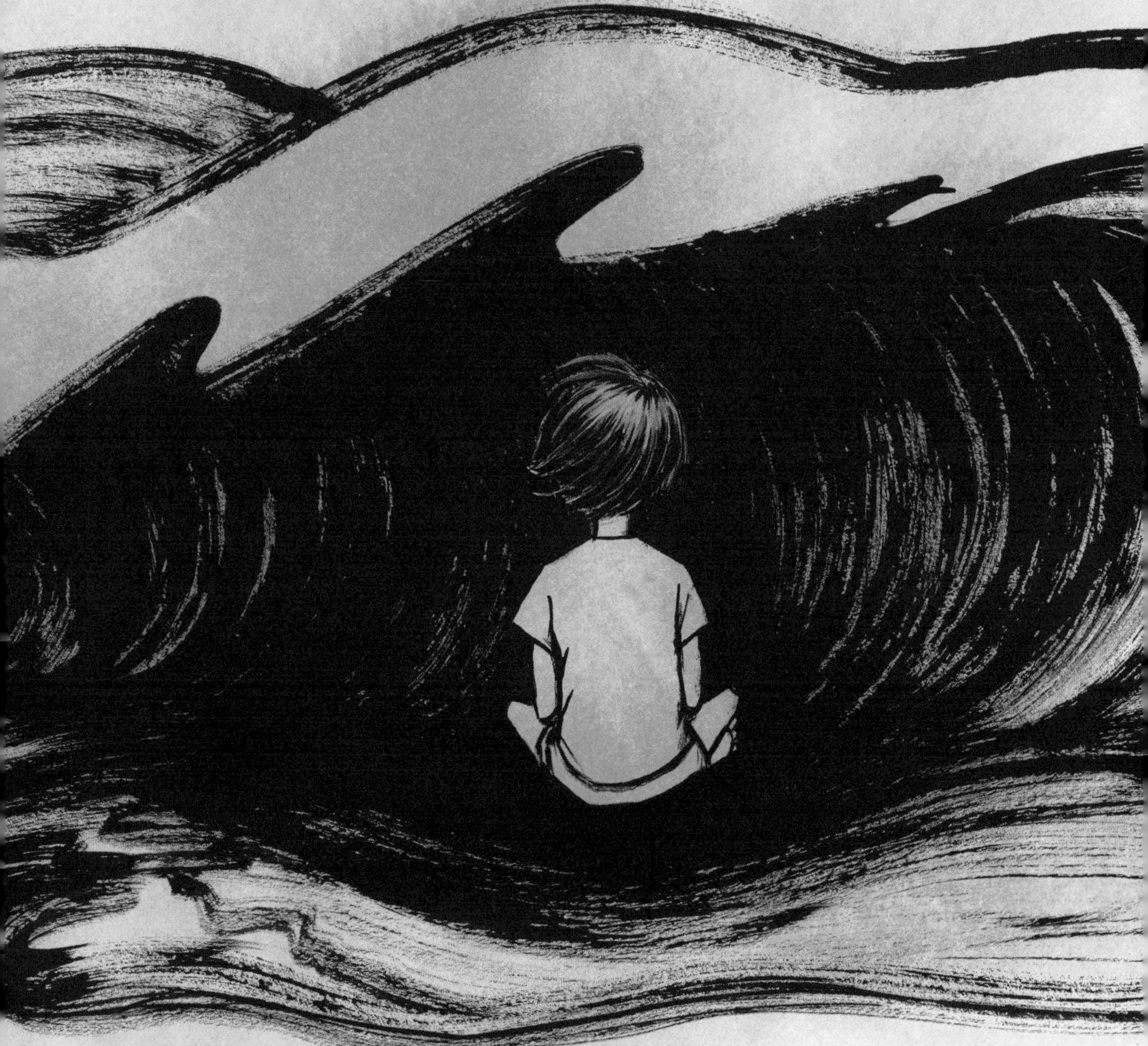

ABRAMS COMICARTS • NEW YORK

Editor: Clarissa Wong
Project Manager: Charles Kochman
Designer: Pamela Notarantonio
Managing Editor: Michael Clark
Production Manager: Kathy Lovisolo

Library of Congress Control Number 2016940170

ISBN 978-1-4197-1878-6

Printed and bound in U.S.A.
13

Abrams ComicArts books are available at special discounts when
purchased in quantity for premiums and promotions as well as fundraising
or educational use. Special editions can also be created to specification.
For details, contact specialsales@abramsbooks.com or the address below.

ABRAMS The Art of Books
195 Broadway, New York, NY 10007
abramsbooks.com

PREFACE

The seeds of this book were planted around 2002, when I was a graduate student and took a detour from my art education training to get lost in the world of oral history. The transcripts of my family's stories (and the clumsy, homemade book that I produced) from that time were more meaningful than any art I had made before. I was trying to understand the forces that caused my family, in the late seventies, to flee one country and start over in another. I titled my project "Buis in Vietnam and America: A Memory Reconstruction." It had photographs and some art, but mostly writing, and it was pretty academic. However, I didn't feel like I had solved the storytelling problem of how to present history in a way that is human and relatable and not oversimplified. I thought that turning it into a graphic novel might help. So then I had to learn how to do comics! I drew the initial draft of the first pages in 2005, and it's been a steep learning curve working in this medium.

For that and other reasons, this book has taken me a very long time to make. When my son was one, and the book was also just a baby, my family and I moved from New York to California. I helped open an alternative public high school for immigrants in Oakland, where I taught for the next seven years. It was difficult to carve out the time and headspace to work on something that not only required a lot of historical research, but was also intensely personal and at times painful. I often wanted to quit. With my mind on current immigration issues and the lives of my students, I gave my book the name *Refugee Reflex* and worked on it during school holidays. Besides sounding an awful lot like "reflux," this title was problematic because it didn't quite encompass everything the book was about. In 2011, while I was reorganizing my life so that my aging parents could be more involved in it, I realized that the book was about parents and children, and it became *The Best We Could Do*.

On the long road to getting this book made, I received many gifts from the people I encountered: The opportunity to pitch this book to a wonderful publisher. Unwavering support and generous guidance from artists, writers, and editors I admire. The camaraderie of storytellers and magic makers. And the unconditional love and trust that were placed in me by my family. My head spins in amazement. My heart swells with gratitude.

—Thi

Thi Bui
Berkeley, California
July 2016

It's been a wild year since *The Best We Could Do* first came out—more than I knew what to do with sometimes. In July 2017, I caught up with Viet Thanh Nguyen, Pulitzer Prize-winning author of *The Sympathizer*, to see if I could glean some wisdom from him. The following four pages contain part of our conversation.

—Thi

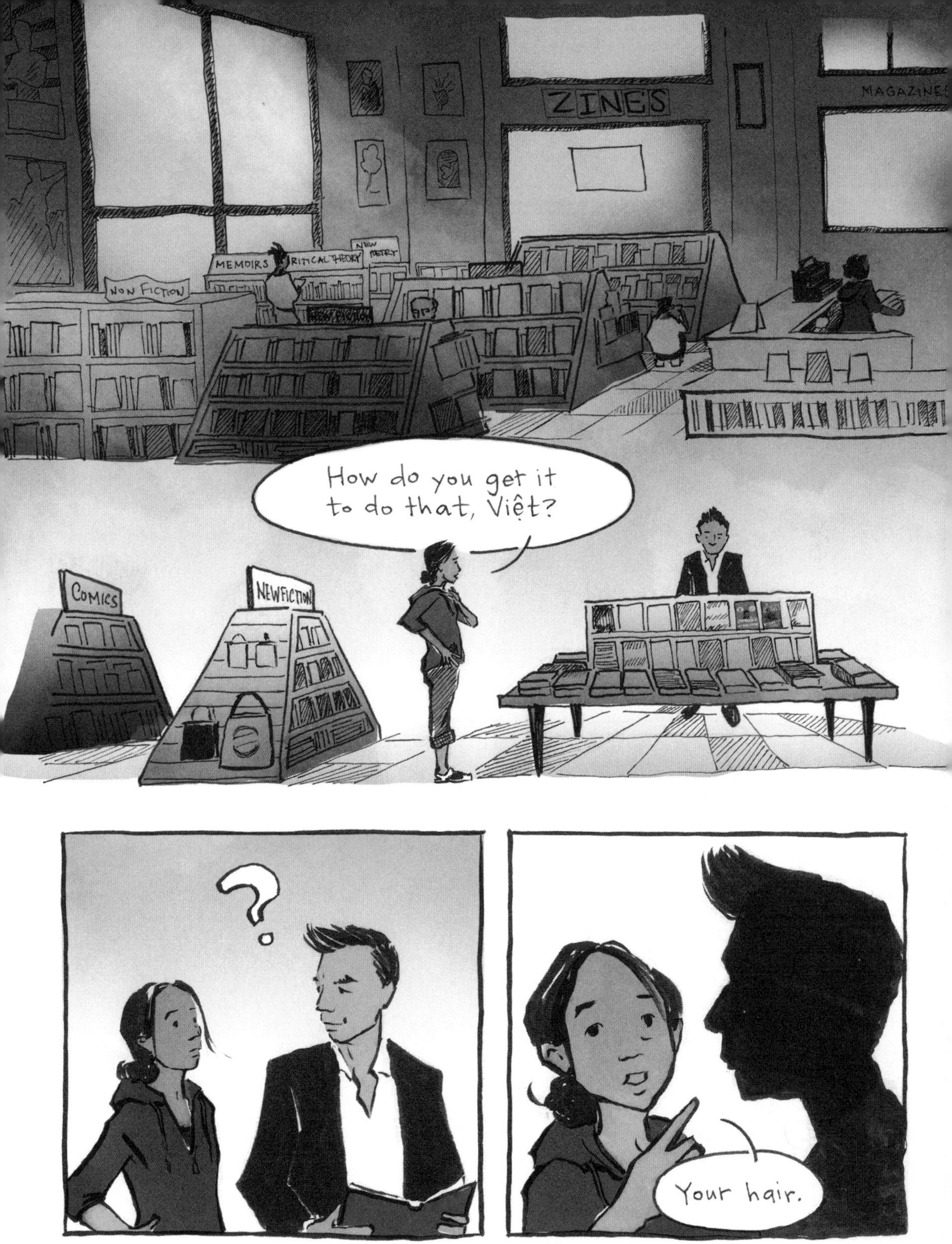
ZINES
MAGAZINES
NON FICTION
MEMOIRS
How do you get it to do that, Việt?
COMICS
NEWFICTION
?
Your hair.

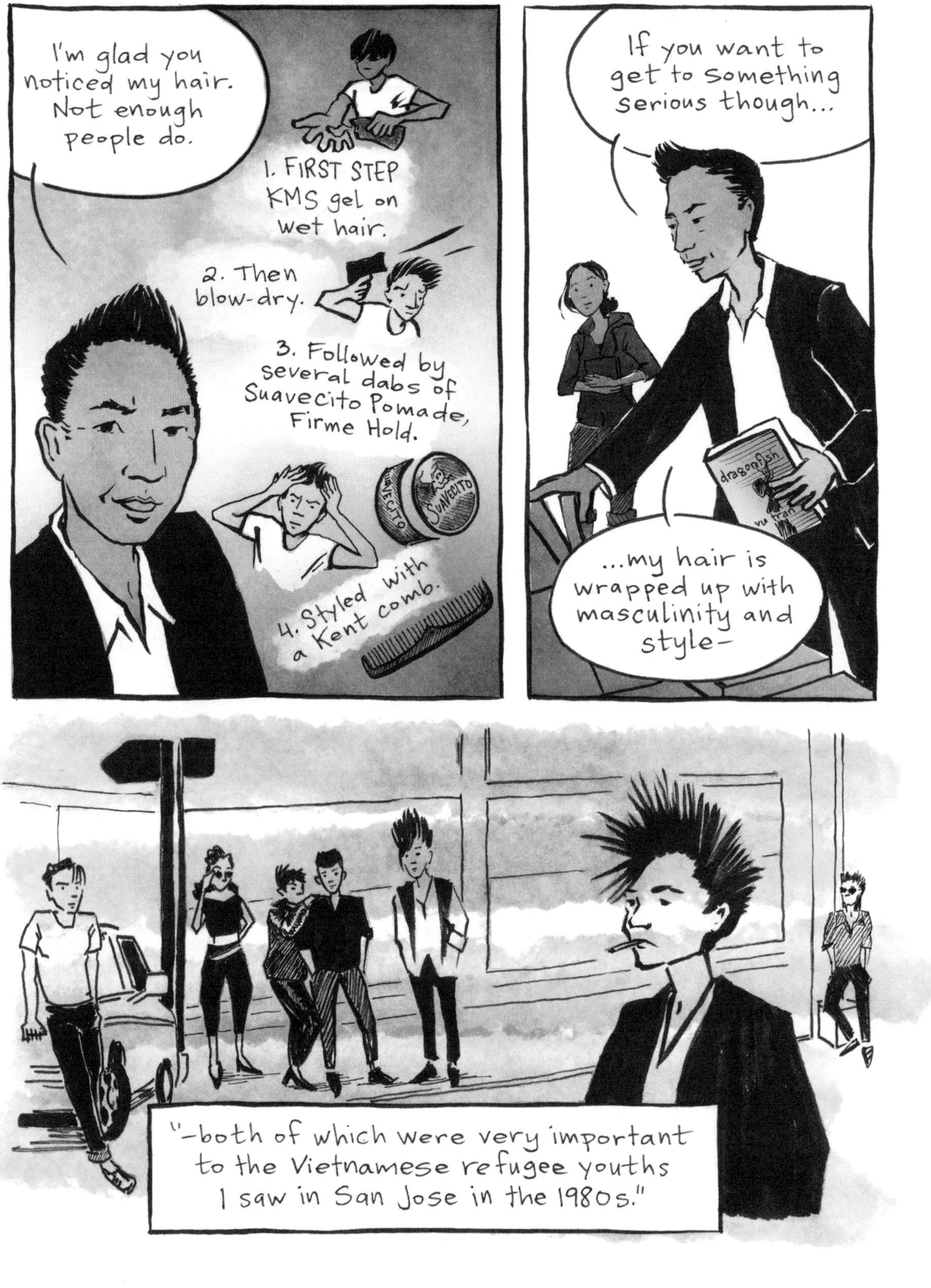
I'm glad you noticed my hair. Not enough people do.
1. FIRST STEP KMS gel on wet hair.
2. Then blow-dry.
3. Followed by several dabs of Suavecito Pomade, Firme Hold.
SUAVECITO
4. Styled with a Kent comb.
If you want to get to something serious though...
dragonfish
vu tran
...my hair is wrapped up with masculinity and style-
"-both of which were very important to the Vietnamese refugee youths I saw in San Jose in the 1980s."

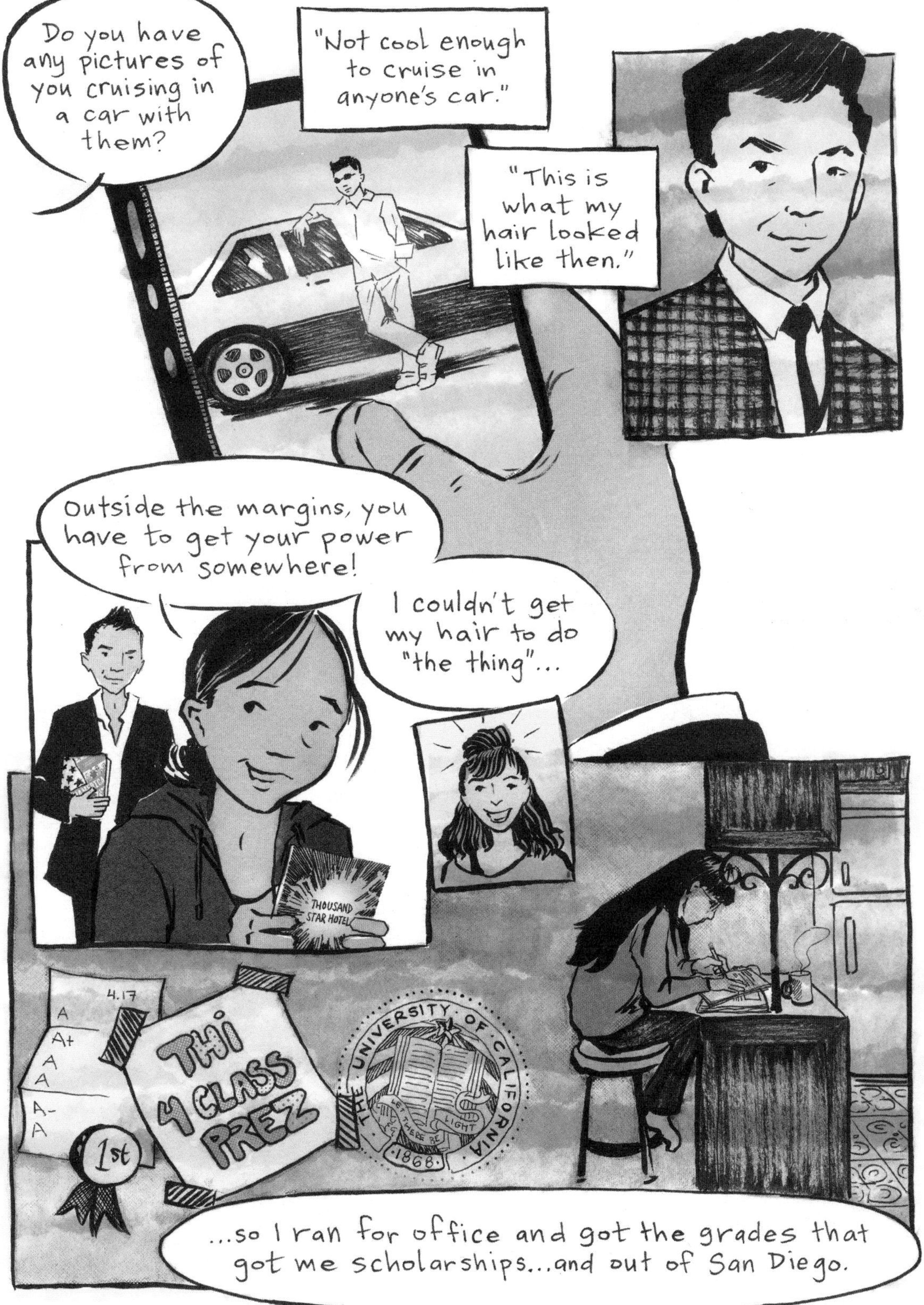

Do you have any pictures of you cruising in a car with them?
"Not cool enough to cruise in anyone's car."
"This is what my hair looked like then."
Outside the margins, you have to get your power from somewhere!
I couldn't get my hair to do "the thing"...
THOUSAND STAR HOTEL
4.17
A
A+
A
A
A-
A
1st
THI 4 CLASS PREZ
THE UNIVERSITY OF CALIFORNIA
LET THERE BE LIGHT
1868
...so I ran for office and got the grades that got me scholarships...and out of San Diego.

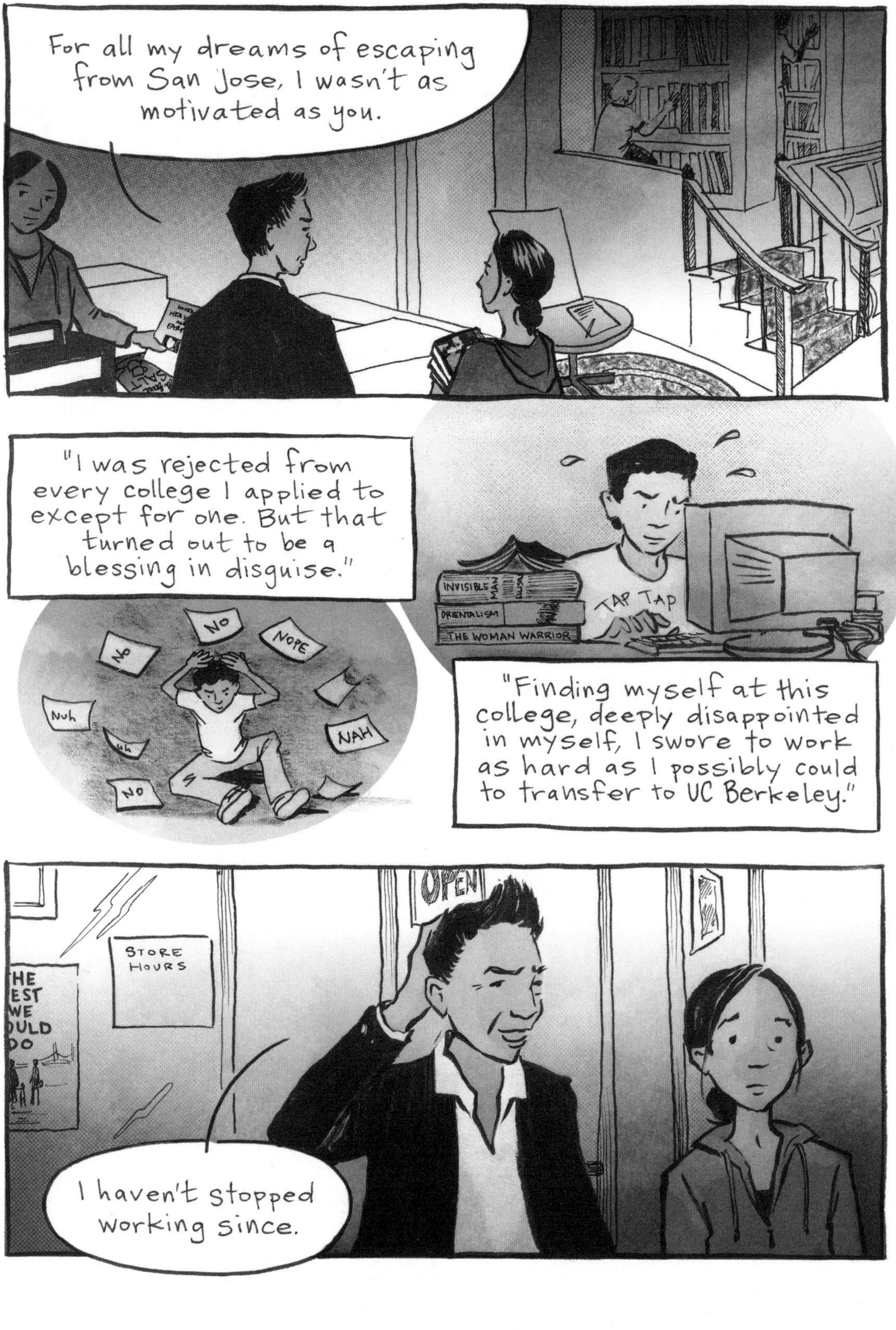
For all my dreams of escaping from San Jose, I wasn't as motivated as you.
"I was rejected from every college I applied to except for one. But that turned out to be a blessing in disguise."
NO
No
NOPE
Nuh
uh
NAH
NO
INVISIBLE MAN
ORIENTALISM
THE WOMAN WARRIOR
TAP TAP
"Finding myself at this college, deeply disappointed in myself, I swore to work as hard as I possibly could to transfer to UC Berkeley."
OPEN
STORE HOURS
I haven't stopped working since.

CONTENTS

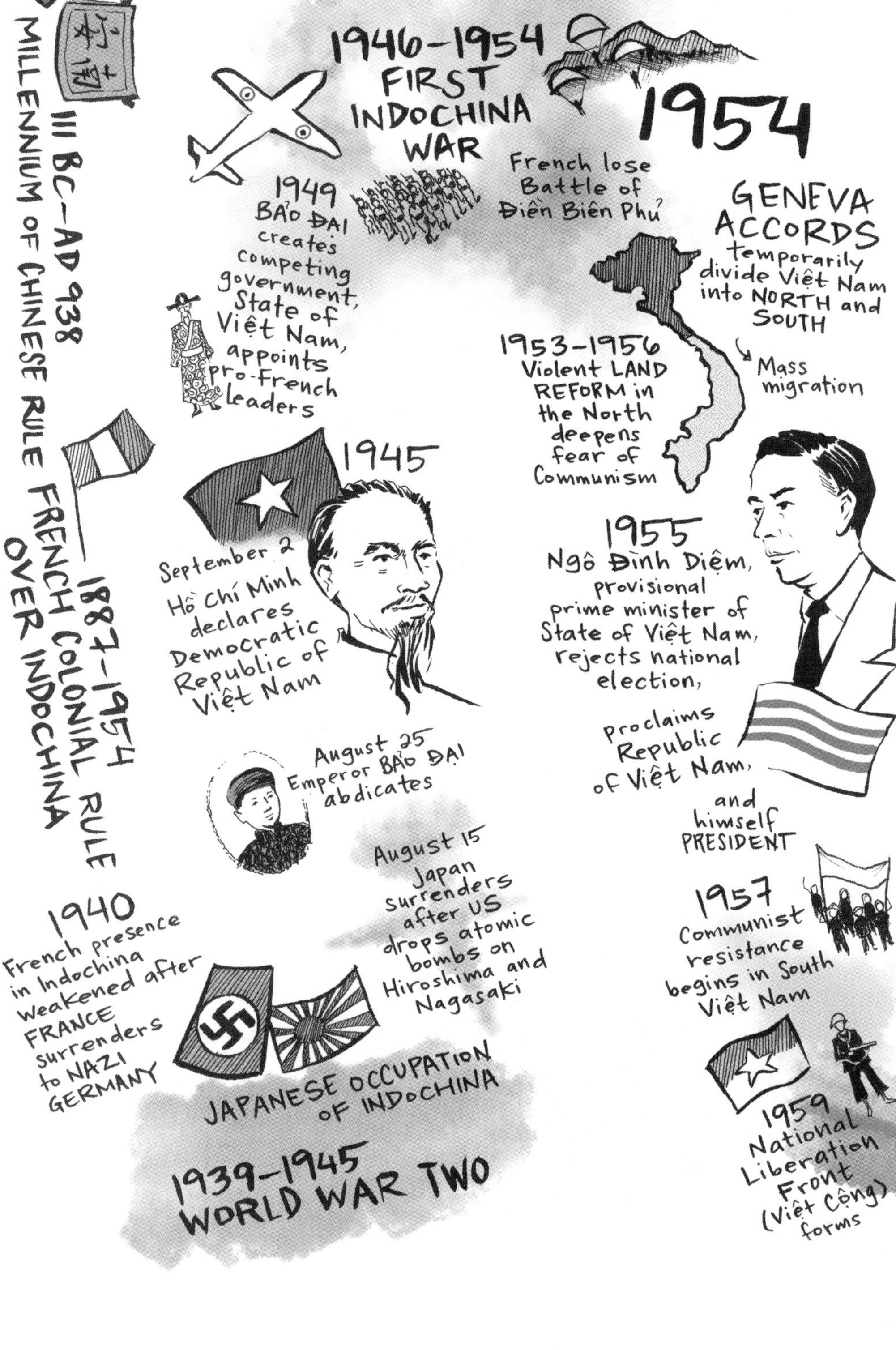
III BC–AD 938
MILLENNIUM OF CHINESE RULE
1887–1954
FRENCH COLONIAL RULE
OVER INDOCHINA
1940
French presence in Indochina weakened after FRANCE surrenders to NAZI GERMANY
1939–1945
WORLD WAR TWO
JAPANESE OCCUPATION OF INDOCHINA
August 15
Japan surrenders after US drops atomic bombs on Hiroshima and Nagasaki
August 25
Emperor BẢO ĐẠI abdicates
1945
September 2
Hồ Chí Minh declares Democratic Republic of Việt Nam
1949
BẢO ĐẠI creates competing government, State of Việt Nam, appoints pro-French leaders
1946–1954
FIRST INDOCHINA WAR
1954
French lose Battle of Điện Biên Phủ
GENEVA ACCORDS
temporarily divide Việt Nam into NORTH and SOUTH
Mass migration
1953–1956
Violent LAND REFORM in the North deepens fear of Communism
1955
Ngô Đình Diệm, provisional prime minister of State of Việt Nam, rejects national election,
proclaims Republic of Việt Nam,
and himself PRESIDENT
1957
Communist resistance begins in South Việt Nam
1959
National Liberation Front (Việt Cộng) forms

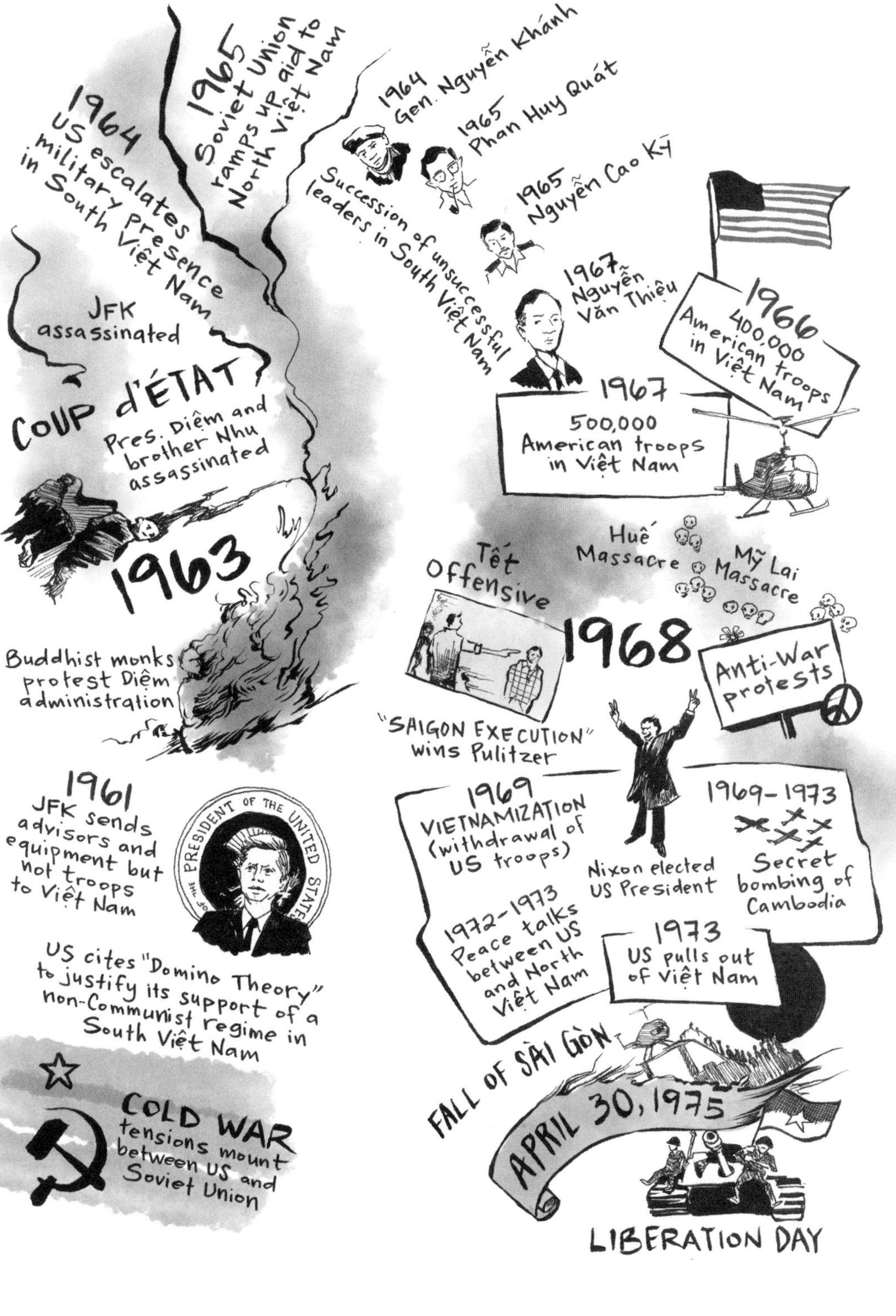
1964
US escalates military presence in South Việt Nam
1965
Soviet Union ramps up aid to North Việt Nam
1964
Gen. Nguyễn Khánh
1965
Phan Huy Quát
1965
Nguyễn Cao Kỳ
Succession of unsuccessful leaders in South Việt Nam
1967
Nguyễn Văn Thiệu
1966
400,000 American troops in Việt Nam
JFK assassinated
COUP d'ÉTAT
Pres. Diệm and brother Nhu assassinated
1963
1967
500,000 American troops in Việt Nam
Buddhist monks protest Diệm administration
Tết Offensive
Huế Massacre
Mỹ Lai Massacre
1968
Anti-War protests
"SAIGON EXECUTION" wins Pulitzer
1961
JFK sends advisors and equipment but not troops to Việt Nam
PRESIDENT OF THE UNITED STATES
1969
VIETNAMIZATION (withdrawal of US troops)
Nixon elected US President
1969–1973
Secret bombing of Cambodia
1972–1973
Peace talks between US and North Việt Nam
1973
US pulls out of Việt Nam
US cites "Domino Theory" to justify its support of a non-Communist regime in South Việt Nam
COLD WAR
tensions mount between US and Soviet Union
FALL OF SÀI GÒN
APRIL 30, 1975
LIBERATION DAY

CHAPTER 1
LABOR

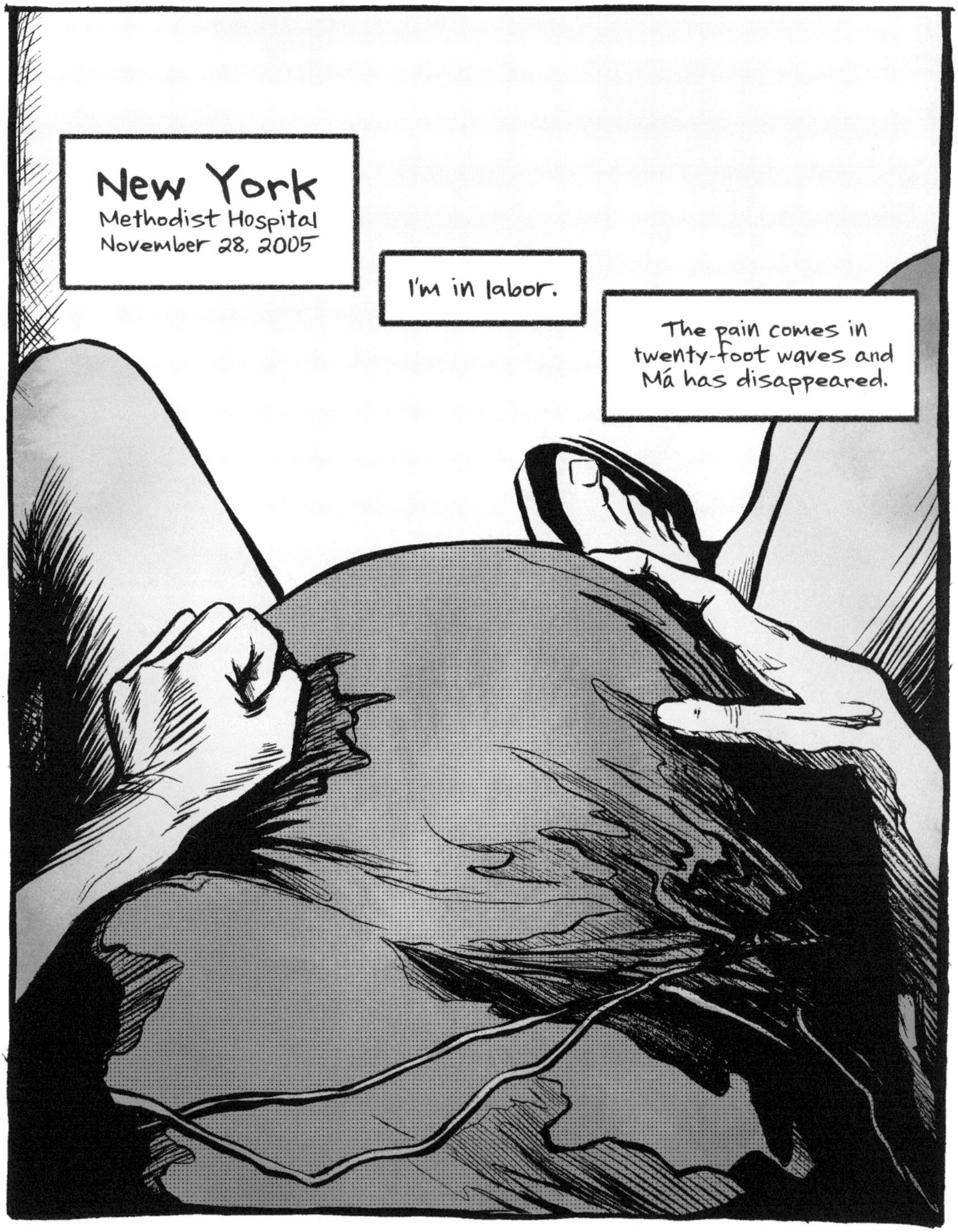
New York
Methodist Hospital
November 28, 2005
I'm in labor.
The pain comes in twenty-foot waves and Má has disappeared.

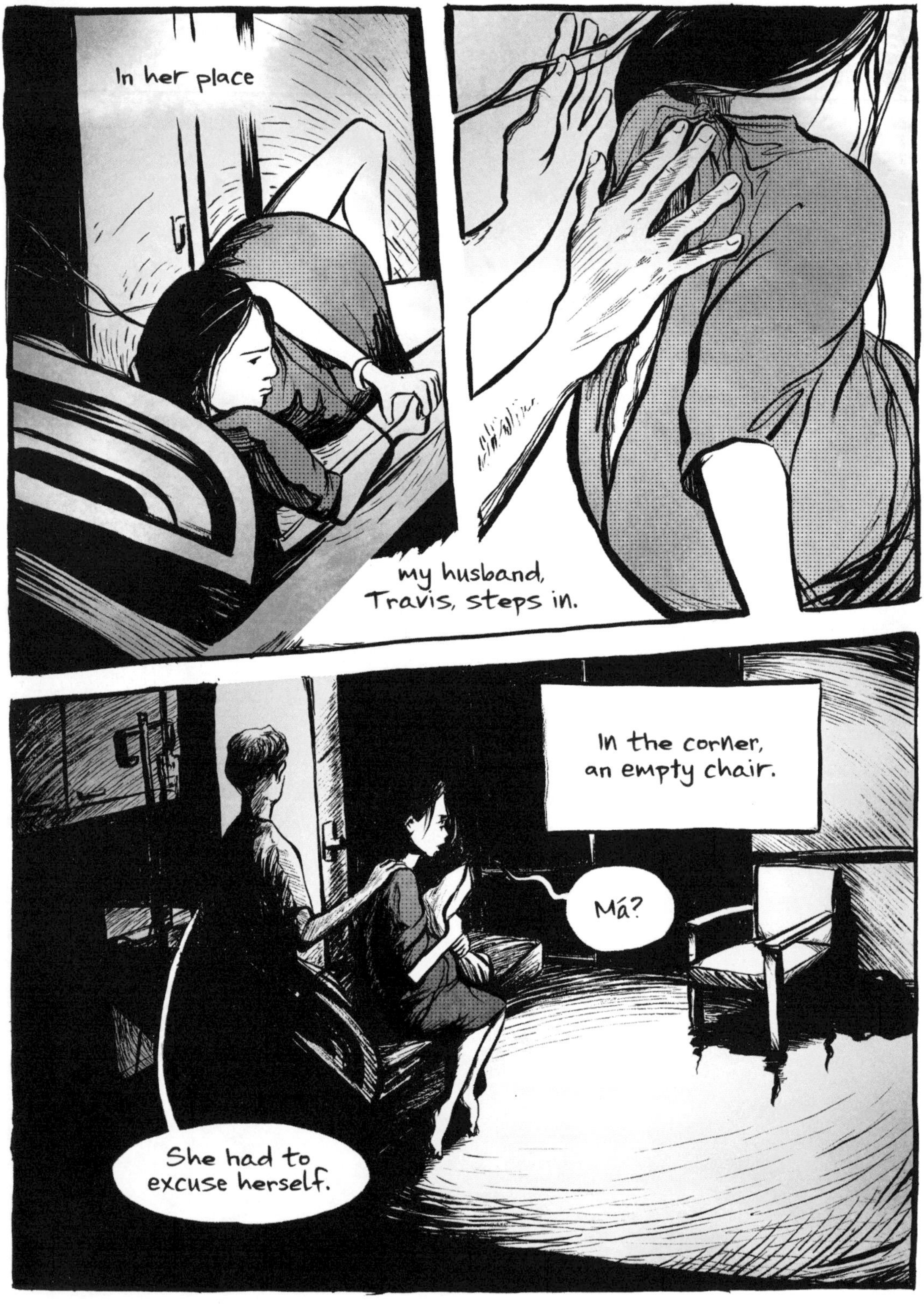
In her place
my husband, Travis, steps in.
In the corner, an empty chair.
Má?
She had to excuse herself.

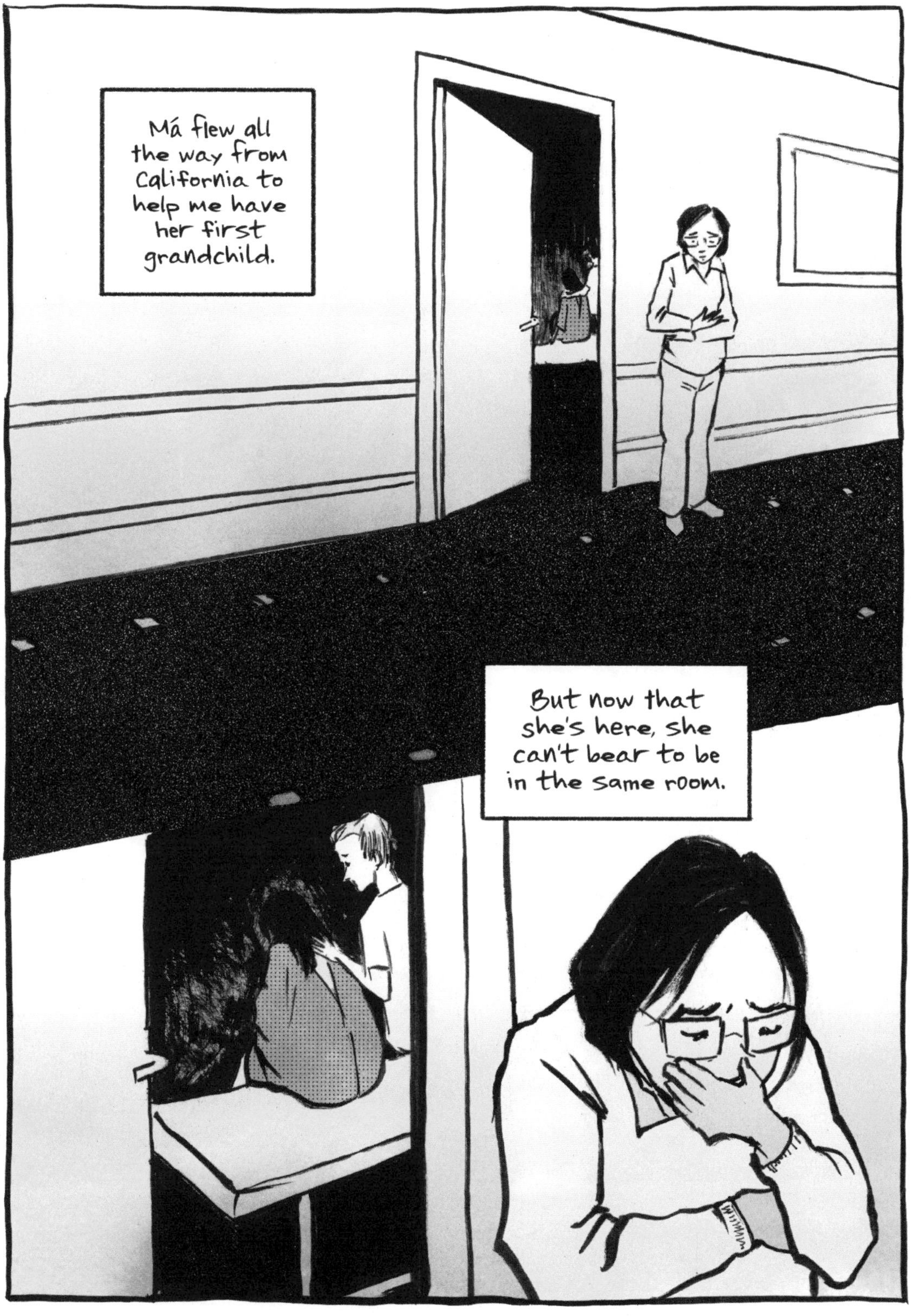
Má flew all the way from California to help me have her first grandchild.
But now that she's here, she can't bear to be in the same room.

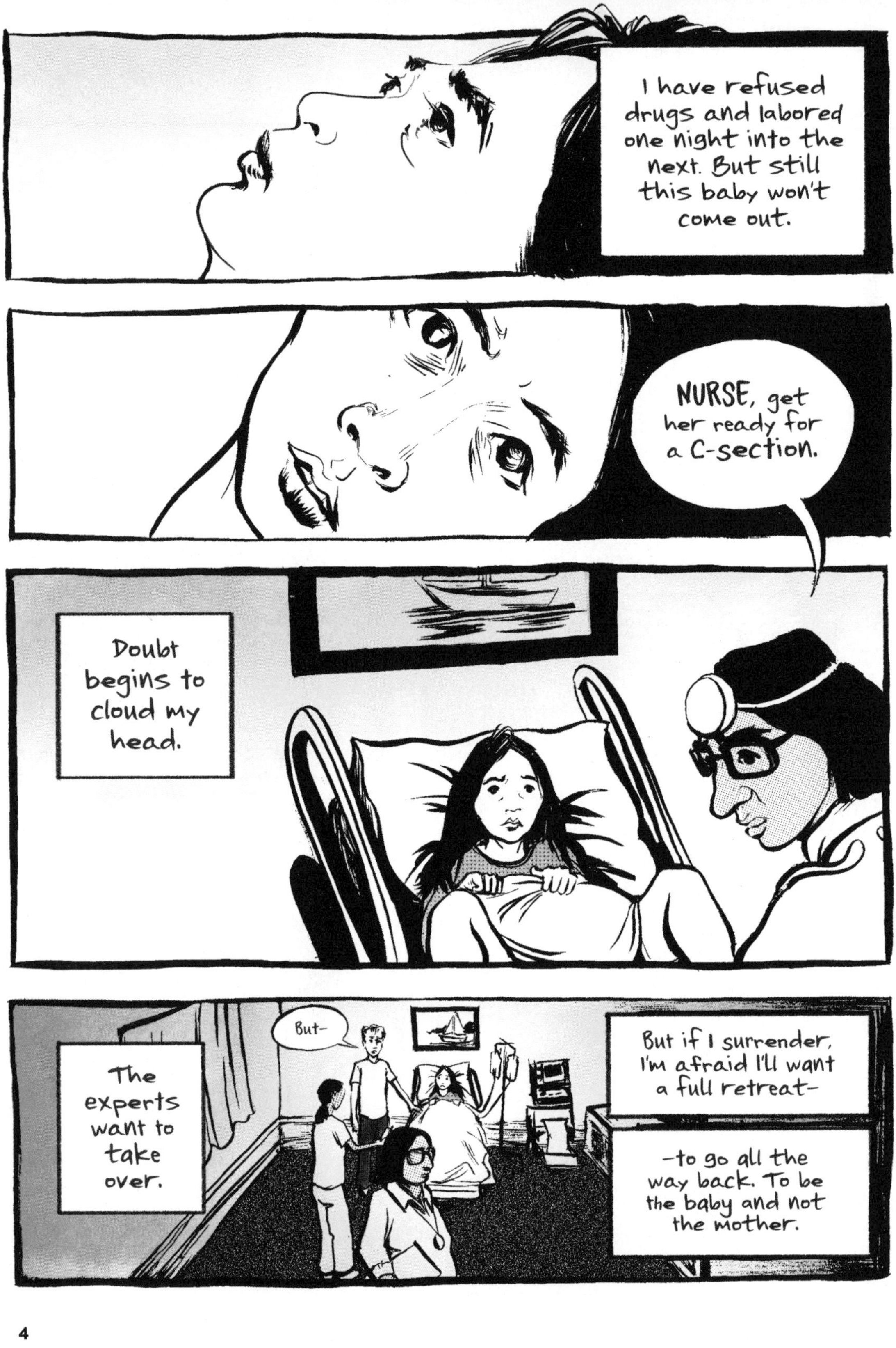

I have refused drugs and labored one night into the next. But still this baby won't come out.
NURSE, get her ready for a C-section.
Doubt begins to cloud my head.
The experts want to take over.
But-
But if I surrender, I'm afraid I'll want a full retreat-
-to go all the way back. To be the baby and not the mother.

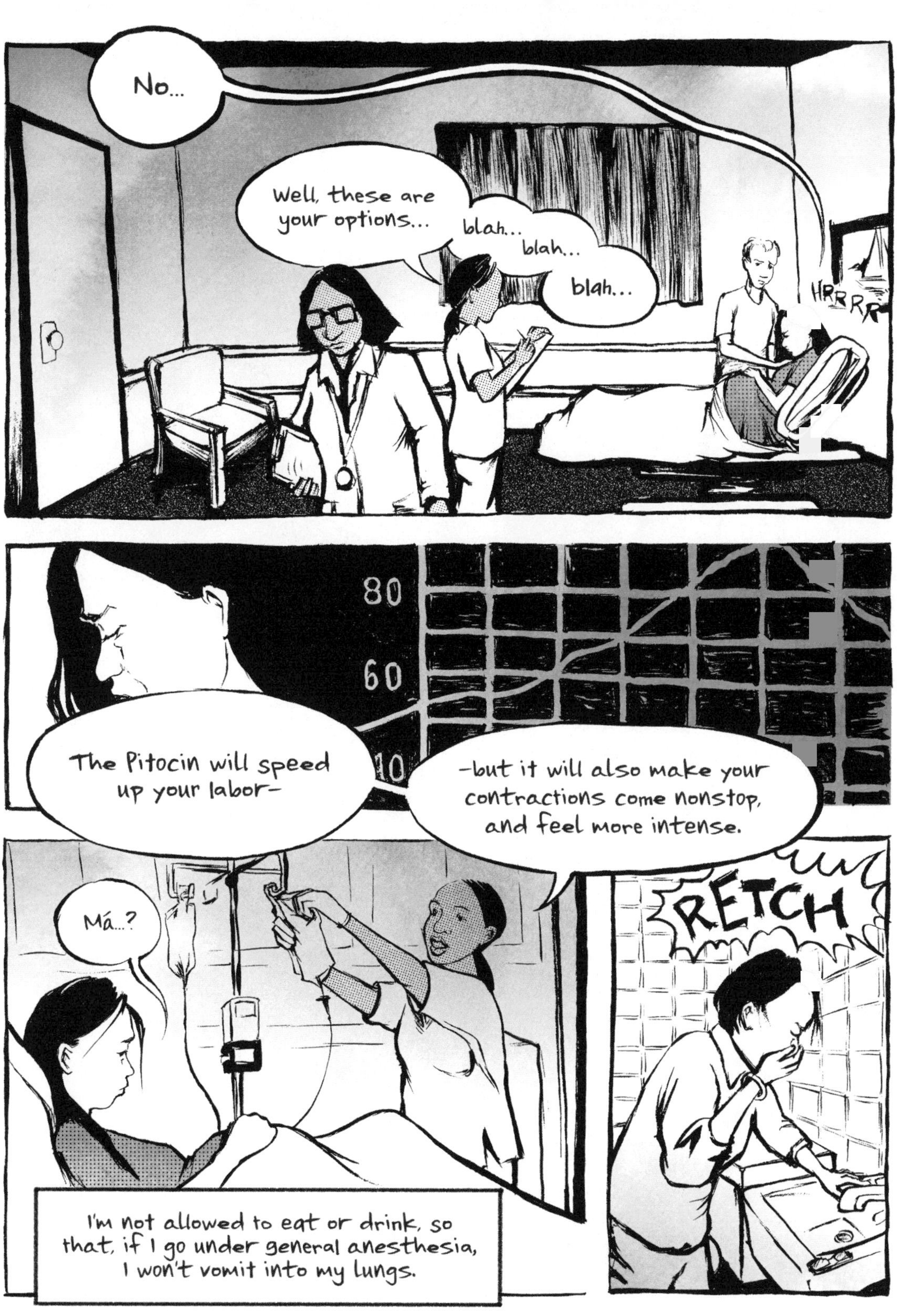
No...
Well, these are your options...
blah...
blah...
blah...
HRRRRR
80
60
10
The Pitocin will speed up your labor–
–but it will also make your contractions come nonstop, and feel more intense.
Má...?
RETCH
I'm not allowed to eat or drink, so that, if I go under general anesthesia, I won't vomit into my lungs.

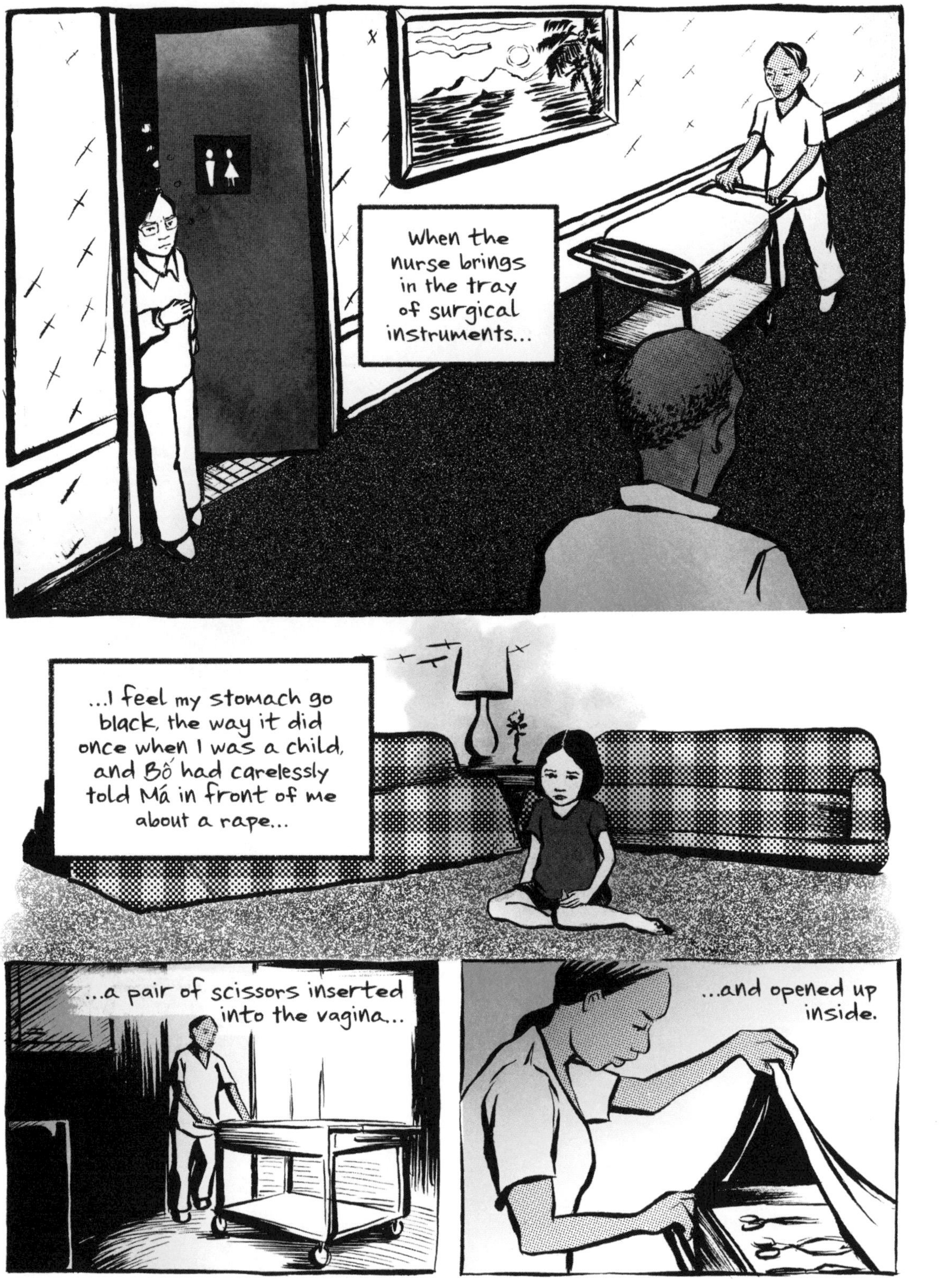
When the nurse brings in the tray of surgical instruments...
...I feel my stomach go black, the way it did once when I was a child, and Bố had carelessly told Má in front of me about a rape...
...a pair of scissors inserted into the vagina...
...and opened up inside.

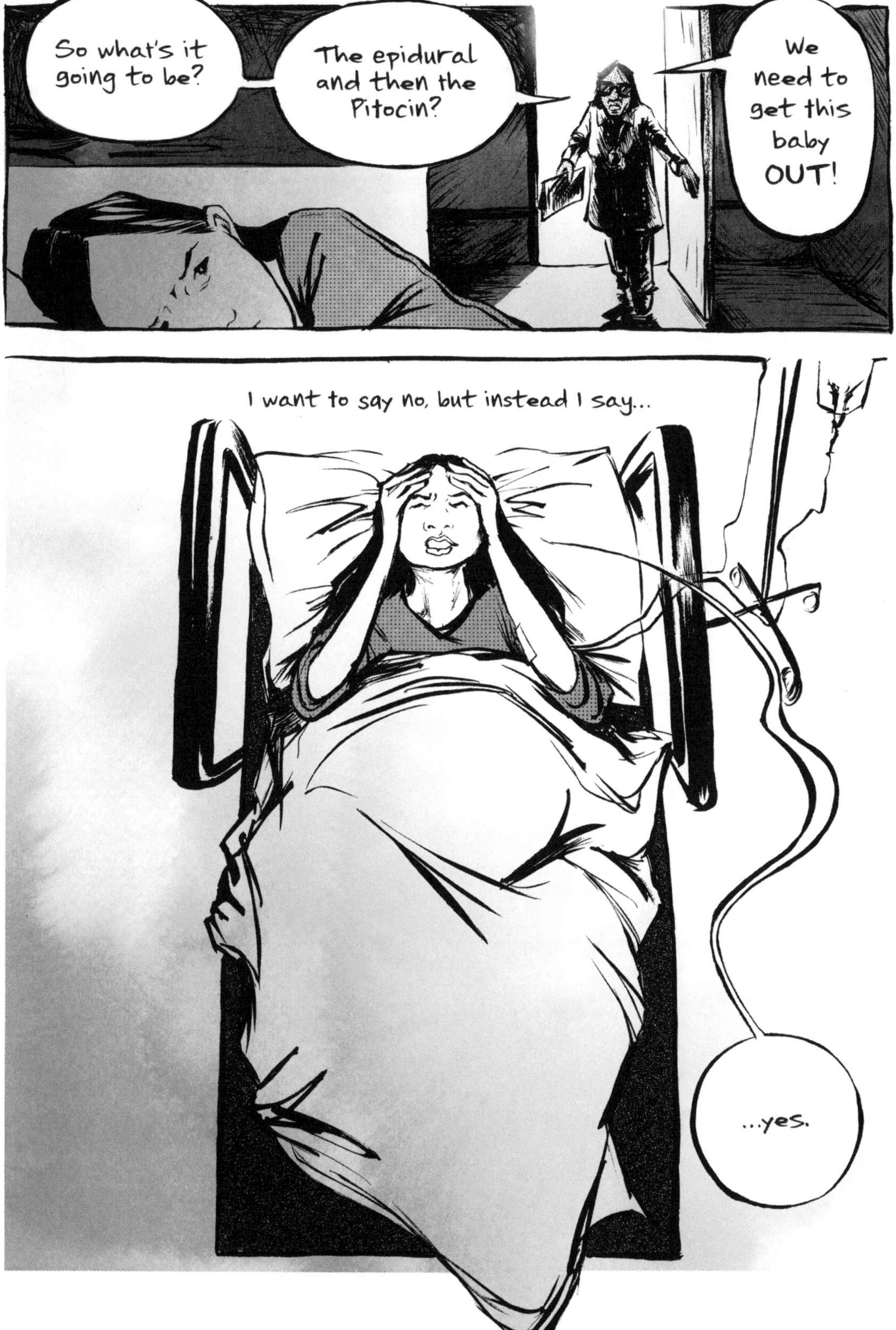
So what's it going to be?
The epidural and then the Pitocin?
We need to get this baby OUT!
I want to say no, but instead I say...
...yes.

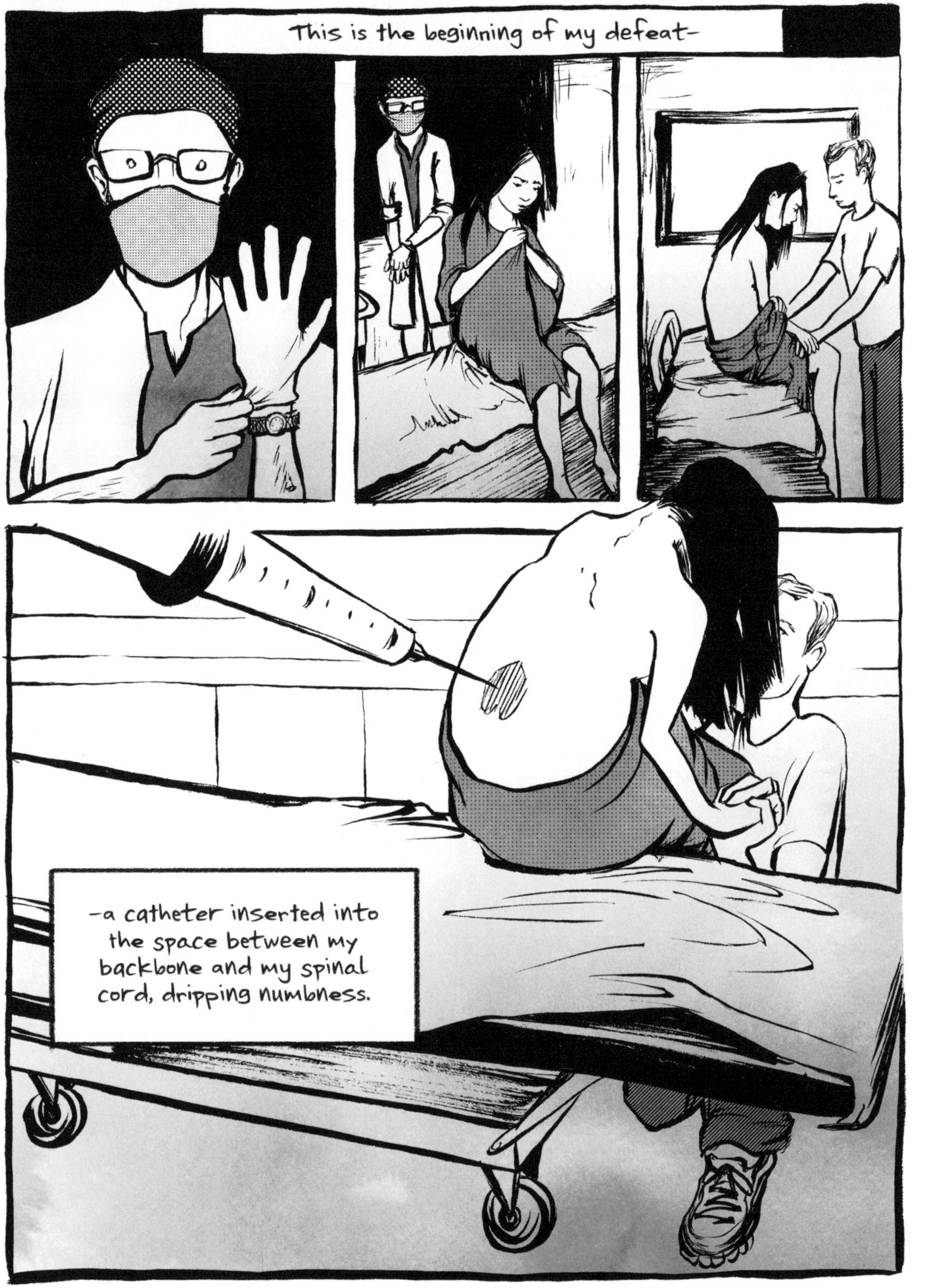
This is the beginning of my defeat-
-a catheter inserted into the space between my backbone and my spinal cord, dripping numbness.

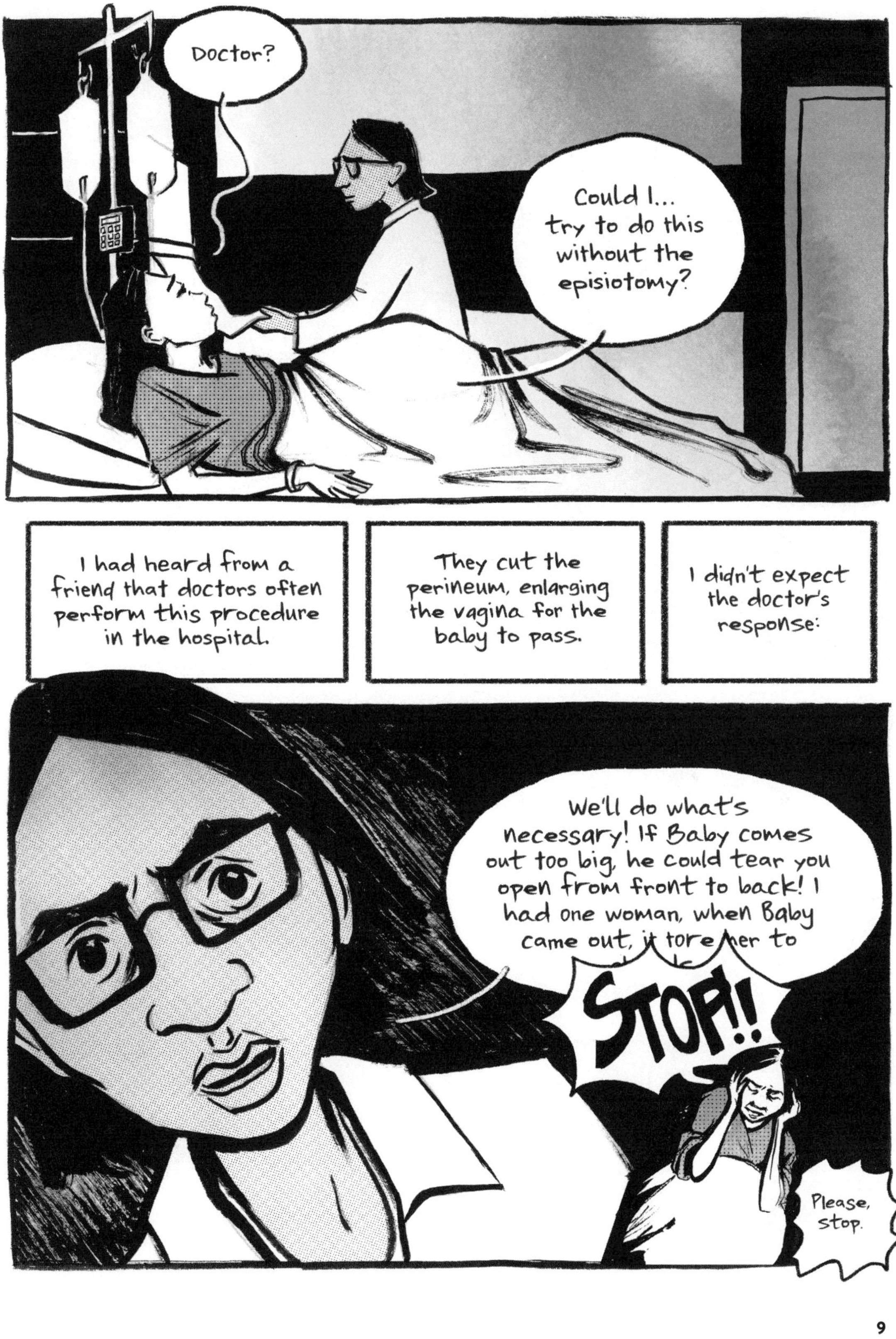
Doctor?
Could I... try to do this without the episiotomy?
I had heard from a friend that doctors often perform this procedure in the hospital.
They cut the perineum, enlarging the vagina for the baby to pass.
I didn't expect the doctor's response:
We'll do what's necessary! If Baby comes out too big, he could tear you open from front to back! I had one woman, when Baby came out, it tore her to
STOP!!
Please, stop.

Wake up. It's time.

But I can't feel anything. I don't know how to push.

Bring in more help.

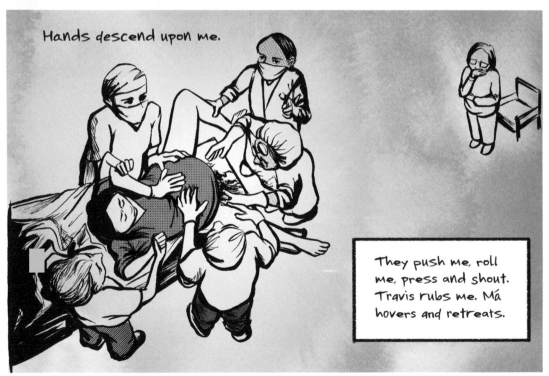

Hands descend upon me.

They push me, roll me, press and shout. Travis rubs me. Má hovers and retreats.

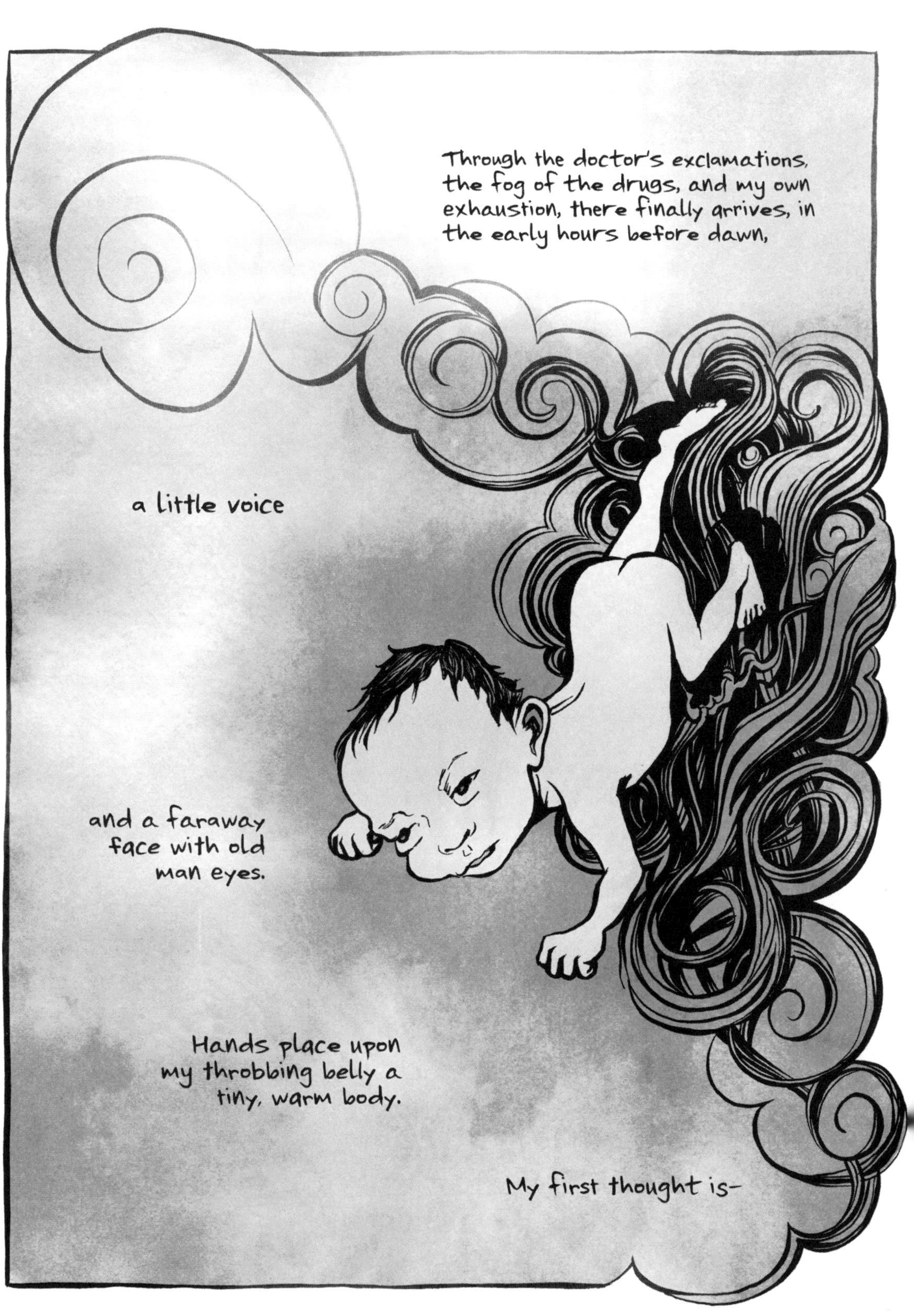
Through the doctor's exclamations, the fog of the drugs, and my own exhaustion, there finally arrives, in the early hours before dawn,
a little voice
and a faraway face with old man eyes.
Hands place upon my throbbing belly a tiny, warm body.
My first thought is-

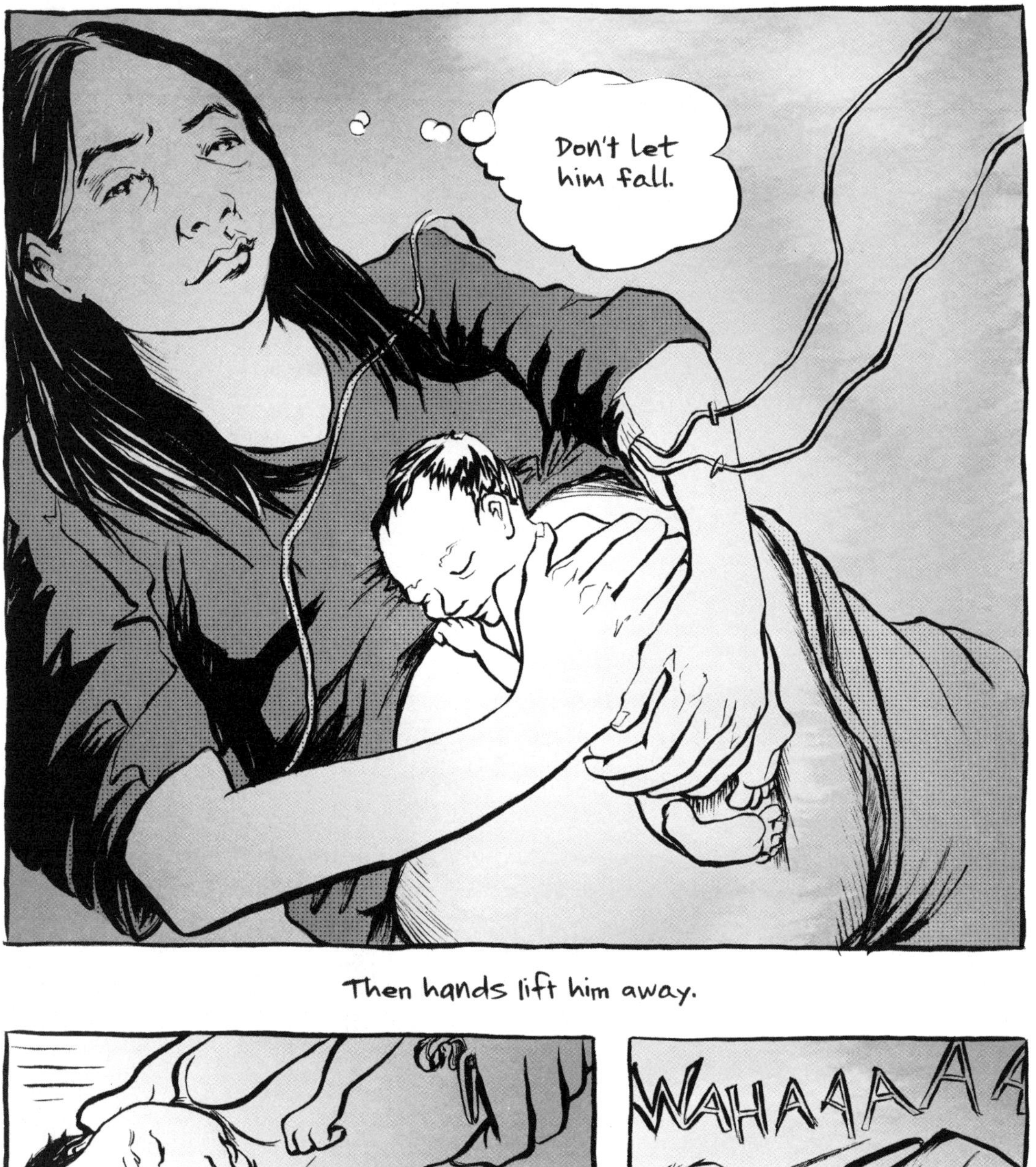
Don't let him fall.

Then hands lift him away.

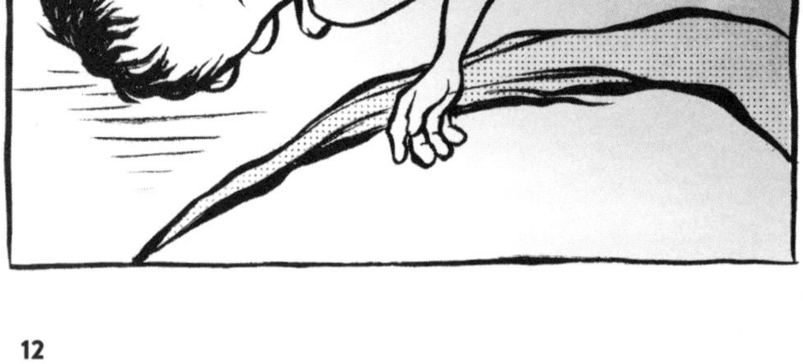

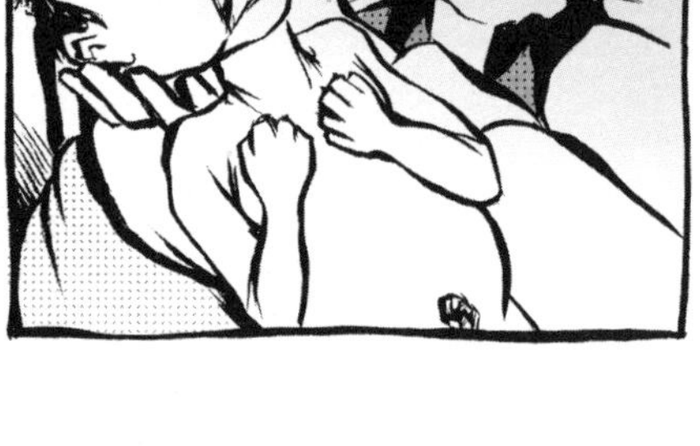
WAHAAAAA

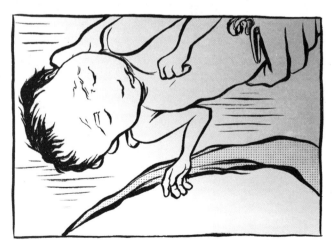

More contractions come.

I am bound to the bed with the remaining business of expelling the placenta—

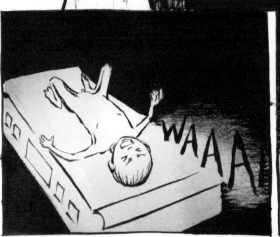

WAAA

—while life comes back to Má.

Do you want to keep this?

Hrmph!

Soon they send Travis and Má away and tell me it is time to...

"Get up."

"Walk."

13

Do you want your baby to room in or stay in the nursery?

710

I'm too tired to speak her hospital lingo.

Here. With me.

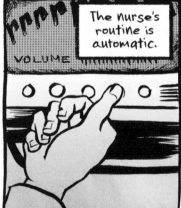

The nurse's routine is automatic.

VOLUME

SHAKEN BABY SYNDRO

Here is your baby. Good night!

And then...

WAAAAAA

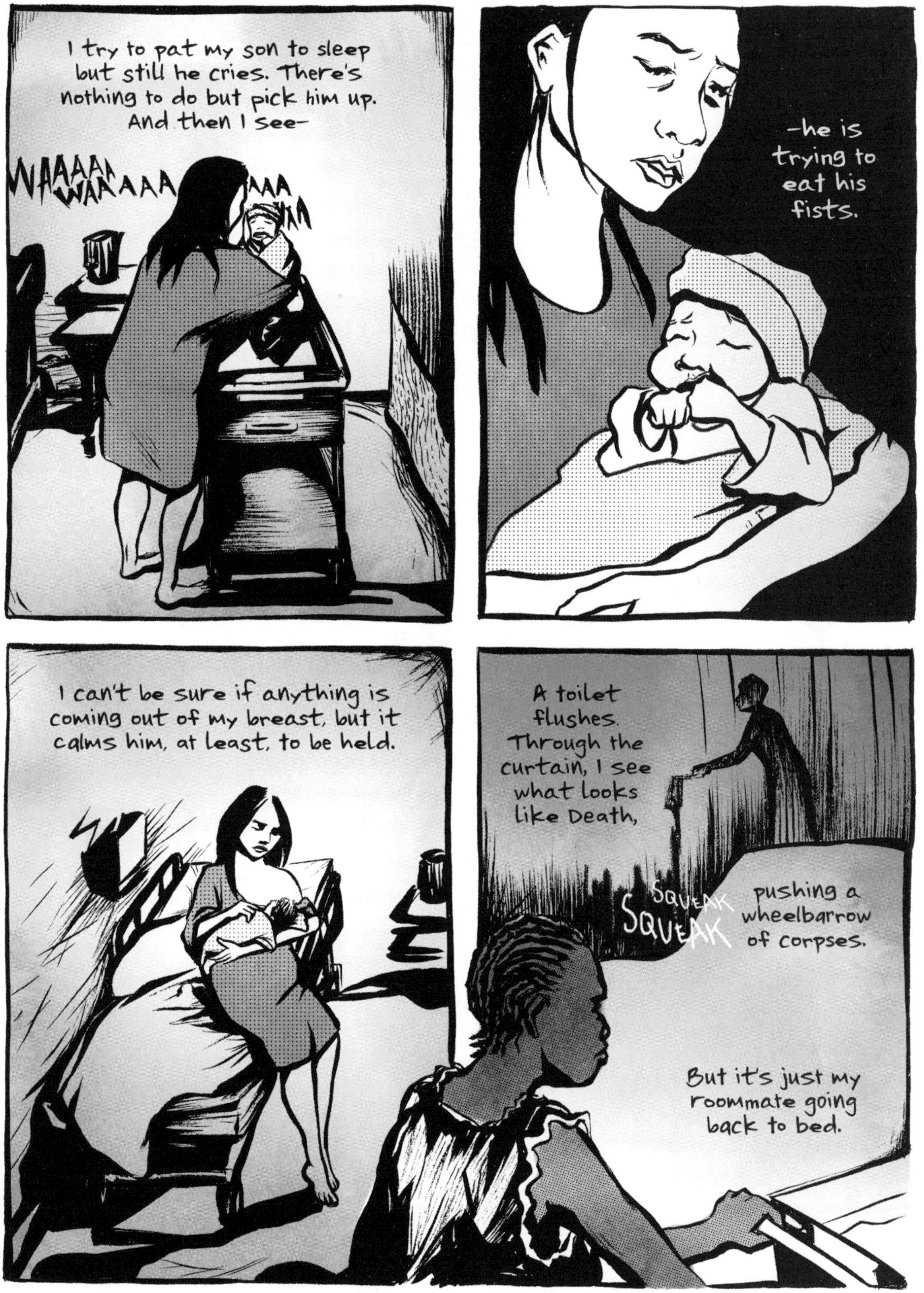
I try to pat my son to sleep but still he cries. There's nothing to do but pick him up. And then I see-
WAAAAA
WAAAAA
AAA
-he is trying to eat his fists.
I can't be sure if anything is coming out of my breast, but it calms him, at least, to be held.
A toilet flushes. Through the curtain, I see what looks like Death,
SQUEAK
SQUEAK
pushing a wheelbarrow of corpses.
But it's just my roommate going back to bed.

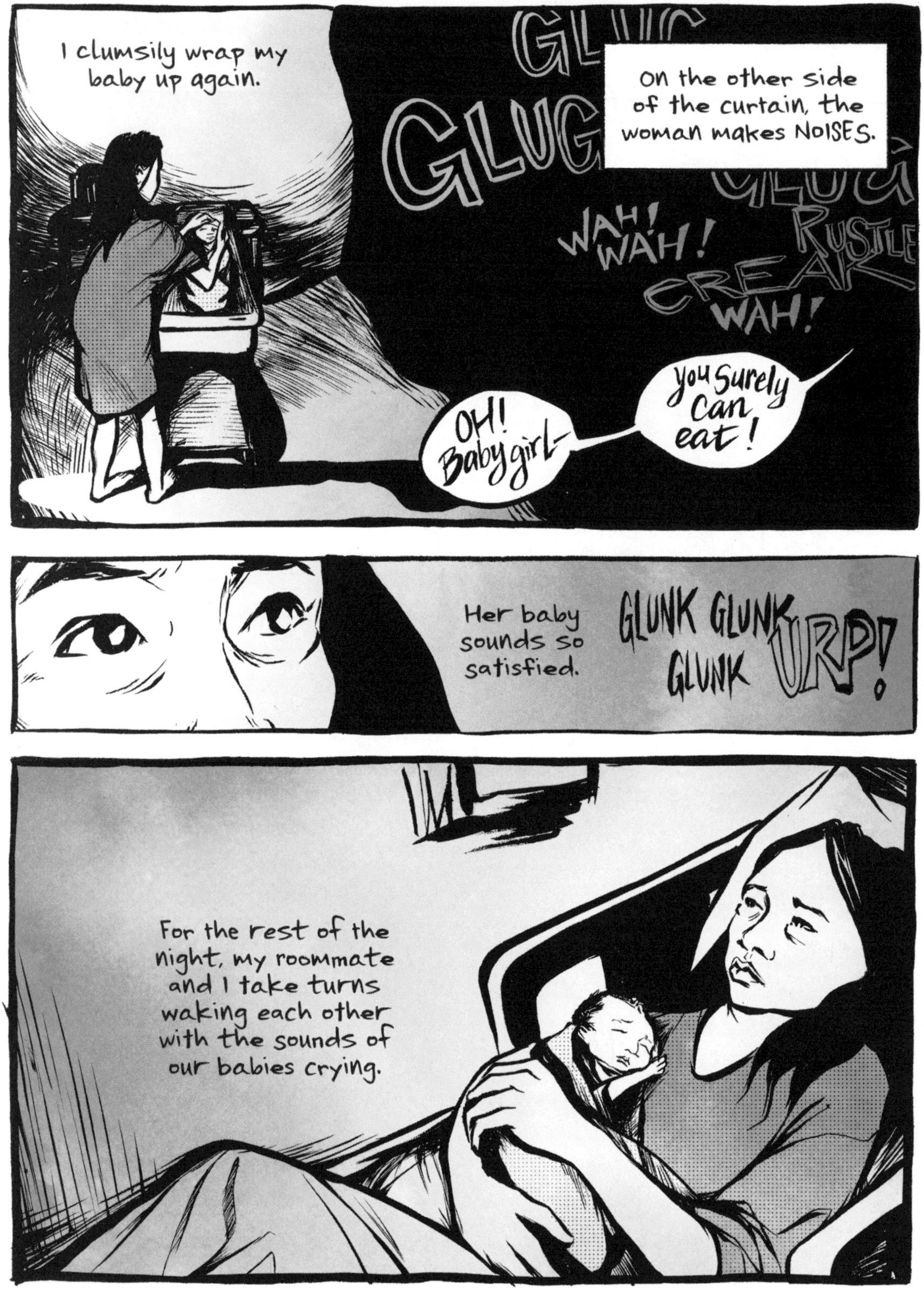

I clumsily wrap my baby up again.
GLUG
GLUG
On the other side of the curtain, the woman makes NOISES.
GLUG
WAH! WAH!
RUSTLE
CREAK
WAH!
OH! Baby girl-
you surely can eat!
Her baby sounds so satisfied.
GLUNK GLUNK GLUNK
URP!
For the rest of the night, my roommate and I take turns waking each other with the sounds of our babies crying.

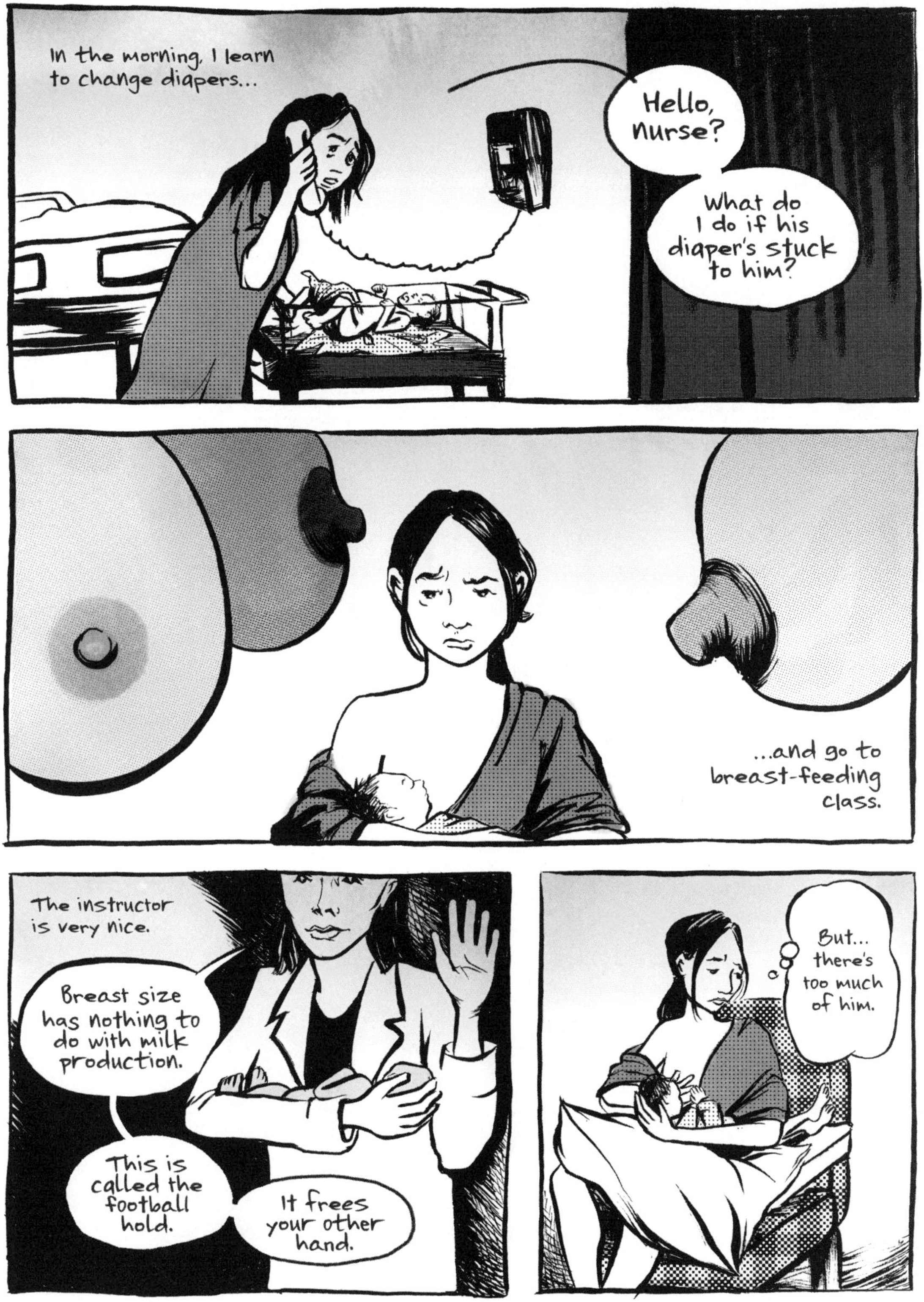

In the morning, I learn to change diapers...
Hello, nurse?
What do I do if his diaper's stuck to him?
...and go to breast-feeding class.
The instructor is very nice.
Breast size has nothing to do with milk production.
This is called the football hold.
It frees your other hand.
But... there's too much of him.

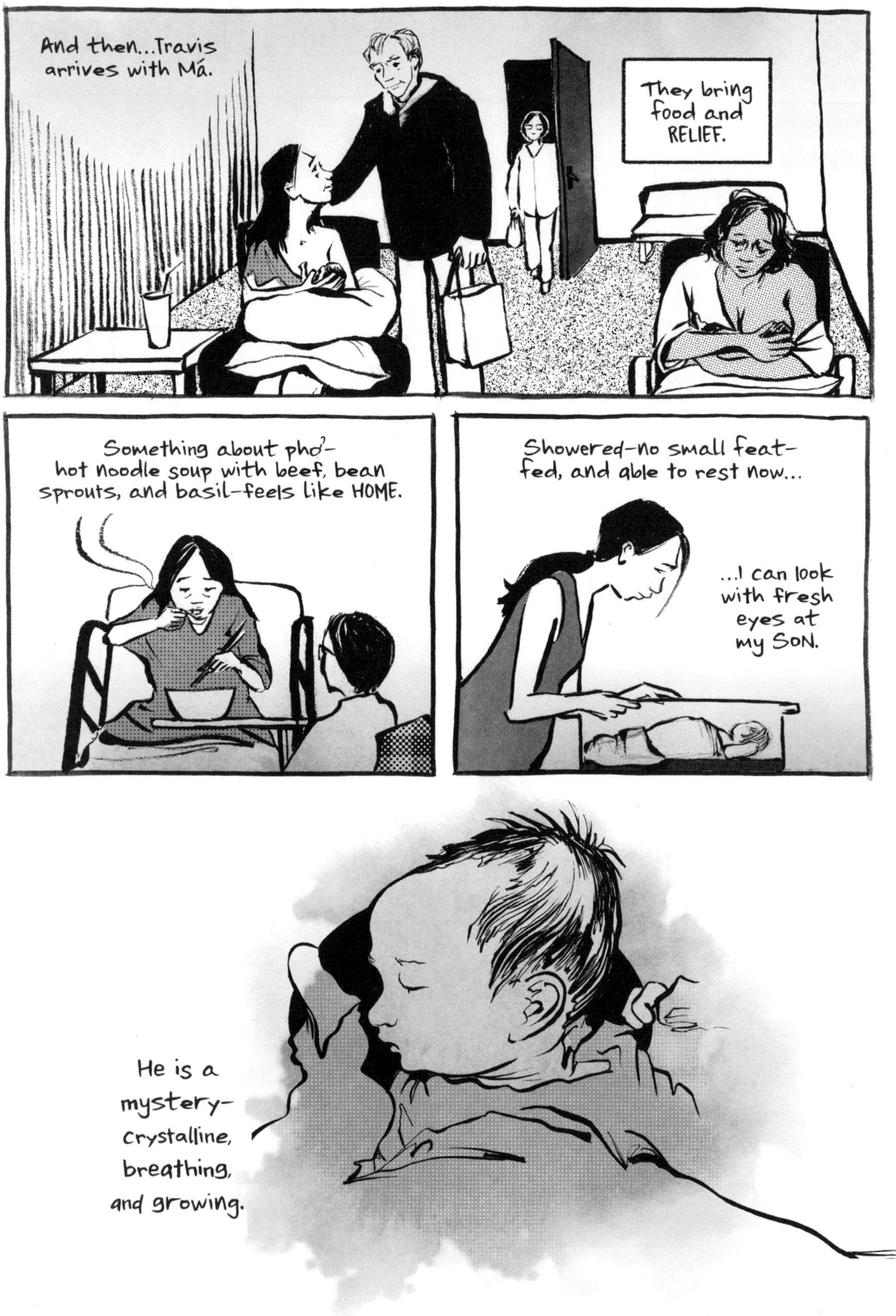
And then...Travis arrives with Má.
They bring food and RELIEF.
Something about phở– hot noodle soup with beef, bean sprouts, and basil–feels like HOME.
Showered–no small feat–fed, and able to rest now...
...I can look with fresh eyes at my SON.
He is a mystery– crystalline, breathing, and growing.

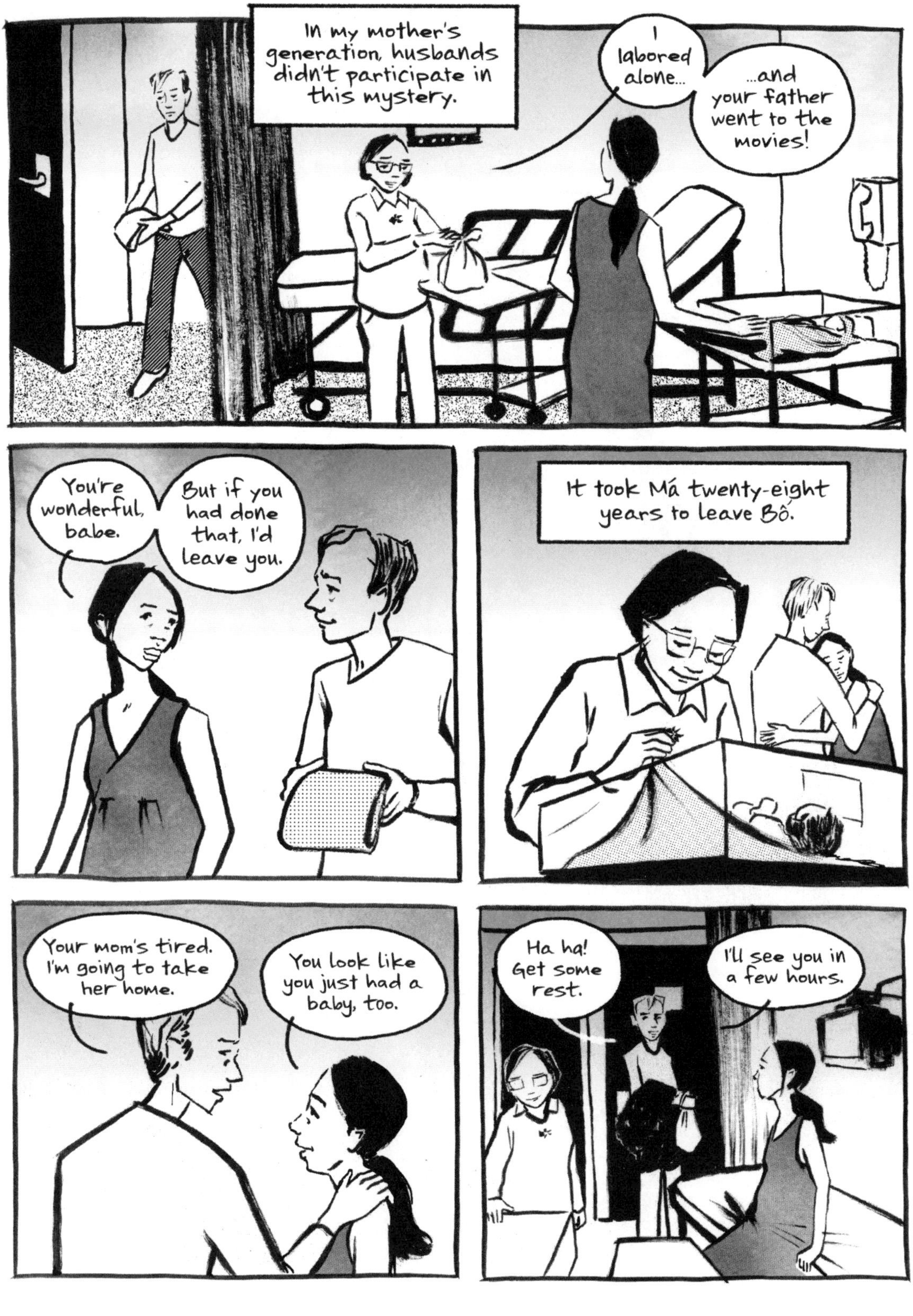
In my mother's generation, husbands didn't participate in this mystery.
I labored alone...
...and your father went to the movies!
You're wonderful, babe.
But if you had done that, I'd leave you.
It took Má twenty-eight years to leave Bố.
Your mom's tired. I'm going to take her home.
You look like you just had a baby, too.
Ha ha! Get some rest.
I'll see you in a few hours.

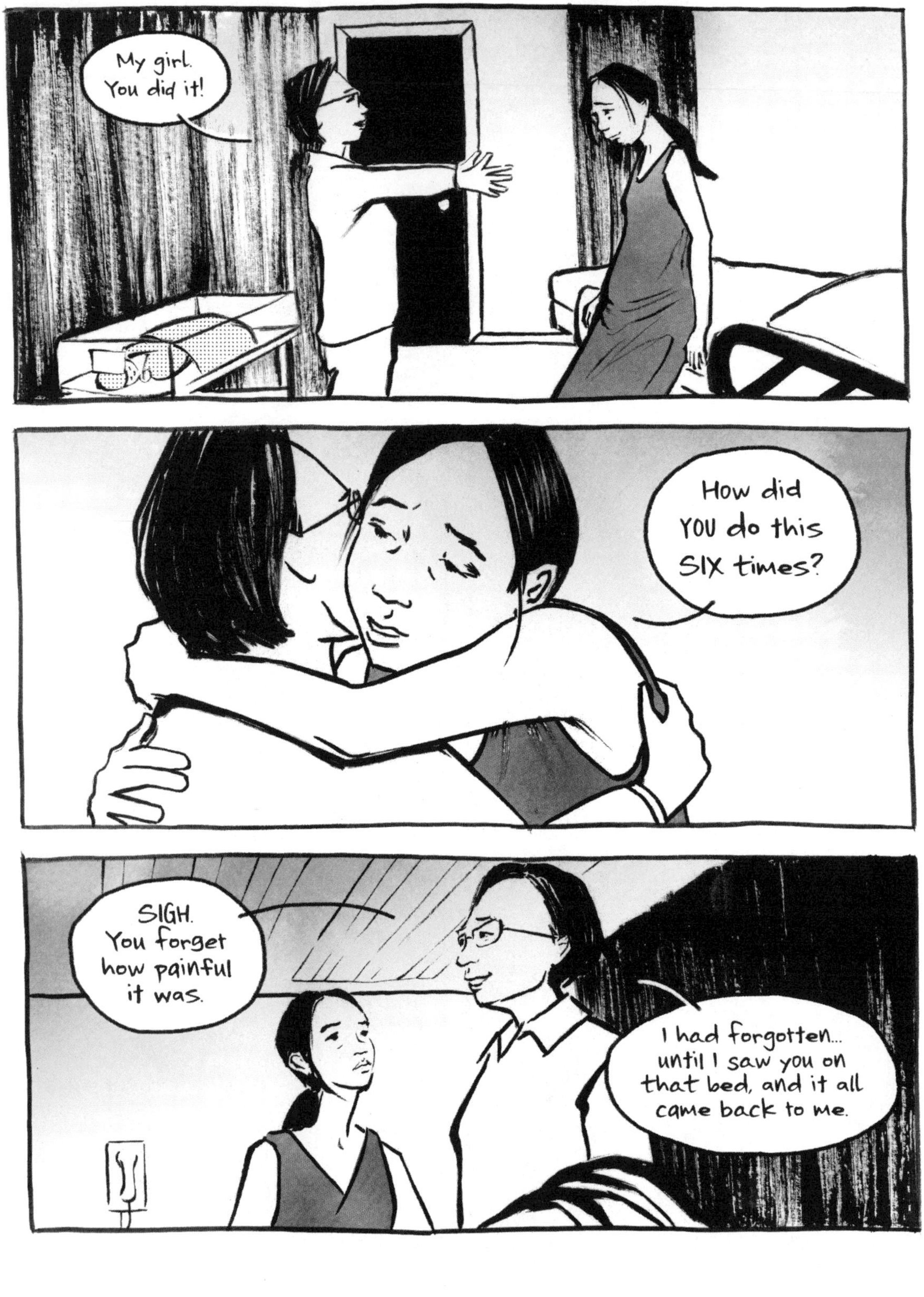
My girl. You did it!
How did YOU do this SIX times?
SIGH. You forget how painful it was.
I had forgotten... until I saw you on that bed, and it all came back to me.

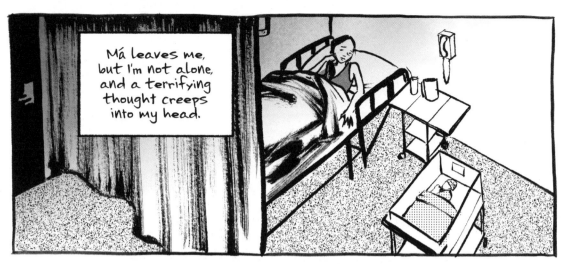

Má leaves me, but I'm not alone, and a terrifying thought creeps into my head.

FAMILY is now something I have created—

—and not just something I was born into.

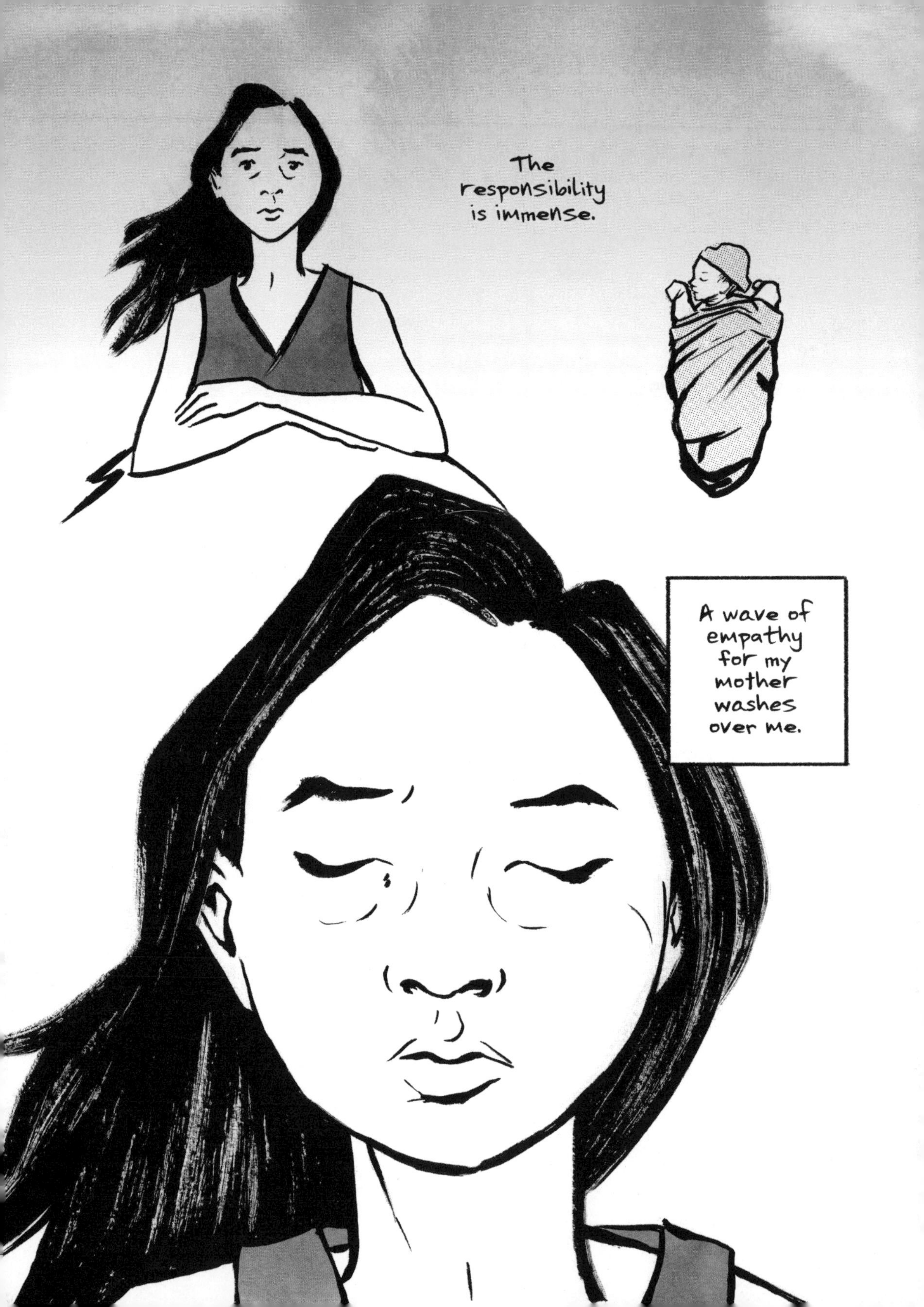
The responsibility is immense.
A wave of empathy for my mother washes over me.

CHAPTER 2

REWIND, REVERSE

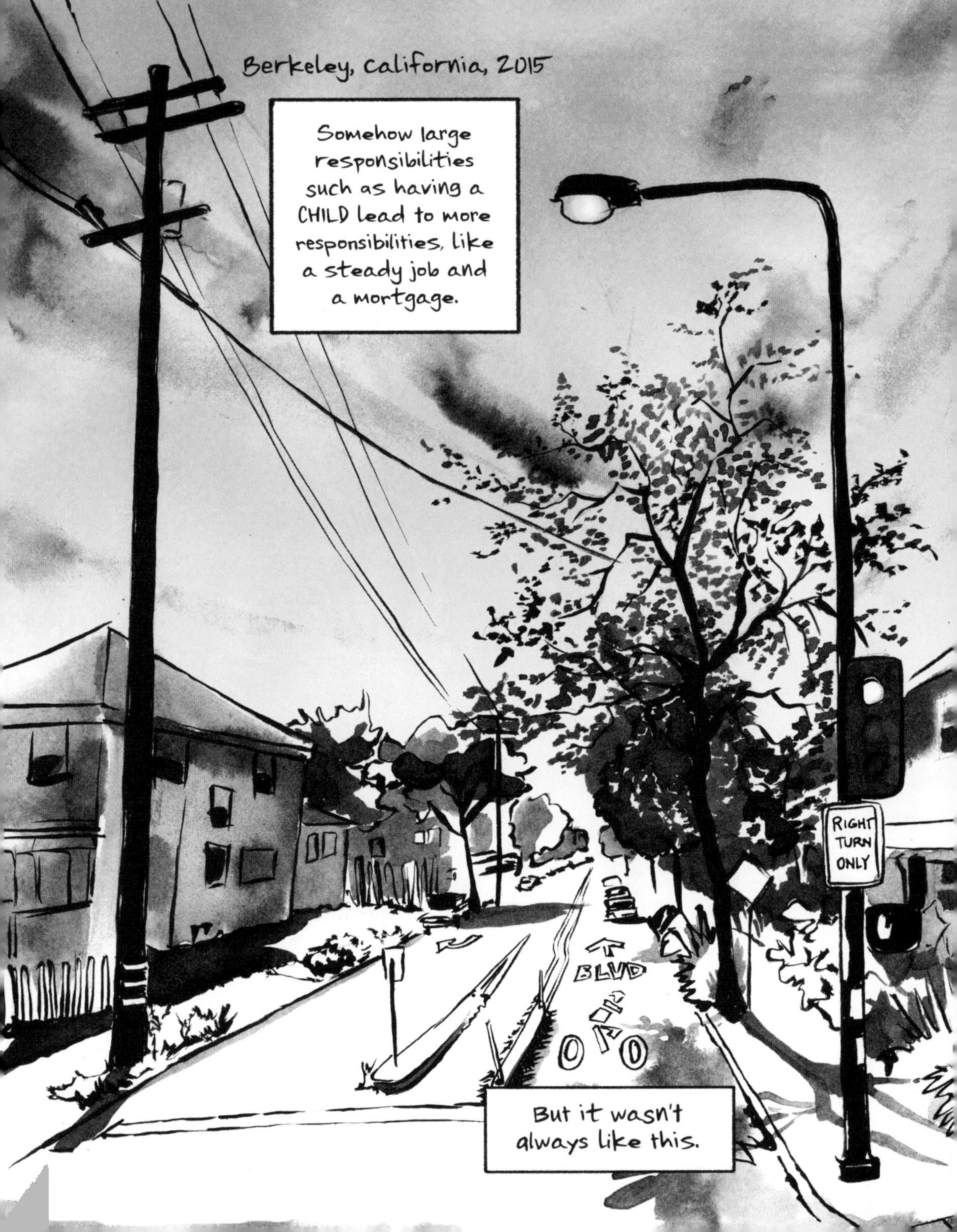
Berkeley, California, 2015
Somehow large responsibilities such as having a CHILD lead to more responsibilities, like a steady job and a mortgage.
RIGHT TURN ONLY
BLVD
But it wasn't always like this.

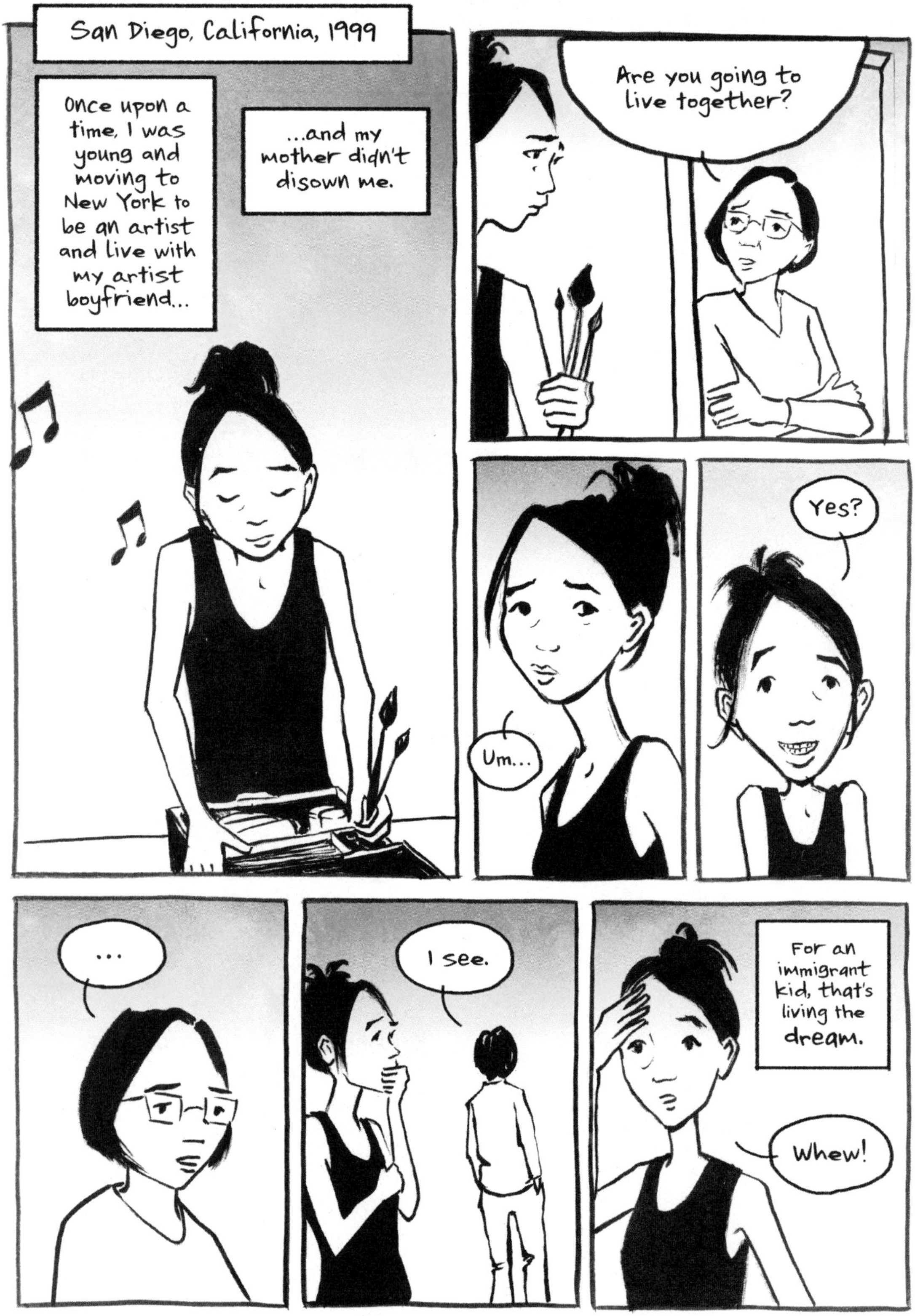
San Diego, California, 1999
Once upon a time, I was young and moving to New York to be an artist and live with my artist boyfriend...
...and my mother didn't disown me.
Are you going to live together?
Um...
Yes?
...
I see.
For an immigrant kid, that's living the dream.
Whew!

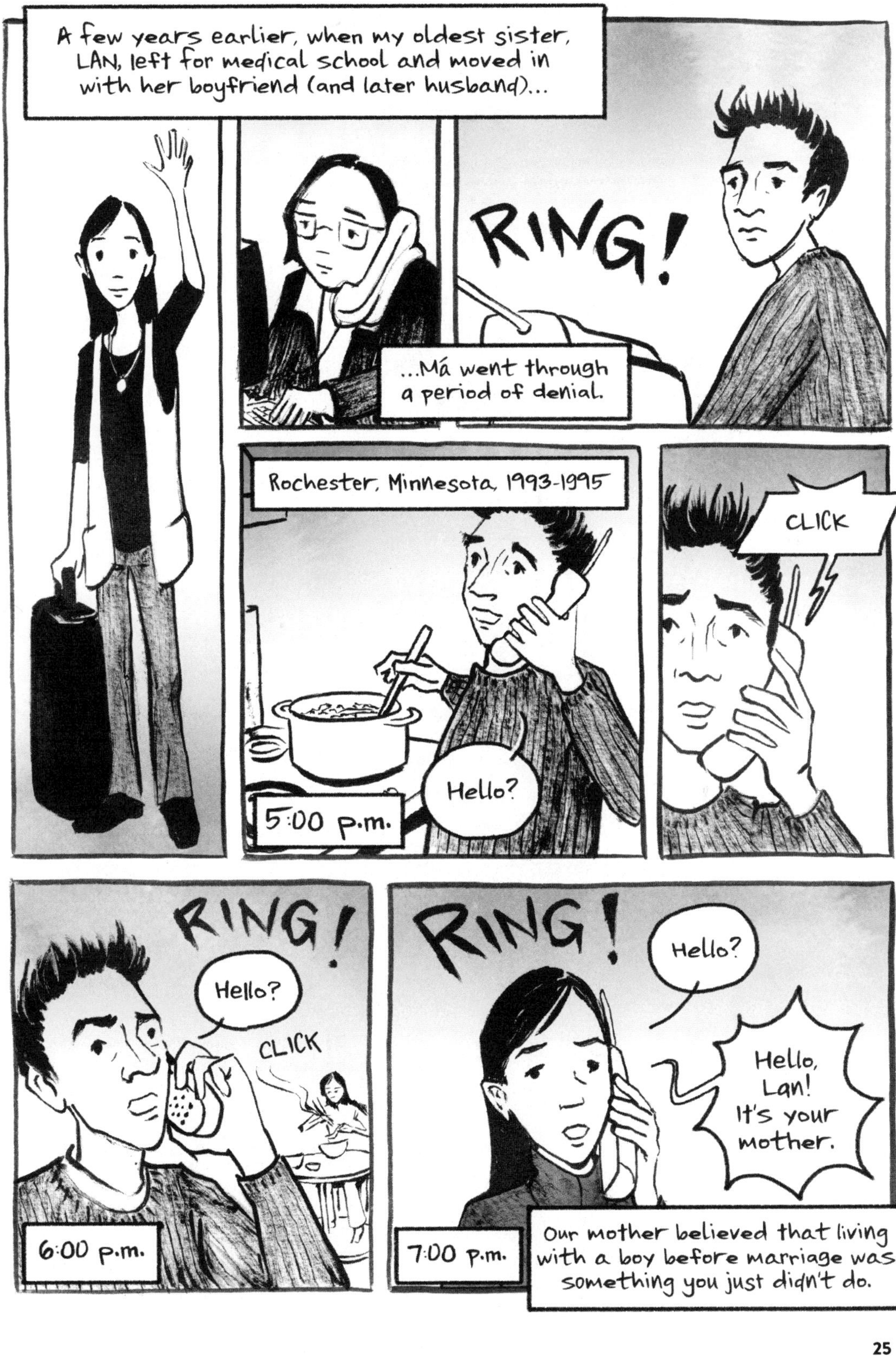

A few years earlier, when my oldest sister, LAN, left for medical school and moved in with her boyfriend (and later husband)...
...Má went through a period of denial.
RING!
Rochester, Minnesota, 1993-1995
5:00 p.m.
Hello?
CLICK
RING!
Hello?
CLICK
6:00 p.m.
RING!
Hello?
Hello, Lan! It's your mother.
7:00 p.m.
Our mother believed that living with a boy before marriage was something you just didn't do.

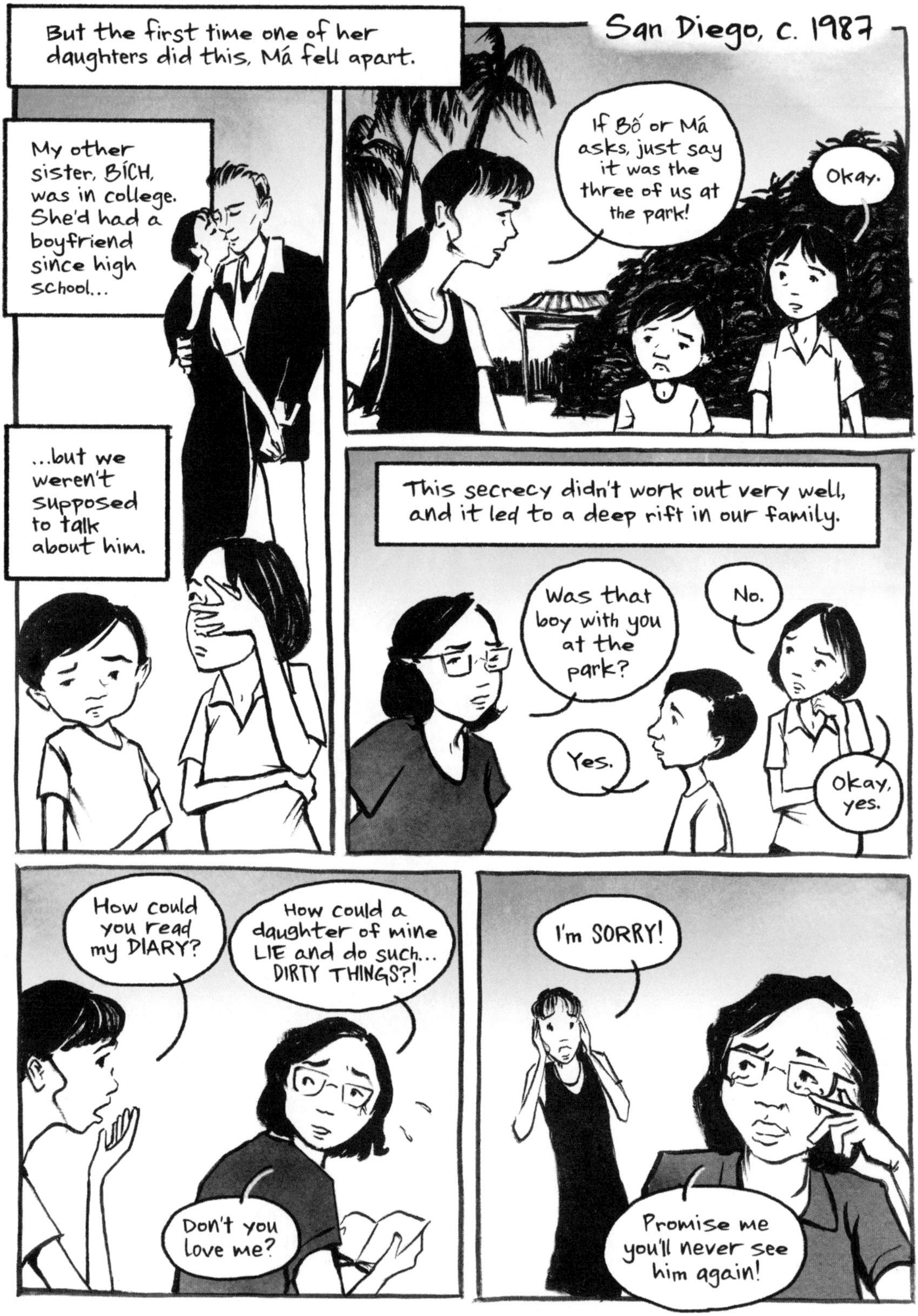

But the first time one of her daughters did this, Má fell apart.
San Diego, c. 1987
My other sister, BÍCH, was in college. She'd had a boyfriend since high school...
...but we weren't supposed to talk about him.
If Bố or Má asks, just say it was the three of us at the park!
Okay.
This secrecy didn't work out very well, and it led to a deep rift in our family.
Was that boy with you at the park?
No.
Yes.
Okay, yes.
How could you read my DIARY?
How could a daughter of mine LIE and do such... DIRTY THINGS?!
Don't you love me?
I'm SORRY!
Promise me you'll never see him again!

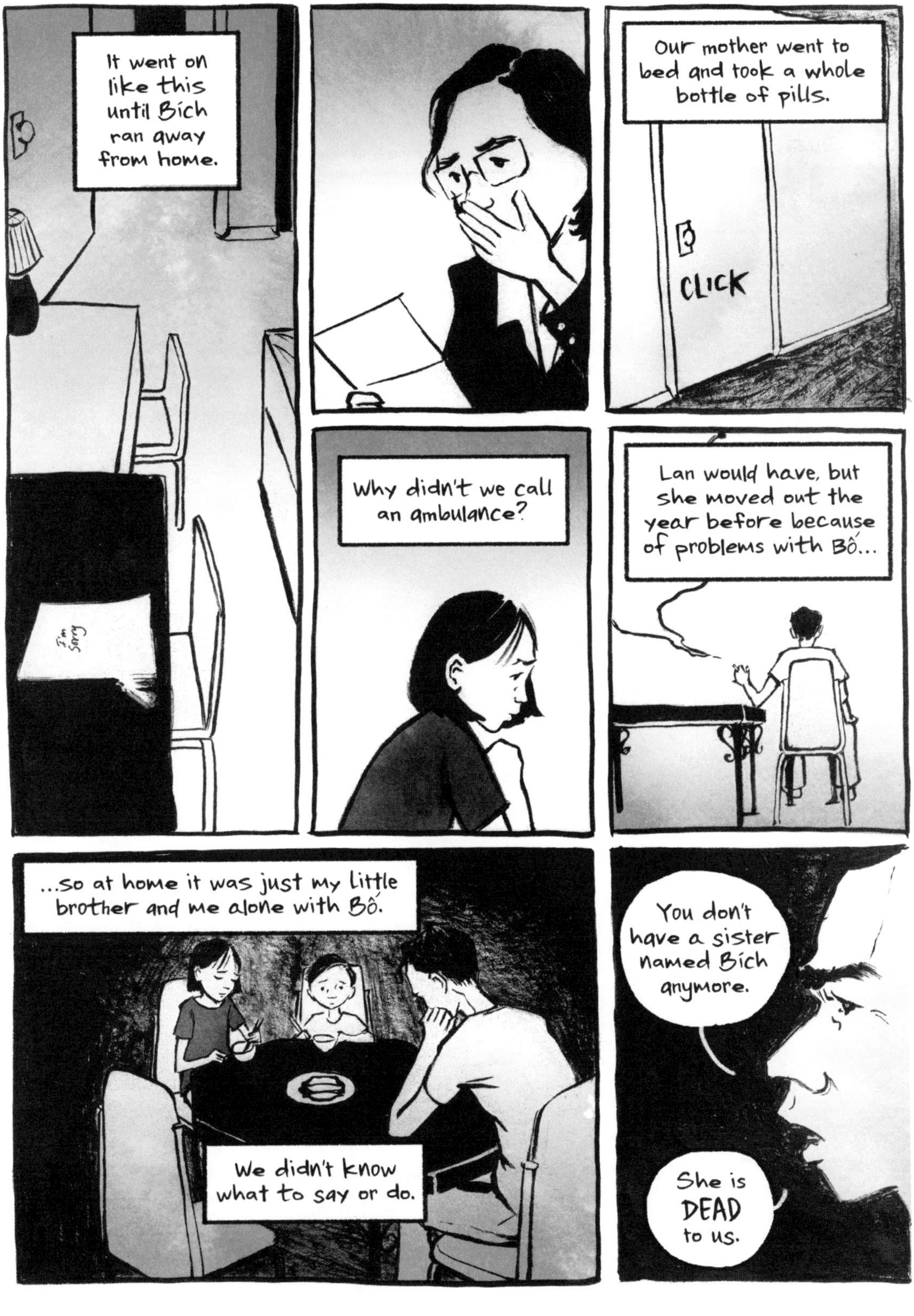
It went on like this until Bích ran away from home.
I'm sorry
Our mother went to bed and took a whole bottle of pills.
CLICK
Why didn't we call an ambulance?
Lan would have, but she moved out the year before because of problems with Bố...
...so at home it was just my little brother and me alone with Bố.
We didn't know what to say or do.
You don't have a sister named Bích anymore.
She is DEAD to us.

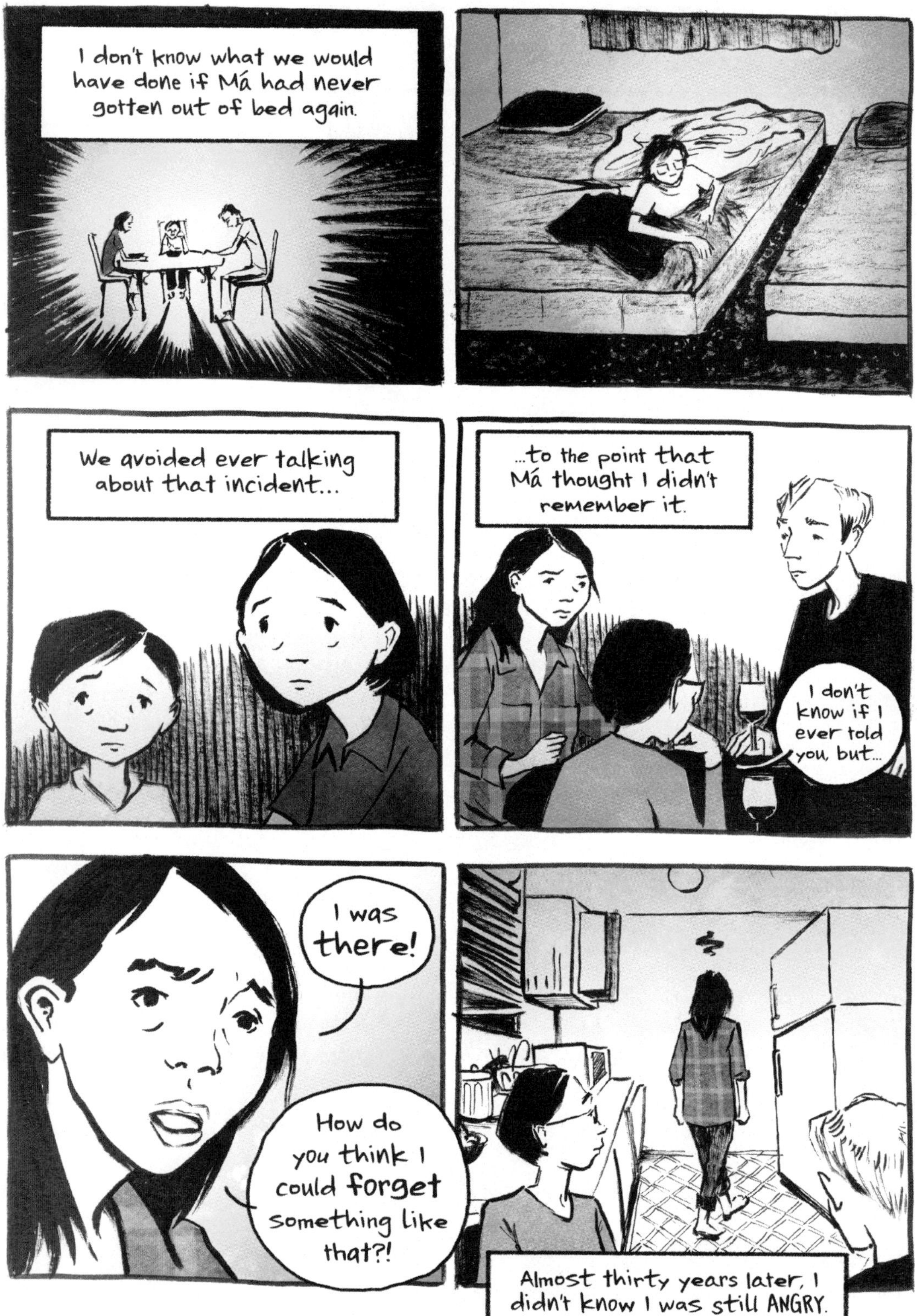
I don't know what we would have done if Má had never gotten out of bed again.
We avoided ever talking about that incident...
...to the point that Má thought I didn't remember it.
I don't know if I ever told you, but...
I was there!
How do you think I could forget something like that?!
Almost thirty years later, I didn't know I was still ANGRY.

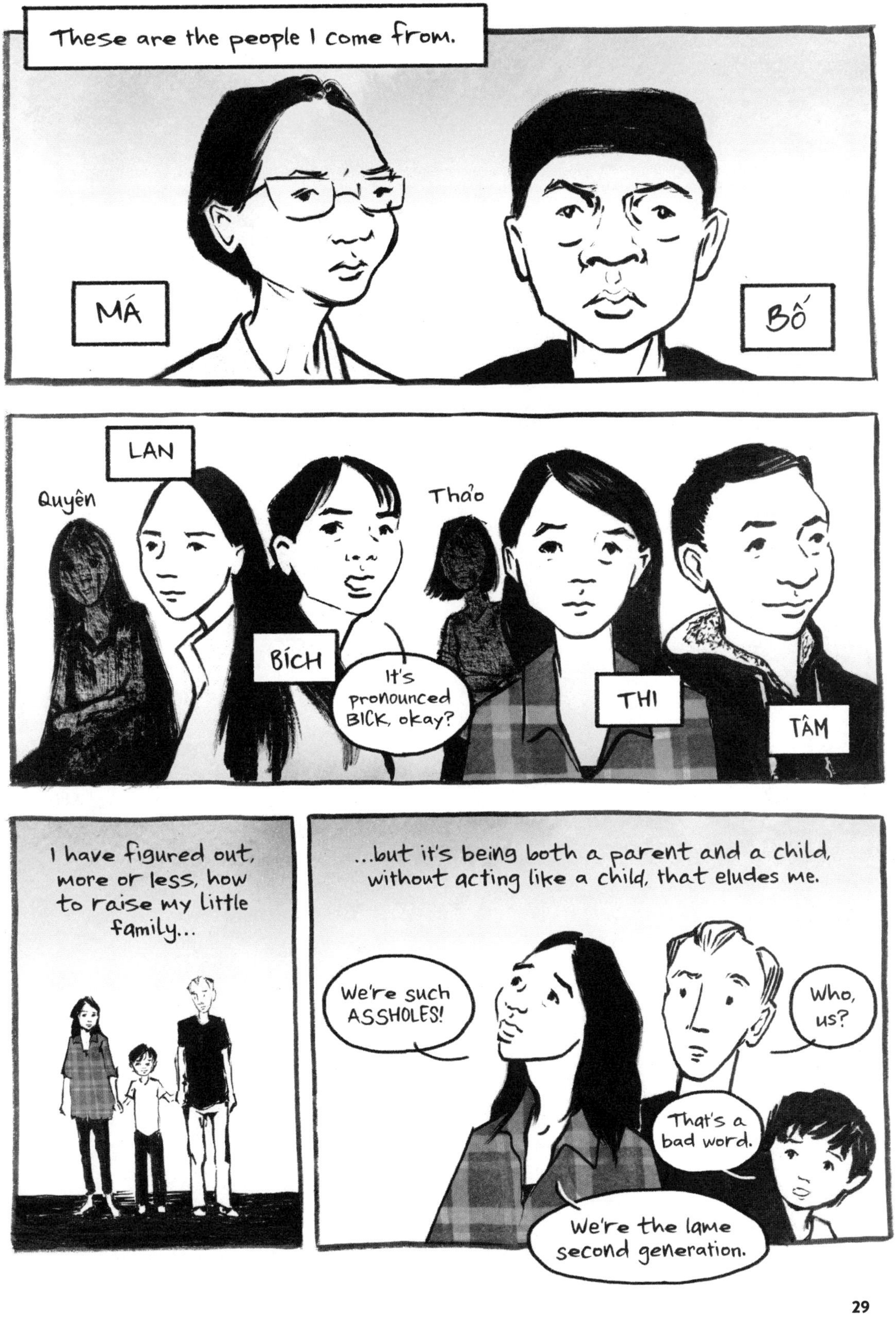
These are the people I come from.
MÁ
BỐ
LAN
Quyên
Thảo
BÍCH
It's pronounced BICK, okay?
THI
TÂM
I have figured out, more or less, how to raise my little family...
...but it's being both a parent and a child, without acting like a child, that eludes me.
We're such ASSHOLES!
Who, us?
That's a bad word.
We're the lame second generation.

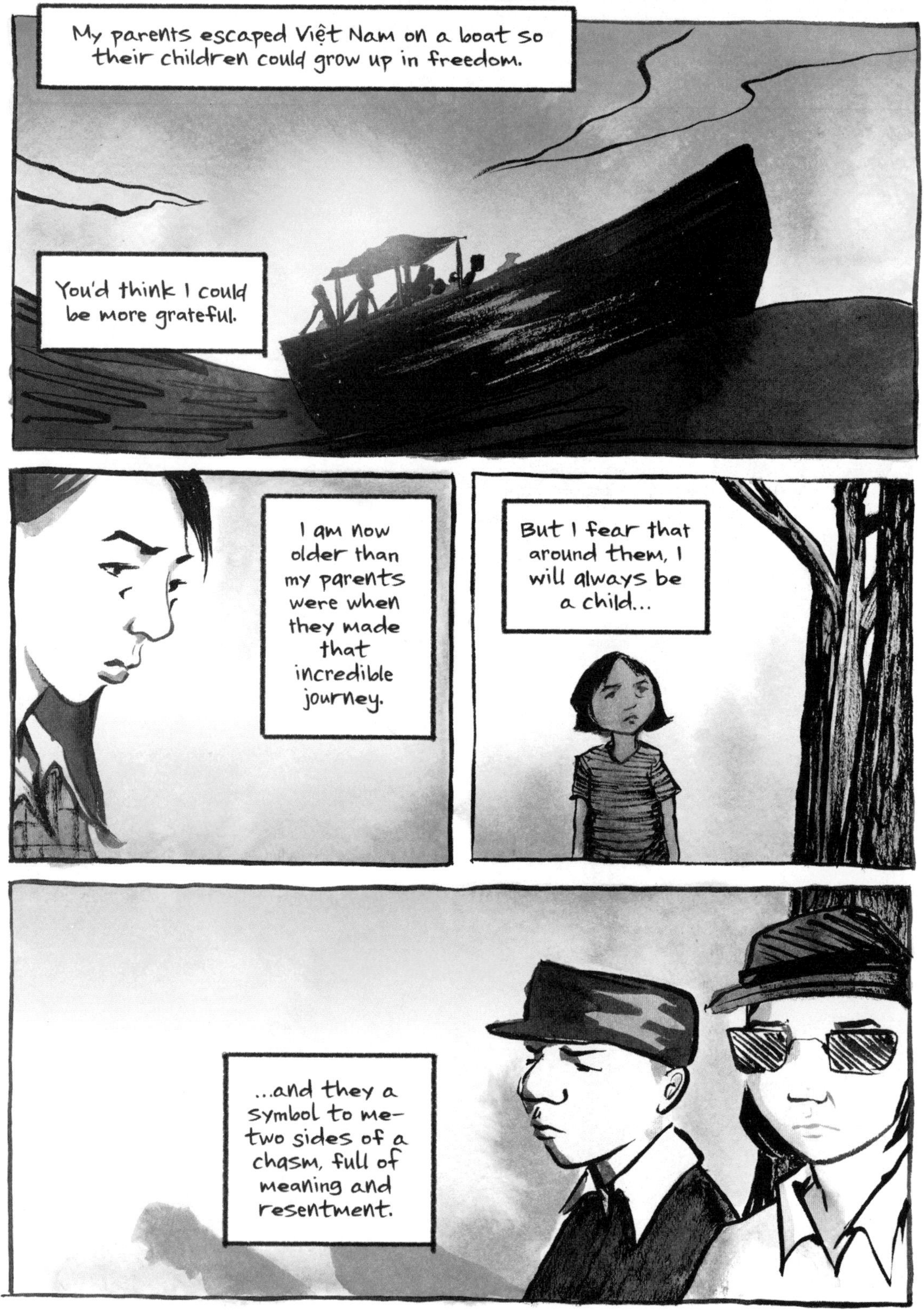
My parents escaped Việt Nam on a boat so their children could grow up in freedom.
You'd think I could be more grateful.
I am now older than my parents were when they made that incredible journey.
But I fear that around them, I will always be a child...
...and they a symbol to me— two sides of a chasm, full of meaning and resentment.

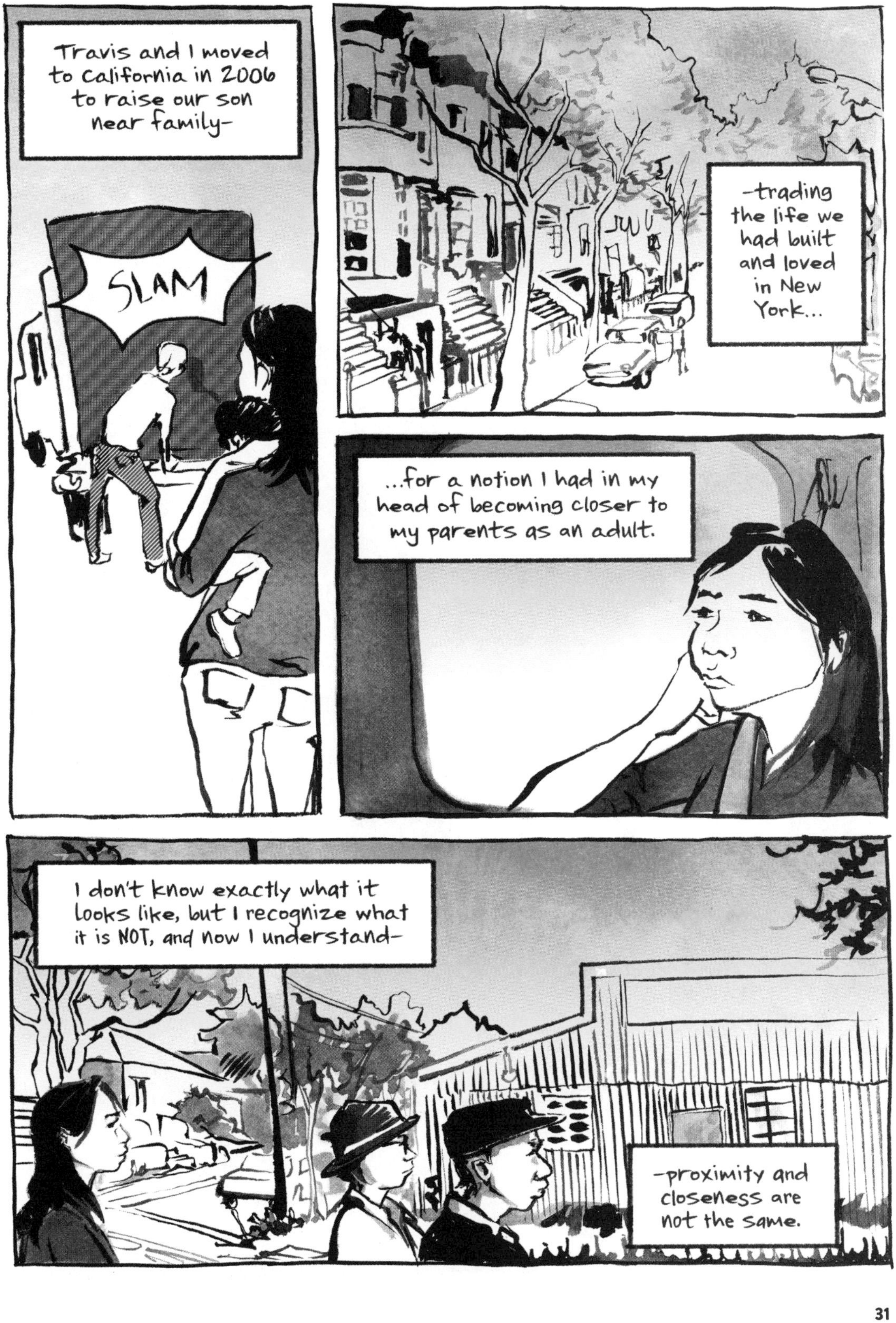
Travis and I moved to California in 2006 to raise our son near family-
SLAM
-trading the life we had built and loved in New York...
...for a notion I had in my head of becoming closer to my parents as an adult.
I don't know exactly what it looks like, but I recognize what it is NOT, and now I understand-
-proximity and closeness are not the same.

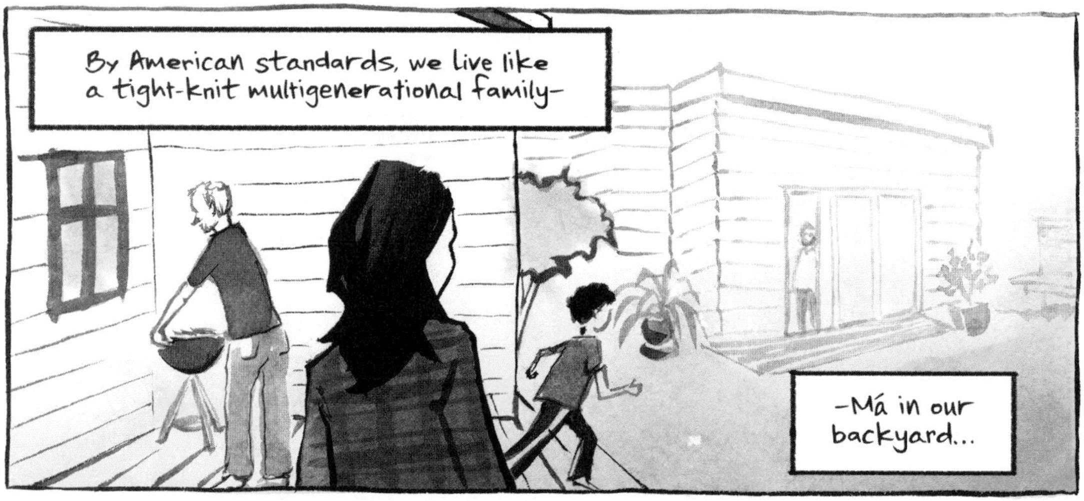
By American standards, we live like a tight-knit multigenerational family-
-Má in our backyard...

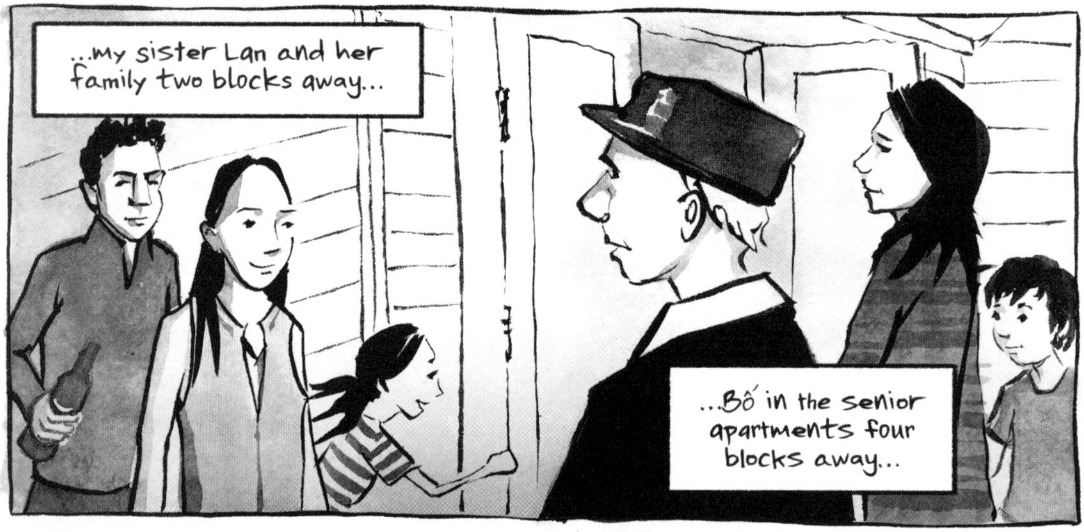
...my sister Lan and her family two blocks away...
...Bố in the senior apartments four blocks away...

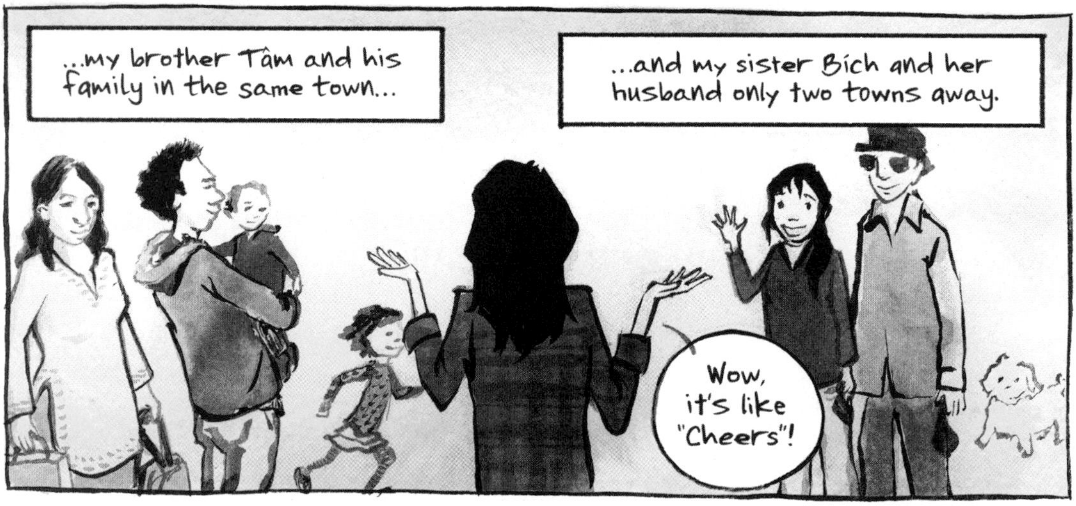
...my brother Tâm and his family in the same town...
...and my sister Bích and her husband only two towns away.
Wow, it's like "Cheers"!

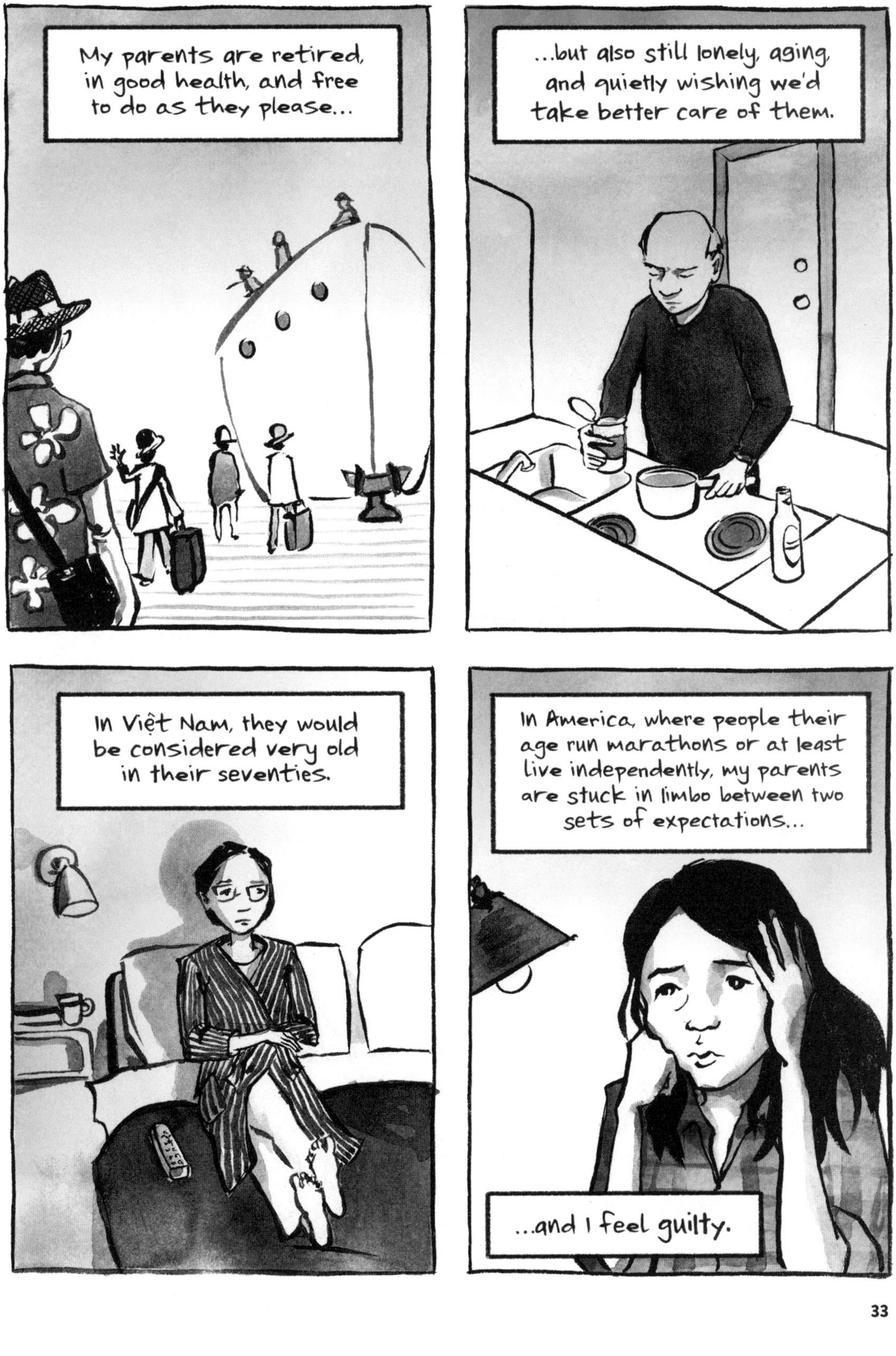
My parents are retired, in good health, and free to do as they please...
...but also still lonely, aging, and quietly wishing we'd take better care of them.
In Việt Nam, they would be considered very old in their seventies.
In America, where people their age run marathons or at least live independently, my parents are stuck in limbo between two sets of expectations...
...and I feel guilty.

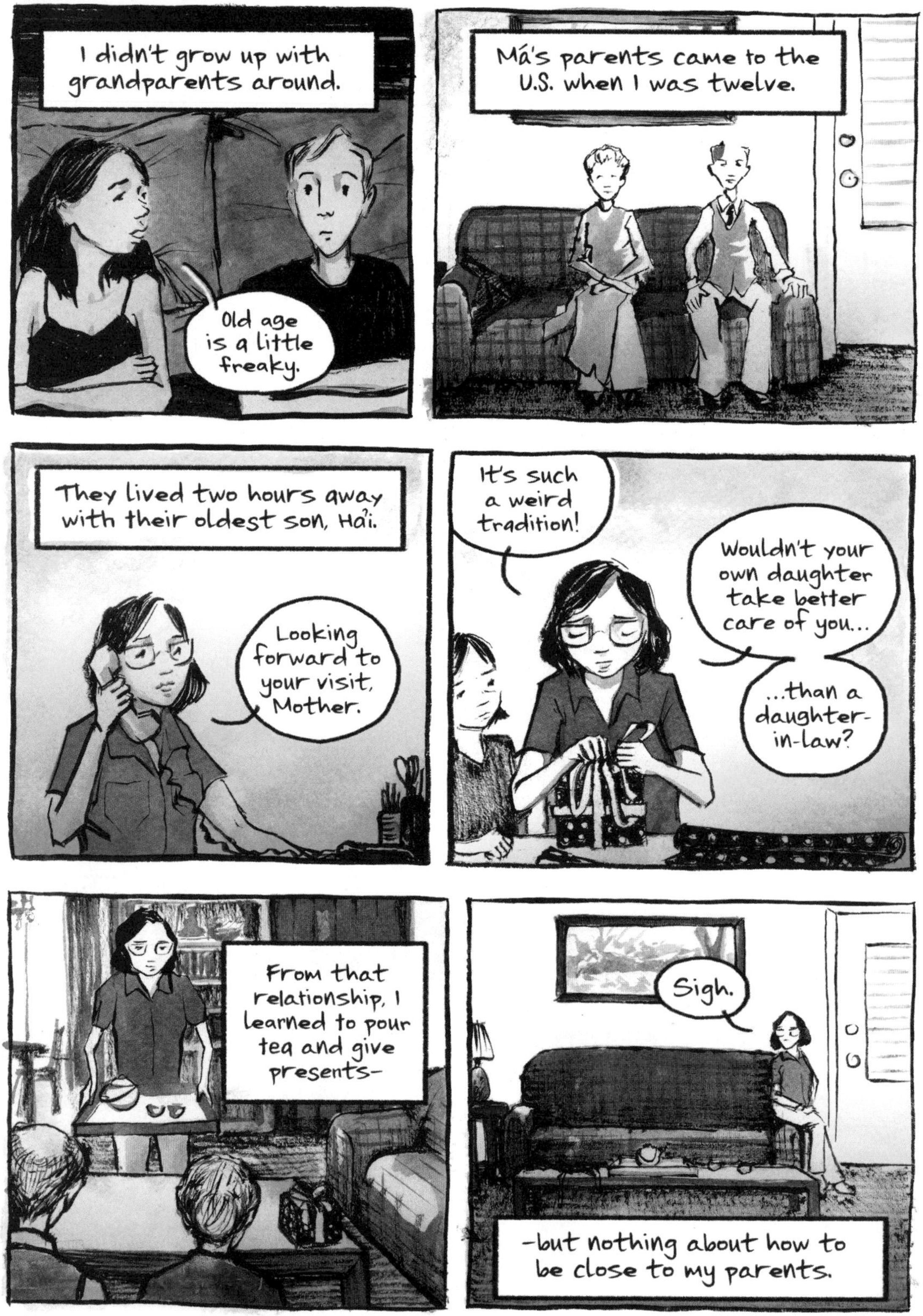
I didn't grow up with grandparents around.
Old age is a little freaky.
Má's parents came to the U.S. when I was twelve.
They lived two hours away with their oldest son, Hải.
Looking forward to your visit, Mother.
It's such a weird tradition!
Wouldn't your own daughter take better care of you...
...than a daughter-in-law?
From that relationship, I learned to pour tea and give presents–
Sigh.
–but nothing about how to be close to my parents.

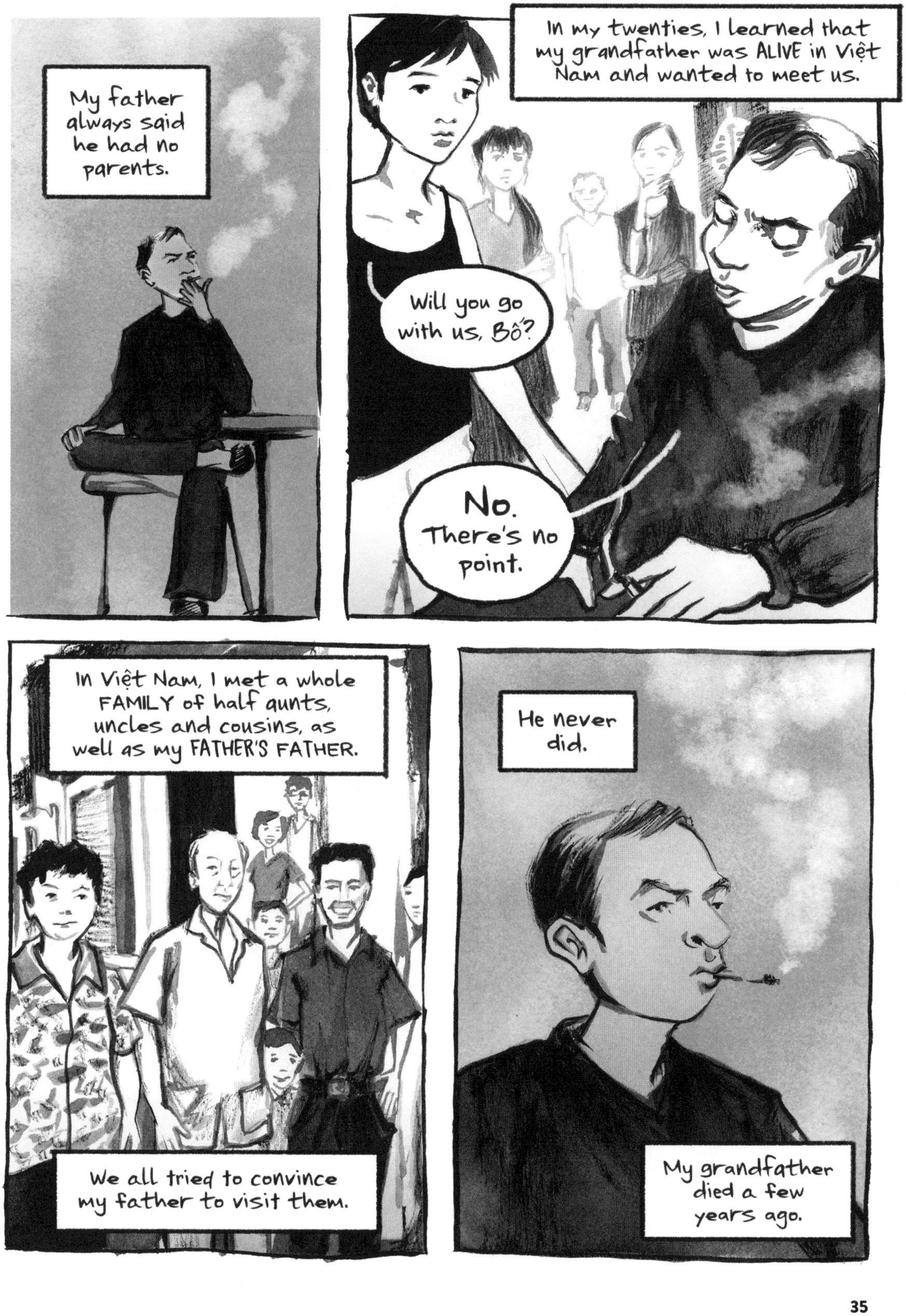
My father always said he had no parents.
In my twenties, I learned that my grandfather was ALIVE in Việt Nam and wanted to meet us.
Will you go with us, Bố?
No. There's no point.
In Việt Nam, I met a whole FAMILY of half aunts, uncles and cousins, as well as my FATHER'S FATHER.
We all tried to convince my father to visit them.
He never did.
My grandfather died a few years ago.

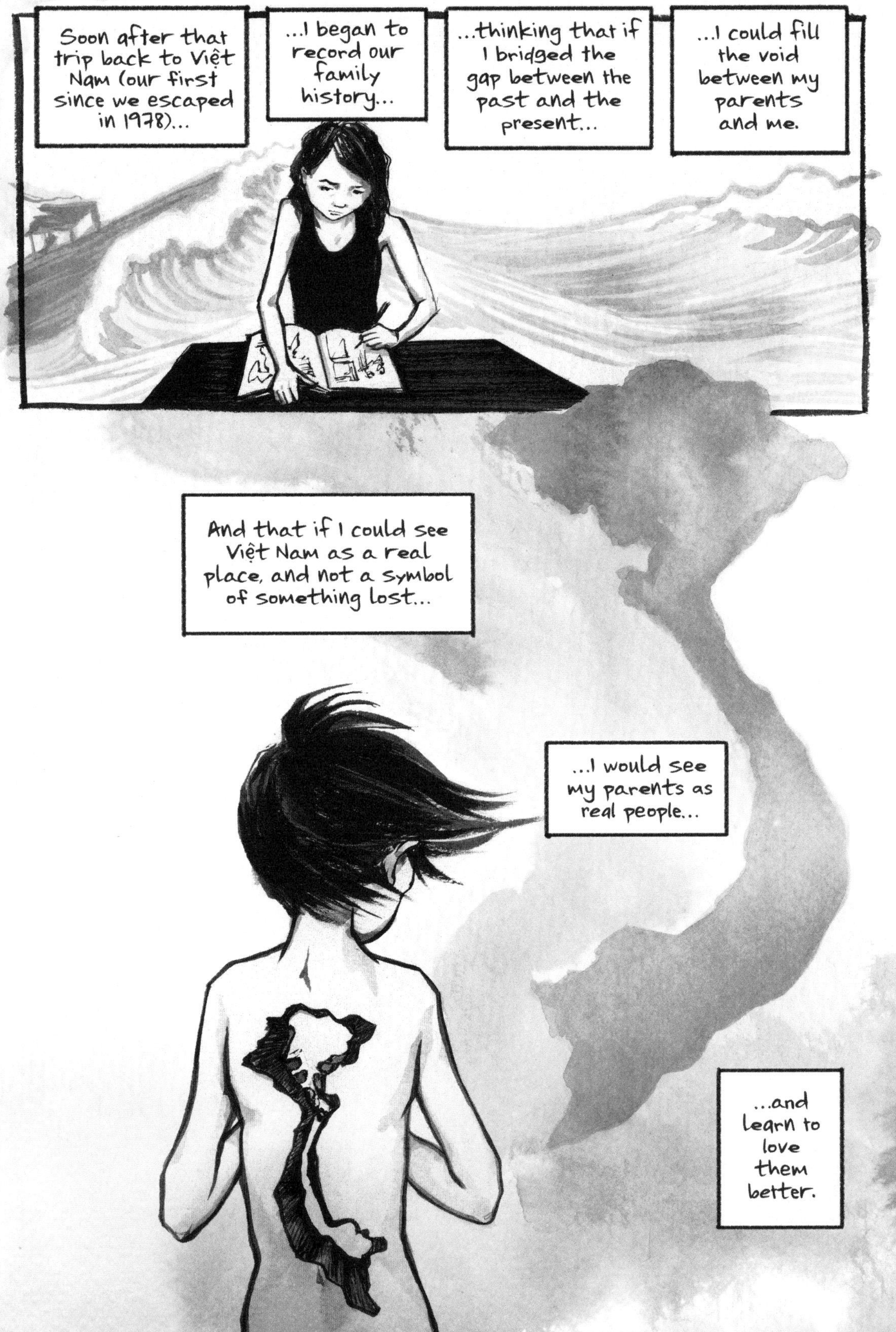
Soon after that trip back to Việt Nam (our first since we escaped in 1978)...
...I began to record our family history...
...thinking that if I bridged the gap between the past and the present...
...I could fill the void between my parents and me.
And that if I could see Việt Nam as a real place, and not a symbol of something lost...
...I would see my parents as real people...
...and learn to love them better.

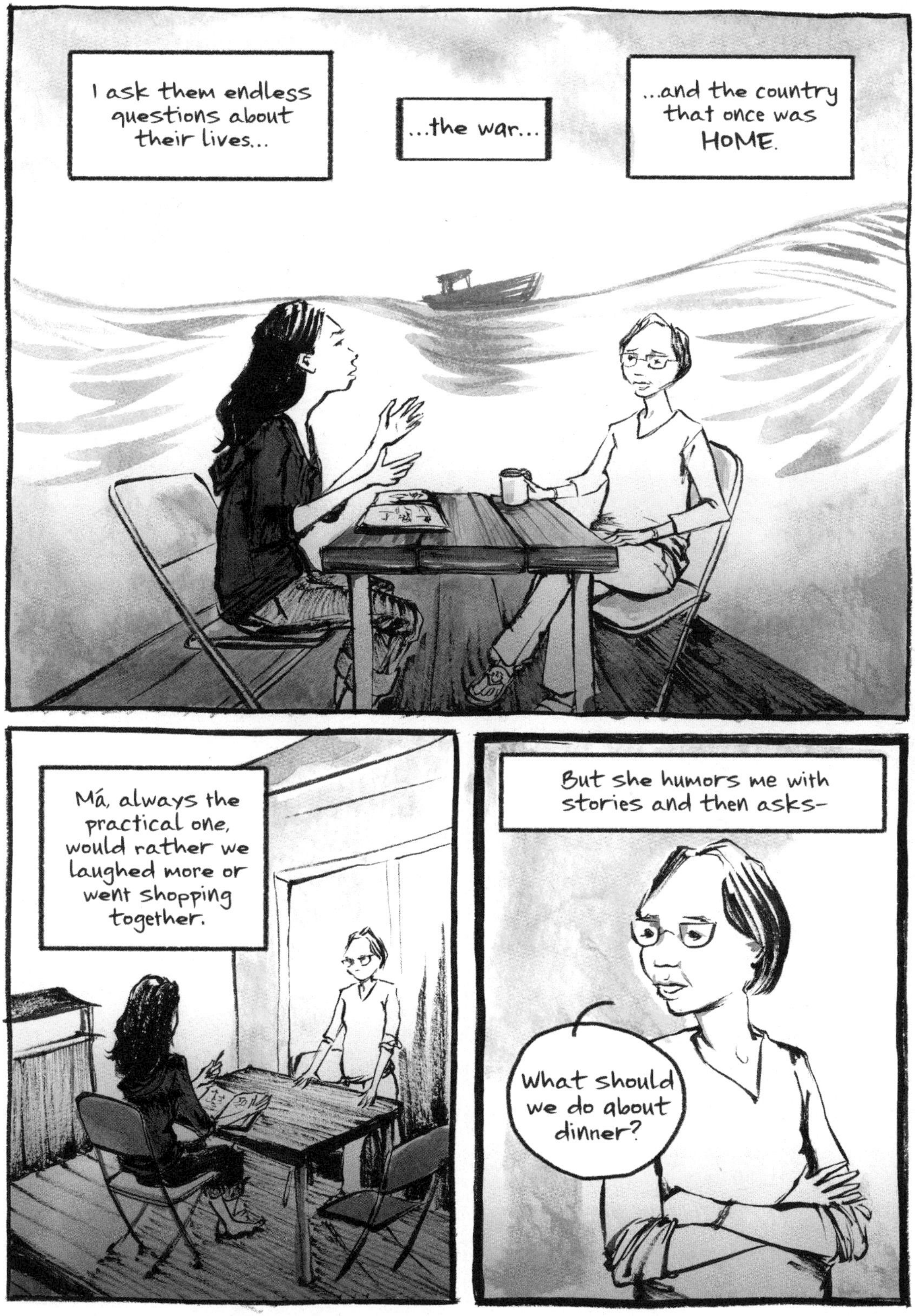
I ask them endless questions about their lives...
...the war...
...and the country that once was HOME.
Má, always the practical one, would rather we laughed more or went shopping together.
But she humors me with stories and then asks-
What should we do about dinner?

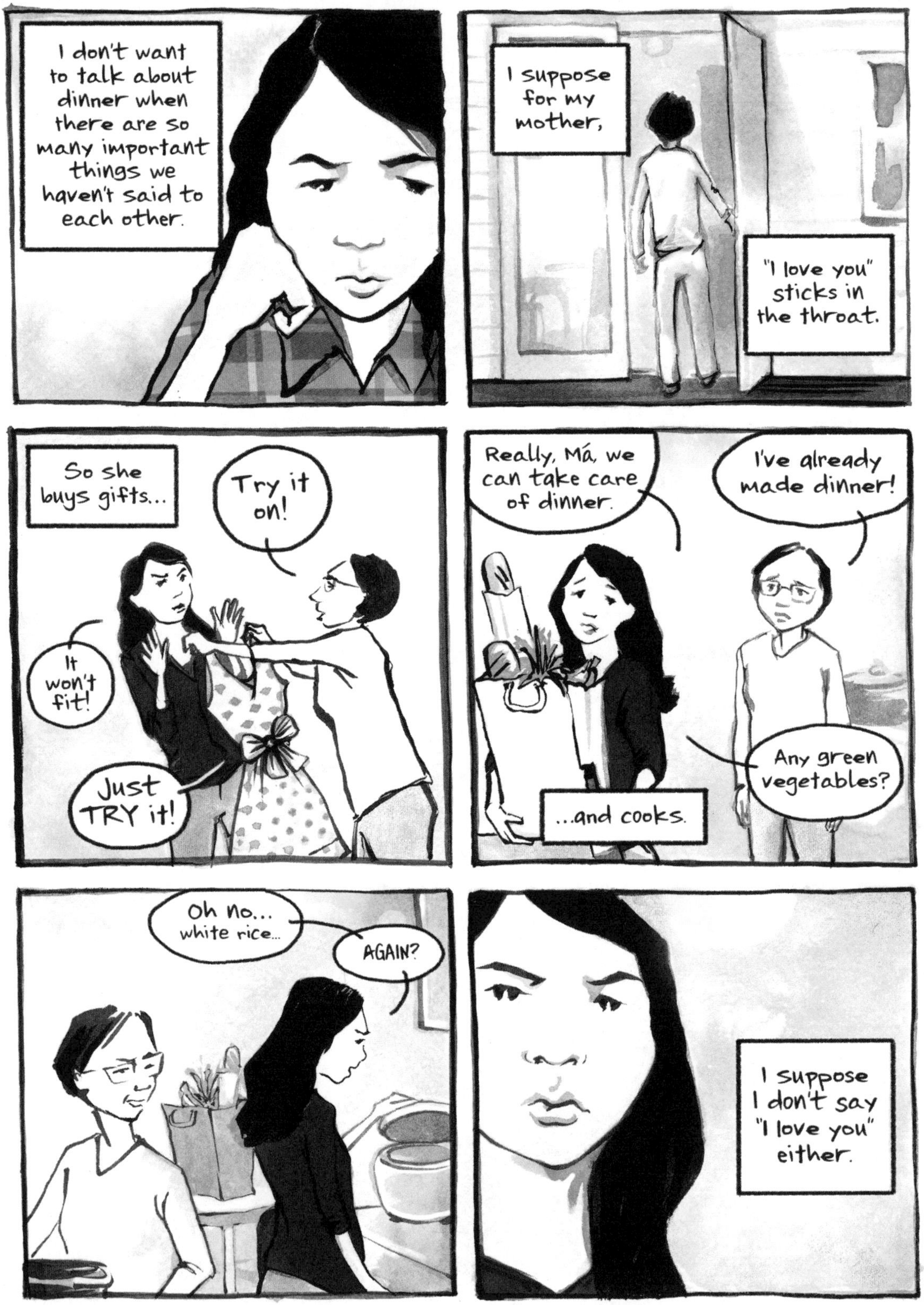
I don't want to talk about dinner when there are so many important things we haven't said to each other.
I suppose for my mother,
"I love you" sticks in the throat.
So she buys gifts...
Try it on!
It won't fit!
Just TRY it!
Really, Má, we can take care of dinner.
I've already made dinner!
Any green vegetables?
...and cooks.
Oh no... white rice...
AGAIN?
I suppose I don't say "I love you" either.

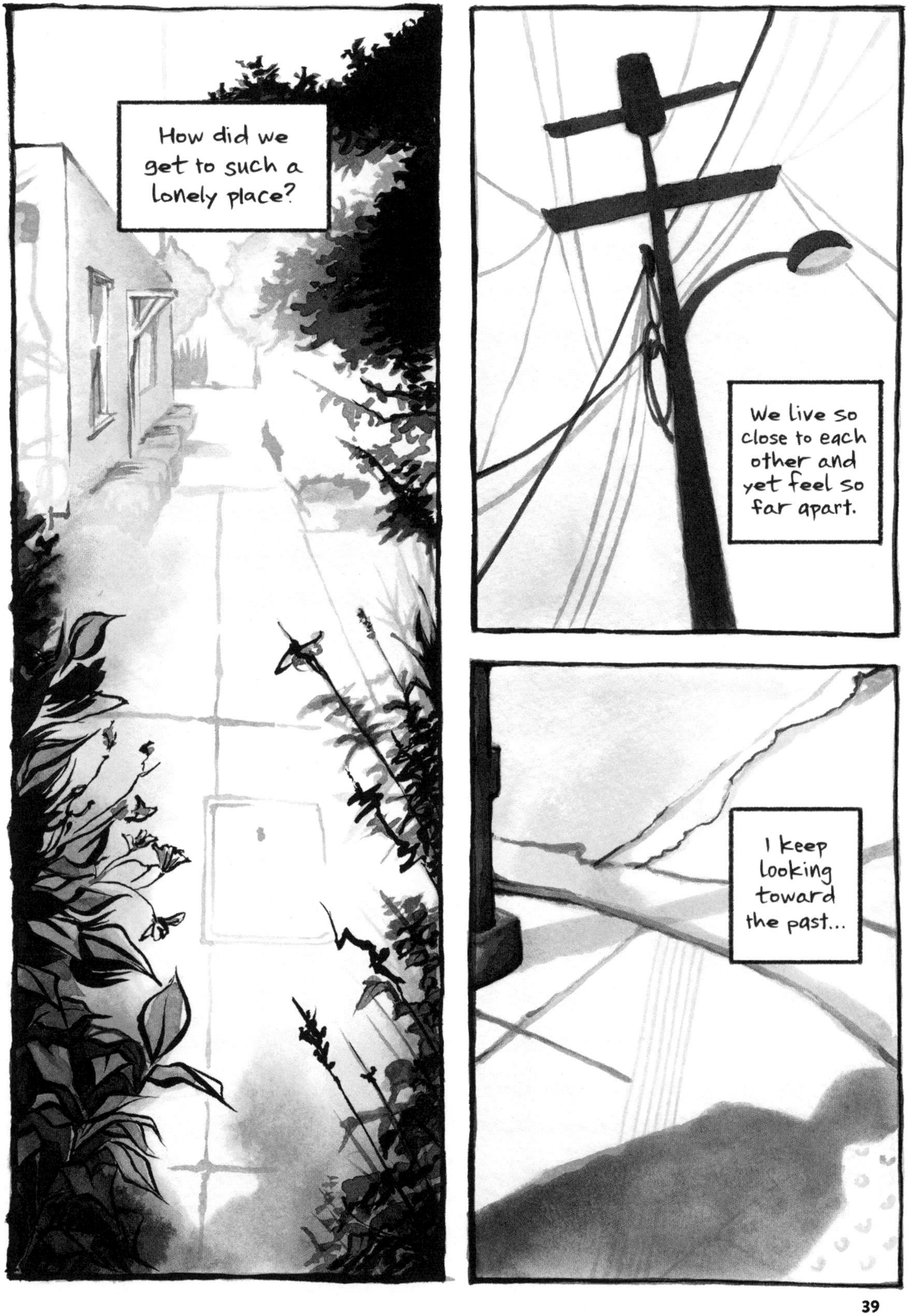
How did we get to such a lonely place?
We live so close to each other and yet feel so far apart.
I keep looking toward the past...

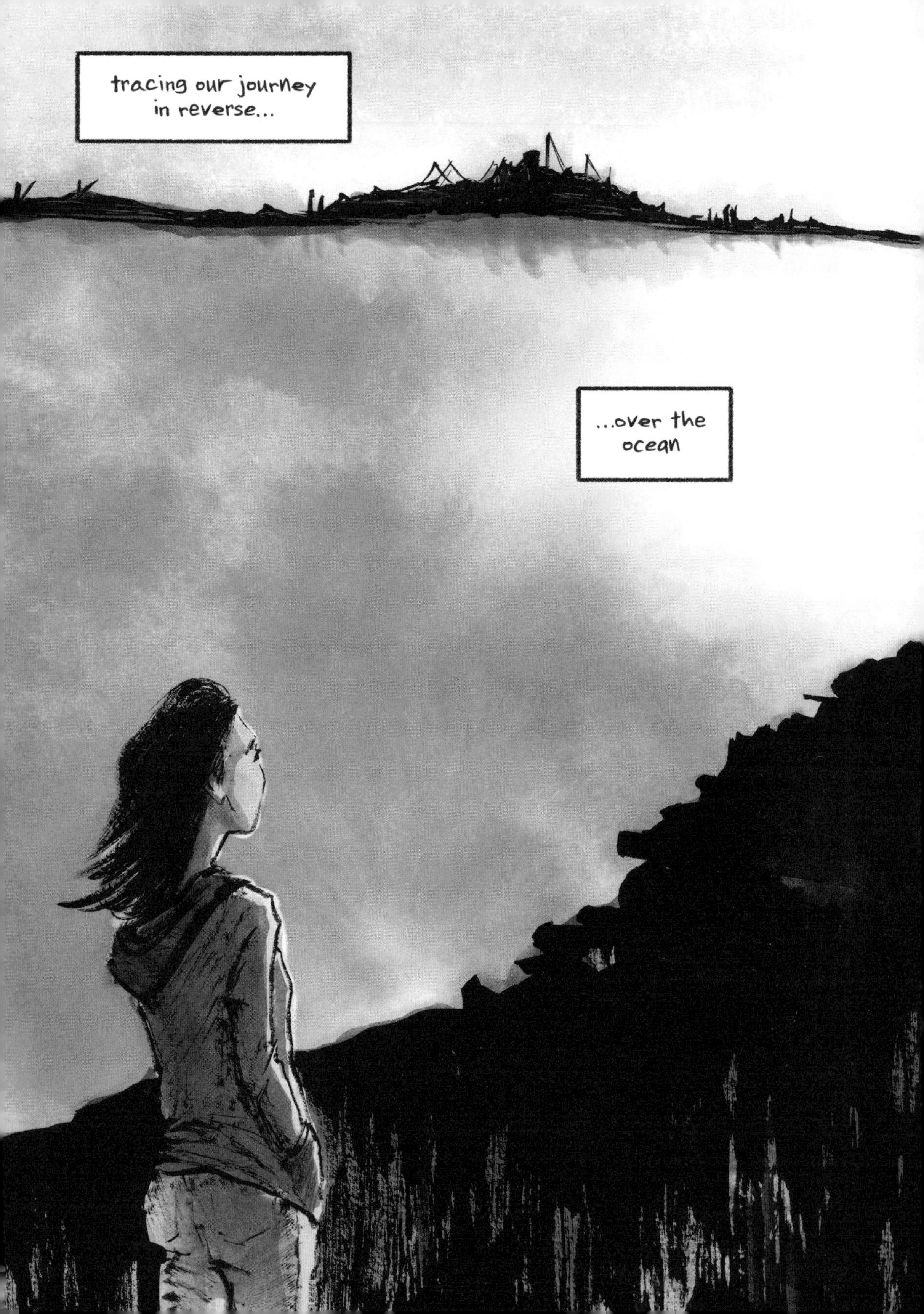
tracing our journey
in reverse...
...over the
ocean

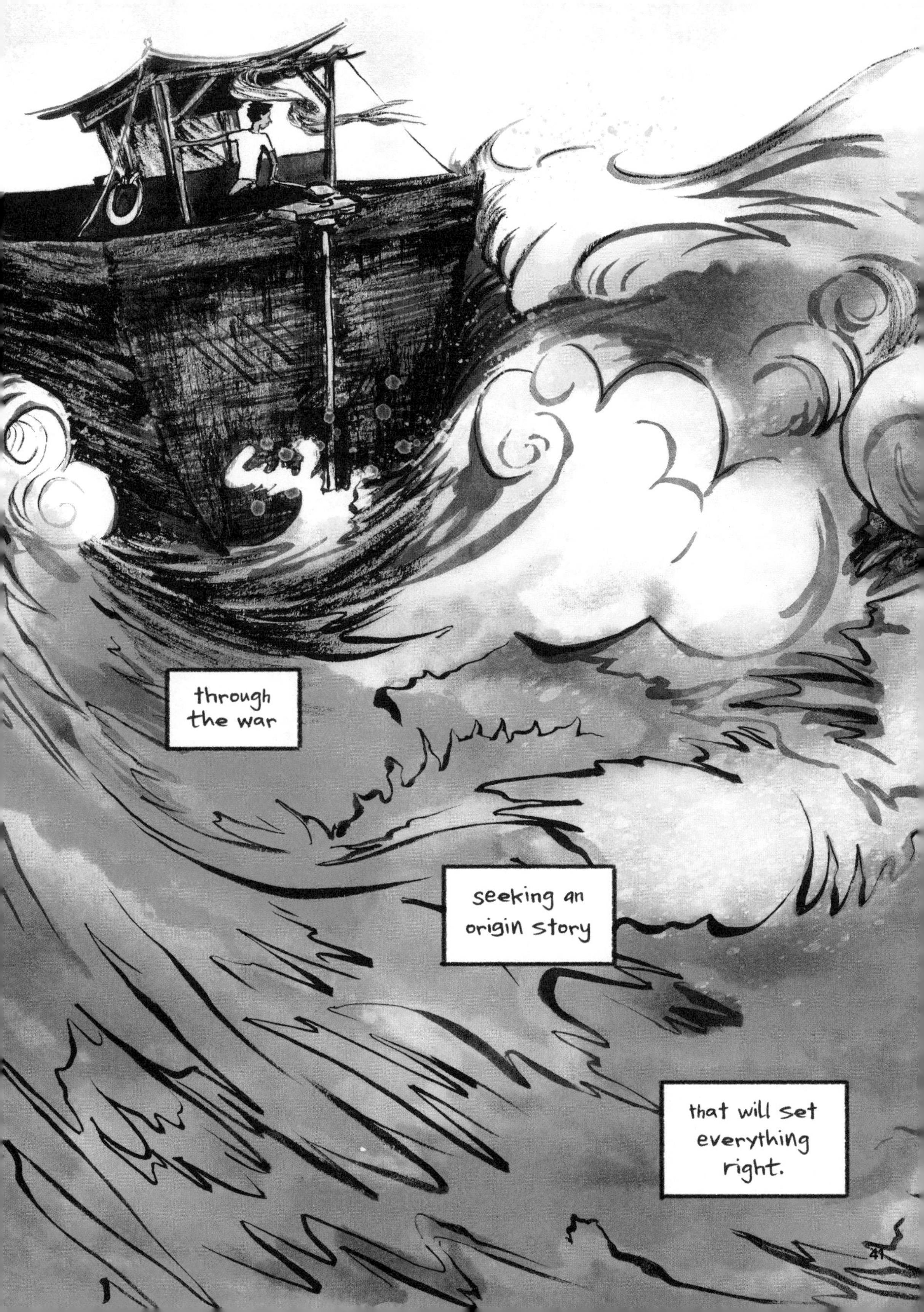
through the war
seeking an origin story
that will set everything right.

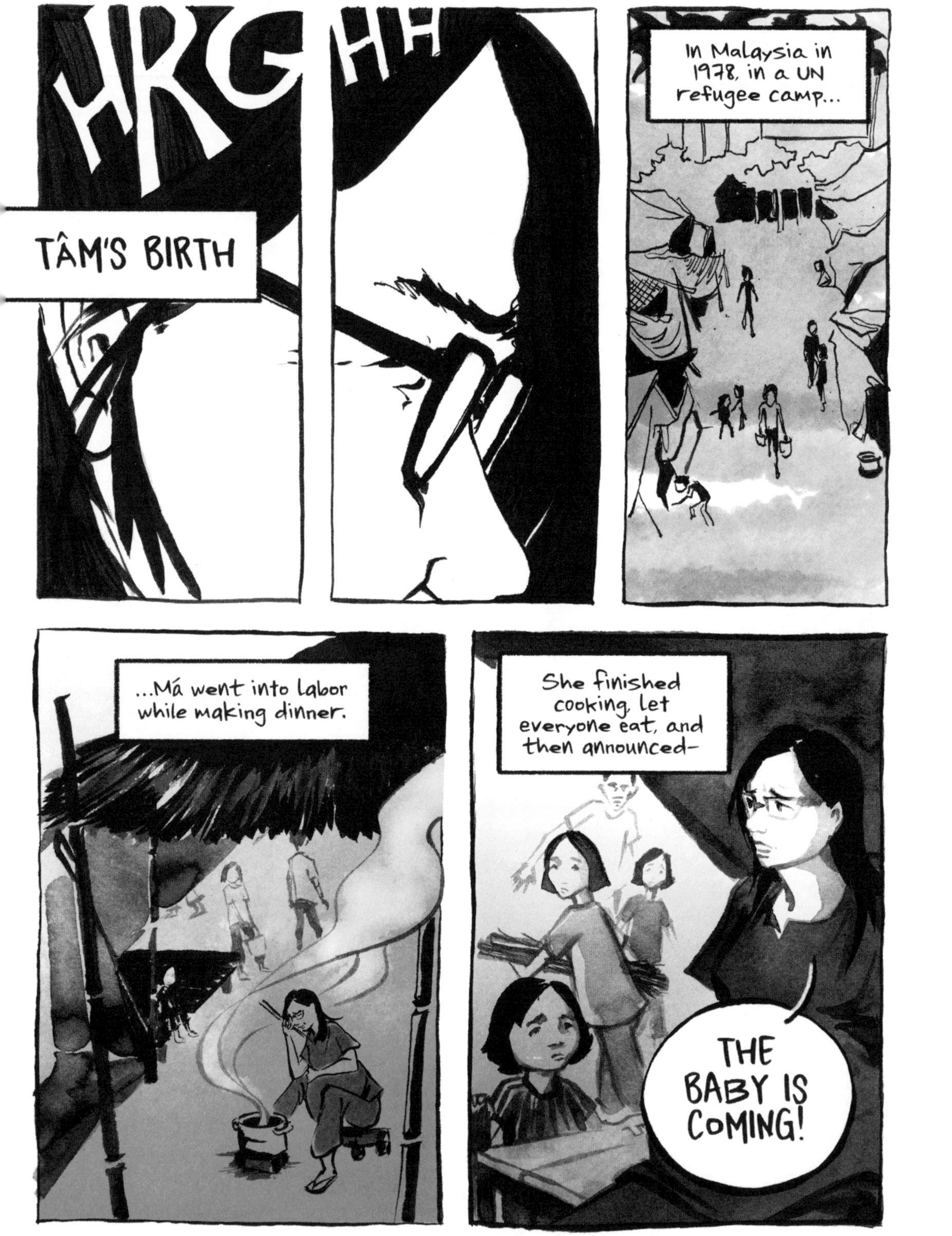
HRGHH
TÂM'S BIRTH
In Malaysia in 1978, in a UN refugee camp...
...Má went into labor while making dinner.
She finished cooking, let everyone eat, and then announced–
THE BABY IS COMING!

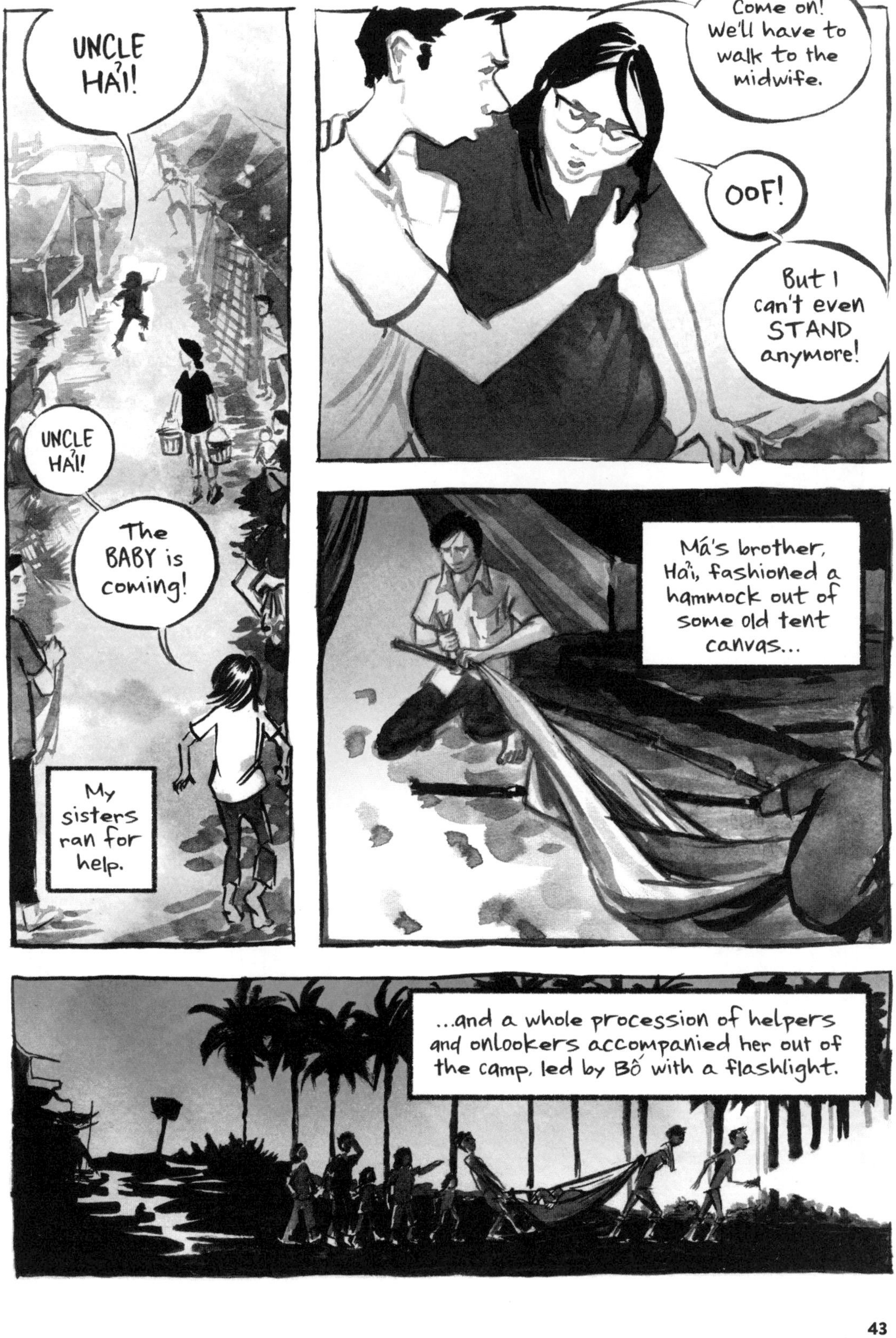

UNCLE HẢI!
UNCLE HẢI!
The BABY is coming!
My sisters ran for help.
Come on! We'll have to walk to the midwife.
OOF!
But I can't even STAND anymore!
Má's brother, Hải, fashioned a hammock out of some old tent canvas...
...and a whole procession of helpers and onlookers accompanied her out of the camp, led by Bố with a flashlight.

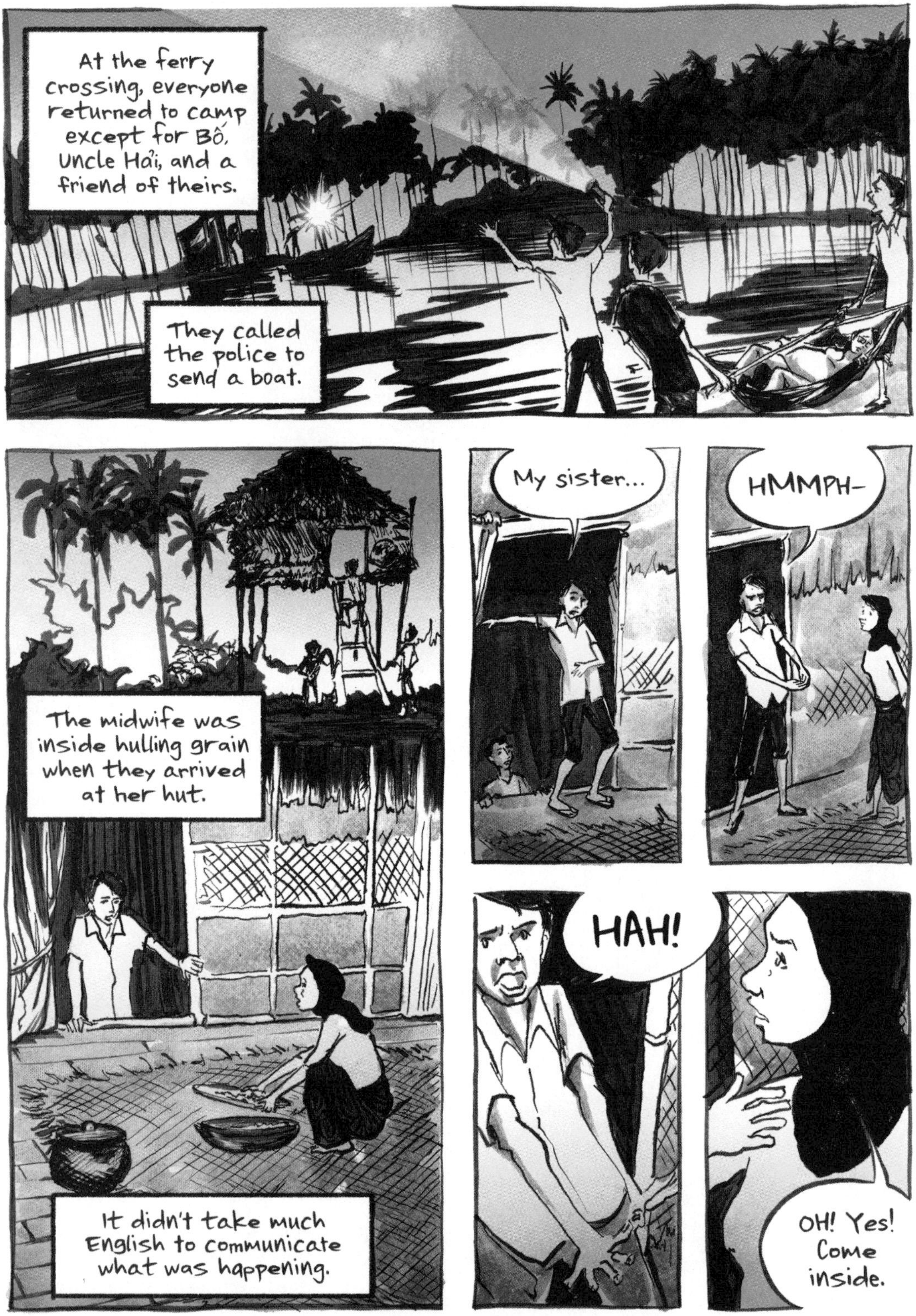

At the ferry crossing, everyone returned to camp except for Bố, Uncle Hải, and a friend of theirs.
They called the police to send a boat.
The midwife was inside hulling grain when they arrived at her hut.
It didn't take much English to communicate what was happening.
My sister...
HMMPH-
HAH!
OH! Yes! Come inside.

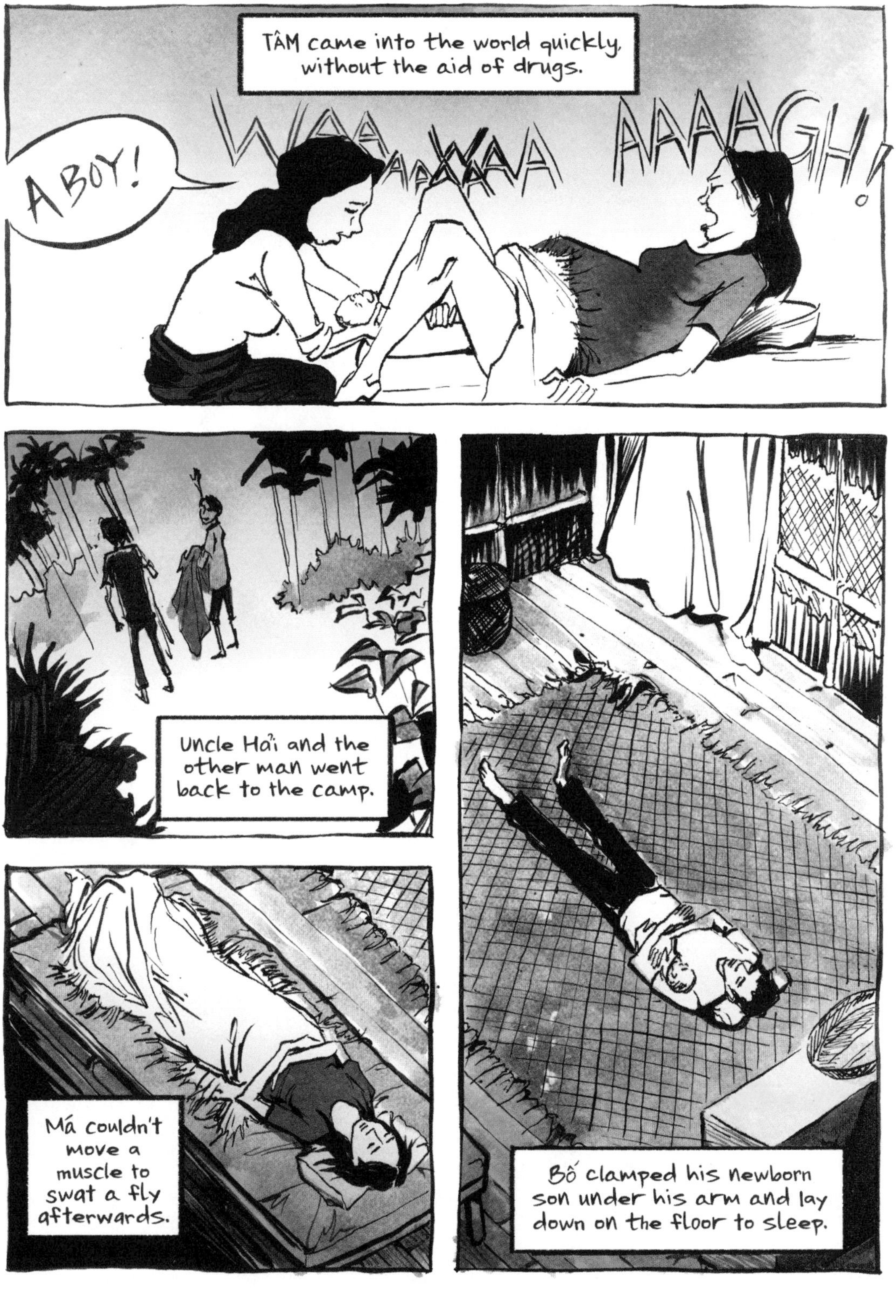
TÂM came into the world quickly, without the aid of drugs.
A BOY!
WAA WAAAAAA
AAAAGH!
Uncle Hải and the other man went back to the camp.
Bố clamped his newborn son under his arm and lay down on the floor to sleep.
Má couldn't move a muscle to swat a fly afterwards.

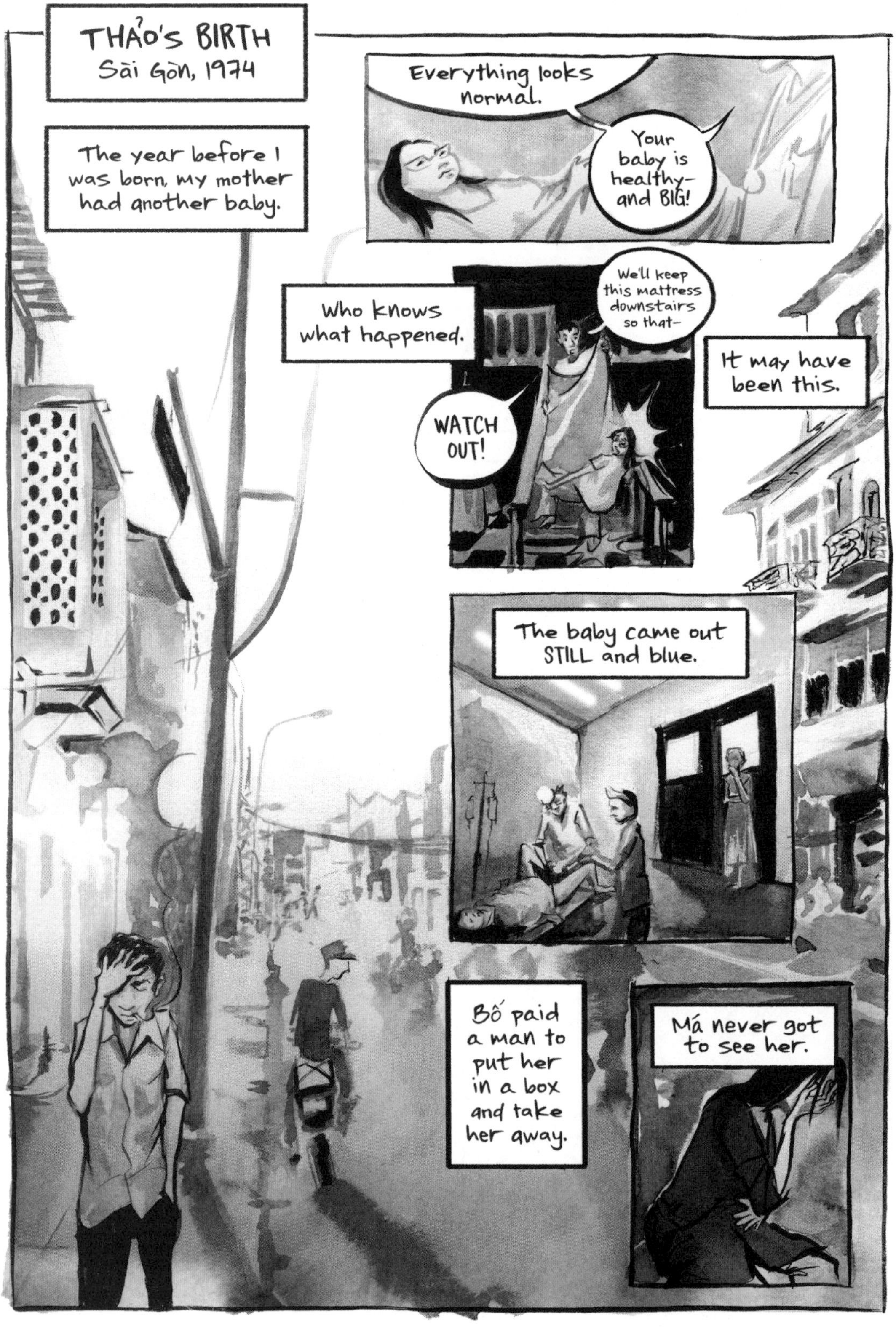
THẢO'S BIRTH
Sài Gòn, 1974
The year before I was born, my mother had another baby.
Everything looks normal.
Your baby is healthy- and BIG!
Who knows what happened.
We'll keep this mattress downstairs so that-
WATCH OUT!
It may have been this.
The baby came out STILL and blue.
Bố paid a man to put her in a box and take her away.
Má never got to see her.

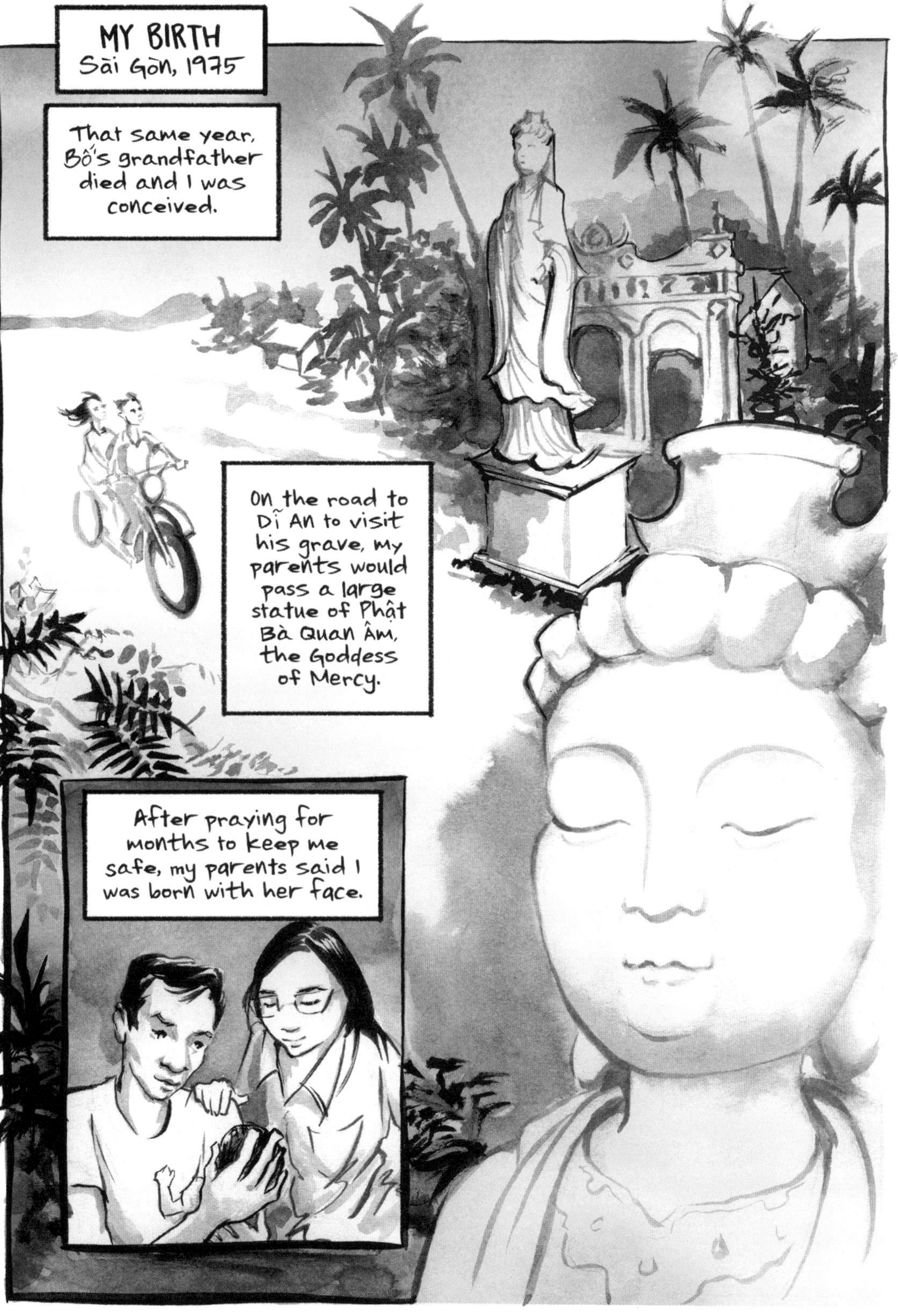
MY BIRTH
Sài Gòn, 1975
That same year, Bố's grandfather died and I was conceived.
On the road to Dĩ An to visit his grave, my parents would pass a large statue of Phật Bà Quan Âm, the Goddess of Mercy.
After praying for months to keep me safe, my parents said I was born with her face.

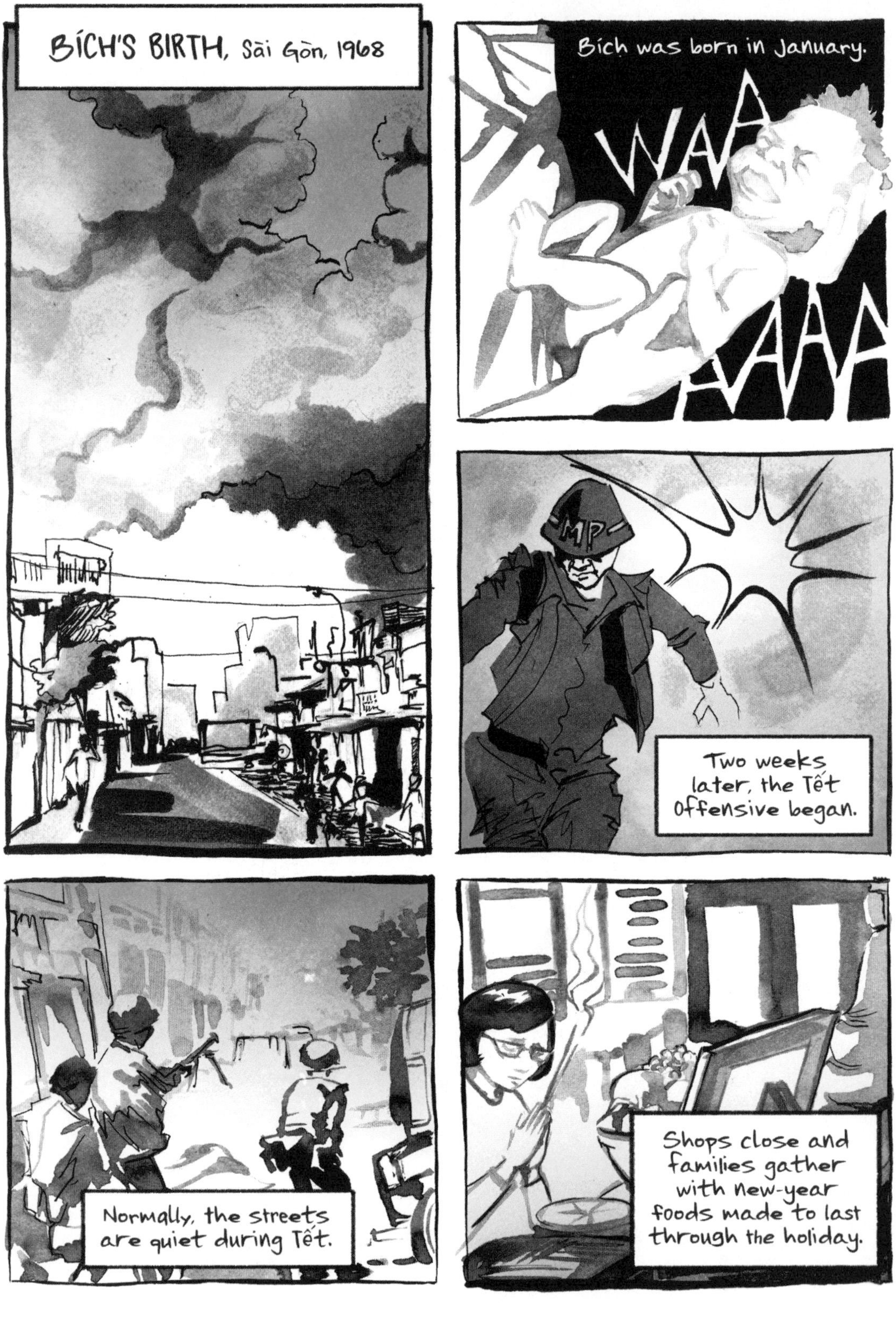
BÍCH'S BIRTH, Sài Gòn, 1968
Bích was born in January.
WAA AAAA
MP
Two weeks later, the Tết Offensive began.
Normally, the streets are quiet during Tết.
Shops close and families gather with new-year foods made to last through the holiday.

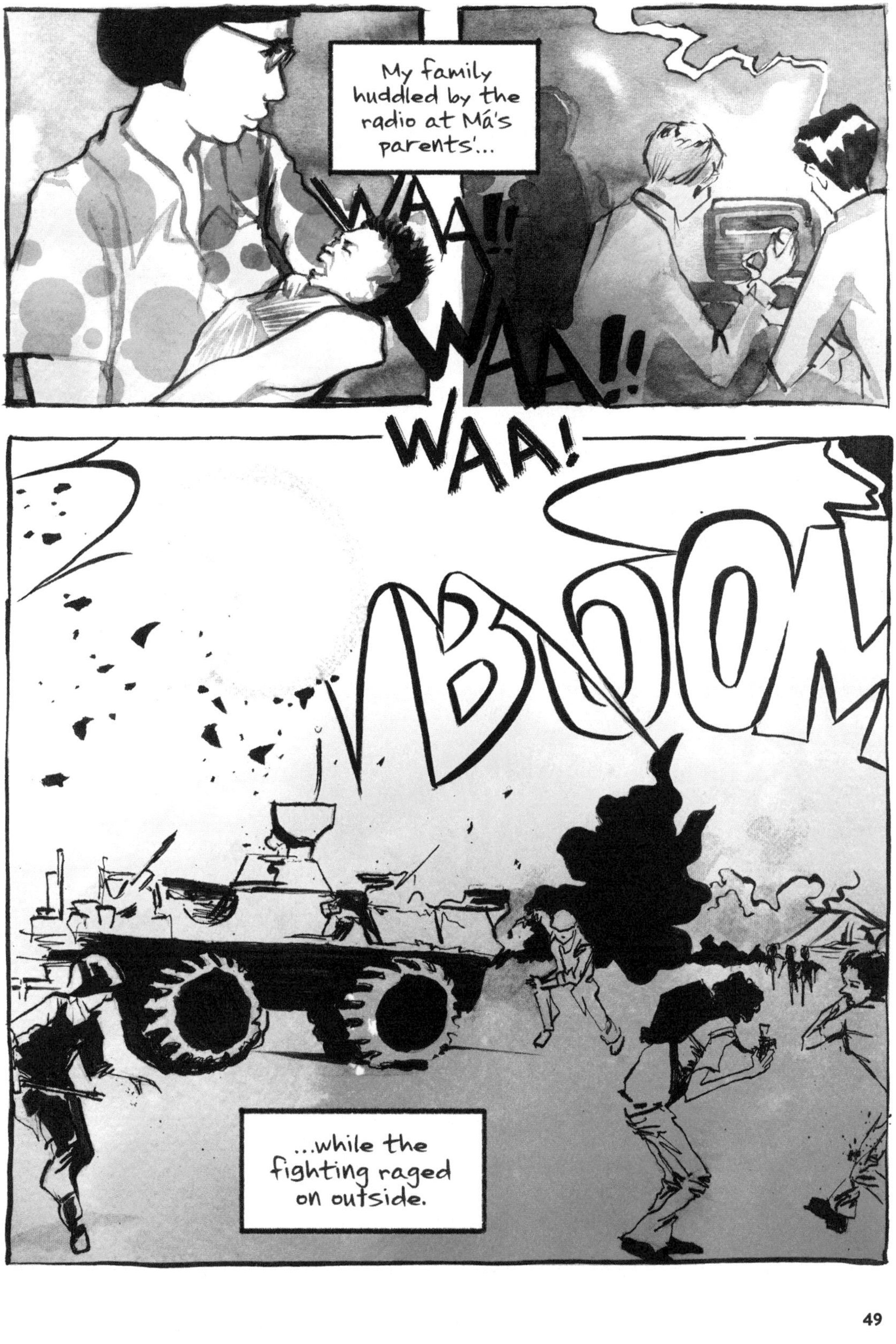

My family huddled by the radio at Má's parents'...
WAA!!
WAA!!
WAA!
BOOOM
...while the fighting raged on outside.

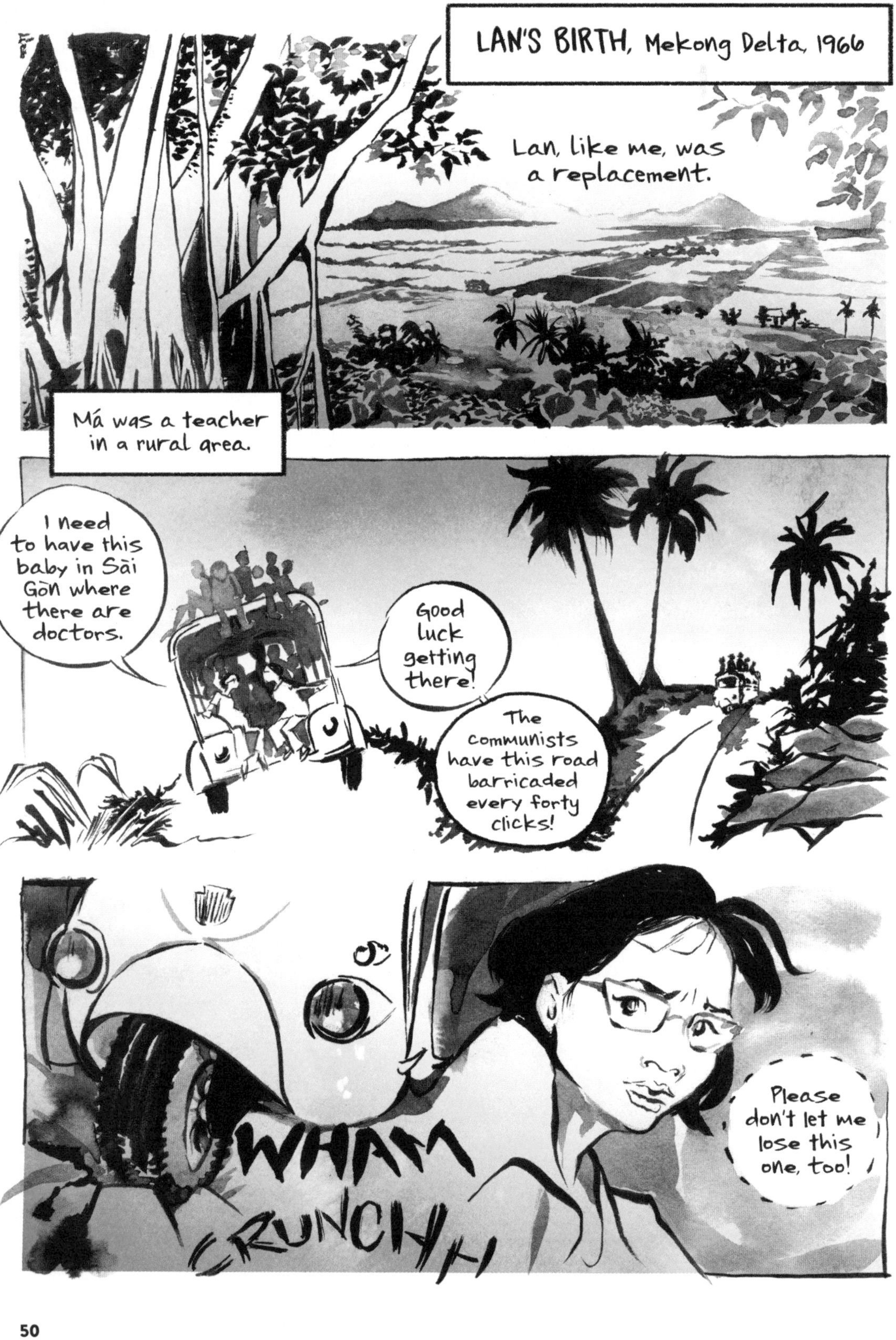
LAN'S BIRTH, Mekong Delta, 1966
Lan, like me, was a replacement.
Má was a teacher in a rural area.
I need to have this baby in Sài Gòn where there are doctors.
Good luck getting there!
The communists have this road barricaded every forty clicks!
WHAM
CRUNCHH
Please don't let me lose this one, too!

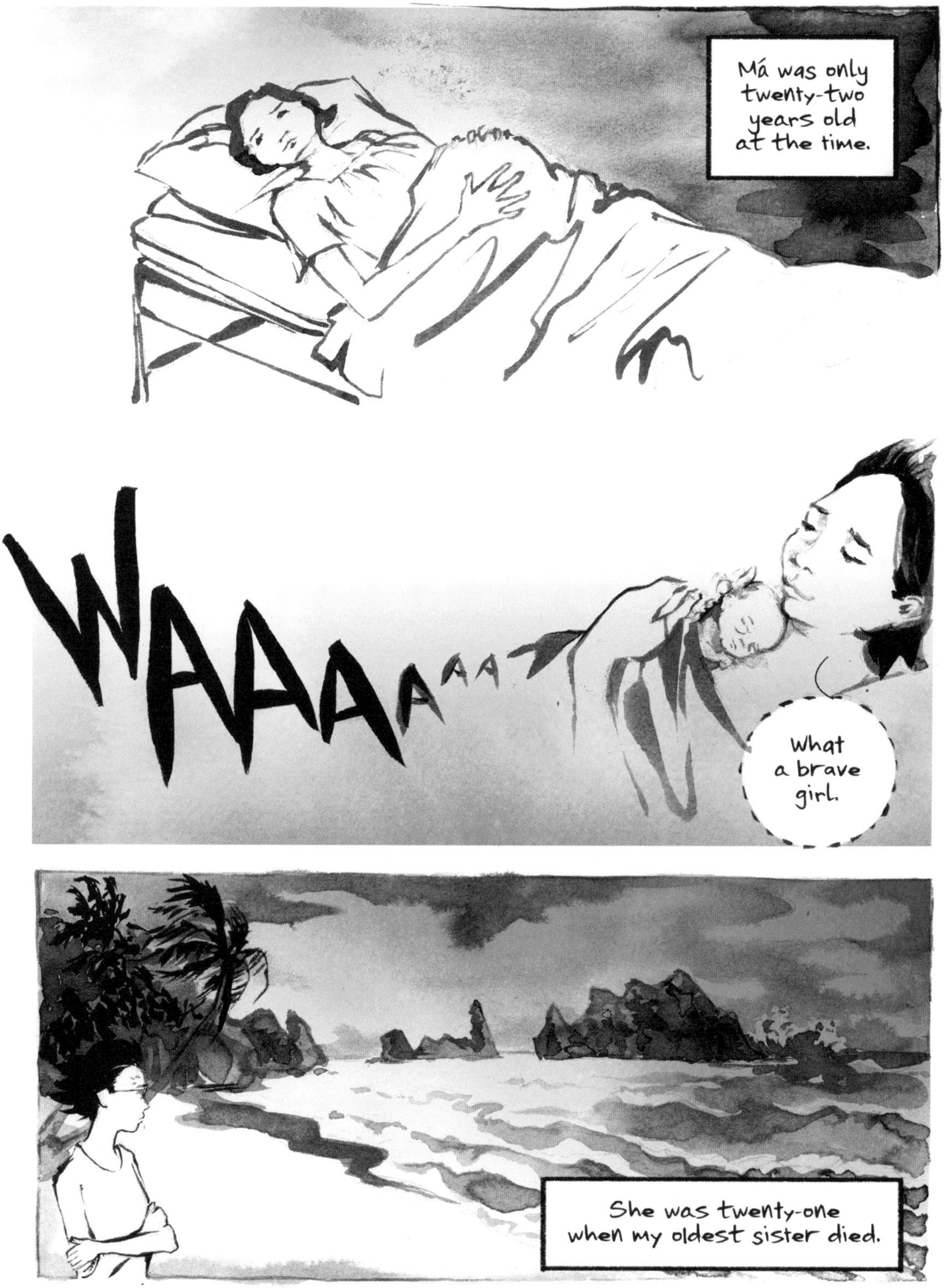
Má was only twenty-two years old at the time.
WAAAAAA
What a brave girl.
She was twenty-one when my oldest sister died.

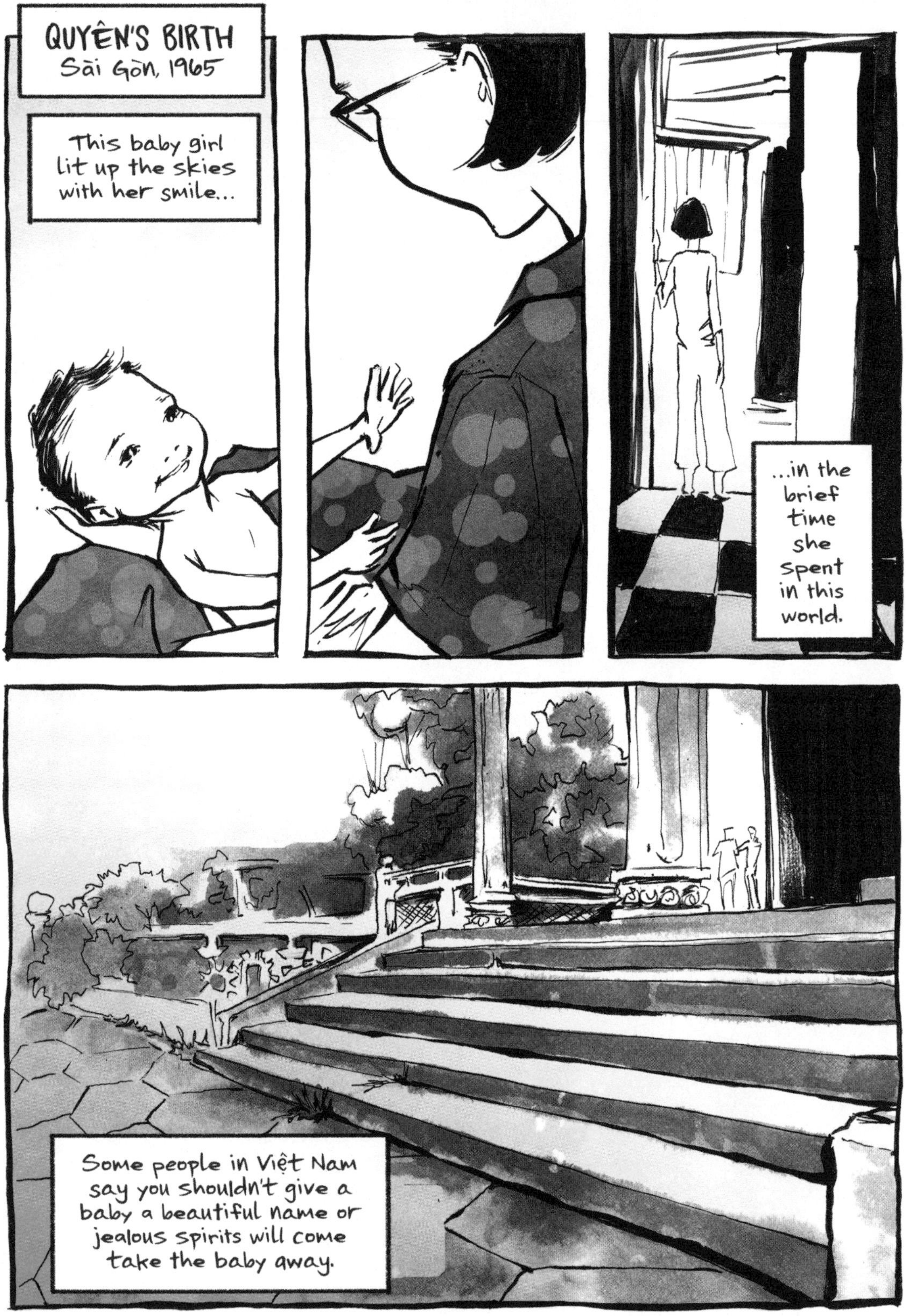
QUYÊN'S BIRTH
Sài Gòn, 1965
This baby girl lit up the skies with her smile...
...in the brief time she spent in this world.
Some people in Việt Nam say you shouldn't give a baby a beautiful name or jealous spirits will come take the baby away.

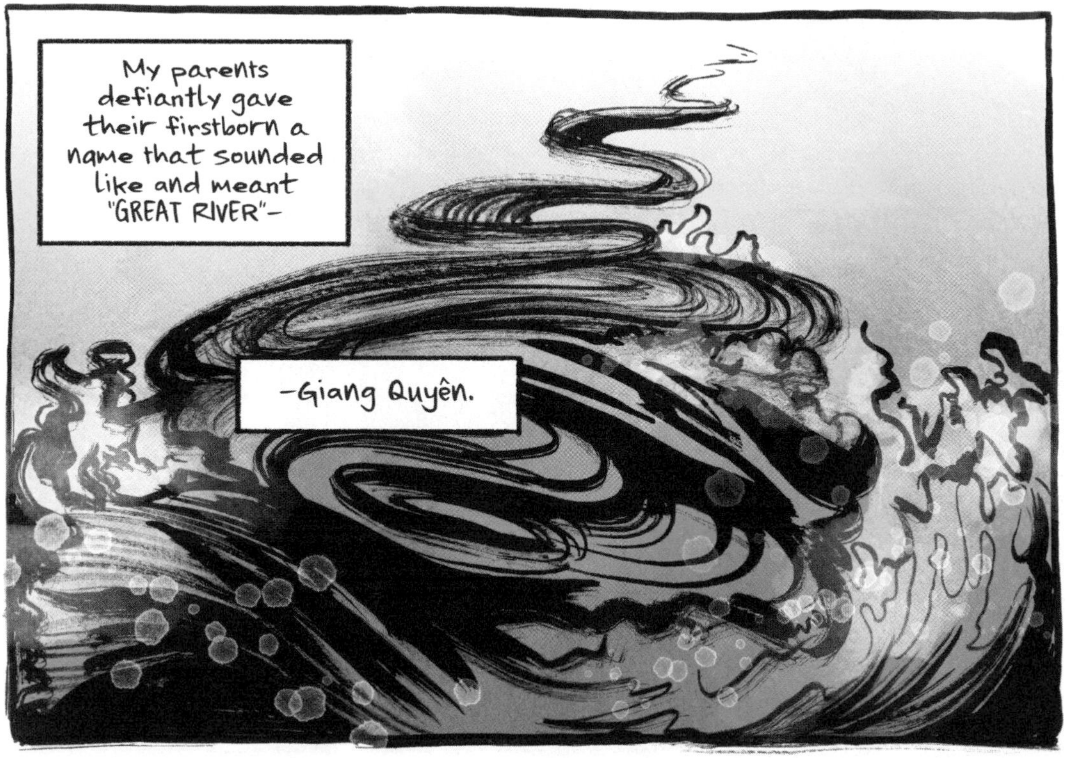
My parents defiantly gave their firstborn a name that sounded like and meant "GREAT RIVER"–
–Giang Quyên.

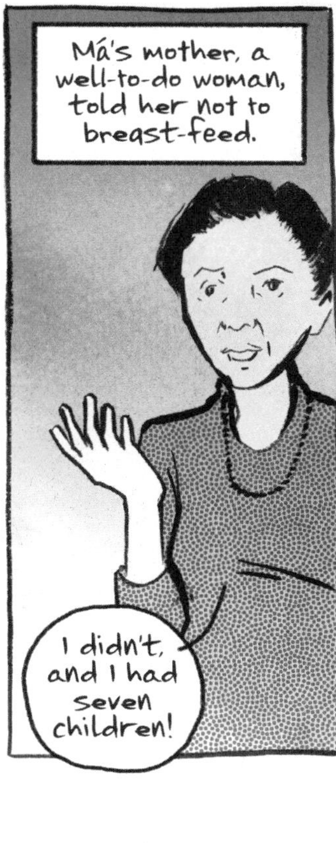
Má's mother, a well-to-do woman, told her not to breast-feed.
I didn't, and I had seven children!

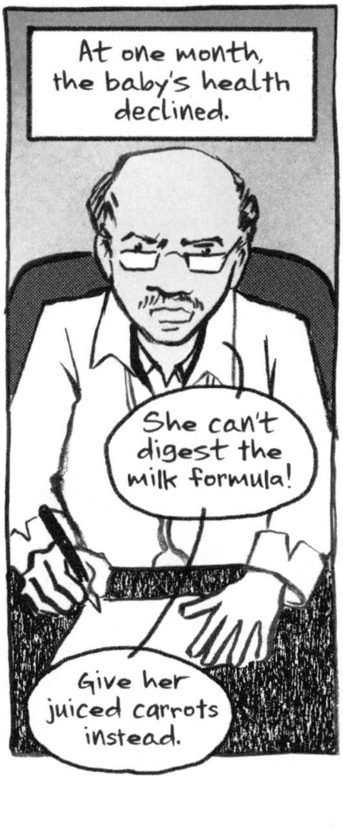
At one month, the baby's health declined.
She can't digest the milk formula!
Give her juiced carrots instead.

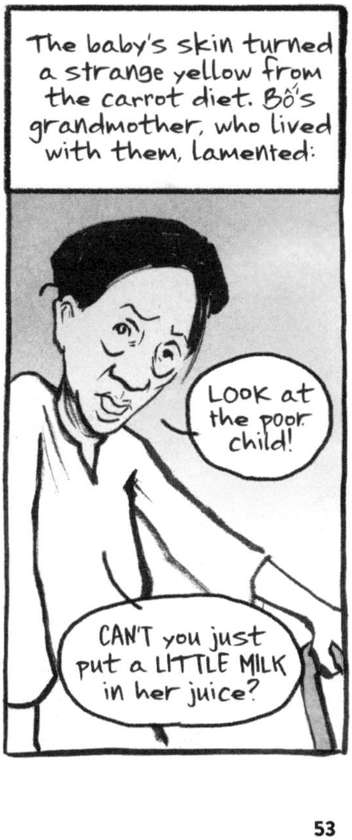
The baby's skin turned a strange yellow from the carrot diet. Bố's grandmother, who lived with them, lamented:
LOOK at the poor child!
CAN'T you just put a LITTLE MILK in her juice?

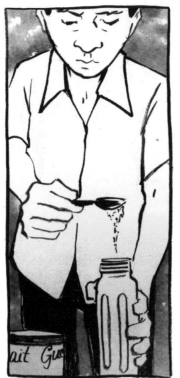

A little while later, the baby got sick again.

PLEASE!

We need a DOCTOR!

You'll have to wait.

We have our hands full here.

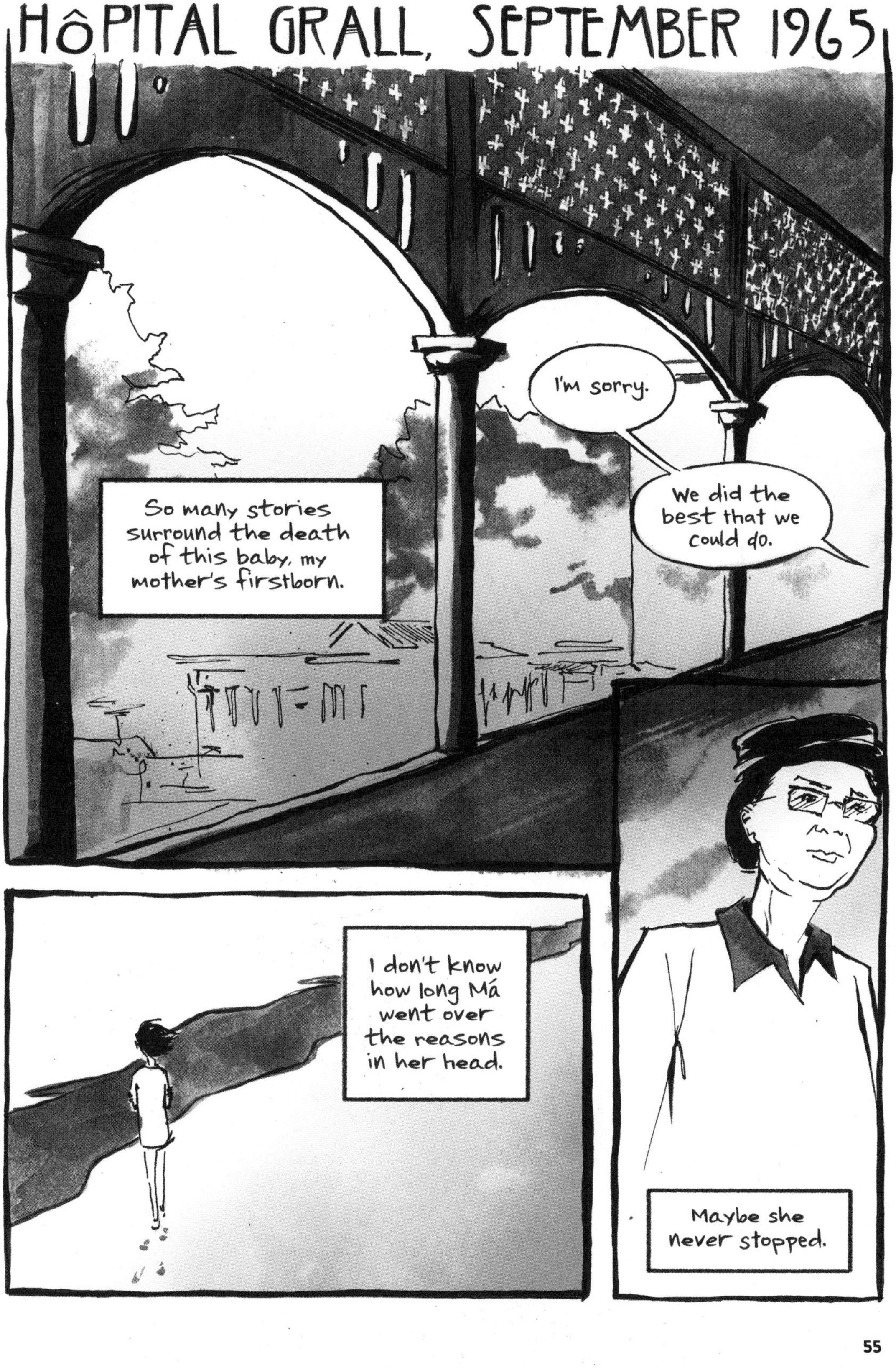

HÔPITAL GRALL, SEPTEMBER 1965
So many stories surround the death of this baby, my mother's firstborn.
I'm sorry.
We did the best that we could do.
I don't know how long Má went over the reasons in her head.
Maybe she never stopped.

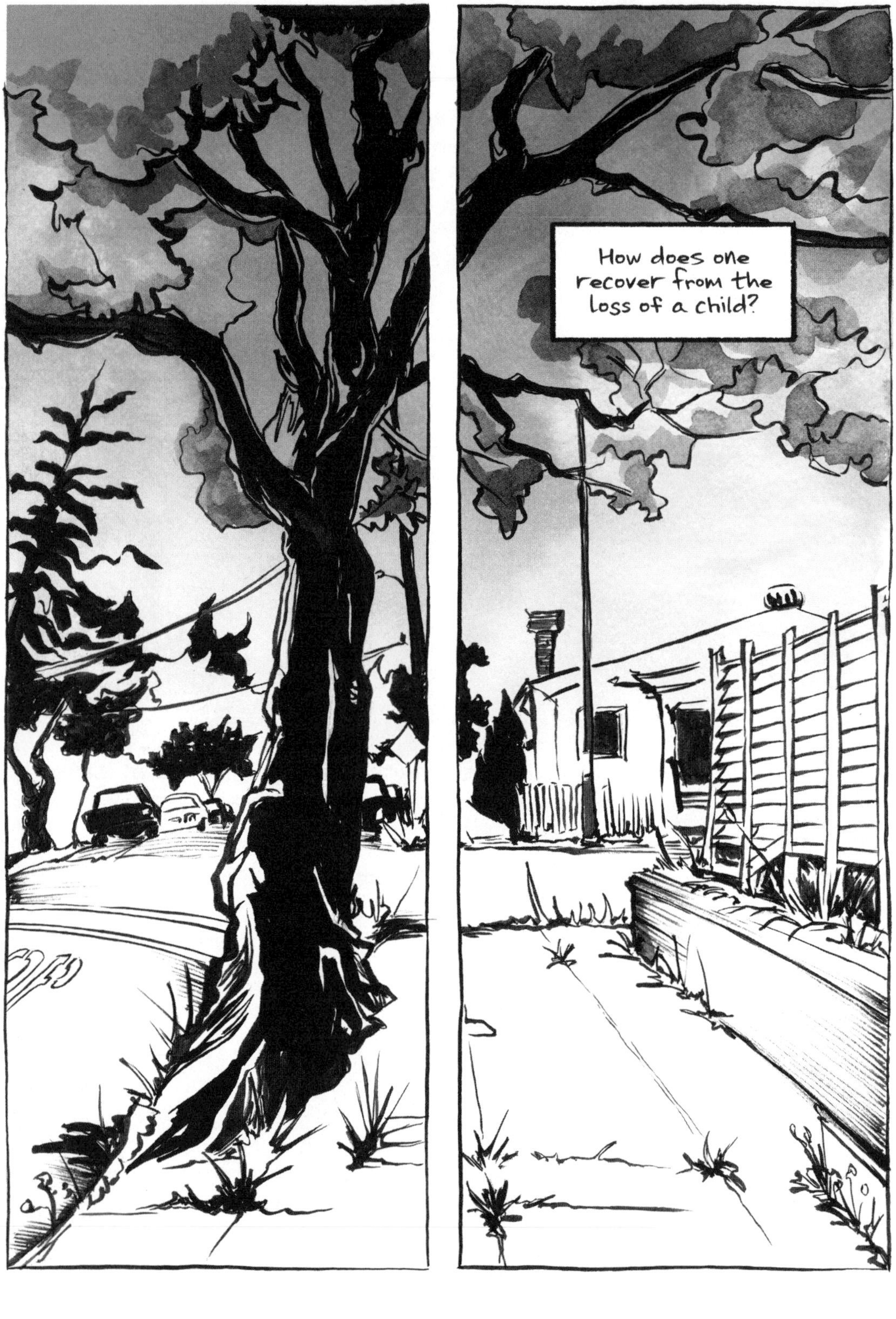
How does one recover from the loss of a child?

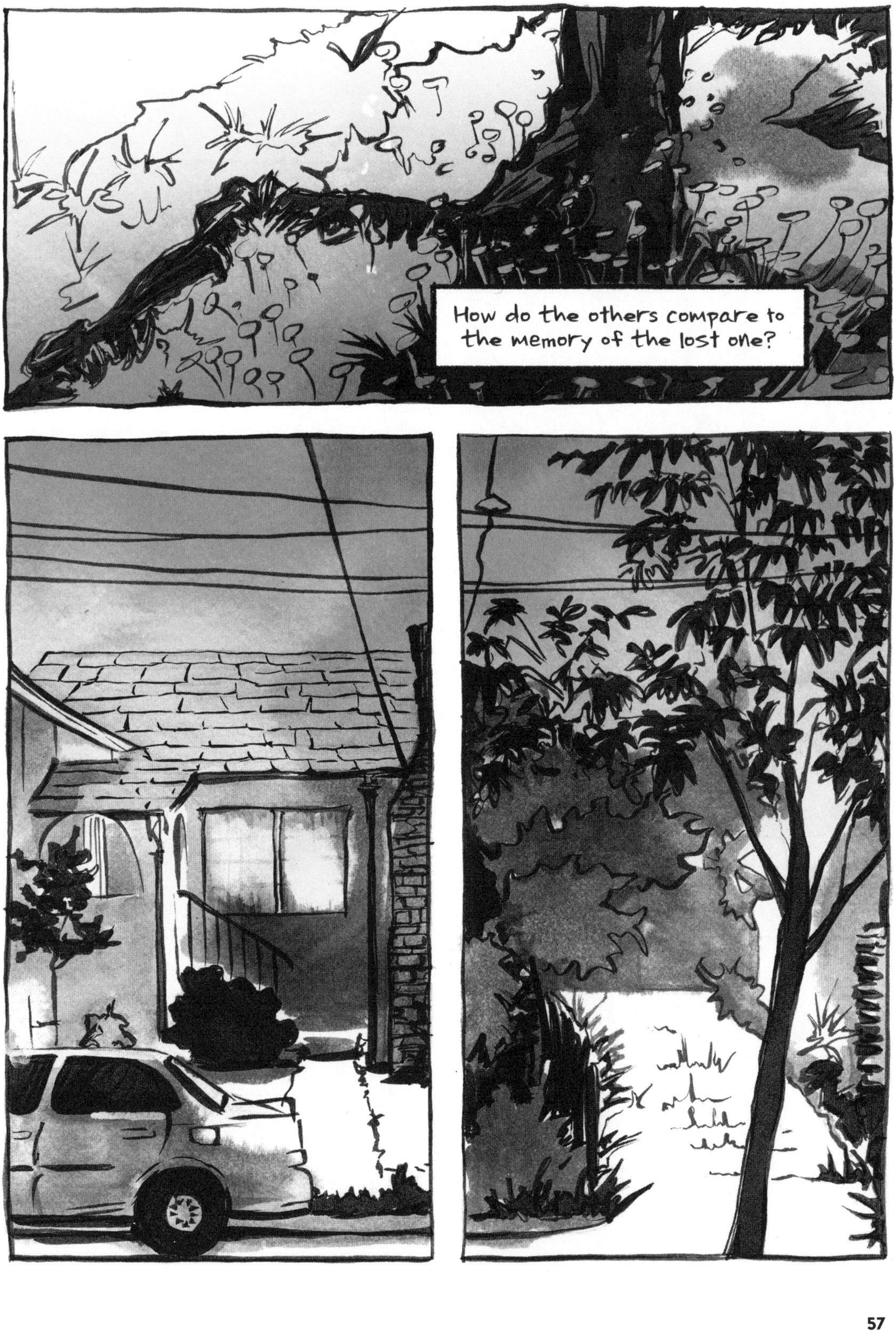
How do the others compare to the memory of the lost one?

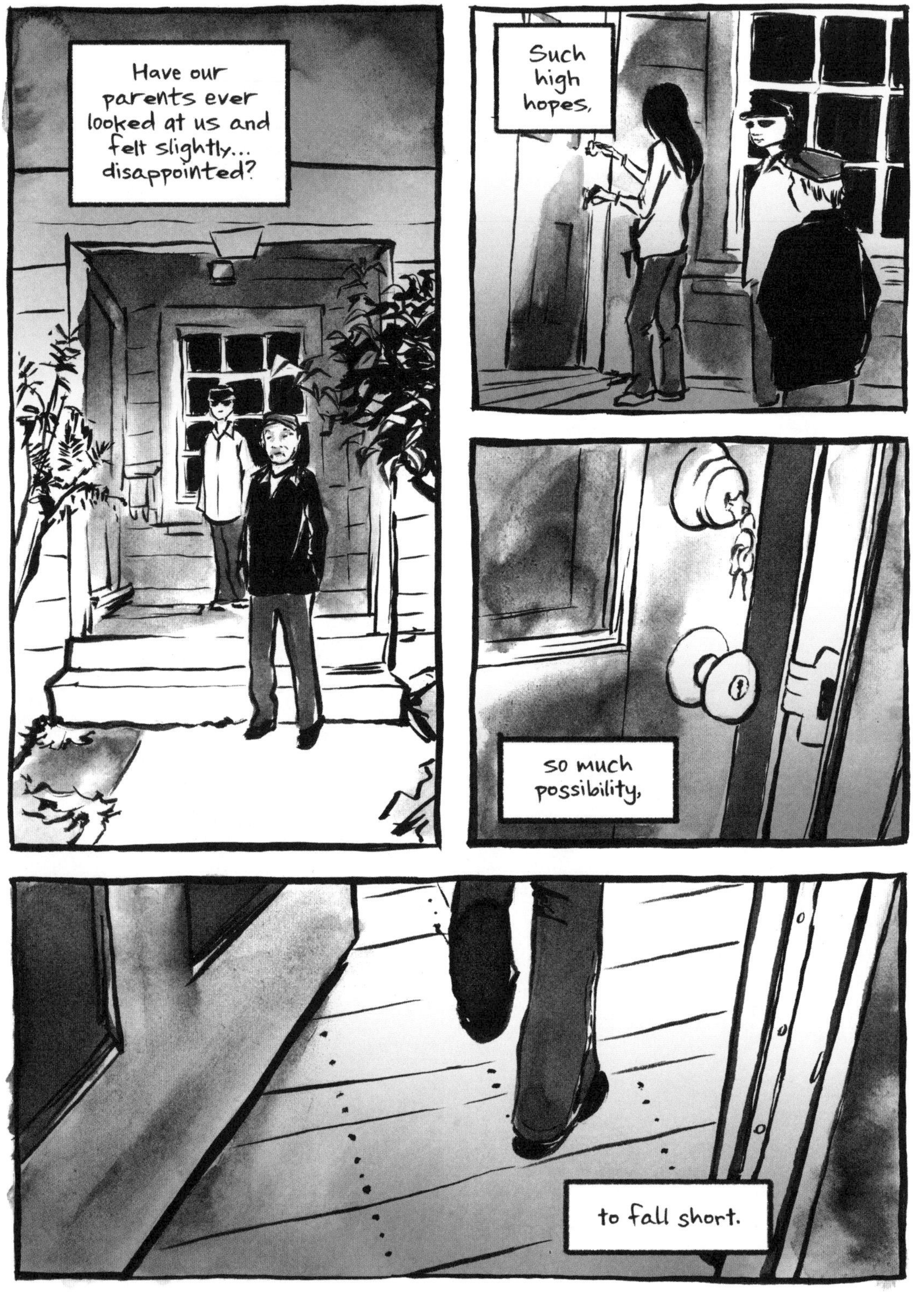

Have our parents ever looked at us and felt slightly... disappointed?
Such high hopes,
so much possibility,
to fall short.

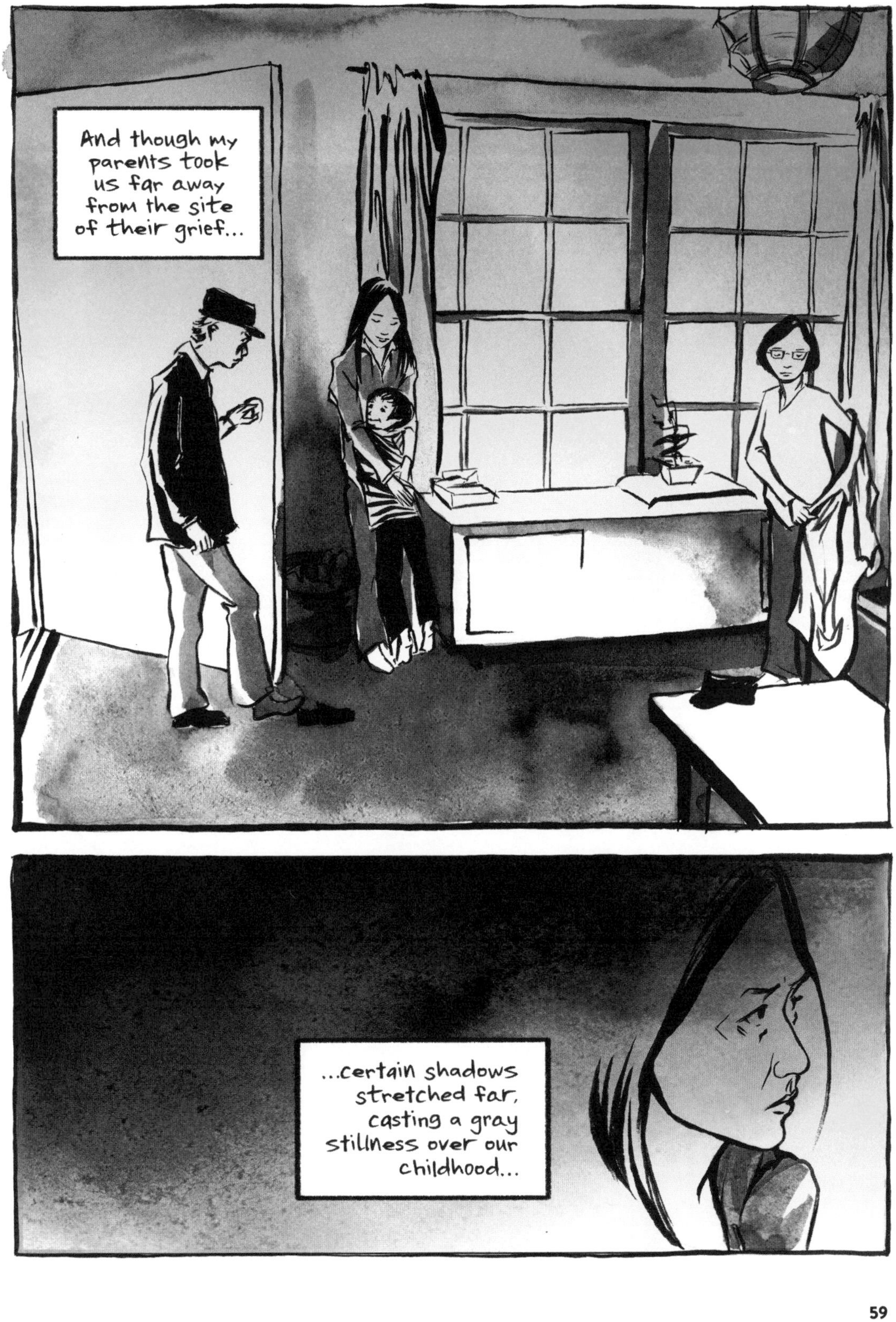
And though my parents took us far away from the site of their grief...
...certain shadows stretched far, casting a gray stillness over our childhood...

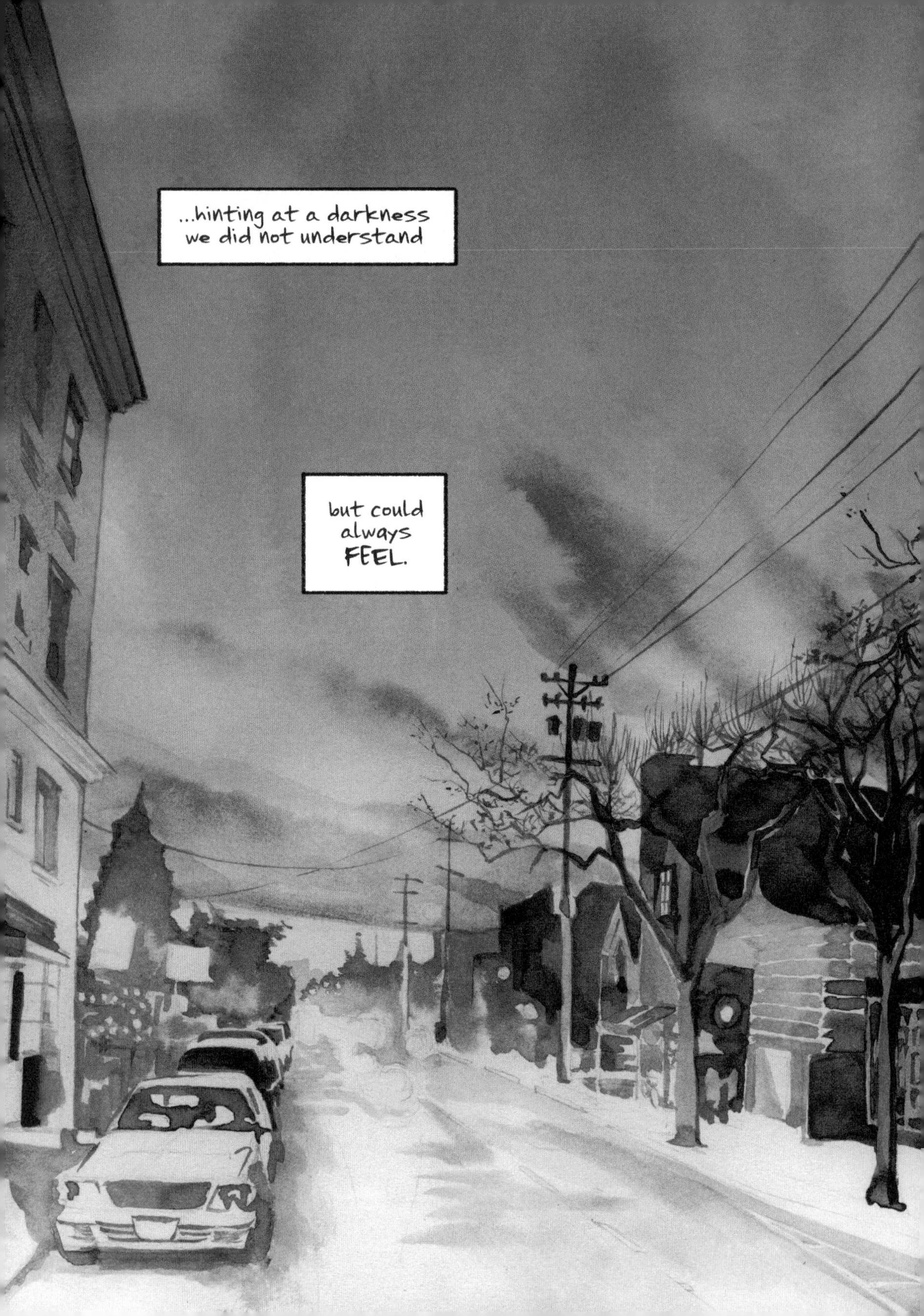
...hinting at a darkness we did not understand
but could always FEEL.

CHAPTER 3

HOME, THE HOLDING PEN

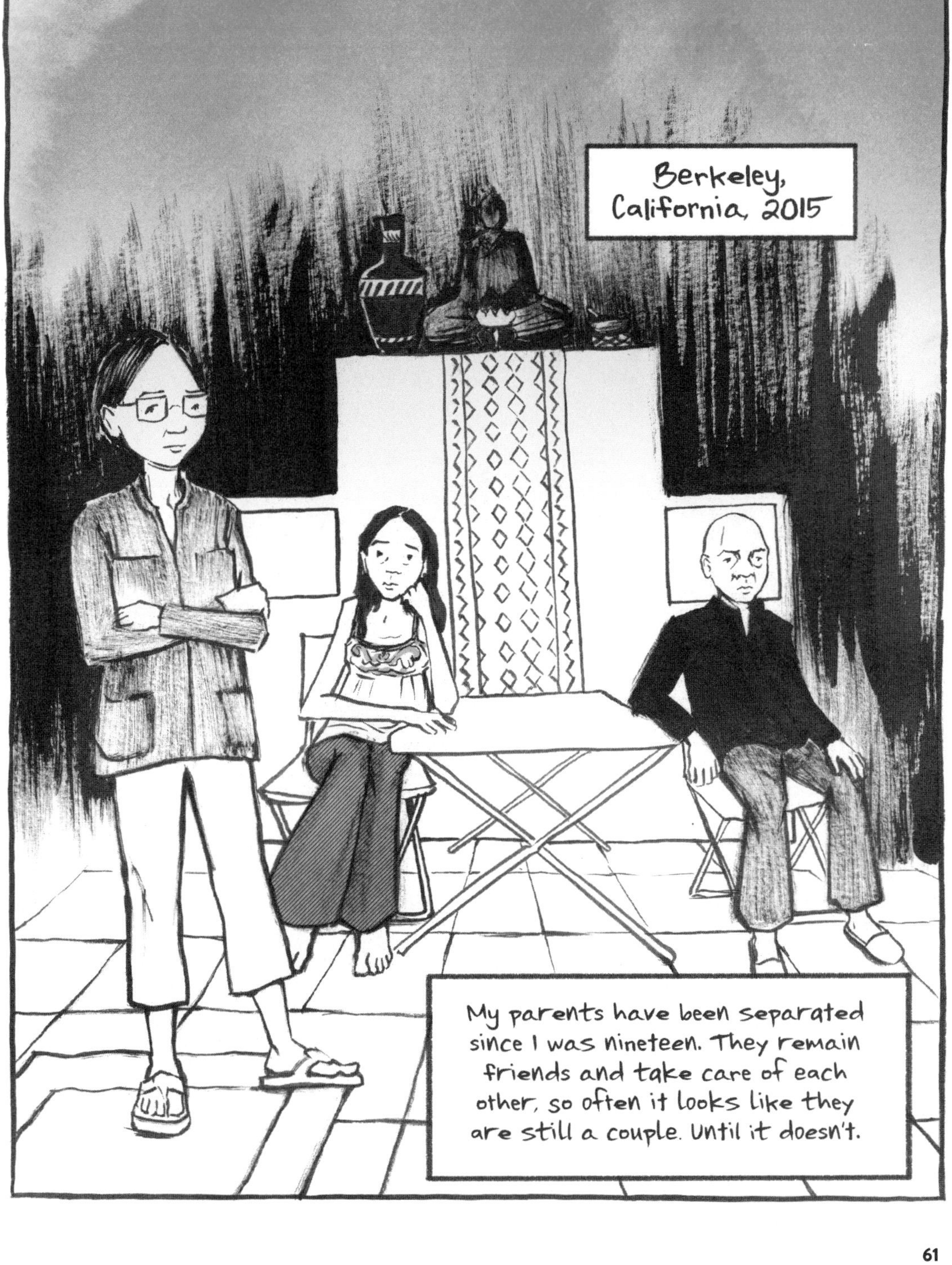
Berkeley, California, 2015
My parents have been separated since I was nineteen. They remain friends and take care of each other, so often it looks like they are still a couple. Until it doesn't.

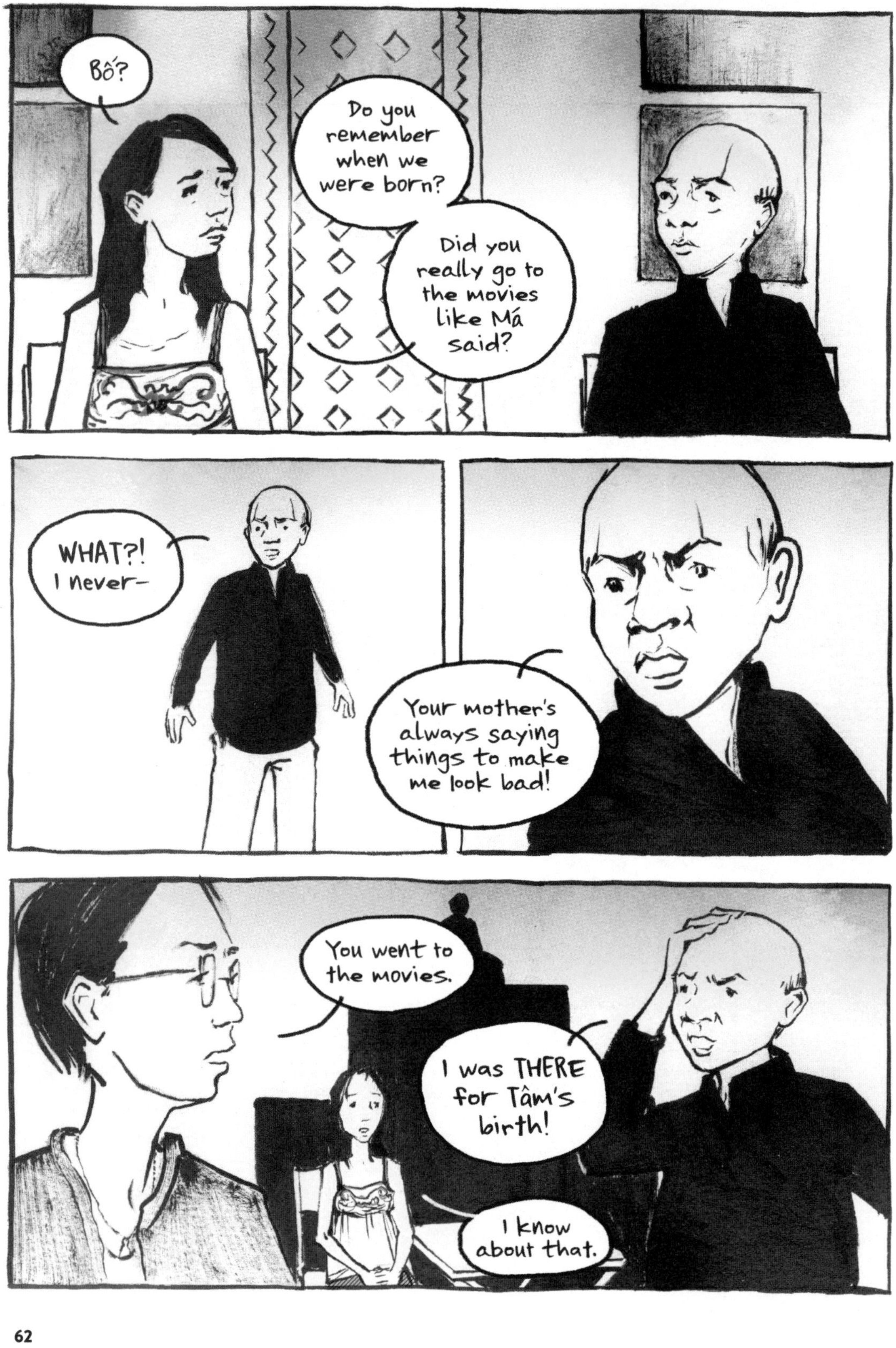
Bố?
Do you remember when we were born?
Did you really go to the movies like Má said?
WHAT?! I never–
Your mother's always saying things to make me look bad!
You went to the movies.
I was THERE for Tâm's birth!
I know about that.

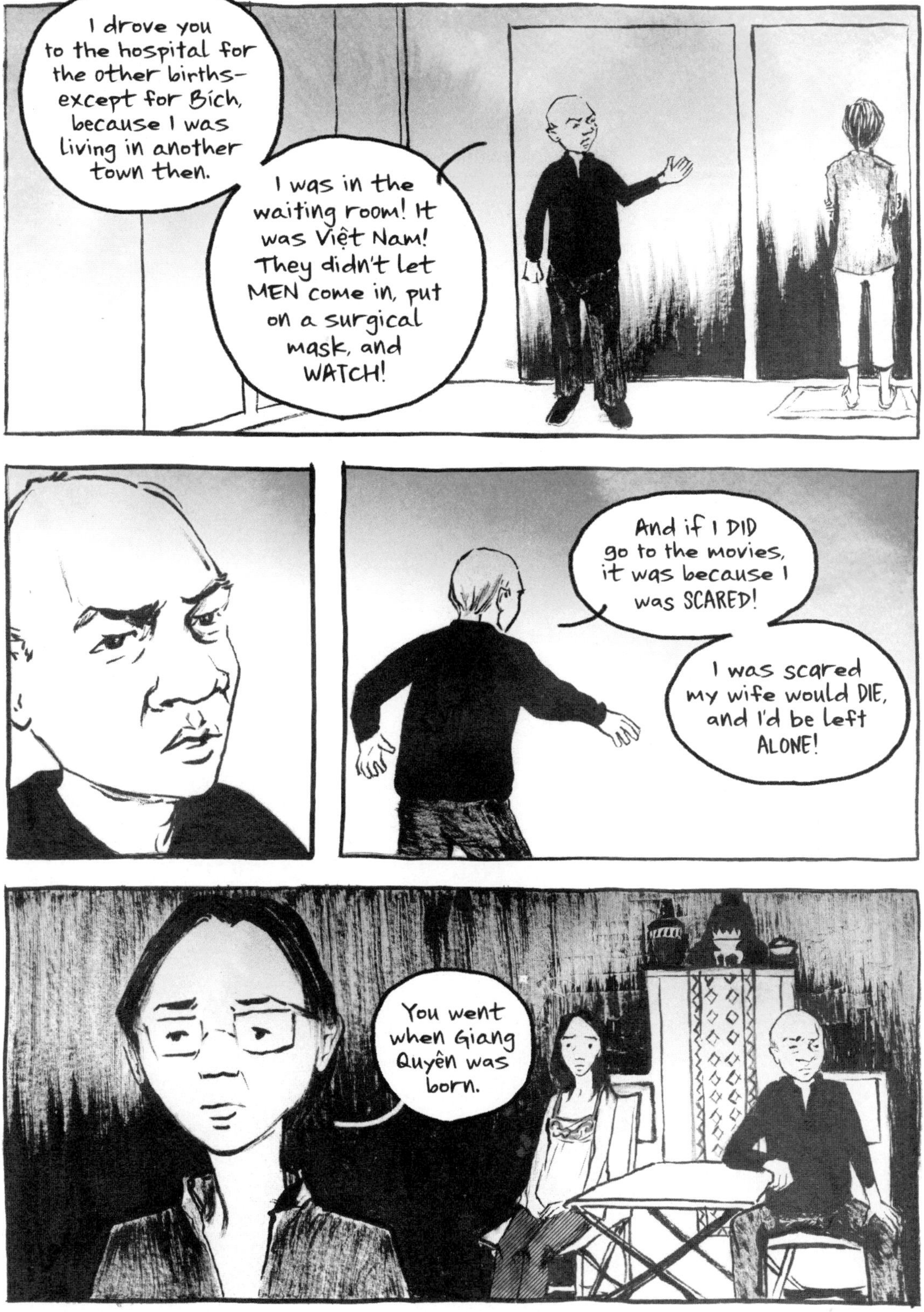
I drove you to the hospital for the other births- except for Bích, because I was living in another town then.
I was in the waiting room! It was Việt Nam! They didn't let MEN come in, put on a surgical mask, and WATCH!
And if I DID go to the movies, it was because I was SCARED!
I was scared my wife would DIE, and I'd be left ALONE!
You went when Giang Quyên was born.

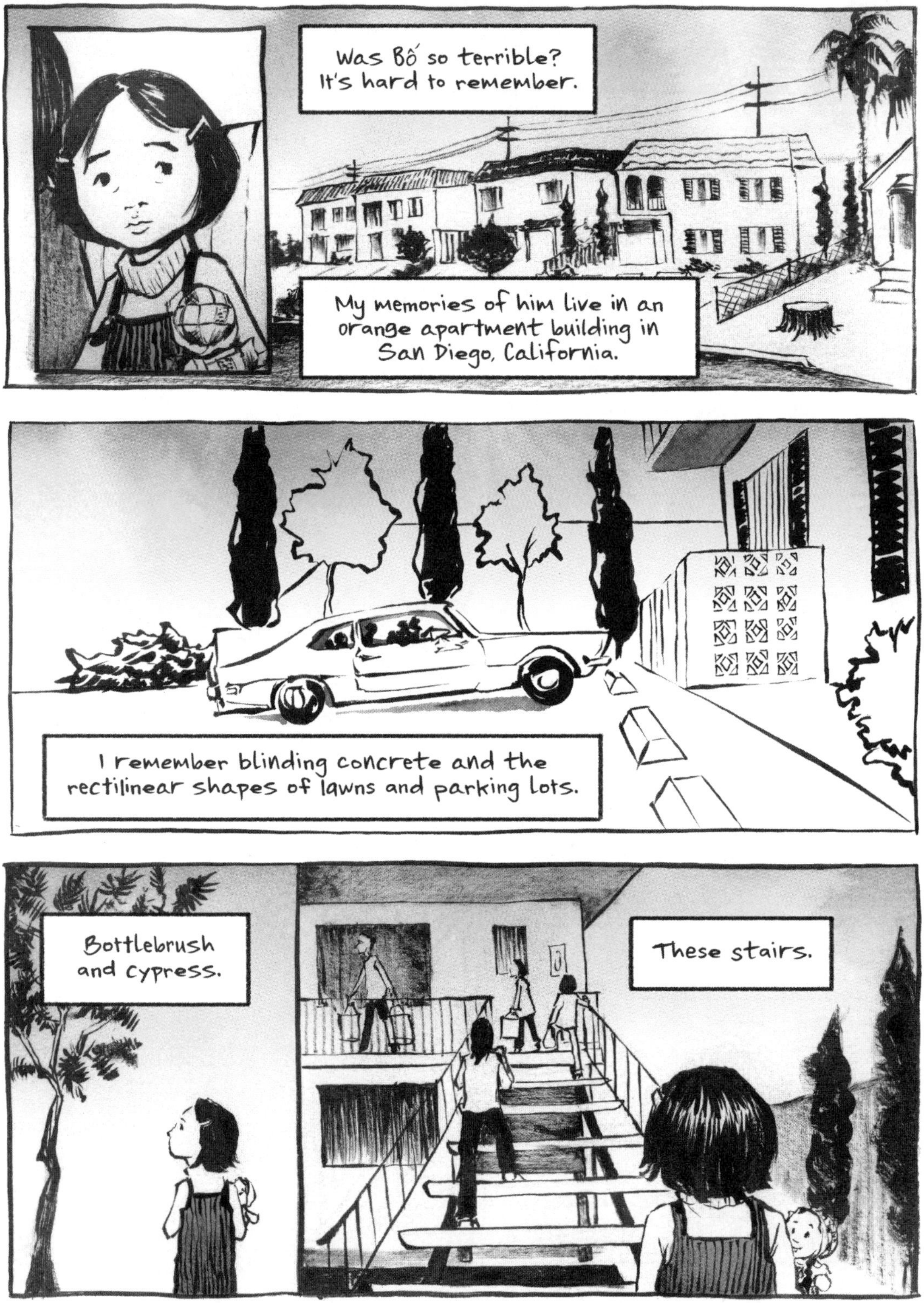
Was Bố so terrible? It's hard to remember.
My memories of him live in an orange apartment building in San Diego, California.
I remember blinding concrete and the rectilinear shapes of lawns and parking lots.
Bottlebrush and cypress.
These stairs.

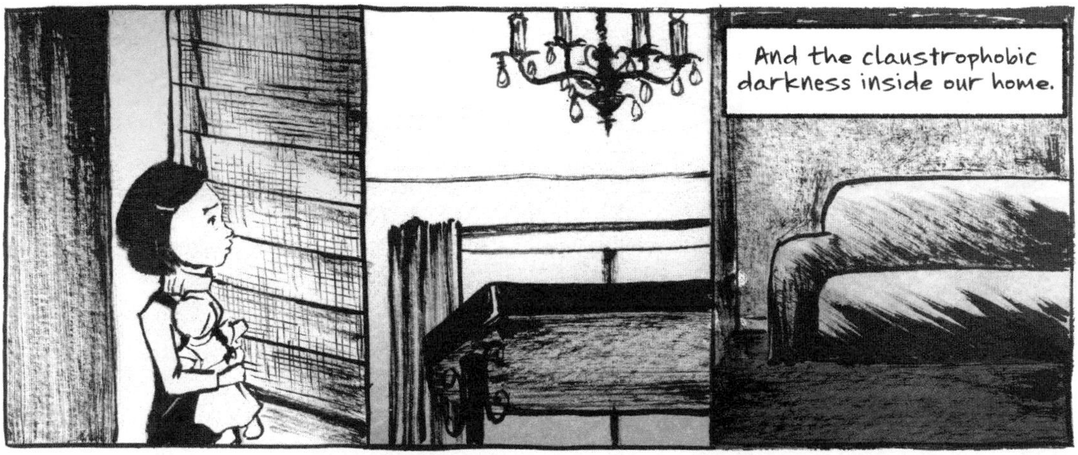
And the claustrophobic darkness inside our home.

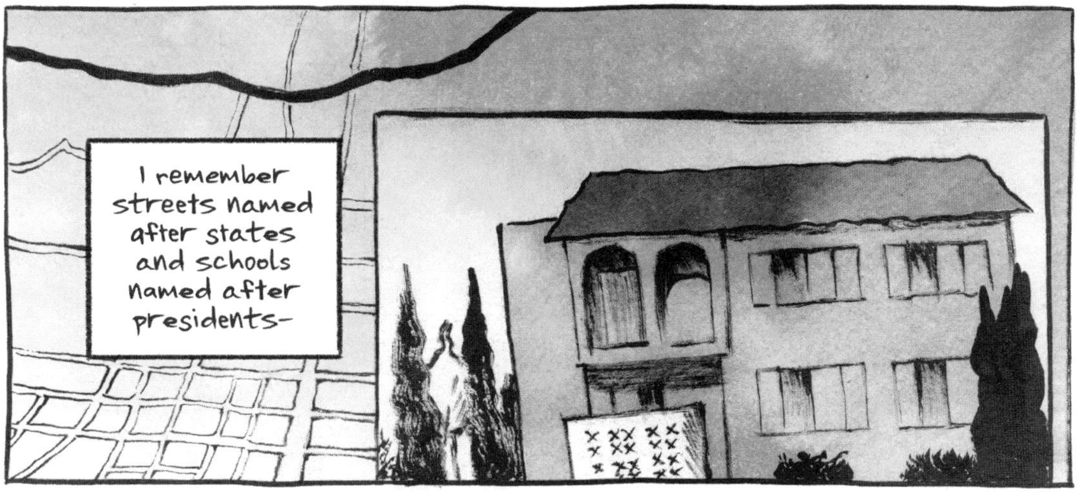
I remember streets named after states and schools named after presidents-

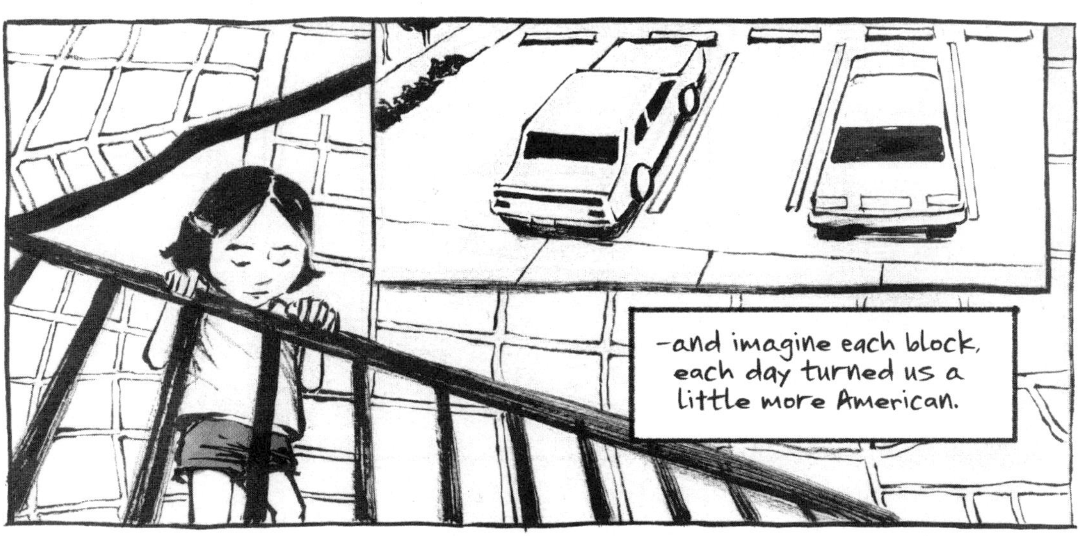
-and imagine each block, each day turned us a little more American.

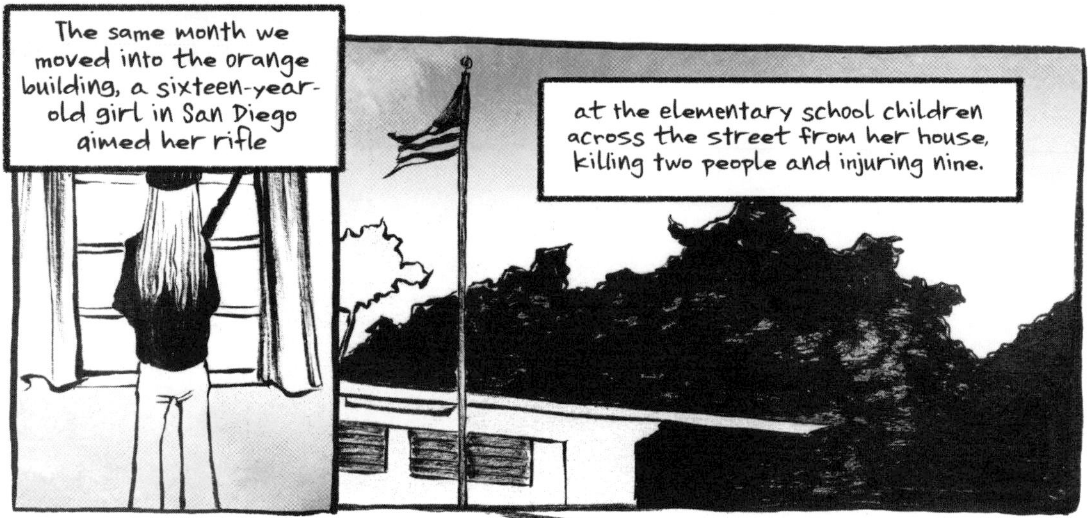
The same month we moved into the orange building, a sixteen-year-old girl in San Diego aimed her rifle
at the elementary school children across the street from her house, killing two people and injuring nine.

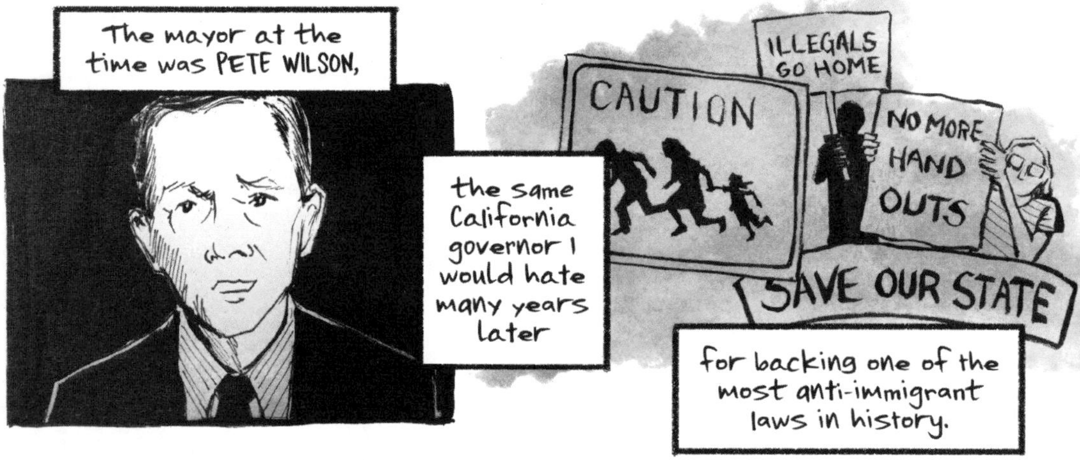
The mayor at the time was PETE WILSON,
the same California governor I would hate many years later
CAUTION
ILLEGALS GO HOME
NO MORE HAND OUTS
SAVE OUR STATE
for backing one of the most anti-immigrant laws in history.

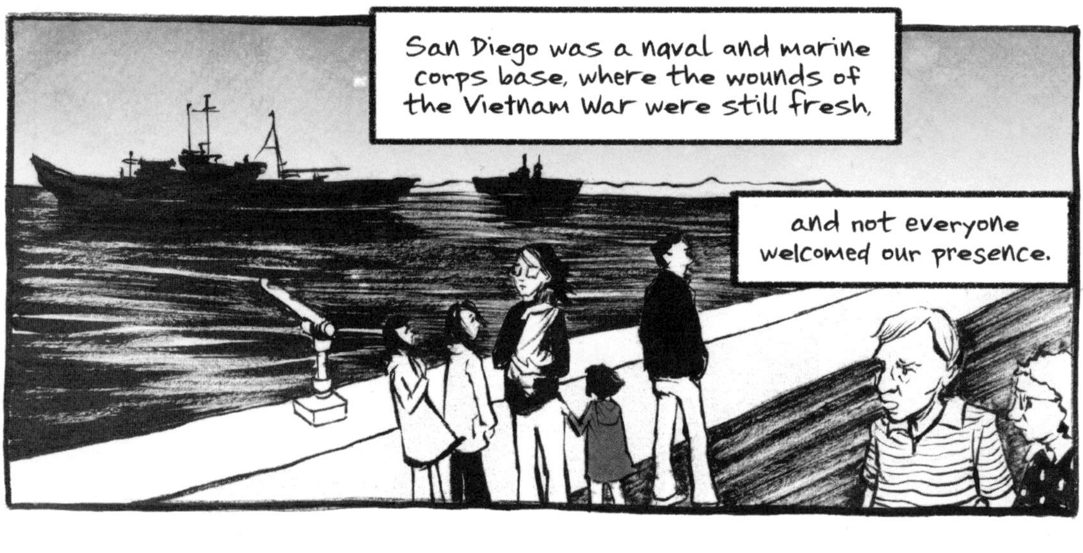
San Diego was a naval and marine corps base, where the wounds of the Vietnam War were still fresh,
and not everyone welcomed our presence.

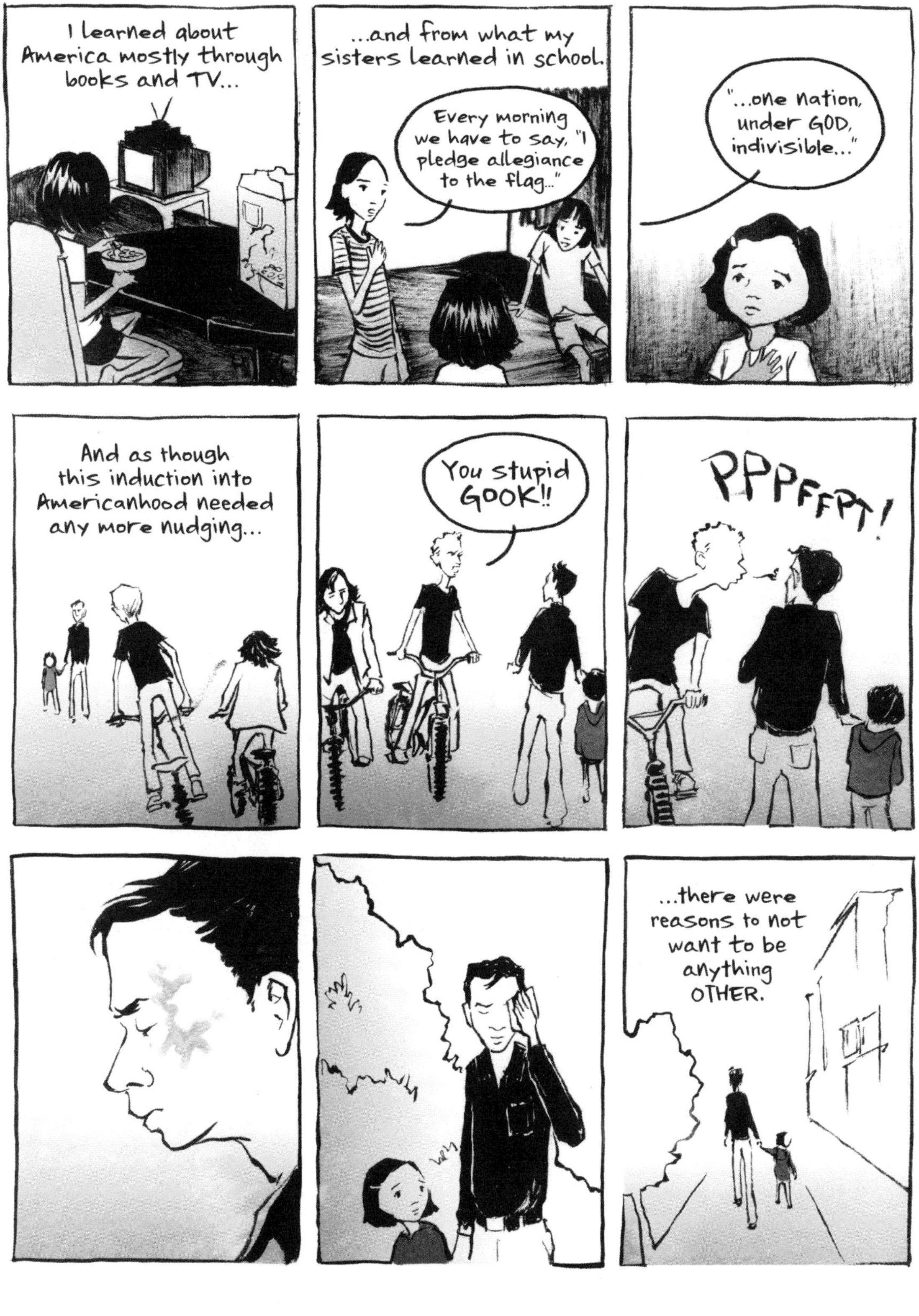
I learned about America mostly through books and TV...
...and from what my sisters learned in school.
Every morning we have to say, "I pledge allegiance to the flag..."
"...one nation, under GOD, indivisible..."
And as though this induction into Americanhood needed any more nudging...
You stupid GOOK!!
PPPFFPT!
...there were reasons to not want to be anything OTHER.

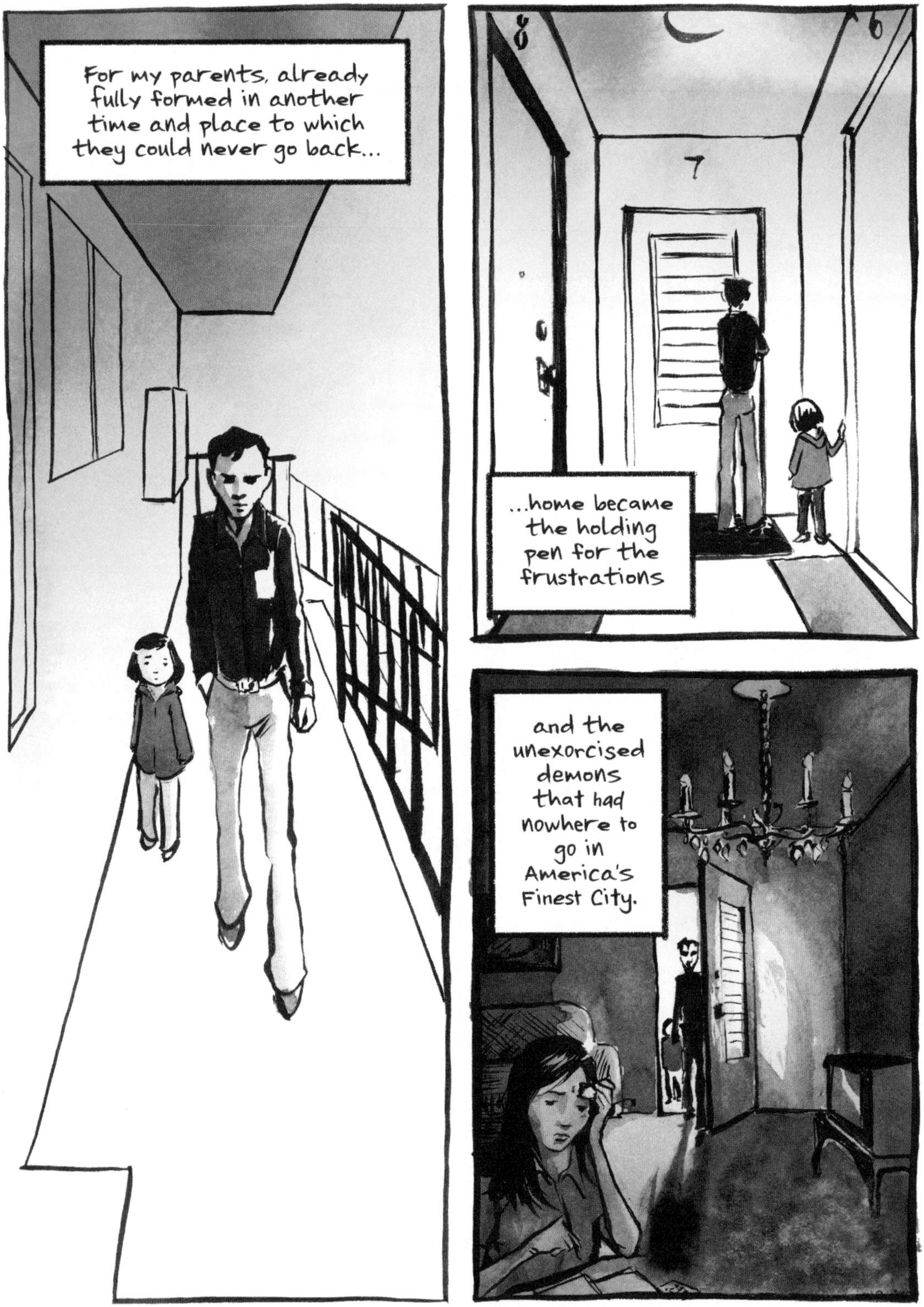
For my parents, already fully formed in another time and place to which they could never go back...
7
...home became the holding pen for the frustrations
and the unexorcised demons that had nowhere to go in America's Finest City.

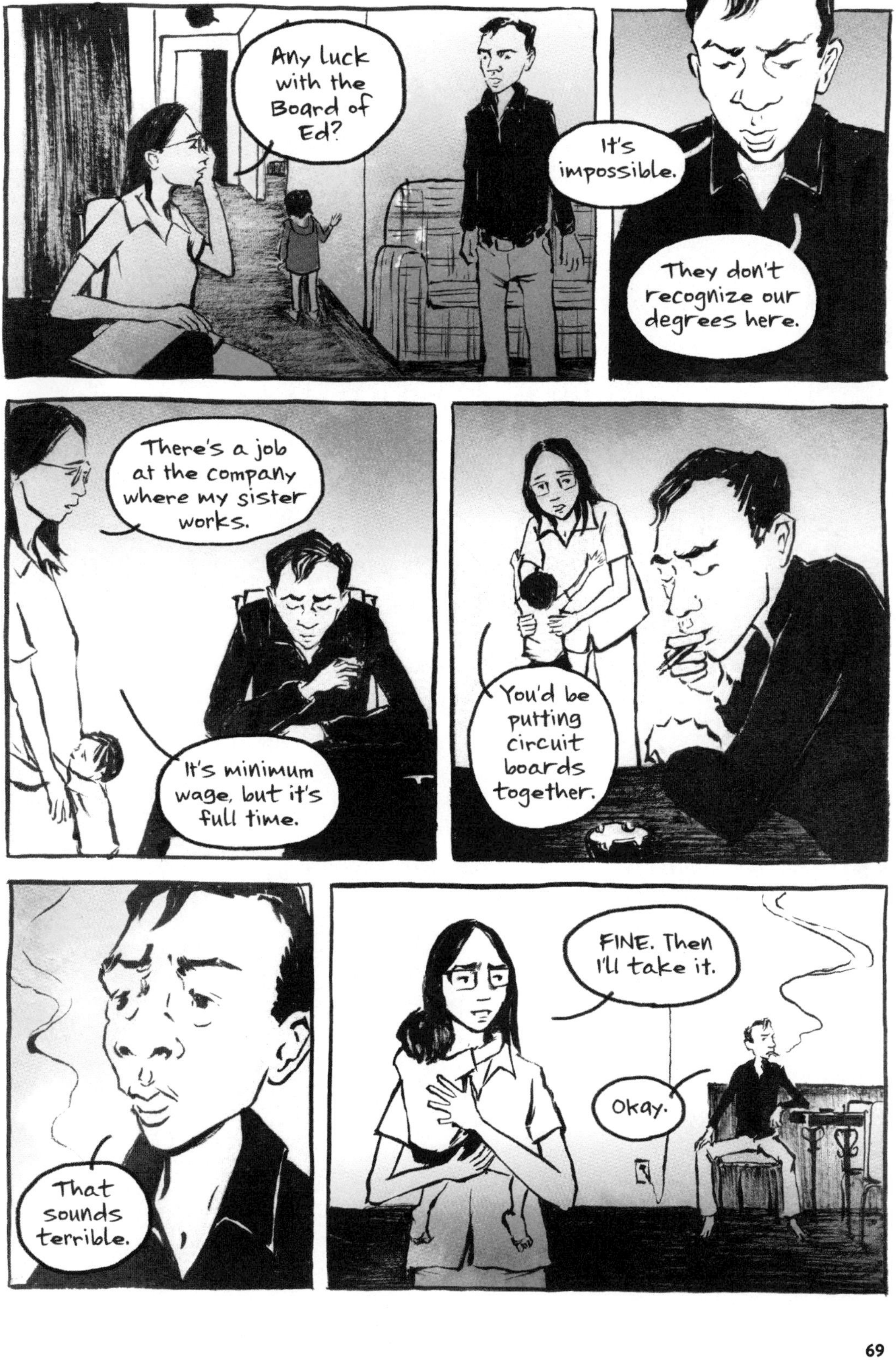
Any luck with the Board of Ed?
It's impossible.
They don't recognize our degrees here.
There's a job at the company where my sister works.
It's minimum wage, but it's full time.
You'd be putting circuit boards together.
That sounds terrible.
FINE. Then I'll take it.
Okay.

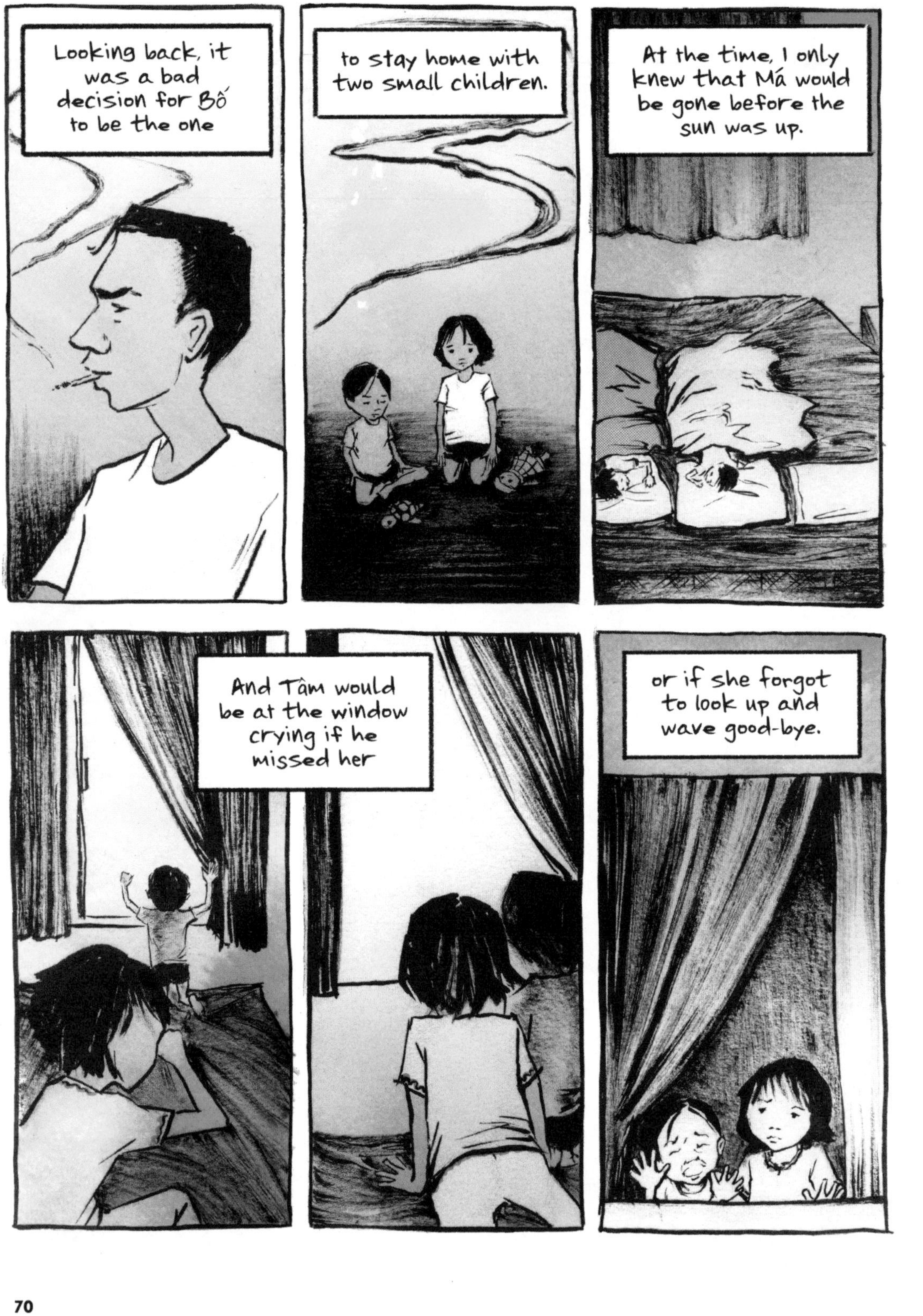
Looking back, it was a bad decision for Bố to be the one
to stay home with two small children.
At the time, I only knew that Má would be gone before the sun was up.
And Tâm would be at the window crying if he missed her
or if she forgot to look up and wave good-bye.

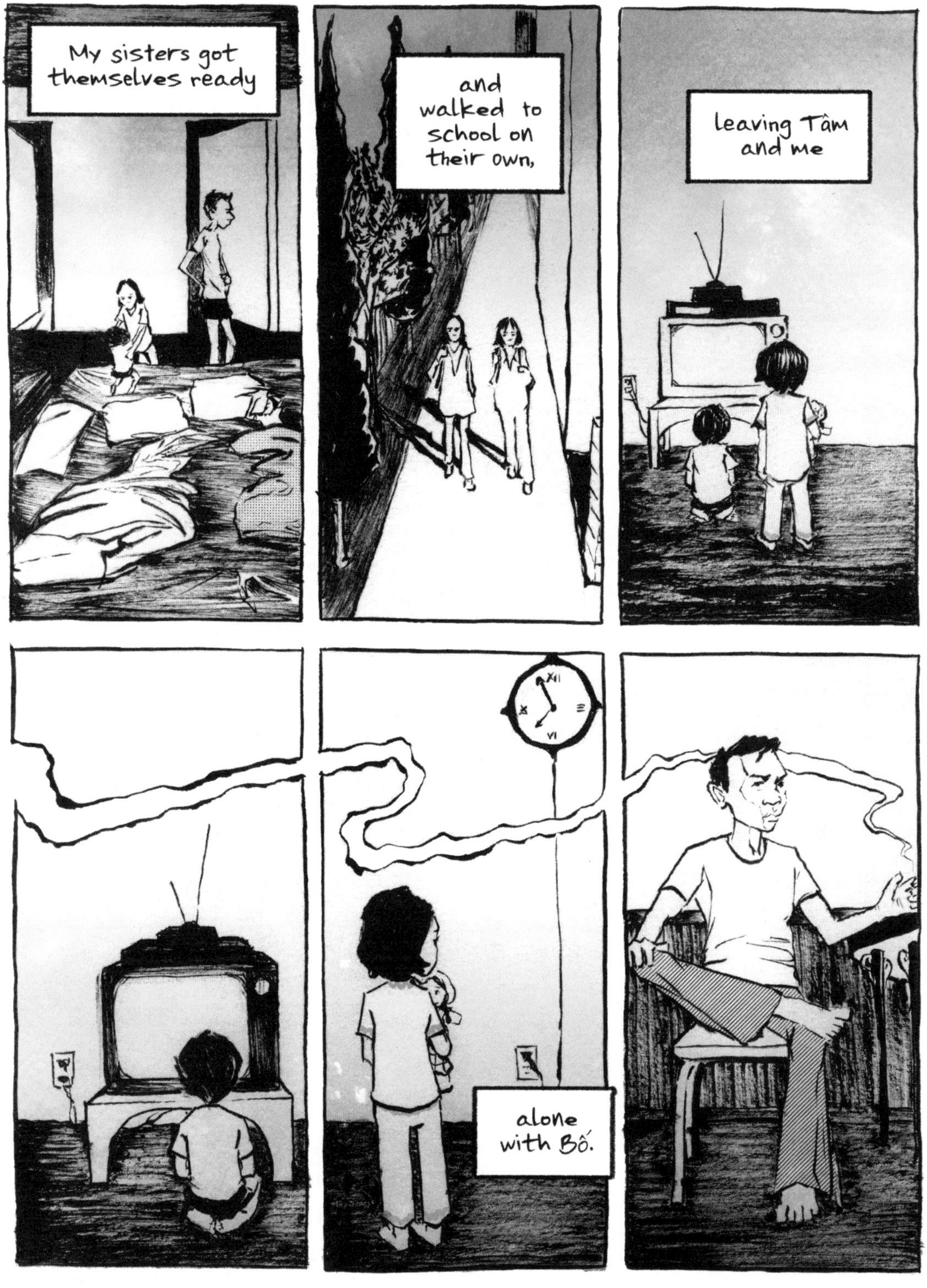
My sisters got themselves ready
and walked to school on their own,
leaving Tâm and me
alone with Bố.

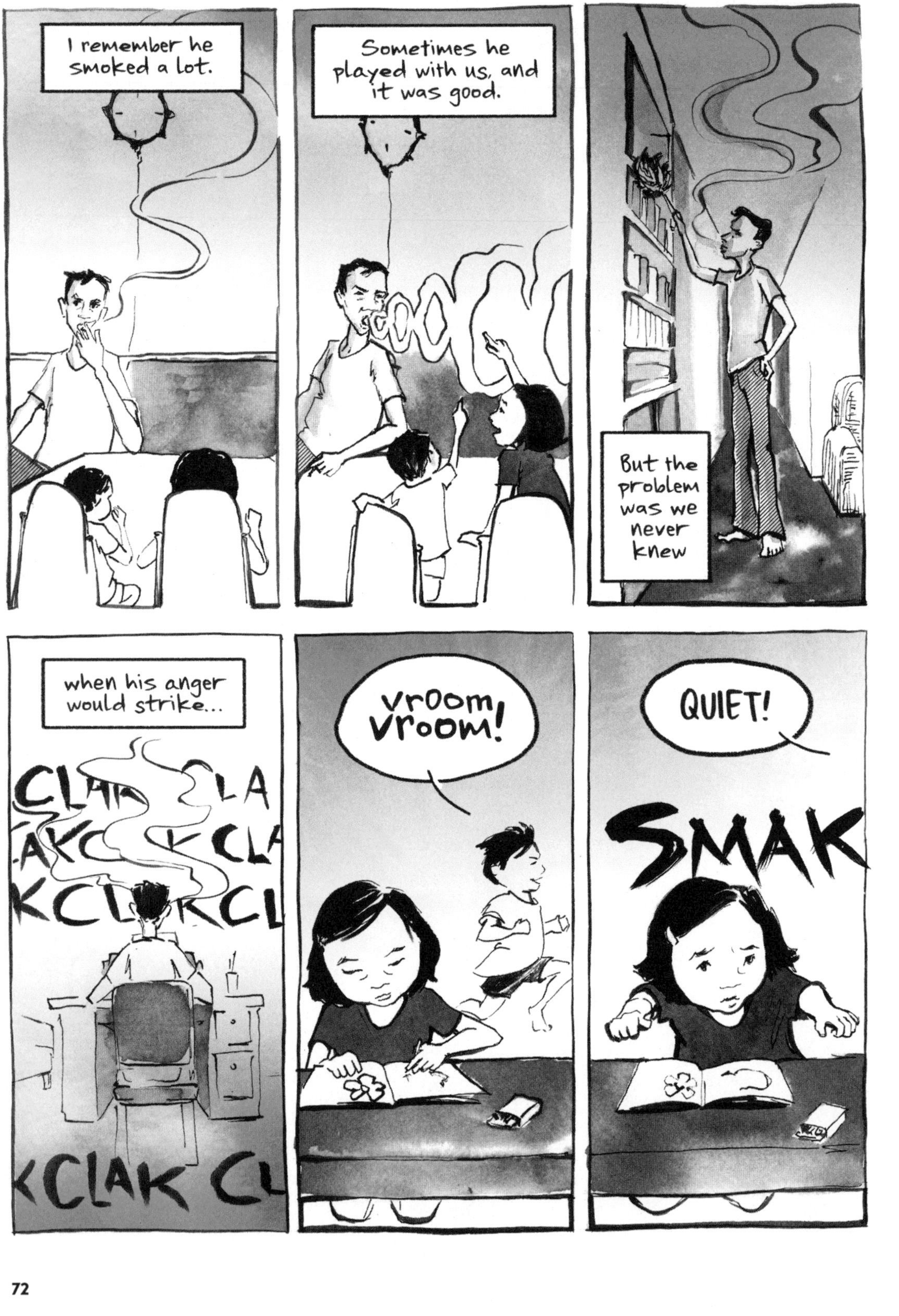
I remember he smoked a lot.
Sometimes he played with us, and it was good.
But the problem was we never knew
when his anger would strike...
CLAK CLA
KCLAKCLA
KCLAKCL
KCLAK CL
vroom vroom!
QUIET!
SMAK

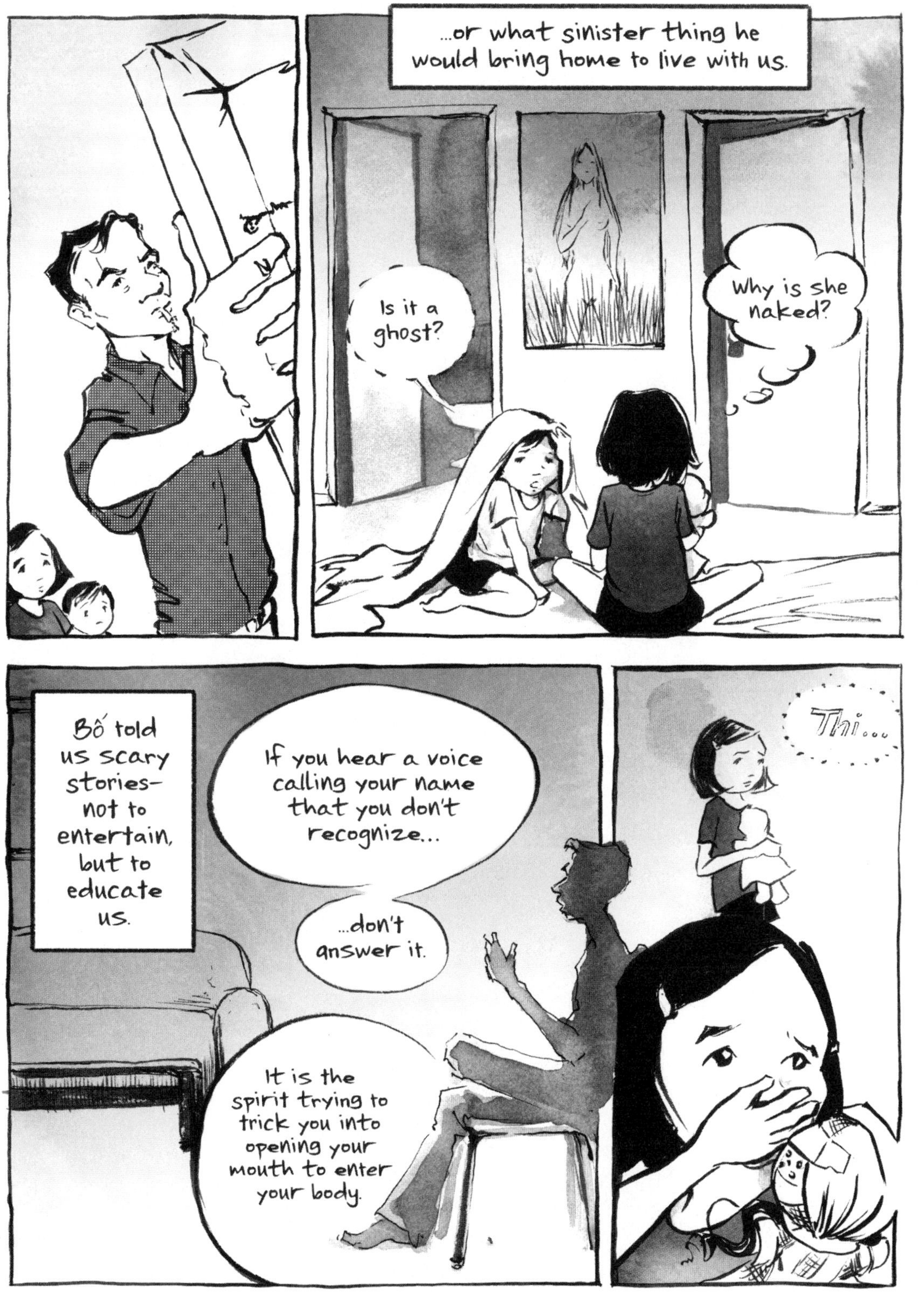
...or what sinister thing he would bring home to live with us.
Is it a ghost?
Why is she naked?
Bố told us scary stories- not to entertain, but to educate us.
If you hear a voice calling your name that you don't recognize...
...don't answer it.
It is the spirit trying to trick you into opening your mouth to enter your body.
Thi...

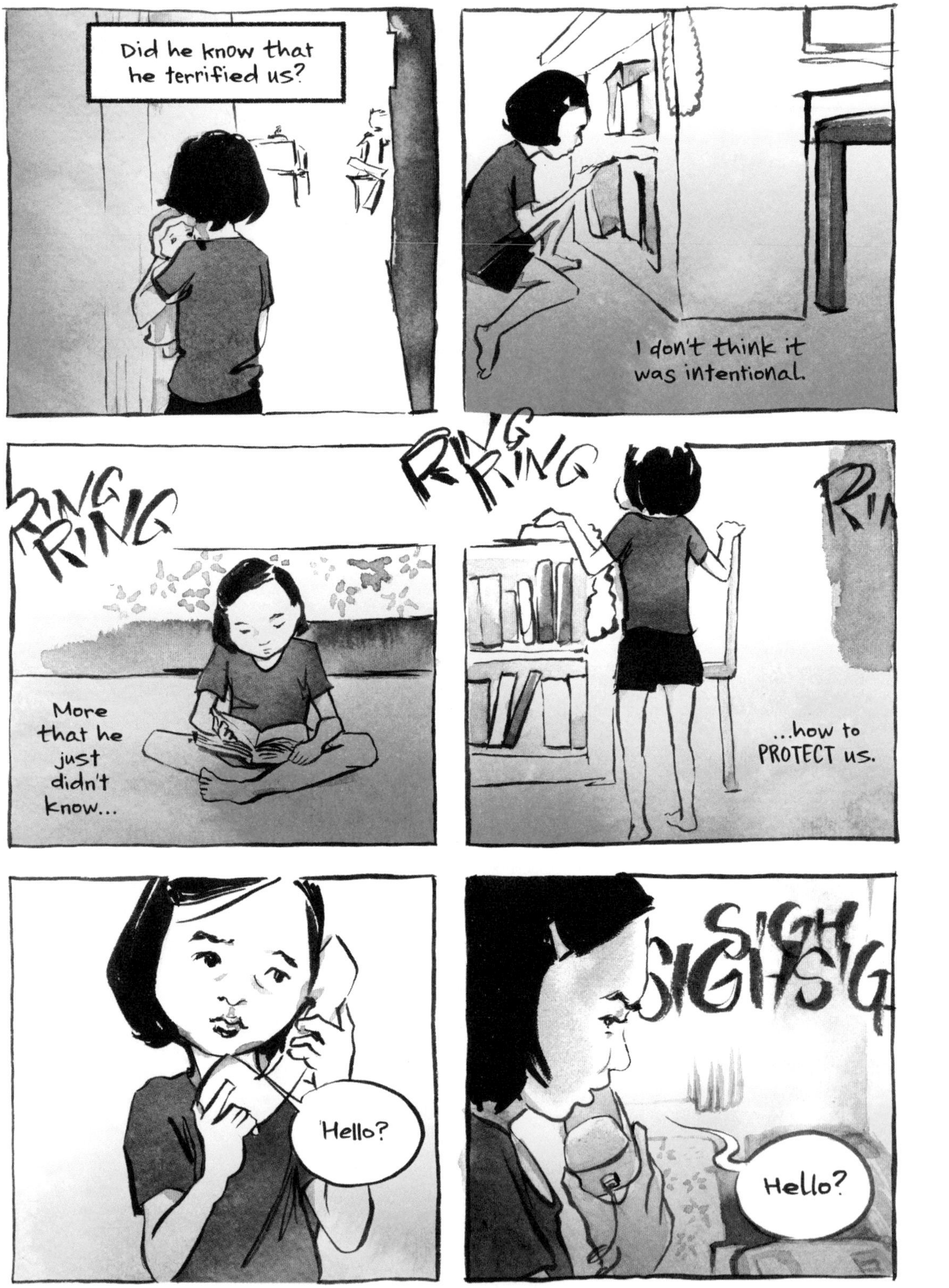
Did he know that he terrified us?
I don't think it was intentional.
RING RING
RING RING
More that he just didn't know...
...how to PROTECT us.
Hello?
SIGH SIGH
Hello?

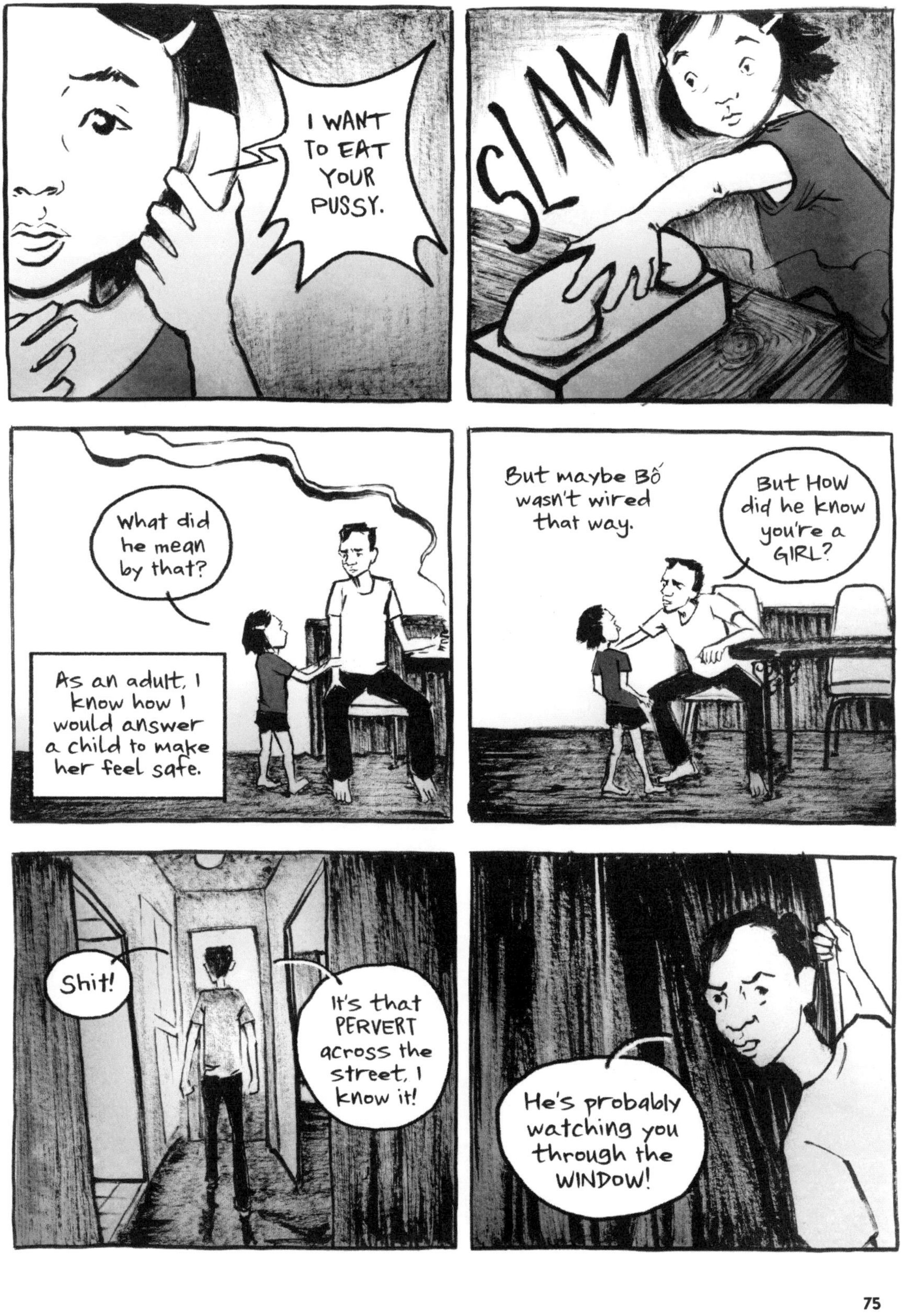
I WANT TO EAT YOUR PUSSY.
SLAM
What did he mean by that?
As an adult, I know how I would answer a child to make her feel safe.
But maybe Bố wasn't wired that way.
But HOW did he know you're a GIRL?
Shit!
It's that PERVERT across the street, I know it!
He's probably watching you through the WINDOW!

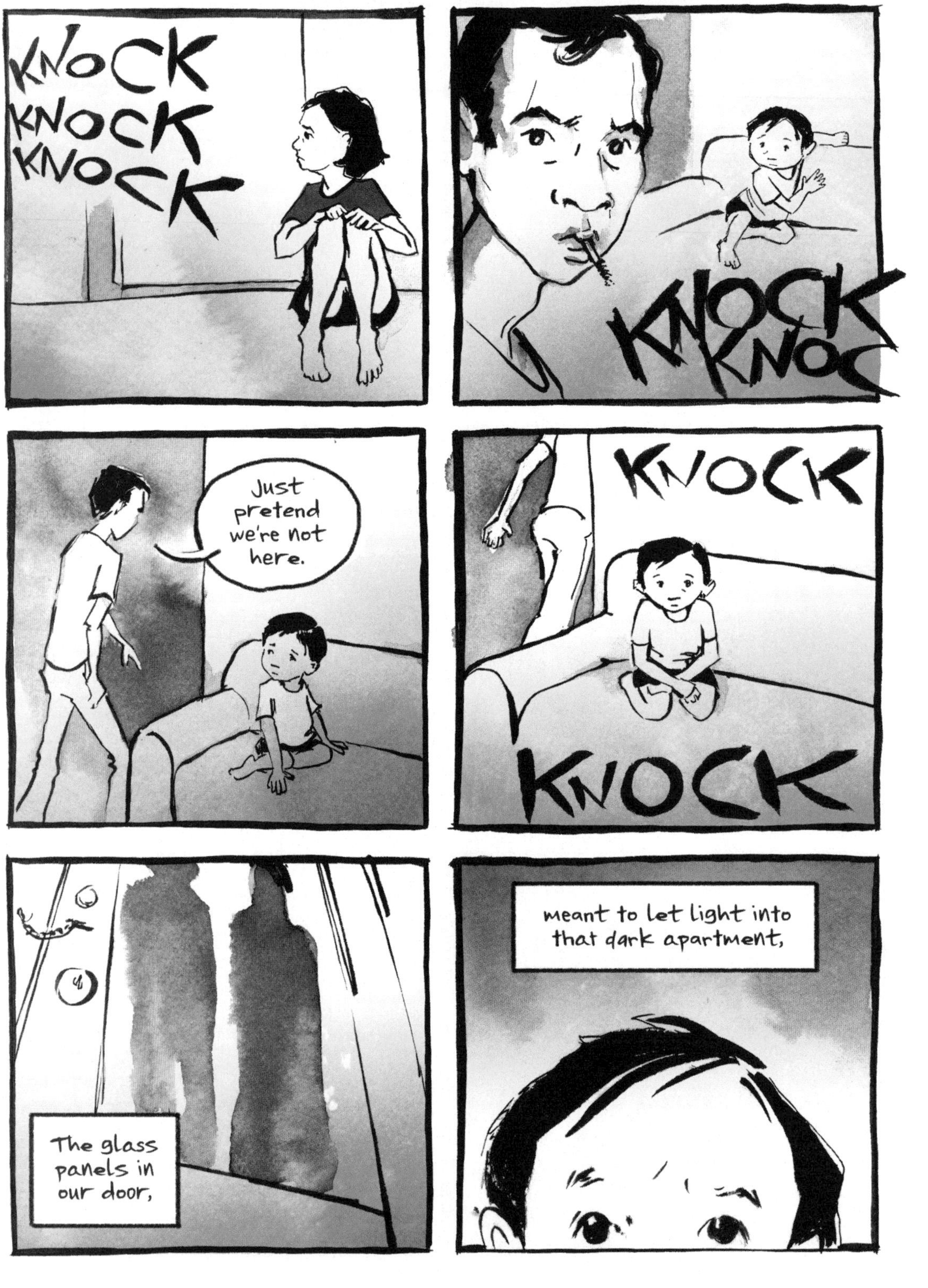
KNOCK
KNOCK
KNOCK
KNOCK
KNOC
Just pretend we're not here.
KNOCK
KNOCK
The glass panels in our door,
meant to let light into that dark apartment,

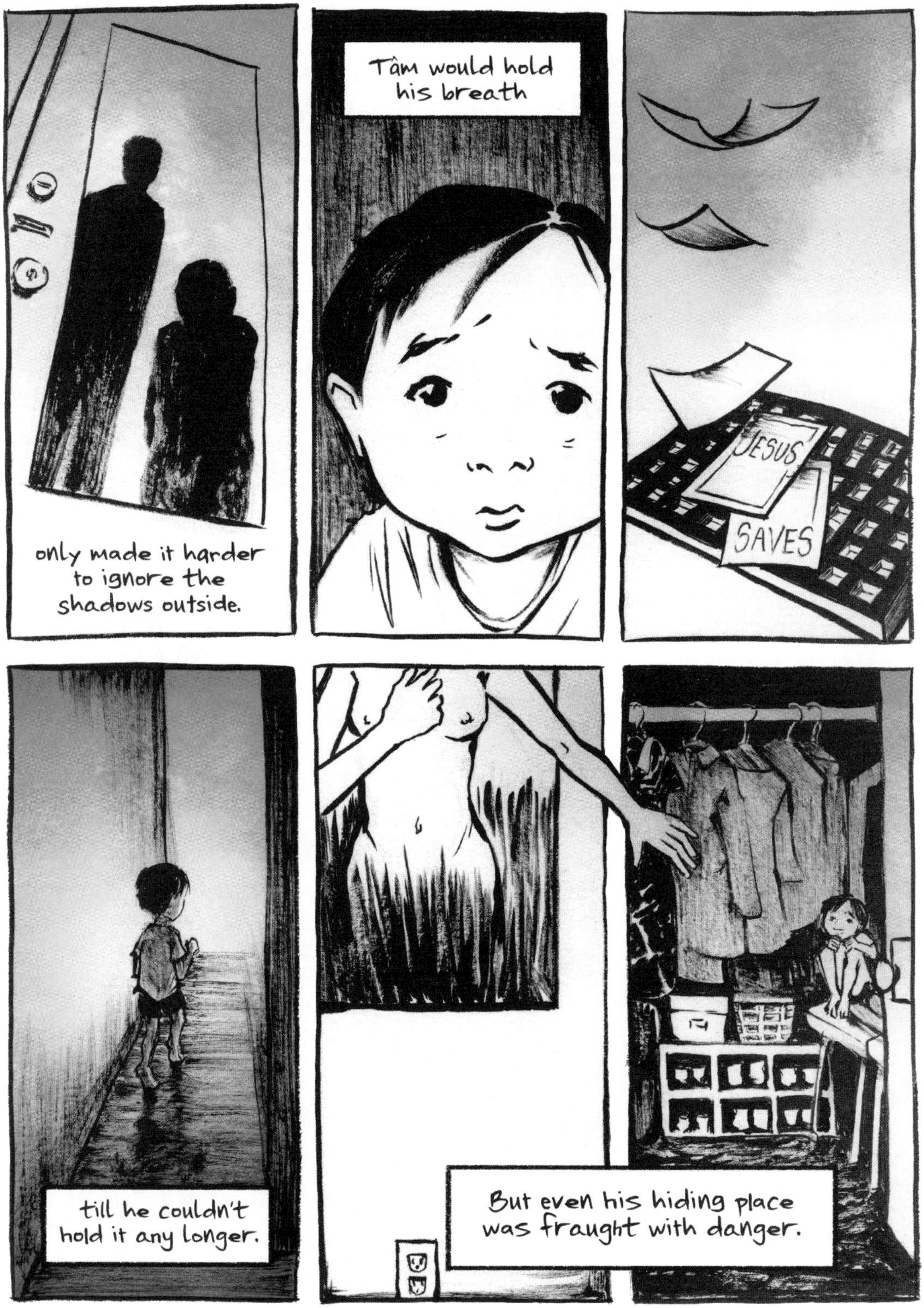
Tâm would hold his breath
only made it harder to ignore the shadows outside.
JESUS
SAVES
till he couldn't hold it any longer.
But even his hiding place was fraught with danger.

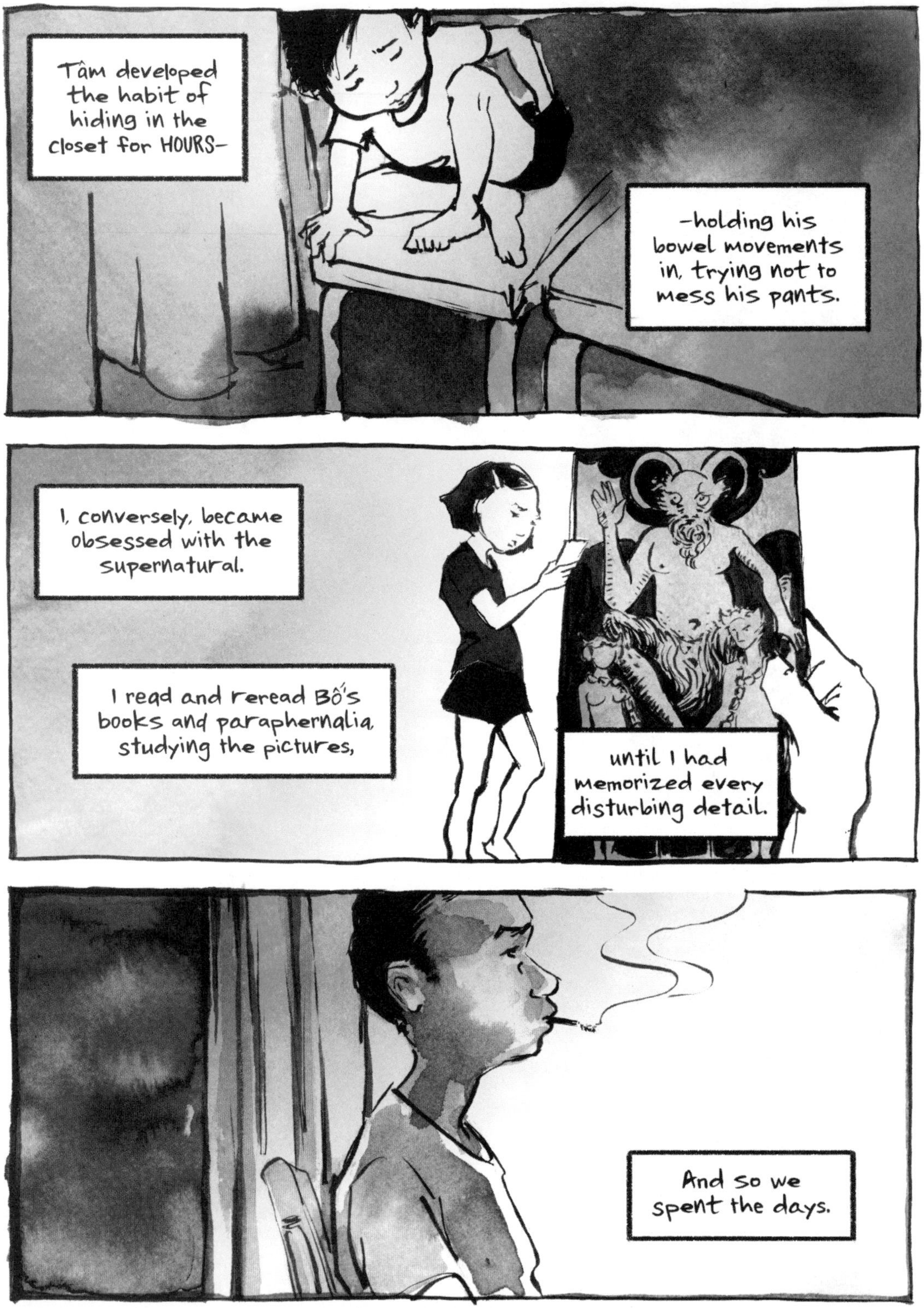
Tâm developed the habit of hiding in the closet for HOURS–
–holding his bowel movements in, trying not to mess his pants.
I, conversely, became obsessed with the supernatural.
I read and reread Bố's books and paraphernalia studying the pictures,
until I had memorized every disturbing detail.
And so we spent the days.

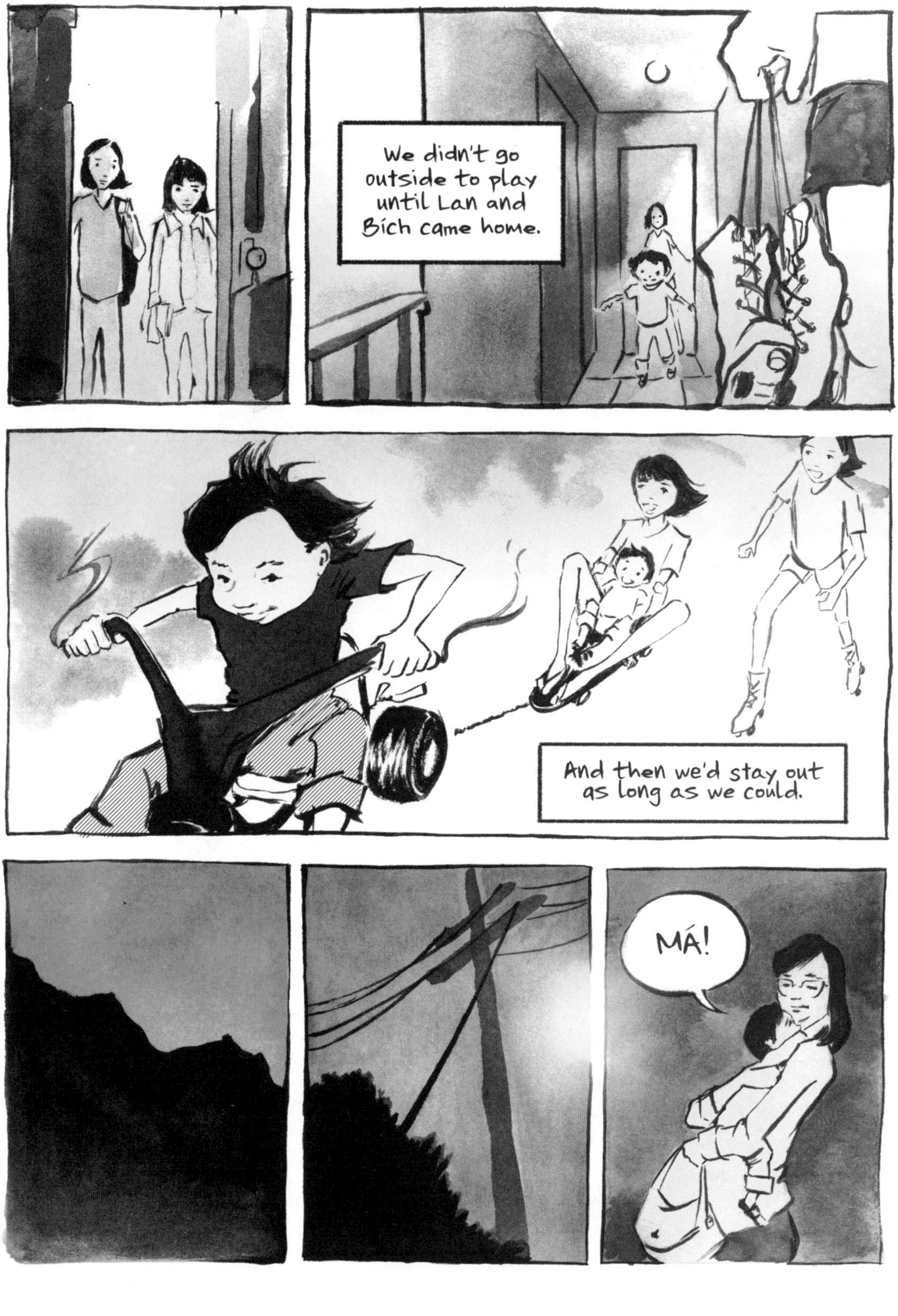
We didn't go outside to play until Lan and Bich came home.
And then we'd stay out as long as we could.
MÁ!

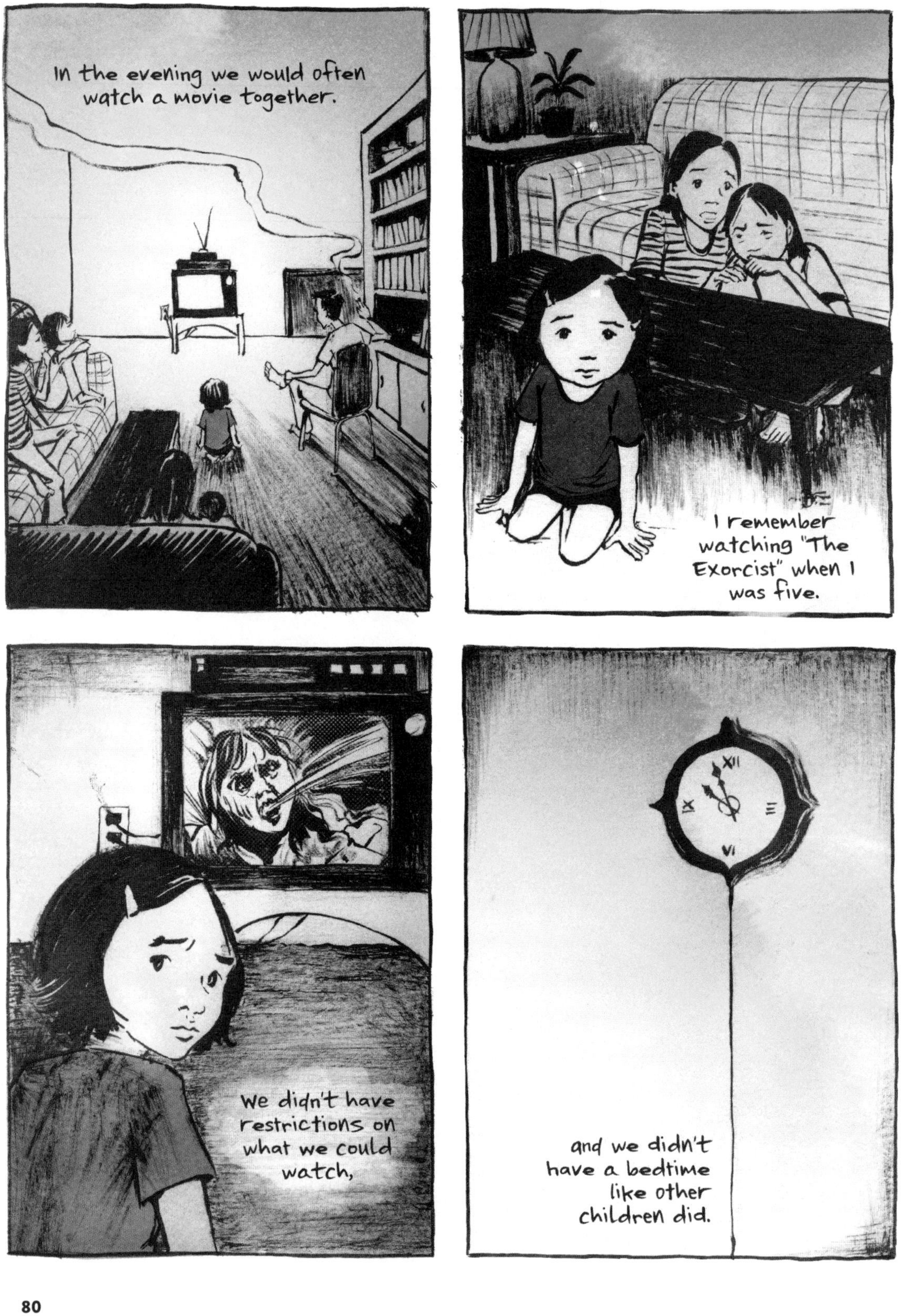
In the evening we would often watch a movie together.
I remember watching "The Exorcist" when I was five.
We didn't have restrictions on what we could watch,
and we didn't have a bedtime like other children did.

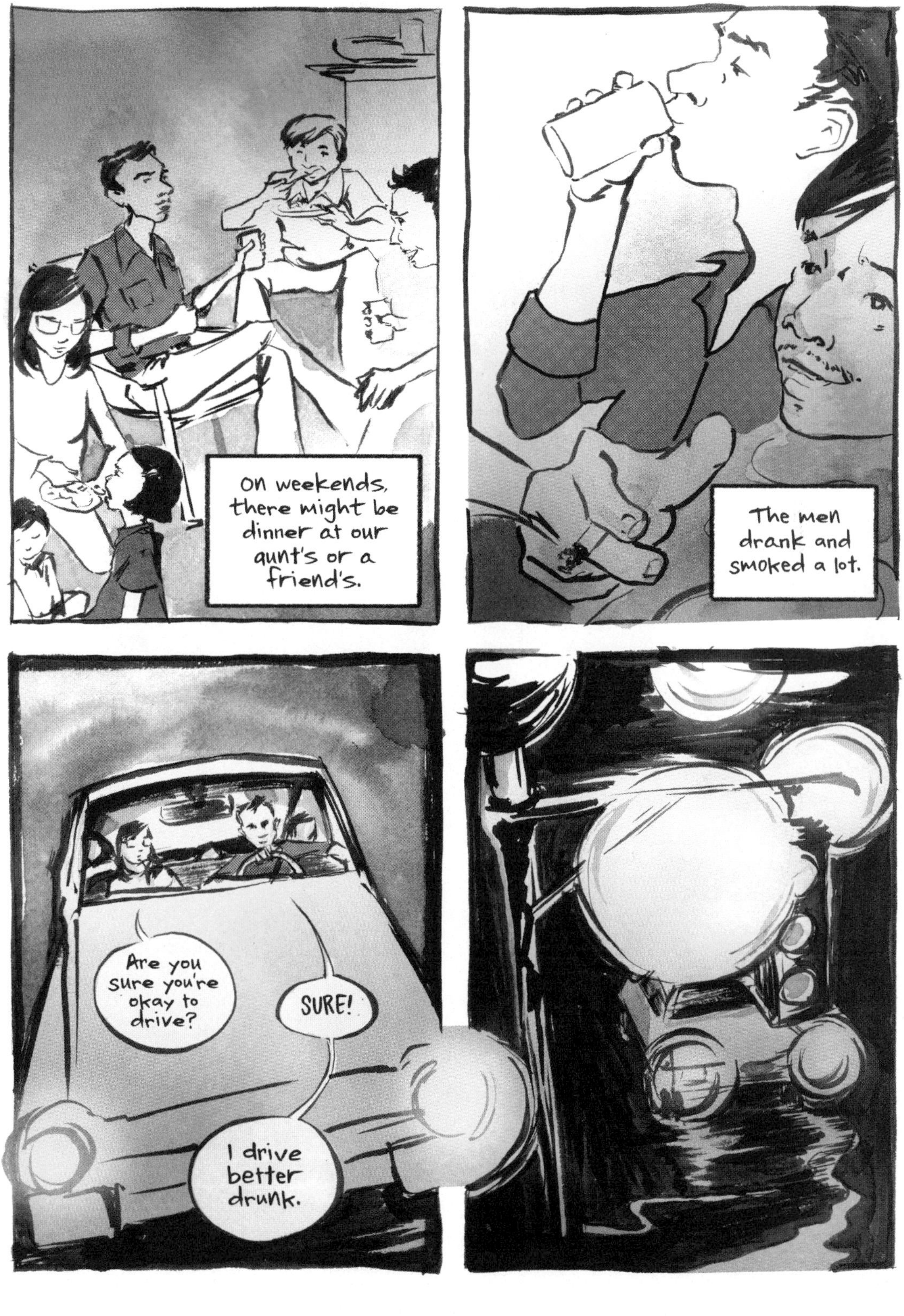
On weekends, there might be dinner at our aunt's or a friend's.
The men drank and smoked a lot.
Are you sure you're okay to drive?
SURE!
I drive better drunk.

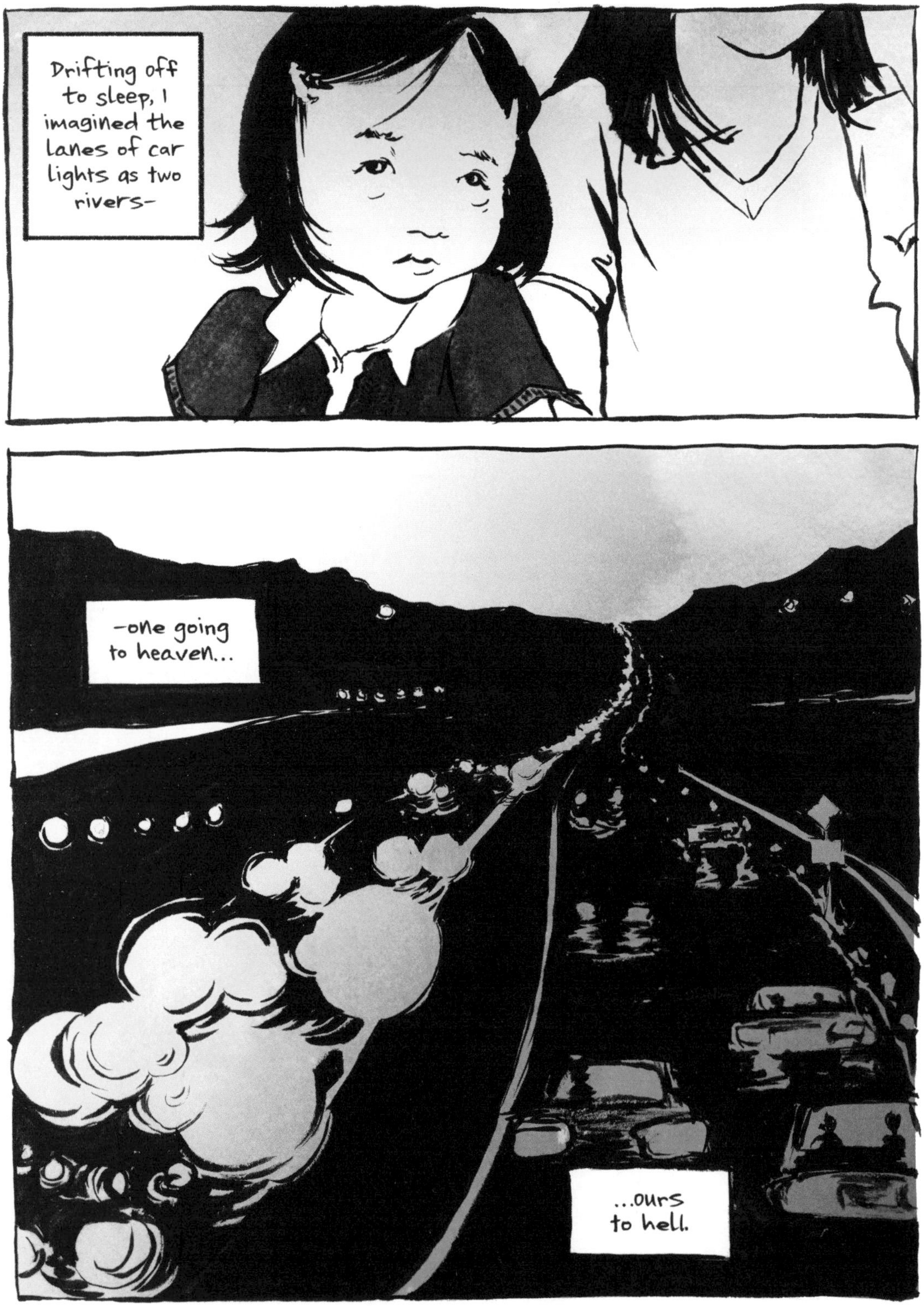
Drifting off to sleep, I imagined the lanes of car lights as two rivers-
-one going to heaven...
...ours to hell.

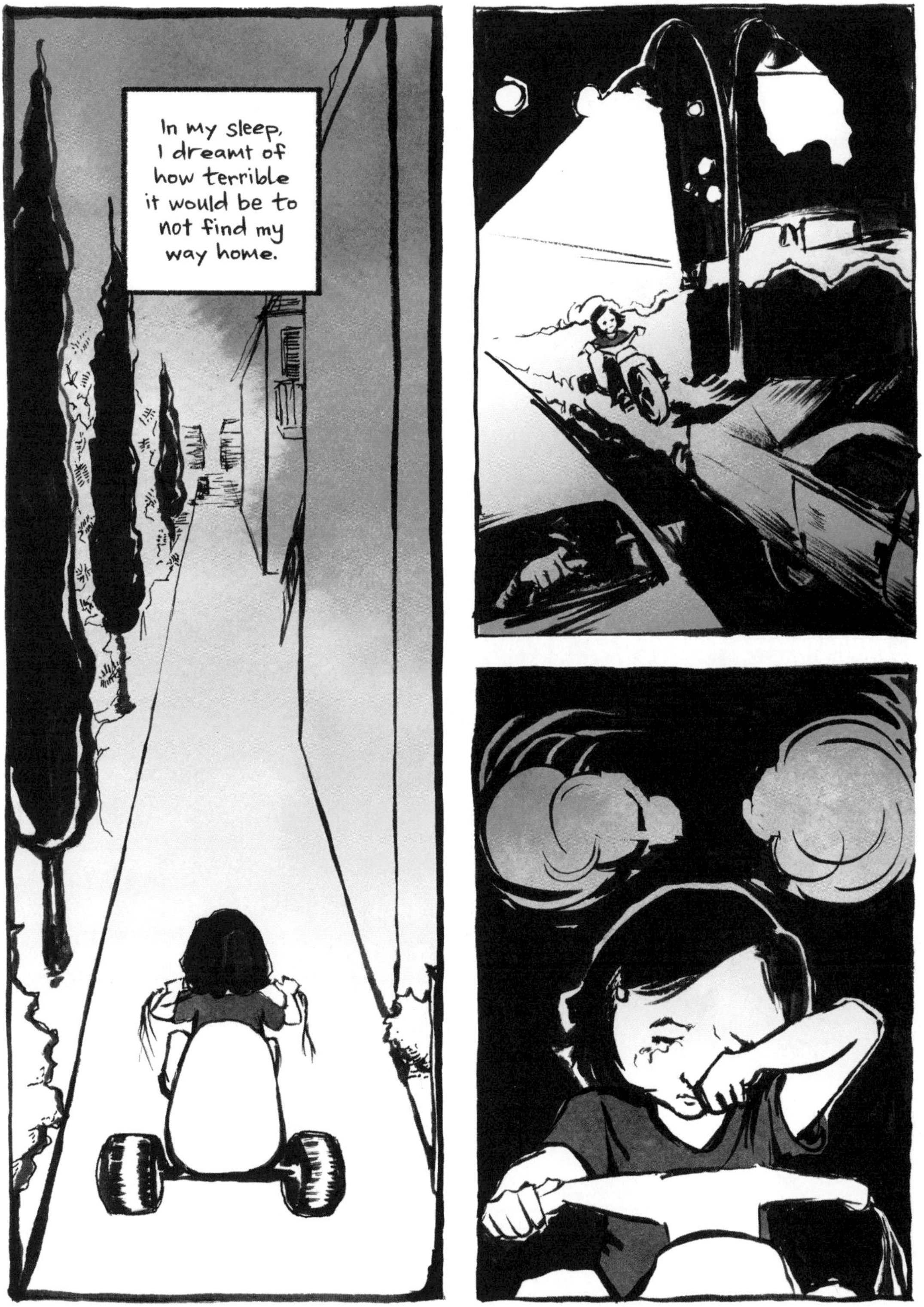
In my sleep, I dreamt of how terrible it would be to not find my way home.

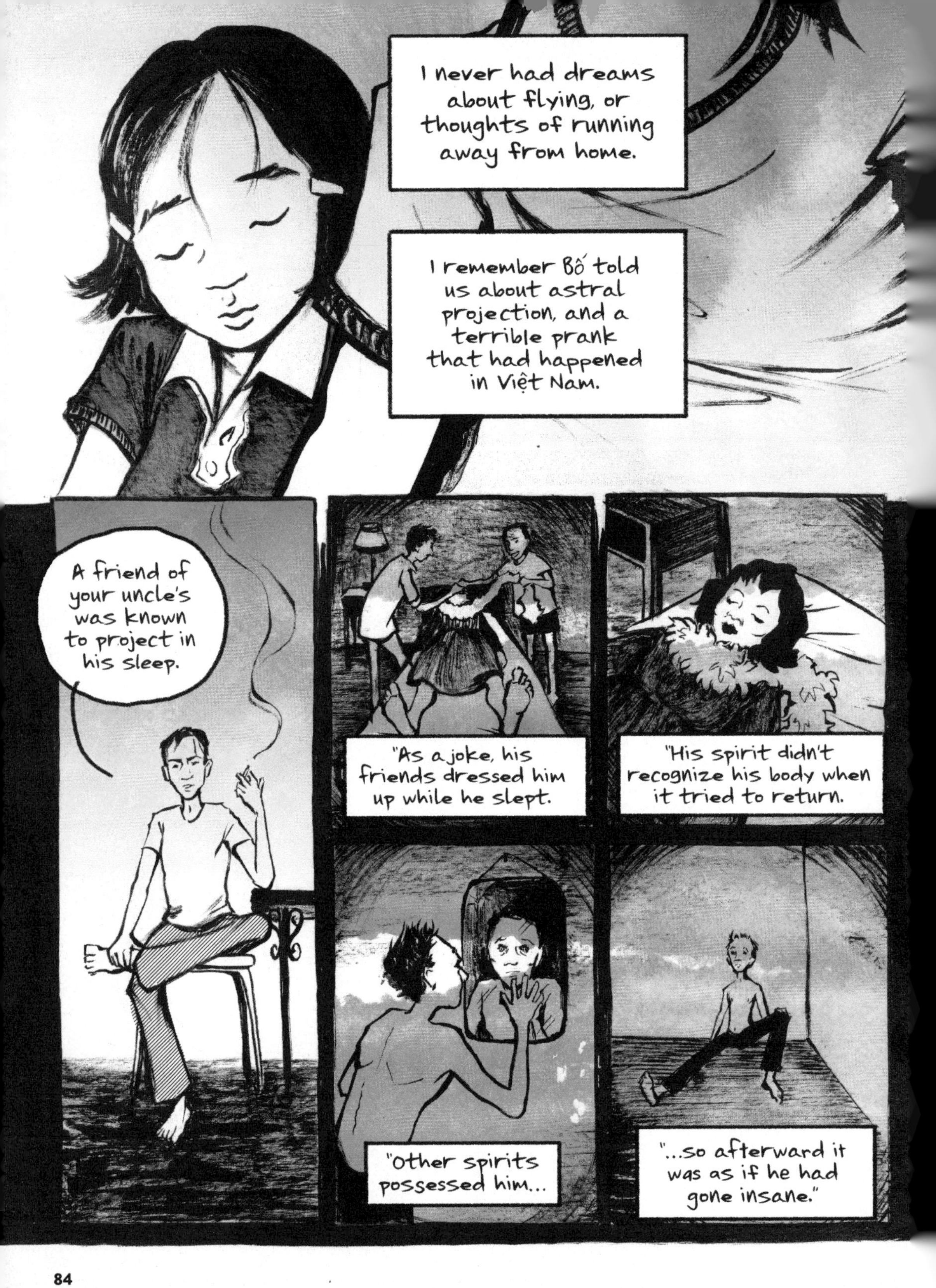
I never had dreams about flying, or thoughts of running away from home.
I remember Bố told us about astral projection, and a terrible prank that had happened in Việt Nam.
A friend of your uncle's was known to project in his sleep.
"As a joke, his friends dressed him up while he slept.
"His spirit didn't recognize his body when it tried to return.
"Other spirits possessed him...
"...so afterward it was as if he had gone insane."

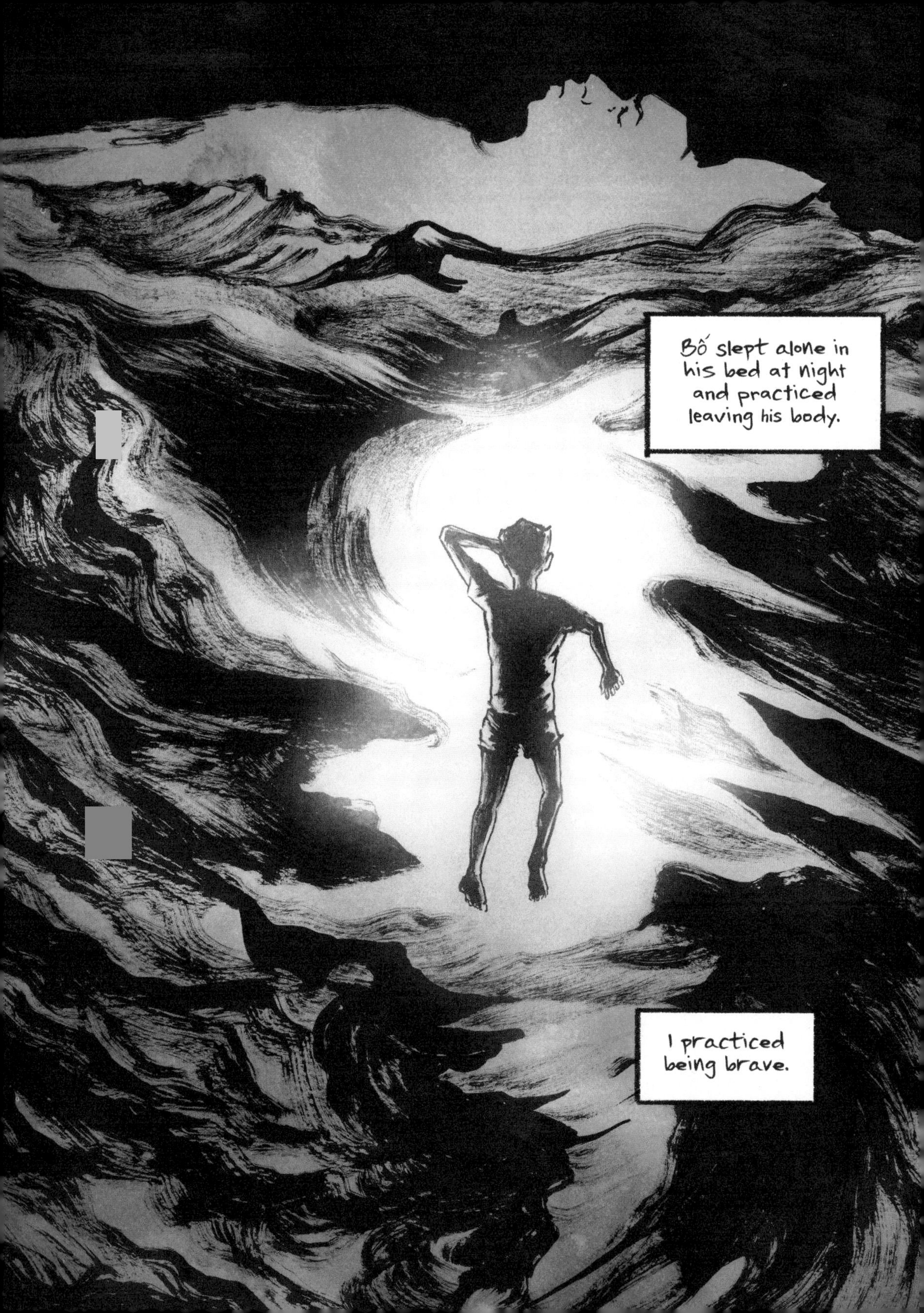
Bố slept alone in his bed at night and practiced leaving his body.
I practiced being brave.

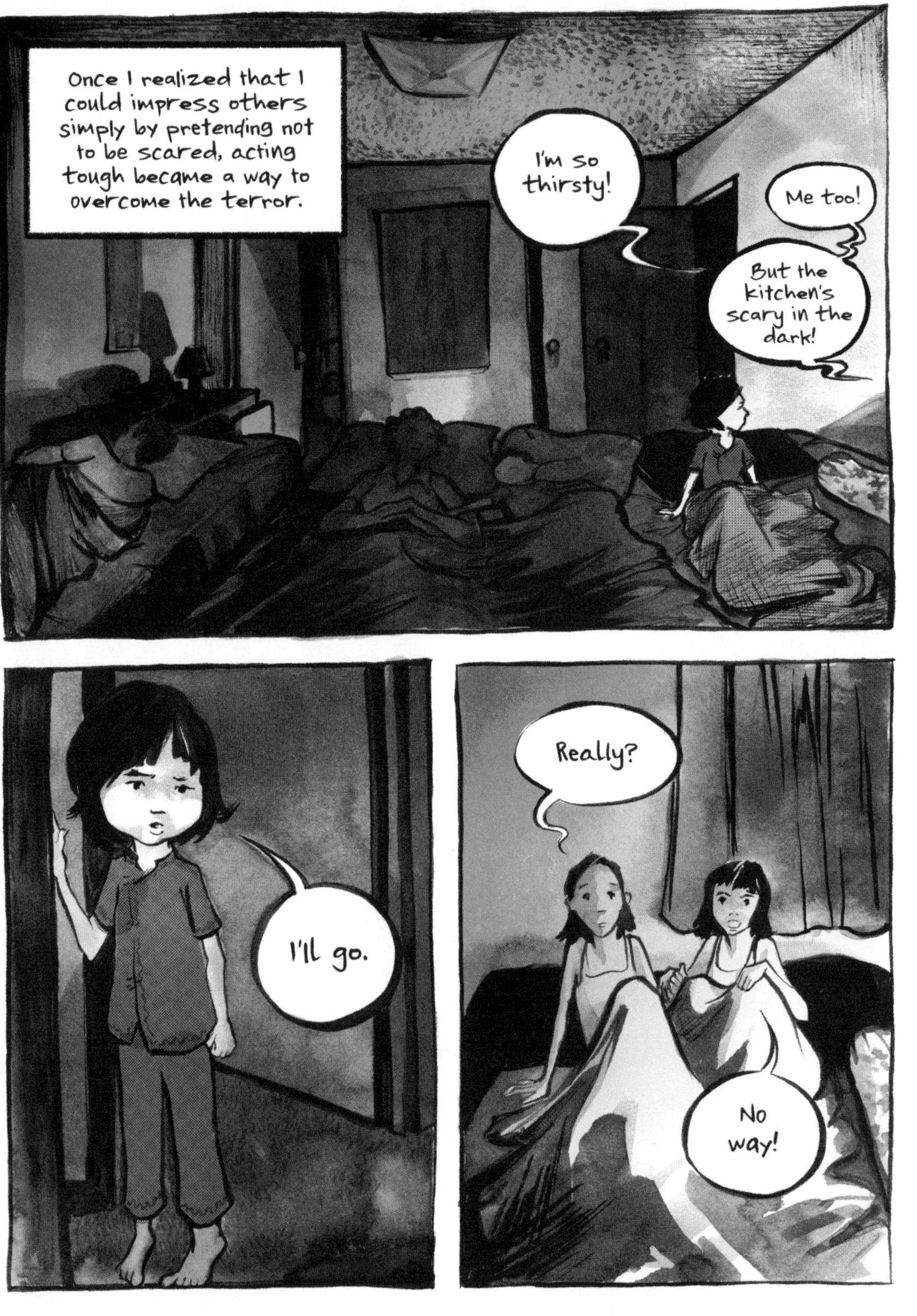
Once I realized that I could impress others simply by pretending not to be scared, acting tough became a way to overcome the terror.
I'm so thirsty!
Me too!
But the kitchen's scary in the dark!
I'll go.
Really?
No way!

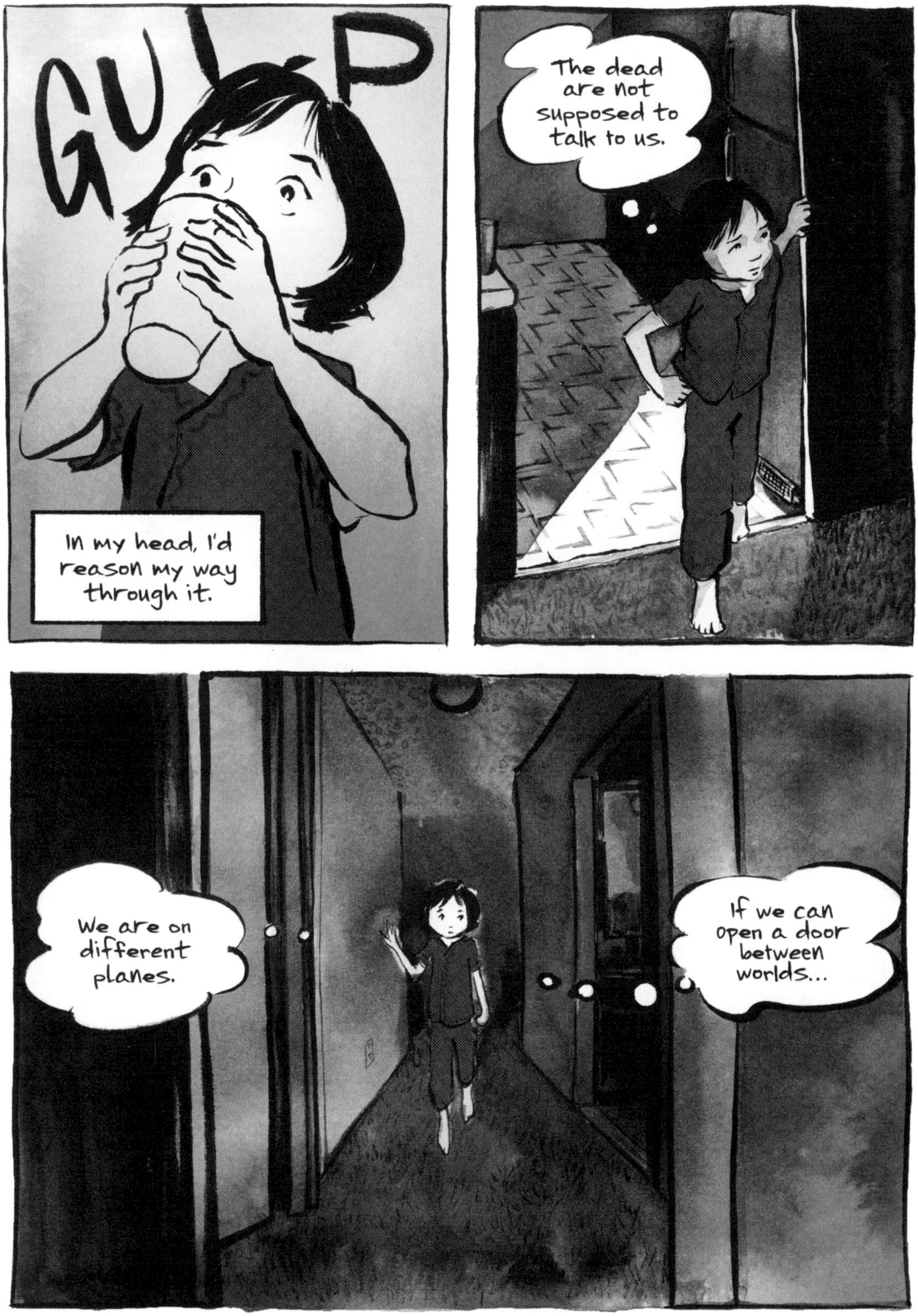
GULP
In my head, I'd reason my way through it.
The dead are not supposed to talk to us.
We are on different planes.
If we can open a door between worlds...

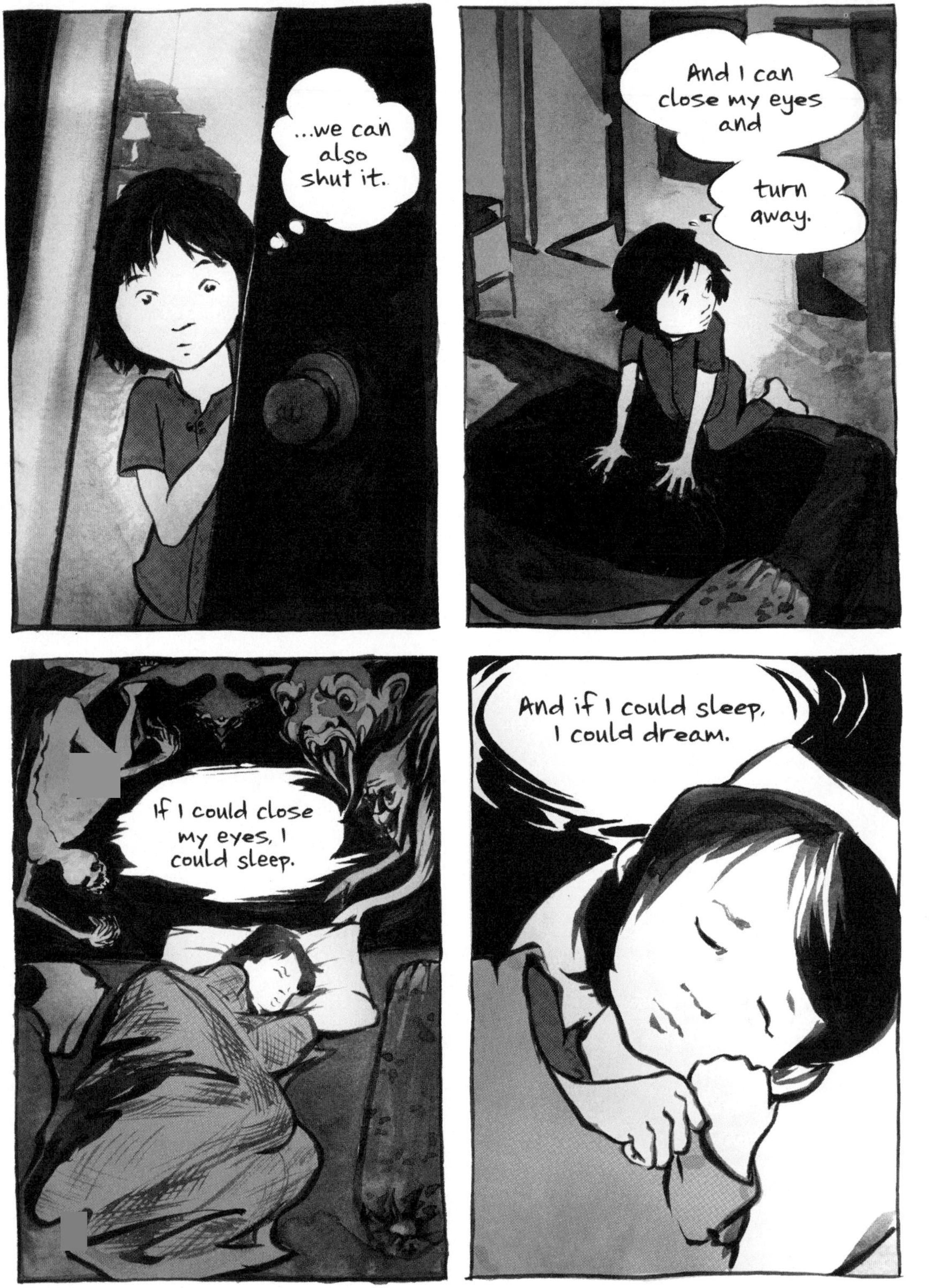
...we can also shut it.
And I can close my eyes and
turn away.
If I could close my eyes, I could sleep.
And if I could sleep, I could dream.

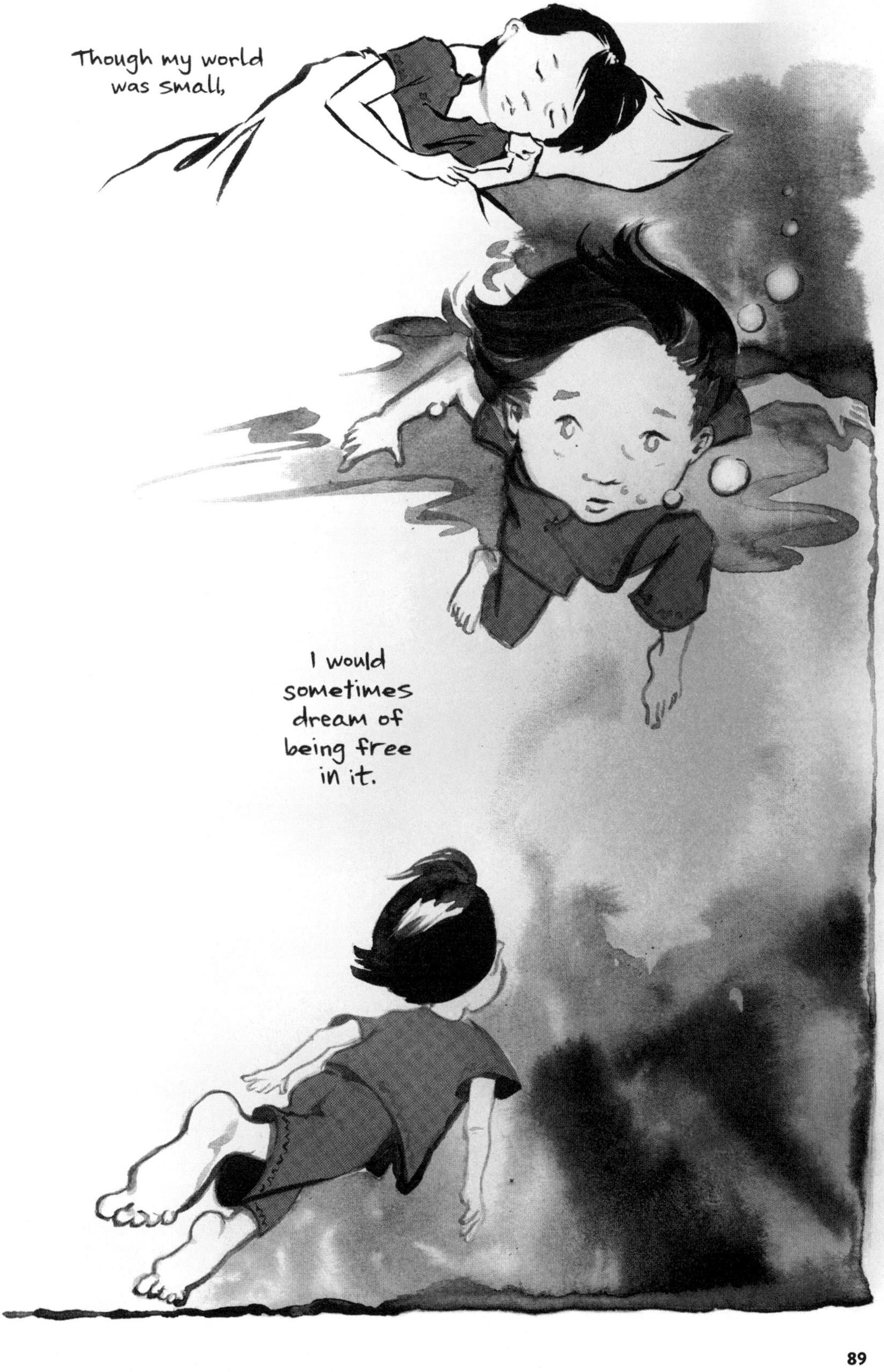
Though my world was small,
I would sometimes dream of being free in it.

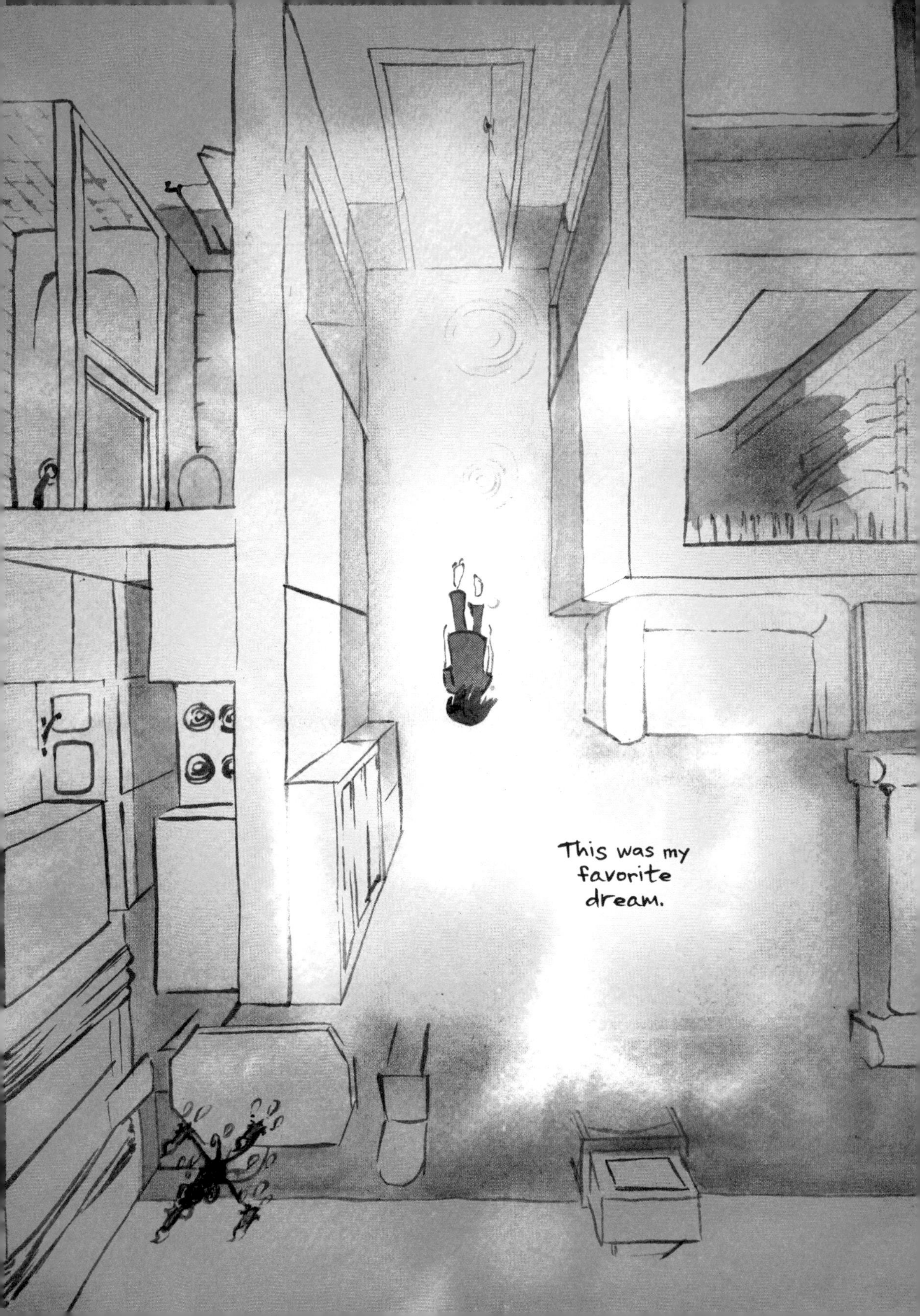
This was my favorite dream.

CHAPTER 4

BLOOD AND RICE

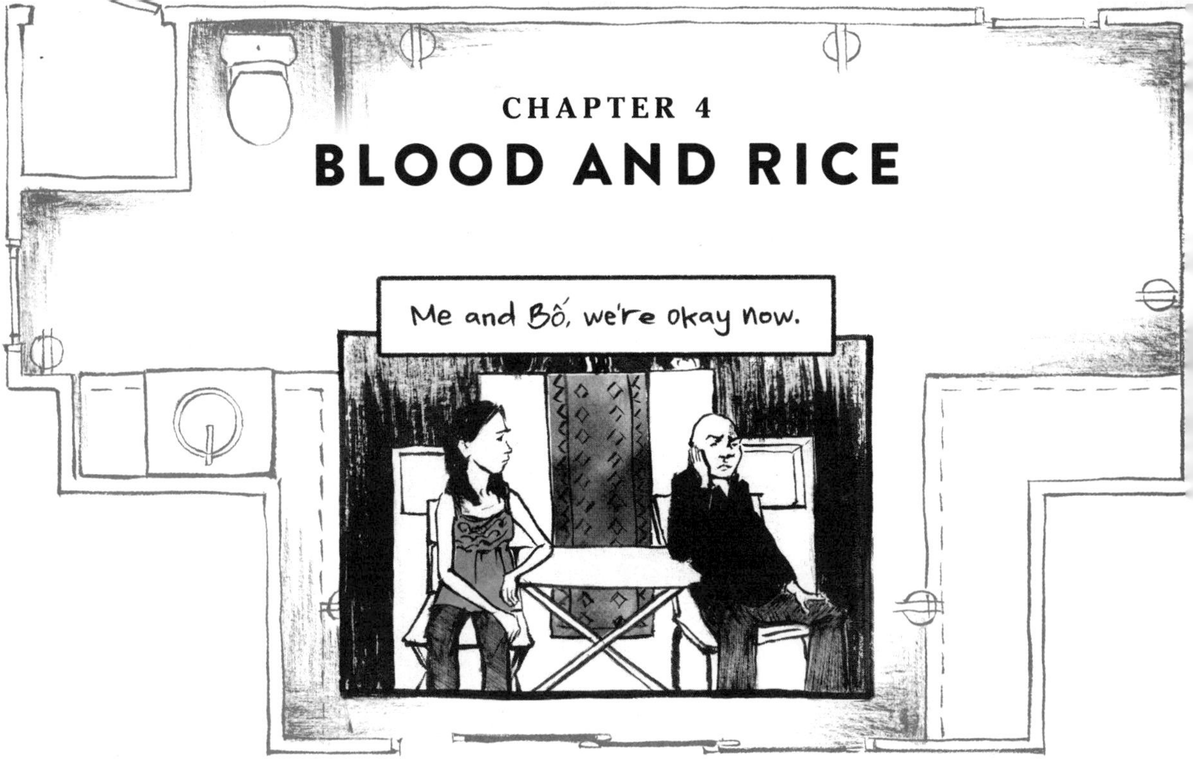
Me and Bố, we're okay now.

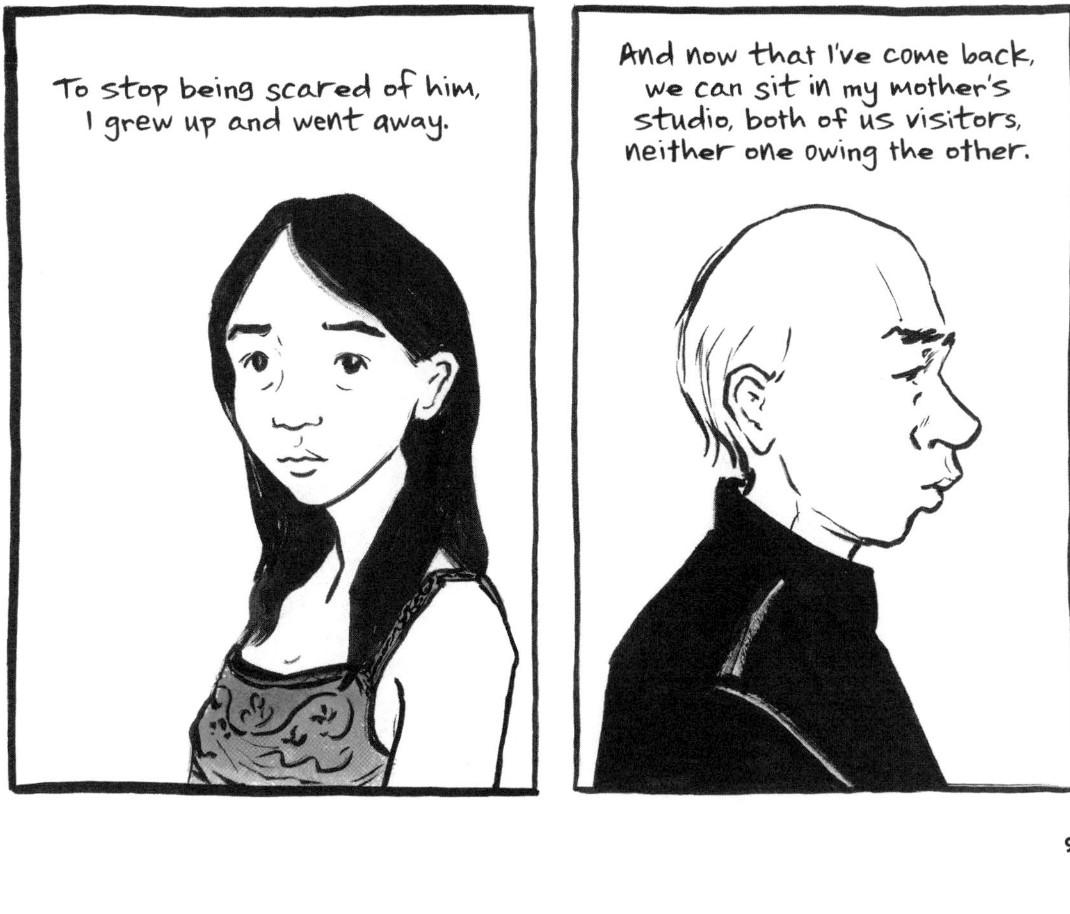
To stop being scared of him, I grew up and went away.
And now that I've come back, we can sit in my mother's studio, both of us visitors, neither one owing the other.

To understand how my father became the way he was,

I had to learn what happened to him as a little boy.

It took a long time

to learn the right questions to ask.

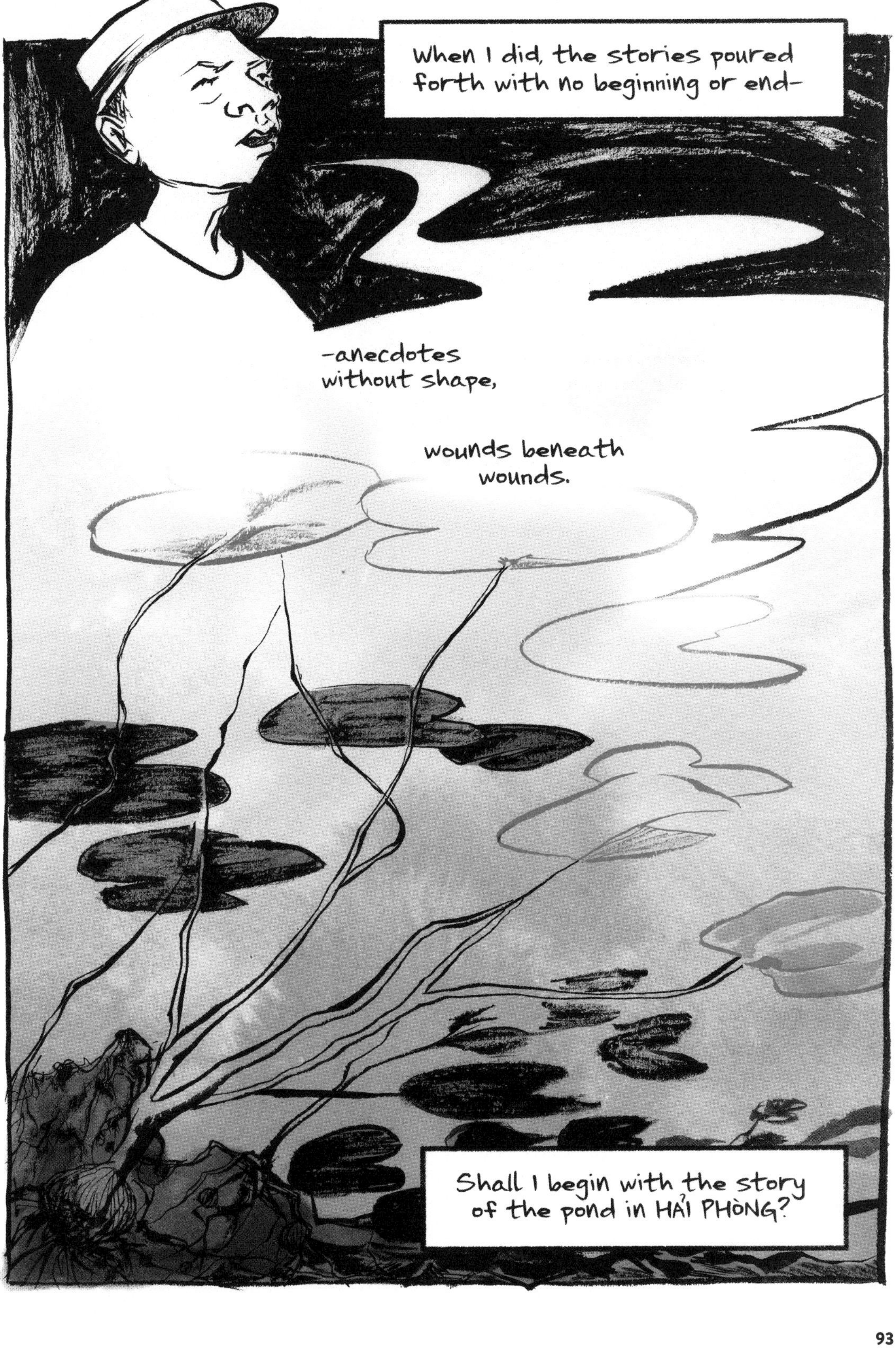
When I did, the stories poured forth with no beginning or end-
-anecdotes without shape,
wounds beneath wounds.
Shall I begin with the story of the pond in HẢI PHÒNG?

In 1951, when Việt Nam was still part of French Indochina,

Bố's grandfather and great-uncle built a street in the northern city of Hải Phòng.

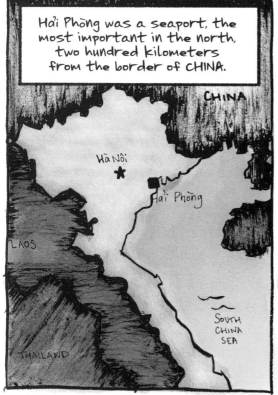

Hải Phòng was a seaport, the most important in the north, two hundred kilometers from the border of CHINA.

CHINA

Hà Nội

Hải Phòng

LAOS

SOUTH CHINA SEA

THAILAND

First they built the road, and named it after themselves.

Ngõ Lâm Tưởng

Boulevard Sadi Carnot

Then they began to dig.

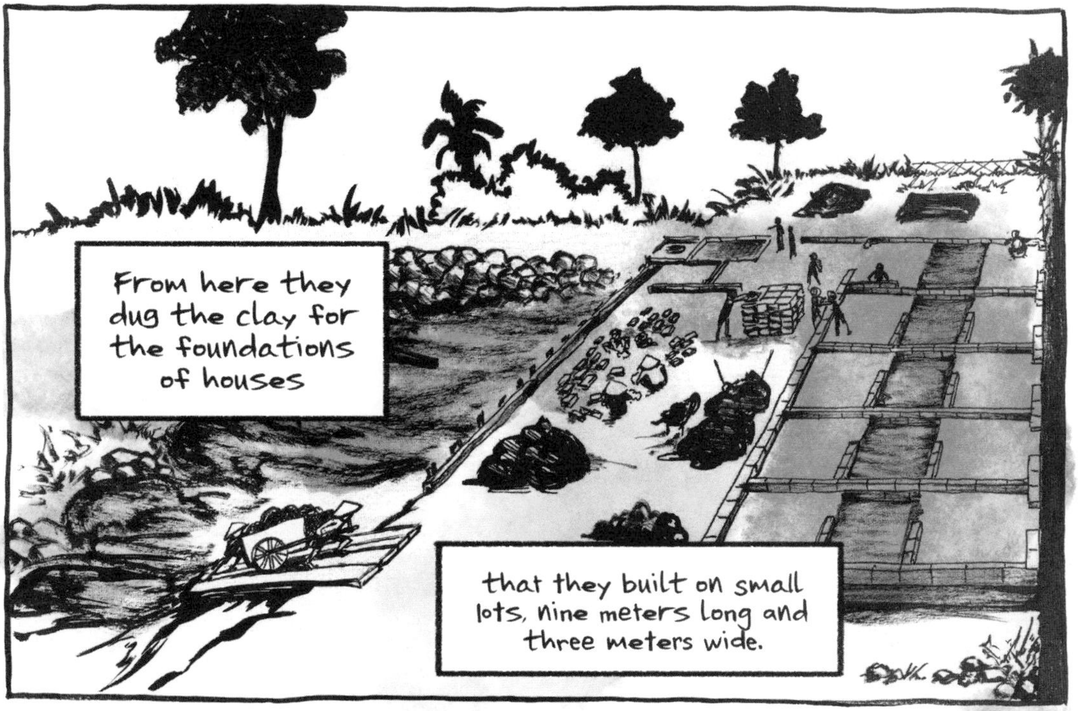
From here they dug the clay for the foundations of houses
that they built on small lots, nine meters long and three meters wide.

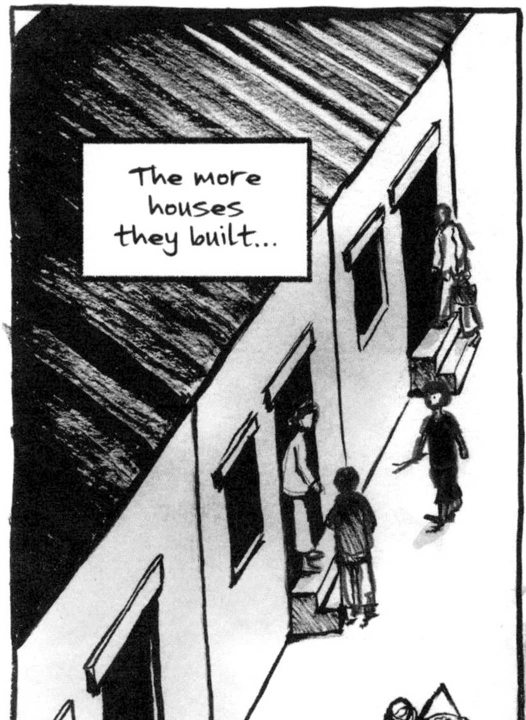
The more houses they built...

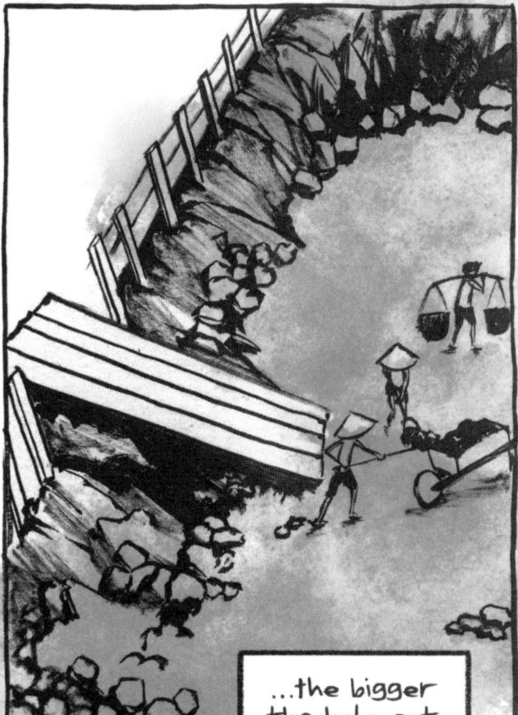
...the bigger the hole got.

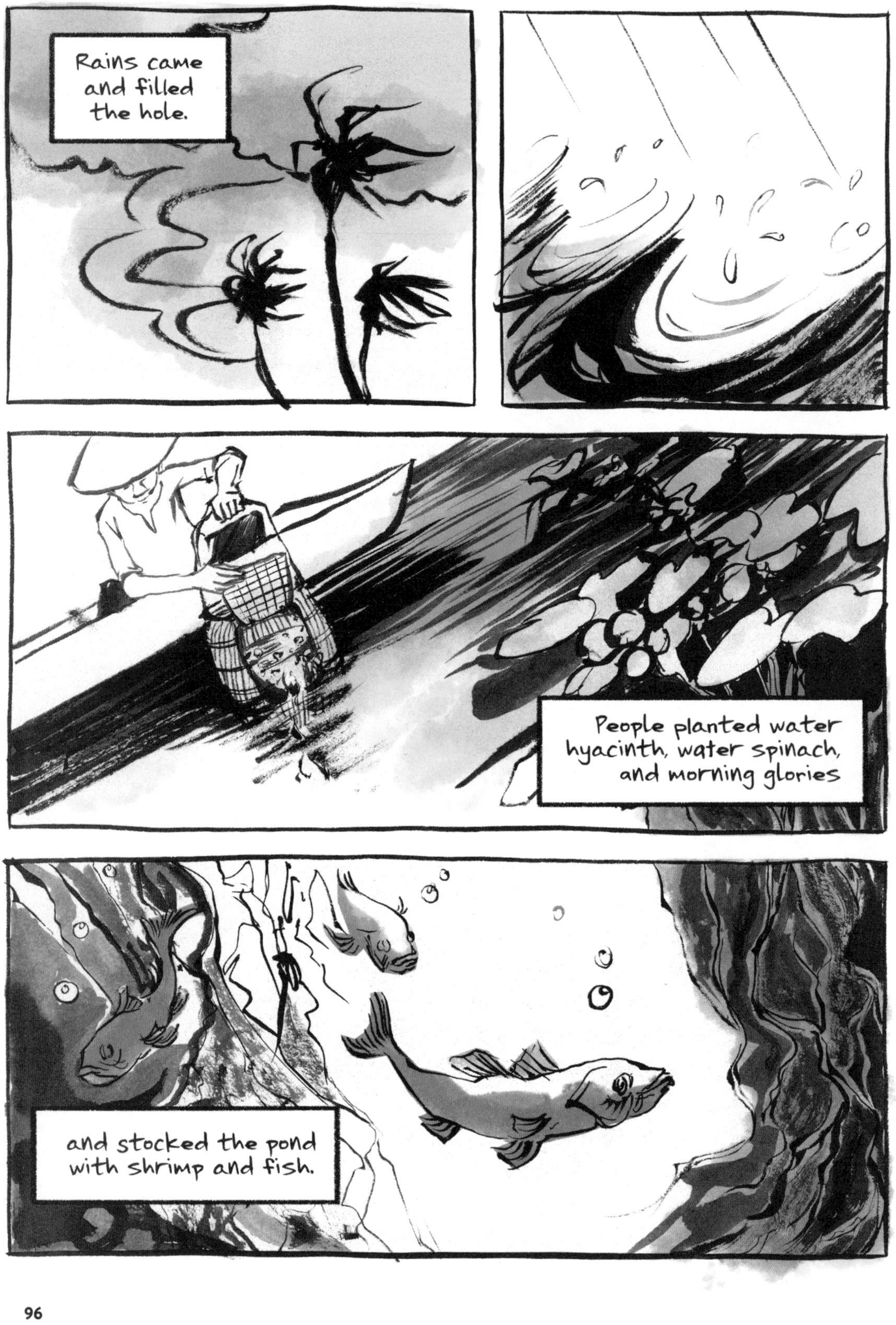
Rains came and filled the hole.
People planted water hyacinth, water spinach, and morning glories
and stocked the pond with shrimp and fish.

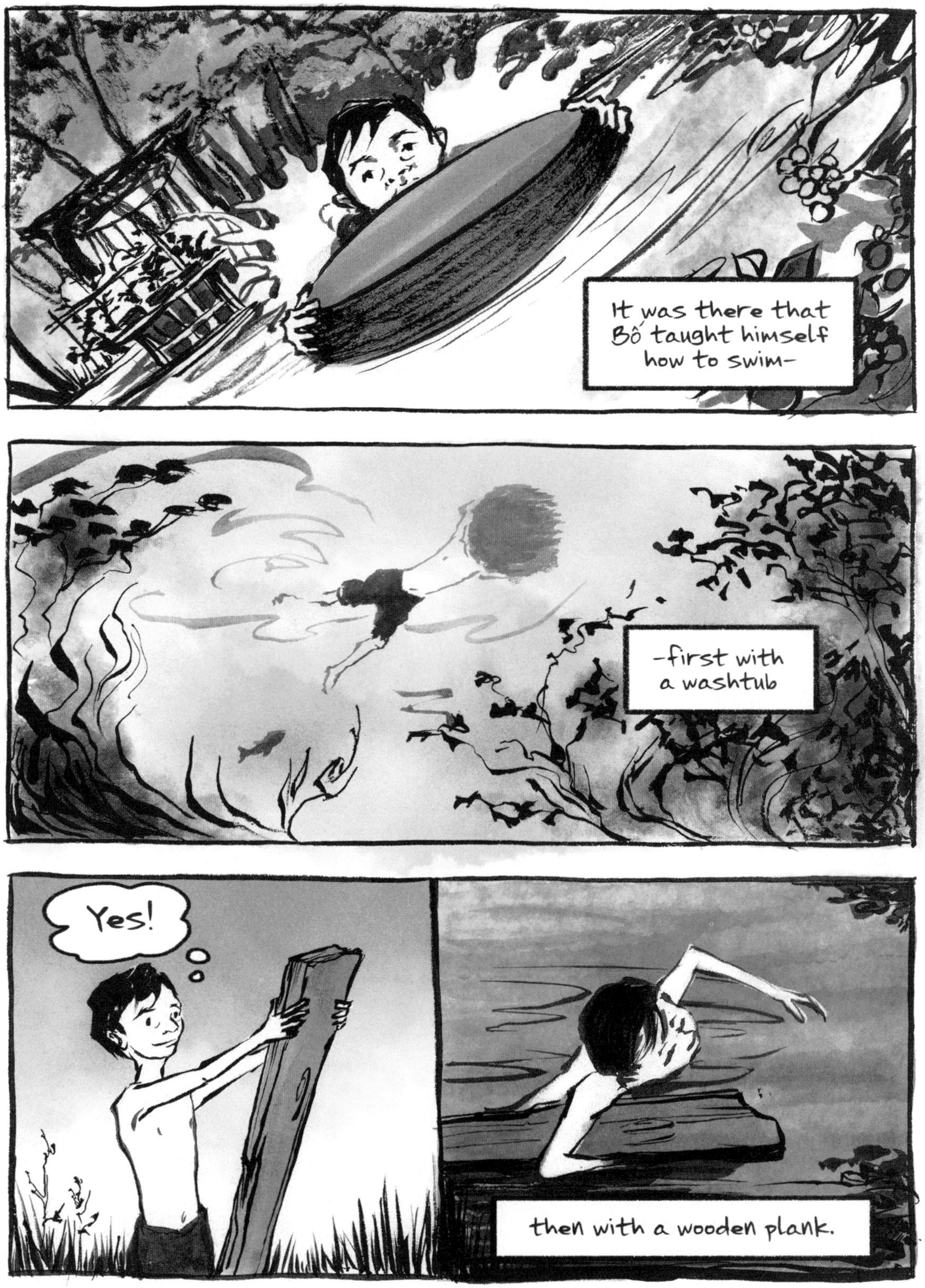
It was there that Bố taught himself how to swim-
-first with a washtub
Yes!
then with a wooden plank.

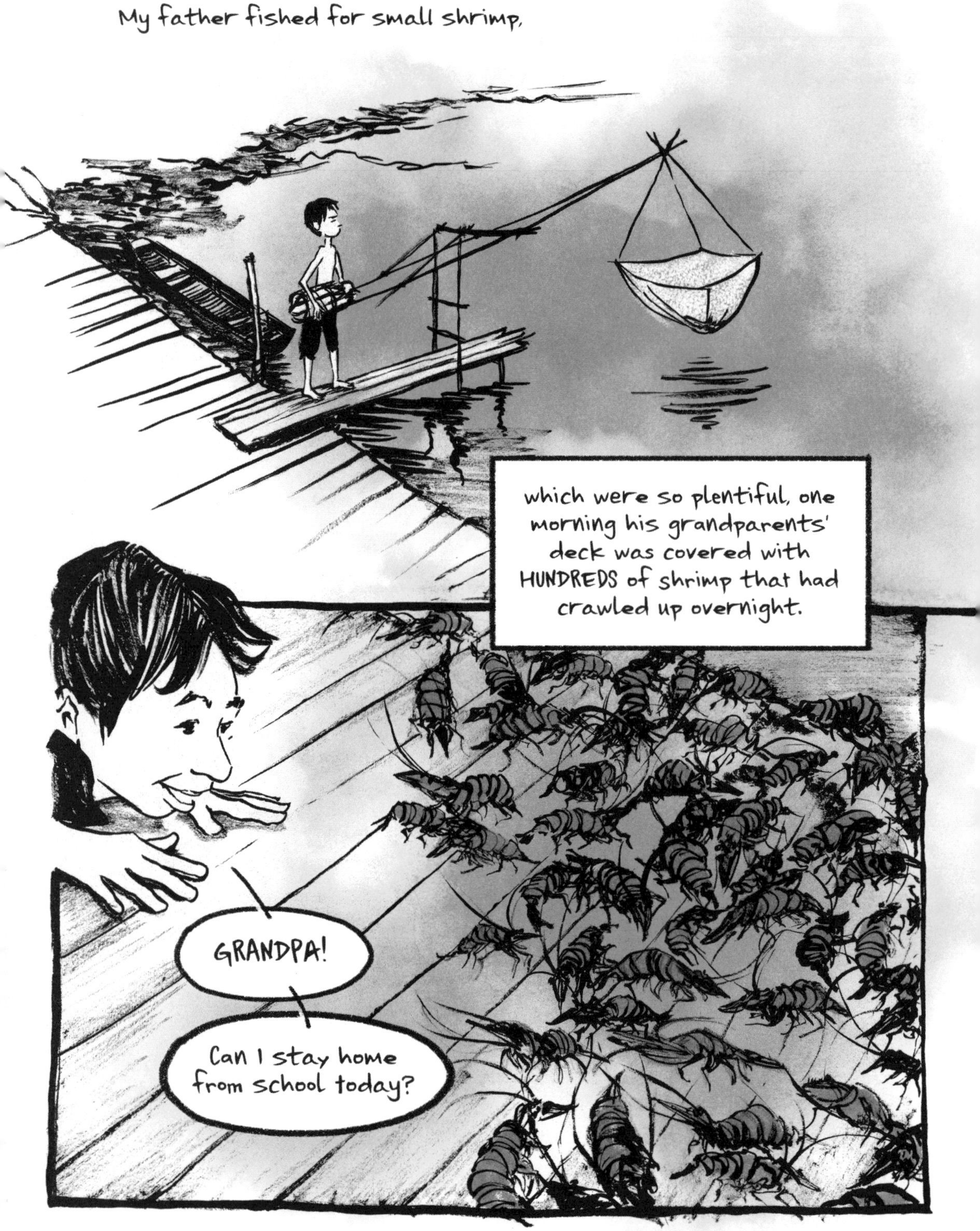
My father fished for small shrimp,
which were so plentiful, one morning his grandparents' deck was covered with HUNDREDS of shrimp that had crawled up overnight.
GRANDPA!
Can I stay home from school today?

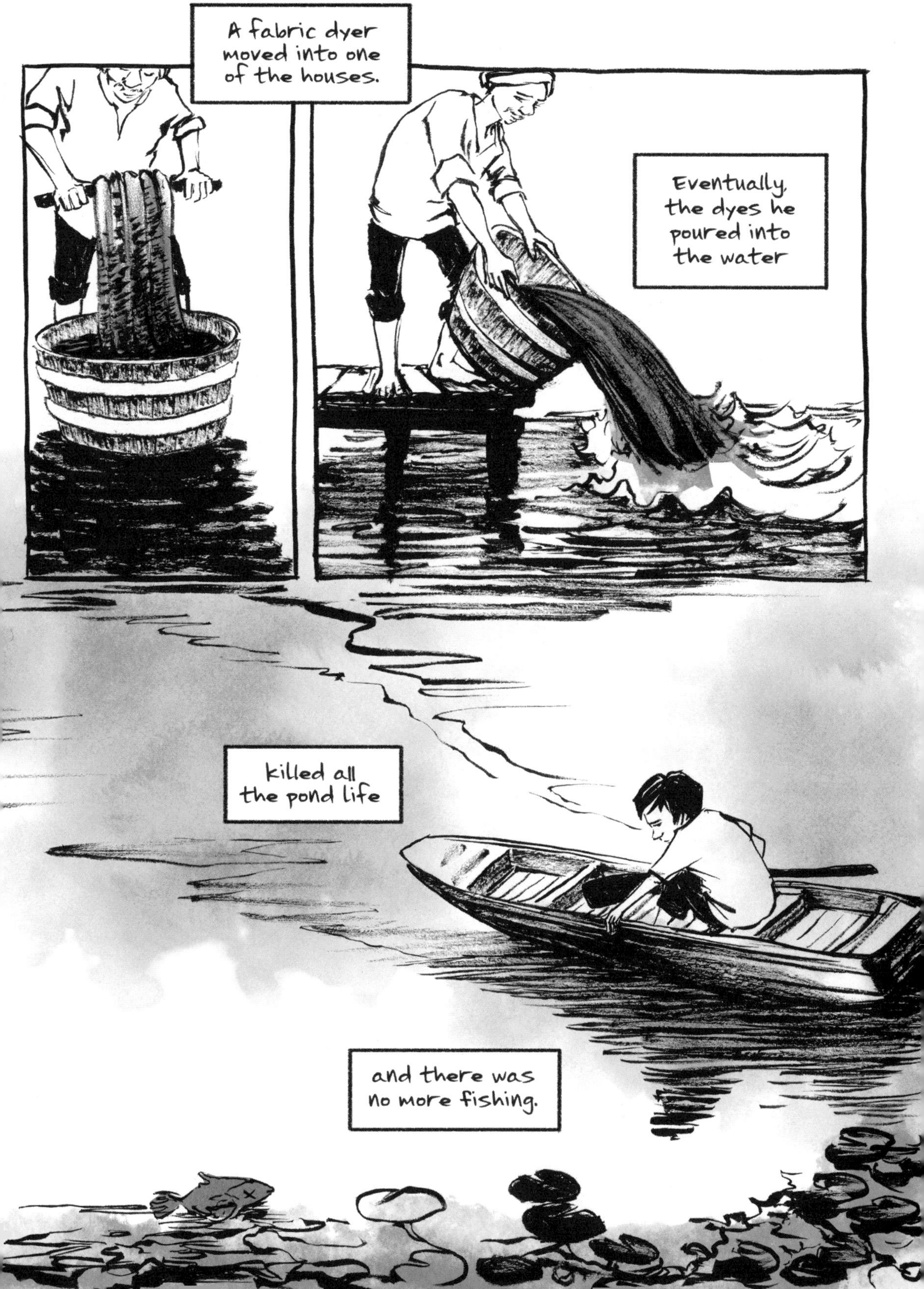
A fabric dyer moved into one of the houses.
Eventually, the dyes he poured into the water
killed all the pond life
and there was no more fishing.

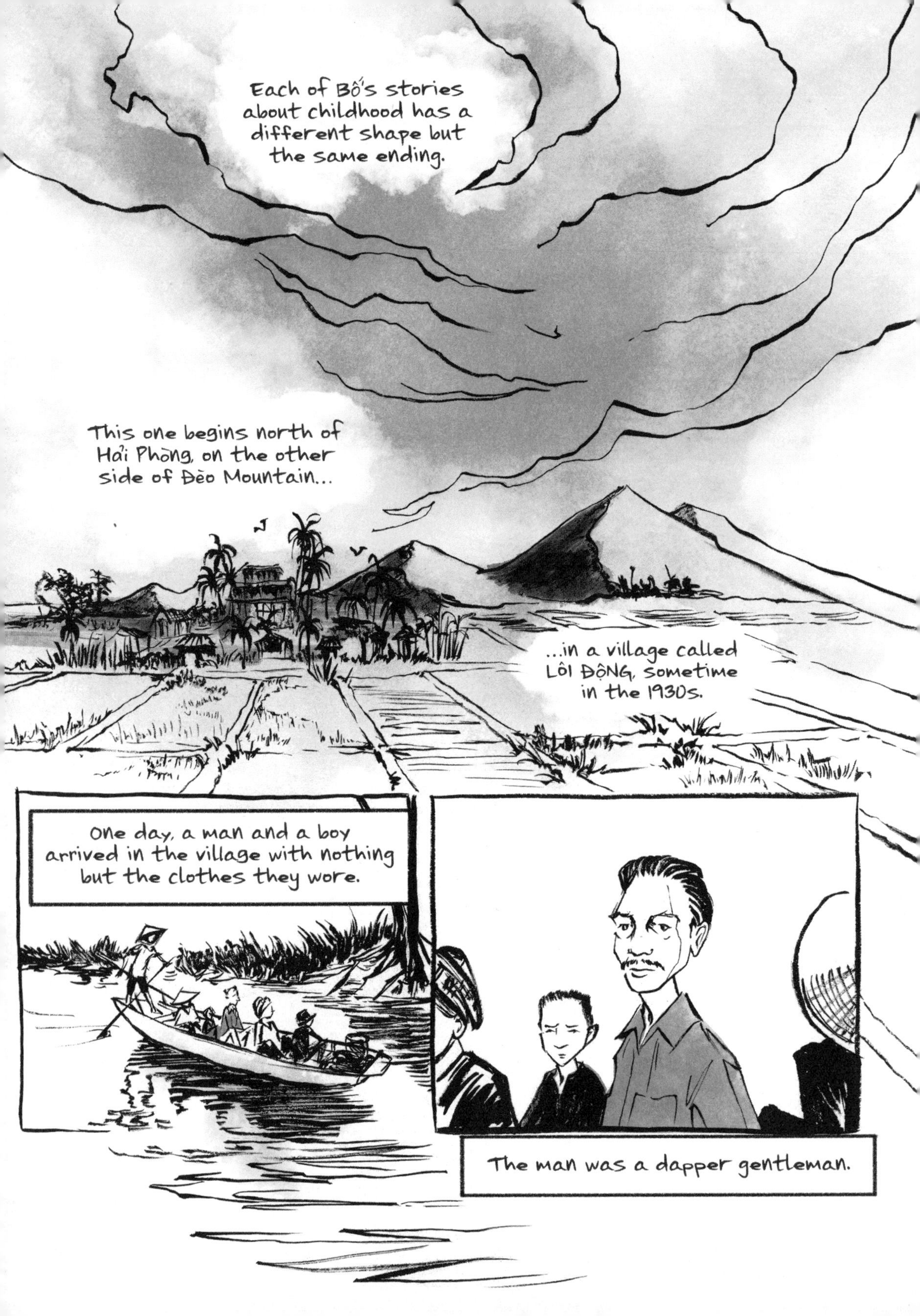
Each of Bố's stories about childhood has a different shape but the same ending.
This one begins north of Hải Phòng, on the other side of Đèo Mountain...
...in a village called LÔI ĐỘNG, sometime in the 1930s.
One day, a man and a boy arrived in the village with nothing but the clothes they wore.
The man was a dapper gentleman.

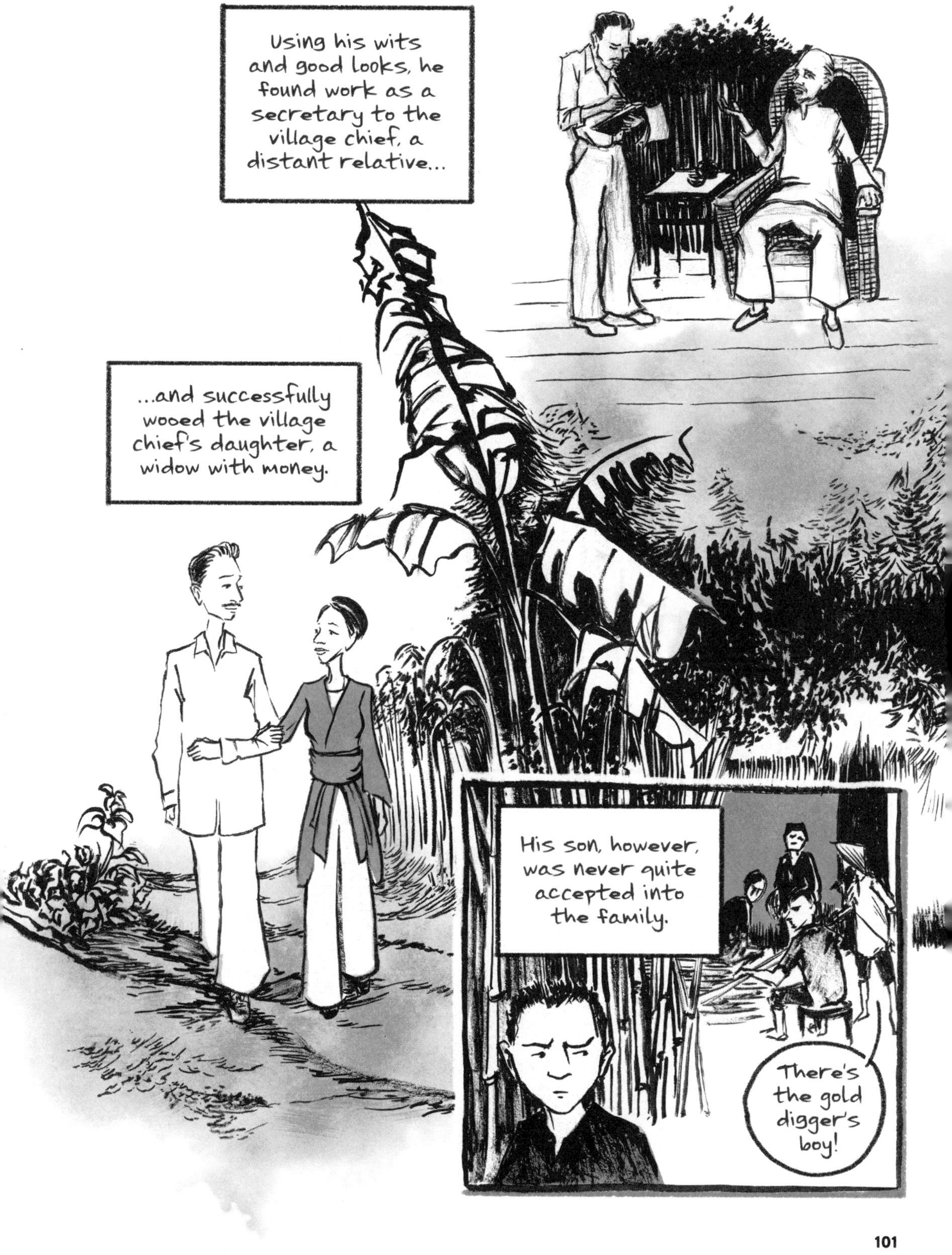
Using his wits and good looks, he found work as a secretary to the village chief, a distant relative...
...and successfully wooed the village chief's daughter, a widow with money.
His son, however, was never quite accepted into the family.
There's the gold digger's boy!

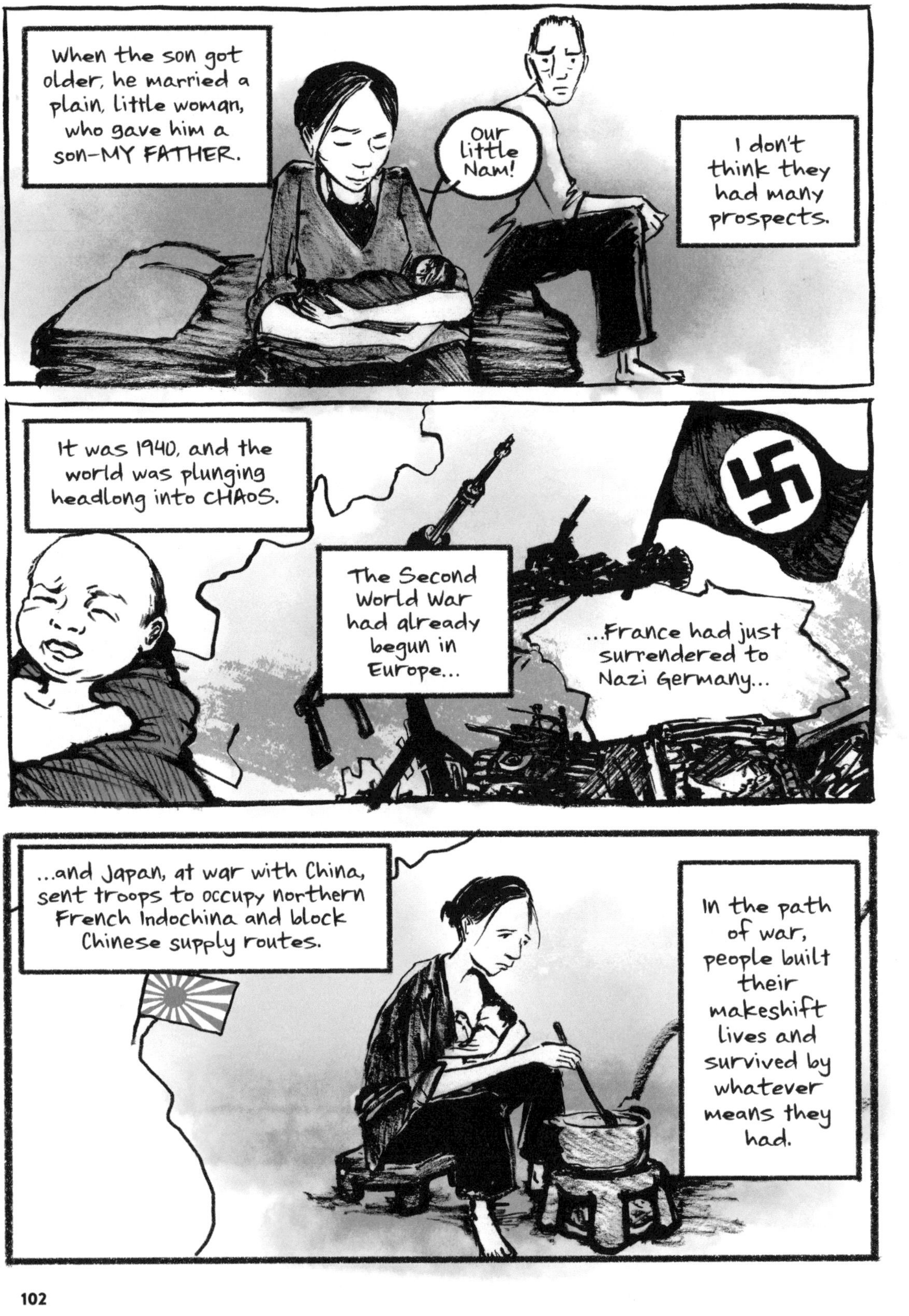
When the son got older, he married a plain, little woman, who gave him a son—MY FATHER.
Our little Nam!
I don't think they had many prospects.
It was 1940, and the world was plunging headlong into CHAOS.
The Second World War had already begun in Europe...
...France had just surrendered to Nazi Germany...
...and Japan, at war with China, sent troops to occupy northern French Indochina and block Chinese supply routes.
In the path of war, people built their makeshift lives and survived by whatever means they had.

When Bố was two, his parents went along with a dubious scheme cooked up by his grandfather.

The dapper gentleman had already begun to cheat on his wife.

He knew she kept jars of opium, which was easy to turn into cash, hidden around the house.

JACKPOT!

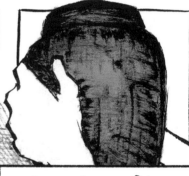

They stole one of the jars, and the three of them ran away together—

—dragging along Bố to the dense forests and mountains of the North—

—to Lạng Sơn, where they hoped to start a lumber business.

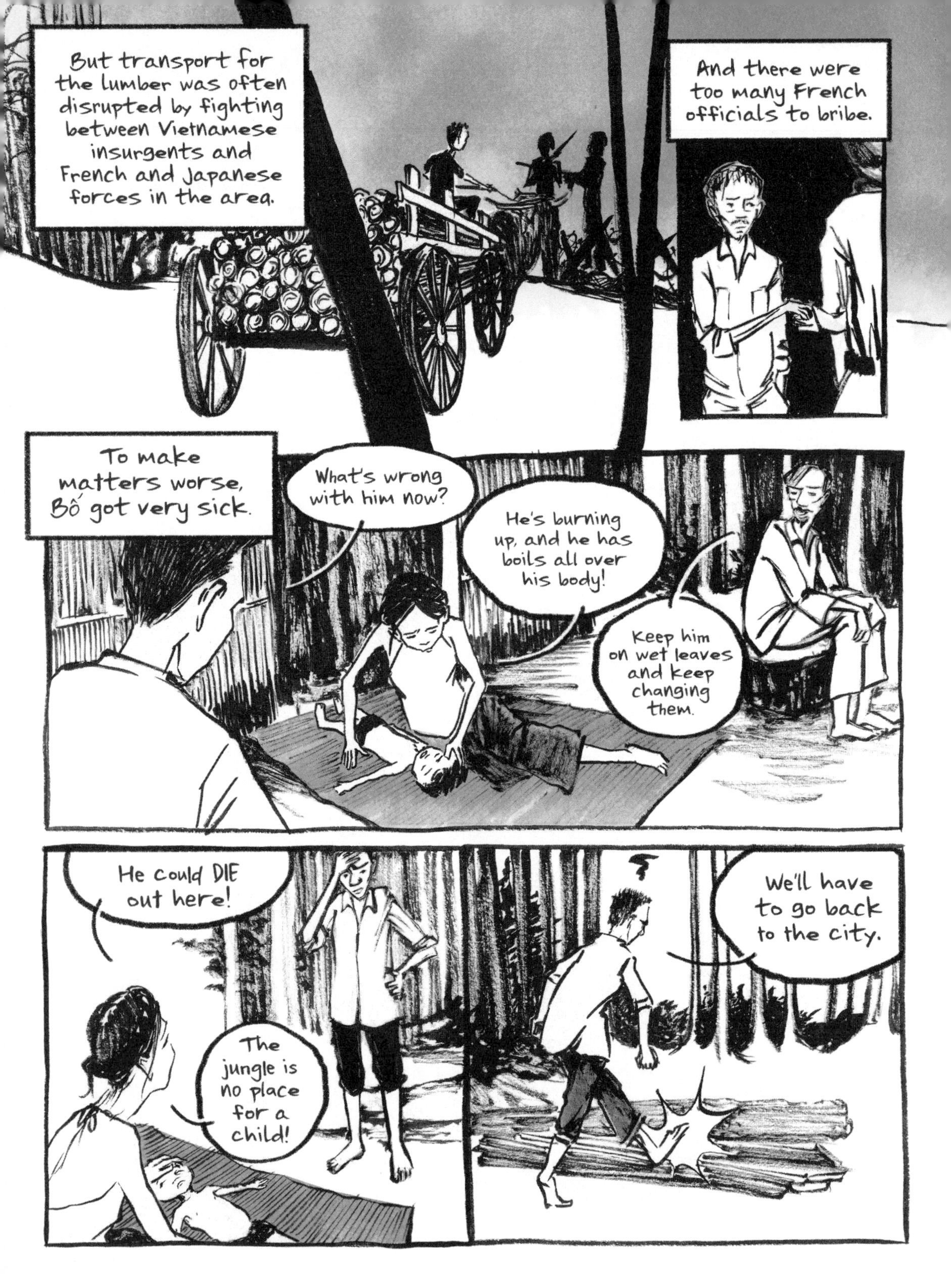
But transport for the lumber was often disrupted by fighting between Vietnamese insurgents and French and Japanese forces in the area.
And there were too many French officials to bribe.
To make matters worse, Bố got very sick.
What's wrong with him now?
He's burning up, and he has boils all over his body!
Keep him on wet leaves and keep changing them.
He could DIE out here!
The jungle is no place for a child!
We'll have to go back to the city.

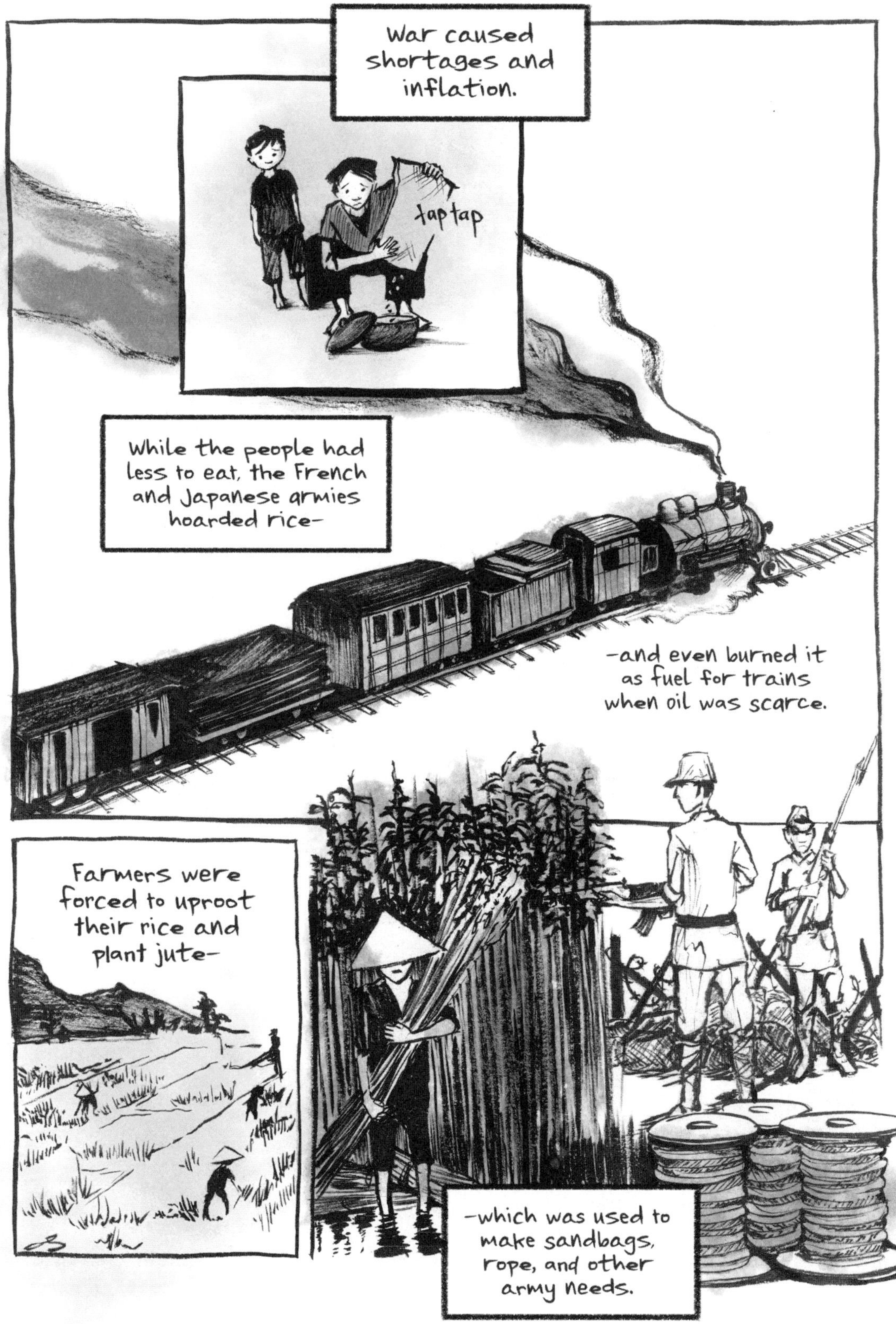
War caused shortages and inflation.
tap tap
While the people had less to eat, the French and Japanese armies hoarded rice-
-and even burned it as fuel for trains when oil was scarce.
Farmers were forced to uproot their rice and plant jute-
-which was used to make sandbags, rope, and other army needs.

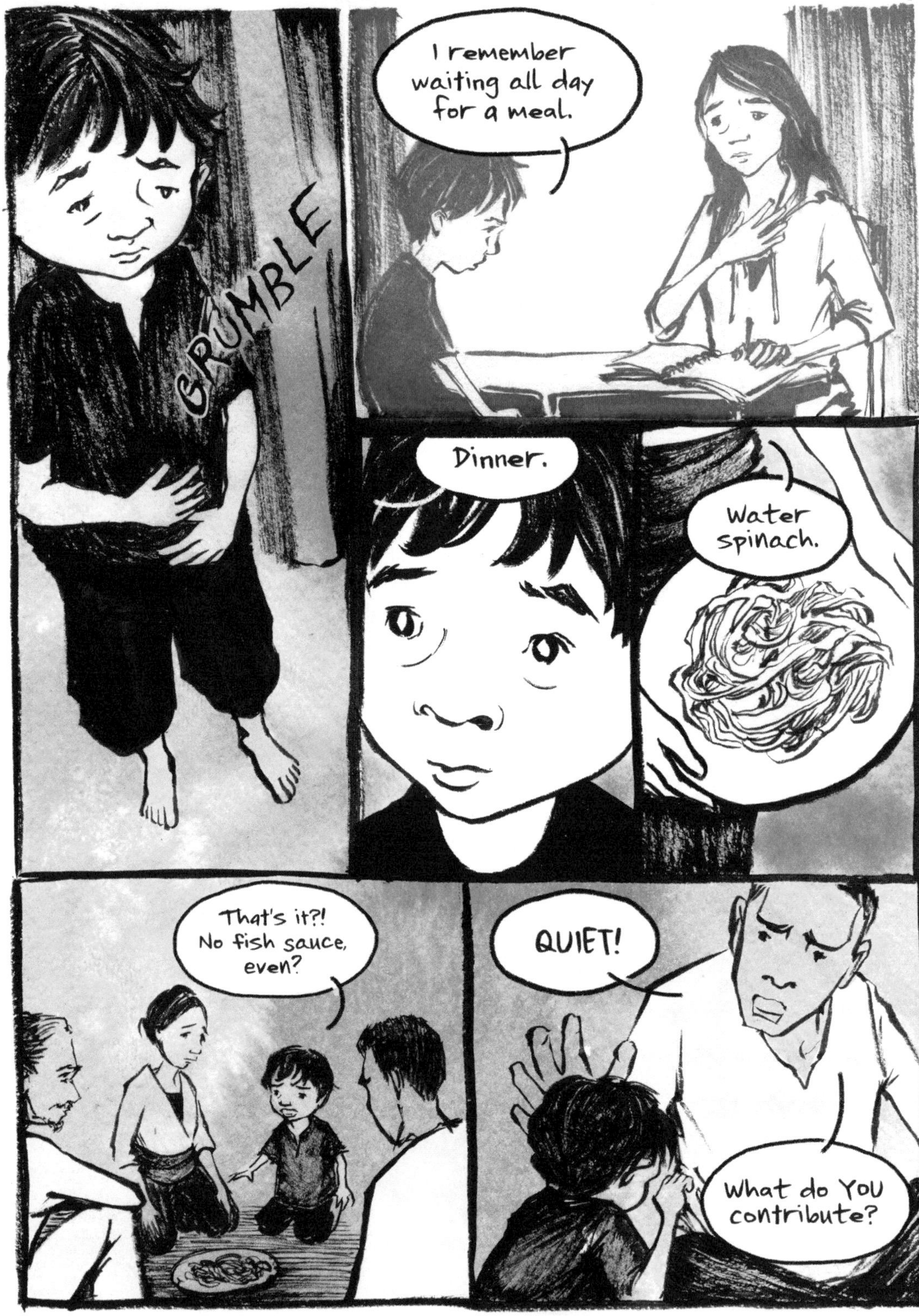
GRUMBLE
I remember waiting all day for a meal.
Dinner.
Water spinach.
That's it?! No fish sauce, even?
QUIET!
What do YOU contribute?

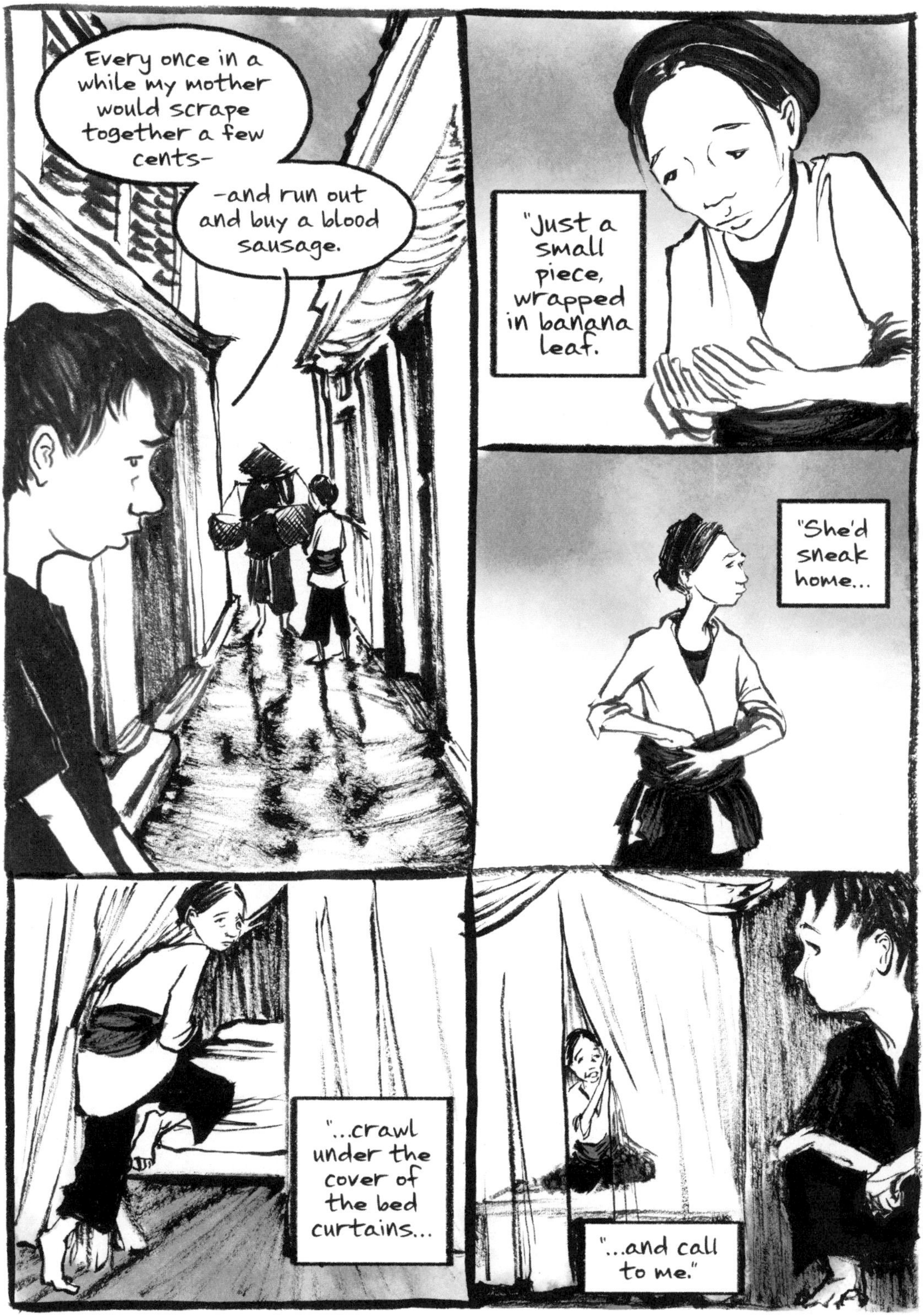

Every once in a while my mother would scrape together a few cents-
-and run out and buy a blood sausage.
"Just a small piece, wrapped in banana leaf.
"She'd sneak home...
"...crawl under the cover of the bed curtains...
"...and call to me."

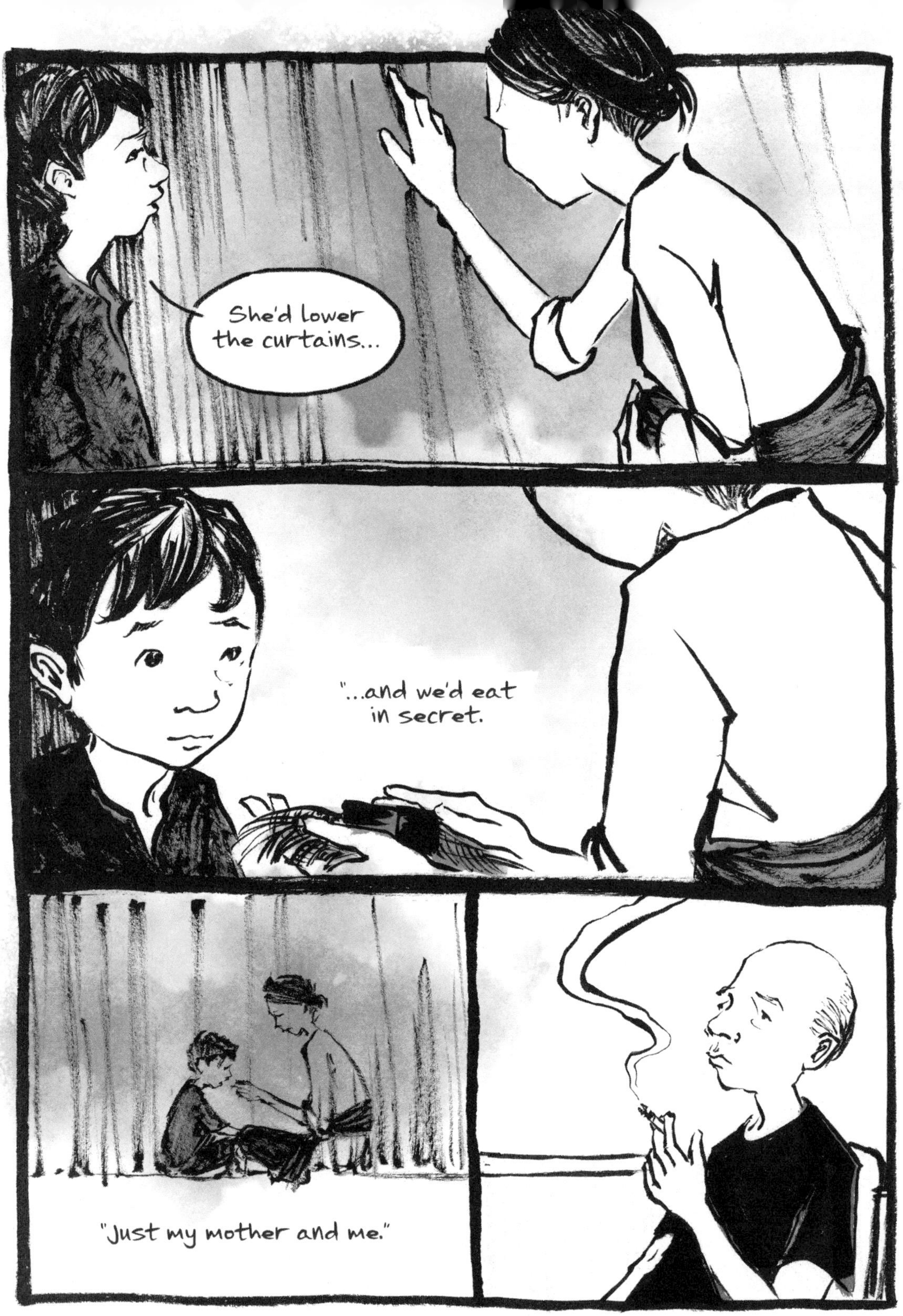
She'd lower the curtains...
"...and we'd eat in secret.
"Just my mother and me."

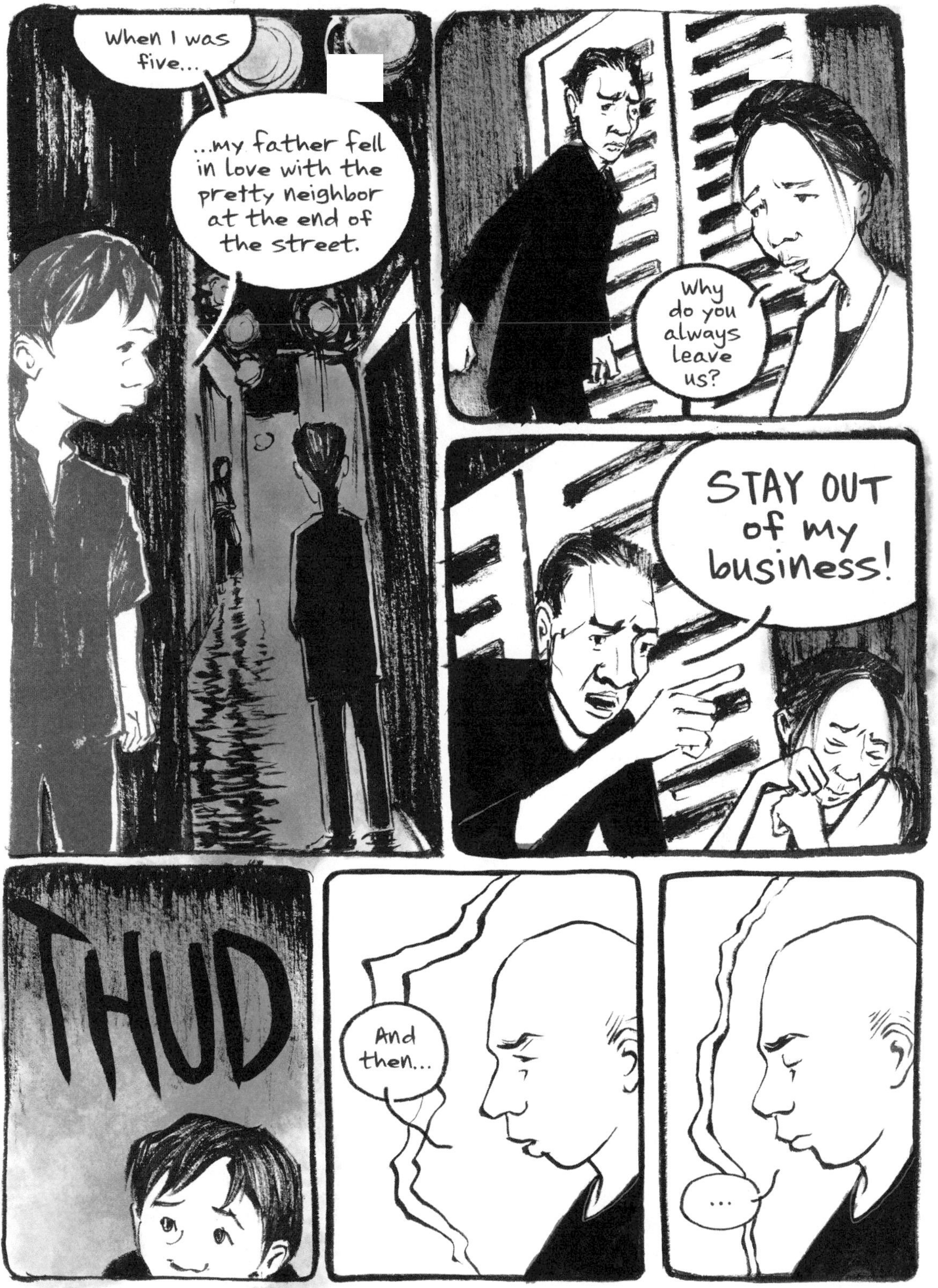
When I was five...
...my father fell in love with the pretty neighbor at the end of the street.
Why do you always leave us?
STAY OUT of my business!
THUD
And then...
...

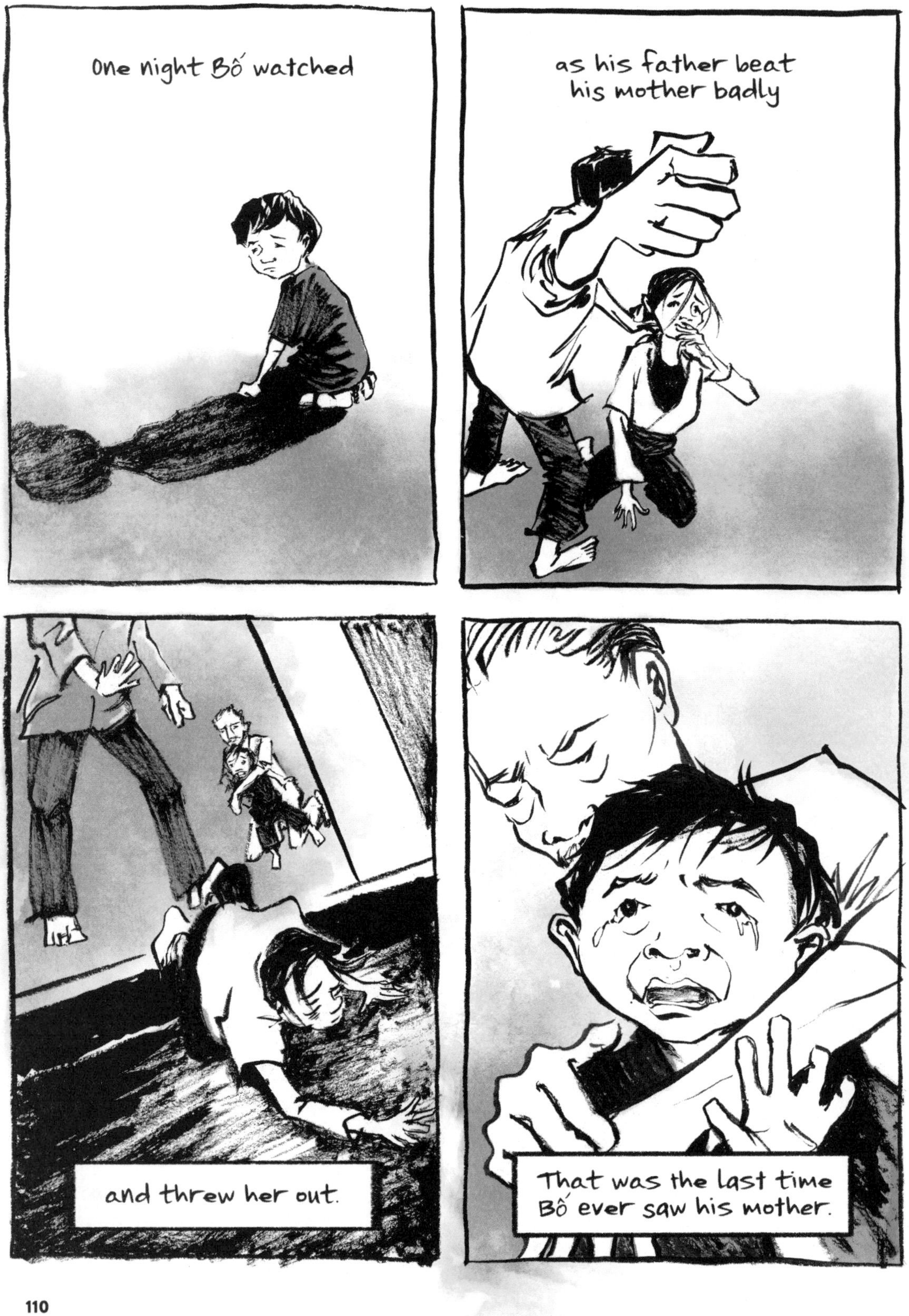
One night Bố watched
as his father beat his mother badly
and threw her out.
That was the last time Bố ever saw his mother.

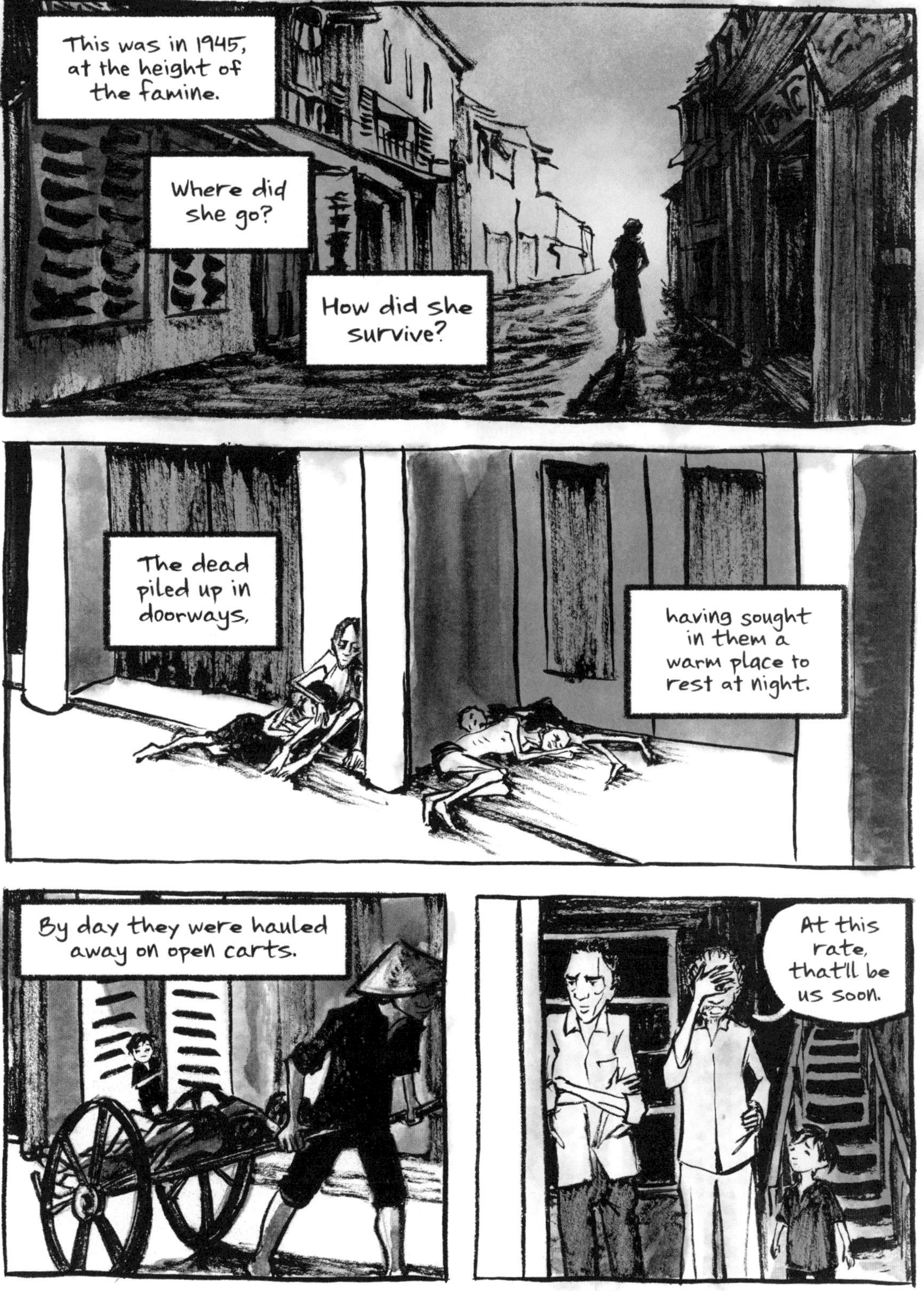
This was in 1945, at the height of the famine.
Where did she go?
How did she survive?
The dead piled up in doorways,
having sought in them a warm place to rest at night.
By day they were hauled away on open carts.
At this rate, that'll be us soon.

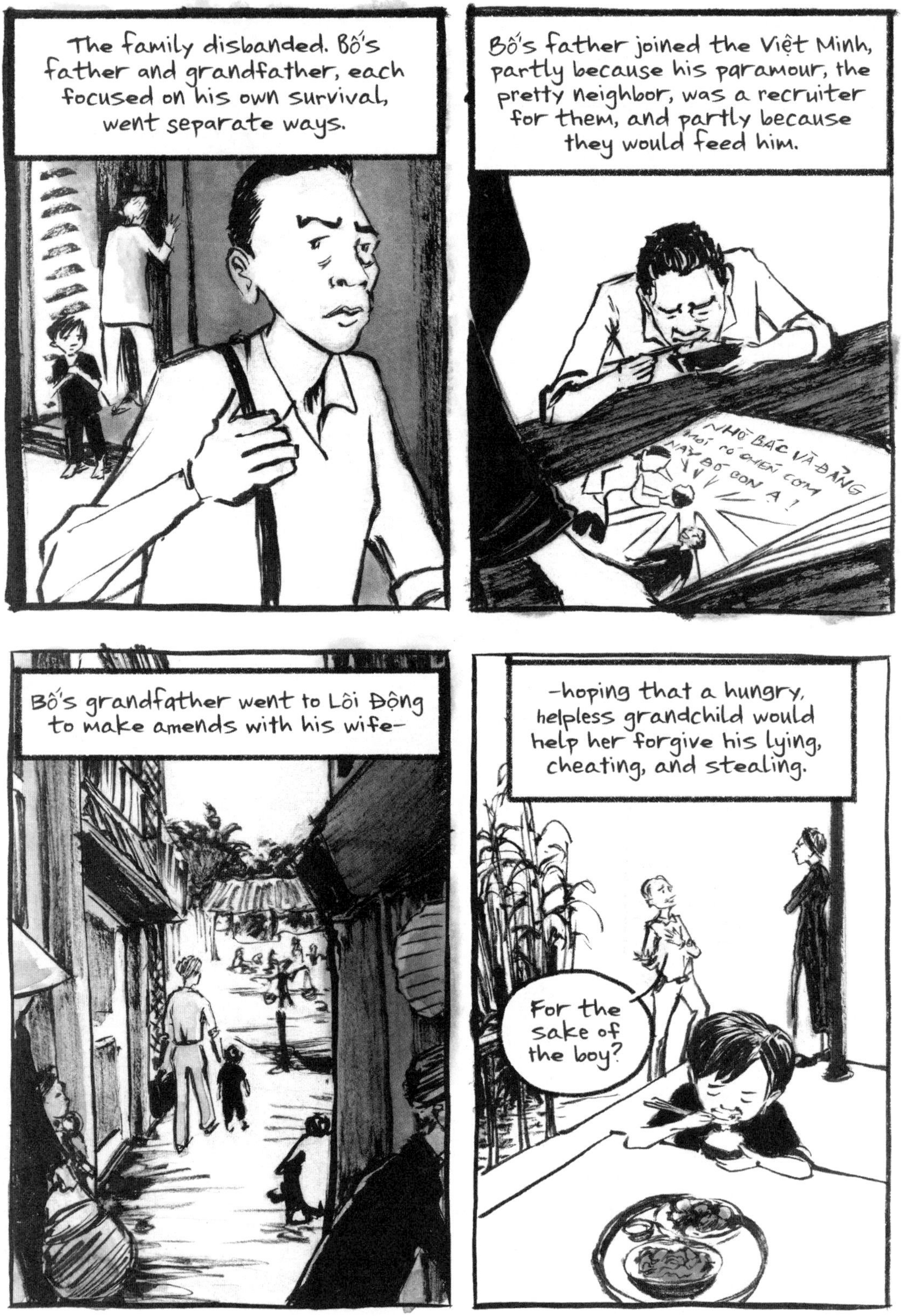

The family disbanded. Bố's father and grandfather, each focused on his own survival, went separate ways.
Bố's father joined the Việt Minh, partly because his paramour, the pretty neighbor, was a recruiter for them, and partly because they would feed him.
NHỜ BÁC VÀ ĐẢNG
MỚI CÓ CHÉN CƠM
NÀY BỐ CON Ạ!
Bố's grandfather went to Lôi Động to make amends with his wife–
–hoping that a hungry, helpless grandchild would help her forgive his lying, cheating, and stealing.
For the sake of the boy?

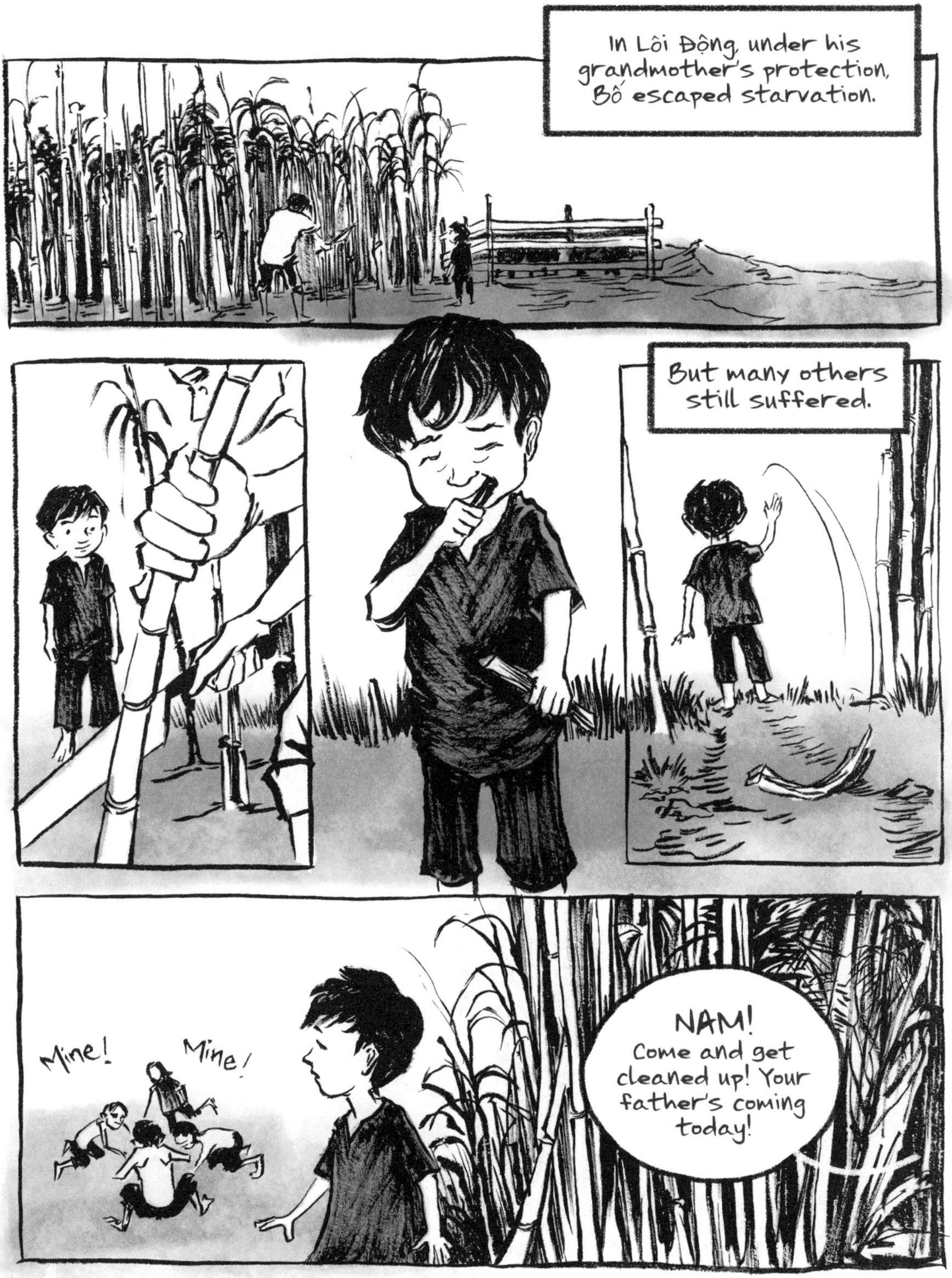
In Lôi Động, under his grandmother's protection, Bố escaped starvation.
But many others still suffered.
Mine!
Mine!
NAM! Come and get cleaned up! Your father's coming today!

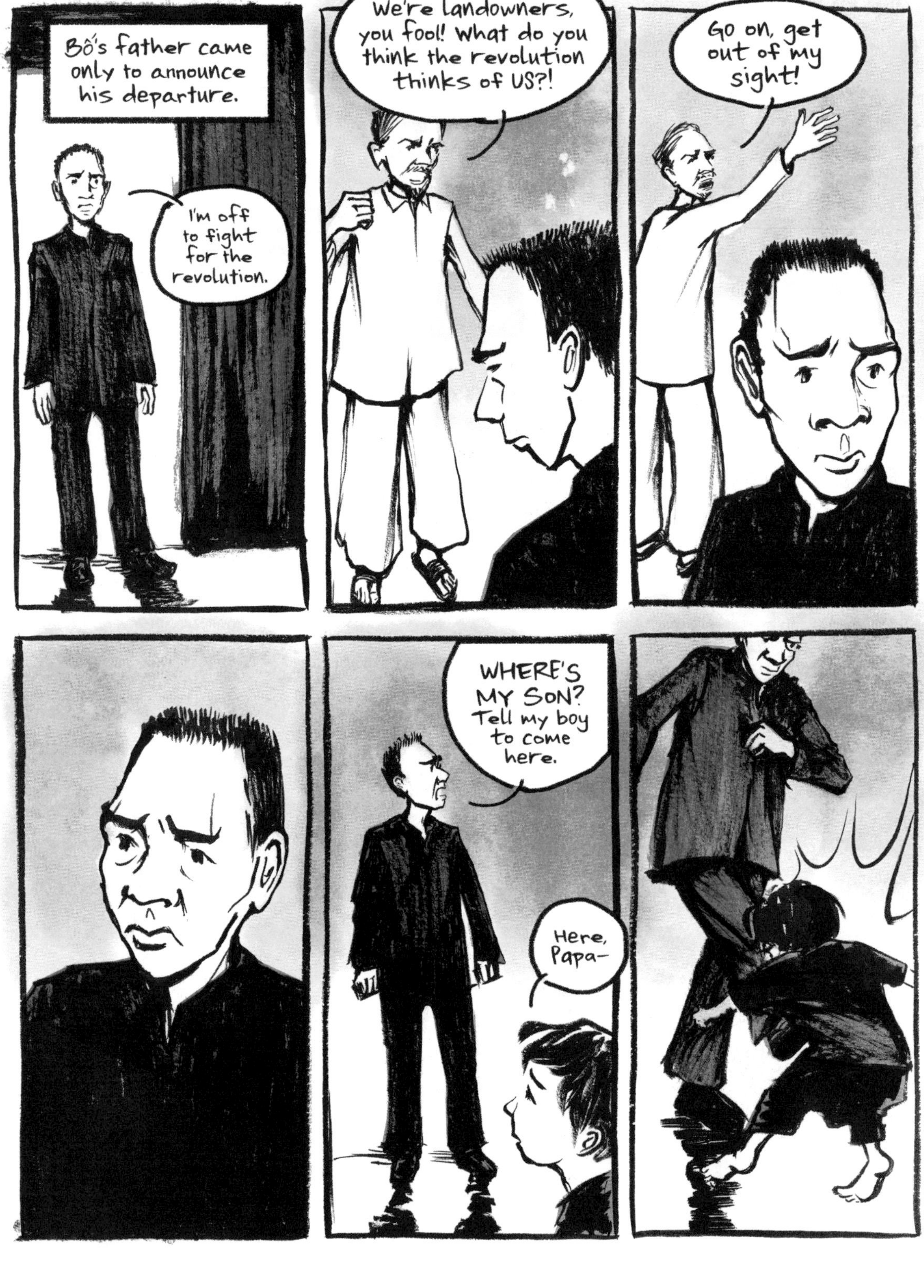

Bố's father came only to announce his departure.
I'm off to fight for the revolution.
We're landowners, you fool! What do you think the revolution thinks of US?!
Go on, get out of my sight!
WHERE'S MY SON? Tell my boy to come here.
Here, Papa–

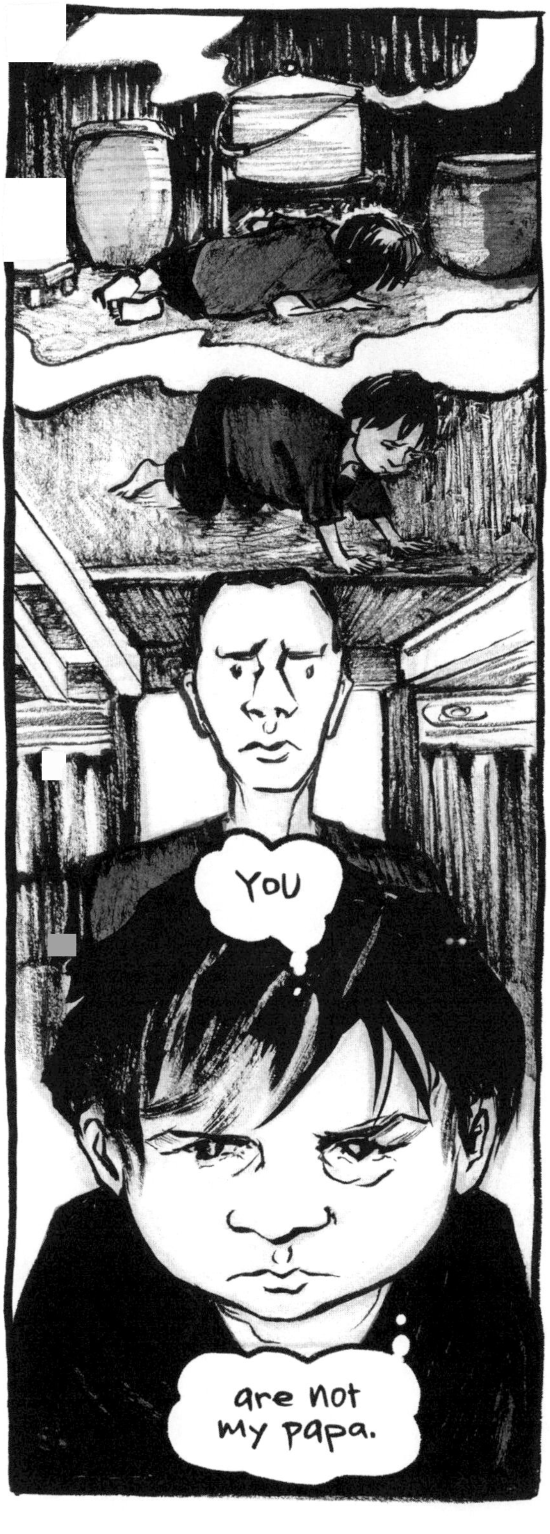
You
are not my papa.

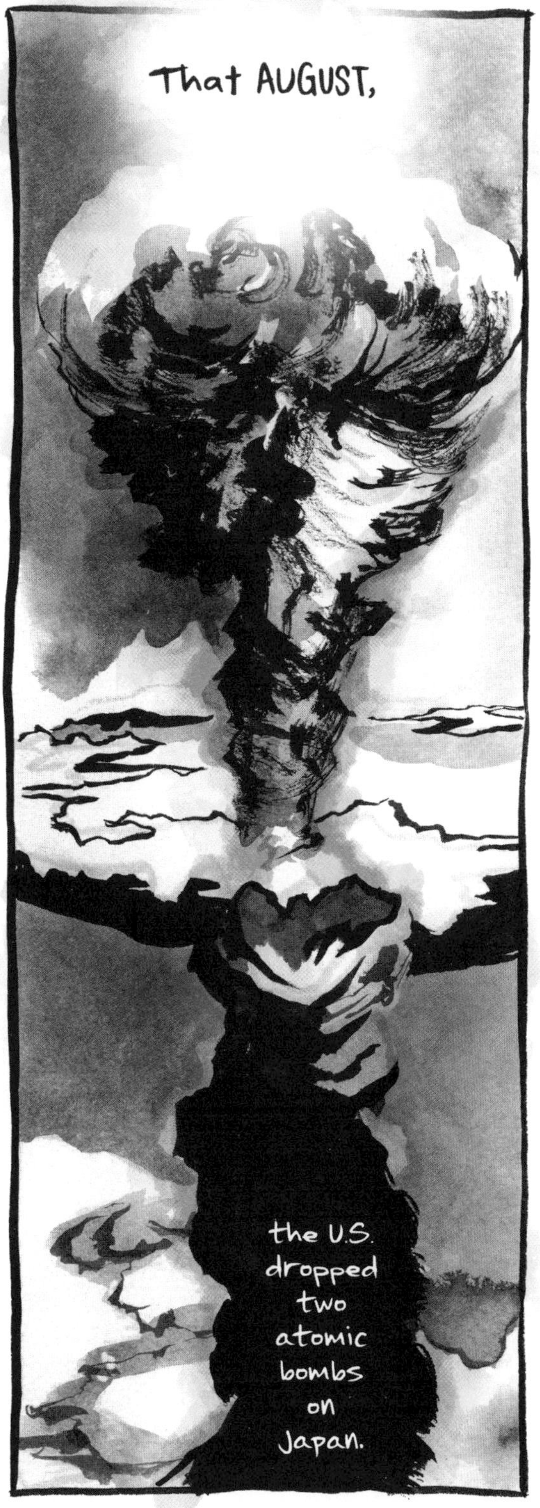
That AUGUST,
the U.S. dropped two atomic bombs on Japan.

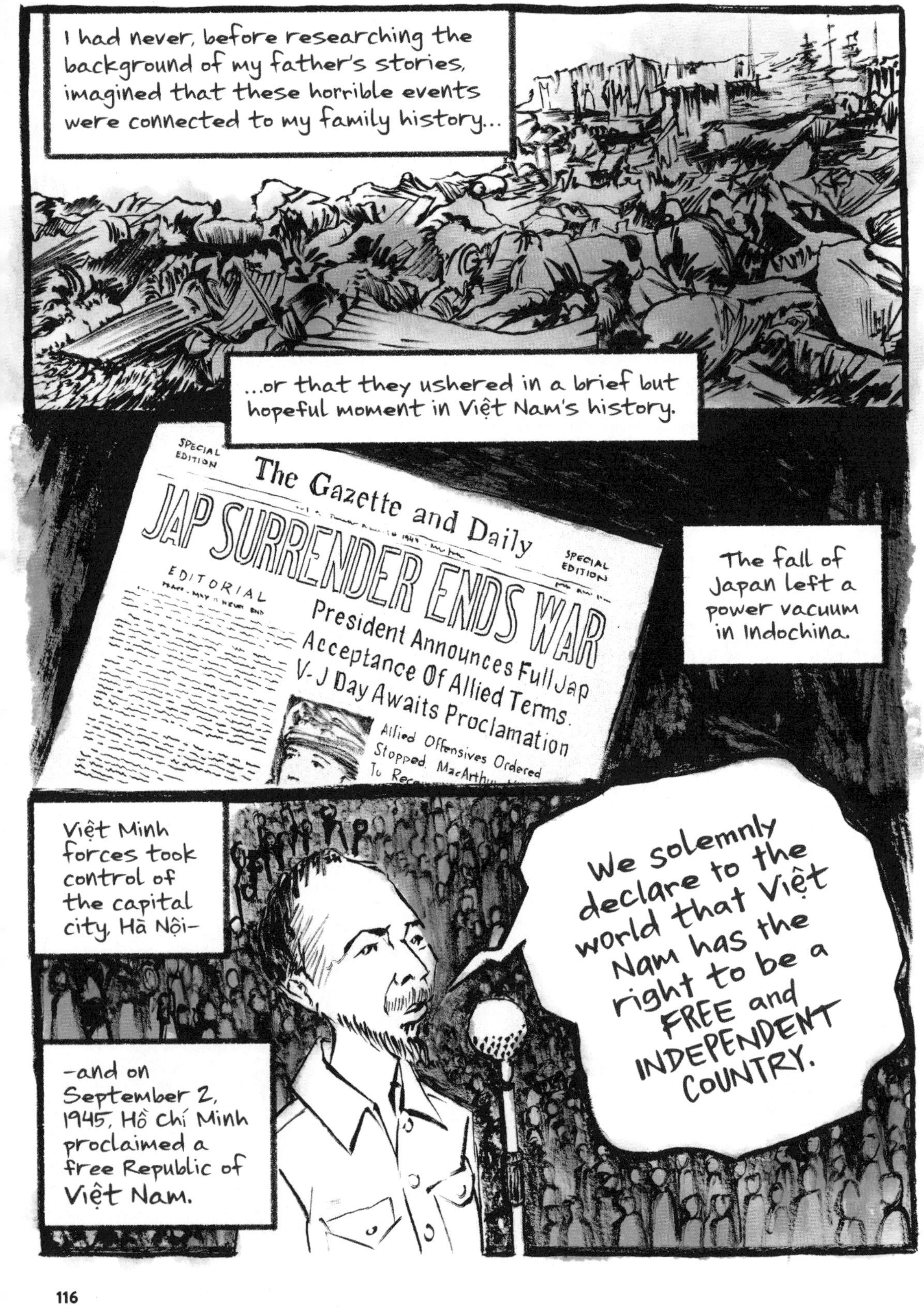
I had never, before researching the background of my father's stories, imagined that these horrible events were connected to my family history...
...or that they ushered in a brief but hopeful moment in Việt Nam's history.
SPECIAL EDITION
The Gazette and Daily
JAP SURRENDER ENDS WAR
SPECIAL EDITION
EDITORIAL
President Announces Full Jap Acceptance Of Allied Terms. V-J Day Awaits Proclamation
Allied Offensives Ordered Stopped. MacArthur
The fall of Japan left a power vacuum in Indochina.
Việt Minh forces took control of the capital city, Hà Nội-
We solemnly declare to the world that Việt Nam has the right to be a FREE and INDEPENDENT COUNTRY.
-and on September 2, 1945, Hồ Chí Minh proclaimed a free Republic of Việt Nam.

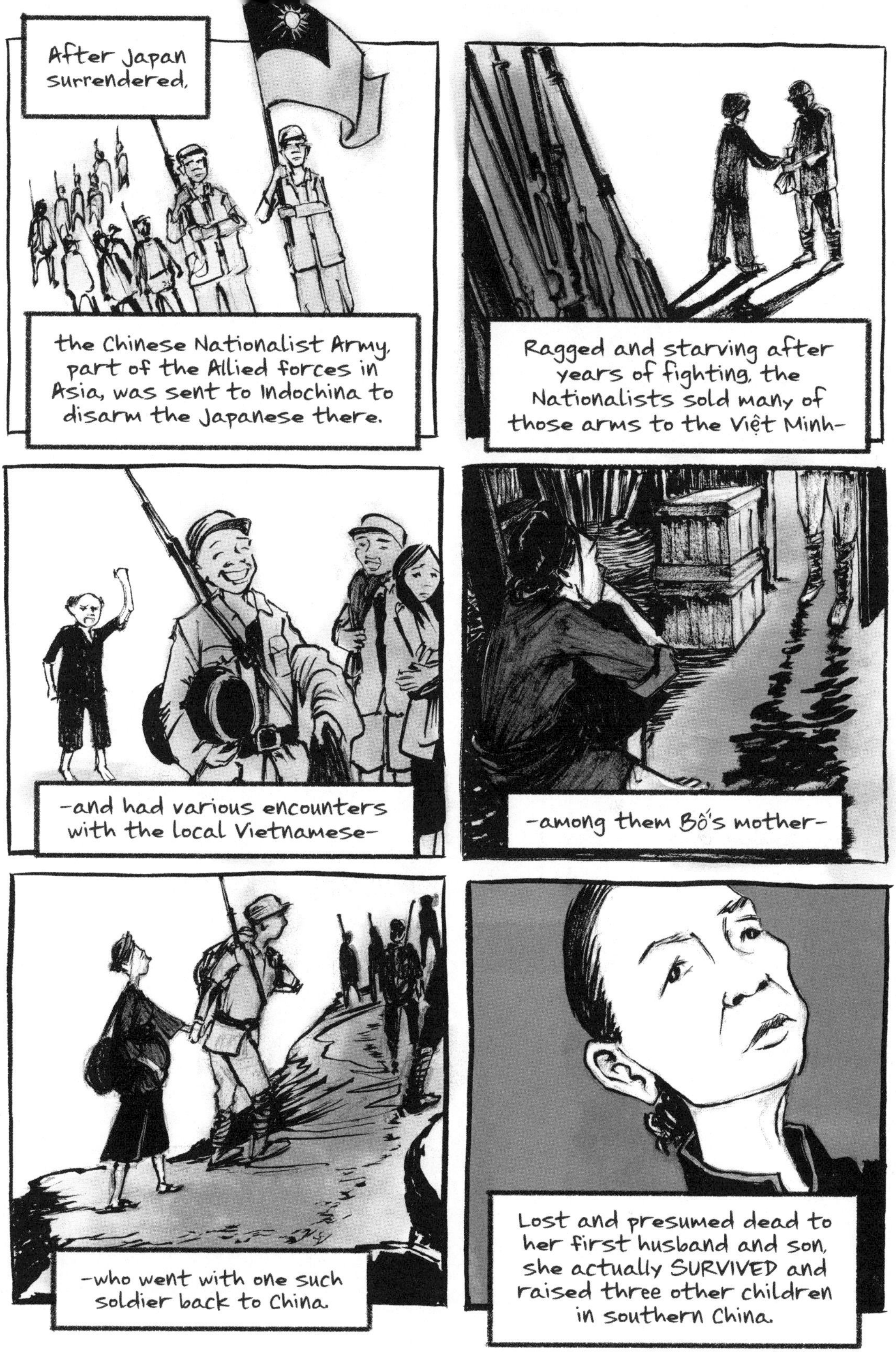
After Japan surrendered,
the Chinese Nationalist Army, part of the Allied forces in Asia, was sent to Indochina to disarm the Japanese there.
Ragged and starving after years of fighting, the Nationalists sold many of those arms to the Việt Minh-
-and had various encounters with the local Vietnamese-
-among them Bố's mother-
-who went with one such soldier back to China.
Lost and presumed dead to her first husband and son, she actually SURVIVED and raised three other children in southern China.

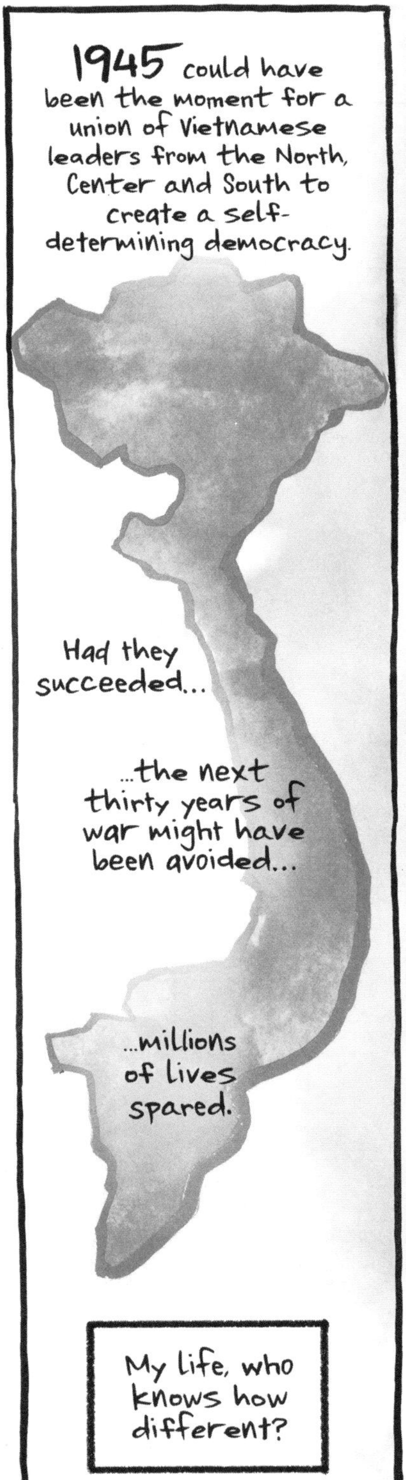
1945 could have been the moment for a union of Vietnamese leaders from the North, Center and South to create a self-determining democracy.
Had they succeeded...
...the next thirty years of war might have been avoided...
...millions of lives spared.
My life, who knows how different?

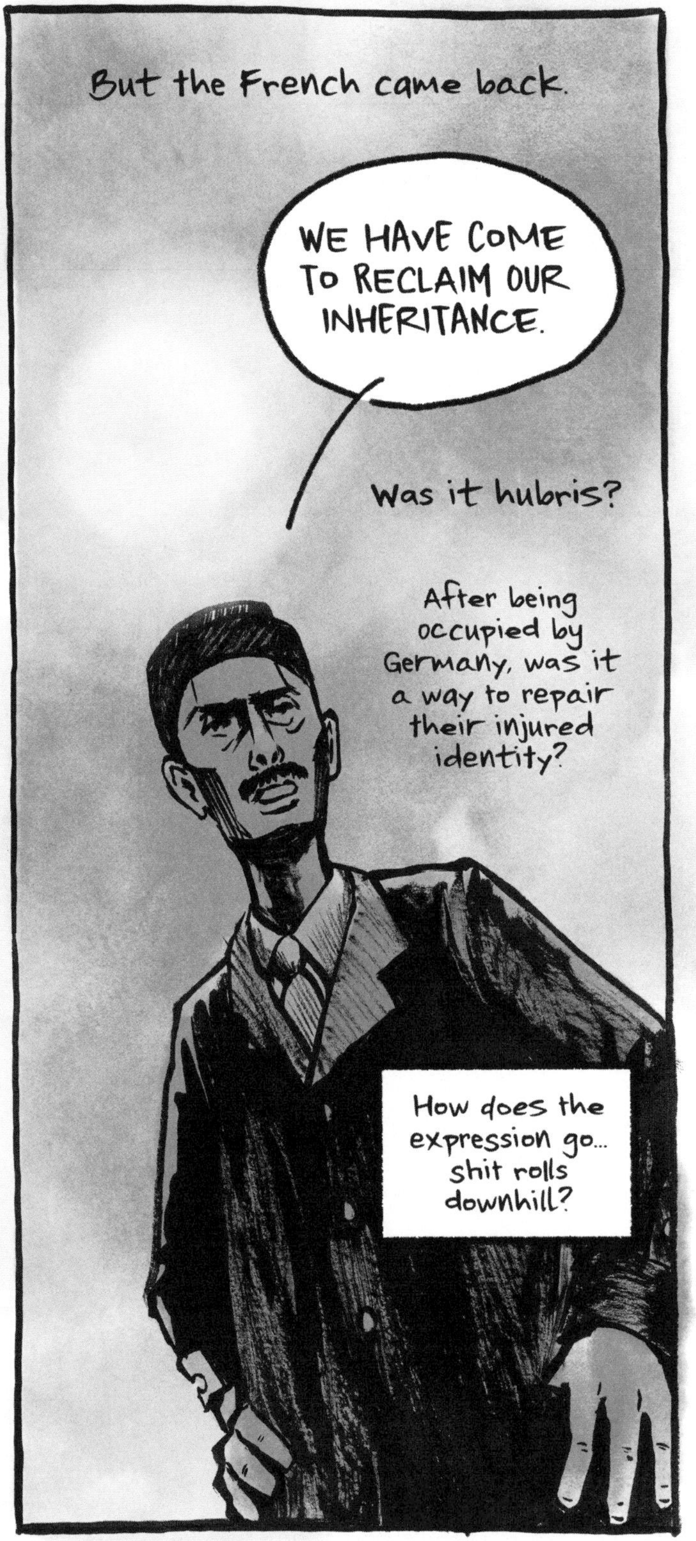
But the French came back.
WE HAVE COME TO RECLAIM OUR INHERITANCE.
Was it hubris?
After being occupied by Germany, was it a way to repair their injured identity?
How does the expression go... shit rolls downhill?

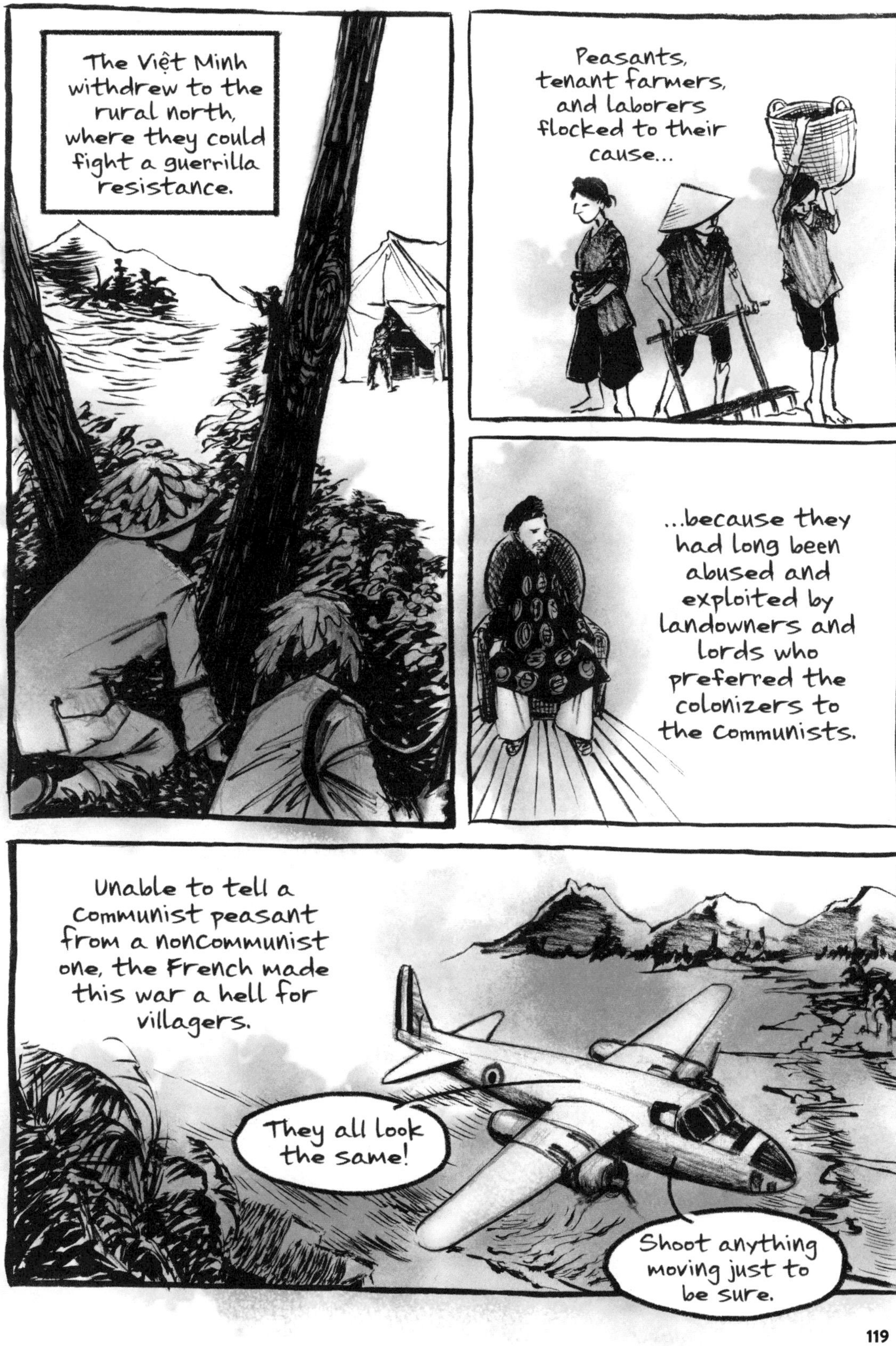

The Việt Minh withdrew to the rural north, where they could fight a guerrilla resistance.
Peasants, tenant farmers, and laborers flocked to their cause...
...because they had long been abused and exploited by landowners and lords who preferred the colonizers to the communists.
Unable to tell a communist peasant from a noncommunist one, the French made this war a hell for villagers.
They all look the same!
Shoot anything moving just to be sure.

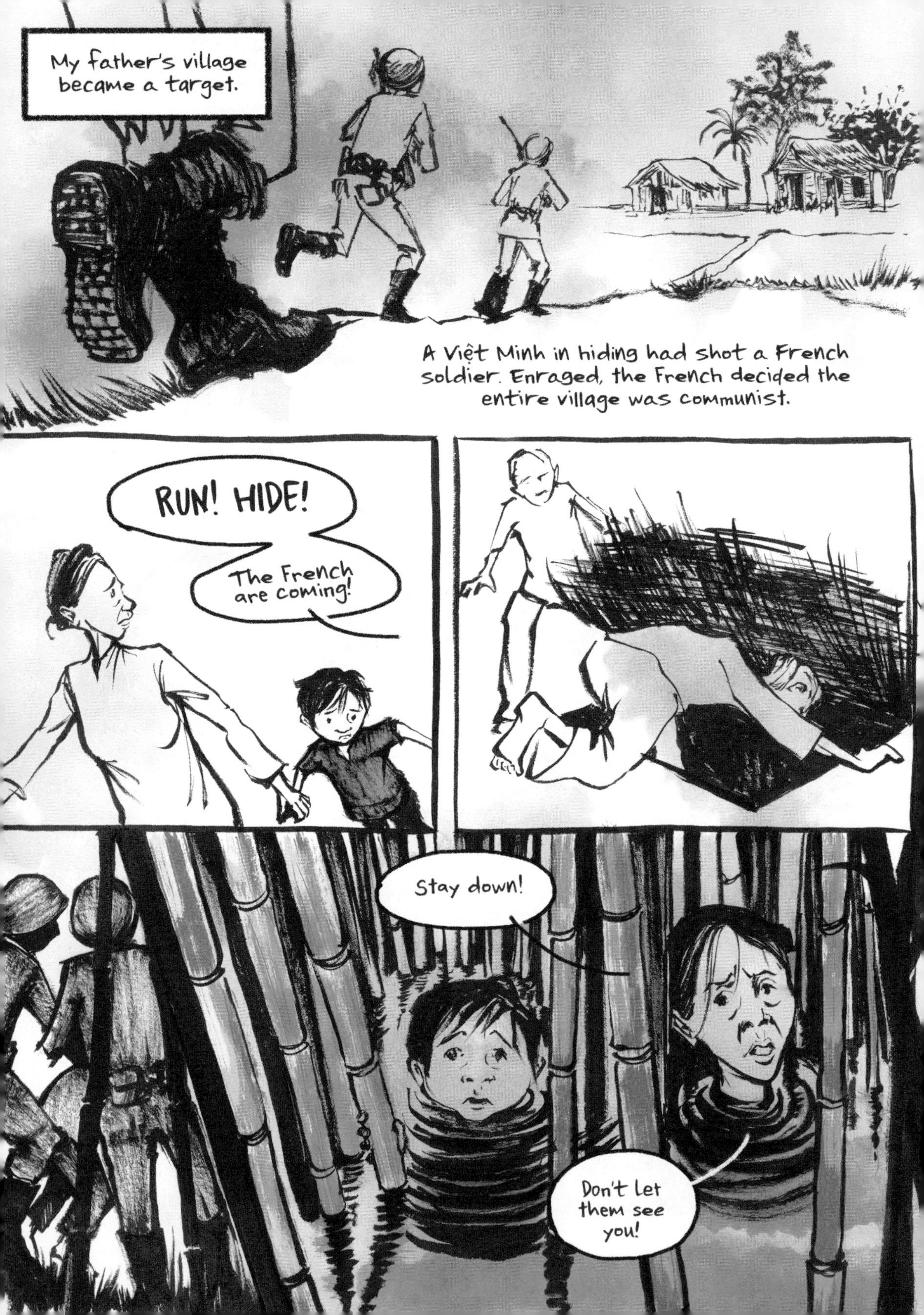
My father's village became a target.
A Việt Minh in hiding had shot a French soldier. Enraged, the French decided the entire village was communist.
RUN! HIDE!
The French are coming!
Stay down!
Don't let them see you!

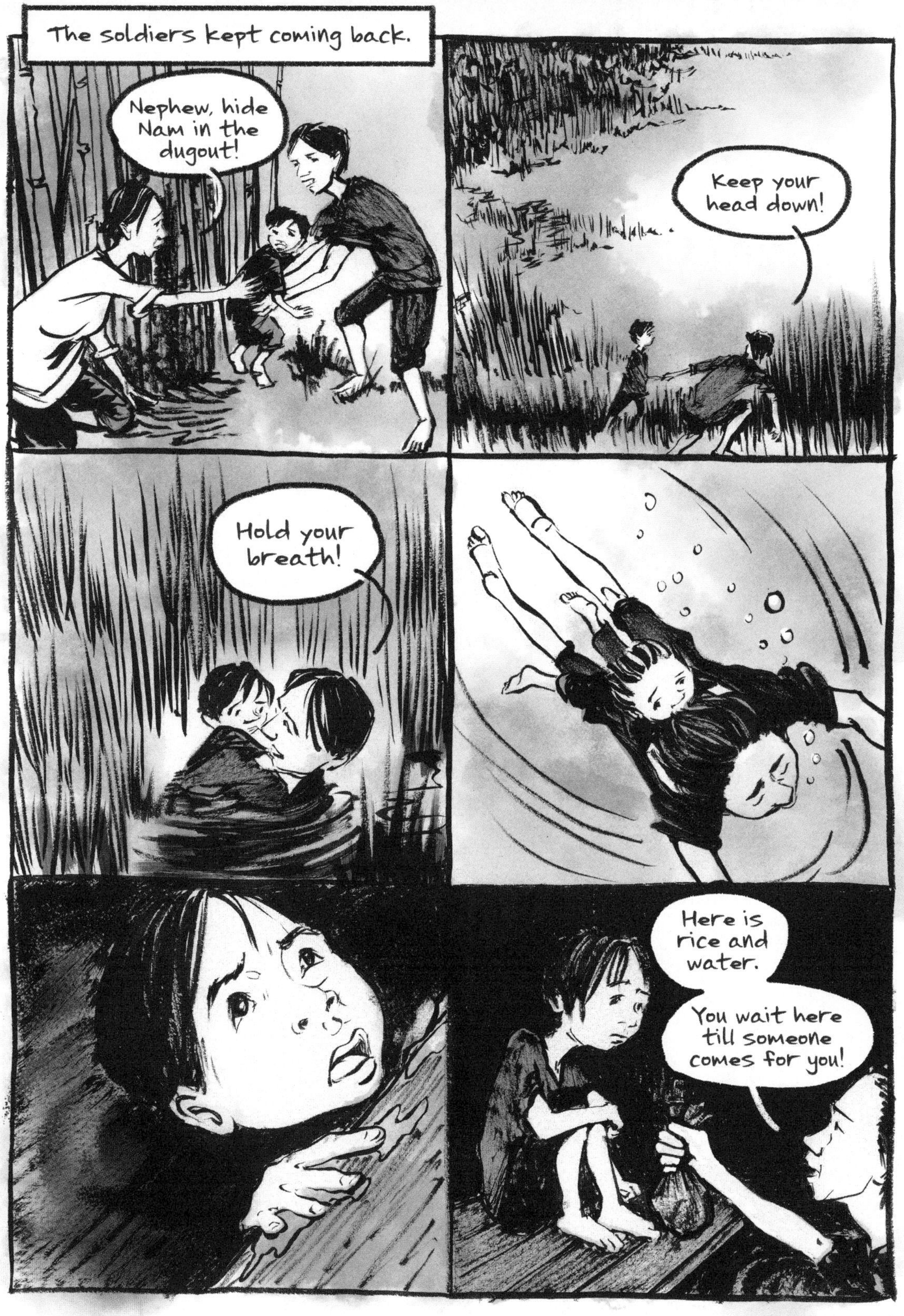
The soldiers kept coming back.
Nephew, hide Nam in the dugout!
Keep your head down!
Hold your breath!
Here is rice and water.
You wait here till someone comes for you!

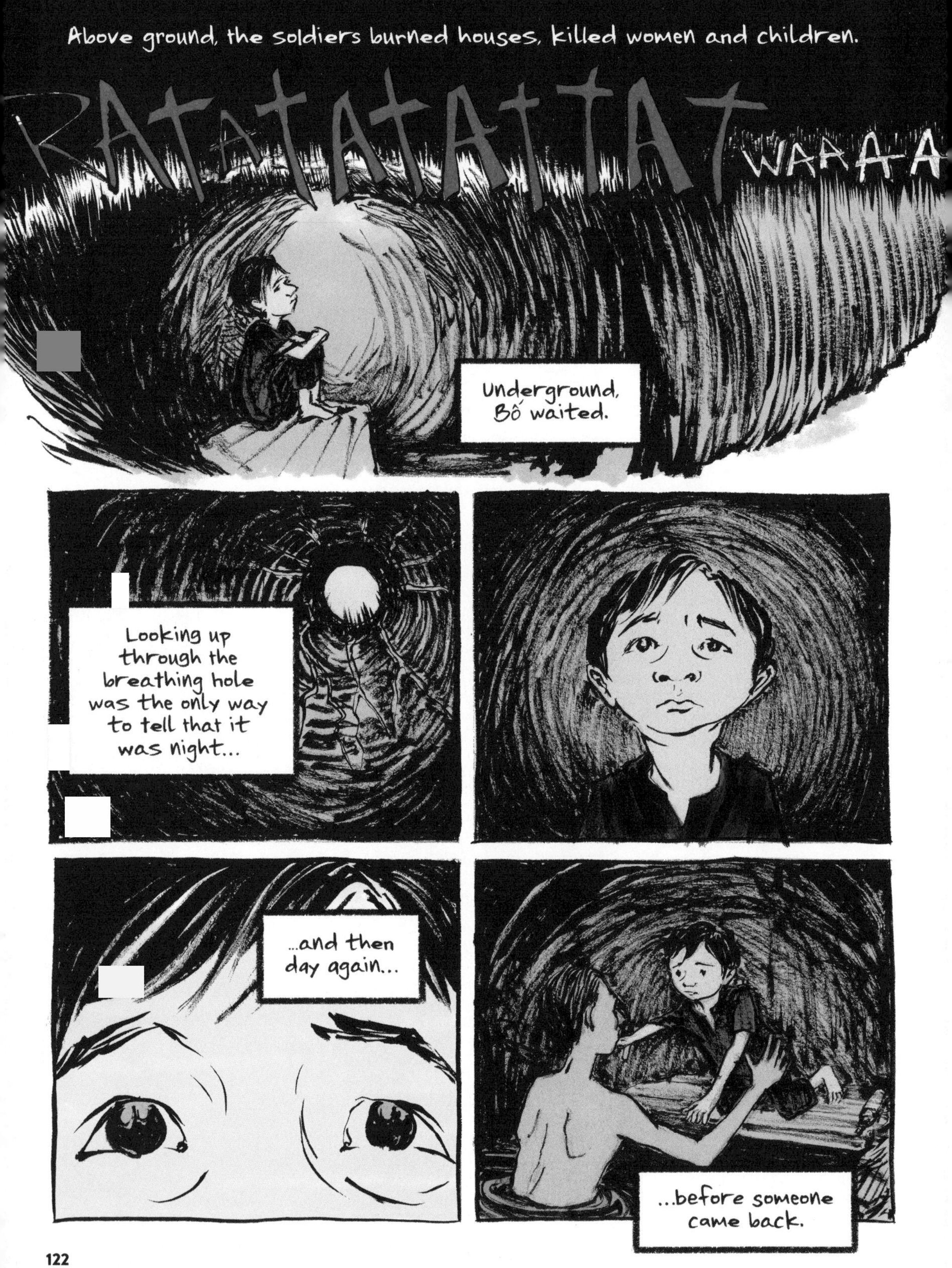

Above ground, the soldiers burned houses, killed women and children.
RATATATATTAT
WARAA
Underground, Bố waited.
Looking up through the breathing hole was the only way to tell that it was night...
...and then day again...
...before someone came back.

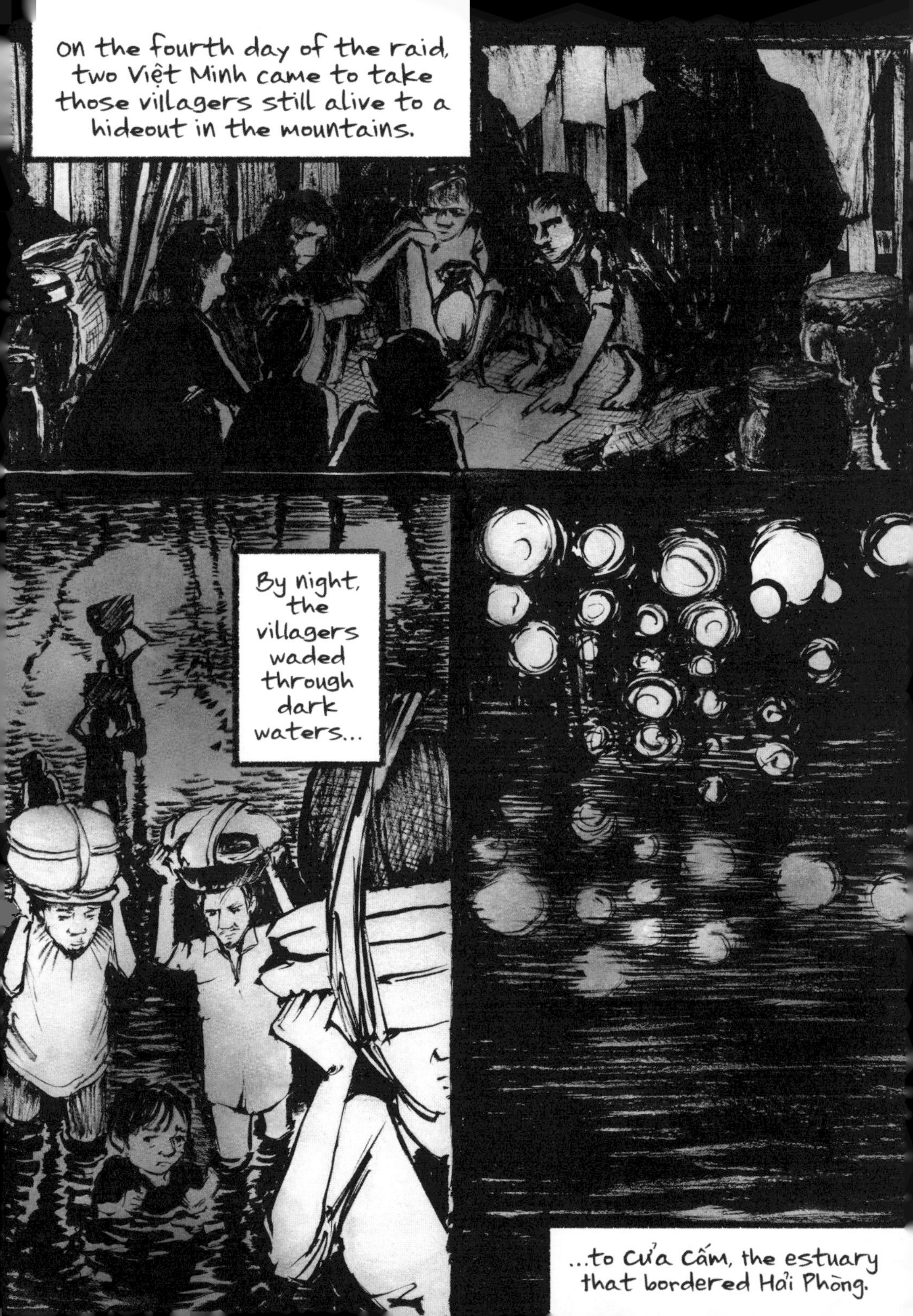
On the fourth day of the raid, two Việt Minh came to take those villagers still alive to a hideout in the mountains.
By night, the villagers waded through dark waters...
...to Cửa Cấm, the estuary that bordered Hải Phòng.

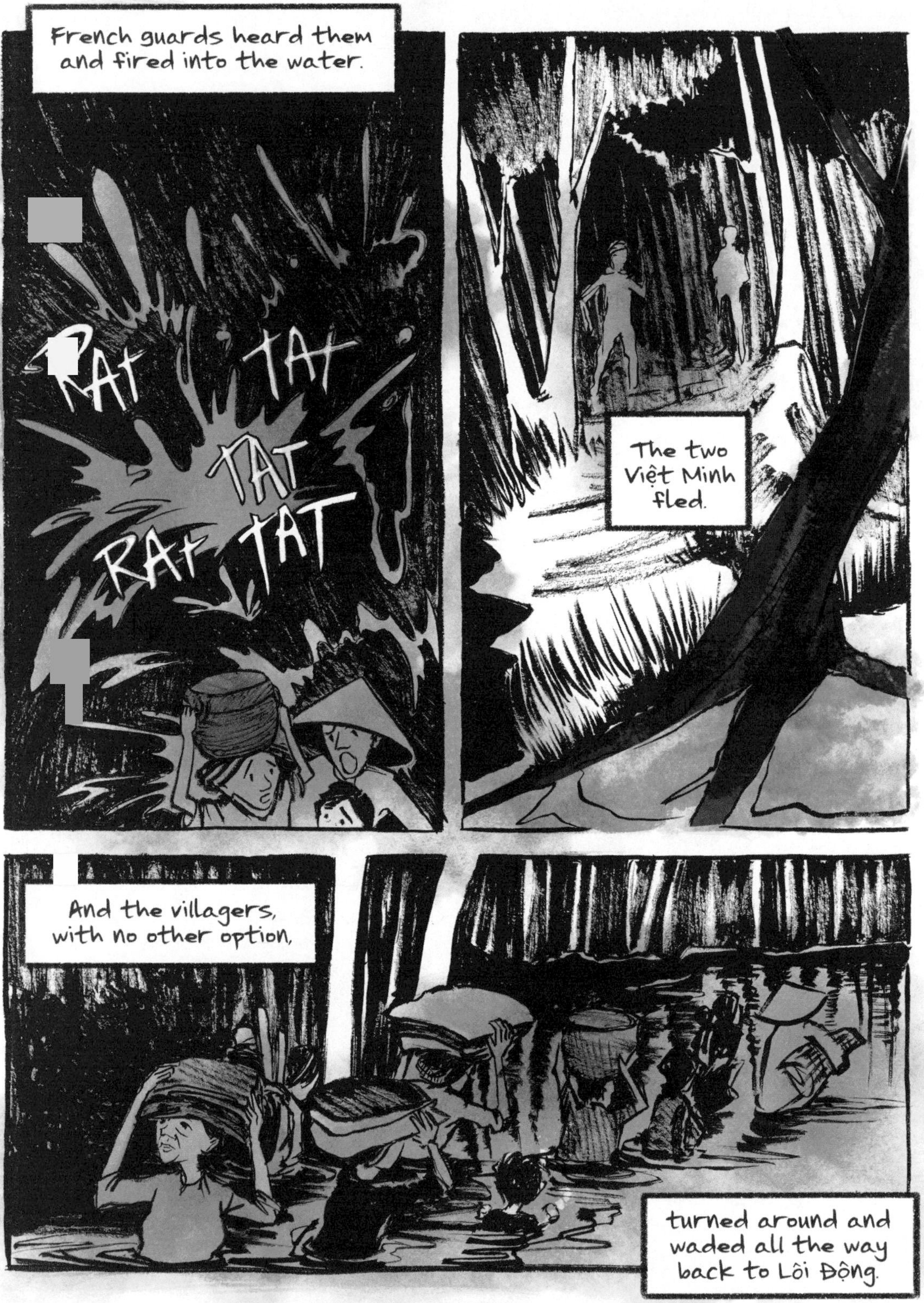
French guards heard them and fired into the water.
RAT TAT
TAT
RAT TAT
The two Việt Minh fled.
And the villagers, with no other option,
turned around and waded all the way back to Lôi Động.

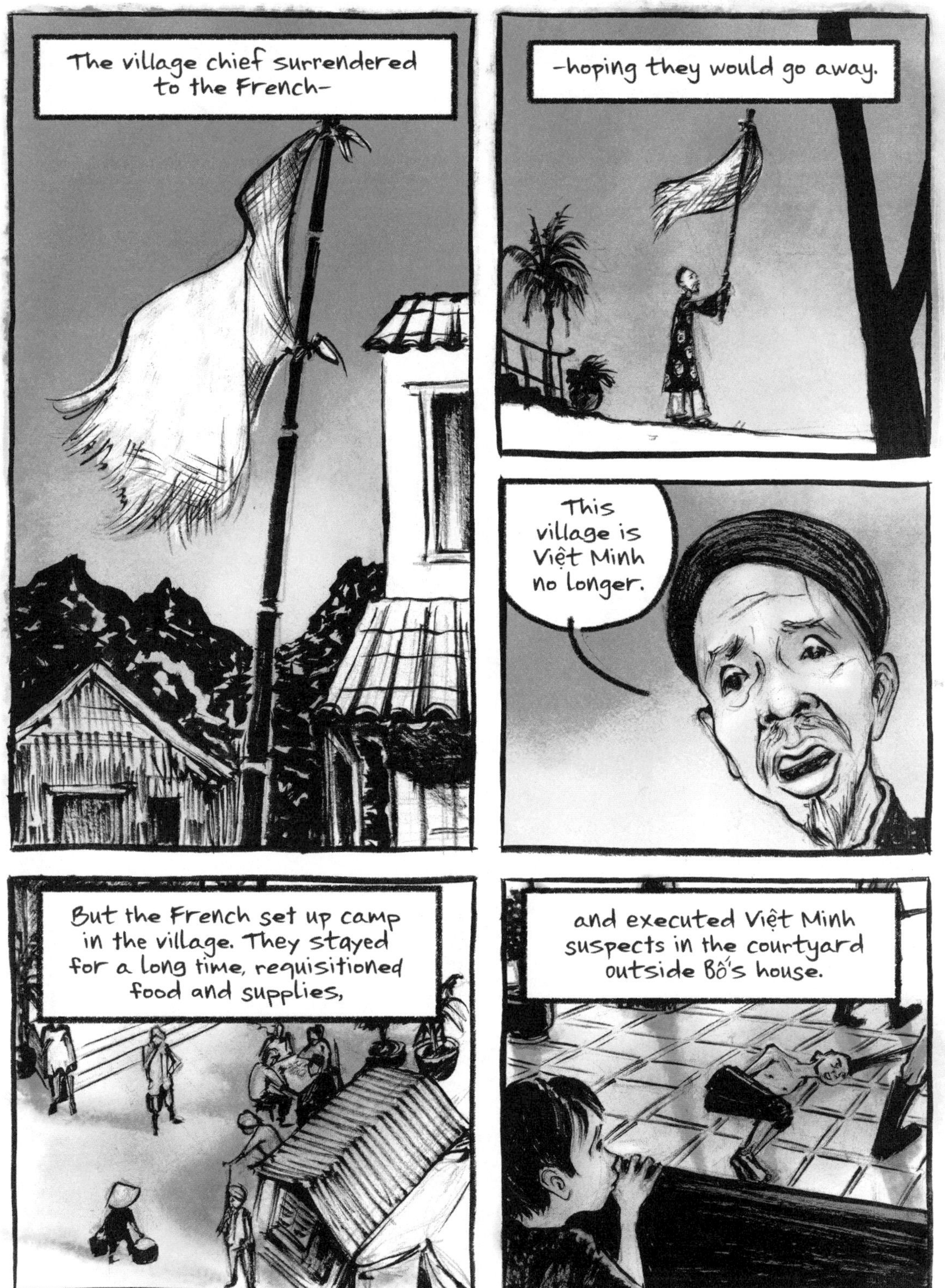
The village chief surrendered to the French-
-hoping they would go away.
This village is Việt Minh no longer.
But the French set up camp in the village. They stayed for a long time, requisitioned food and supplies,
and executed Việt Minh suspects in the courtyard outside Bố's house.

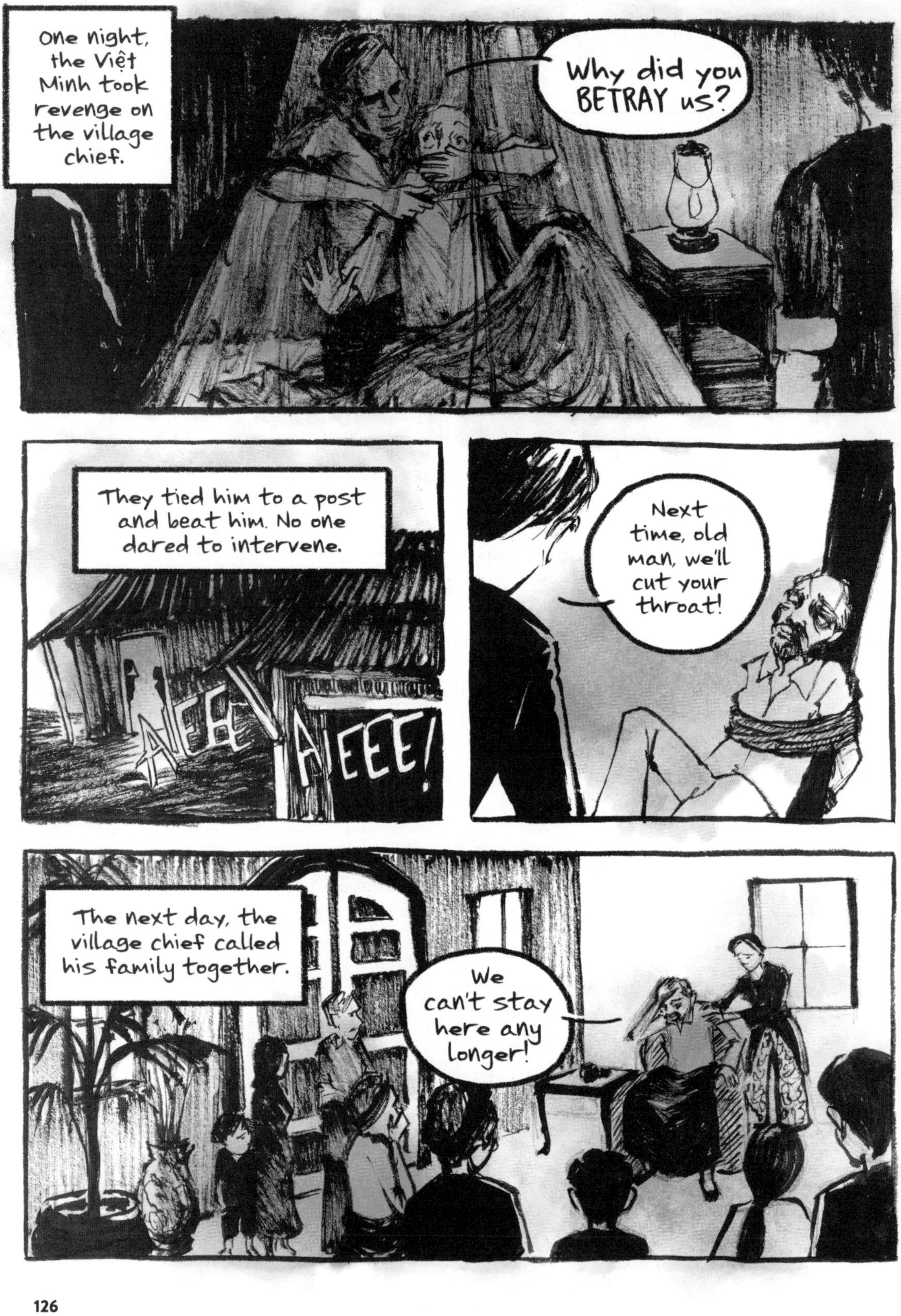
One night, the Việt Minh took revenge on the village chief.
Why did you BETRAY us?
They tied him to a post and beat him. No one dared to intervene.
AIEEE
AIEEE!
Next time, old man, we'll cut your throat!
The next day, the village chief called his family together.
We can't stay here any longer!

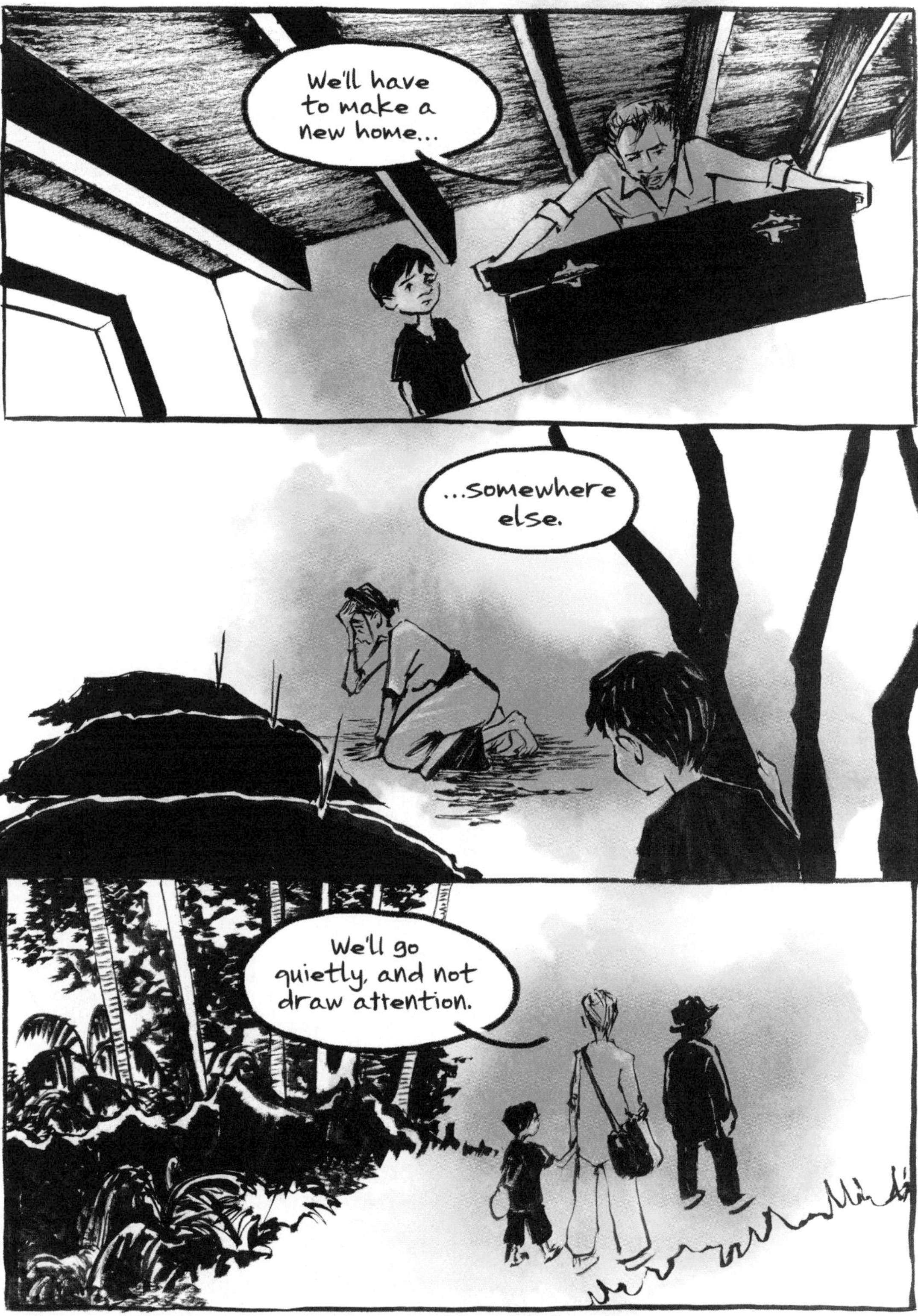
We'll have to make a new home...
...somewhere else.
We'll go quietly, and not draw attention.

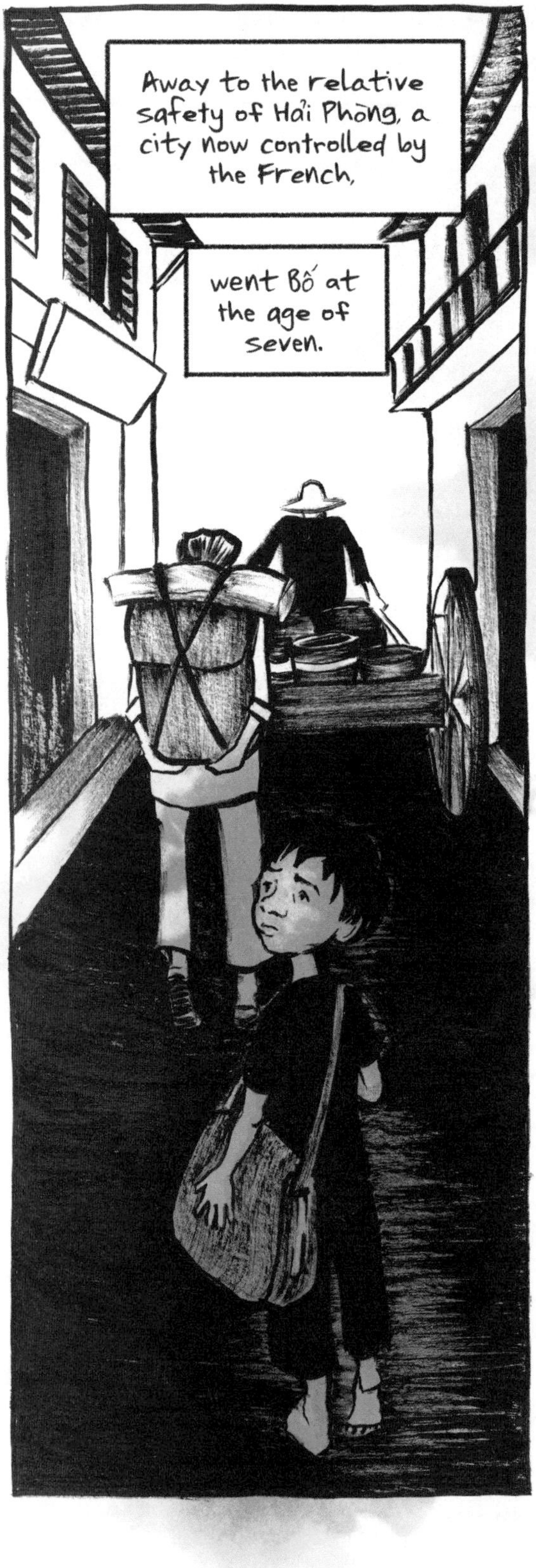
Away to the relative safety of Hải Phòng, a city now controlled by the French,
went Bố at the age of seven.

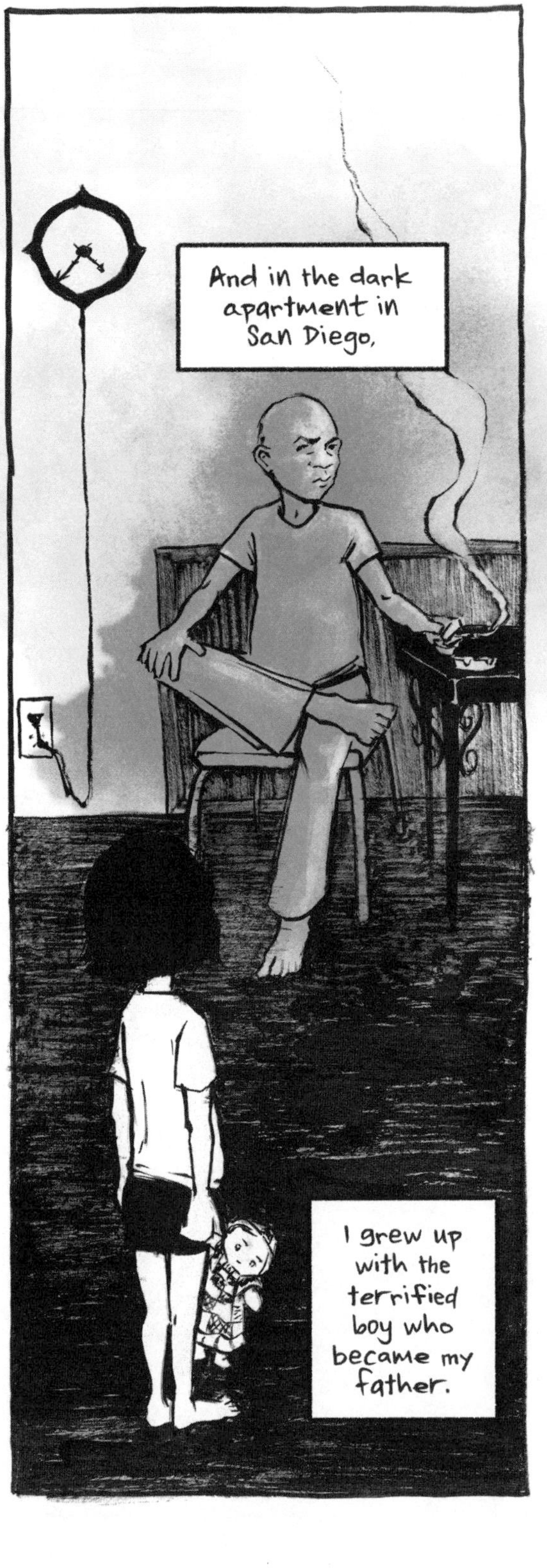
And in the dark apartment in San Diego,
I grew up with the terrified boy who became my father.

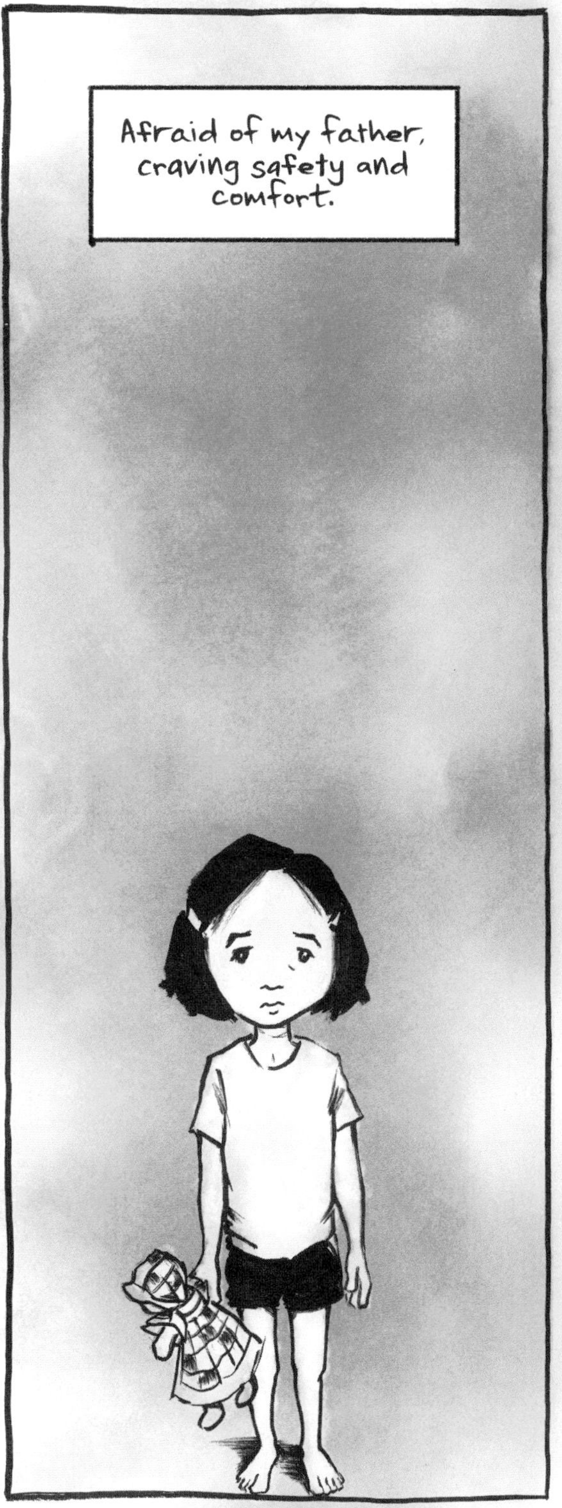
Afraid of my father, craving safety and comfort.

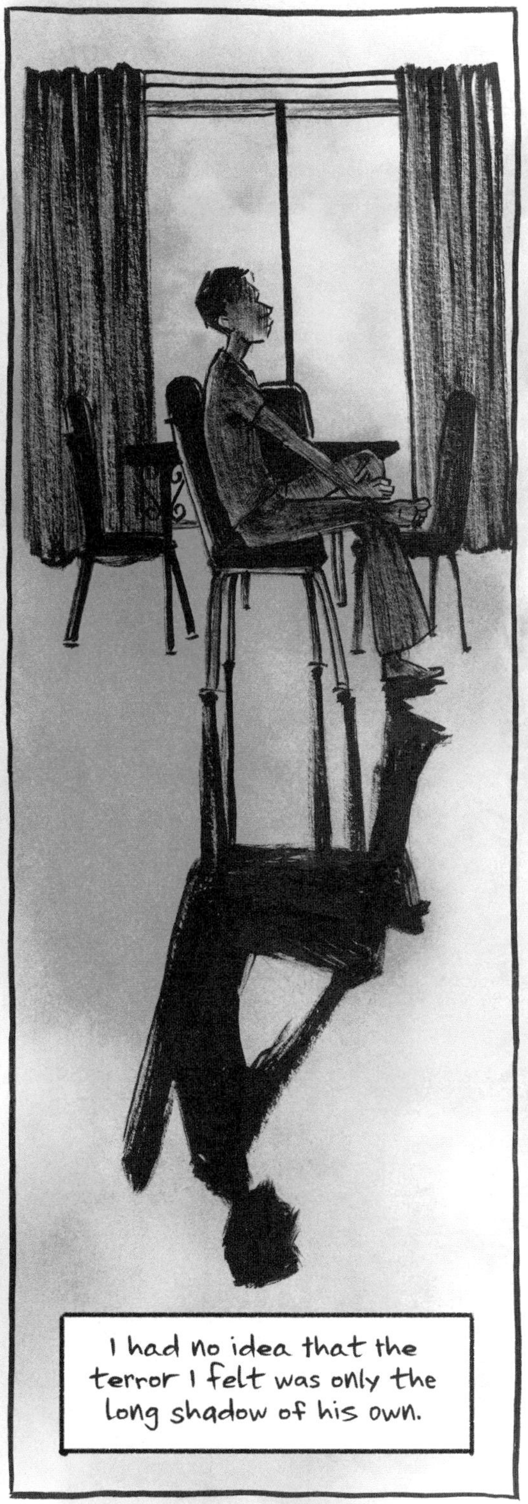
I had no idea that the terror I felt was only the long shadow of his own.

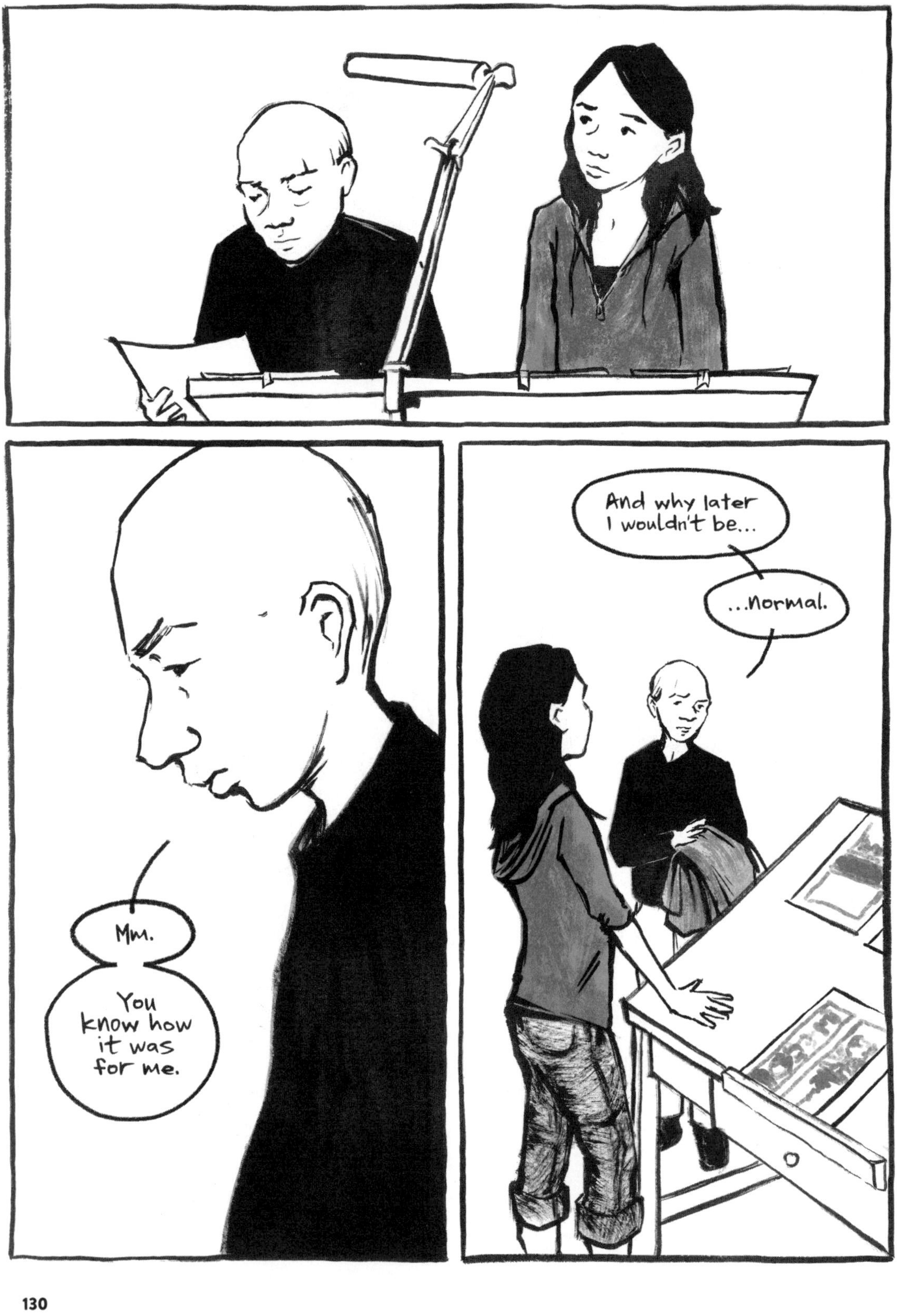
Mm.
You know how it was for me.
And why later I wouldn't be...
...normal.

CHAPTER 5

EITHER, OR

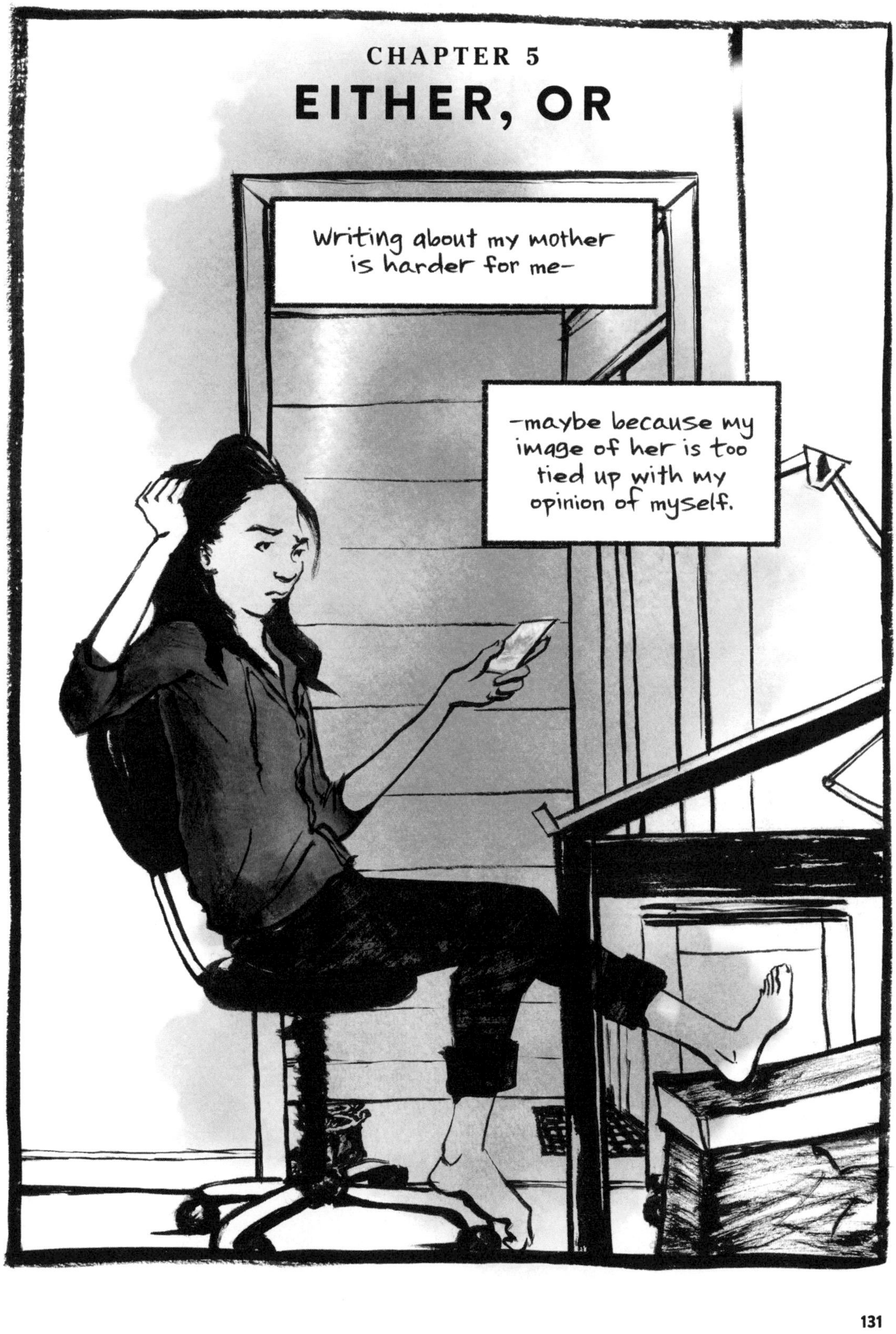
Writing about my mother is harder for me-
-maybe because my image of her is too tied up with my opinion of myself.

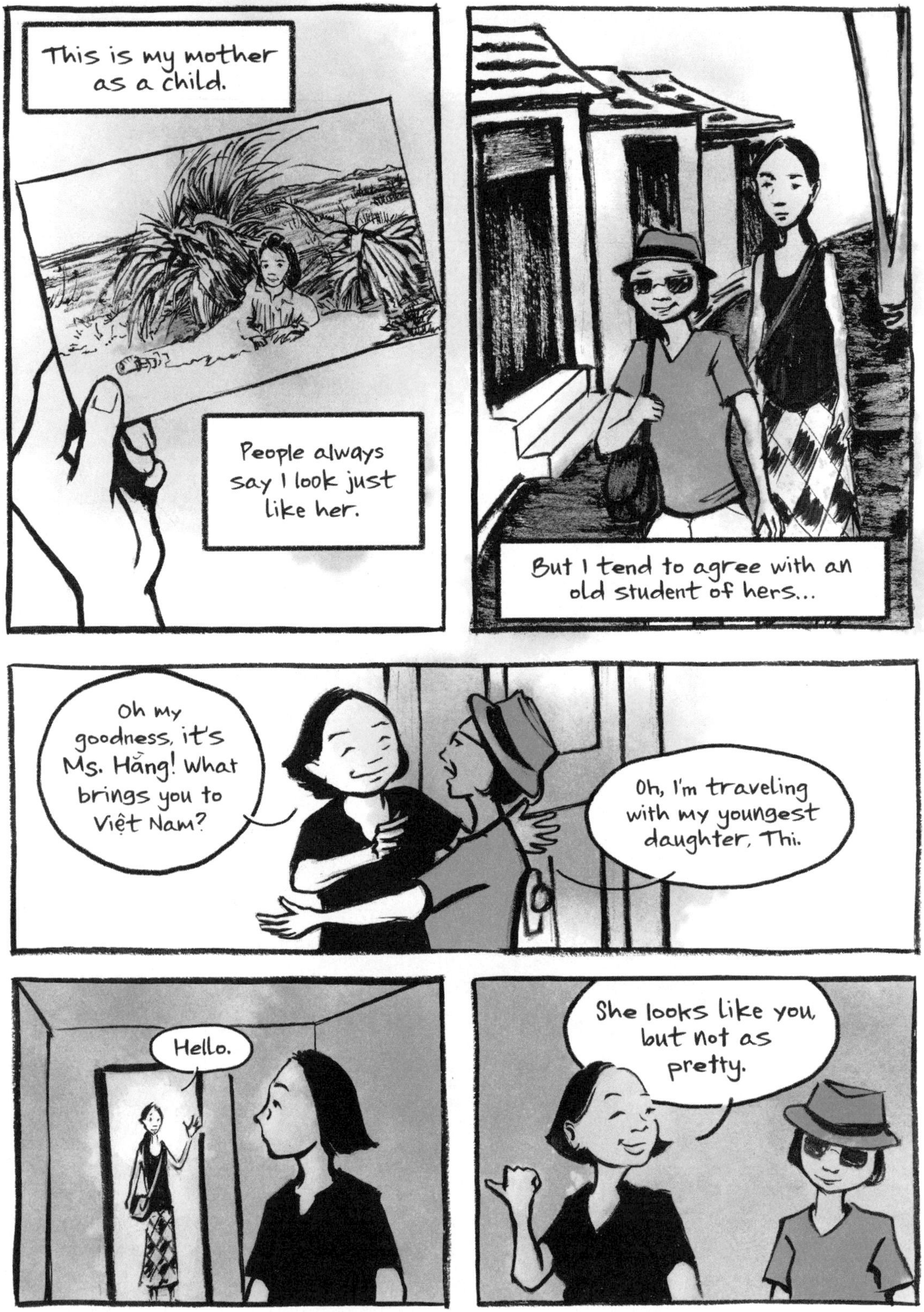
This is my mother as a child.
People always say I look just like her.
But I tend to agree with an old student of hers...
Oh my goodness, it's Ms. Hằng! What brings you to Việt Nam?
Oh, I'm traveling with my youngest daughter, Thi.
Hello.
She looks like you, but not as pretty.

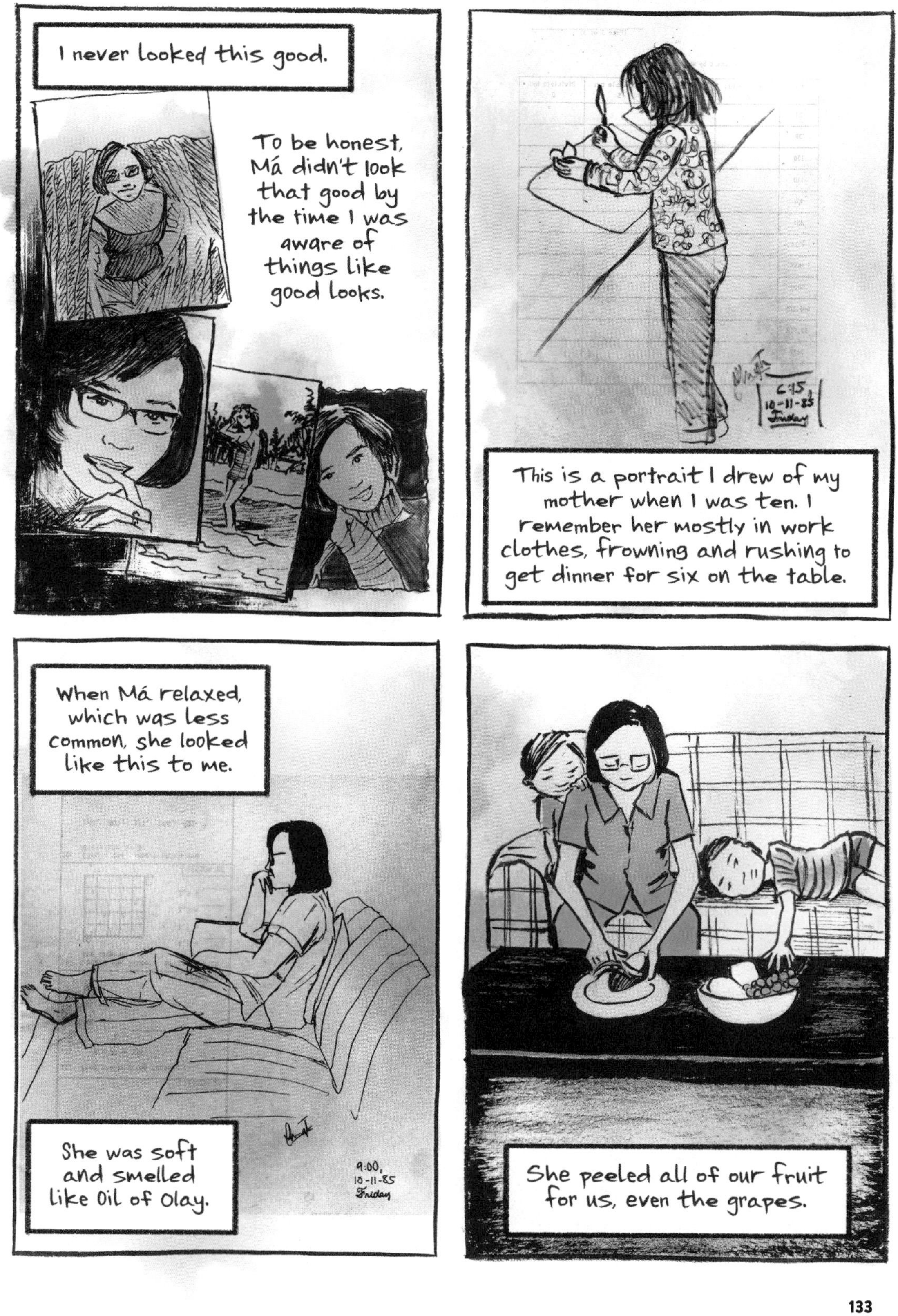
I never looked this good.
To be honest, Má didn't look that good by the time I was aware of things like good looks.
6:15 10-11-85 Friday
This is a portrait I drew of my mother when I was ten. I remember her mostly in work clothes, frowning and rushing to get dinner for six on the table.
When Má relaxed, which was less common, she looked like this to me.
She was soft and smelled like Oil of Olay.
9:00, 10-11-85 Friday
She peeled all of our fruit for us, even the grapes.

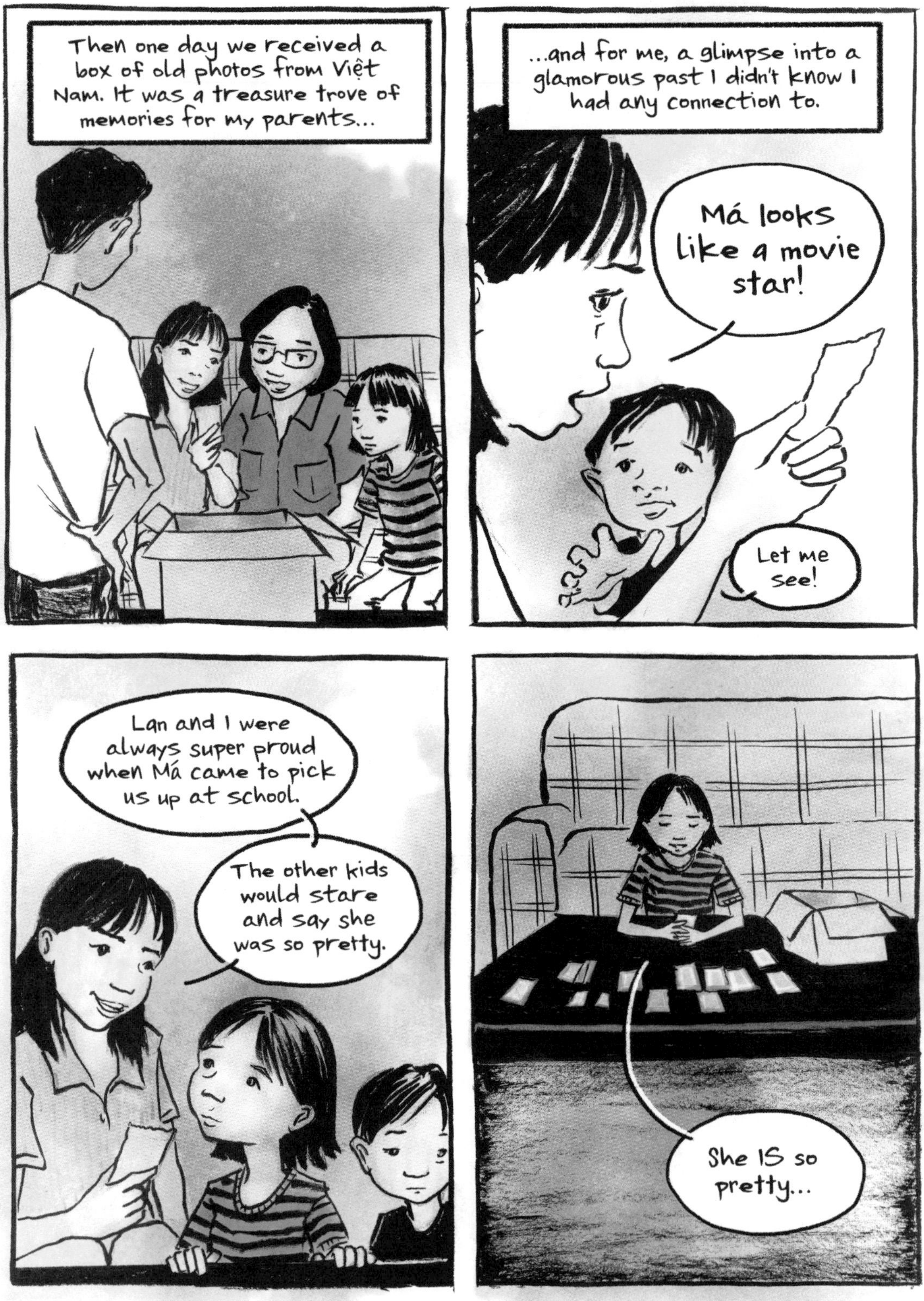
Then one day we received a box of old photos from Việt Nam. It was a treasure trove of memories for my parents...
...and for me, a glimpse into a glamorous past I didn't know I had any connection to.
Má looks like a movie star!
Let me see!
Lan and I were always super proud when Má came to pick us up at school.
The other kids would stare and say she was so pretty.
She IS so pretty...

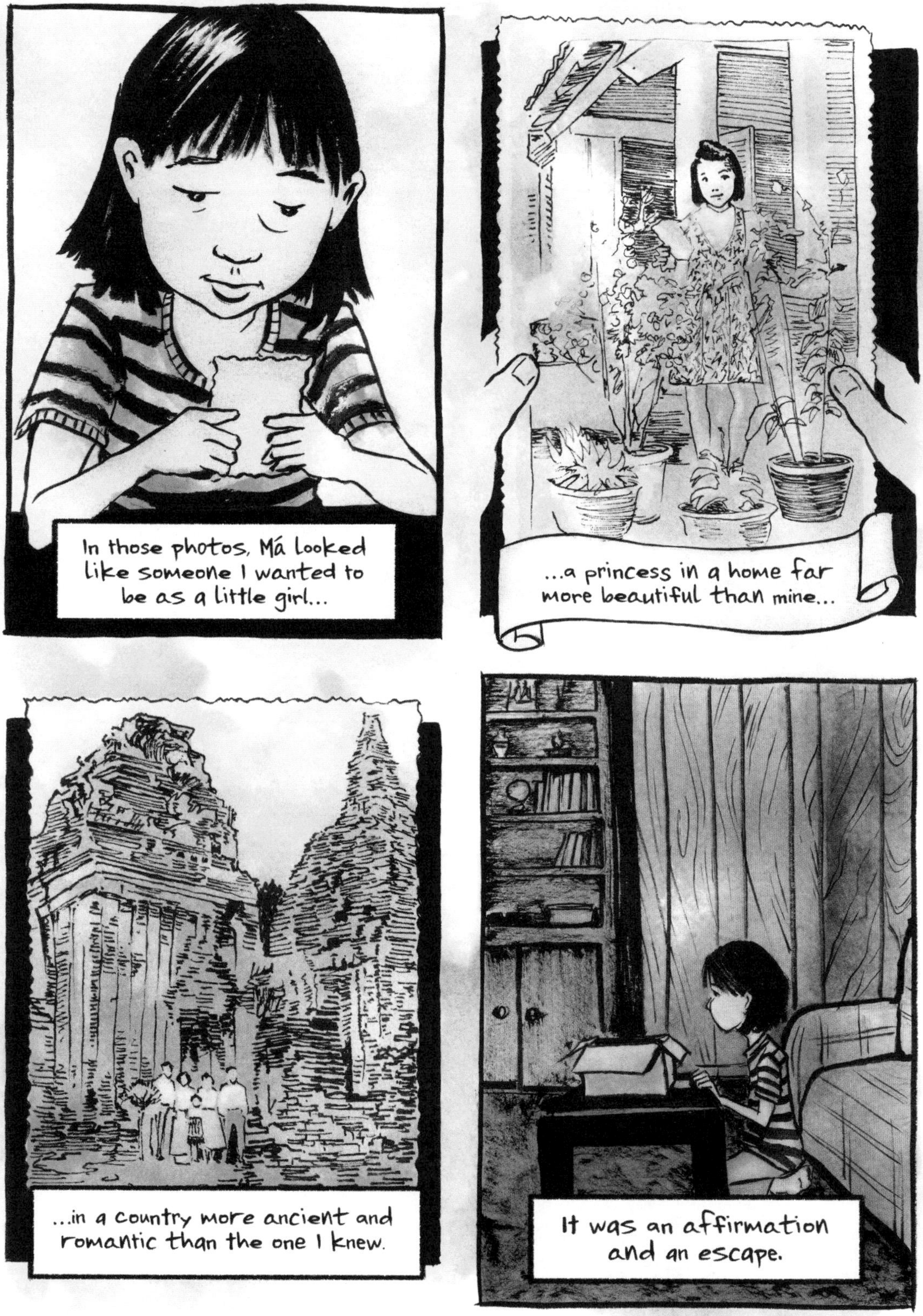
In those photos, Má looked like someone I wanted to be as a little girl...
...a princess in a home far more beautiful than mine...
...in a country more ancient and romantic than the one I knew.
It was an affirmation and an escape.

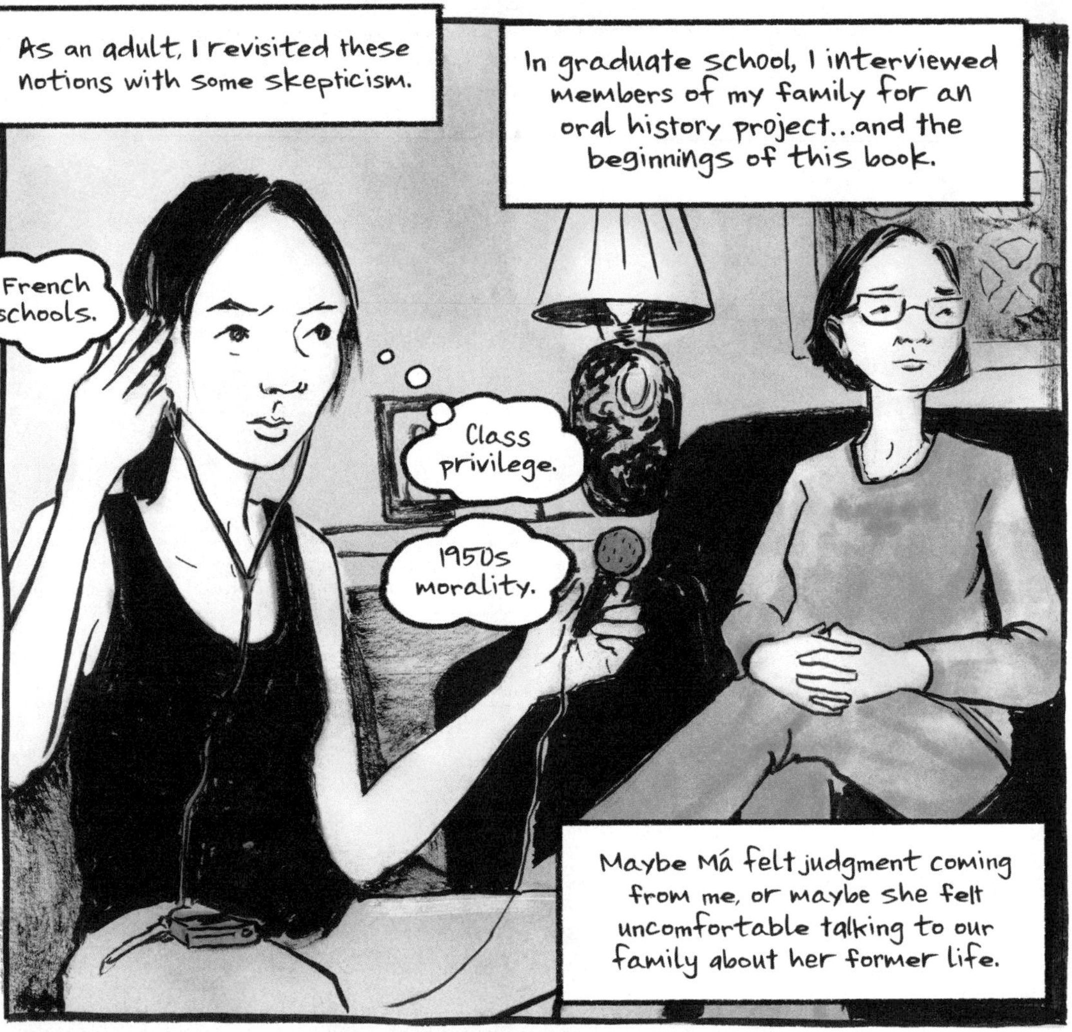
As an adult, I revisited these notions with some skepticism.
In graduate school, I interviewed members of my family for an oral history project...and the beginnings of this book.
French schools.
Class privilege.
1950s morality.
Maybe Má felt judgment coming from me, or maybe she felt uncomfortable talking to our family about her former life.

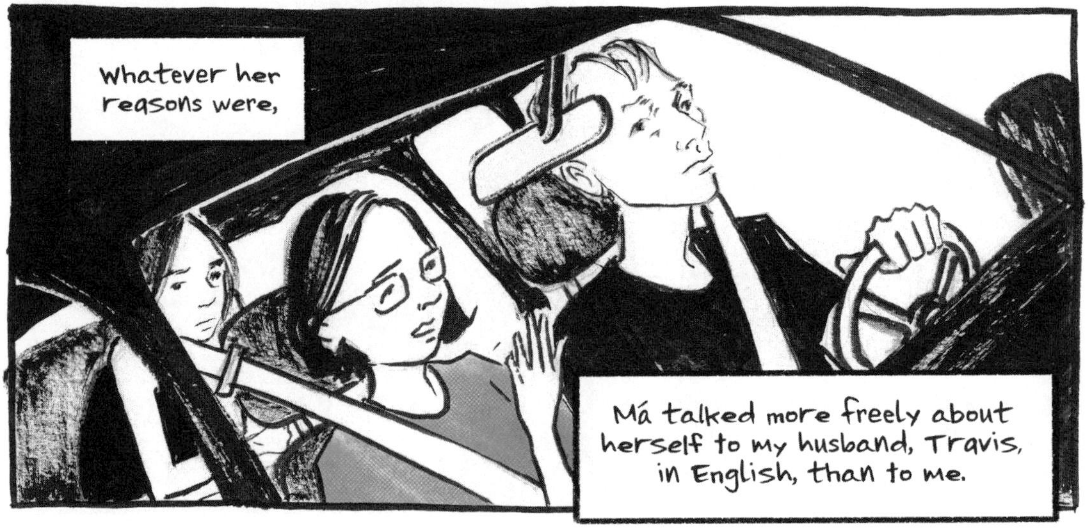
Whatever her reasons were,
Má talked more freely about herself to my husband, Travis, in English, than to me.

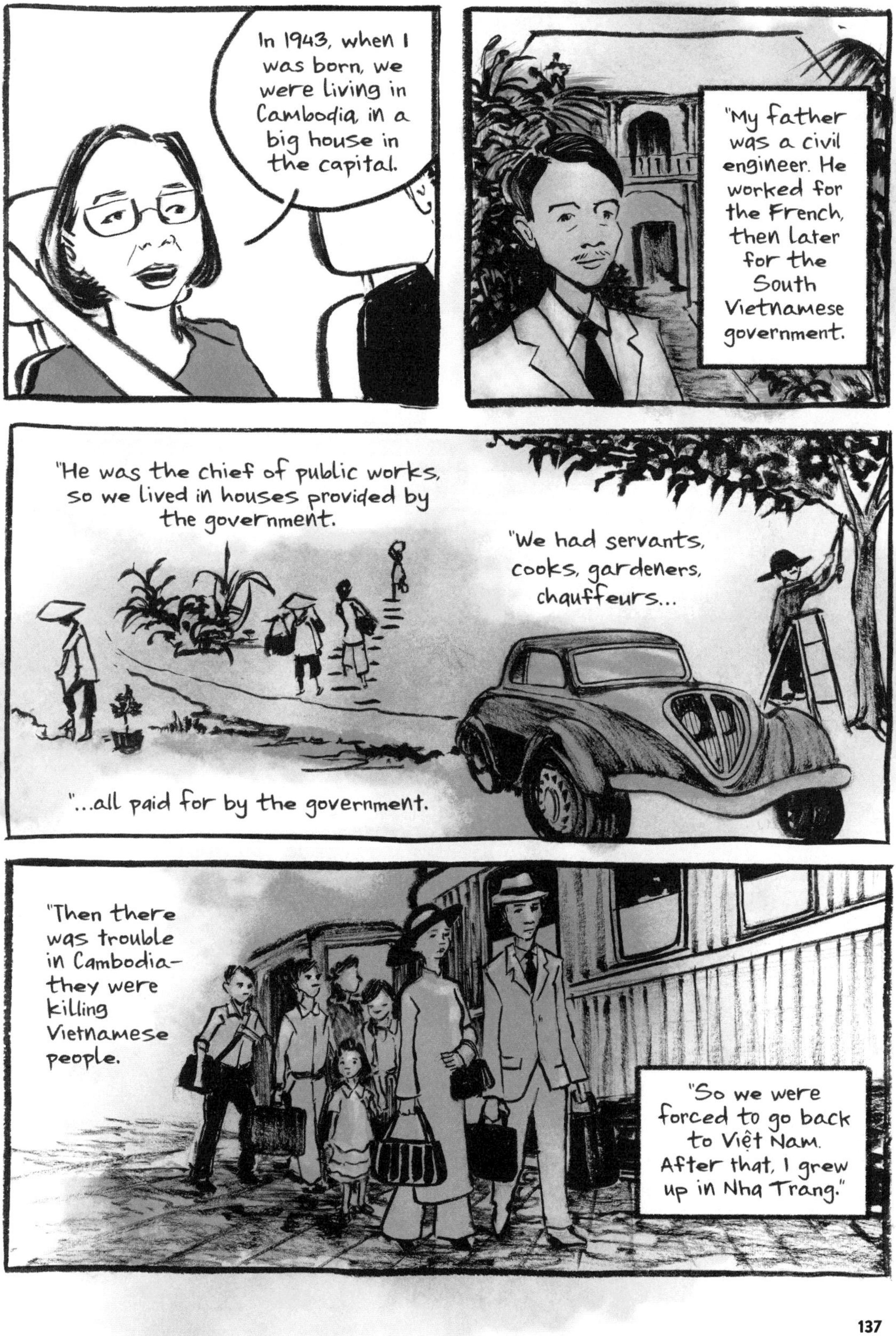
In 1943, when I was born, we were living in Cambodia, in a big house in the capital.
"My father was a civil engineer. He worked for the French, then later for the South Vietnamese government.
"He was the chief of public works, so we lived in houses provided by the government.
"We had servants, cooks, gardeners, chauffeurs...
"...all paid for by the government.
"Then there was trouble in Cambodia-they were killing Vietnamese people.
"So we were forced to go back to Việt Nam. After that, I grew up in Nha Trang."

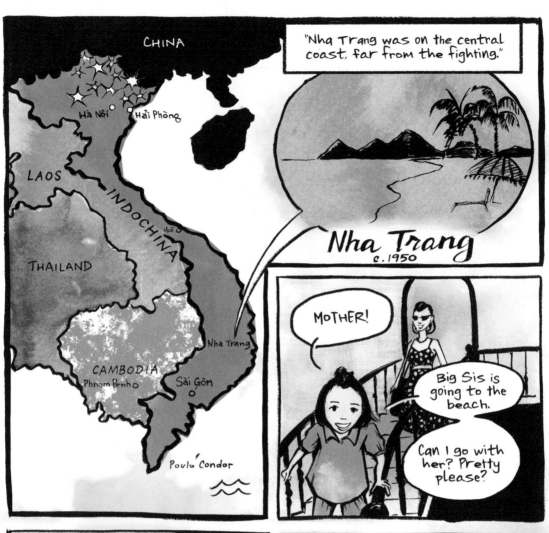

CHINA

Hà Nội · Hải Phòng

LAOS

INDOCHINA

Huế

THAILAND

Nha Trang

CAMBODIA

Phnom Penho · Sài Gòn

Poulo Condor

"Nha Trang was on the central coast, far from the fighting."

Nha Trang
c. 1950

MOTHER!

Big Sis is going to the beach.

Can I go with her? Pretty please?

Wear a hat, and don't stay out in the sun too long!

Thank you! Thank you!

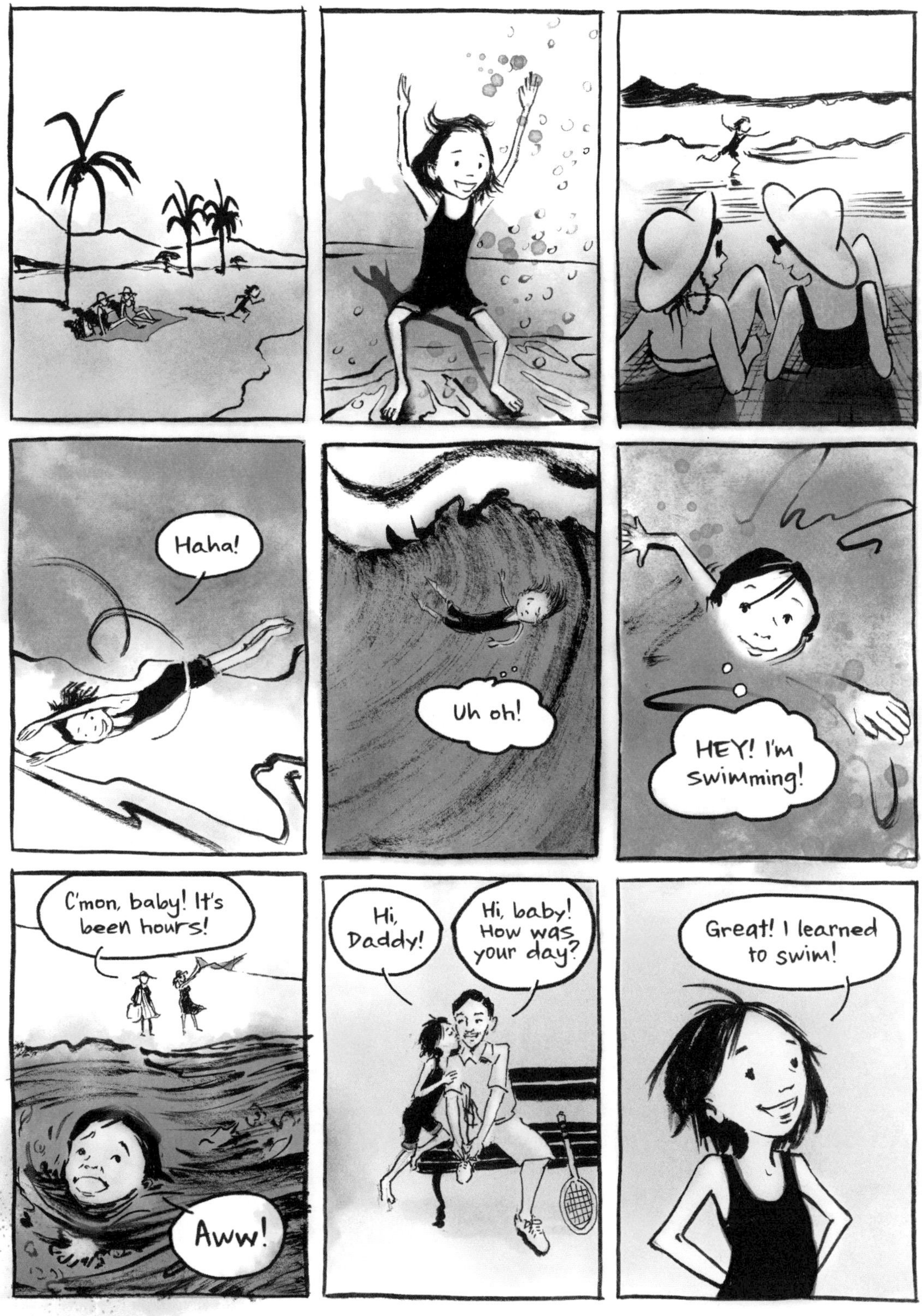
Haha!
Uh oh!
HEY! I'm swimming!
C'mon, baby! It's been hours!
Aww!
Hi, Daddy!
Hi, baby! How was your day?
Great! I learned to swim!

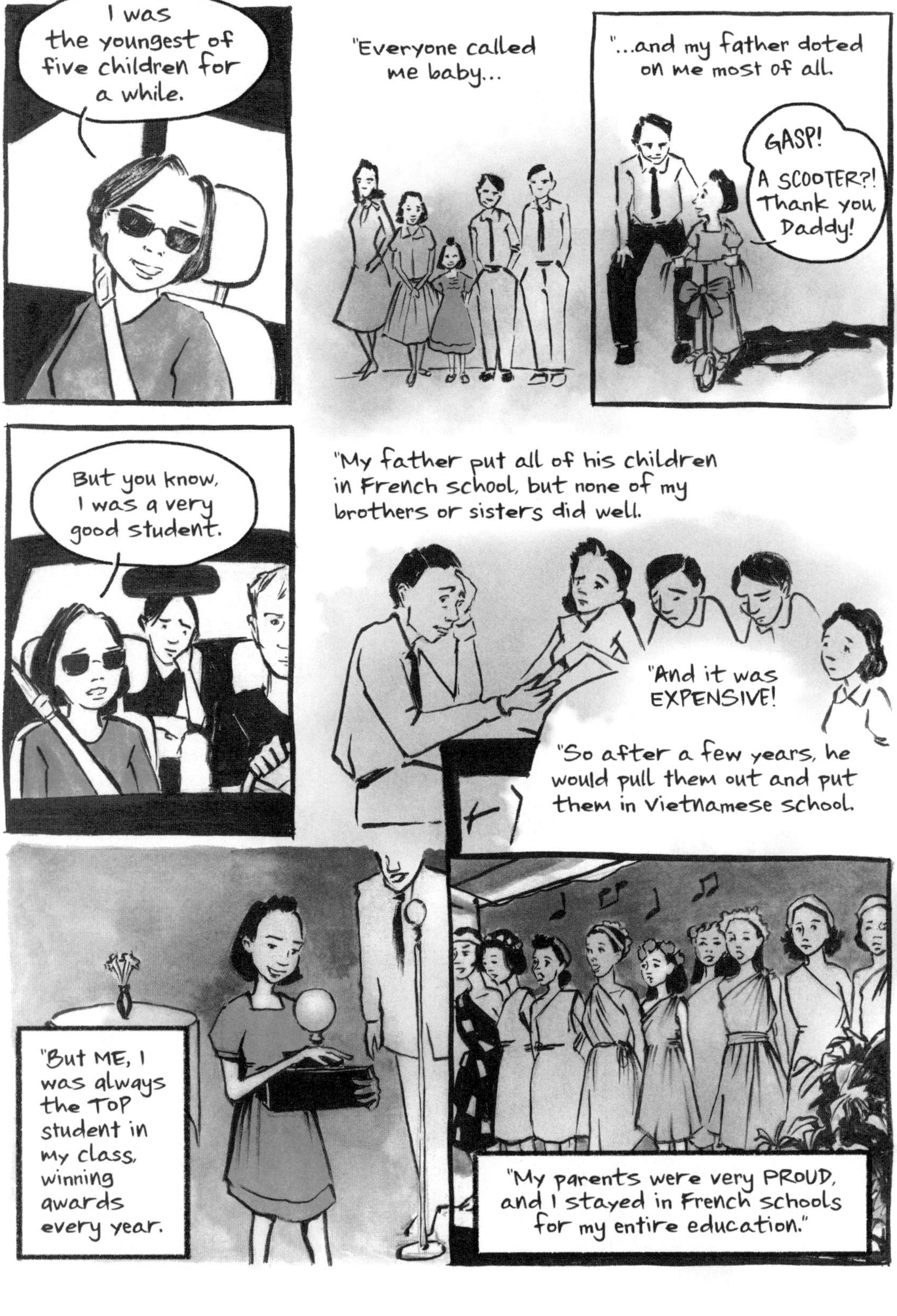
I was the youngest of five children for a while.
"Everyone called me baby...
"...and my father doted on me most of all.
GASP!
A SCOOTER?! Thank you, Daddy!
But you know, I was a very good student.
"My father put all of his children in French school, but none of my brothers or sisters did well.
"And it was EXPENSIVE!
"So after a few years, he would pull them out and put them in Vietnamese school.
"But ME, I was always the TOP student in my class, winning awards every year.
"My parents were very PROUD, and I stayed in French schools for my entire education."

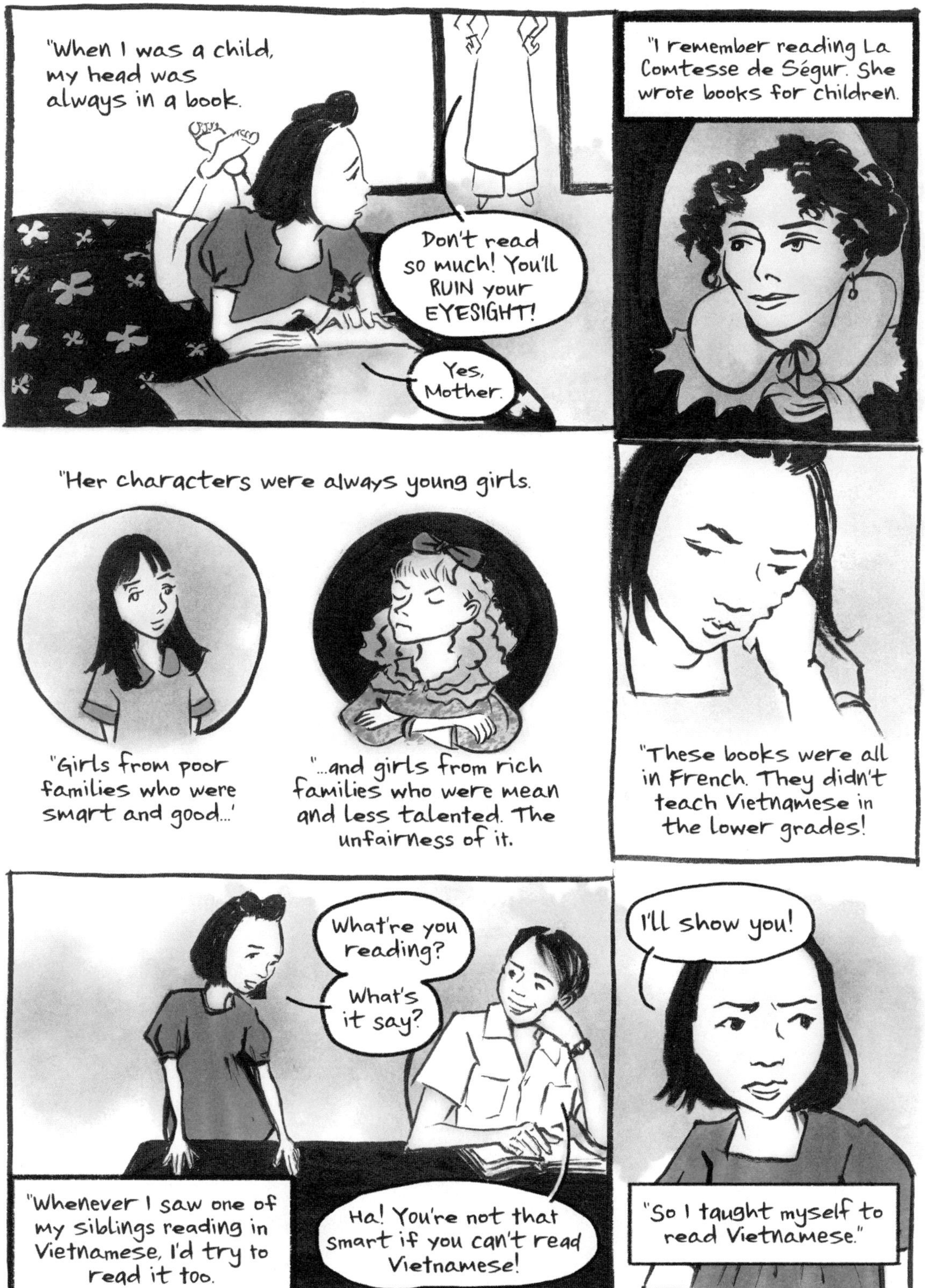
"When I was a child, my head was always in a book.
Don't read so much! You'll RUIN your EYESIGHT!
Yes, Mother.
"I remember reading La Comtesse de Ségur. She wrote books for children.
"Her characters were always young girls.
"Girls from poor families who were smart and good...'
"...and girls from rich families who were mean and less talented. The unfairness of it.
"These books were all in French. They didn't teach Vietnamese in the lower grades!
What're you reading?
What's it say?
"Whenever I saw one of my siblings reading in Vietnamese, I'd try to read it too.
Ha! You're not that smart if you can't read Vietnamese!
I'll show you!
"So I taught myself to read Vietnamese."

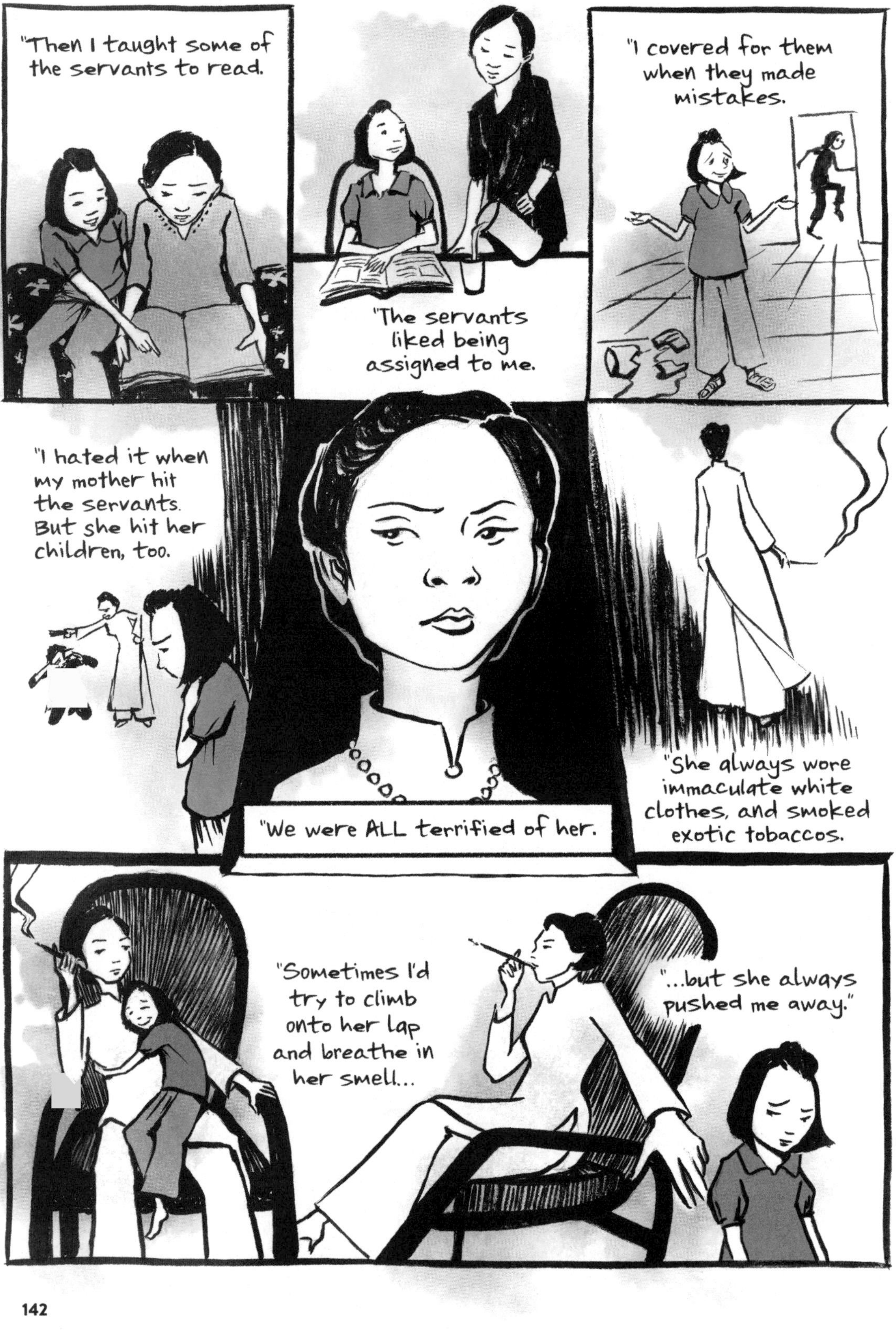
"Then I taught some of the servants to read.
"The servants liked being assigned to me.
"I covered for them when they made mistakes.
"I hated it when my mother hit the servants. But she hit her children, too.
"We were ALL terrified of her.
"She always wore immaculate white clothes, and smoked exotic tobaccos.
"Sometimes I'd try to climb onto her lap and breathe in her smell...
"...but she always pushed me away."

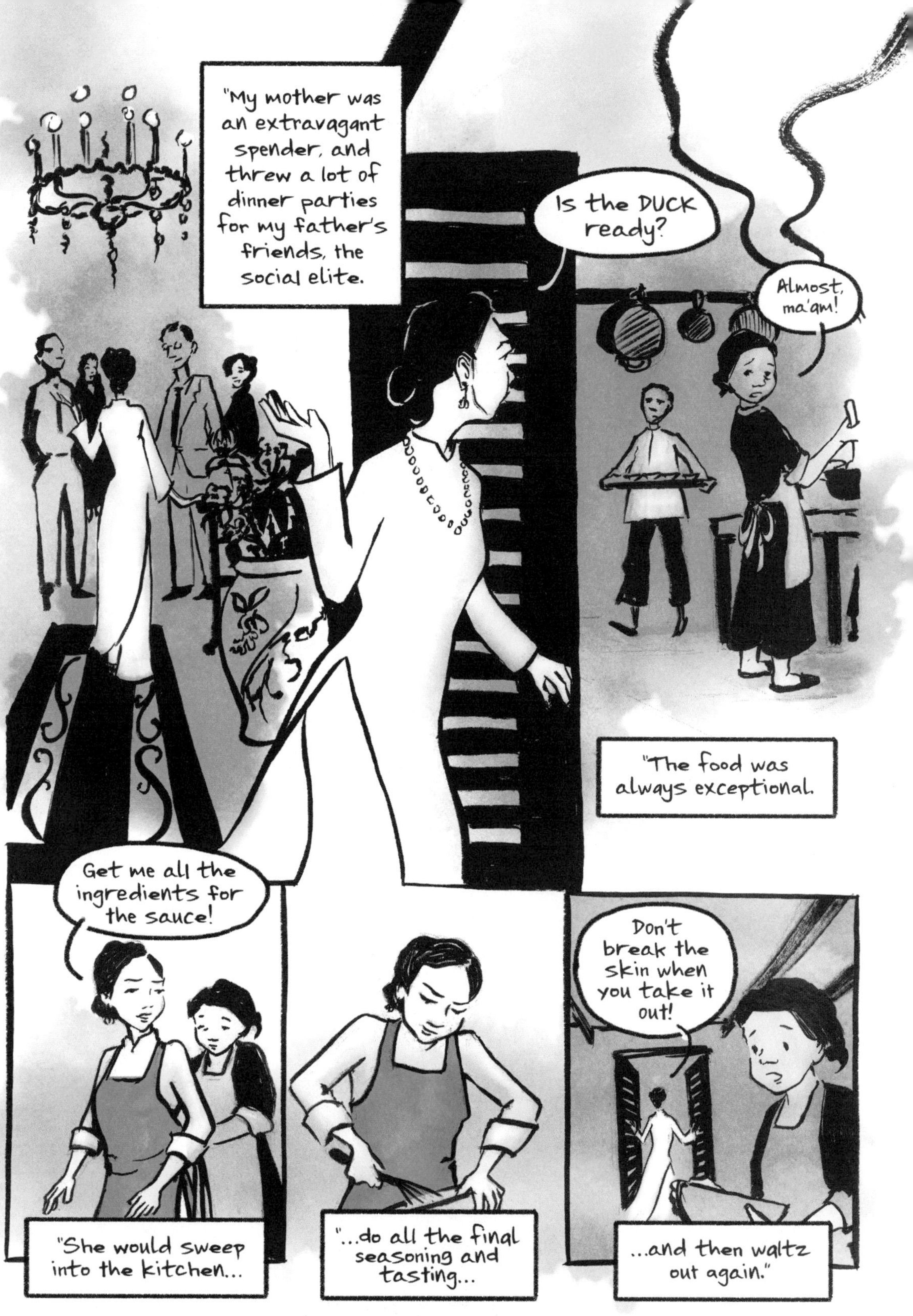
"My mother was an extravagant spender, and threw a lot of dinner parties for my father's friends, the social elite.
Is the DUCK ready?
Almost, ma'am!
"The food was always exceptional.
Get me all the ingredients for the sauce!
"She would sweep into the kitchen...
"...do all the final seasoning and tasting...
Don't break the skin when you take it out!
...and then waltz out again."

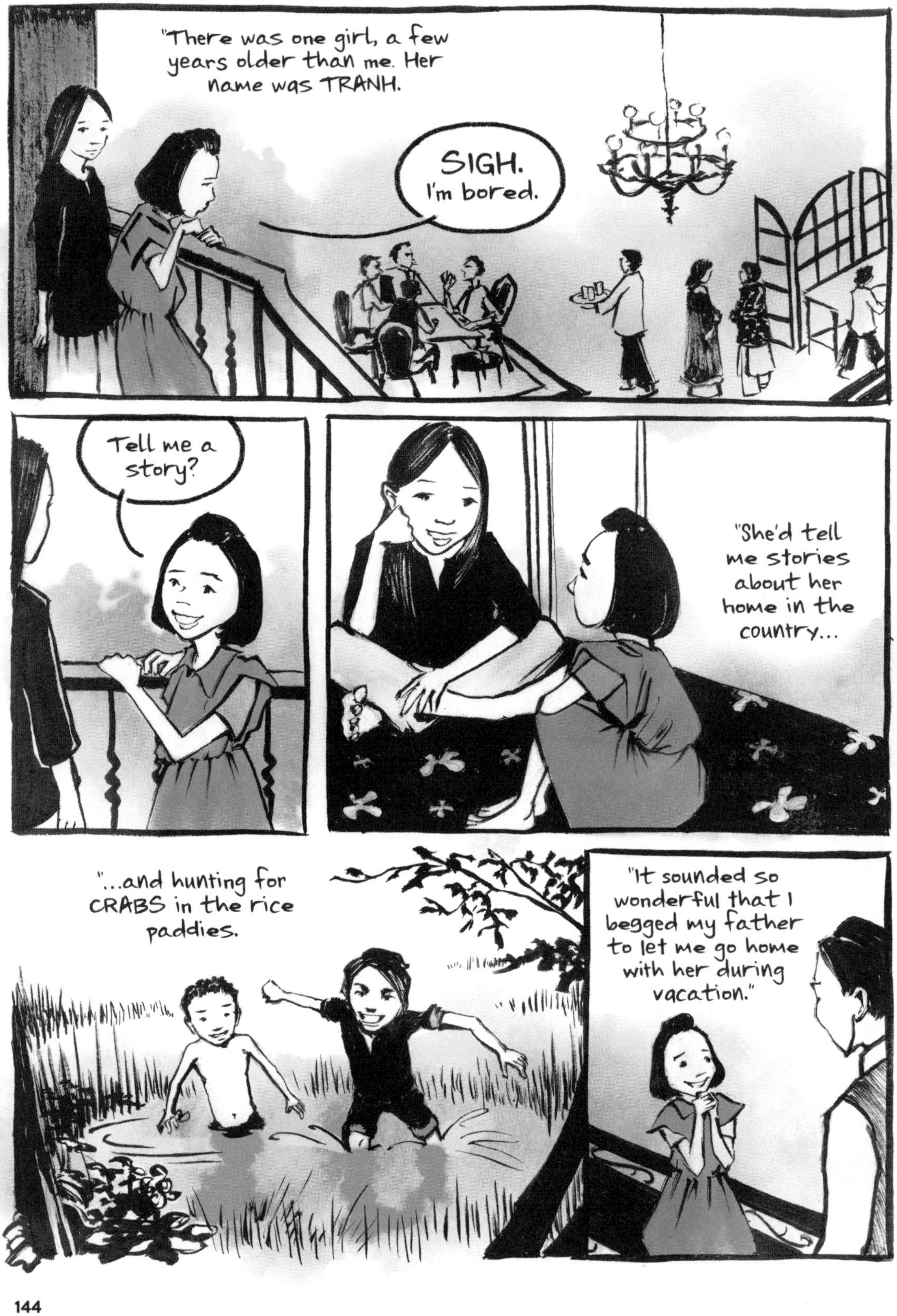
"There was one girl, a few years older than me. Her name was TRANH.
SIGH. I'm bored.
Tell me a story?
"She'd tell me stories about her home in the country...
"...and hunting for CRABS in the rice paddies.
"It sounded so wonderful that I begged my father to let me go home with her during vacation."

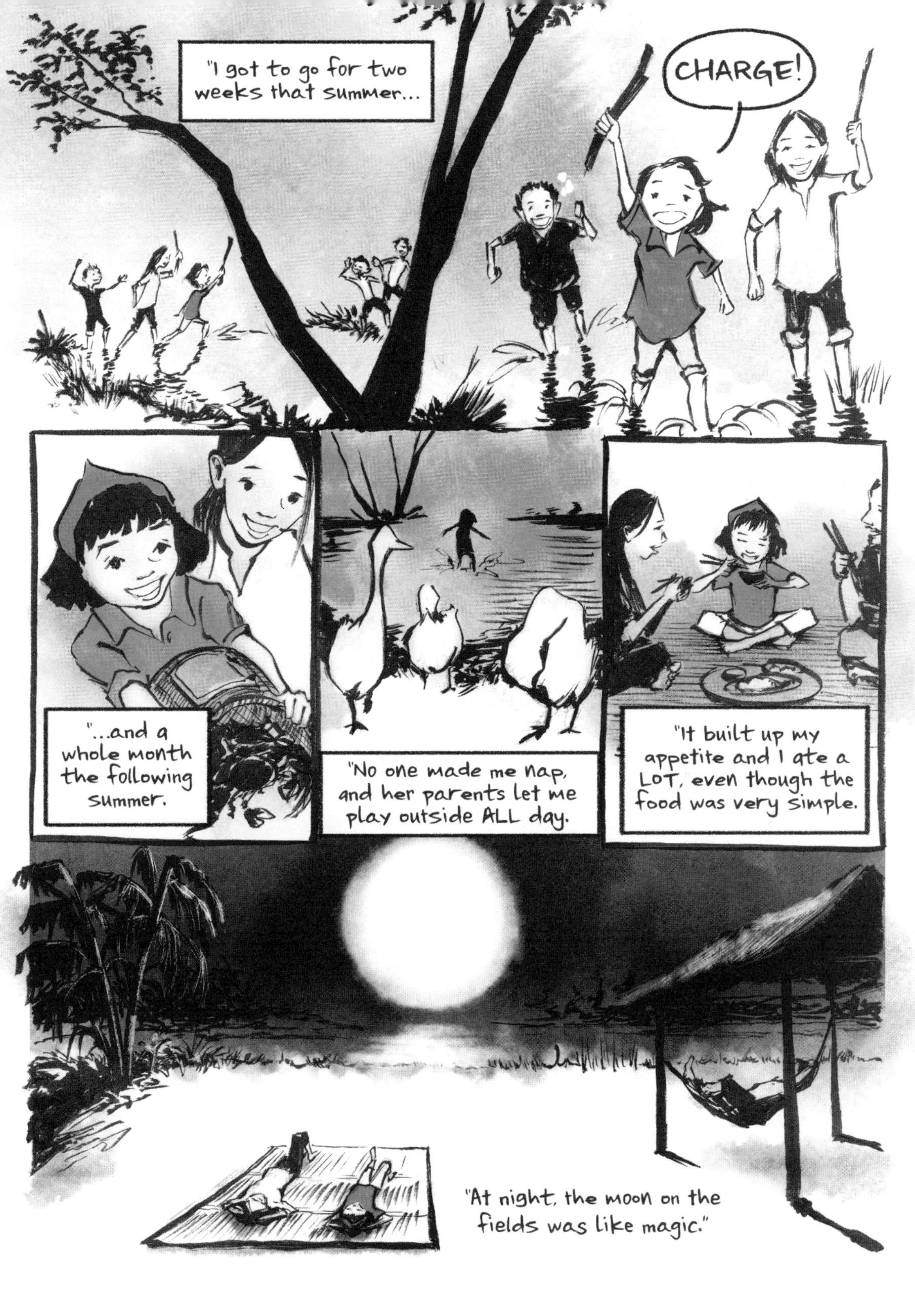
"I got to go for two weeks that summer...
CHARGE!
"...and a whole month the following summer.
"No one made me nap, and her parents let me play outside ALL day.
"It built up my appetite and I ate a LOT, even though the food was very simple.
"At night, the moon on the fields was like magic."

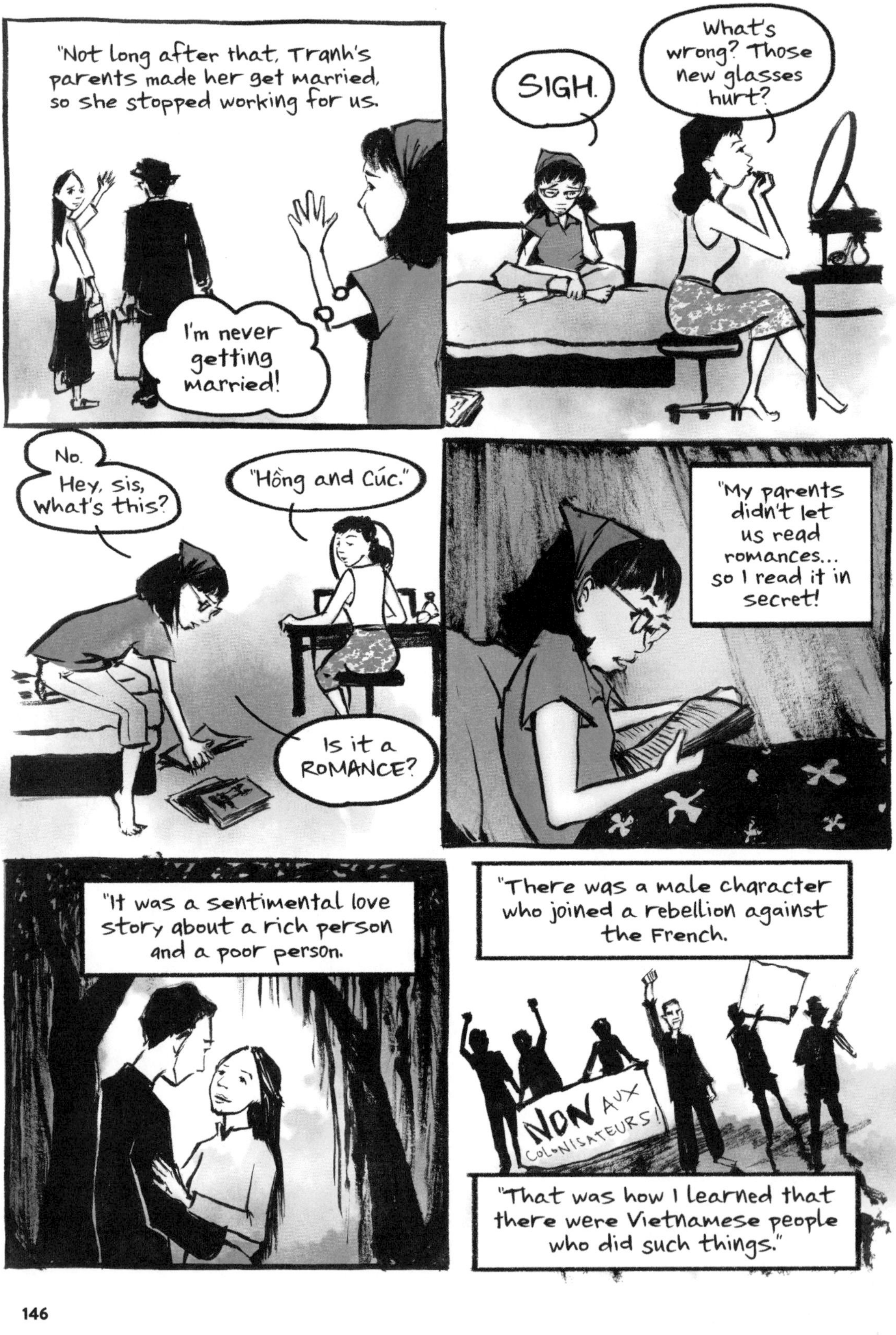
"Not long after that, Tranh's parents made her get married, so she stopped working for us.
I'm never getting married!
SIGH.
What's wrong? Those new glasses hurt?
No. Hey, sis, what's this?
"Hồng and Cúc."
Is it a ROMANCE?
"My parents didn't let us read romances... so I read it in secret!
"It was a sentimental love story about a rich person and a poor person.
"There was a male character who joined a rebellion against the French.
NON AUX COLONISATEURS!
"That was how I learned that there were Vietnamese people who did such things."

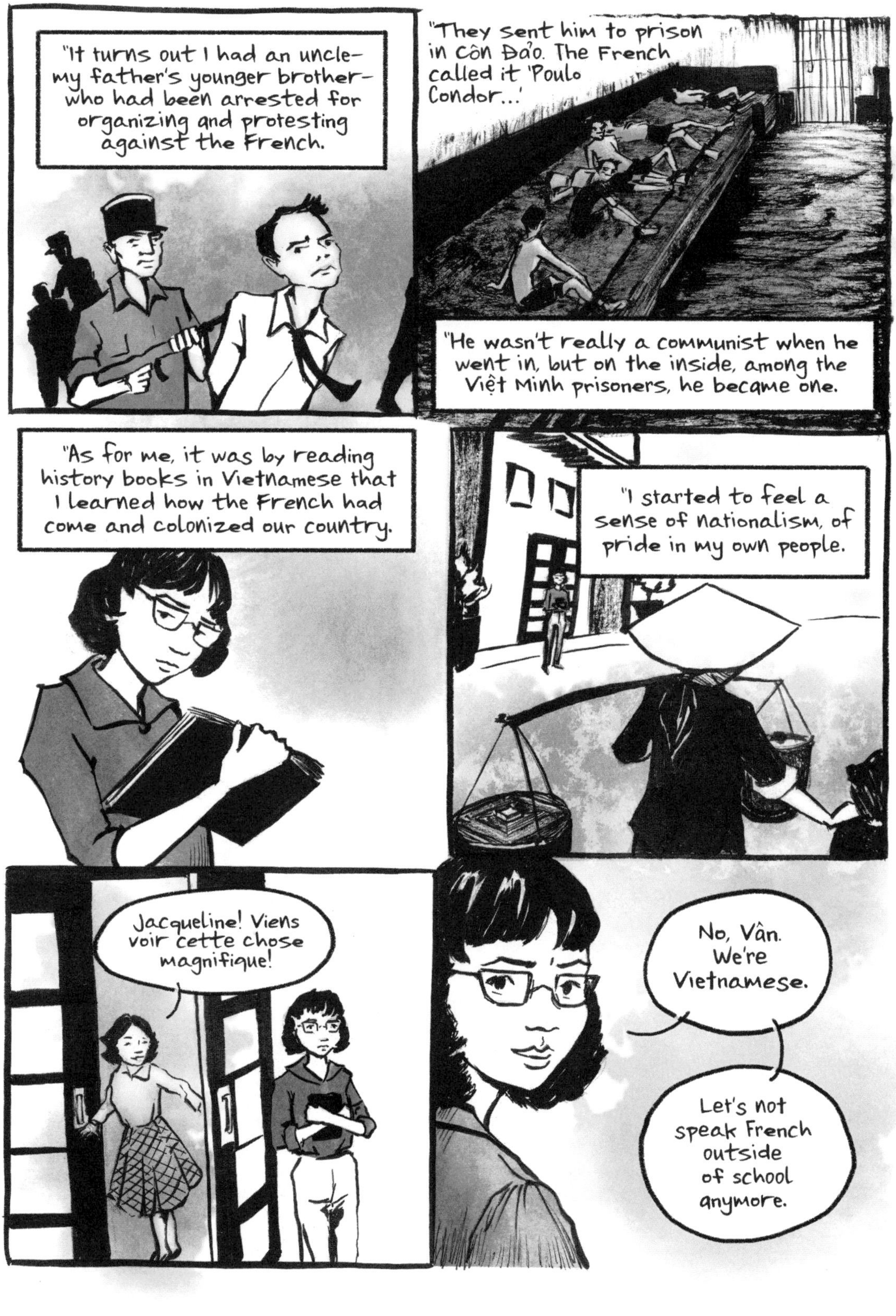
"It turns out I had an uncle—my father's younger brother—who had been arrested for organizing and protesting against the French.
"They sent him to prison in Côn Đảo. The French called it 'Poulo Condor...'
"He wasn't really a communist when he went in, but on the inside, among the Việt Minh prisoners, he became one.
"As for me, it was by reading history books in Vietnamese that I learned how the French had come and colonized our country.
"I started to feel a sense of nationalism, of pride in my own people.
Jacqueline! Viens voir cette chose magnifique!
No, Vân. We're Vietnamese.
Let's not speak French outside of school anymore.

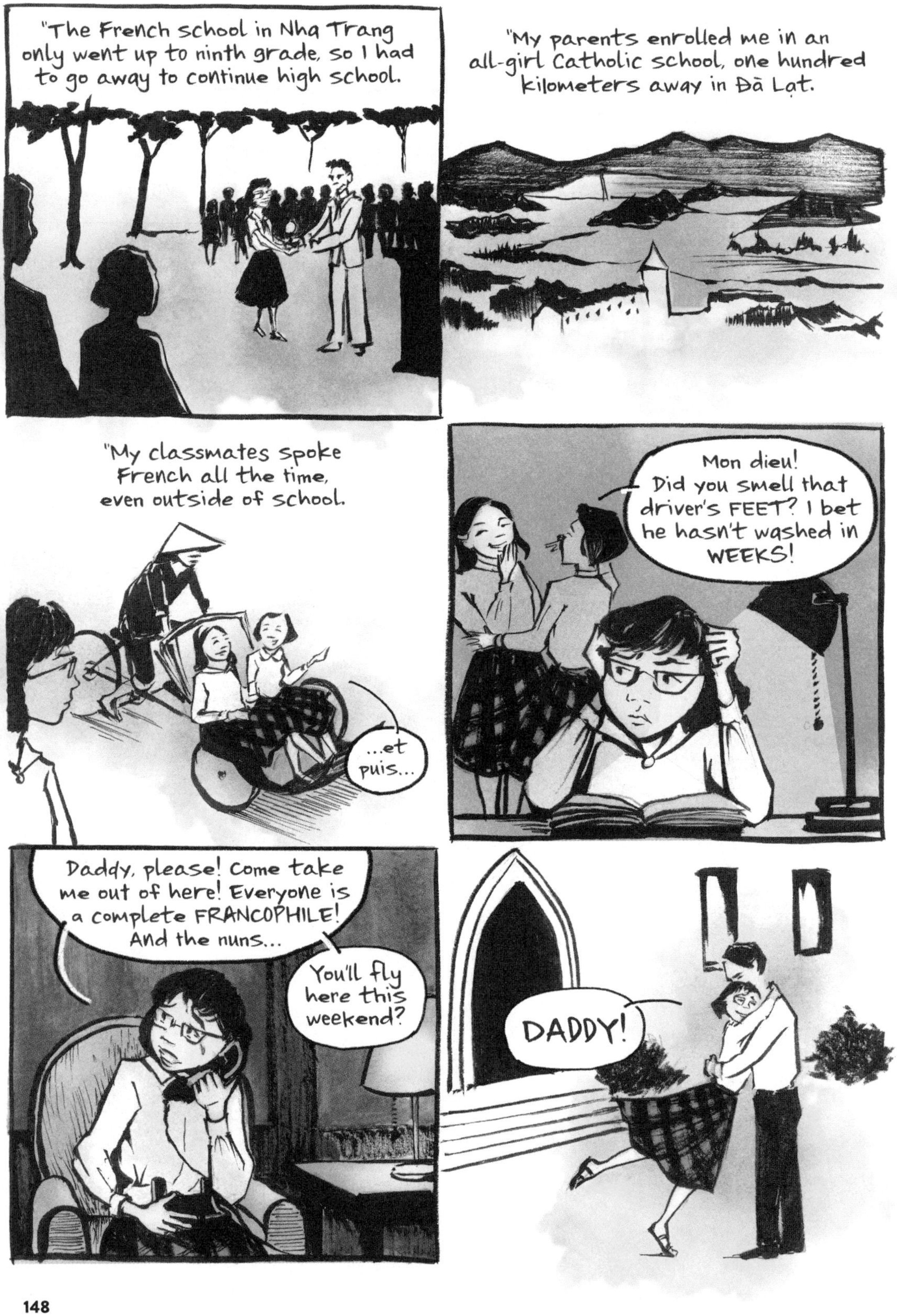
"The French school in Nha Trang only went up to ninth grade, so I had to go away to continue high school.
"My parents enrolled me in an all-girl Catholic school, one hundred kilometers away in Đà Lạt.
"My classmates spoke French all the time, even outside of school.
...et puis...
Mon dieu! Did you smell that driver's FEET? I bet he hasn't washed in WEEKS!
Daddy, please! Come take me out of here! Everyone is a complete FRANCOPHILE! And the nuns...
You'll fly here this weekend?
DADDY!

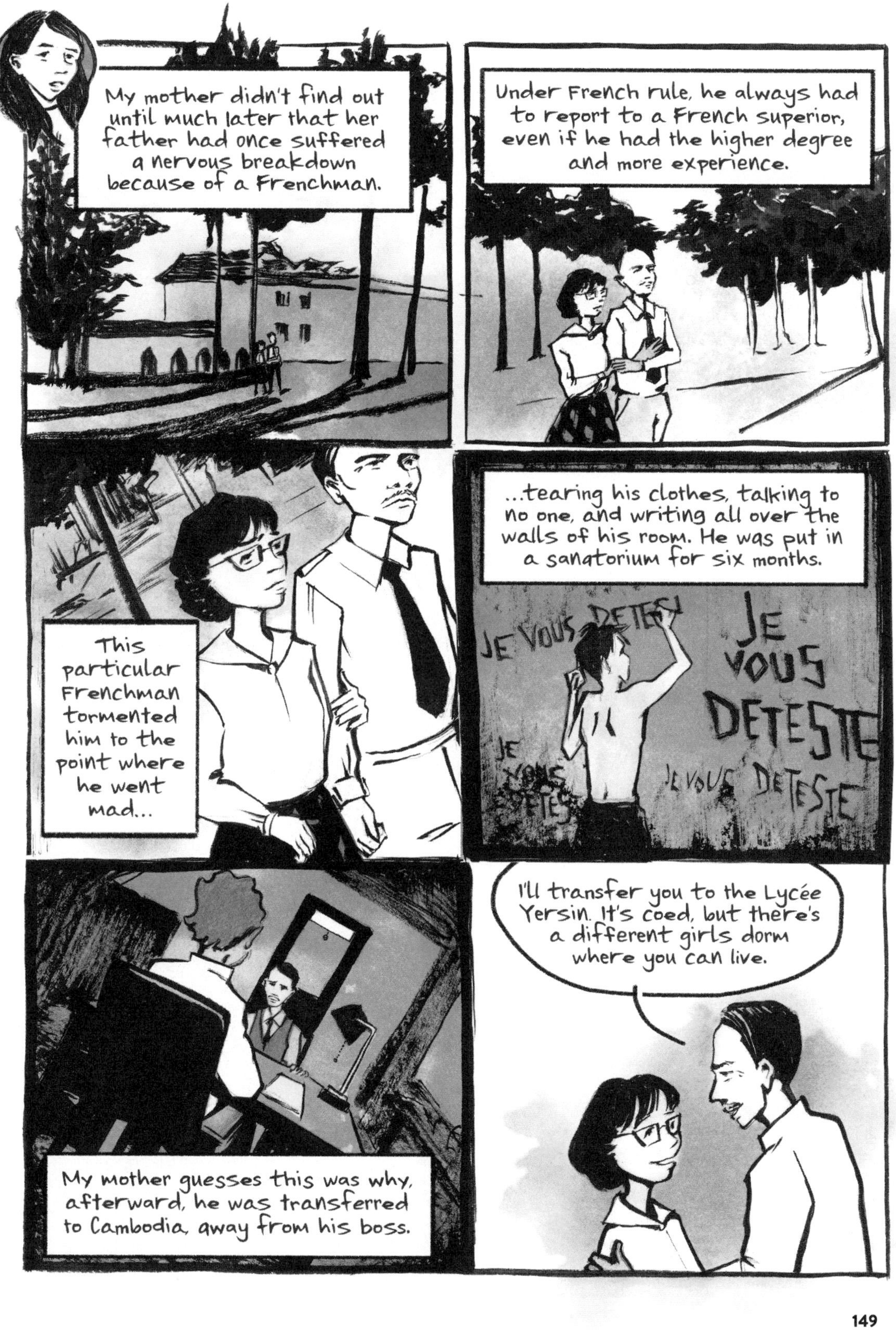

My mother didn't find out until much later that her father had once suffered a nervous breakdown because of a Frenchman.
Under French rule, he always had to report to a French superior, even if he had the higher degree and more experience.
This particular Frenchman tormented him to the point where he went mad...
...tearing his clothes, talking to no one, and writing all over the walls of his room. He was put in a sanatorium for six months.
JE VOUS DETESTE
My mother guesses this was why, afterward, he was transferred to Cambodia, away from his boss.
I'll transfer you to the Lycée Yersin. It's coed, but there's a different girls dorm where you can live.

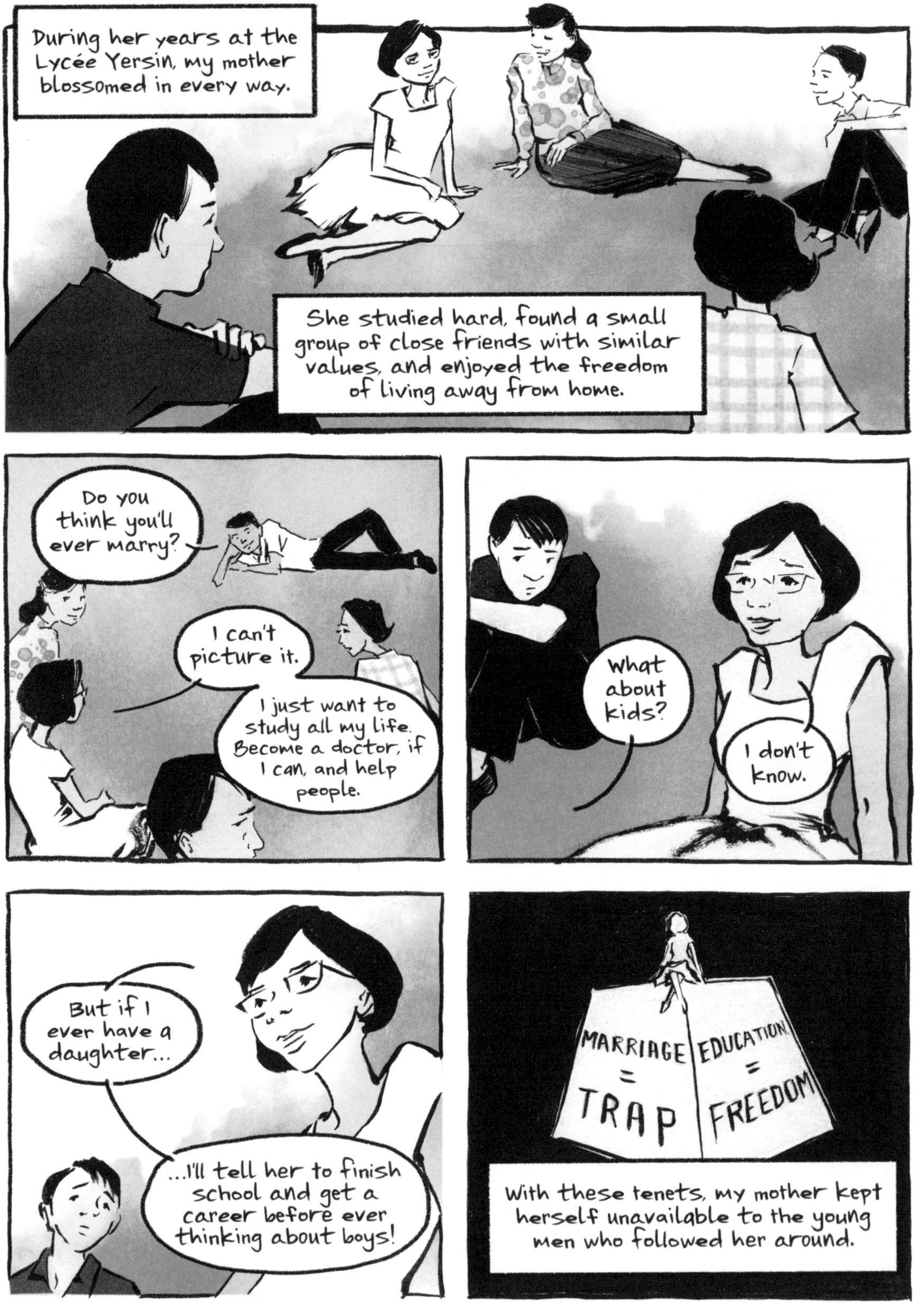
During her years at the Lycée Yersin, my mother blossomed in every way.
She studied hard, found a small group of close friends with similar values, and enjoyed the freedom of living away from home.
Do you think you'll ever marry?
I can't picture it.
I just want to study all my life. Become a doctor, if I can, and help people.
What about kids?
I don't know.
But if I ever have a daughter...
...I'll tell her to finish school and get a career before ever thinking about boys!
MARRIAGE = TRAP
EDUCATION = FREEDOM
With these tenets, my mother kept herself unavailable to the young men who followed her around.

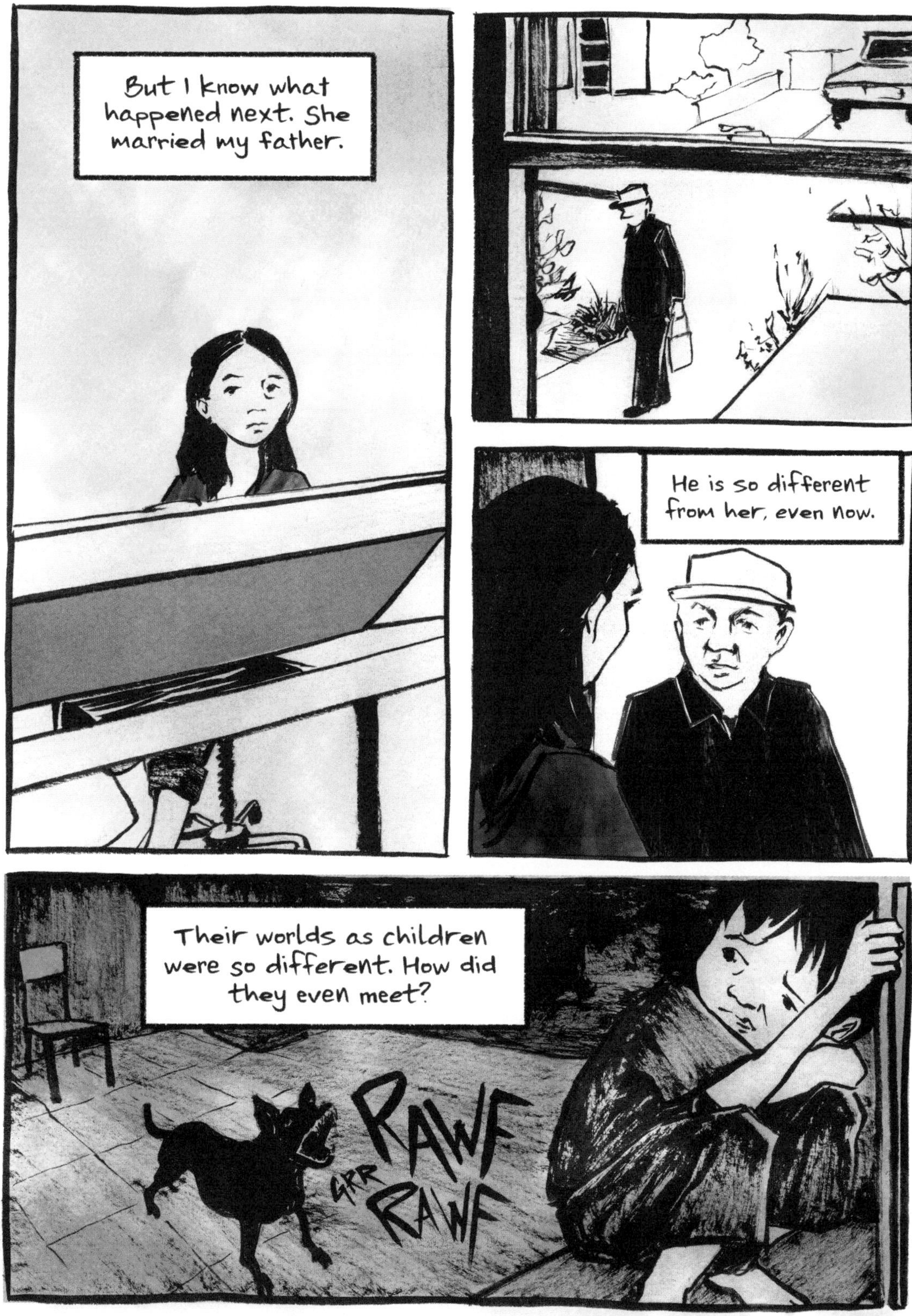
But I know what happened next. She married my father.
He is so different from her, even now.
Their worlds as children were so different. How did they even meet?
RAWF
GRR
RAWF

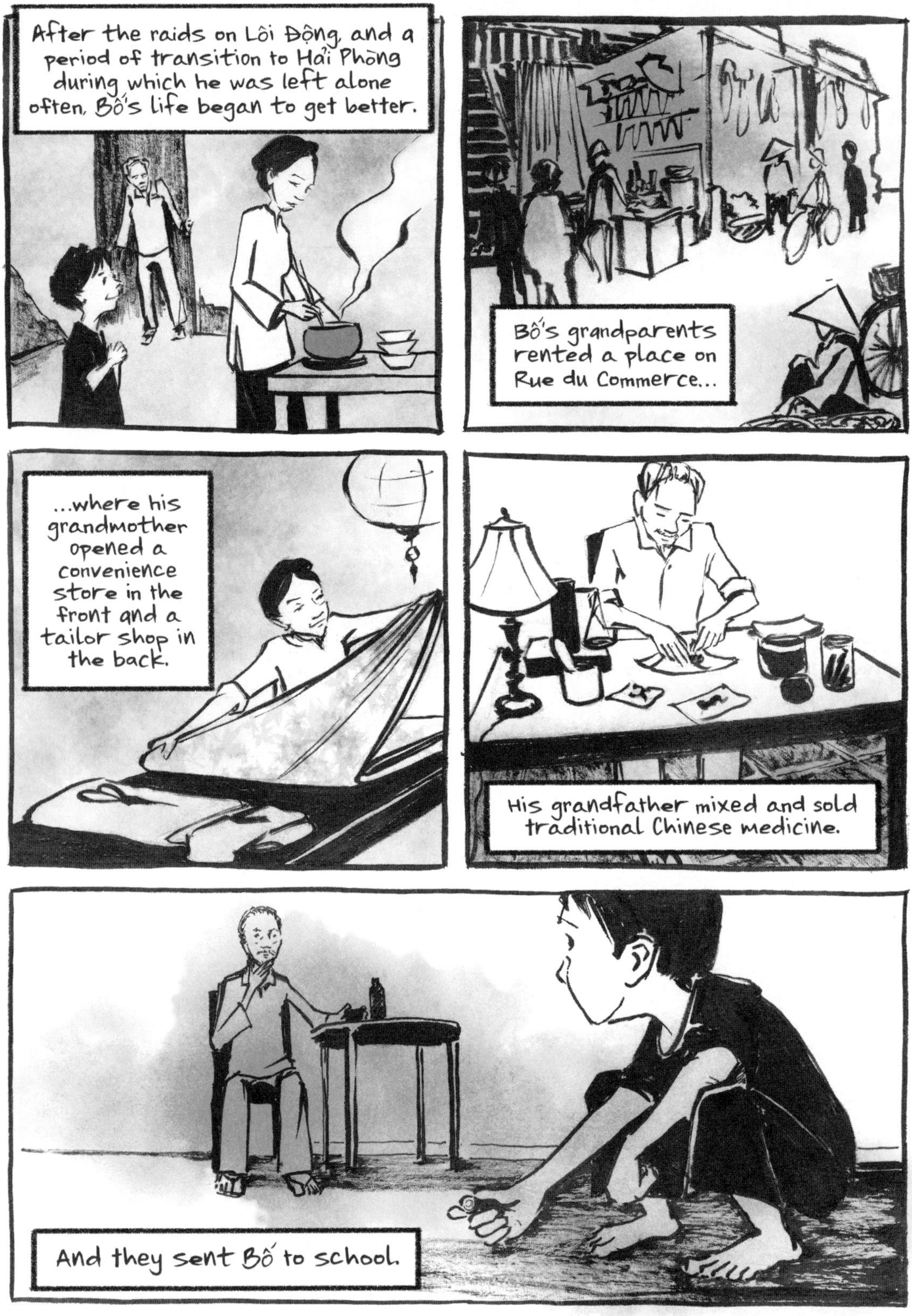
After the raids on Lôi Động, and a period of transition to Hải Phòng during which he was left alone often, Bố's life began to get better.
Bố's grandparents rented a place on Rue du Commerce...
...where his grandmother opened a convenience store in the front and a tailor shop in the back.
His grandfather mixed and sold traditional Chinese medicine.
And they sent Bố to school.

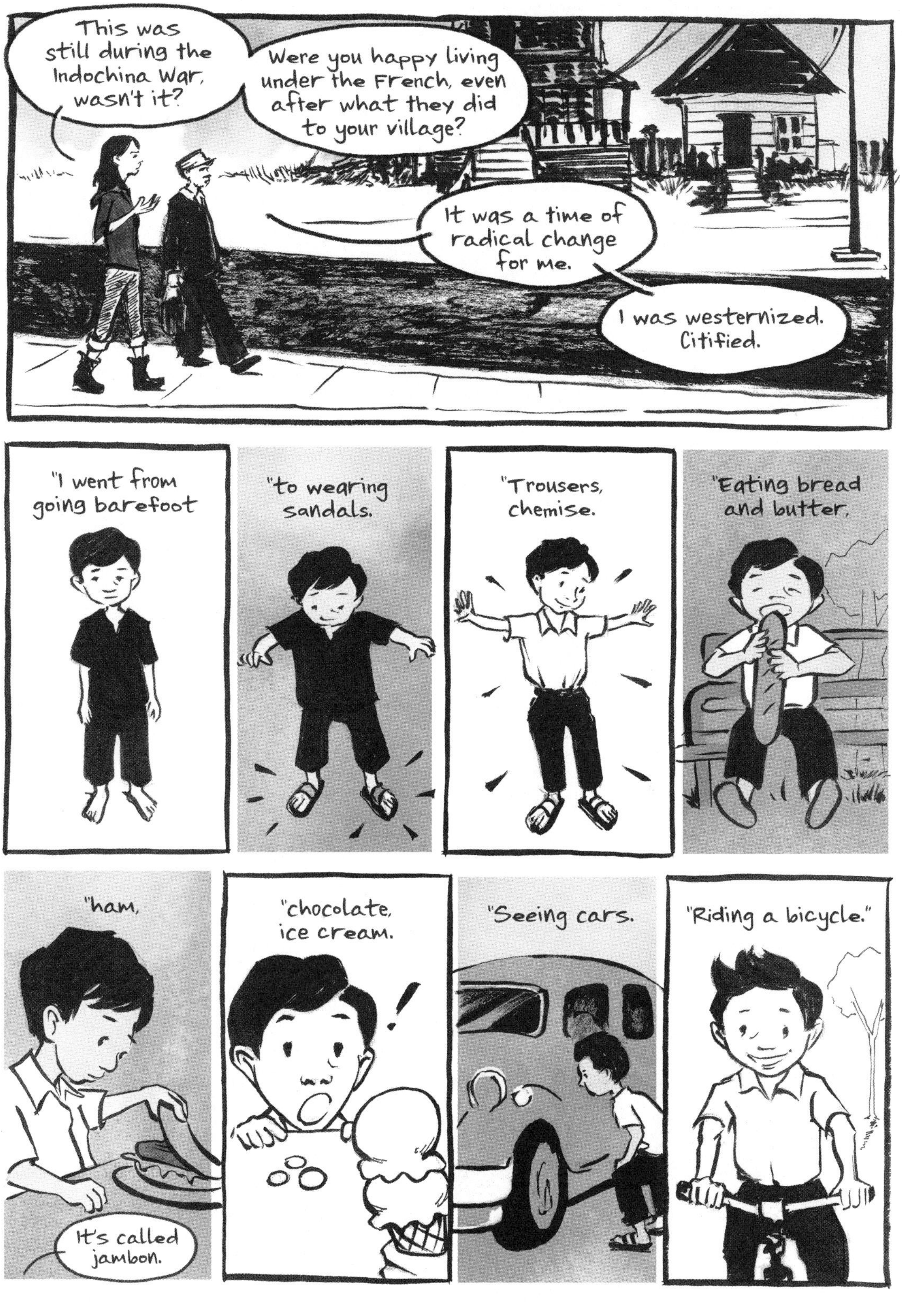
This was still during the Indochina War, wasn't it?
Were you happy living under the French, even after what they did to your village?
It was a time of radical change for me.
I was westernized. Citified.
"I went from going barefoot
"to wearing sandals.
"Trousers, chemise.
"Eating bread and butter,
"ham,
It's called jambon.
"chocolate, ice cream.
!
"Seeing cars.
"Riding a bicycle."

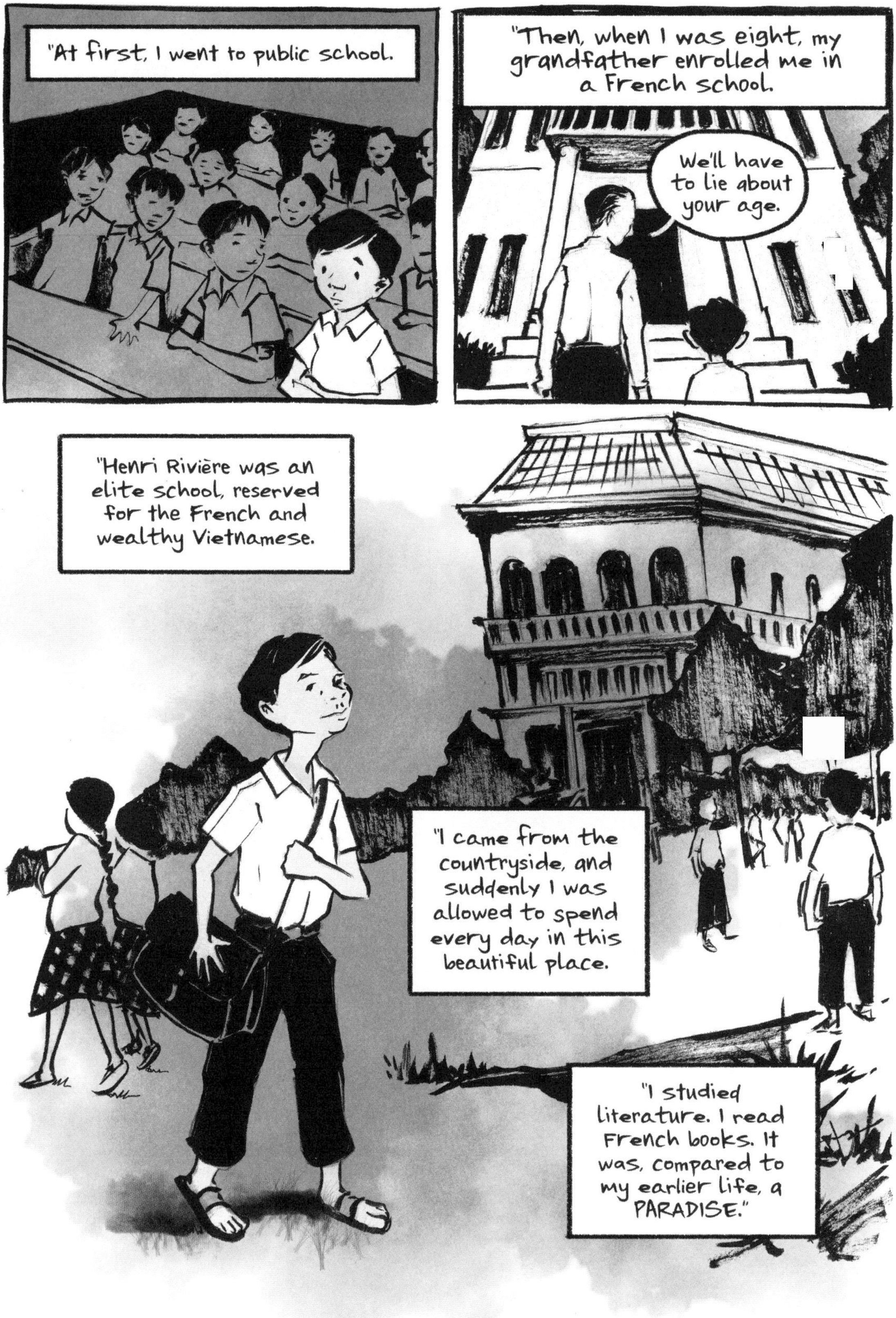
"At first, I went to public school.
"Then, when I was eight, my grandfather enrolled me in a French school.
We'll have to lie about your age.
"Henri Rivière was an elite school, reserved for the French and wealthy Vietnamese.
"I came from the countryside, and suddenly I was allowed to spend every day in this beautiful place.
"I studied literature. I read French books. It was, compared to my earlier life, a PARADISE."

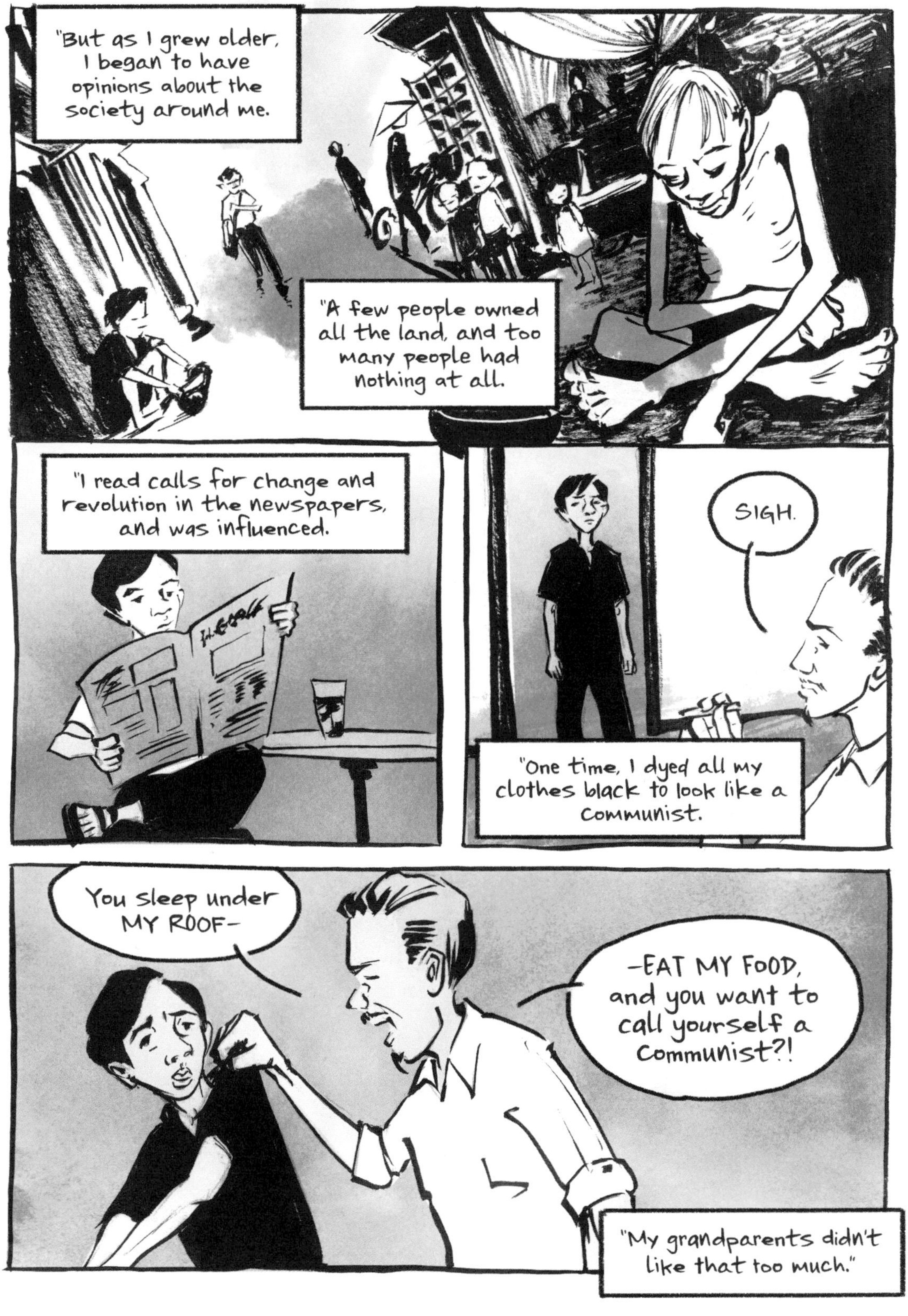
"But as I grew older, I began to have opinions about the society around me.
"A few people owned all the land, and too many people had nothing at all.
"I read calls for change and revolution in the newspapers, and was influenced.
SIGH.
"One time, I dyed all my clothes black to look like a communist.
You sleep under MY ROOF–
–EAT MY FOOD, and you want to call yourself a communist?!
"My grandparents didn't like that too much."

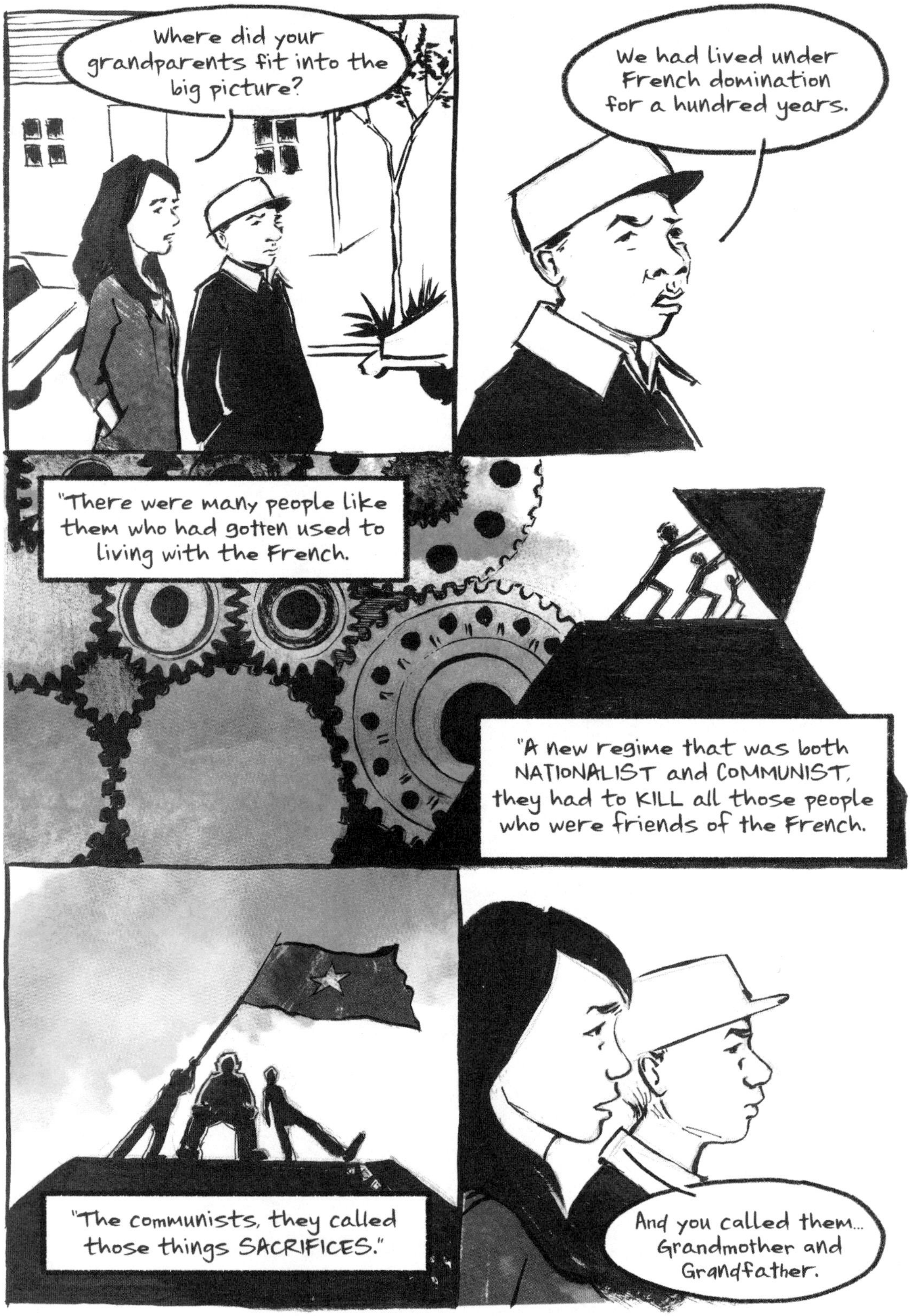
Where did your grandparents fit into the big picture?
We had lived under French domination for a hundred years.
"There were many people like them who had gotten used to living with the French.
"A new regime that was both NATIONALIST and COMMUNIST, they had to KILL all those people who were friends of the French.
"The communists, they called those things SACRIFICES."
And you called them... Grandmother and Grandfather.

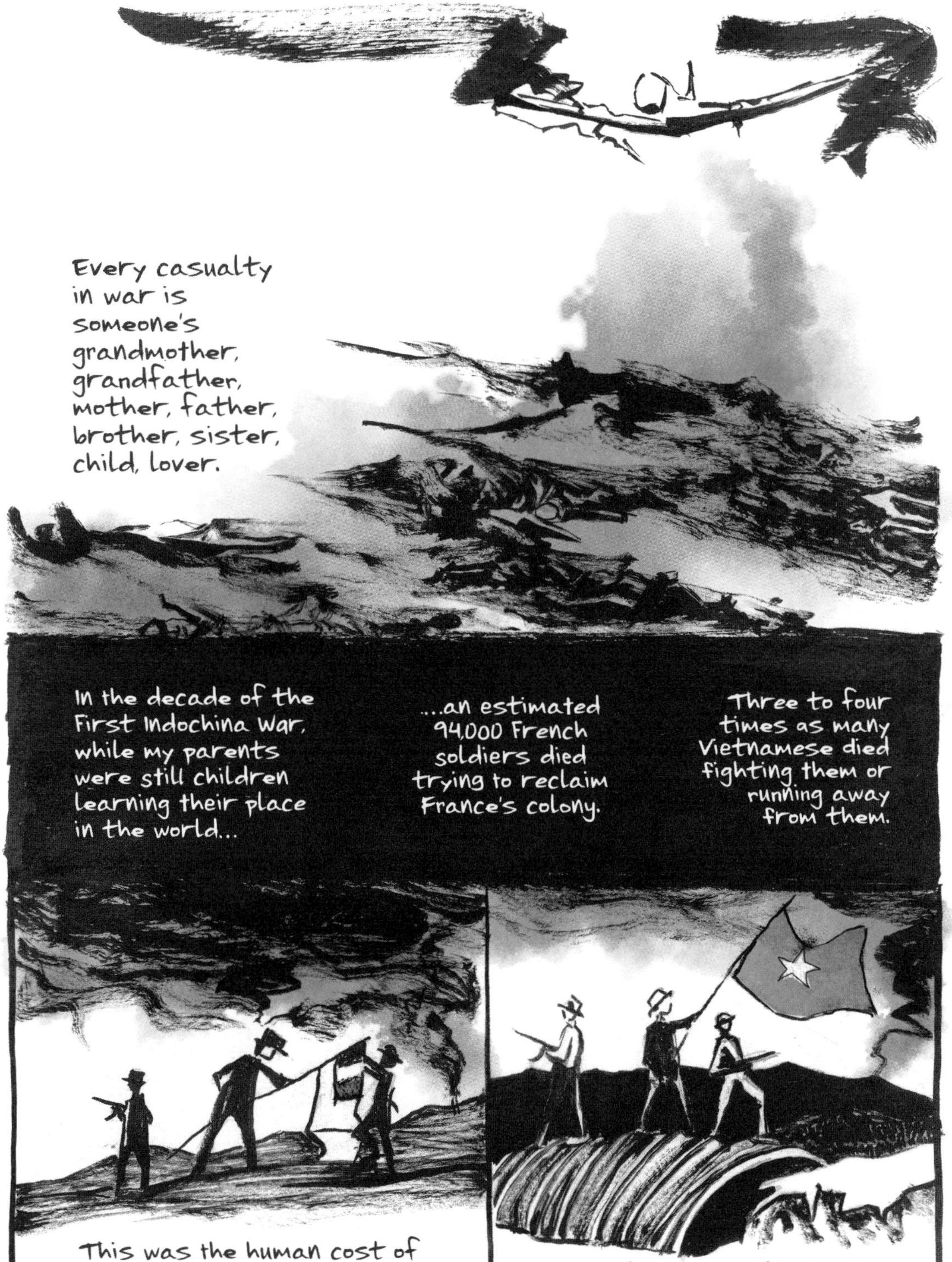
Every casualty in war is someone's grandmother, grandfather, mother, father, brother, sister, child, lover.
In the decade of the First Indochina War, while my parents were still children learning their place in the world...
...an estimated 94,000 French soldiers died trying to reclaim France's colony.
Three to four times as many Vietnamese died fighting them or running away from them.
This was the human cost of ending France's colonial rule in Southeast Asia...
...and winning Việt Nam's independence.

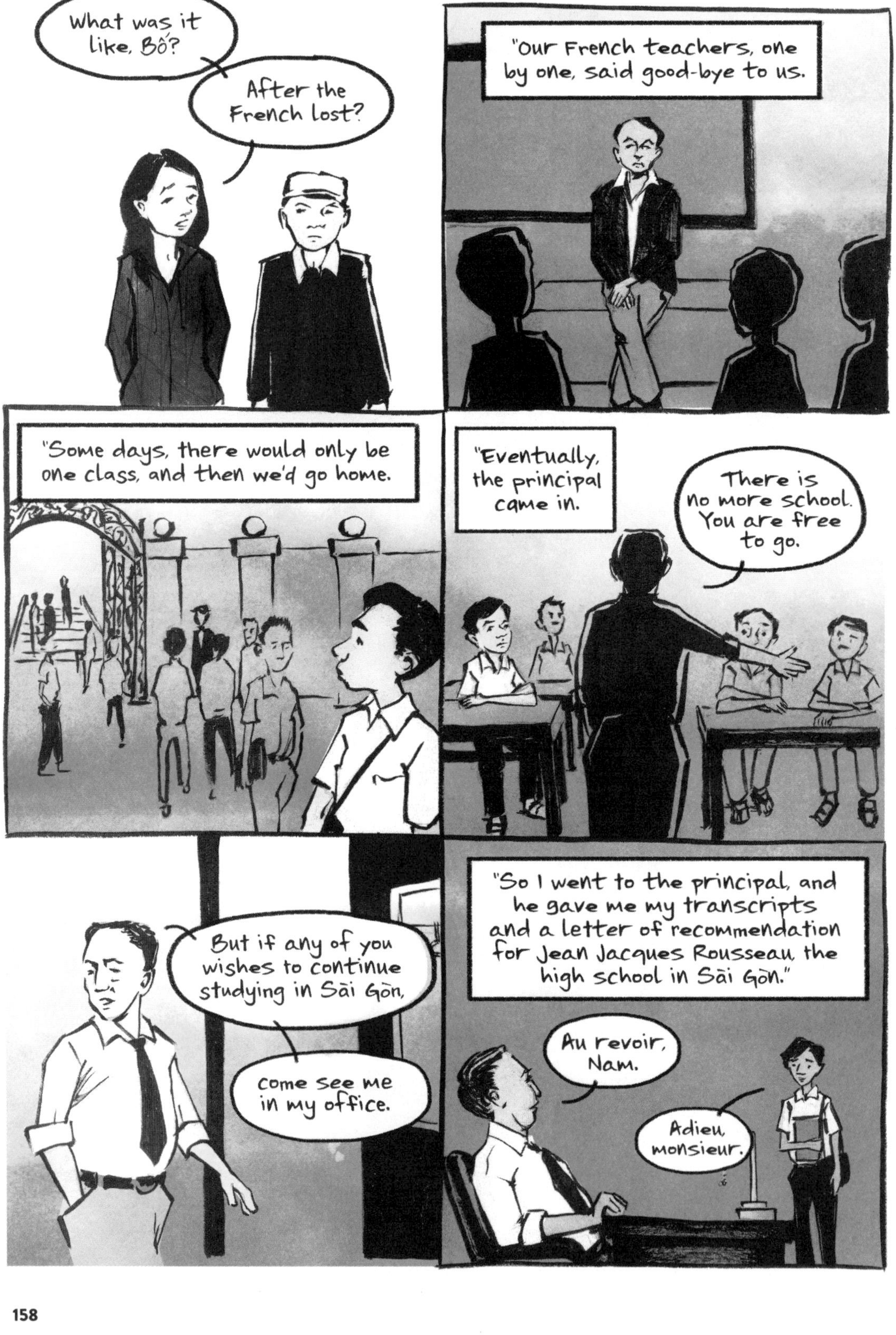
What was it like, Bố?
After the French lost?
"Our French teachers, one by one, said good-bye to us.
"Some days, there would only be one class, and then we'd go home.
"Eventually, the principal came in.
There is no more school. You are free to go.
But if any of you wishes to continue studying in Sài Gòn,
come see me in my office.
"So I went to the principal, and he gave me my transcripts and a letter of recommendation for Jean Jacques Rousseau, the high school in Sài Gòn."
Au revoir, Nam.
Adieu, monsieur.

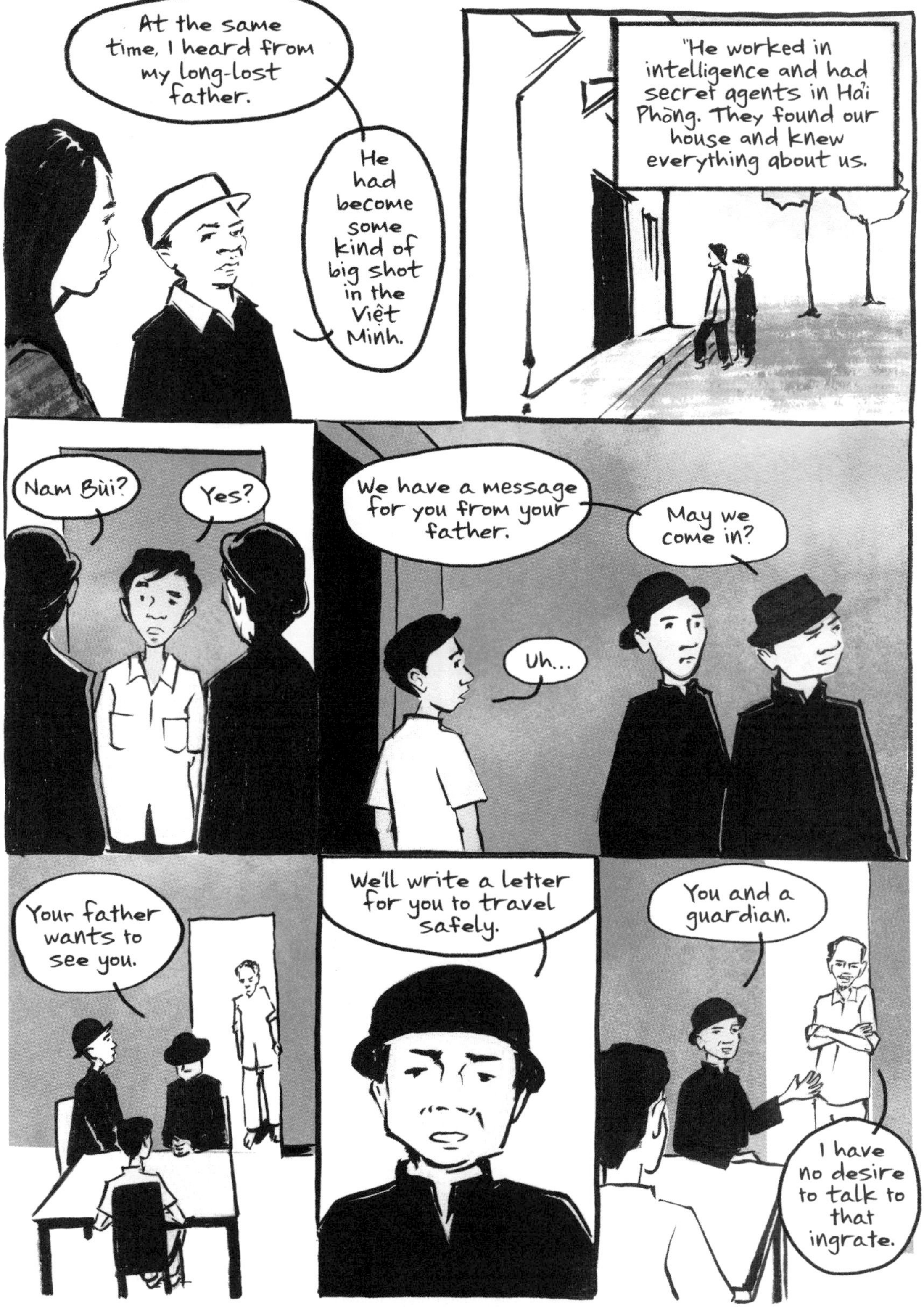
At the same time, I heard from my long-lost father.
He had become some kind of big shot in the Việt Minh.
"He worked in intelligence and had secret agents in Hải Phòng. They found our house and knew everything about us.
Nam Bùi?
Yes?
We have a message for you from your father.
May we come in?
Uh...
Your father wants to see you.
We'll write a letter for you to travel safely.
You and a guardian.
I have no desire to talk to that ingrate.

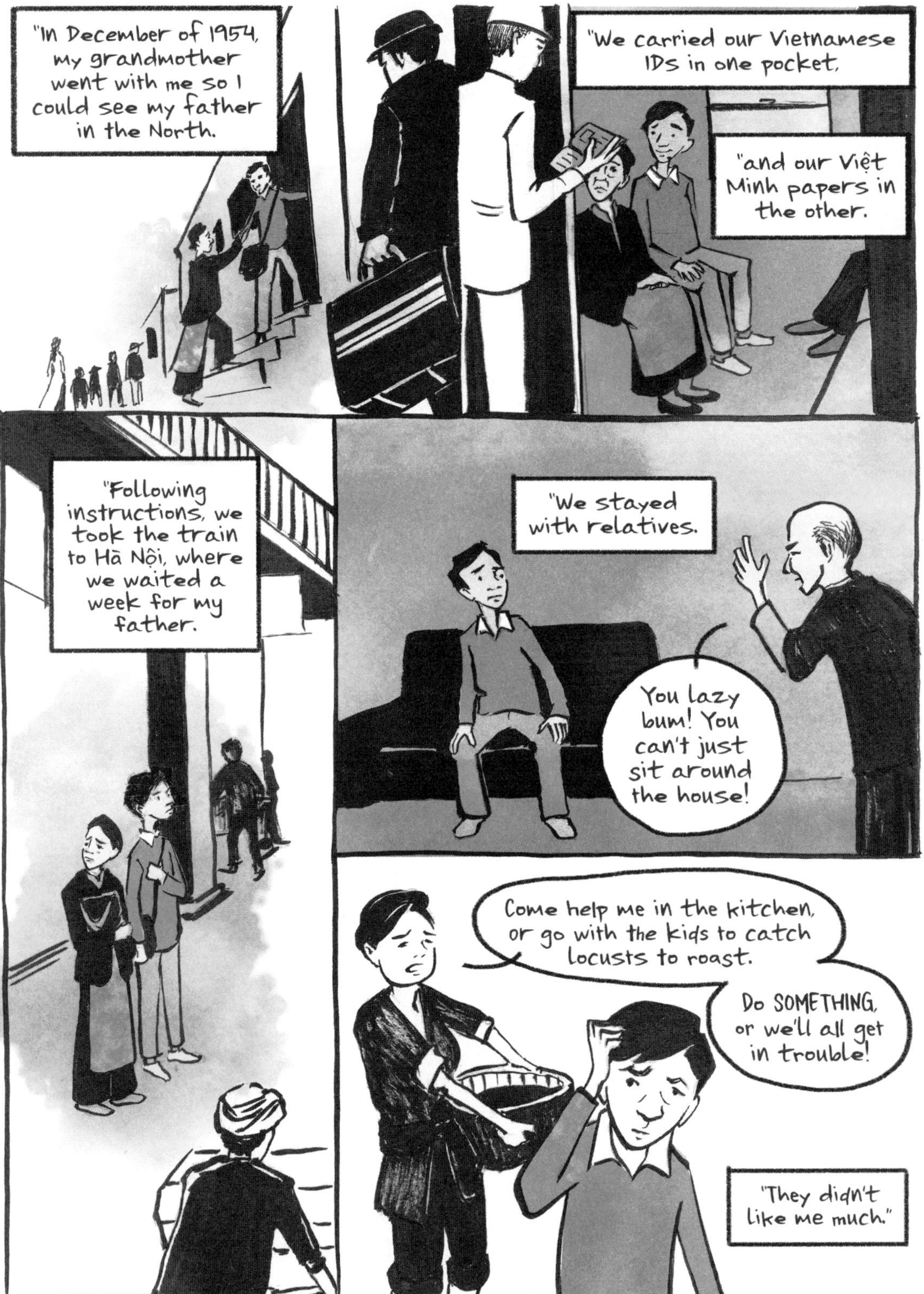
"In December of 1954, my grandmother went with me so I could see my father in the North.
"We carried our Vietnamese IDs in one pocket,
"and our Việt Minh papers in the other.
"Following instructions, we took the train to Hà Nội, where we waited a week for my father.
"We stayed with relatives.
You lazy bum! You can't just sit around the house!
Come help me in the kitchen, or go with the kids to catch locusts to roast.
Do SOMETHING, or we'll all get in trouble!
"They didn't like me much."

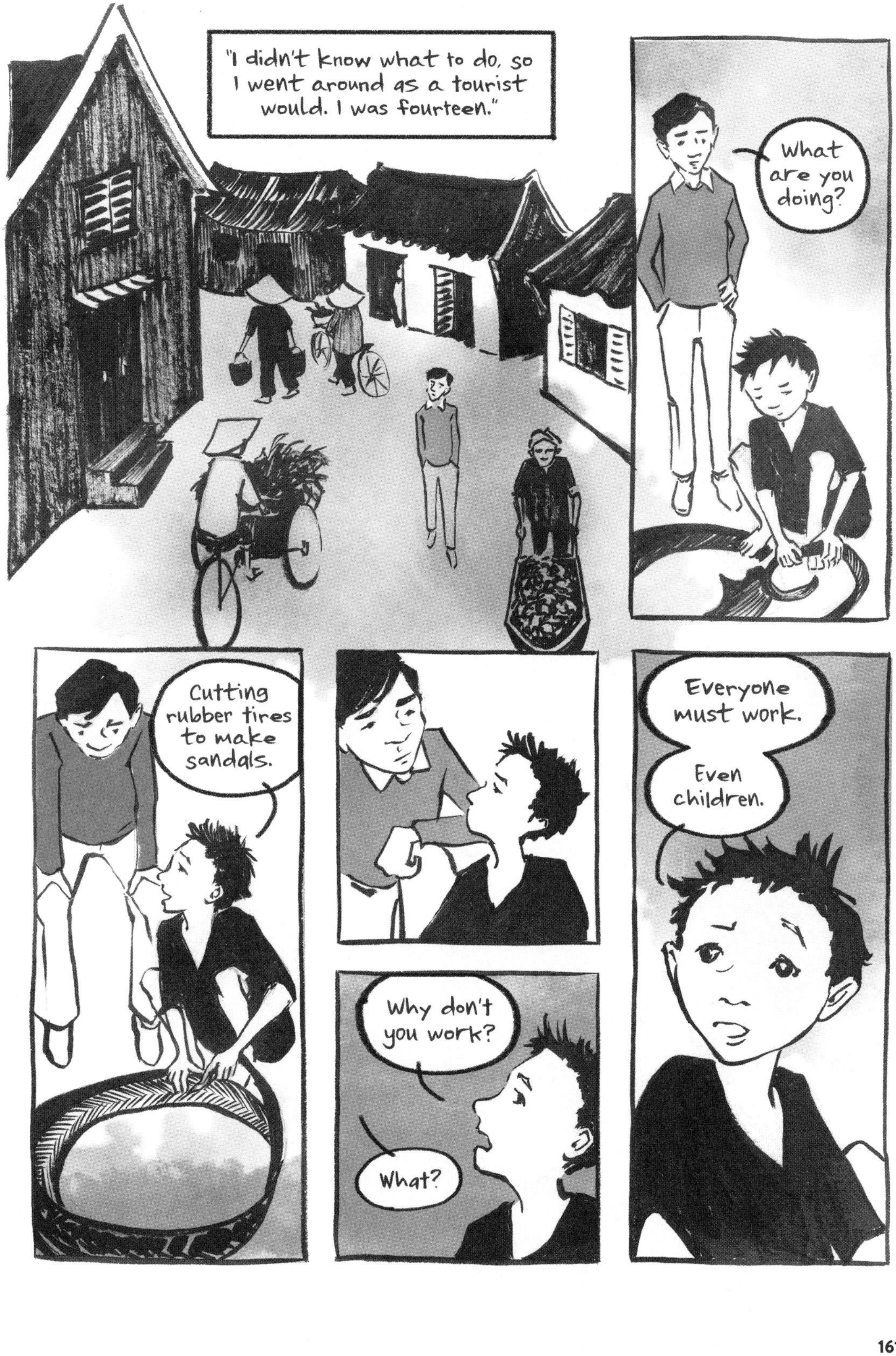
"I didn't know what to do, so I went around as a tourist would. I was fourteen."
What are you doing?
Cutting rubber tires to make sandals.
Why don't you work?
What?
Everyone must work.
Even children.

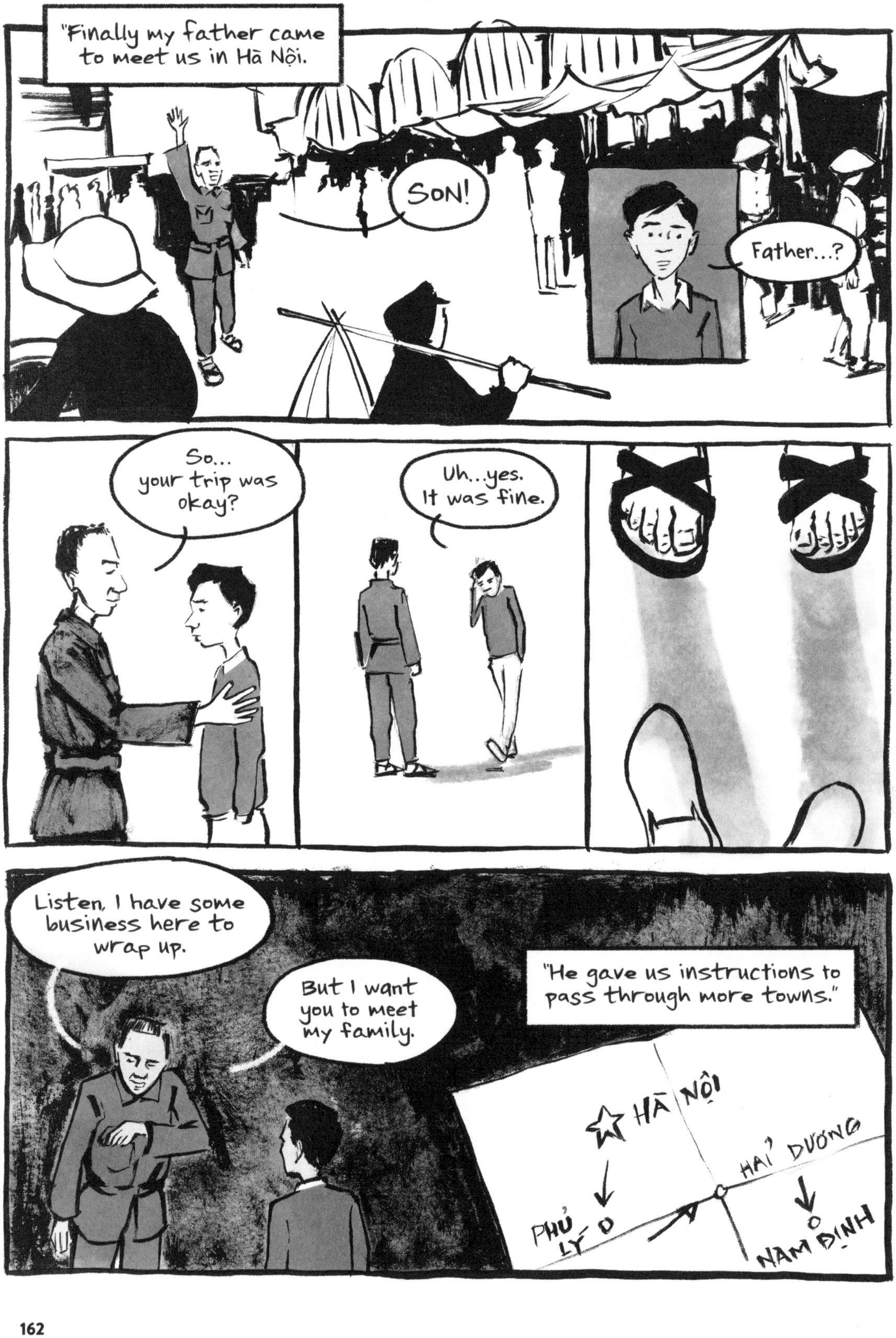
"Finally my father came to meet us in Hà Nội.
SON!
Father...?
So... your trip was okay?
Uh...yes. It was fine.
Listen, I have some business here to wrap up.
But I want you to meet my family.
"He gave us instructions to pass through more towns."
HÀ NỘI
HẢI DƯƠNG
PHỦ LÝ
NAM ĐỊNH

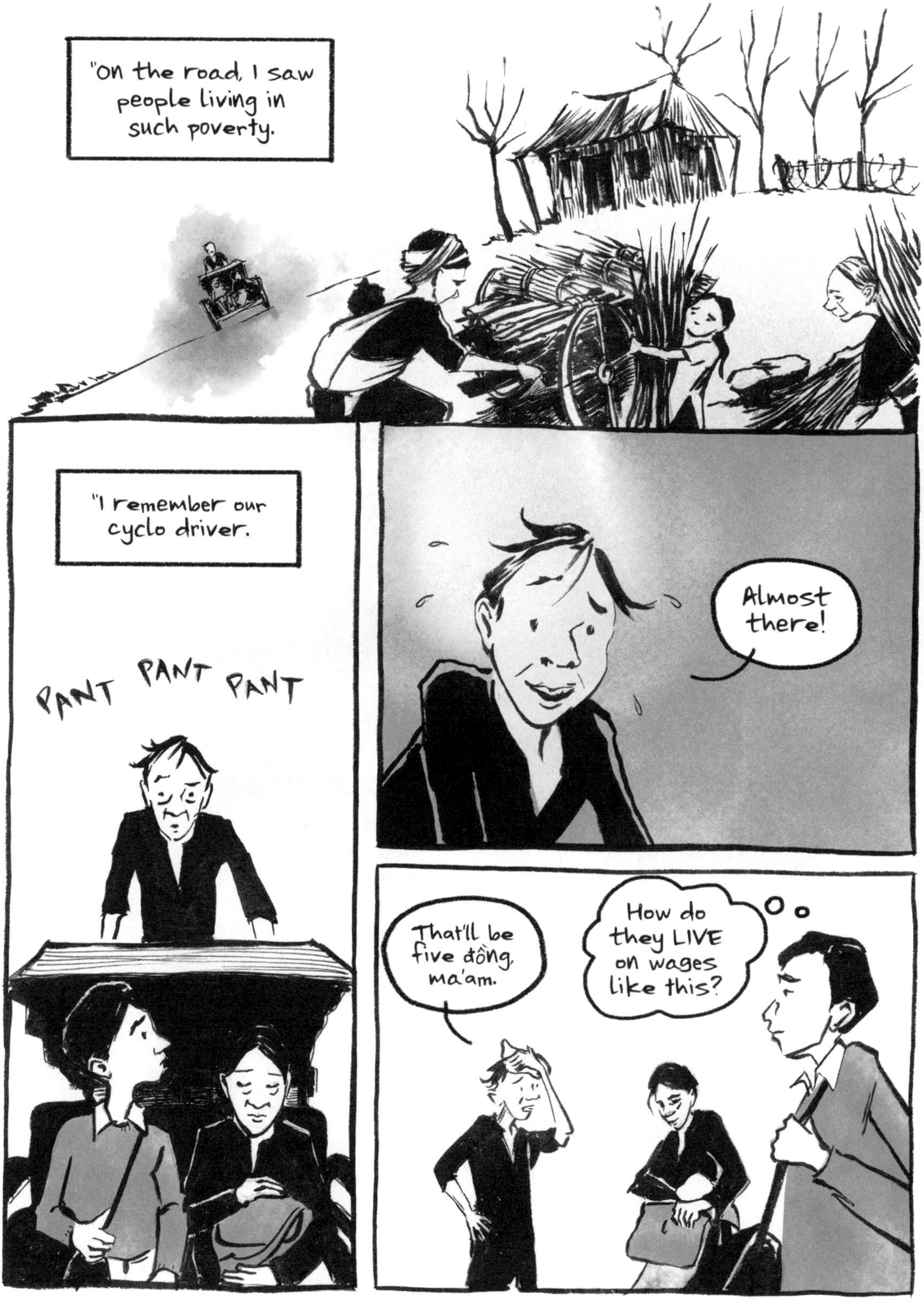
"On the road, I saw people living in such poverty.
"I remember our cyclo driver.
PANT PANT PANT
Almost there!
That'll be five đồng, ma'am.
How do they LIVE on wages like this?

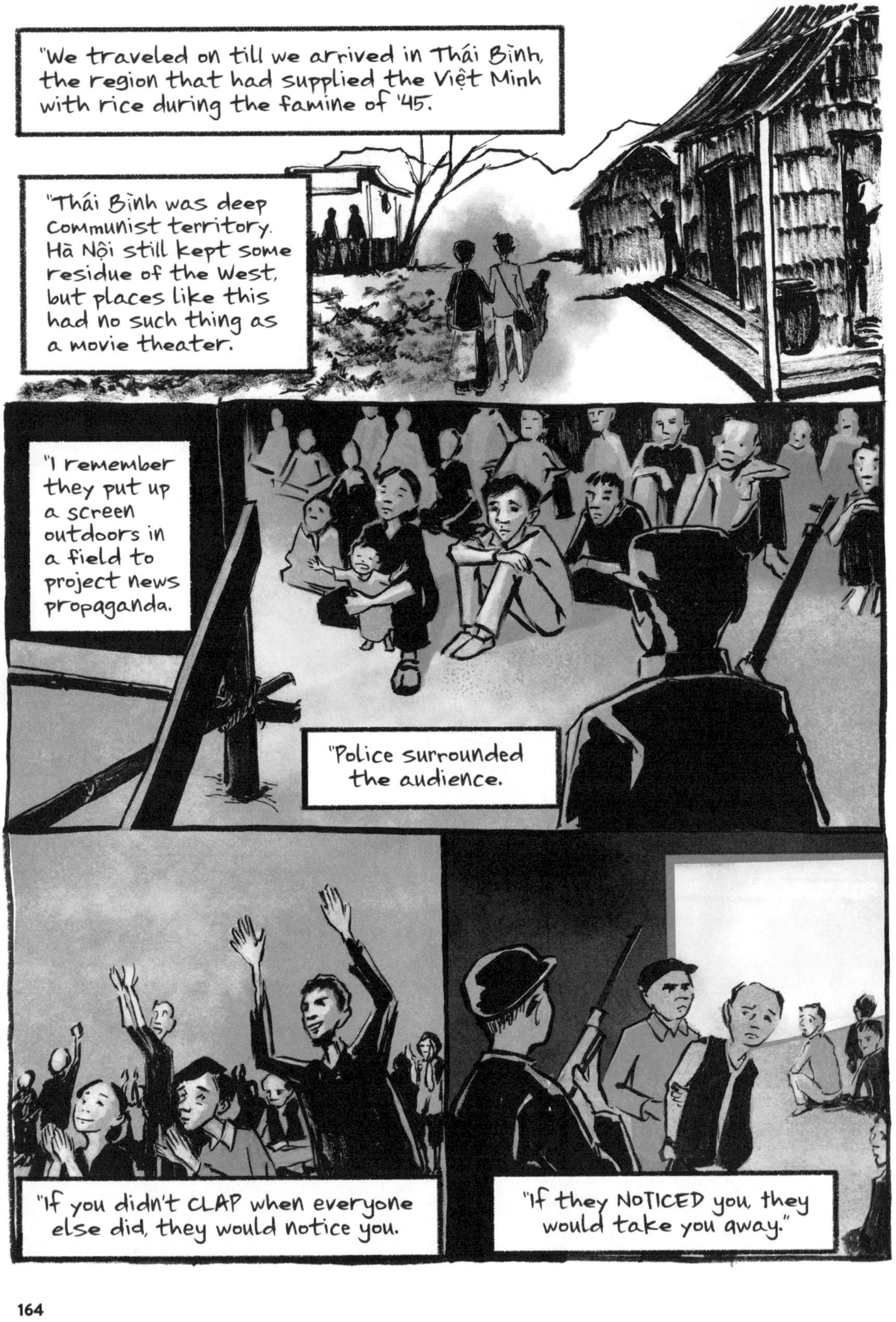
"We traveled on till we arrived in Thái Bình, the region that had supplied the Việt Minh with rice during the famine of '45.
"Thái Bình was deep Communist territory. Hà Nội still kept some residue of the West, but places like this had no such thing as a movie theater.
"I remember they put up a screen outdoors in a field to project news propaganda.
"Police surrounded the audience.
"If you didn't CLAP when everyone else did, they would notice you.
"If they NOTICED you, they would take you away."

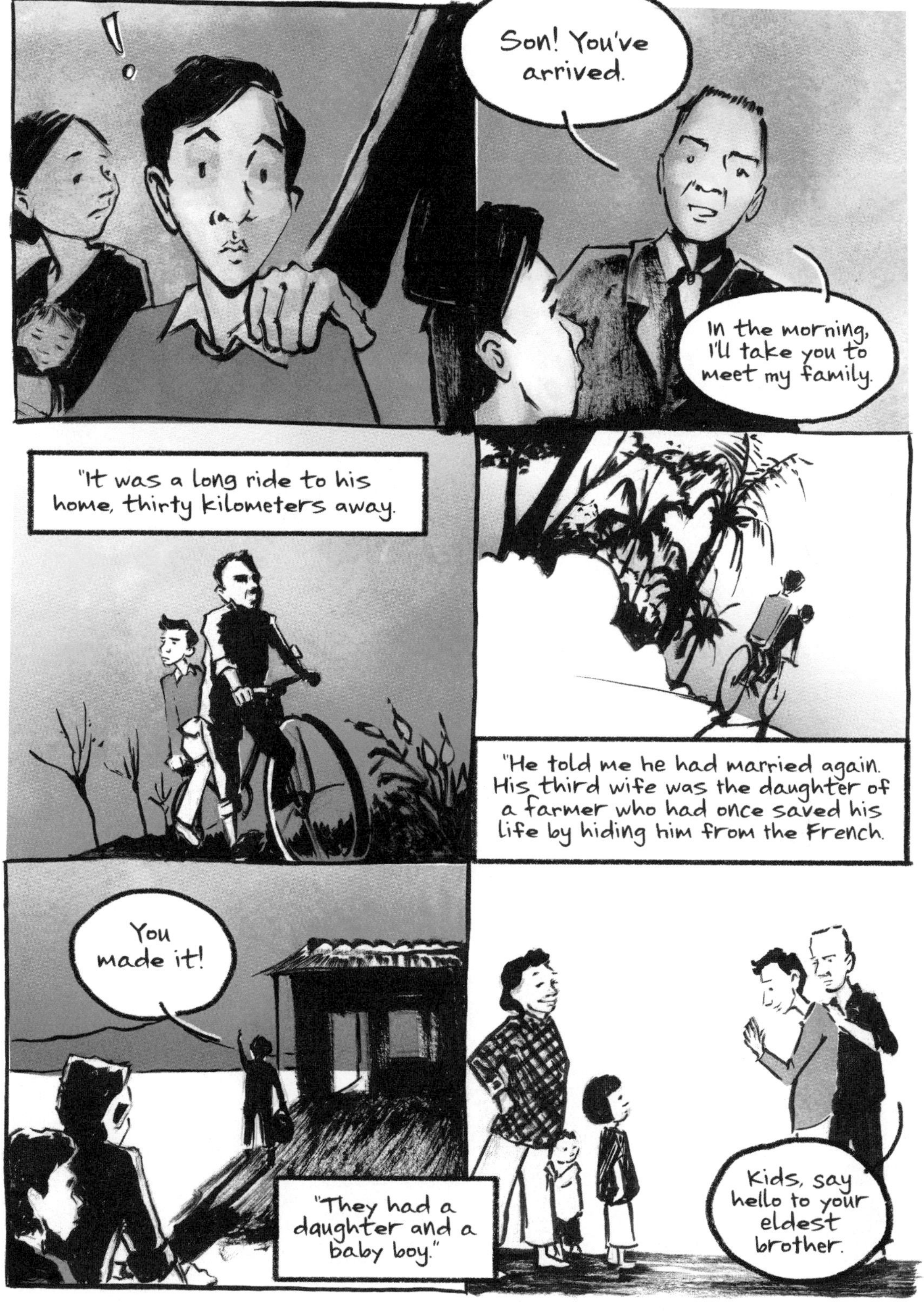
!
Son! You've arrived.
In the morning, I'll take you to meet my family.
"It was a long ride to his home, thirty kilometers away.
"He told me he had married again. His third wife was the daughter of a farmer who had once saved his life by hiding him from the French.
You made it!
"They had a daughter and a baby boy."
Kids, say hello to your eldest brother.

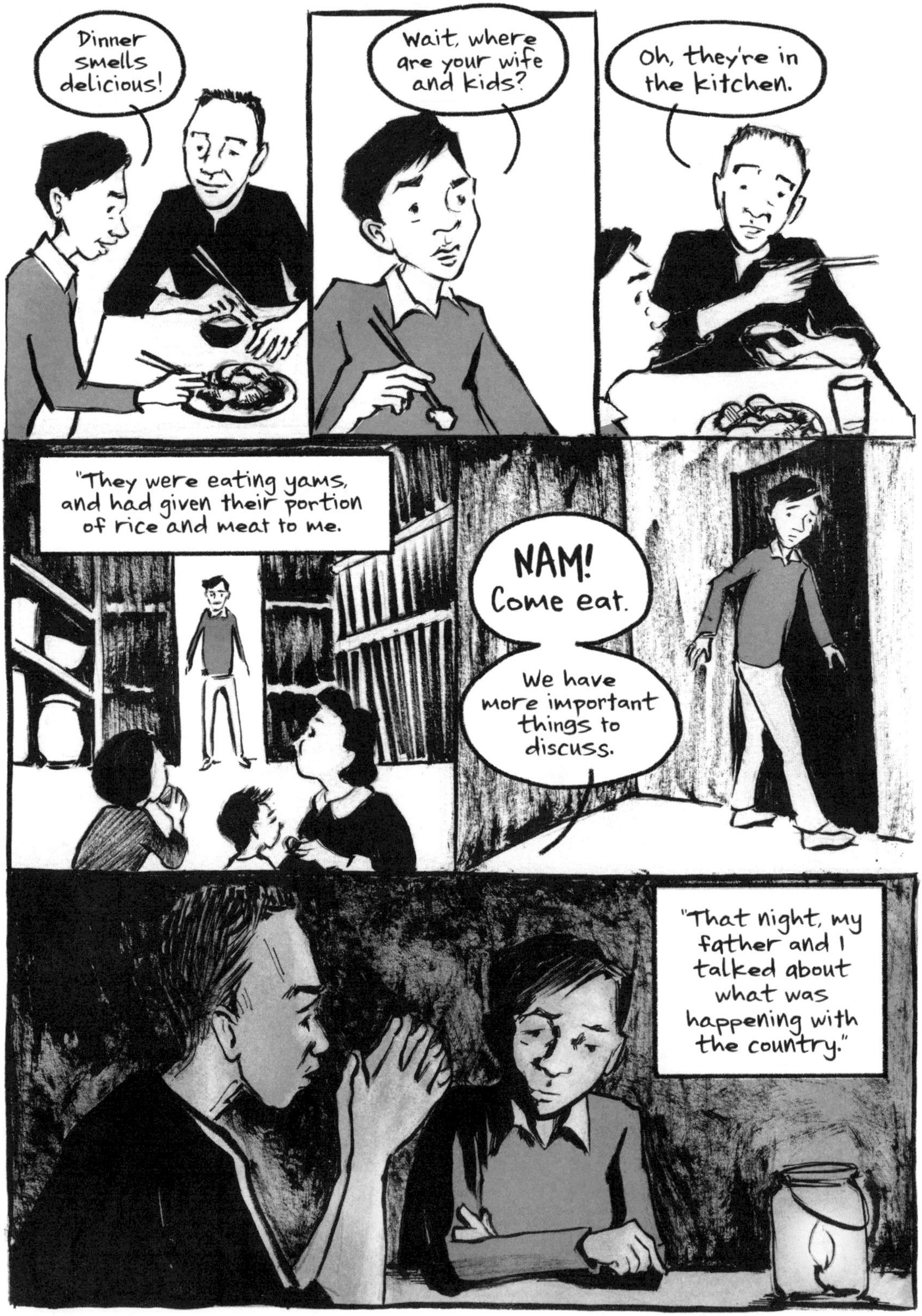
Dinner smells delicious!
Wait, where are your wife and kids?
Oh, they're in the kitchen.
"They were eating yams, and had given their portion of rice and meat to me.
NAM! Come eat.
We have more important things to discuss.
"That night, my father and I talked about what was happening with the country."

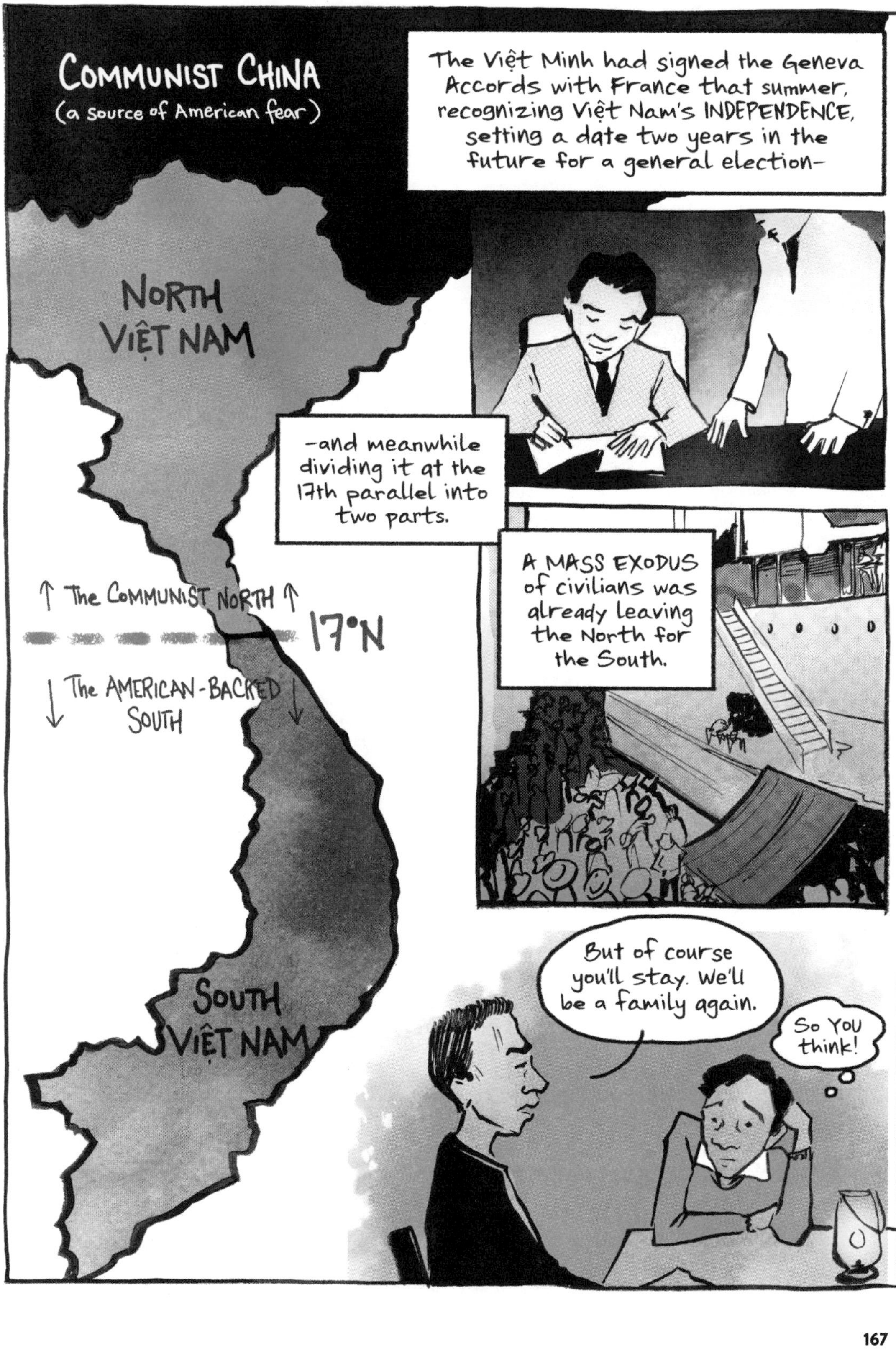
COMMUNIST CHINA
(a source of American fear)
NORTH VIỆT NAM
↑ The COMMUNIST NORTH ↑
17°N
↓ The AMERICAN-BACKED SOUTH ↓
SOUTH VIỆT NAM
The Việt Minh had signed the Geneva Accords with France that summer, recognizing Việt Nam's INDEPENDENCE, setting a date two years in the future for a general election-
-and meanwhile dividing it at the 17th parallel into two parts.
A MASS EXODUS of civilians was already leaving the North for the South.
But of course you'll stay. We'll be a family again.
So YOU think!

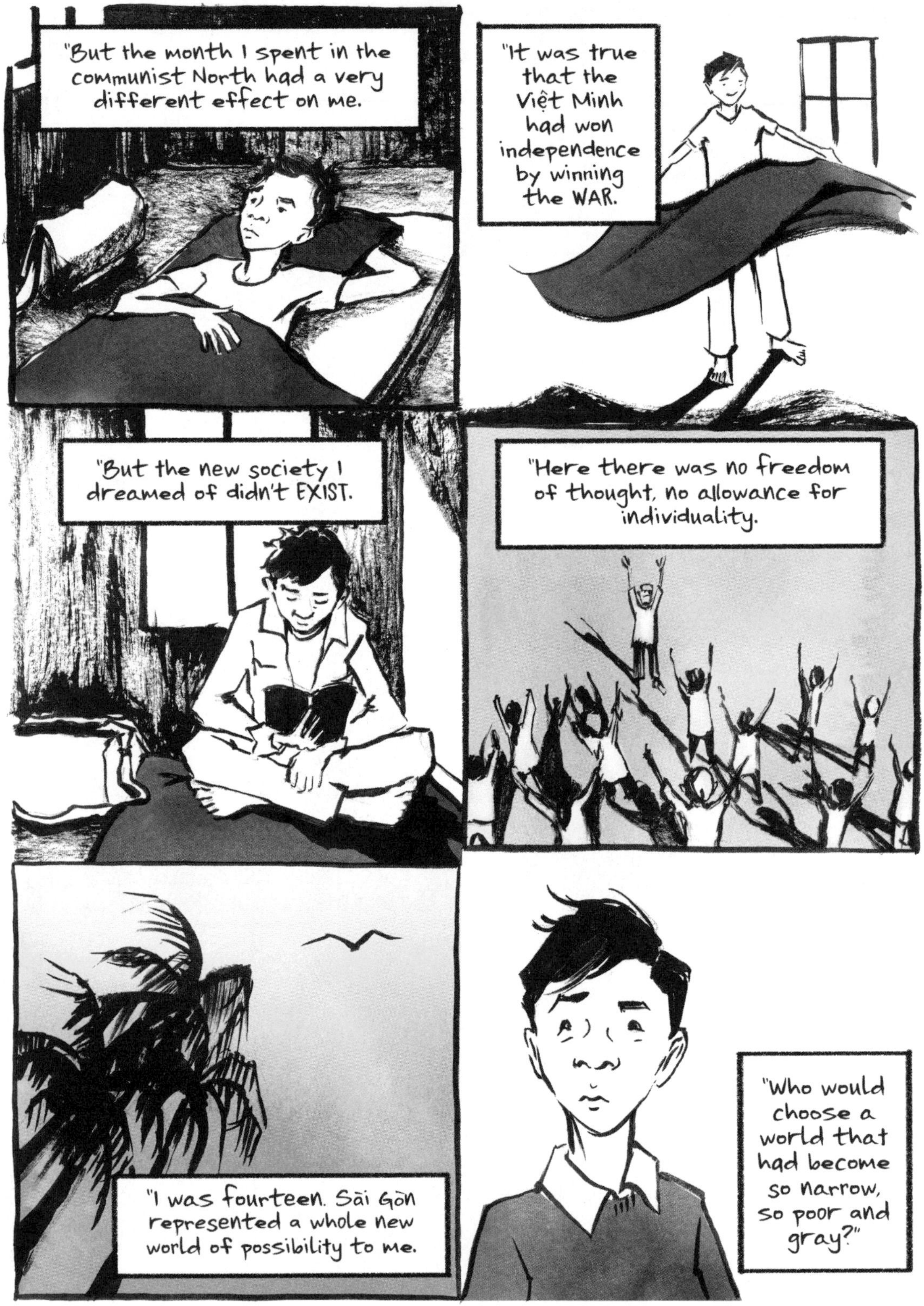
"But the month I spent in the communist North had a very different effect on me.
"It was true that the Việt Minh had won independence by winning the WAR.
"But the new society I dreamed of didn't EXIST.
"Here there was no freedom of thought, no allowance for individuality.
"I was fourteen. Sài Gòn represented a whole new world of possibility to me.
"Who would choose a world that had become so narrow, so poor and gray?"

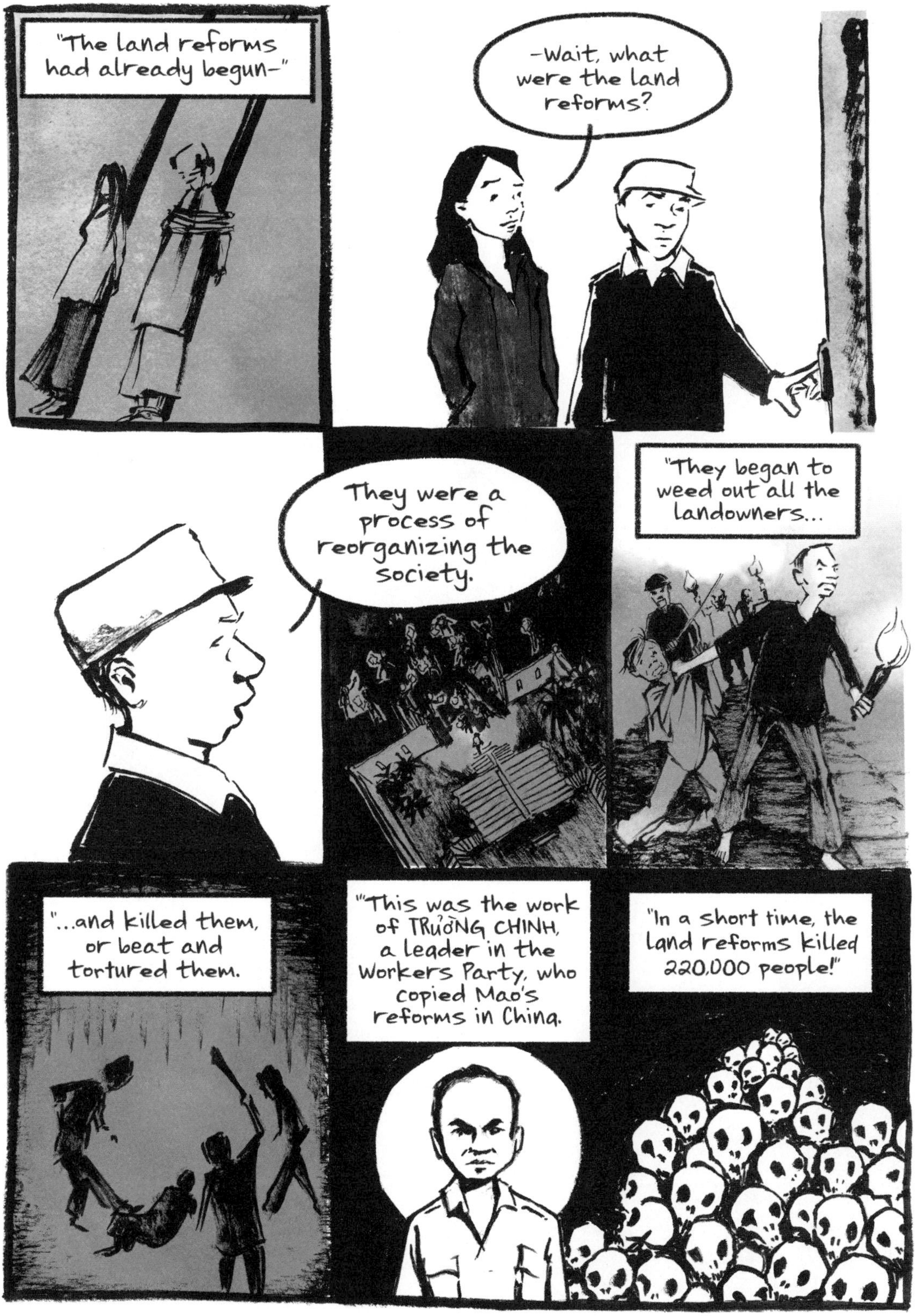

"The land reforms had already begun-"
-Wait, what were the land reforms?
They were a process of reorganizing the society.
"They began to weed out all the landowners...
"...and killed them, or beat and tortured them.
"This was the work of TRƯỜNG CHINH, a leader in the Workers Party, who copied Mao's reforms in China.
"In a short time, the land reforms killed 220,000 people!"

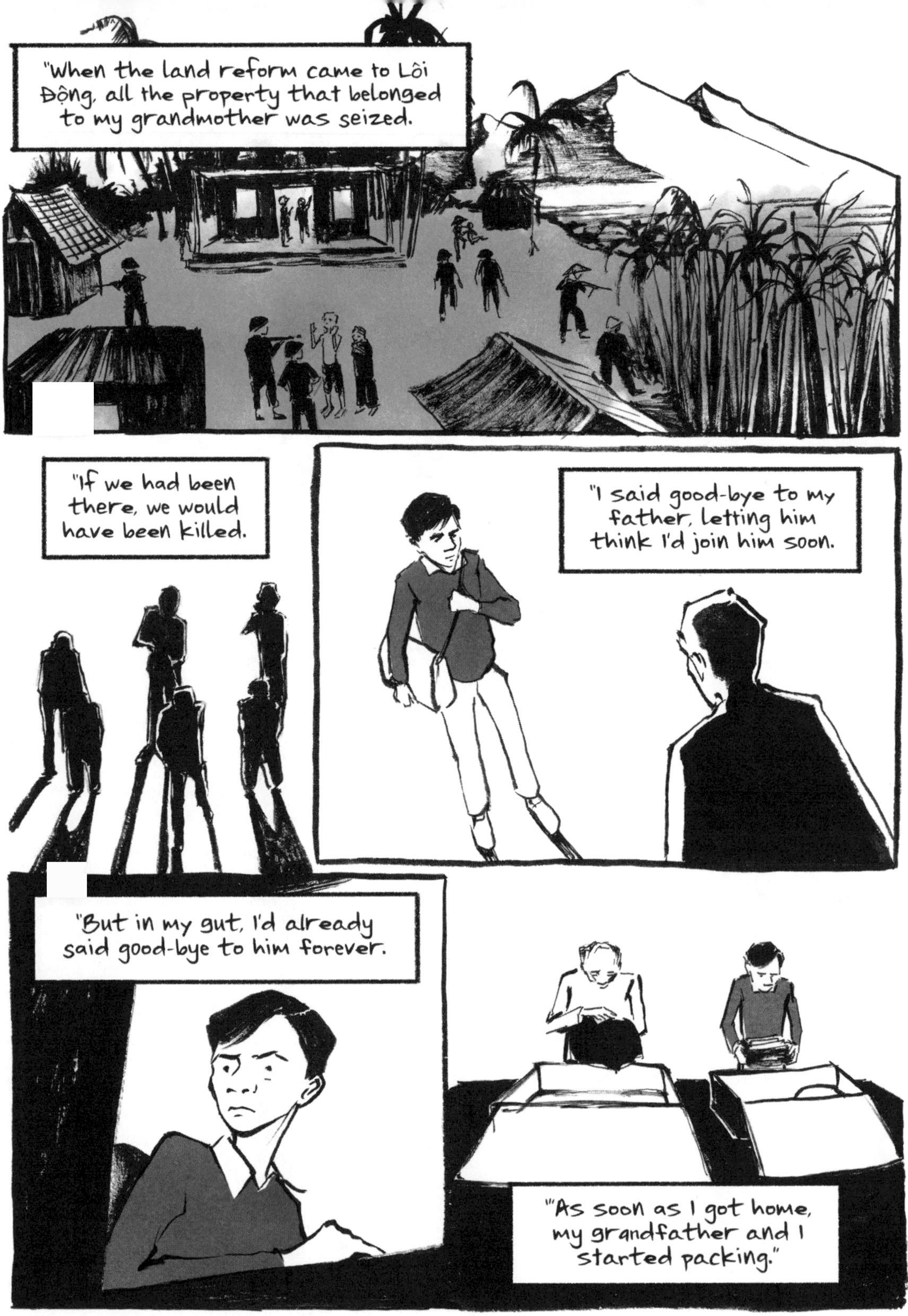
"When the land reform came to Lôi Động, all the property that belonged to my grandmother was seized.
"If we had been there, we would have been killed.
"I said good-bye to my father, letting him think I'd join him soon.
"But in my gut, I'd already said good-bye to him forever.
"As soon as I got home, my grandfather and I started packing."

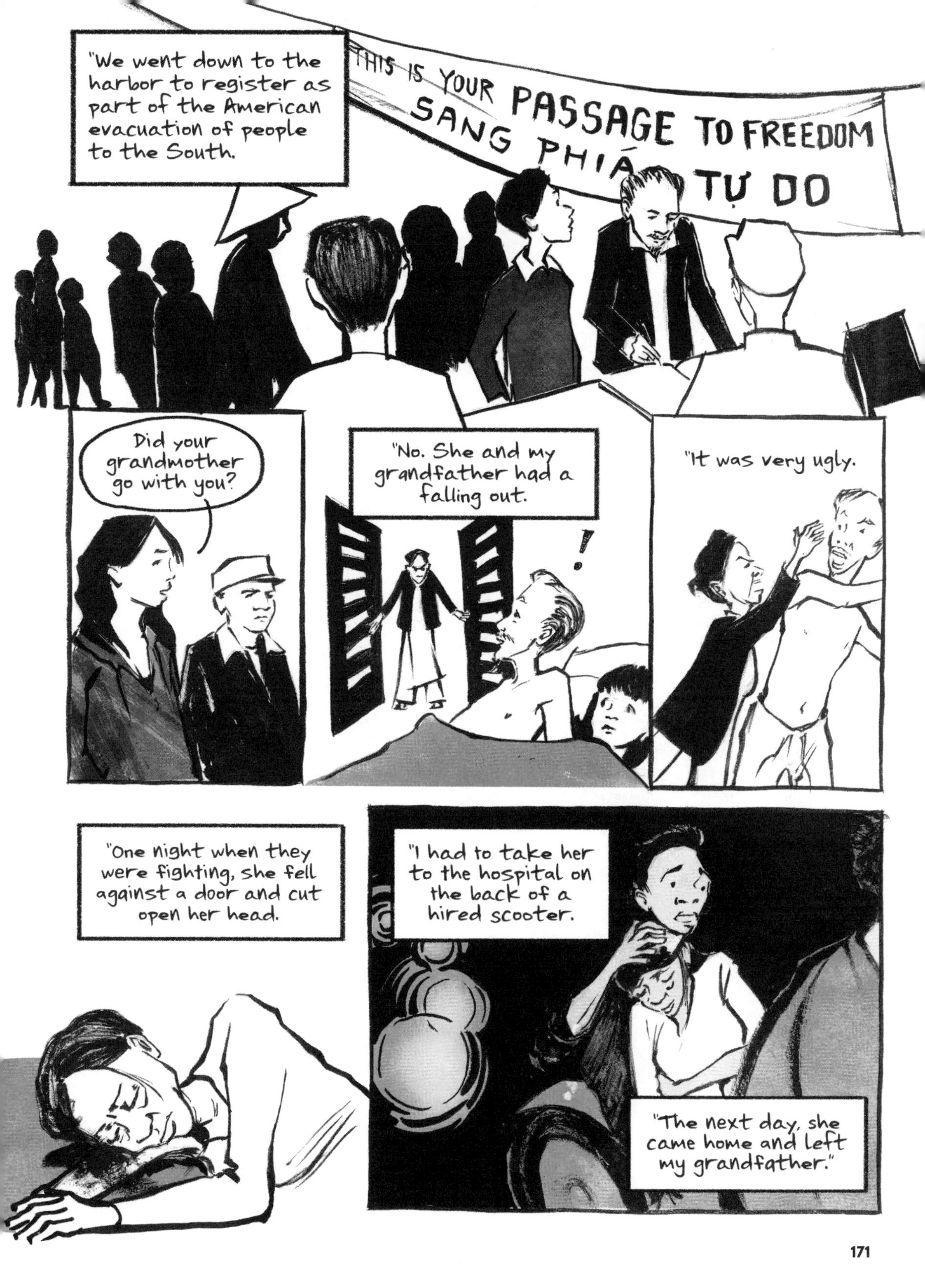
"We went down to the harbor to register as part of the American evacuation of people to the South.
THIS IS YOUR PASSAGE TO FREEDOM
SANG PHIÁ TỰ DO
Did your grandmother go with you?
"No. She and my grandfather had a falling out.
!
"It was very ugly.
"One night when they were fighting, she fell against a door and cut open her head.
"I had to take her to the hospital on the back of a hired scooter.
"The next day, she came home and left my grandfather."

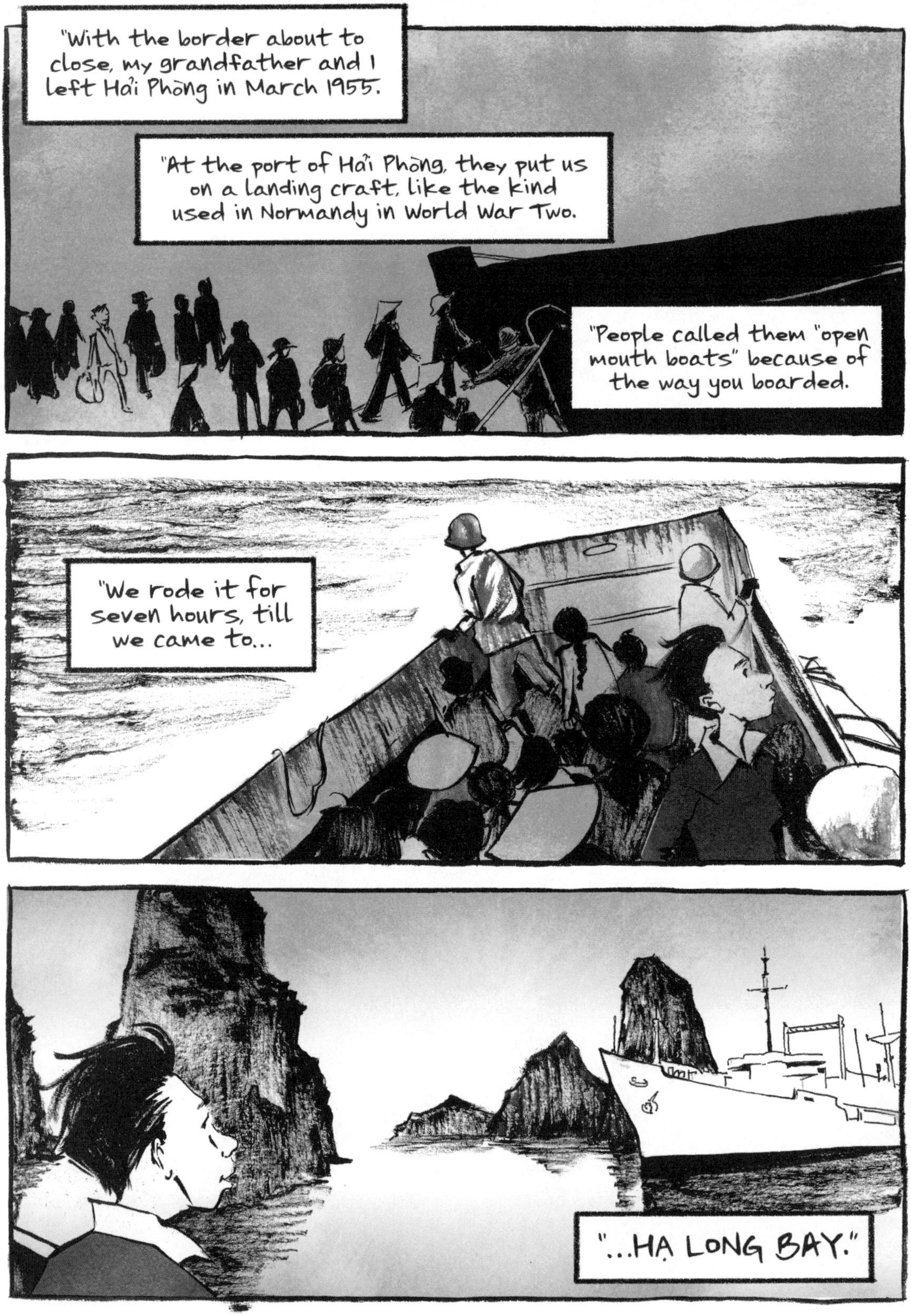
"With the border about to close, my grandfather and I left Hải Phòng in March 1955.
"At the port of Hải Phòng, they put us on a landing craft, like the kind used in Normandy in World War Two.
"People called them "open mouth boats" because of the way you boarded.
"We rode it for seven hours, till we came to...
"...HẠ LONG BAY."

CHAPTER 6
THE CHESSBOARD

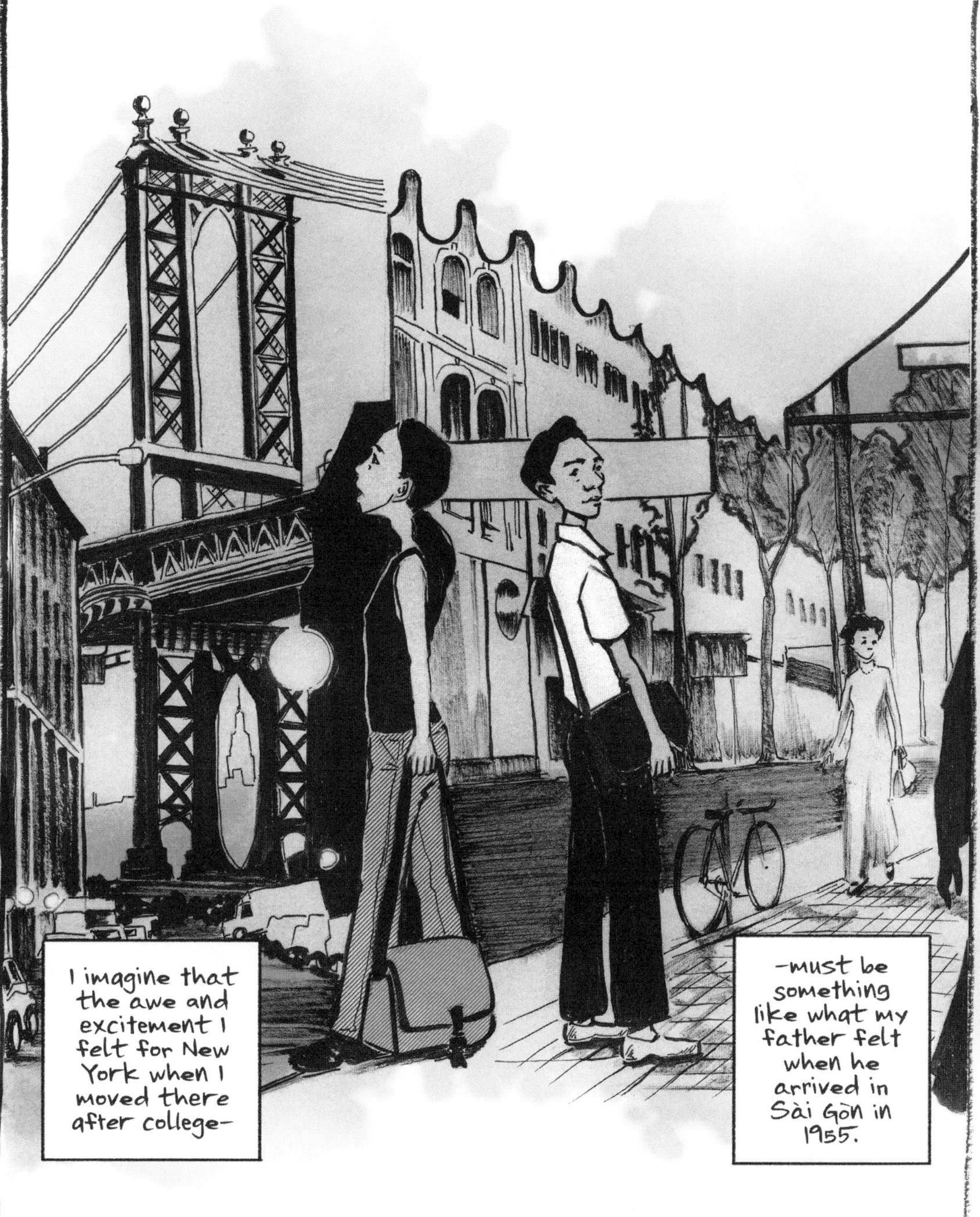
I imagine that the awe and excitement I felt for New York when I moved there after college-
-must be something like what my father felt when he arrived in Sài Gòn in 1955.

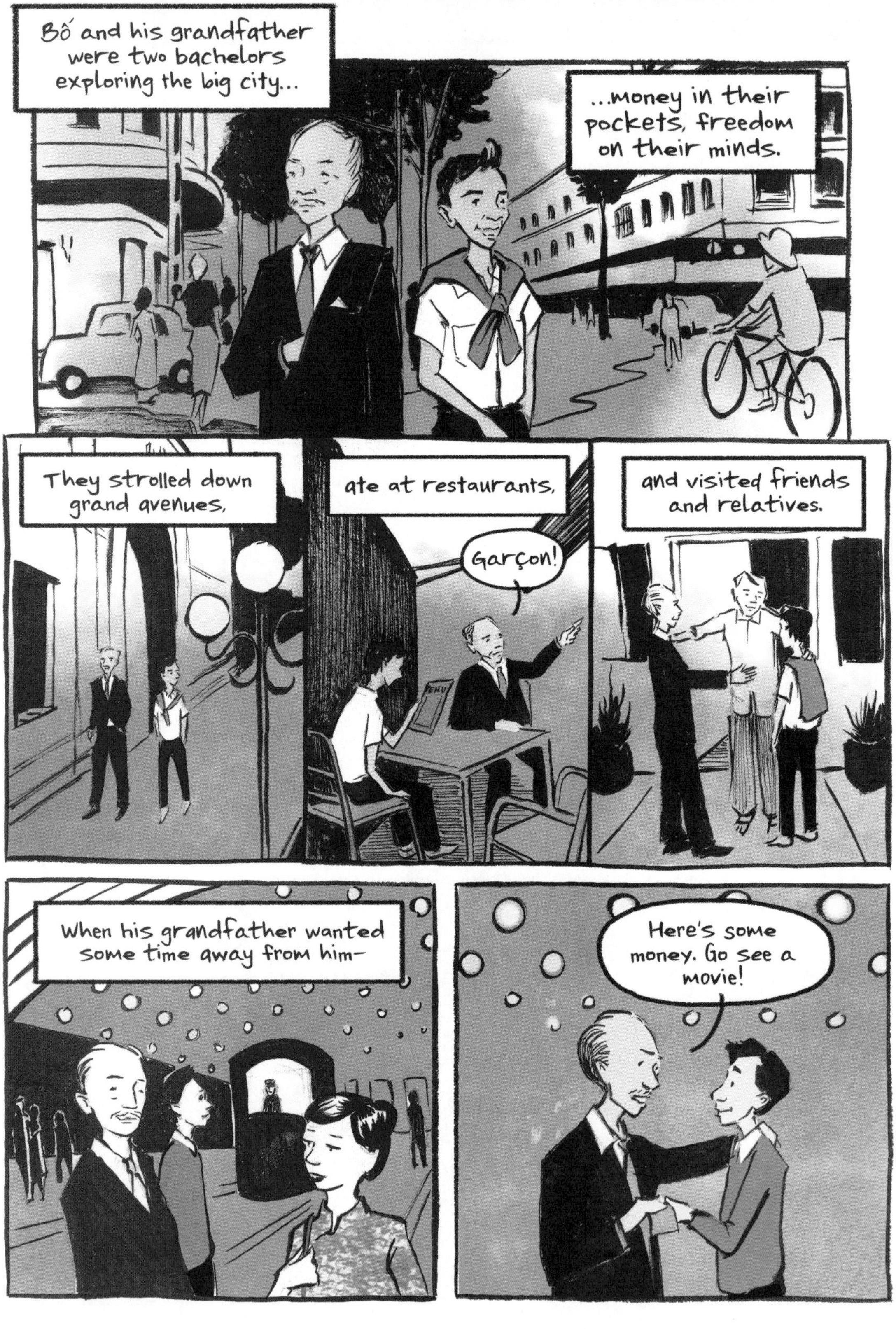
Bố and his grandfather were two bachelors exploring the big city...
...money in their pockets, freedom on their minds.
They strolled down grand avenues,
ate at restaurants,
Garçon!
MENU
and visited friends and relatives.
When his grandfather wanted some time away from him–
Here's some money. Go see a movie!

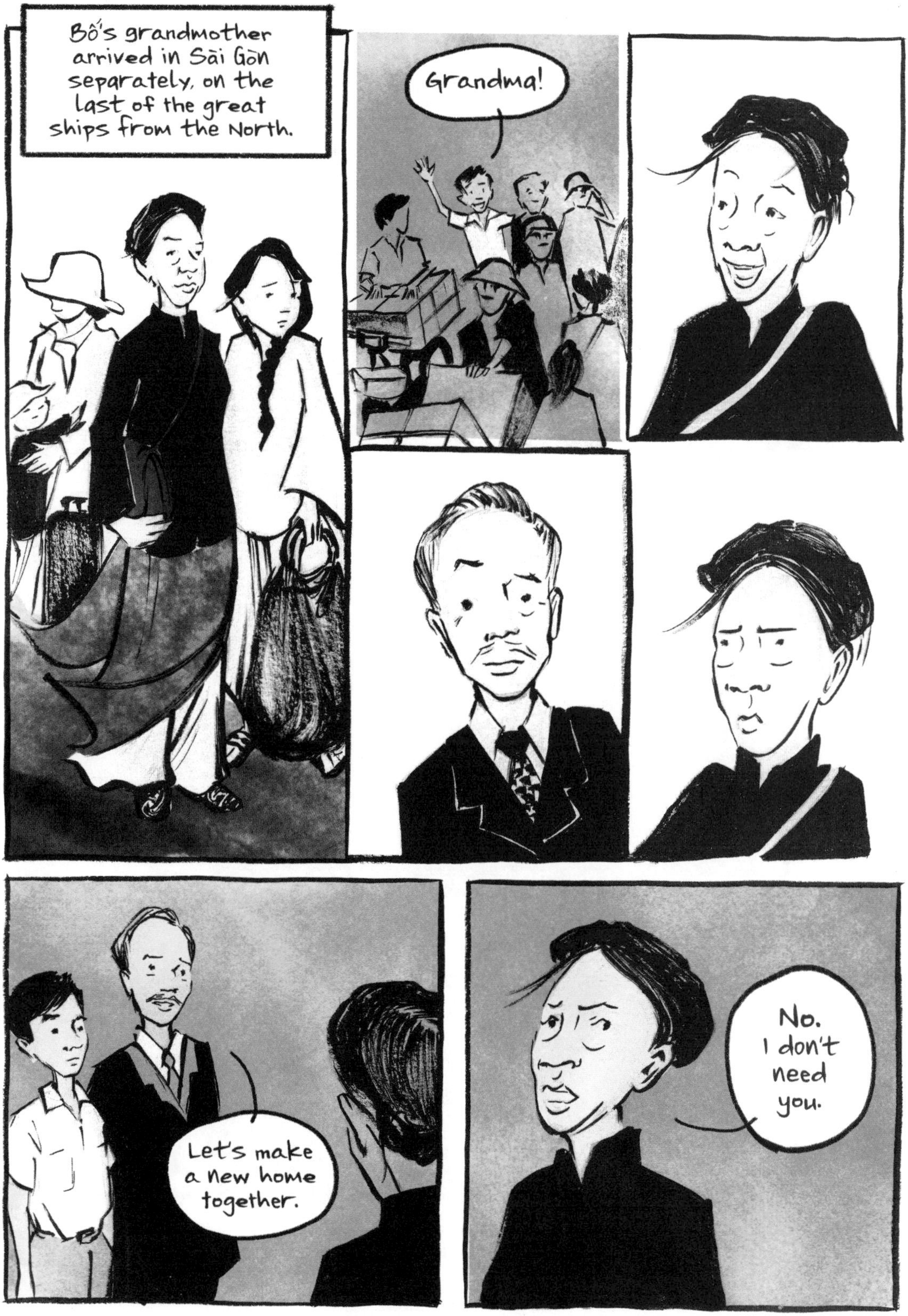
Bố's grandmother arrived in Sài Gòn separately, on the last of the great ships from the North.
Grandma!
Let's make a new home together.
No. I don't need you.

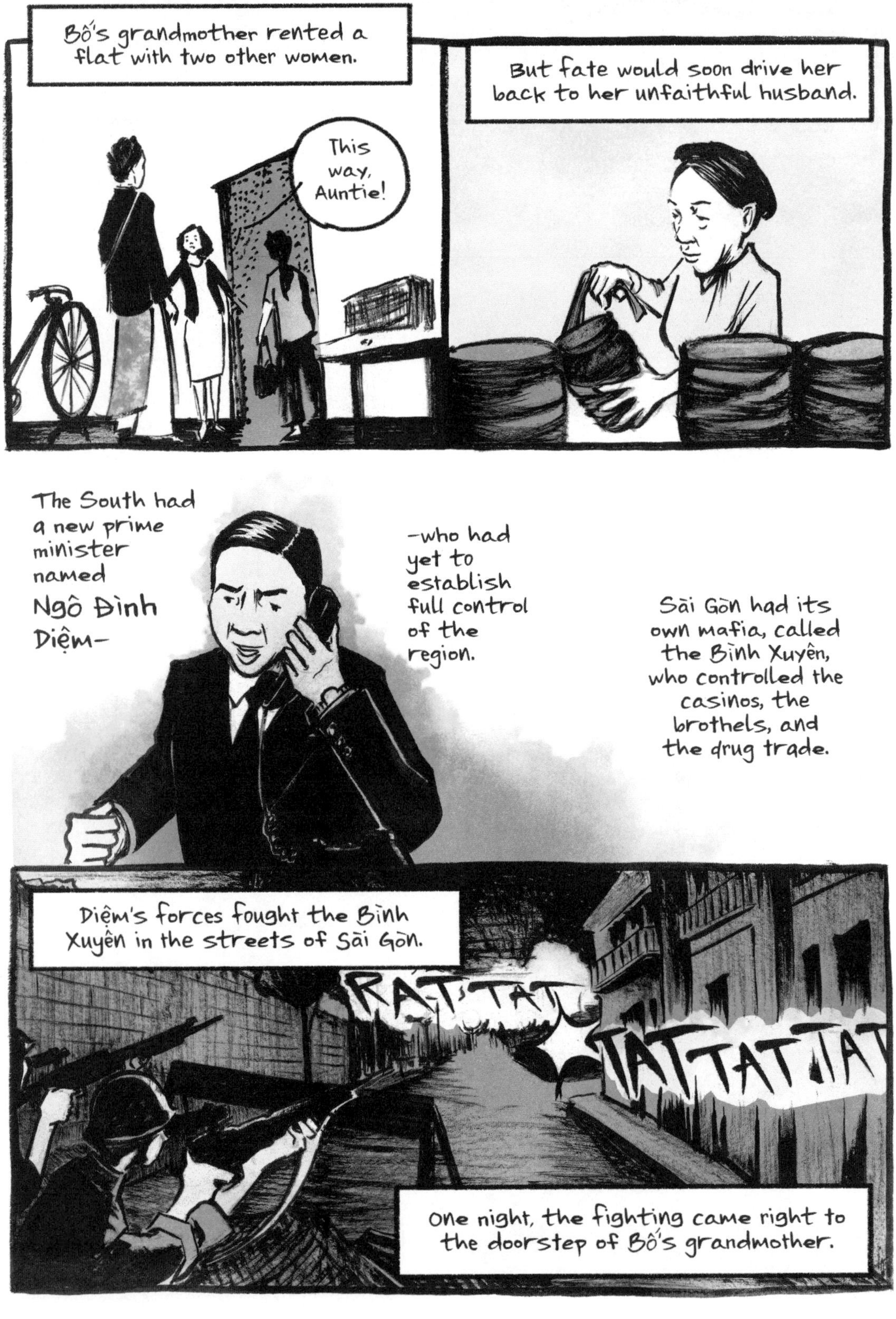
Bố's grandmother rented a flat with two other women.
This way, Auntie!
But fate would soon drive her back to her unfaithful husband.
The South had a new prime minister named Ngô Đình Diệm—
—who had yet to establish full control of the region.
Sài Gòn had its own mafia, called the Bình Xuyên, who controlled the casinos, the brothels, and the drug trade.
Diệm's forces fought the Bình Xuyên in the streets of Sài Gòn.
RAT TAT
TAT TAT TAT
One night, the fighting came right to the doorstep of Bố's grandmother.

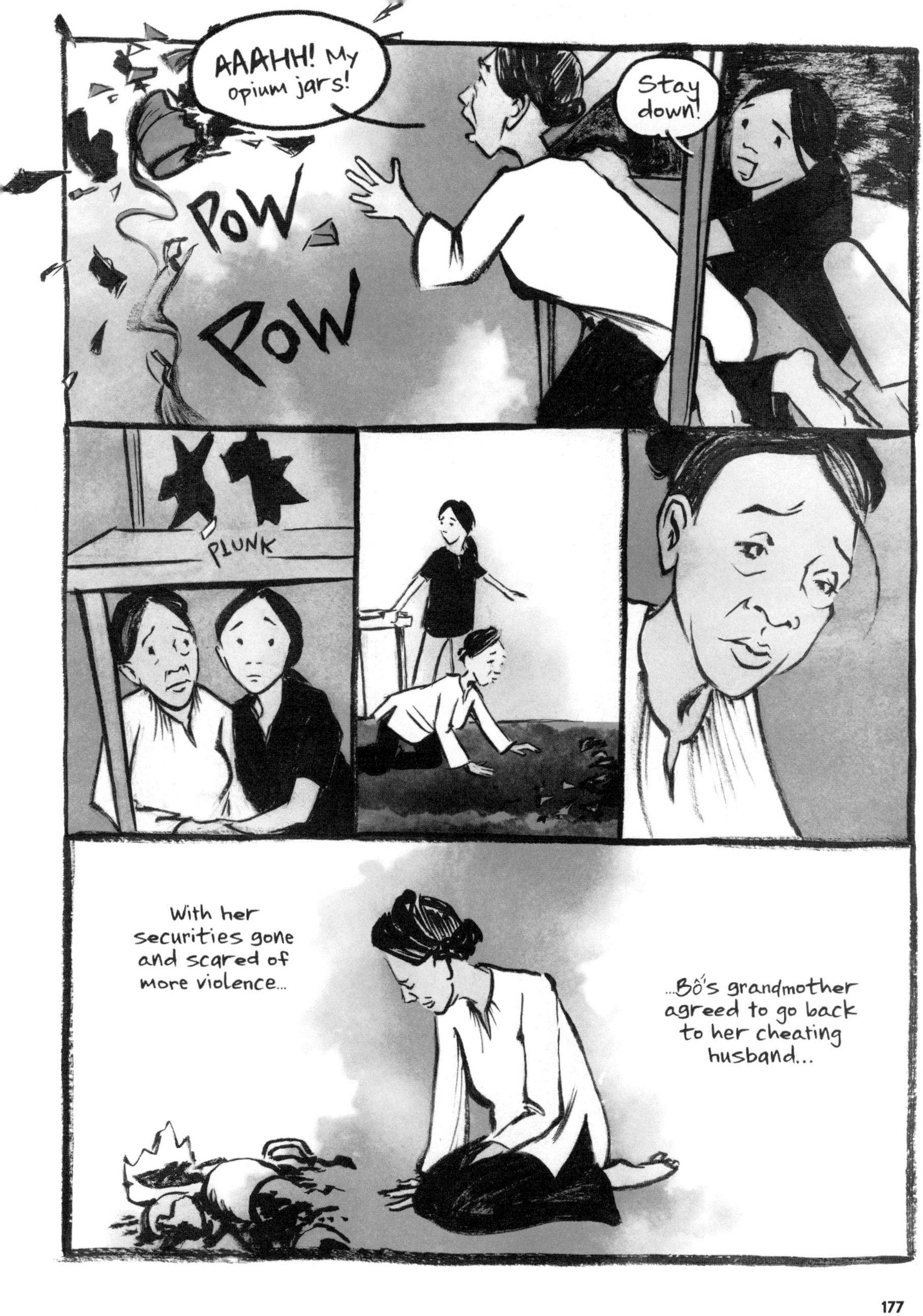

AAAHH! My opium jars!
POW
POW
Stay down!
PLUNK
With her securities gone and scared of more violence...
...Bố's grandmother agreed to go back to her cheating husband...

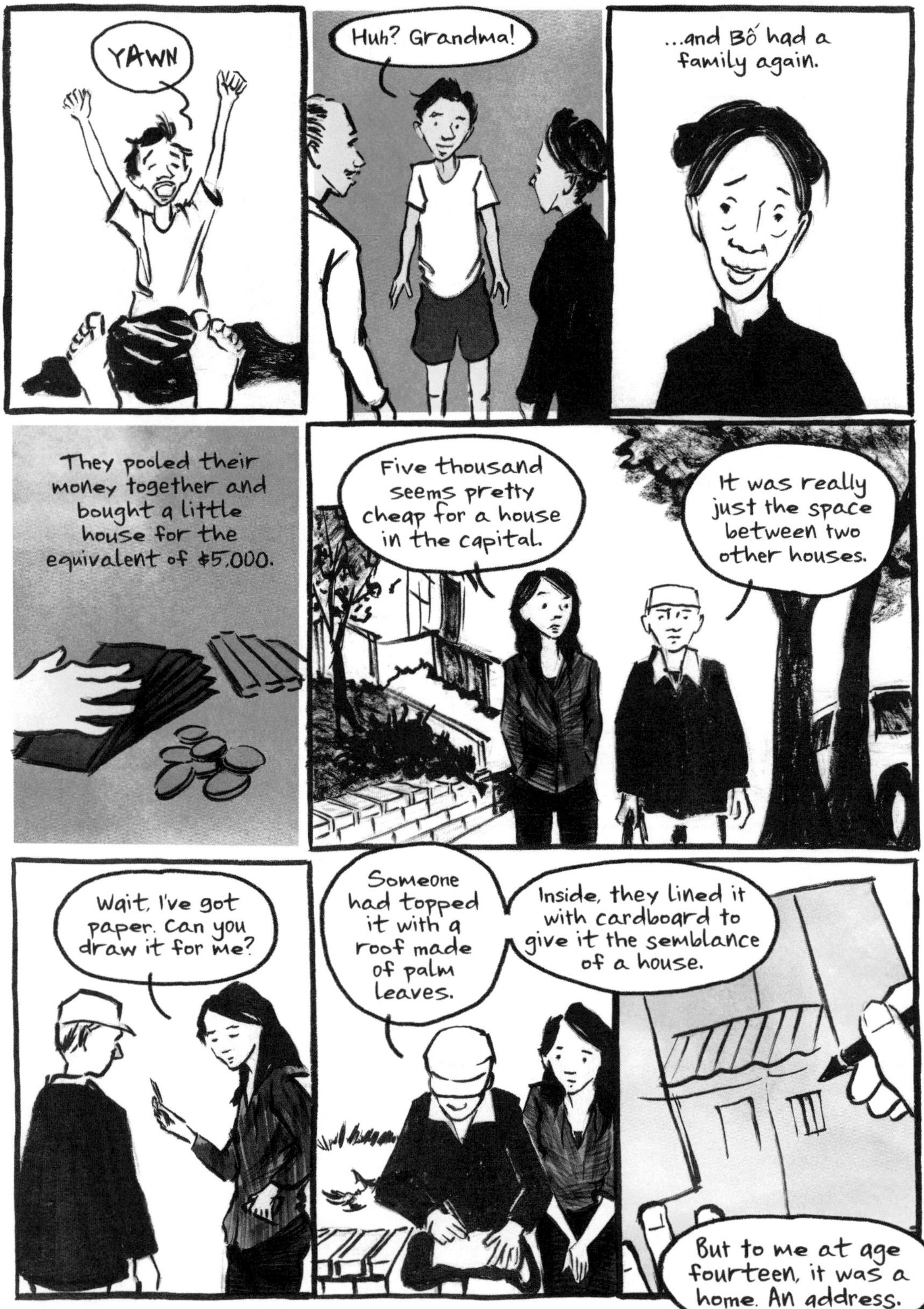
YAWN
Huh? Grandma!
...and Bố had a family again.
They pooled their money together and bought a little house for the equivalent of $5,000.
Five thousand seems pretty cheap for a house in the capital.
It was really just the space between two other houses.
Wait, I've got paper. Can you draw it for me?
Someone had topped it with a roof made of palm leaves.
Inside, they lined it with cardboard to give it the semblance of a house.
But to me at age fourteen, it was a home. An address.

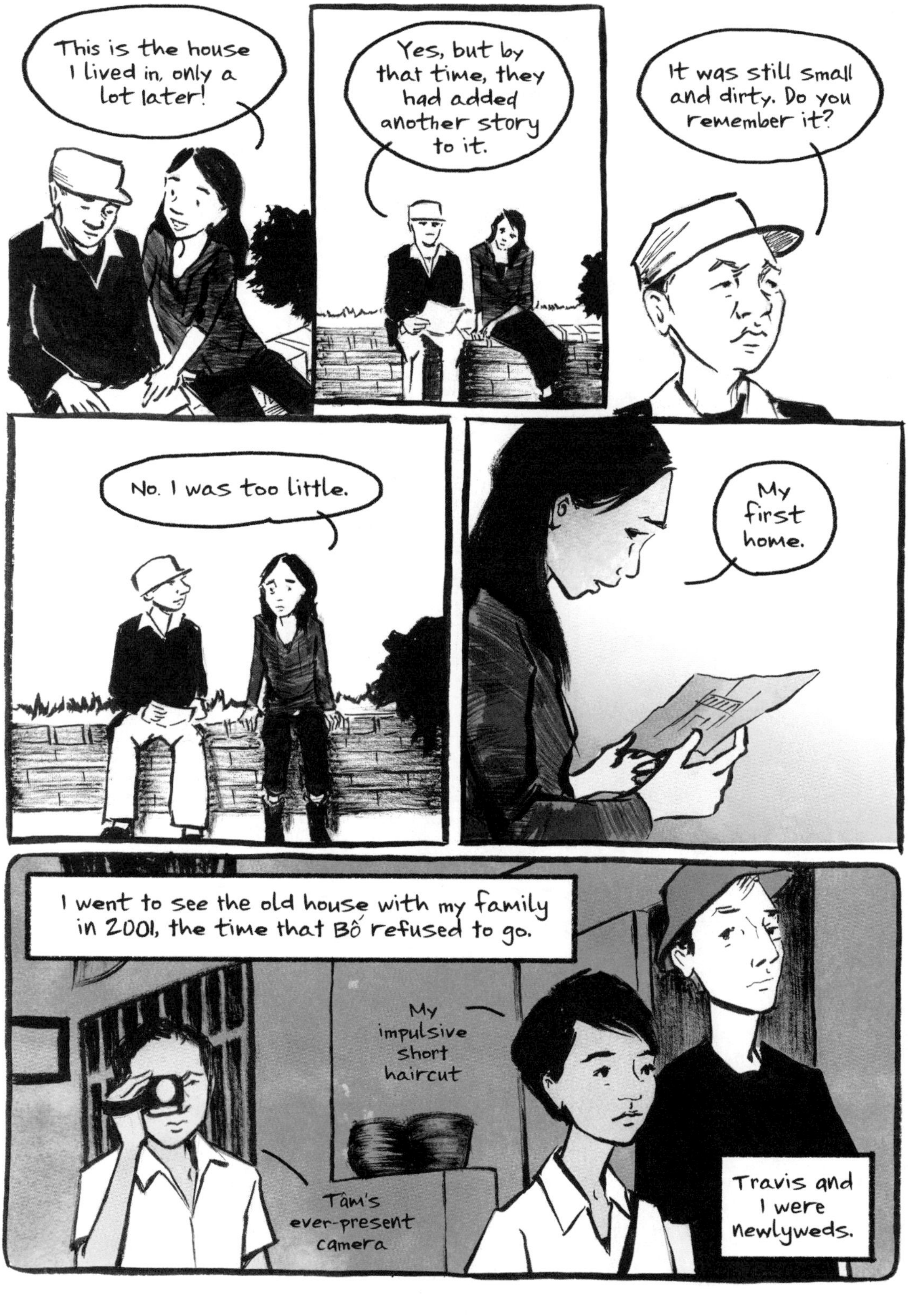
This is the house I lived in, only a lot later!
Yes, but by that time, they had added another story to it.
It was still small and dirty. Do you remember it?
No. I was too little.
My first home.
I went to see the old house with my family in 2001, the time that Bố refused to go.
My impulsive short haircut
Tâm's ever-present camera
Travis and I were newlyweds.

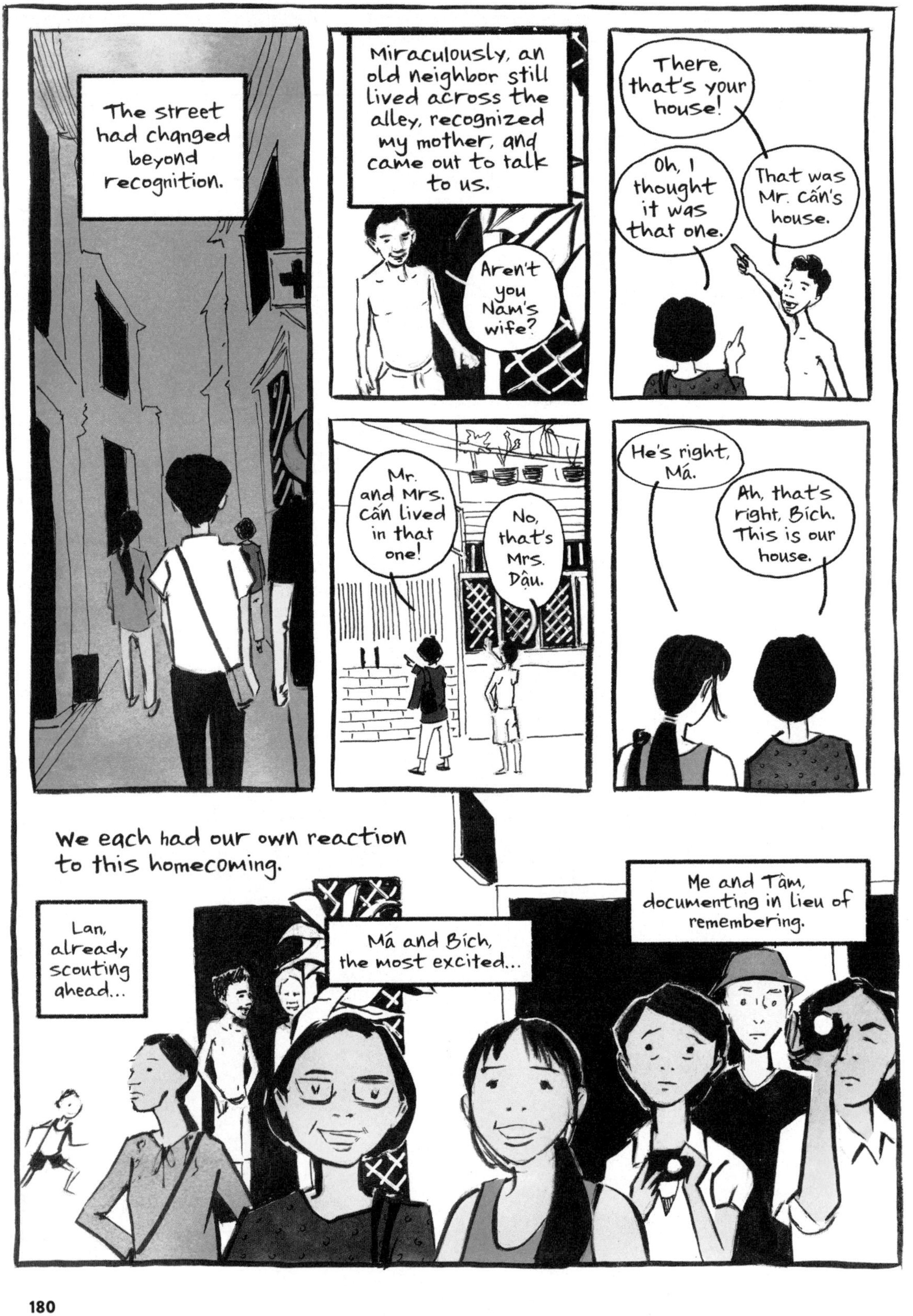
The street had changed beyond recognition.
Miraculously, an old neighbor still lived across the alley, recognized my mother, and came out to talk to us.
Aren't you Nam's wife?
There, that's your house!
Oh, I thought it was that one.
That was Mr. Cấn's house.
Mr. and Mrs. Cấn lived in that one!
No, that's Mrs. Dậu.
He's right, Má.
Ah, that's right, Bích. This is our house.
We each had our own reaction to this homecoming.
Lan, already scouting ahead...
Má and Bích, the most excited...
Me and Tâm, documenting in lieu of remembering.

We didn't know the people who lived there and didn't go inside.

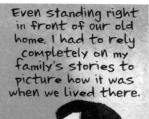
Even standing right in front of our old home, I had to rely completely on my family's stories to picture how it was when we lived there.

I think this is the same shop where occasionally we would get a cigarette or two for Dad.

This is where we learned to ride our bikes!

From there...

...all the way to the end—

—without hitting any of the vendors!

This is the old coffeehouse where we would go out every day

with our little glass, and bring back some coffee for Dad—

—with the condensed milk—

—laced with opium!

Smelled really GOOD!

CLICK

Lan and Bích remembered the alley where a friend lived,

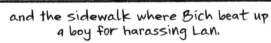

a lamppost that Lan walked into while reading,

and the sidewalk where Bích beat up a boy for harassing Lan.

Lacking memories of my own, I do research.

CLICK

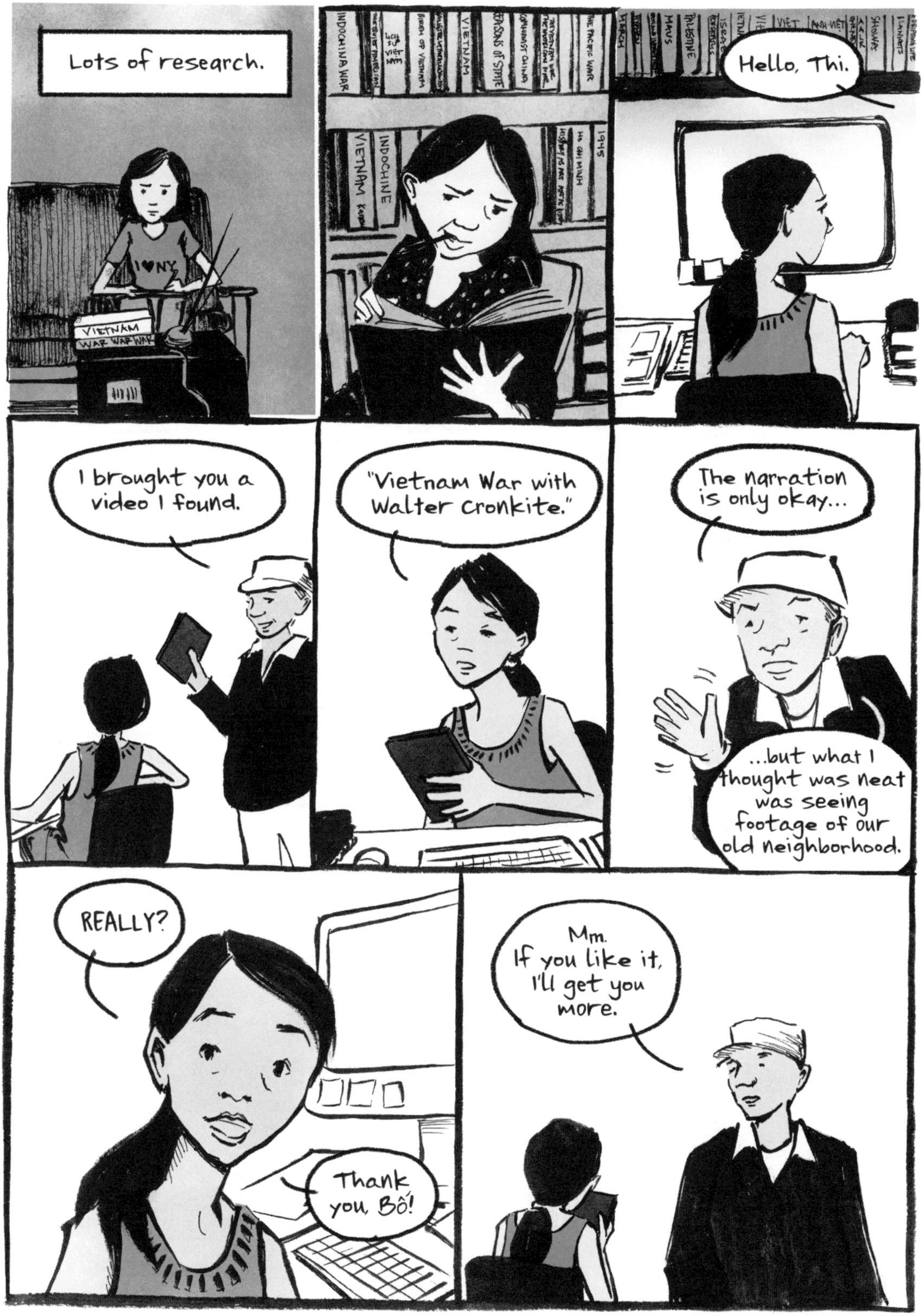
Lots of research.
Hello, Thi.
I brought you a video I found.
"Vietnam War with Walter Cronkite."
The narration is only okay...
...but what I thought was neat was seeing footage of our old neighborhood.
REALLY?
Thank you, Bố!
Mm. If you like it, I'll get you more.

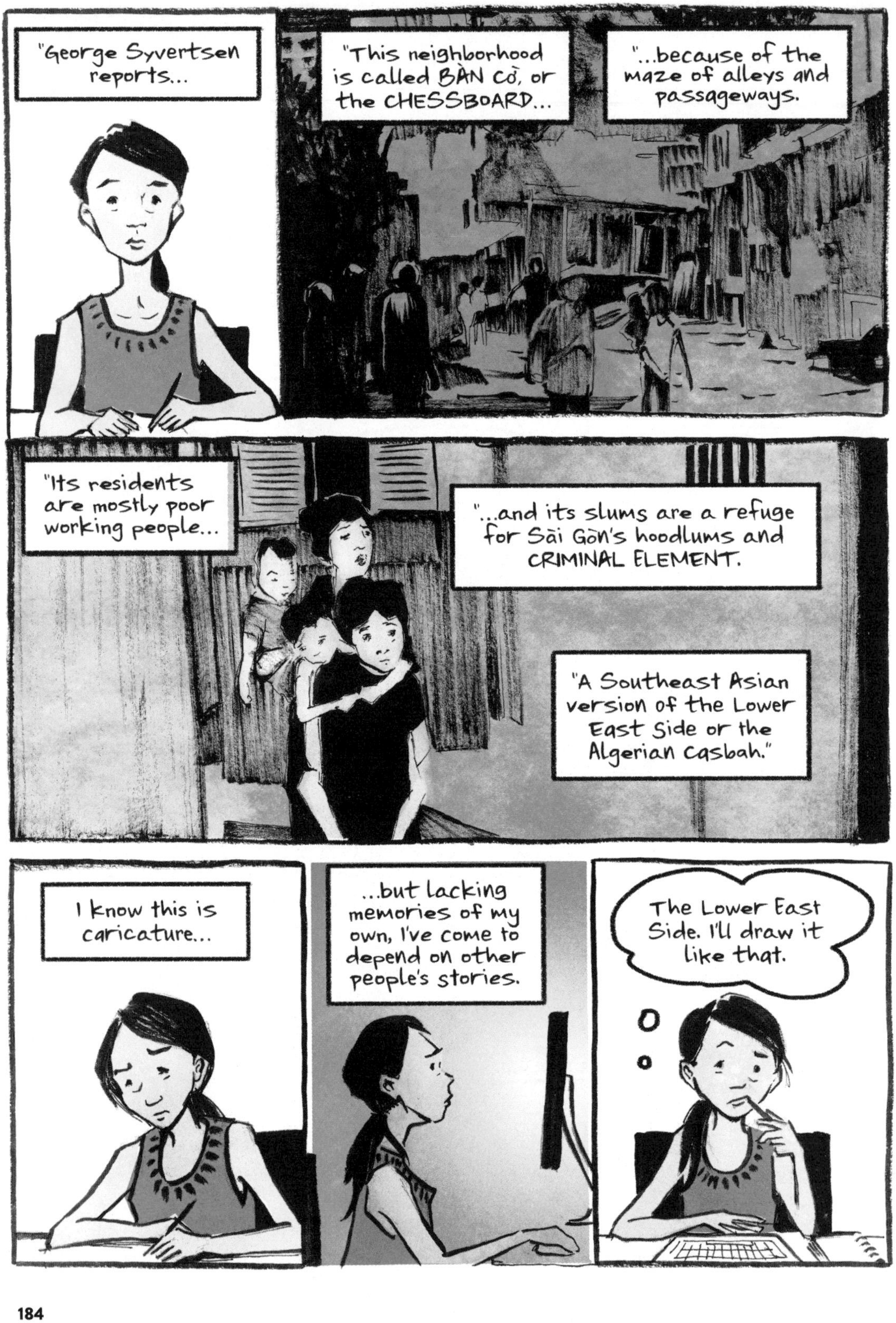
"George Syvertsen reports...
"This neighborhood is called BÀN CỜ, or the CHESSBOARD...
"...because of the maze of alleys and passageways.
"Its residents are mostly poor working people...
"...and its slums are a refuge for Sài Gòn's hoodlums and CRIMINAL ELEMENT.
"A Southeast Asian version of the Lower East Side or the Algerian casbah."
I know this is caricature...
...but lacking memories of my own, I've come to depend on other people's stories.
The Lower East Side. I'll draw it like that.

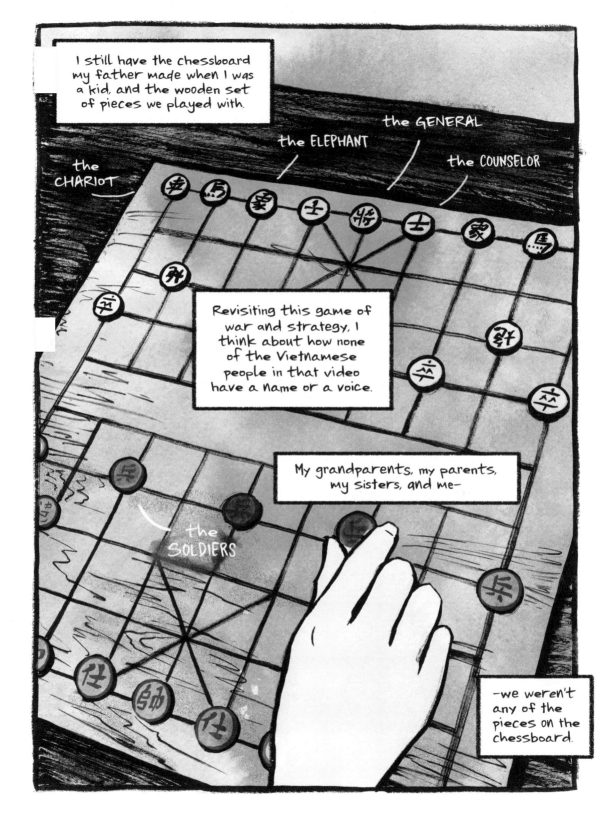

I still have the chessboard my father made when I was a kid, and the wooden set of pieces we played with.

the GENERAL

the ELEPHANT

the COUNSELOR

the CHARIOT

Revisiting this game of war and strategy, I think about how none of the Vietnamese people in that video have a name or a voice.

My grandparents, my parents, my sisters, and me—

the SOLDIERS

—we weren't any of the pieces on the chessboard.

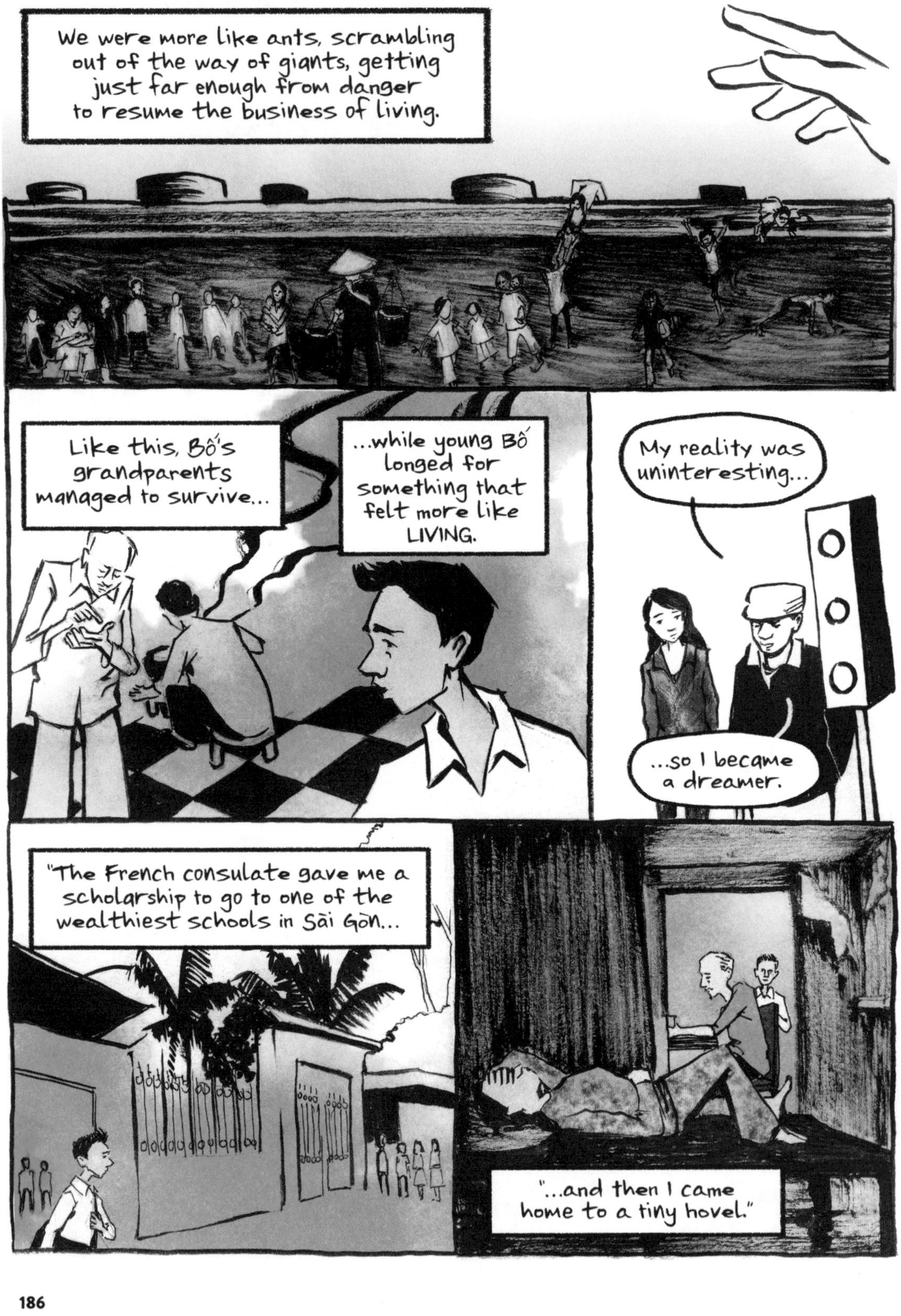

We were more like ants, scrambling out of the way of giants, getting just far enough from danger to resume the business of living.
Like this, Bố's grandparents managed to survive...
...while young Bố longed for something that felt more like LIVING.
My reality was uninteresting...
...so I became a dreamer.
"The French consulate gave me a scholarship to go to one of the wealthiest schools in Sài Gòn...
"...and then I came home to a tiny hovel."

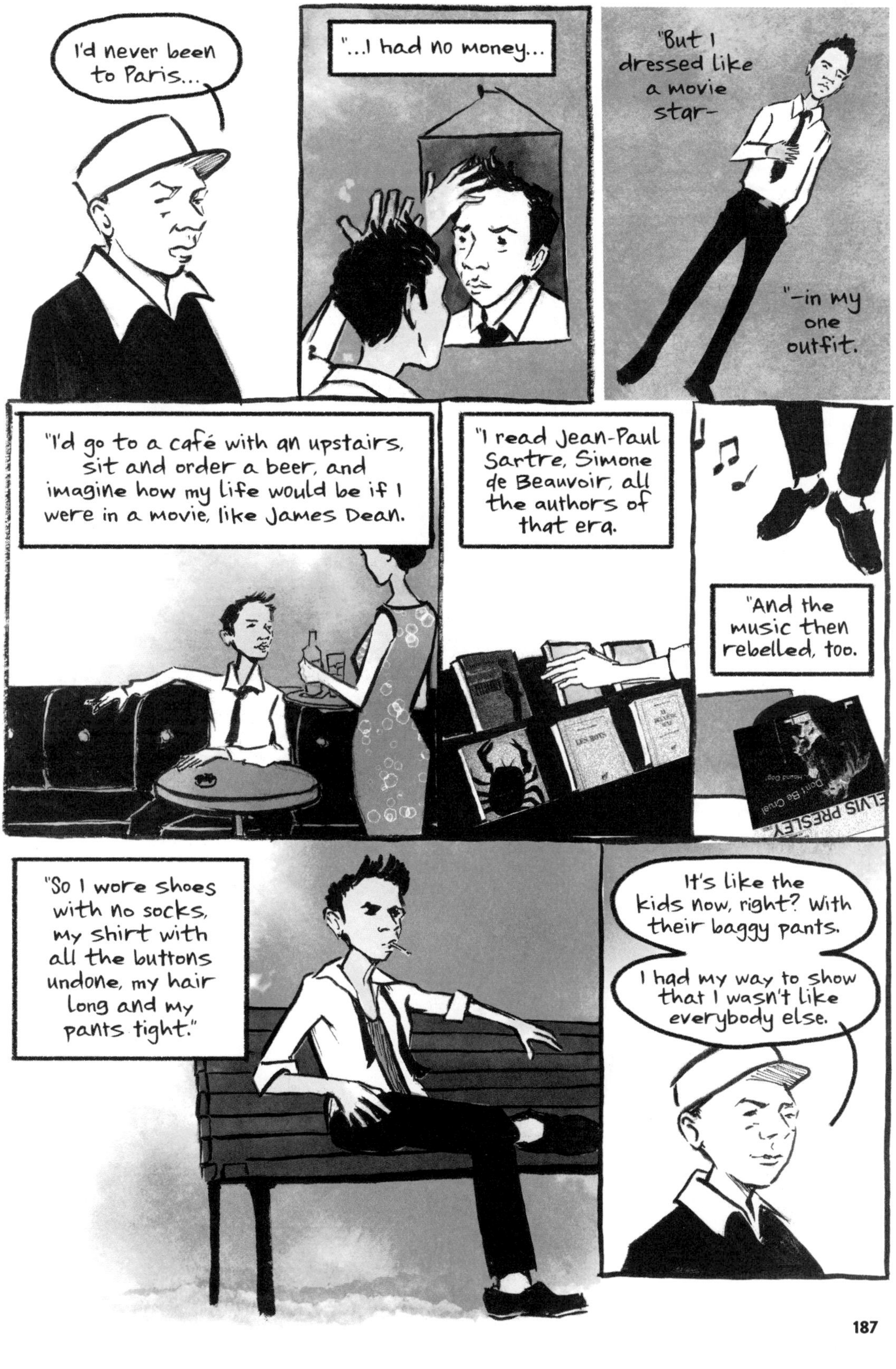
I'd never been to Paris...
"...I had no money...
"But I dressed like a movie star-
"-in my one outfit.
"I'd go to a café with an upstairs, sit and order a beer, and imagine how my life would be if I were in a movie, like James Dean.
"I read Jean-Paul Sartre, Simone de Beauvoir, all the authors of that era.
"And the music then rebelled, too.
ELVIS PRESLEY
Don't Be Cruel
Hound Dog
"So I wore shoes with no socks, my shirt with all the buttons undone, my hair long and my pants tight."
It's like the kids now, right? With their baggy pants.
I had my way to show that I wasn't like everybody else.

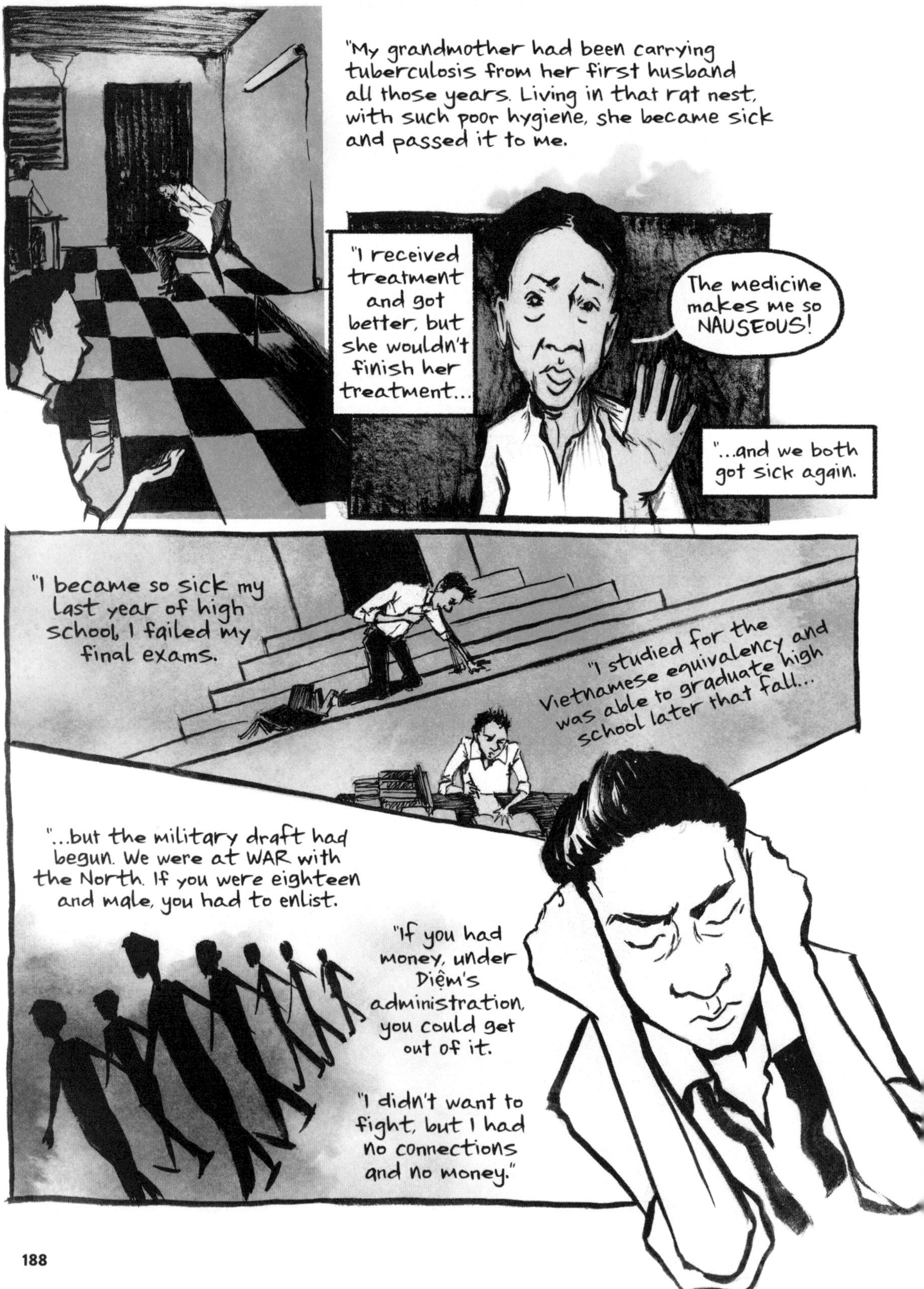
"My grandmother had been carrying tuberculosis from her first husband all those years. Living in that rat nest, with such poor hygiene, she became sick and passed it to me.
"I received treatment and got better, but she wouldn't finish her treatment...
The medicine makes me so NAUSEOUS!
"...and we both got sick again.
"I became so sick my last year of high school, I failed my final exams.
"I studied for the Vietnamese equivalency and was able to graduate high school later that fall...
"...but the military draft had begun. We were at WAR with the North. If you were eighteen and male, you had to enlist.
"If you had money, under Diệm's administration, you could get out of it.
"I didn't want to fight, but I had no connections and no money."

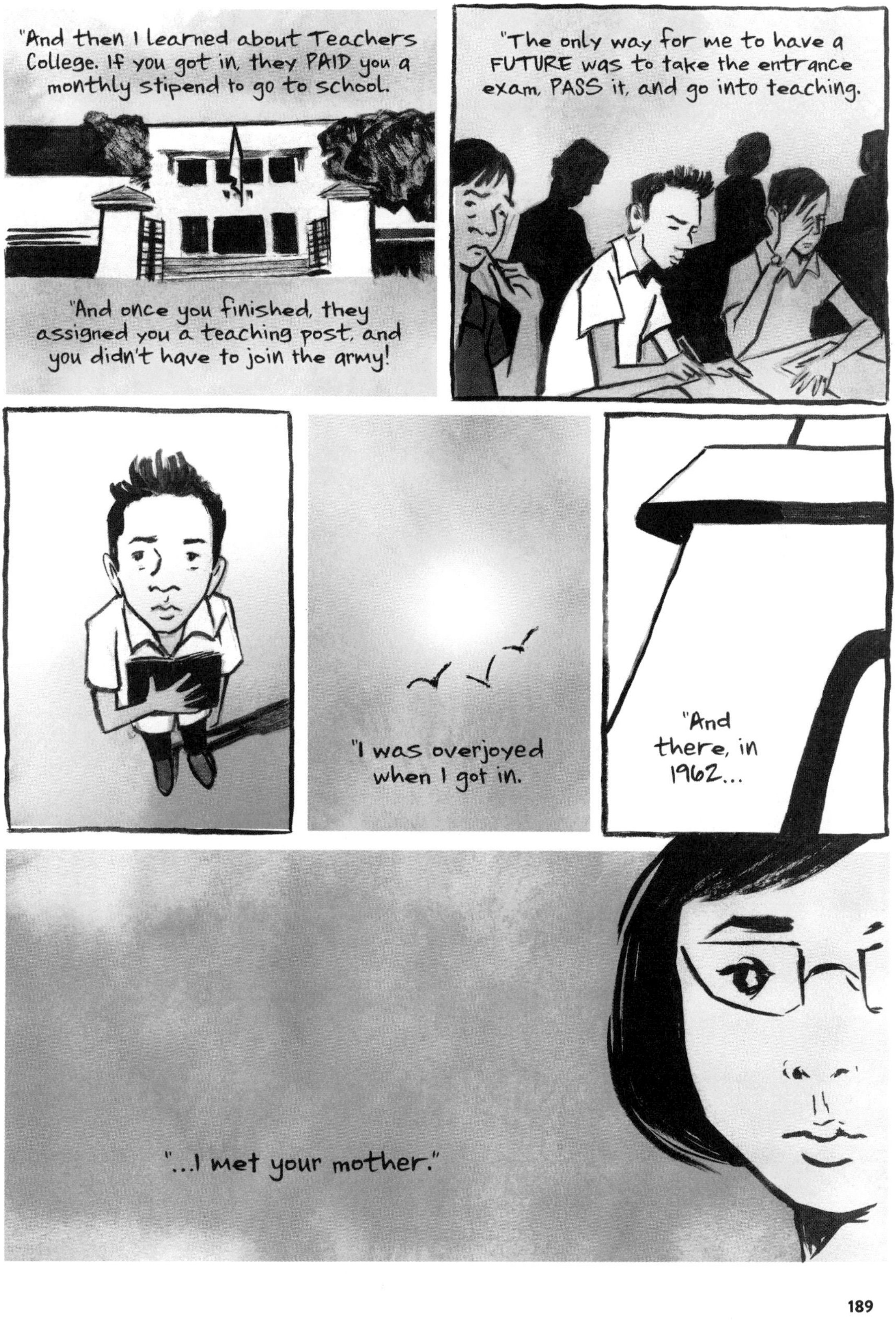
"And then I learned about Teachers College. If you got in, they PAID you a monthly stipend to go to school.
"And once you finished, they assigned you a teaching post, and you didn't have to join the army!
"The only way for me to have a FUTURE was to take the entrance exam, PASS it, and go into teaching.
"I was overjoyed when I got in.
"And there, in 1962...
"...I met your mother."

 I'd like to tell this as a happy story, in which a young man, my father, meets a young woman, my mother.

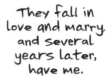 They fall in love and marry, and several years later, have me.

But my mother's version of the story foils it.

 When I was a young girl going to school at the Lycée Yersin in Đà Lạt...

 ...those three years were the best of my life.

 Really?

You know all my HAPPIEST moments... always go back to that time.

 The friends I have now—they were all very close friends I had in Việt Nam.

They all came from that time.

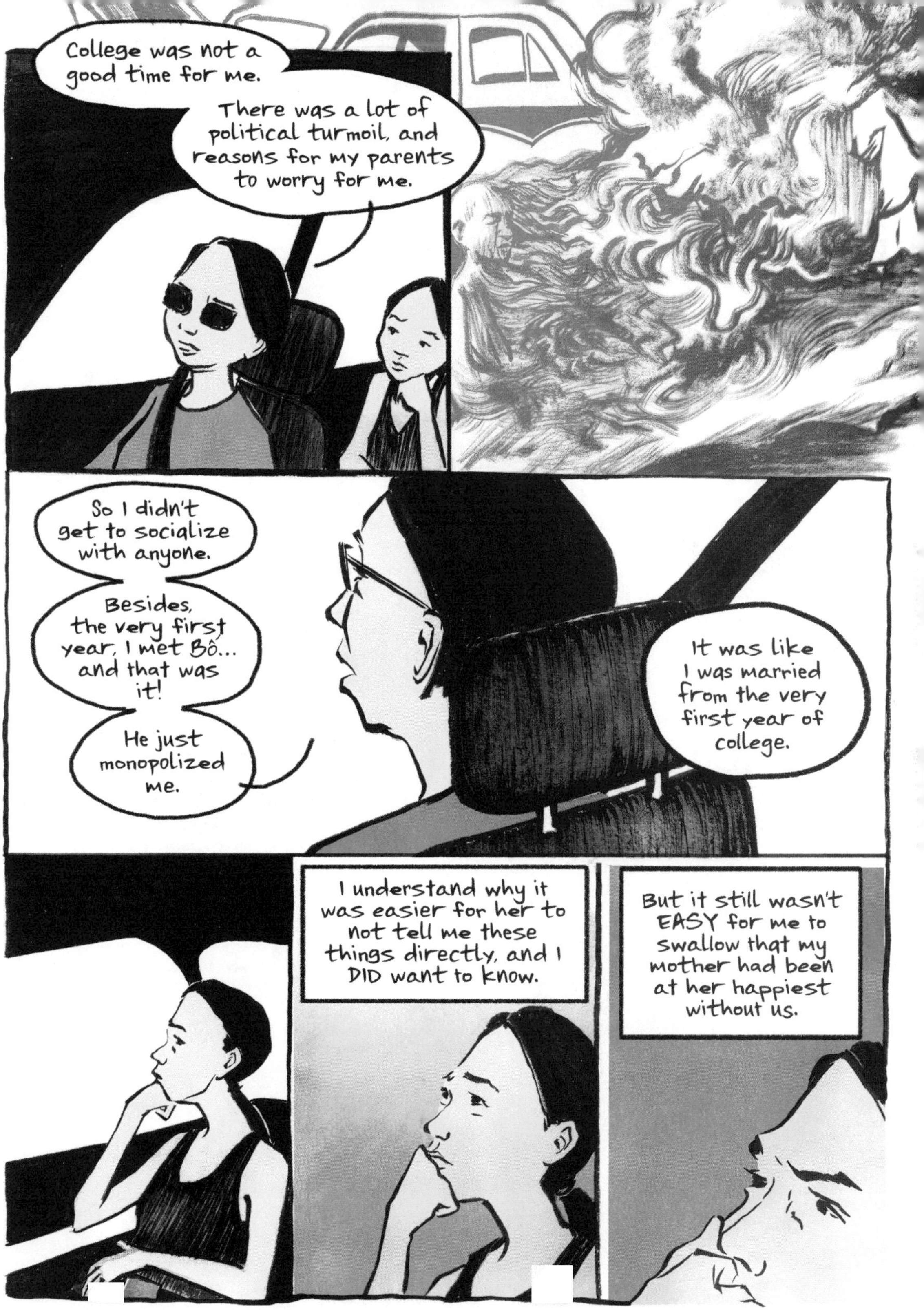

College was not a good time for me.
There was a lot of political turmoil, and reasons for my parents to worry for me.
So I didn't get to socialize with anyone.
Besides, the very first year, I met Bô... and that was it!
He just monopolized me.
It was like I was married from the very first year of college.
I understand why it was easier for her to not tell me these things directly, and I DID want to know.
But it still wasn't EASY for me to swallow that my mother had been at her happiest without us.

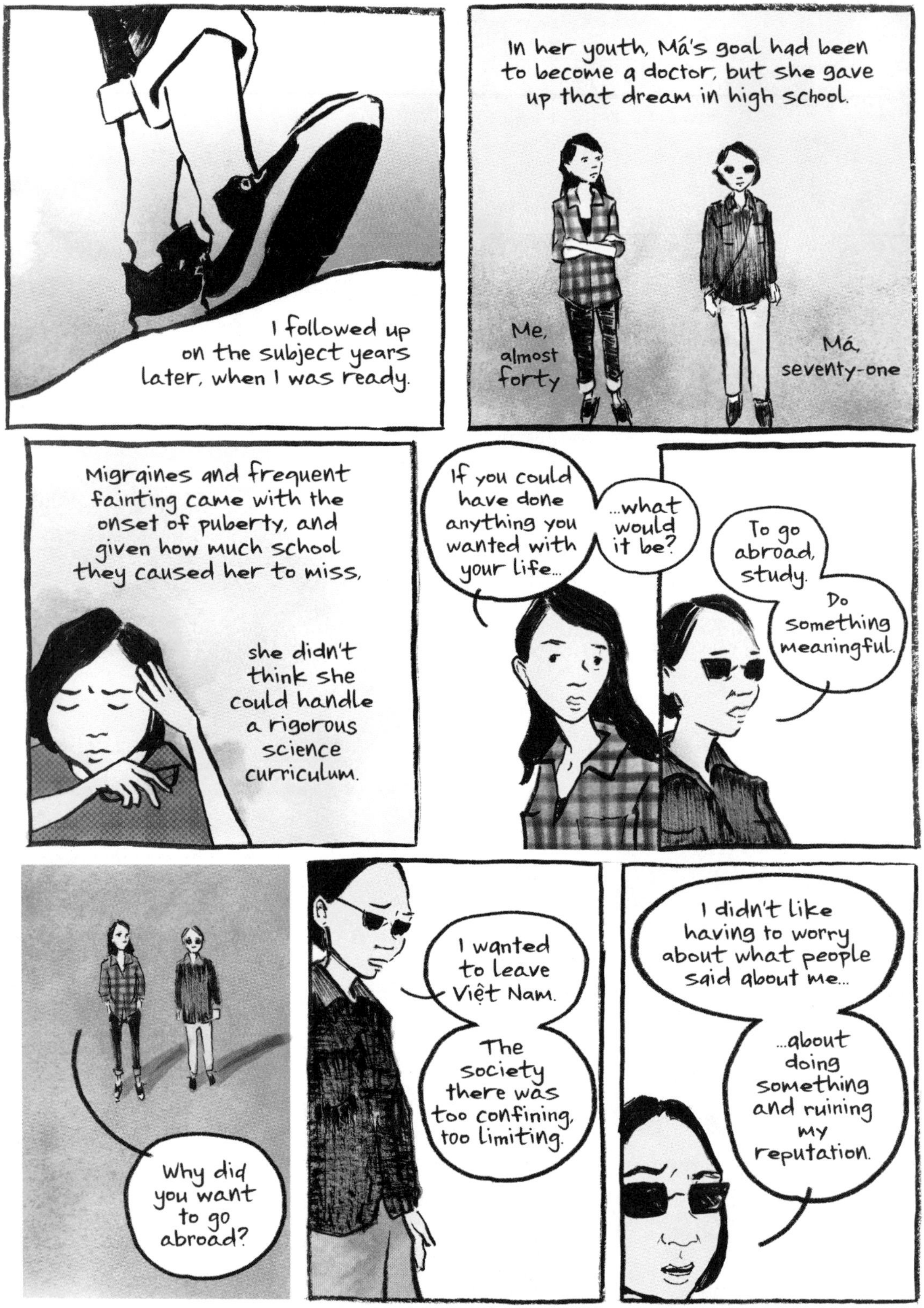
I followed up on the subject years later, when I was ready.
In her youth, Má's goal had been to become a doctor, but she gave up that dream in high school.
Me, almost forty
Má, seventy-one
Migraines and frequent fainting came with the onset of puberty, and given how much school they caused her to miss,
she didn't think she could handle a rigorous science curriculum.
If you could have done anything you wanted with your life...
...what would it be?
To go abroad, study.
Do something meaningful.
Why did you want to go abroad?
I wanted to leave Việt Nam.
The society there was too confining, too limiting.
I didn't like having to worry about what people said about me...
...about doing something and ruining my reputation.

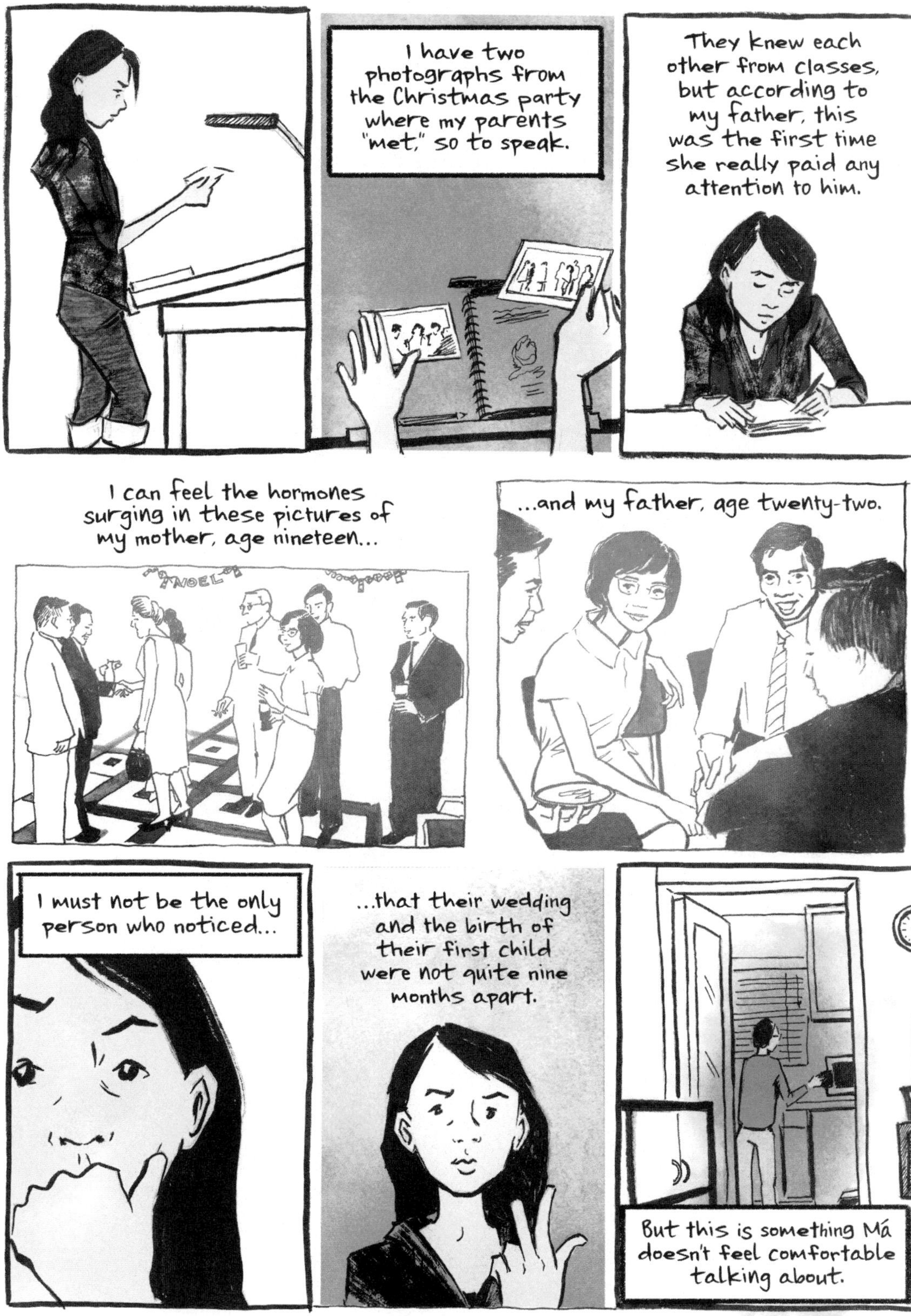

I have two photographs from the Christmas party where my parents "met," so to speak.
They knew each other from classes, but according to my father, this was the first time she really paid any attention to him.
I can feel the hormones surging in these pictures of my mother, age nineteen...
NOEL
...and my father, age twenty-two.
I must not be the only person who noticed...
...that their wedding and the birth of their first child were not quite nine months apart.
But this is something Má doesn't feel comfortable talking about.

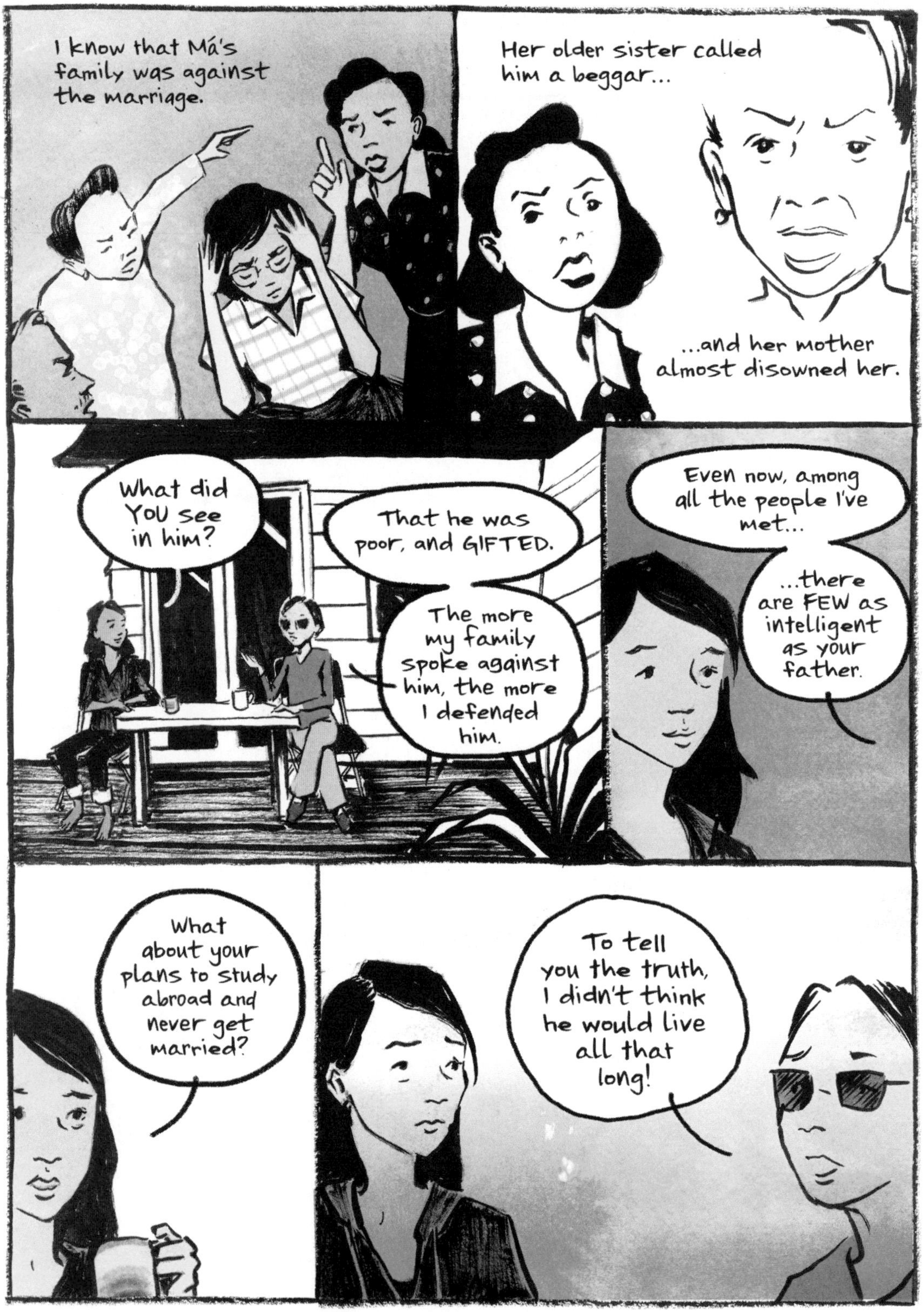

I know that Má's family was against the marriage.
Her older sister called him a beggar...
...and her mother almost disowned her.
What did YOU see in him?
That he was poor, and GIFTED.
The more my family spoke against him, the more I defended him.
Even now, among all the people I've met...
...there are FEW as intelligent as your father.
What about your plans to study abroad and never get married?
To tell you the truth, I didn't think he would live all that long!

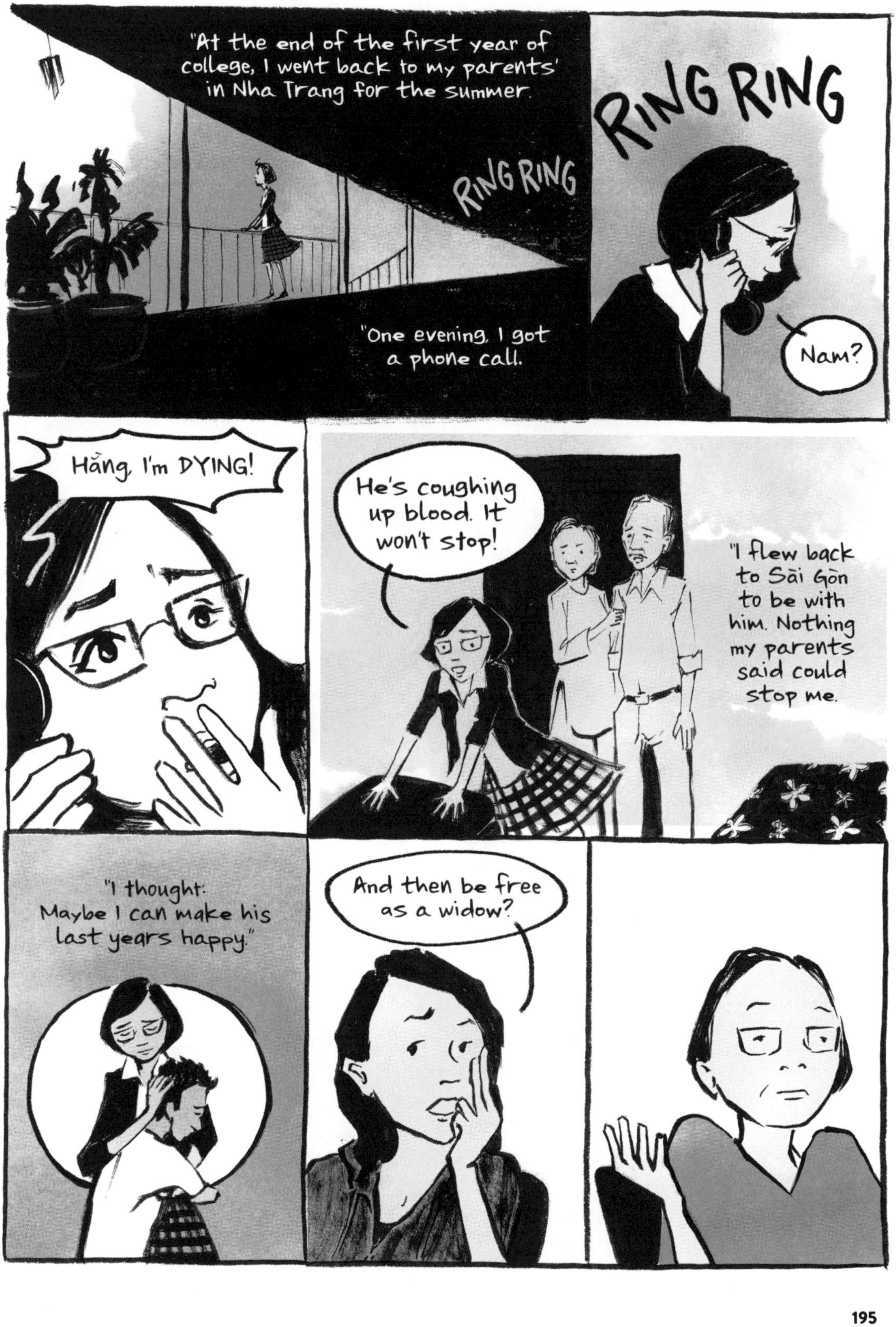
"At the end of the first year of college, I went back to my parents' in Nha Trang for the summer.
RING RING
"One evening, I got a phone call.
RING RING
Nam?
Hằng, I'm DYING!
He's coughing up blood. It won't stop!
"I flew back to Sài Gòn to be with him. Nothing my parents said could stop me.
"I thought: Maybe I can make his last years happy."
And then be free as a widow?

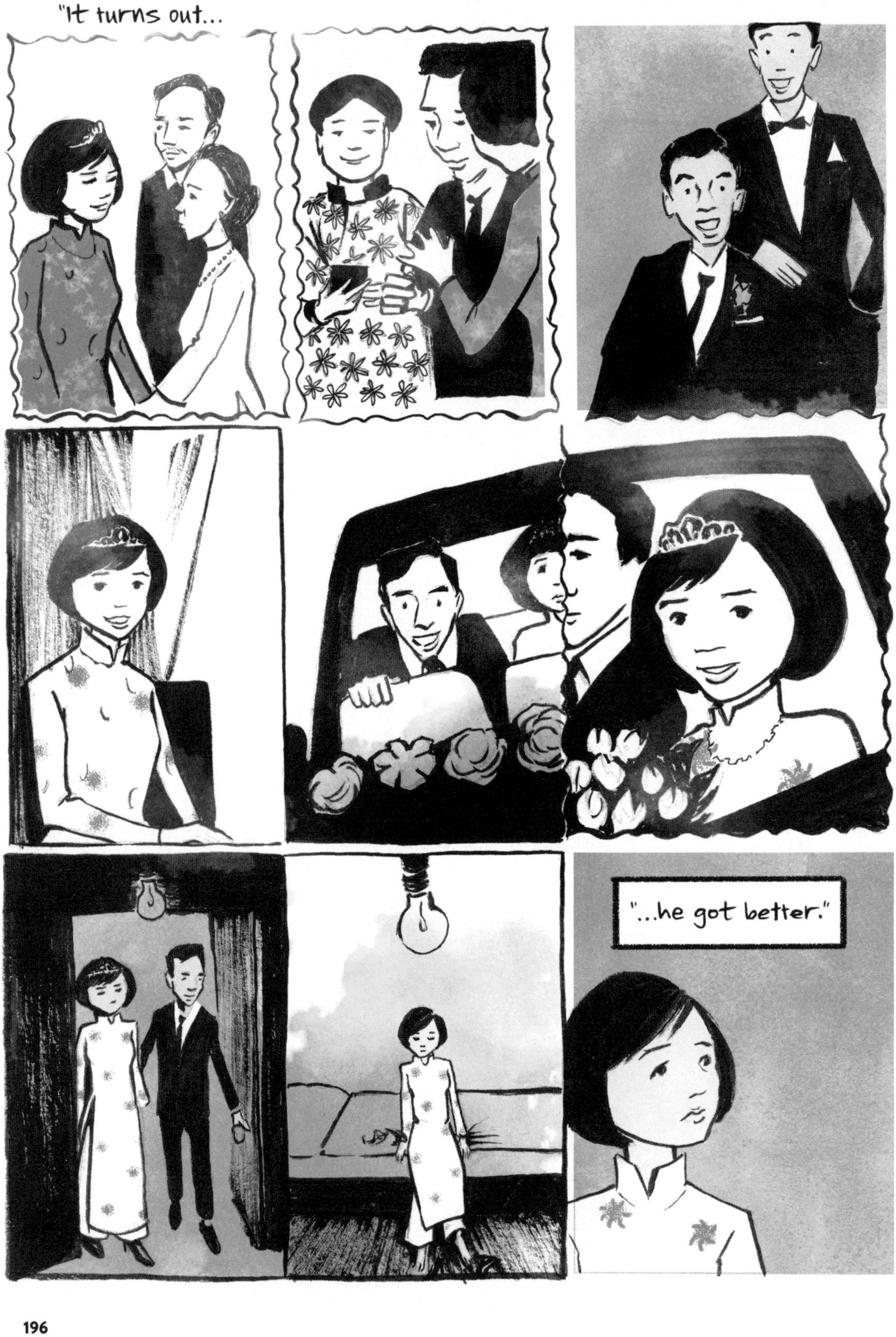
"It turns out...
"...he got better."

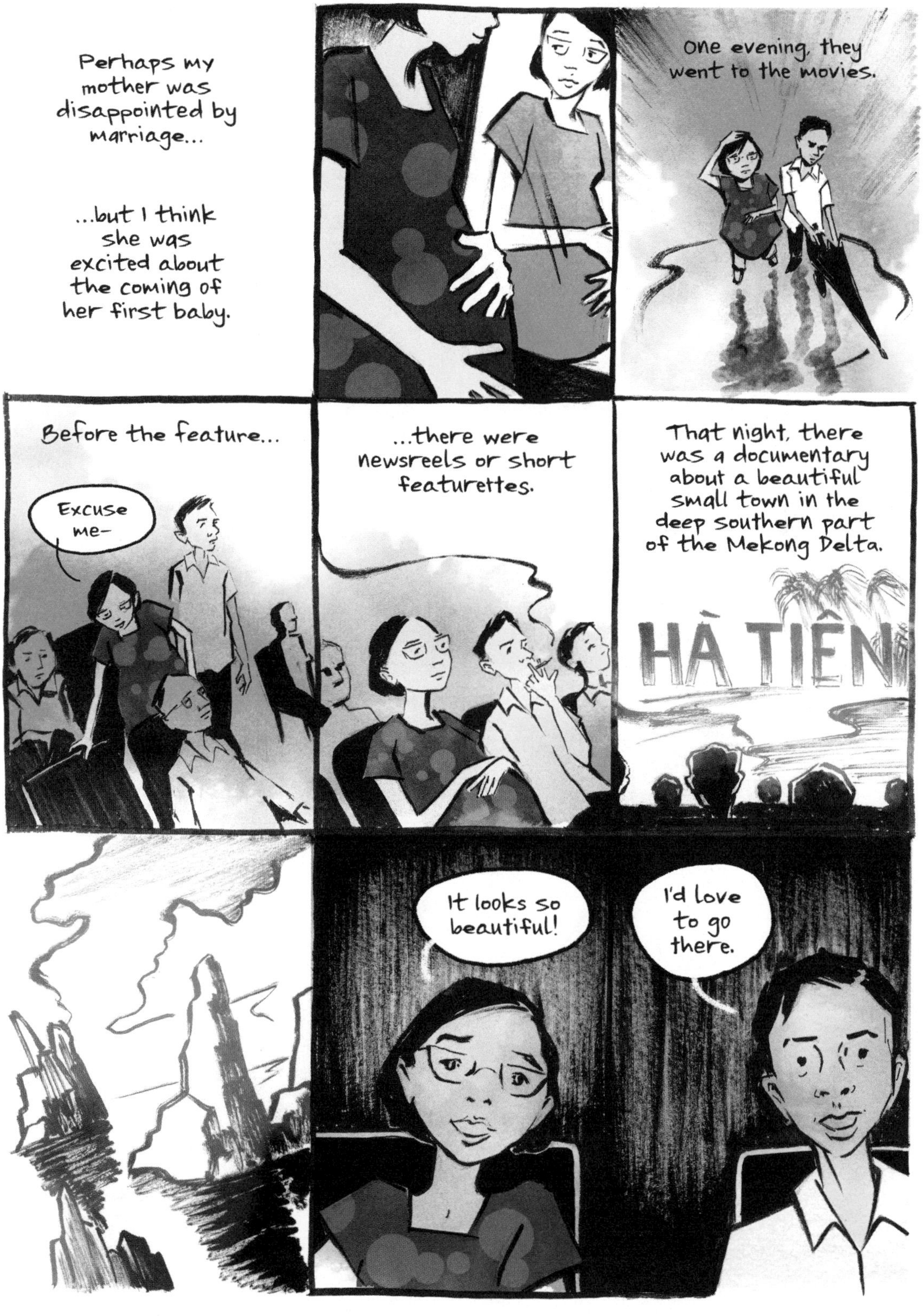
Perhaps my mother was disappointed by marriage...
...but I think she was excited about the coming of her first baby.
One evening, they went to the movies.
Before the feature...
Excuse me-
...there were newsreels or short featurettes.
That night, there was a documentary about a beautiful small town in the deep southern part of the Mekong Delta.
HÀ TIÊN
It looks so beautiful!
I'd love to go there.

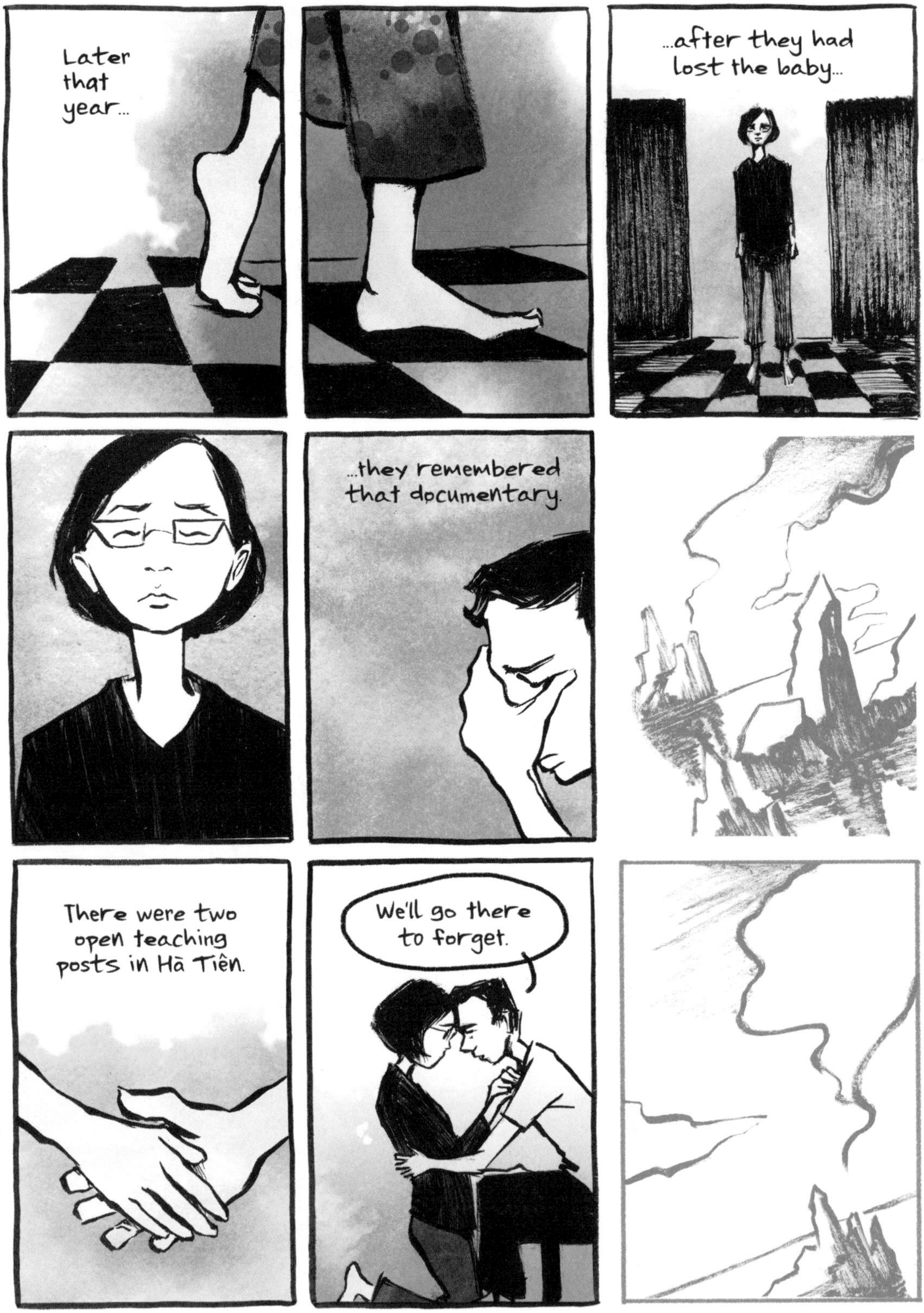
Later that year...
...after they had lost the baby...
...they remembered that documentary.
There were two open teaching posts in Hà Tiên.
We'll go there to forget.

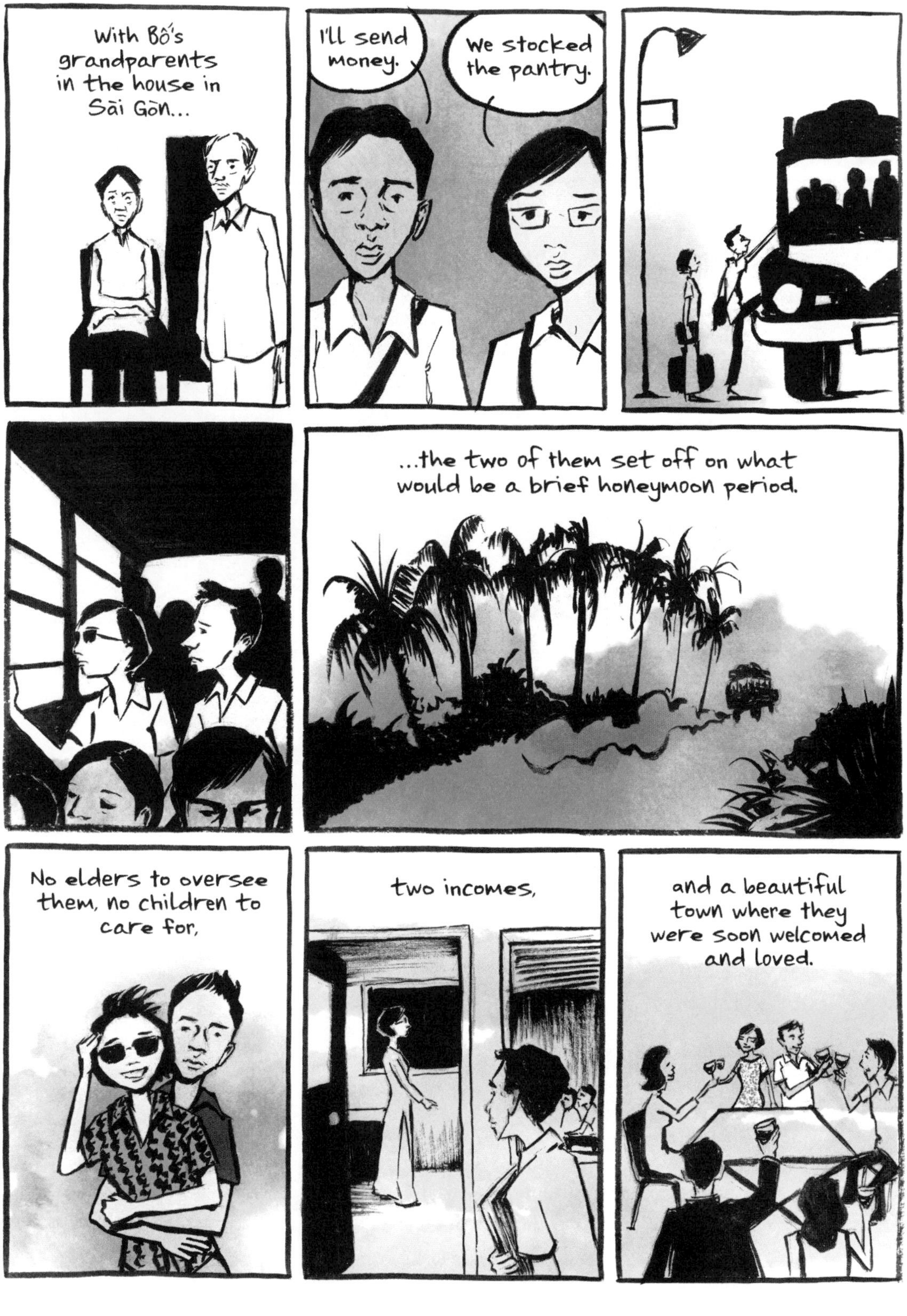
With Bố's grandparents in the house in Sài Gòn...
I'll send money.
We stocked the pantry.
...the two of them set off on what would be a brief honeymoon period.
No elders to oversee them, no children to care for,
two incomes,
and a beautiful town where they were soon welcomed and loved.

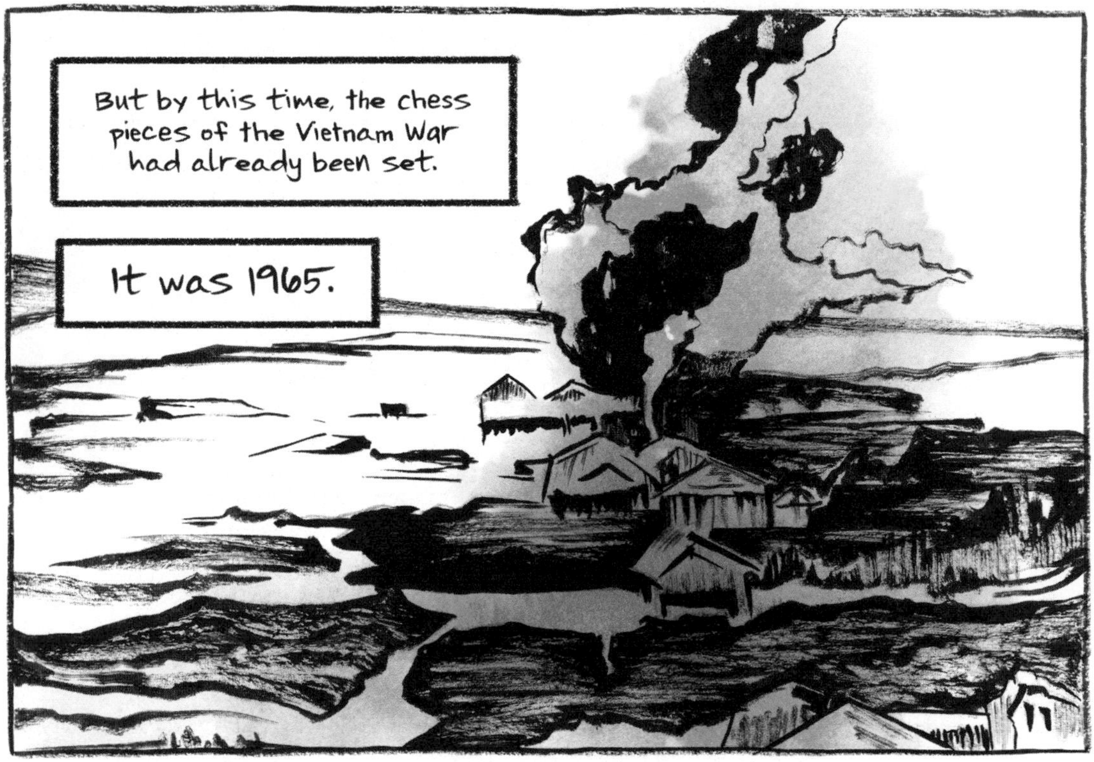
But by this time, the chess pieces of the Vietnam War had already been set.
It was 1965.

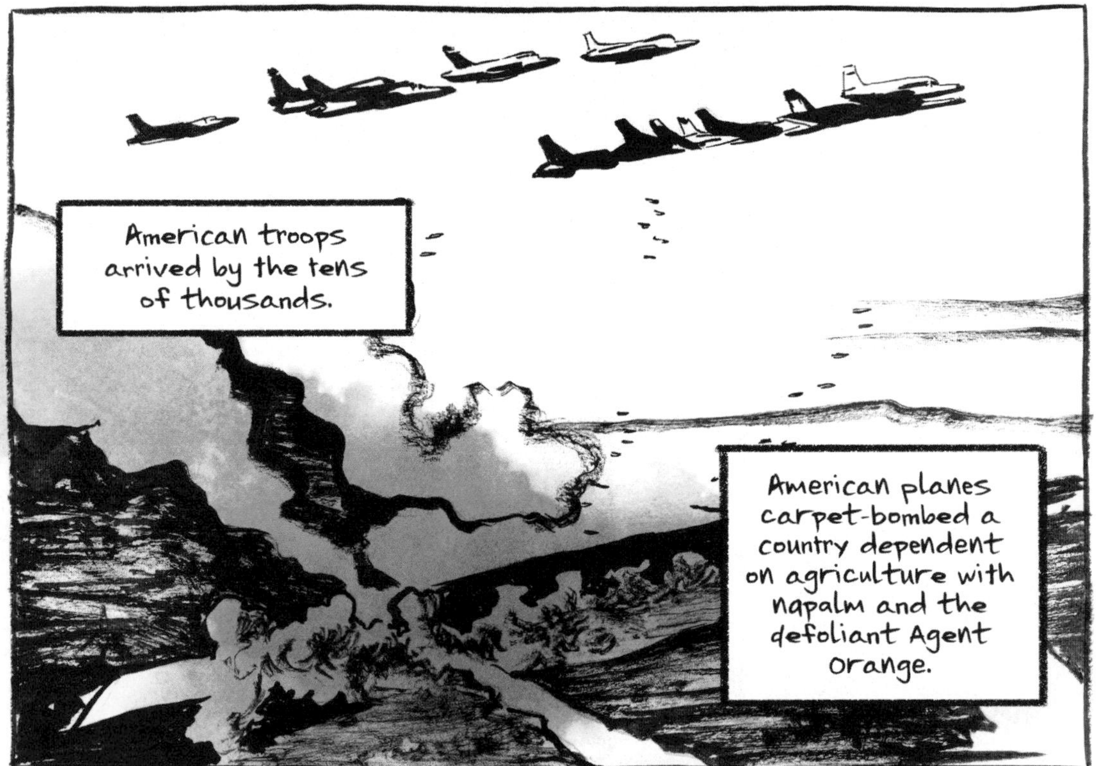
American troops arrived by the tens of thousands.
American planes carpet-bombed a country dependent on agriculture with napalm and the defoliant Agent Orange.

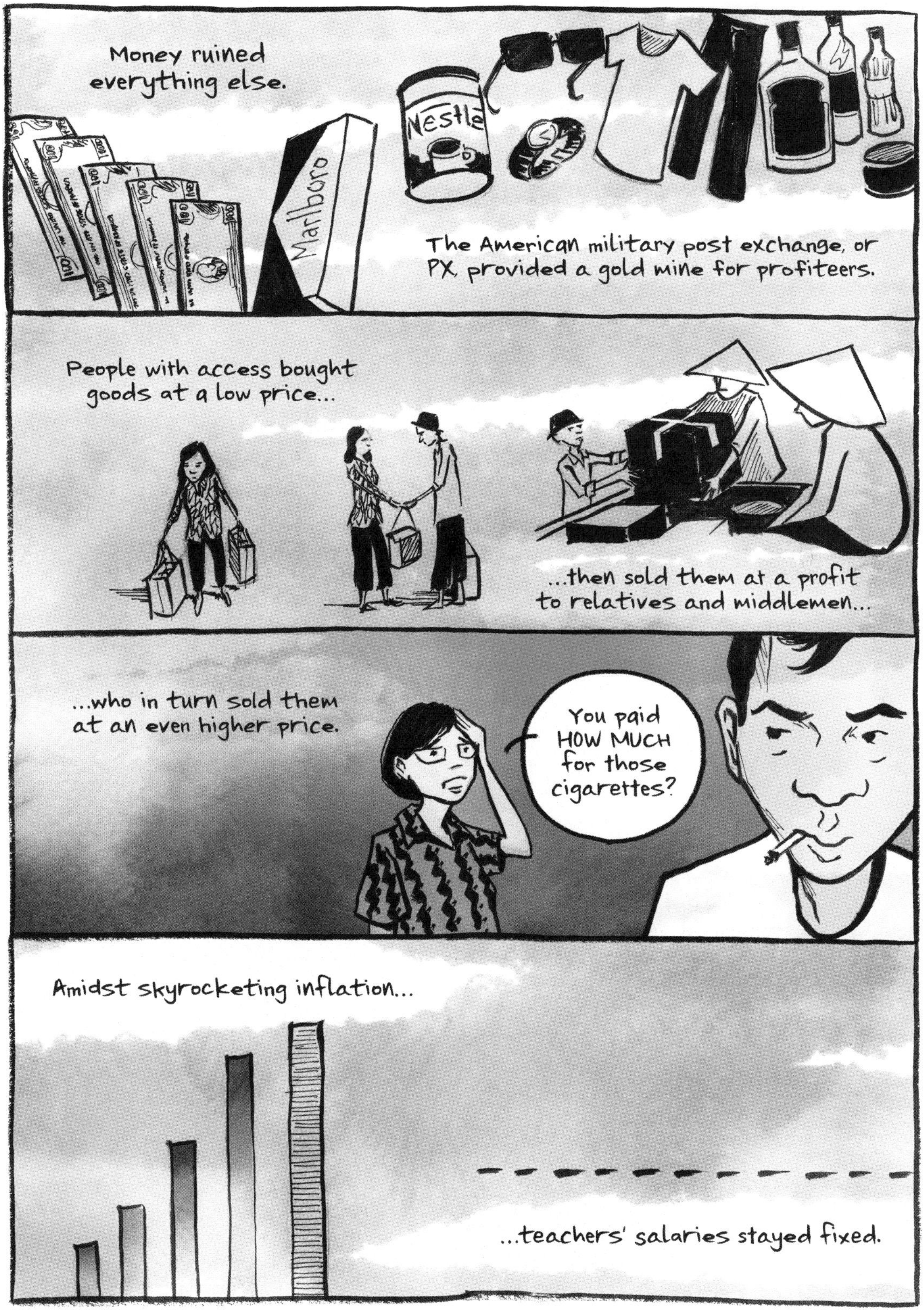

Money ruined everything else.
Nestle
Marlboro
The American military post exchange, or PX, provided a gold mine for profiteers.
People with access bought goods at a low price...
...then sold them at a profit to relatives and middlemen...
...who in turn sold them at an even higher price.
You paid HOW MUCH for those cigarettes?
Amidst skyrocketing inflation...
...teachers' salaries stayed fixed.

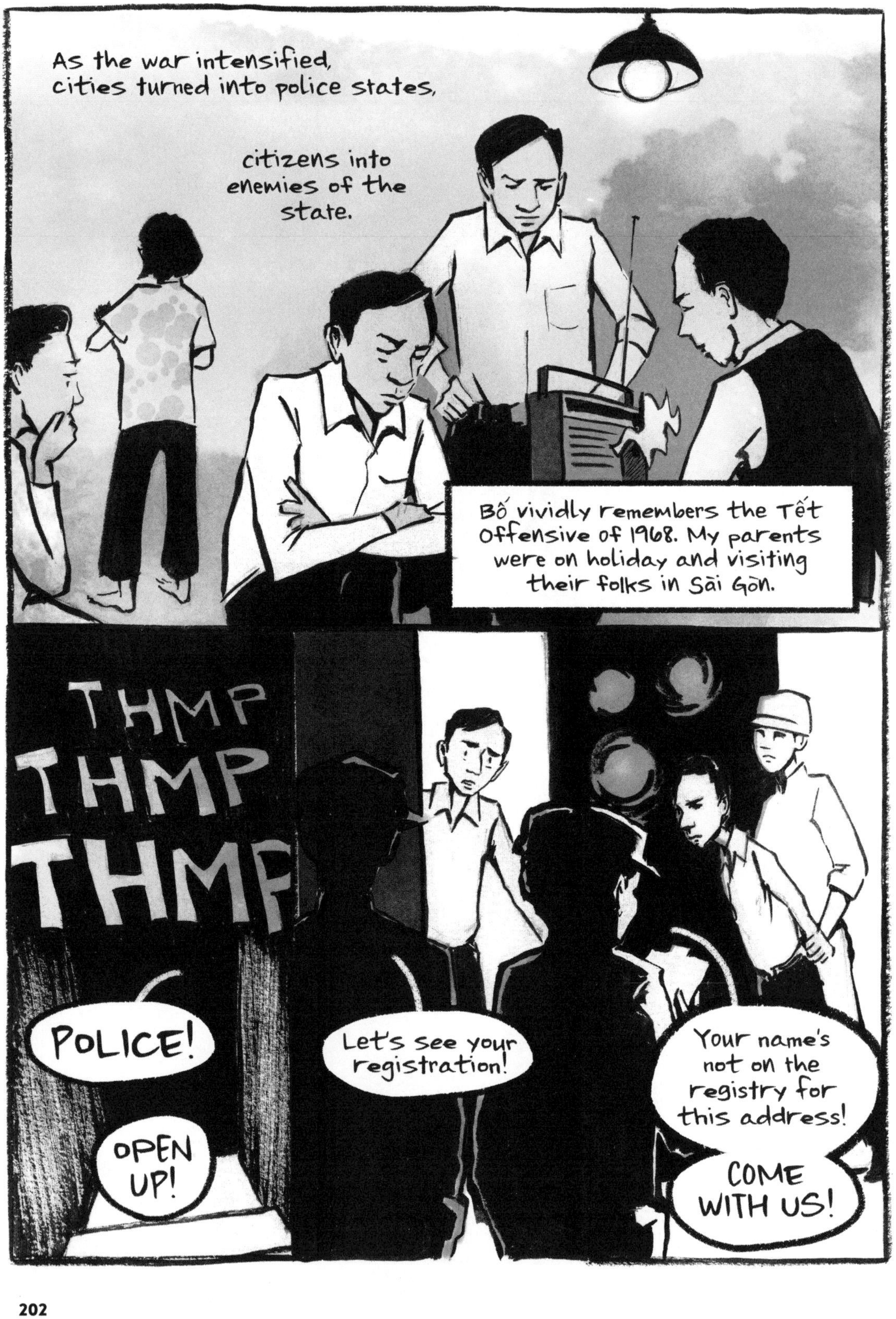
As the war intensified, cities turned into police states,
citizens into enemies of the state.
Bố vividly remembers the Tết Offensive of 1968. My parents were on holiday and visiting their folks in Sài Gòn.
THMP
THMP
THMP
POLICE!
OPEN UP!
Let's see your registration!
Your name's not on the registry for this address!
COME WITH US!

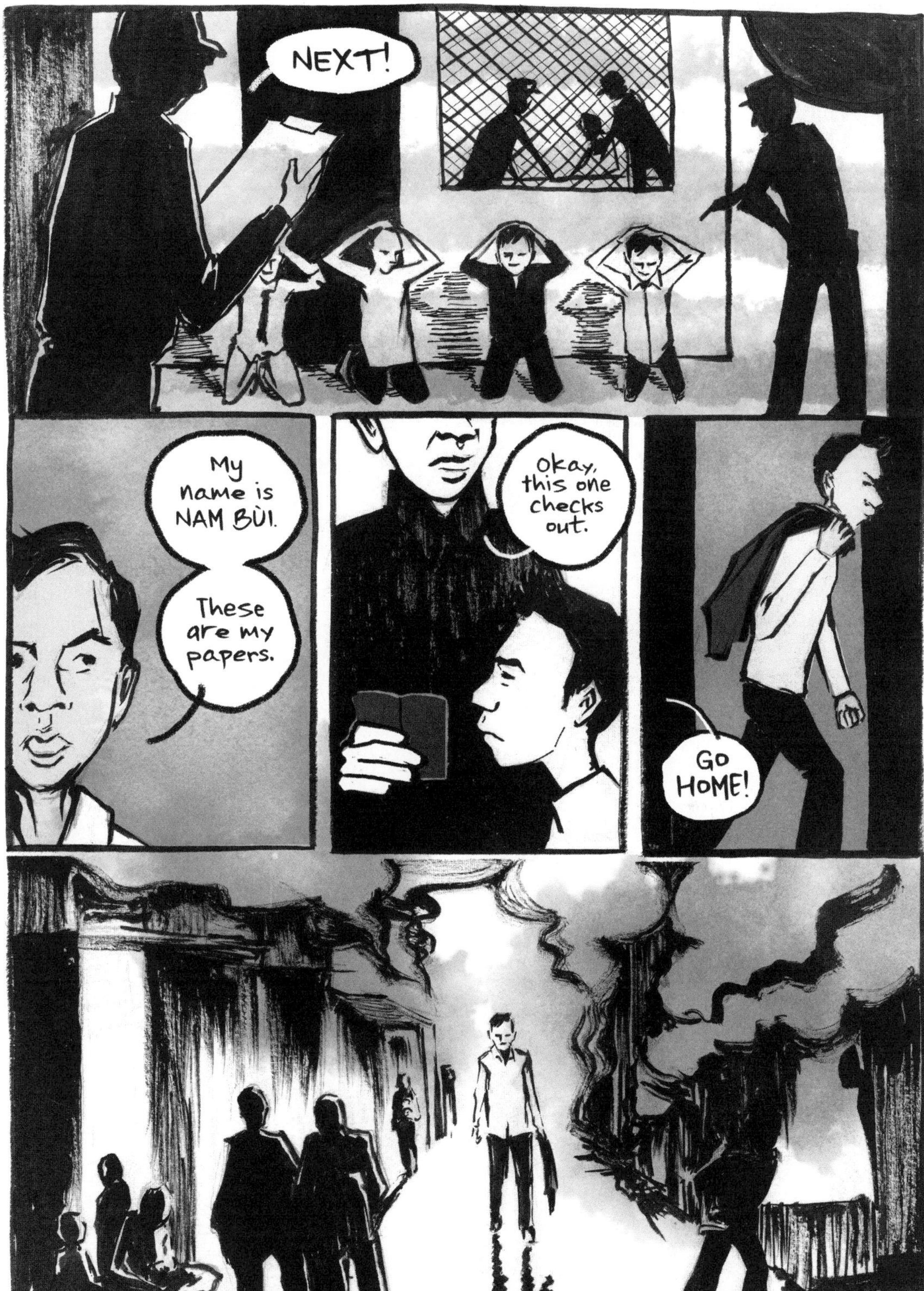
NEXT!
My name is NAM BÙI.
These are my papers.
Okay, this one checks out.
GO HOME!

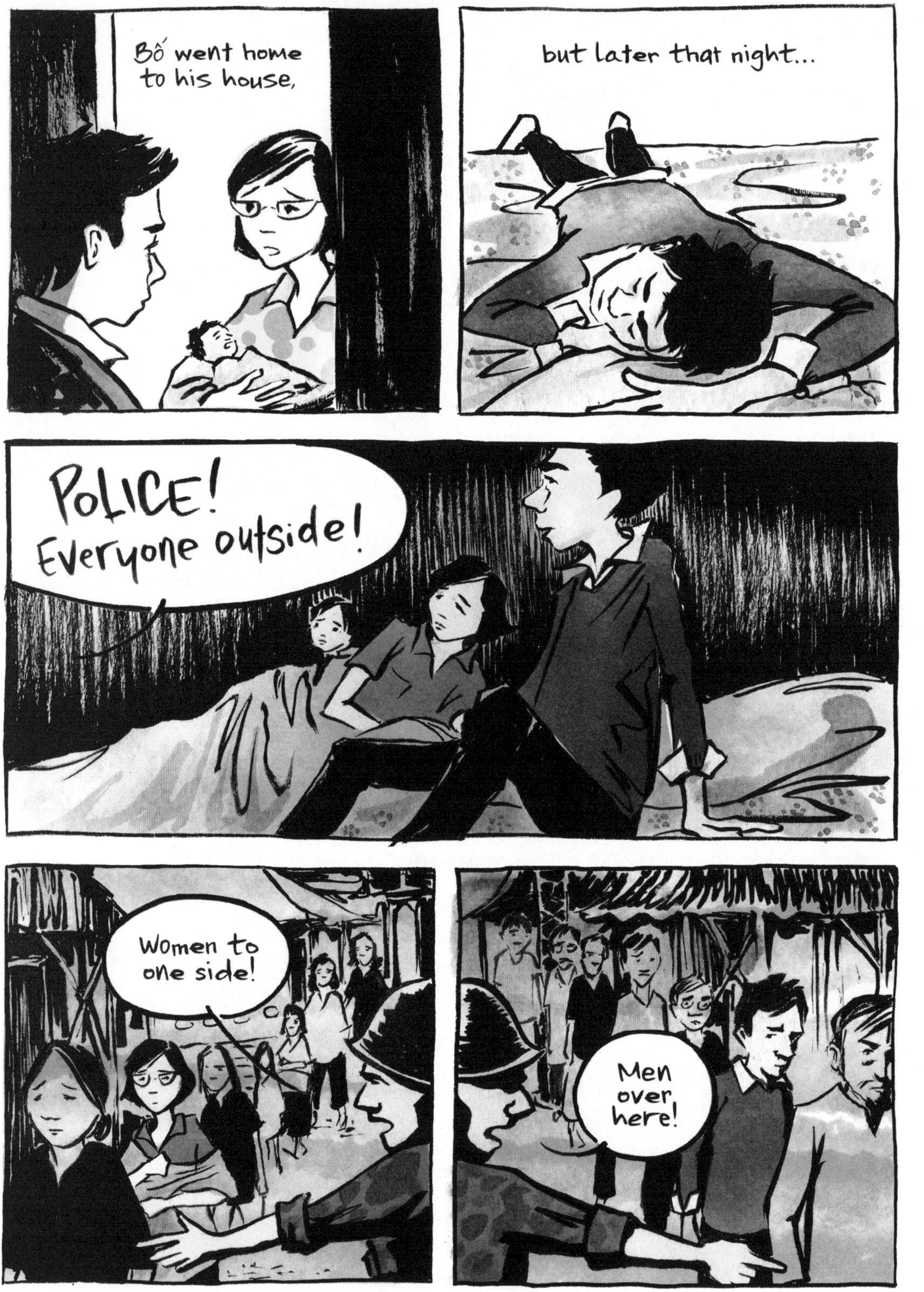
Bố went home to his house,
but later that night...
POLICE! Everyone outside!
Women to one side!
Men over here!

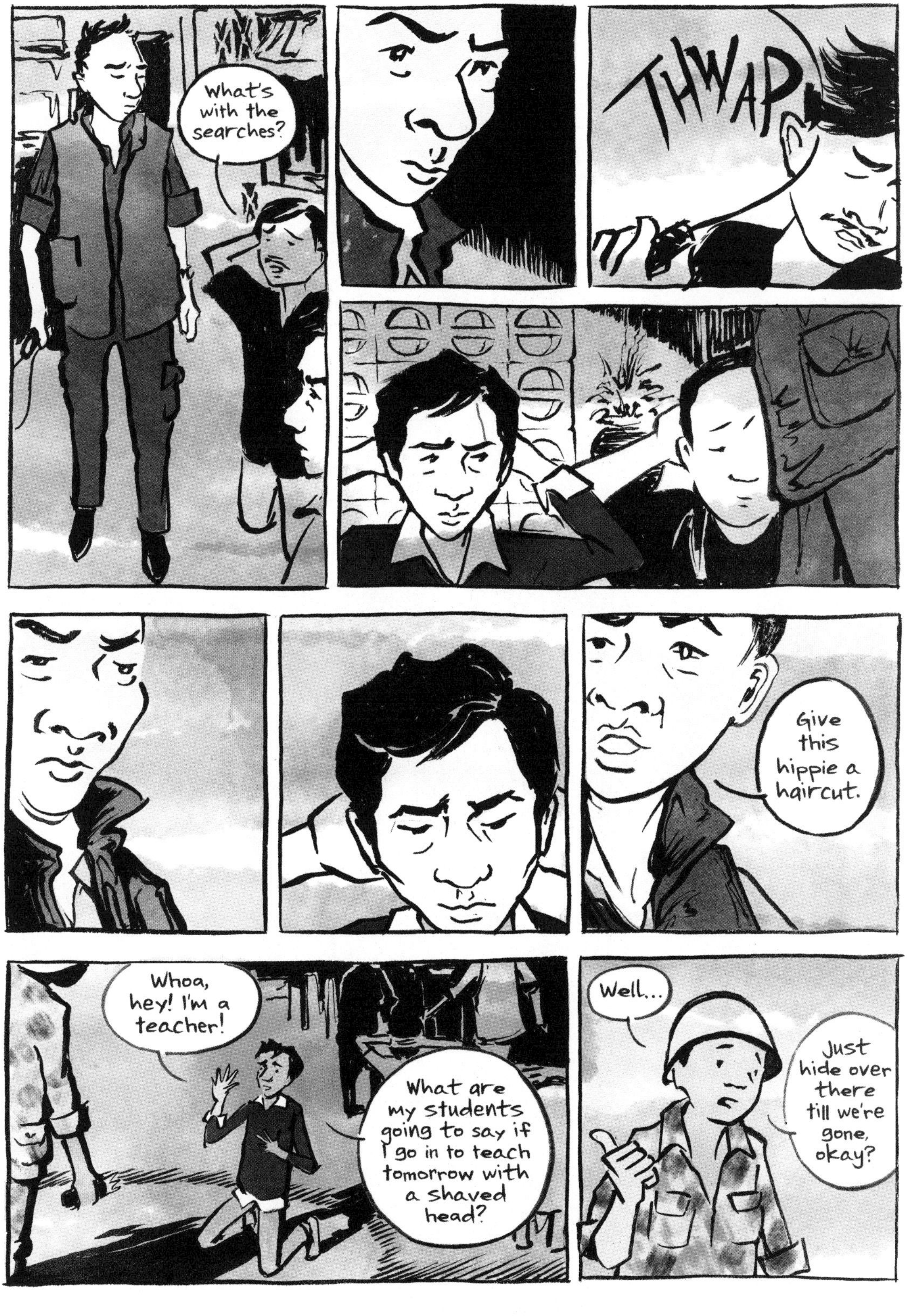
What's with the searches?
THWAP
Give this hippie a haircut.
Whoa, hey! I'm a teacher!
What are my students going to say if I go in to teach tomorrow with a shaved head?
Well...
Just hide over there till we're gone, okay?

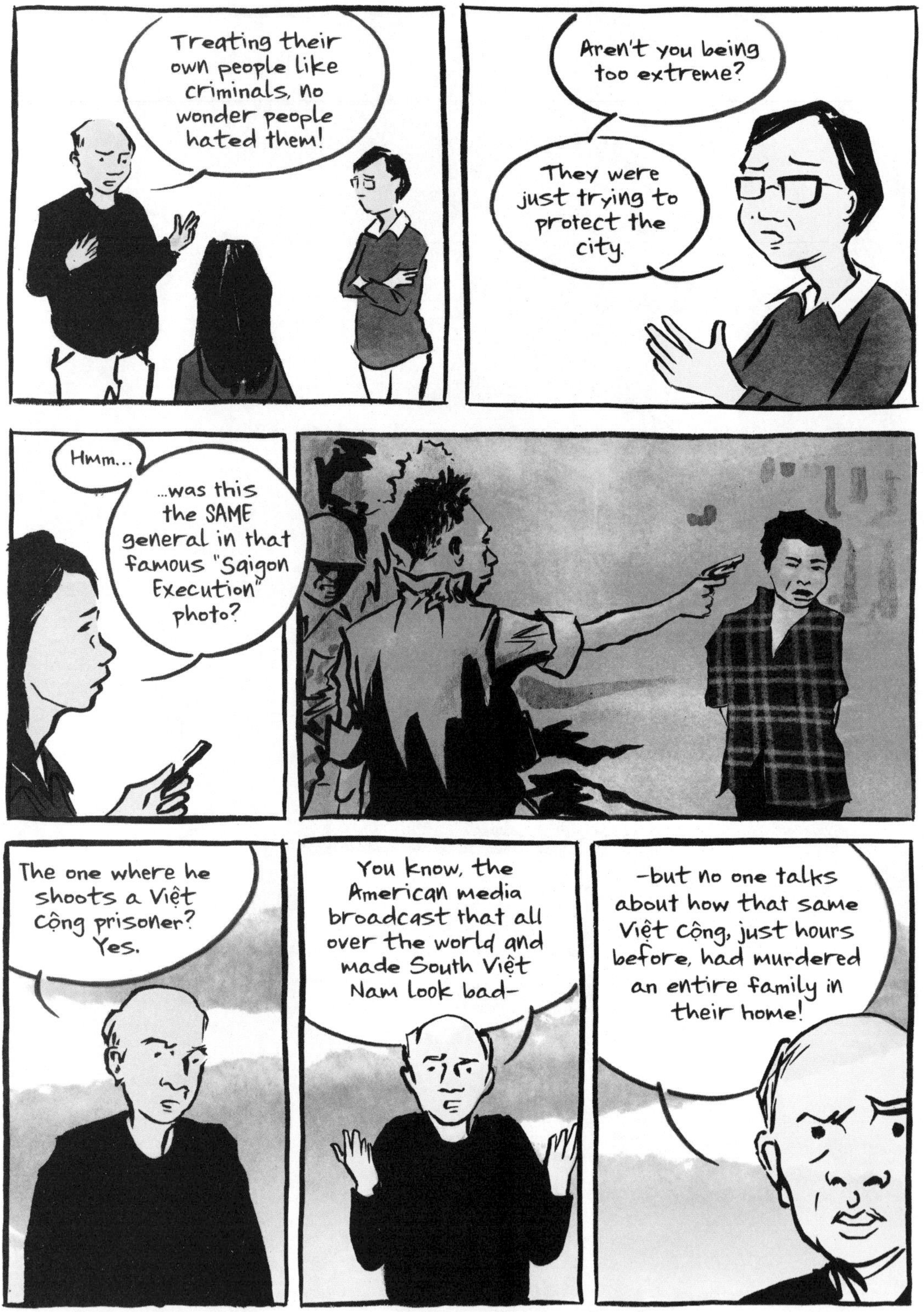
Treating their own people like criminals, no wonder people hated them!
Aren't you being too extreme?
They were just trying to protect the city.
Hmm...
...was this the SAME general in that famous "Saigon Execution" photo?
The one where he shoots a Việt Cộng prisoner? Yes.
You know, the American media broadcast that all over the world and made South Việt Nam look bad-
-but no one talks about how that same Việt Cộng, just hours before, had murdered an entire family in their home!

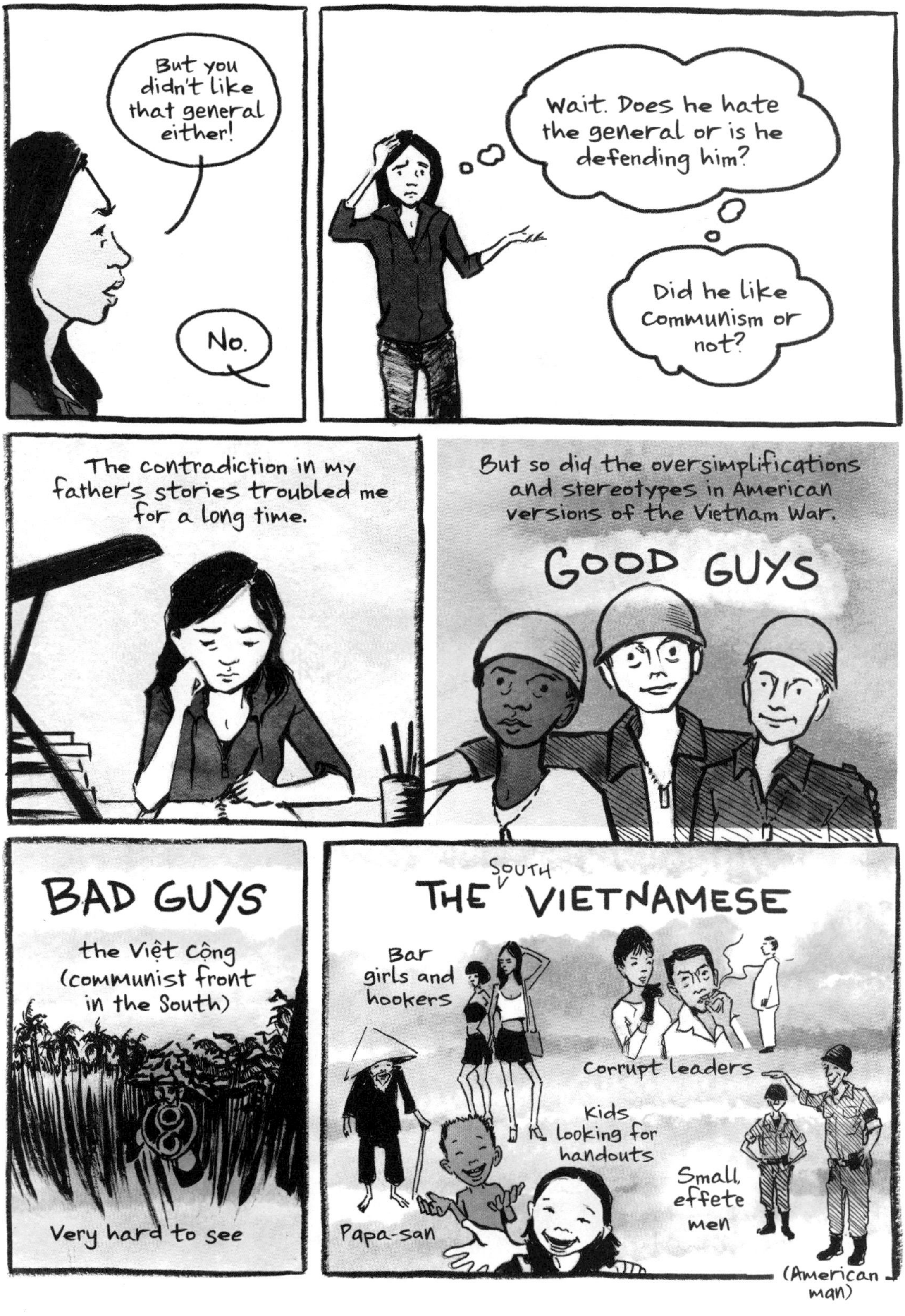

But you didn't like that general either!
No.
Wait. Does he hate the general or is he defending him?
Did he like Communism or not?
The contradiction in my father's stories troubled me for a long time.
But so did the oversimplifications and stereotypes in American versions of the Vietnam War.
GOOD GUYS
BAD GUYS
the Việt Cộng (communist front in the South)
Very hard to see
THE SOUTH VIETNAMESE
Bar girls and hookers
Corrupt leaders
Papa-san
Kids looking for handouts
Small, effete men
(American man)

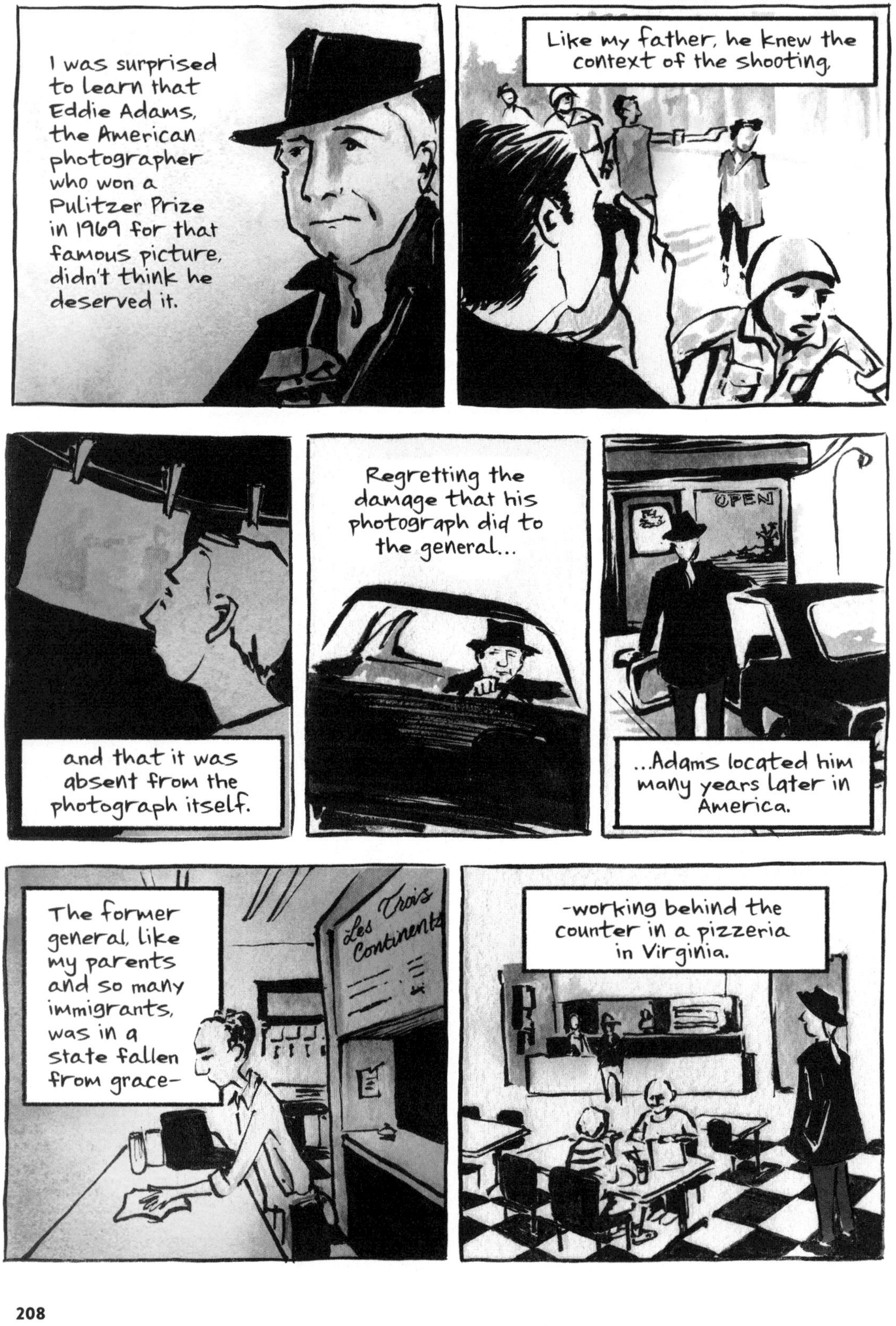
I was surprised to learn that Eddie Adams, the American photographer who won a Pulitzer Prize in 1969 for that famous picture, didn't think he deserved it.
Like my father, he knew the context of the shooting,
and that it was absent from the photograph itself.
Regretting the damage that his photograph did to the general...
OPEN
...Adams located him many years later in America.
The former general, like my parents and so many immigrants, was in a state fallen from grace-
Les Trois
Continent
-working behind the counter in a pizzeria in Virginia.

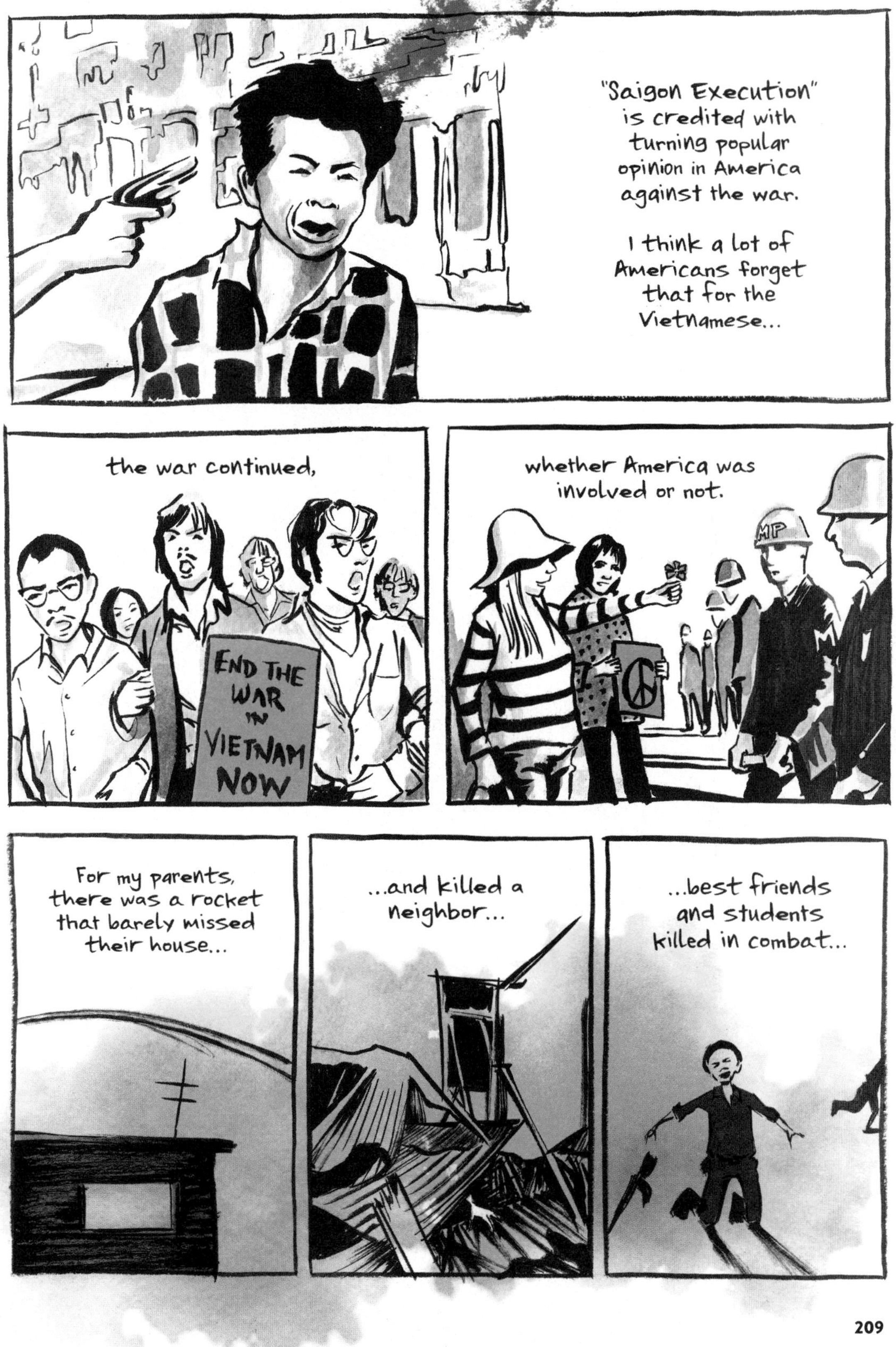
"Saigon Execution" is credited with turning popular opinion in America against the war.
I think a lot of Americans forget that for the Vietnamese...
the war continued,
END THE WAR IN VIETNAM NOW
whether America was involved or not.
MP
For my parents, there was a rocket that barely missed their house...
...and killed a neighbor...
...best friends and students killed in combat...

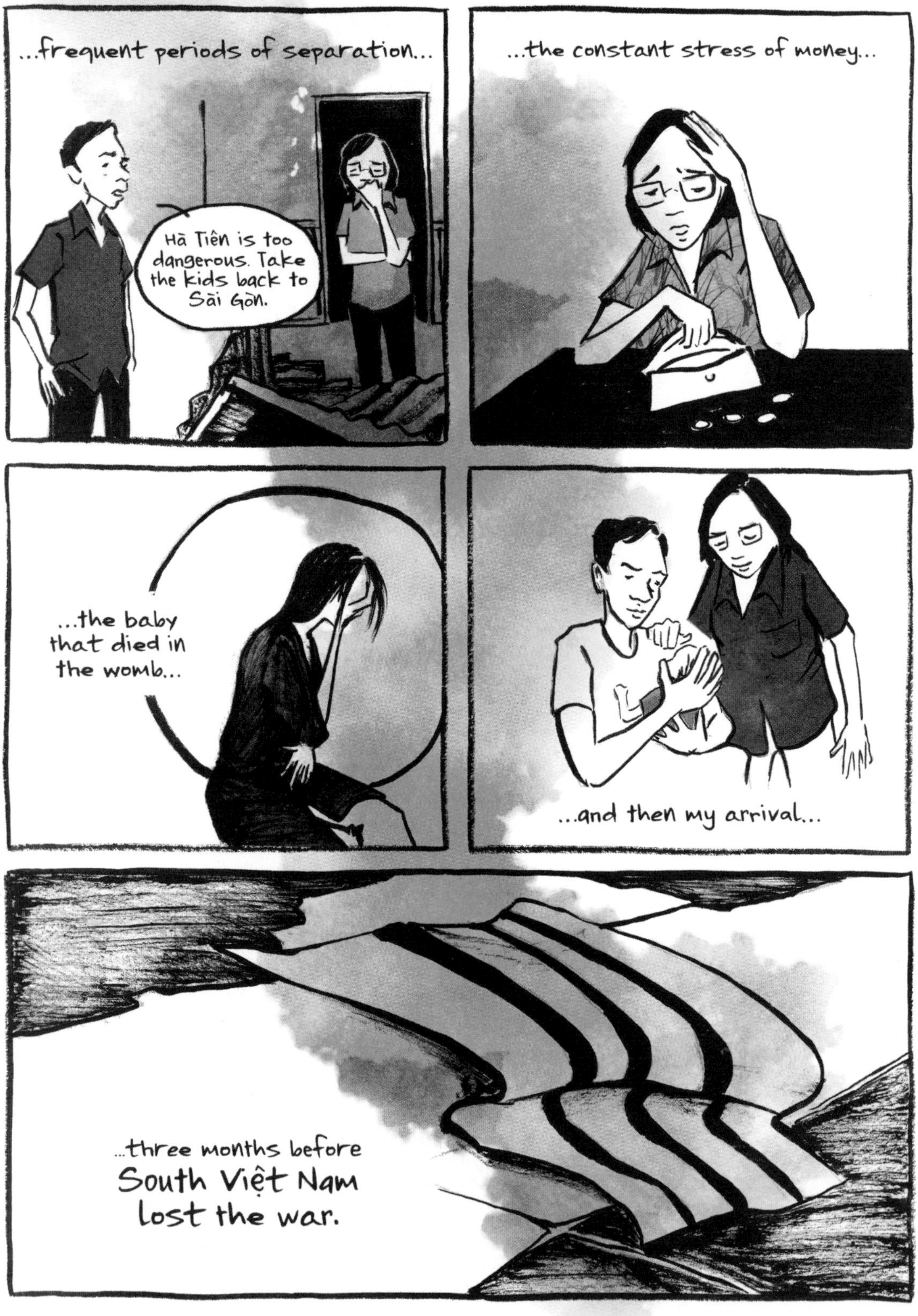
...frequent periods of separation...
Hà Tiên is too dangerous. Take the kids back to Sài Gòn.
...the constant stress of money...
...the baby that died in the womb...
...and then my arrival...
...three months before South Việt Nam lost the war.

CHAPTER 7

HEROES AND LOSERS

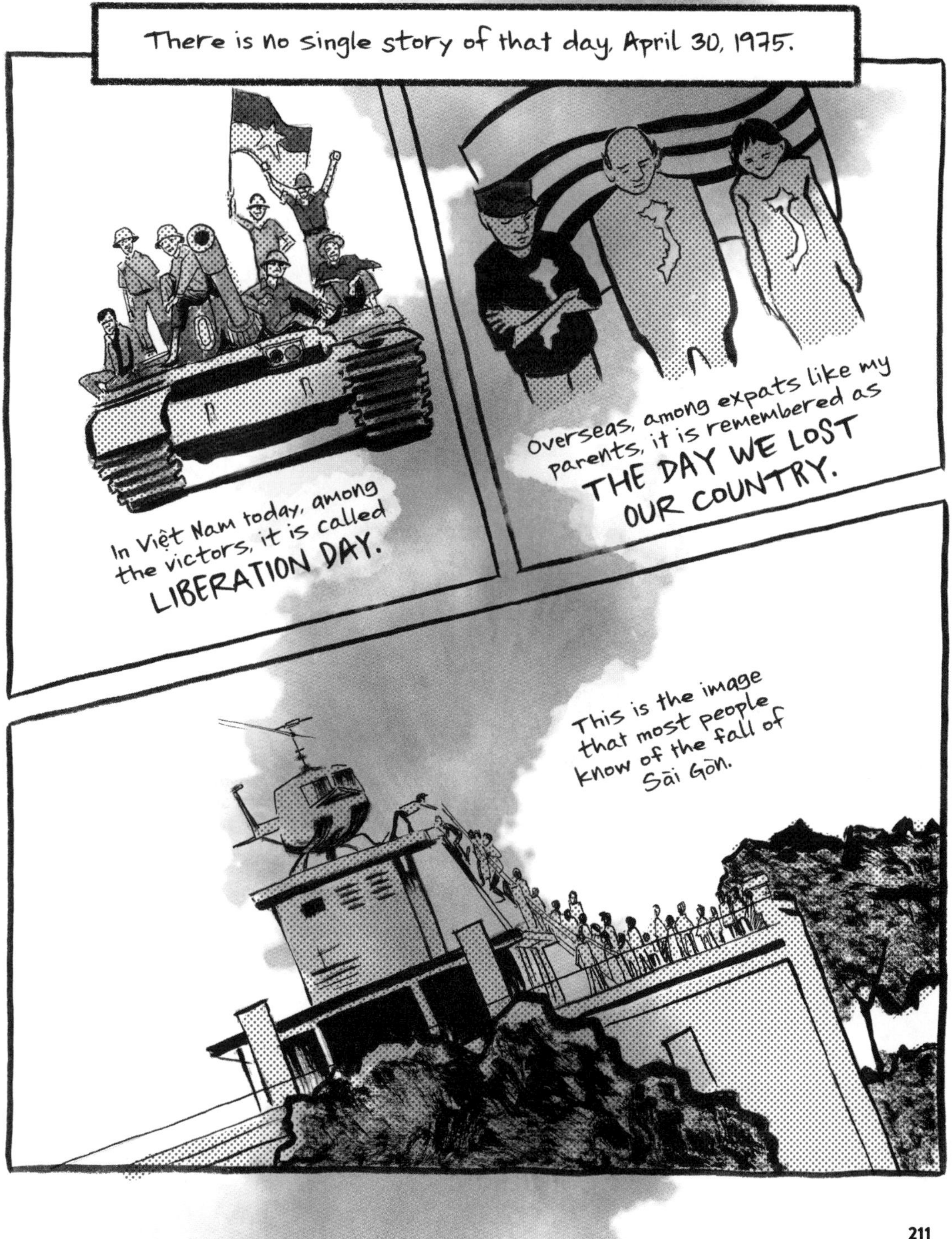
There is no single story of that day, April 30, 1975.
In Việt Nam today, among the victors, it is called LIBERATION DAY.
Overseas, among expats like my parents, it is remembered as THE DAY WE LOST OUR COUNTRY.
This is the image that most people know of the fall of Sài Gòn.

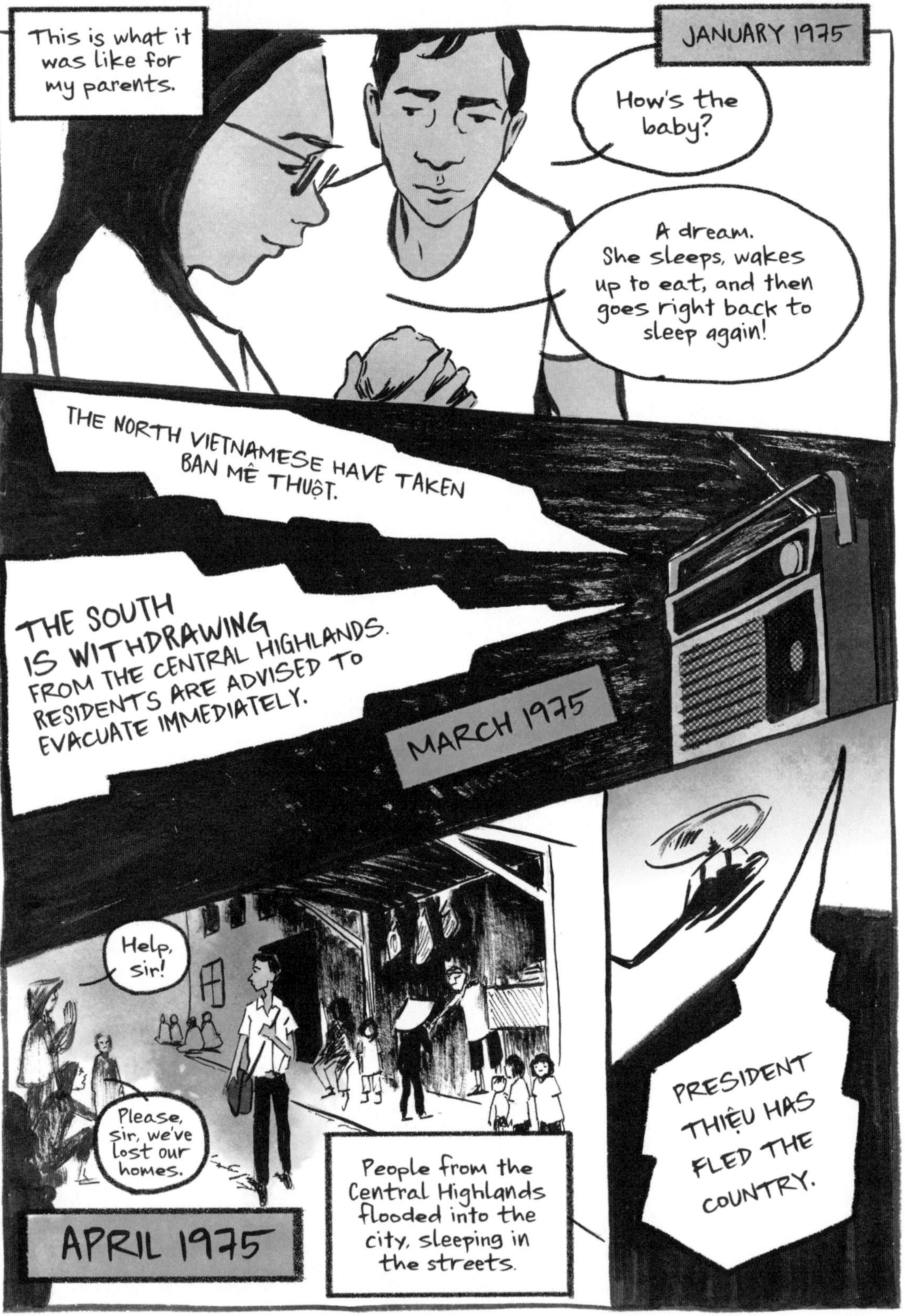
This is what it was like for my parents.
JANUARY 1975
How's the baby?
A dream. She sleeps, wakes up to eat, and then goes right back to sleep again!
THE NORTH VIETNAMESE HAVE TAKEN BAN MÊ THUỘT.
THE SOUTH IS WITHDRAWING FROM THE CENTRAL HIGHLANDS. RESIDENTS ARE ADVISED TO EVACUATE IMMEDIATELY.
MARCH 1975
Help, sir!
Please, sir, we've lost our homes.
APRIL 1975
People from the Central Highlands flooded into the city, sleeping in the streets.
PRESIDENT THIỆU HAS FLED THE COUNTRY.

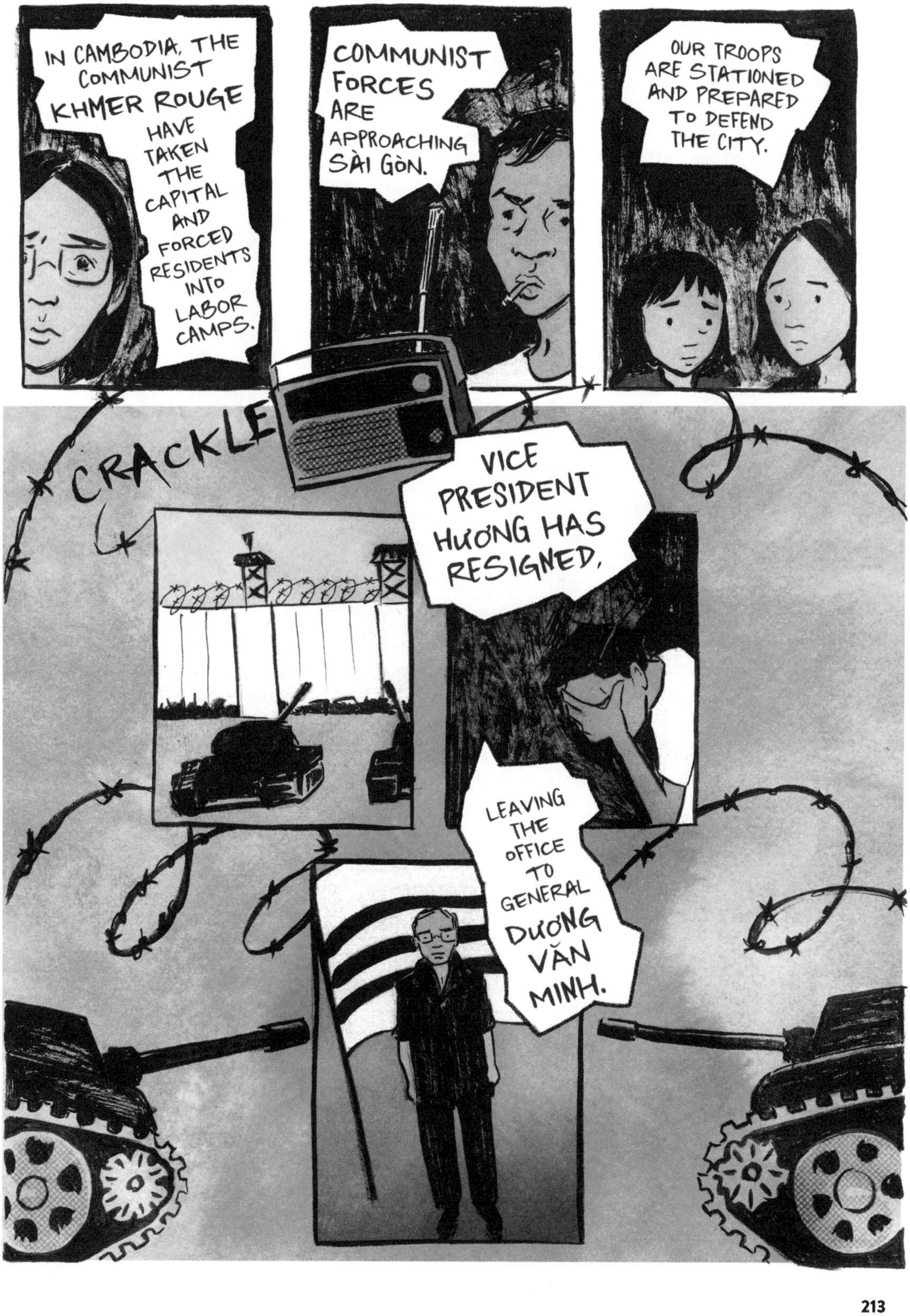
IN CAMBODIA, THE COMMUNIST KHMER ROUGE HAVE TAKEN THE CAPITAL AND FORCED RESIDENTS INTO LABOR CAMPS.
COMMUNIST FORCES ARE APPROACHING SÀI GÒN.
OUR TROOPS ARE STATIONED AND PREPARED TO DEFEND THE CITY.
CRACKLE
VICE PRESIDENT HƯƠNG HAS RESIGNED,
LEAVING THE OFFICE TO GENERAL DƯƠNG VĂN MINH.

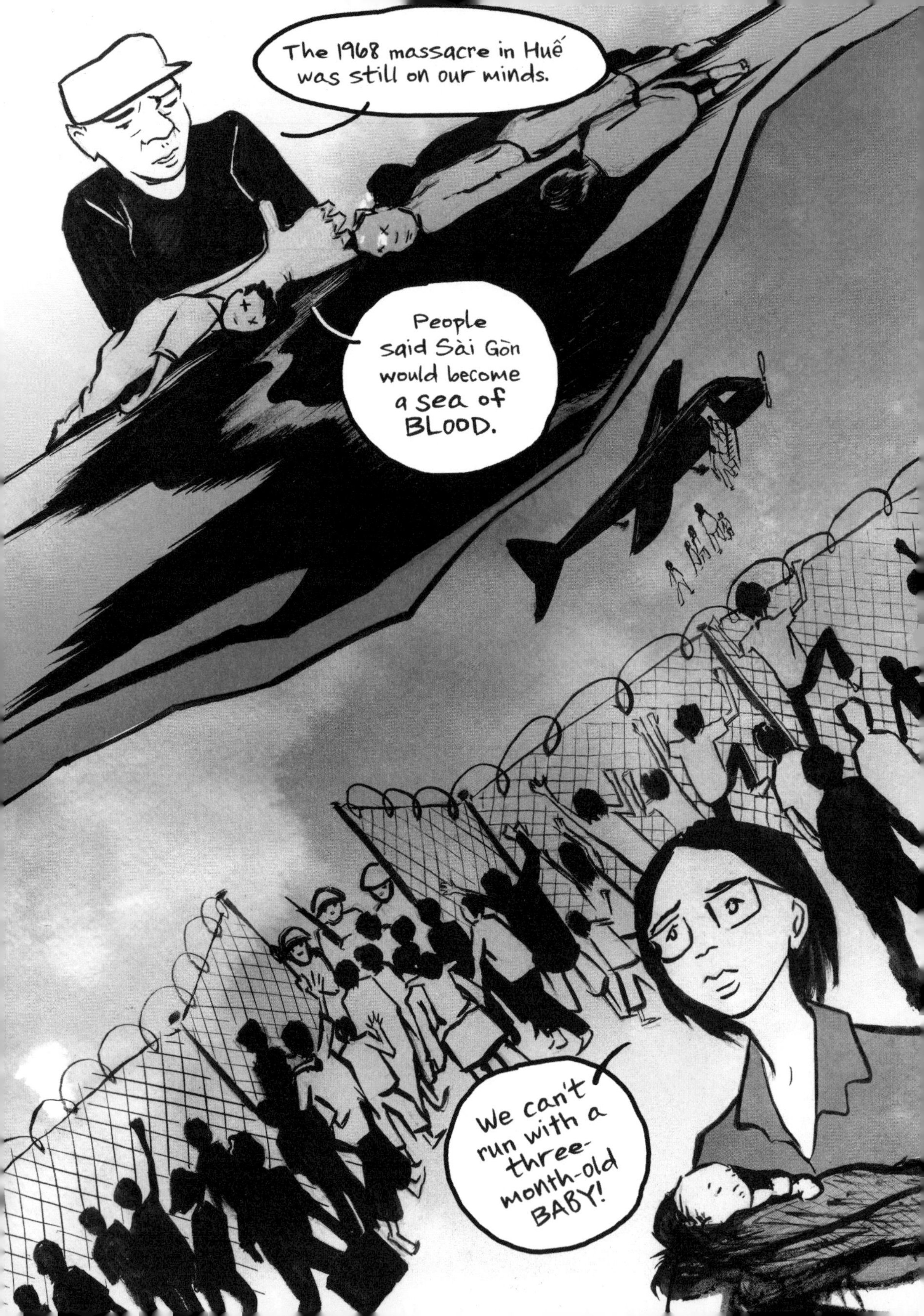
The 1968 massacre in Huế was still on our minds.
People said Sài Gòn would become a sea of BLOOD.
We can't run with a three-month-old BABY!

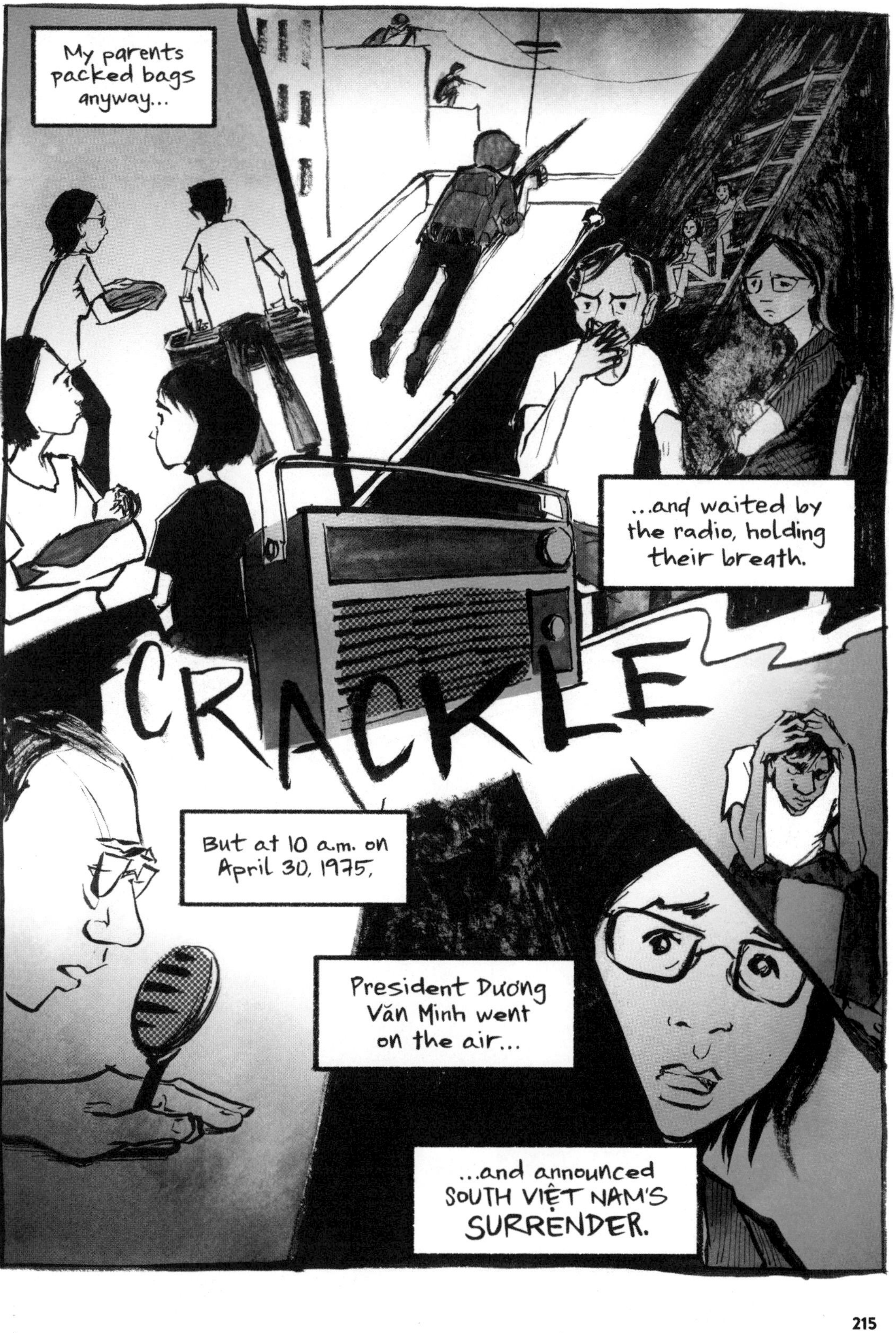
My parents packed bags anyway...
...and waited by the radio, holding their breath.
CRACKLE
But at 10 a.m. on April 30, 1975,
President Dương Văn Minh went on the air...
...and announced SOUTH VIỆT NAM'S SURRENDER.

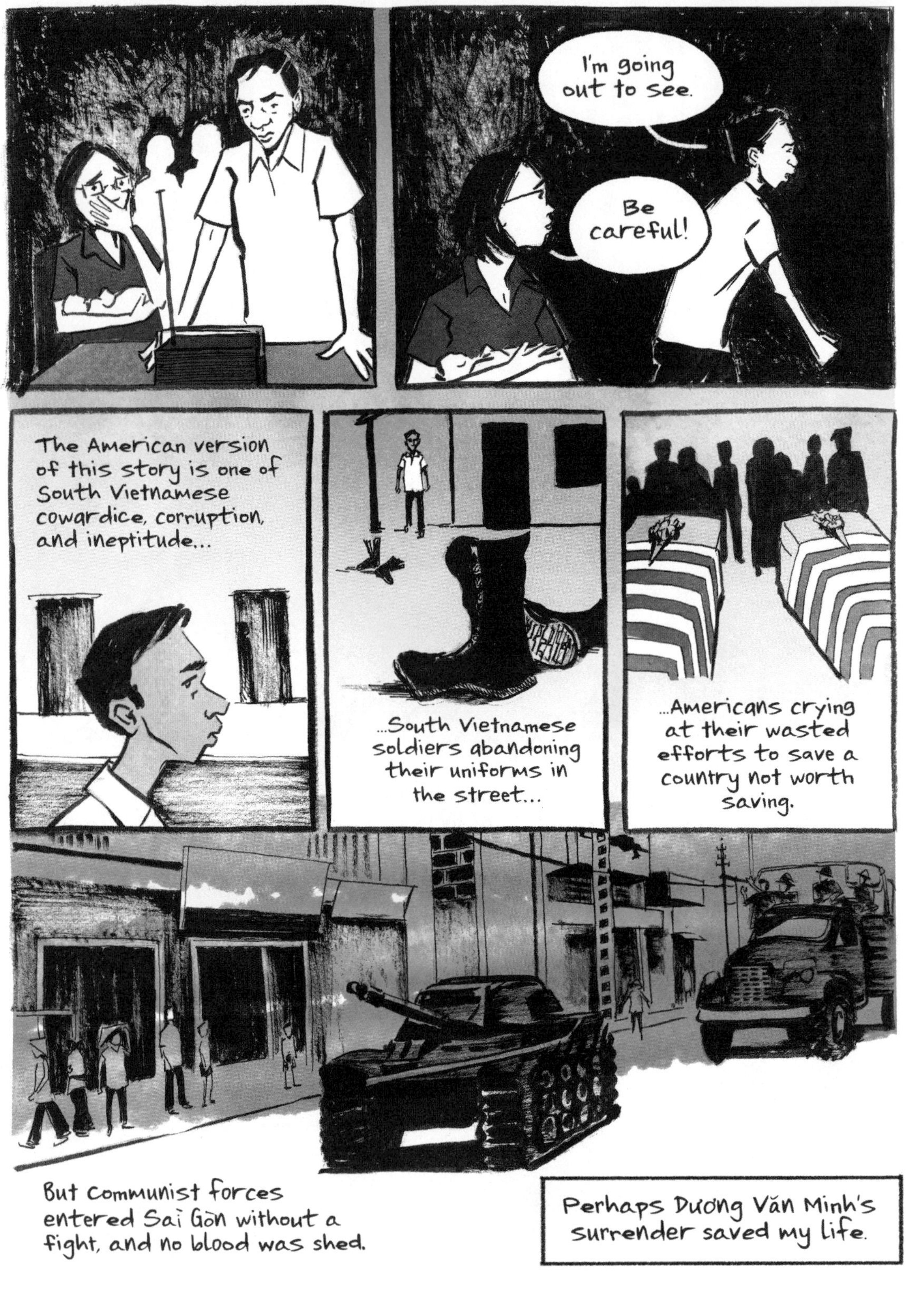
I'm going out to see.
Be careful!
The American version of this story is one of South Vietnamese cowardice, corruption, and ineptitude...
...South Vietnamese soldiers abandoning their uniforms in the street...
...Americans crying at their wasted efforts to save a country not worth saving.
But Communist forces entered Sài Gòn without a fight, and no blood was shed.
Perhaps Dương Văn Minh's surrender saved my life.

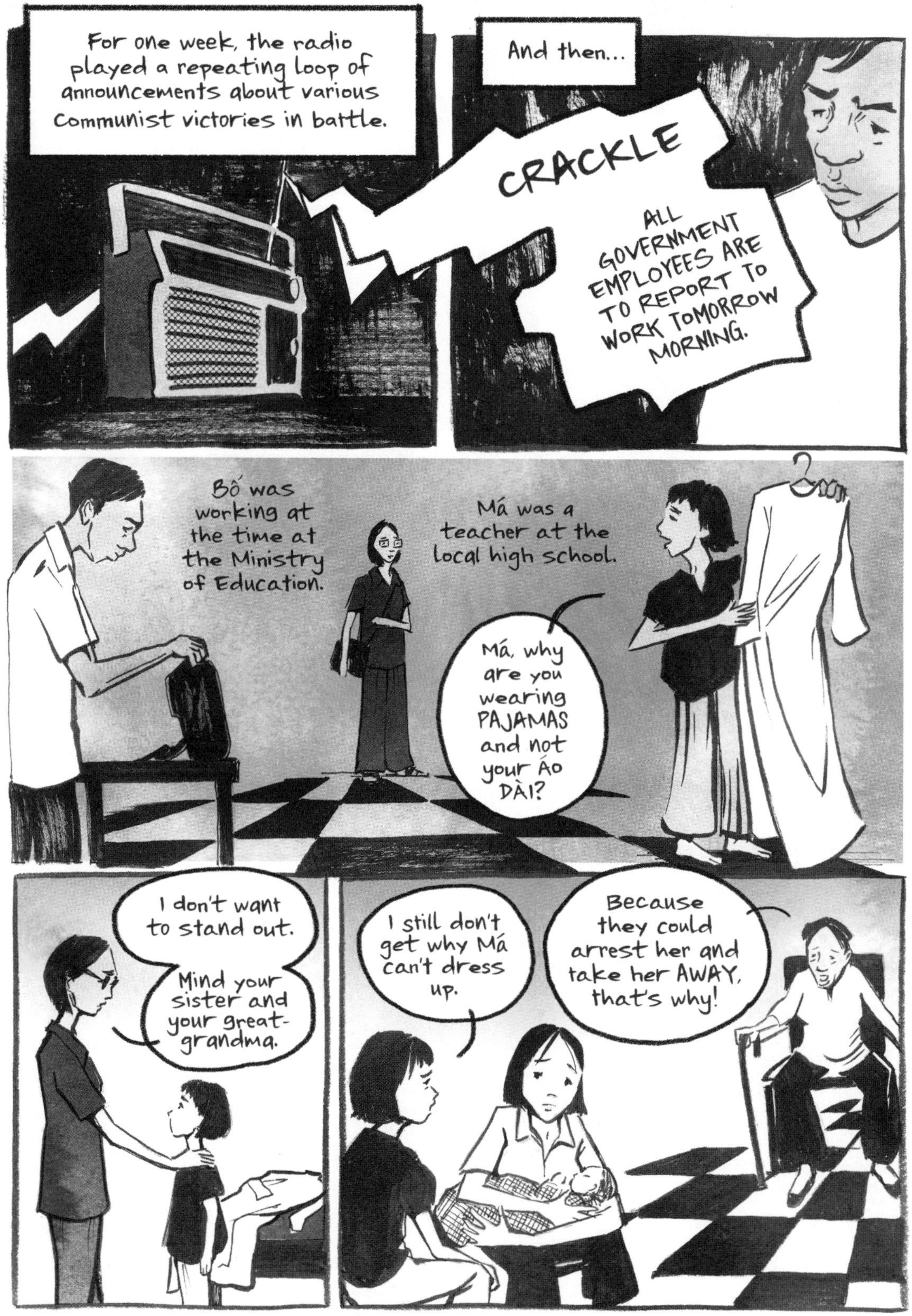
For one week, the radio played a repeating loop of announcements about various Communist victories in battle.
And then...
CRACKLE
ALL GOVERNMENT EMPLOYEES ARE TO REPORT TO WORK TOMORROW MORNING.
Bố was working at the time at the Ministry of Education.
Má was a teacher at the local high school.
Má, why are you wearing PAJAMAS and not your ÁO DÀI?
I don't want to stand out.
Mind your sister and your great-grandma.
I still don't get why Má can't dress up.
Because they could arrest her and take her AWAY, that's why!

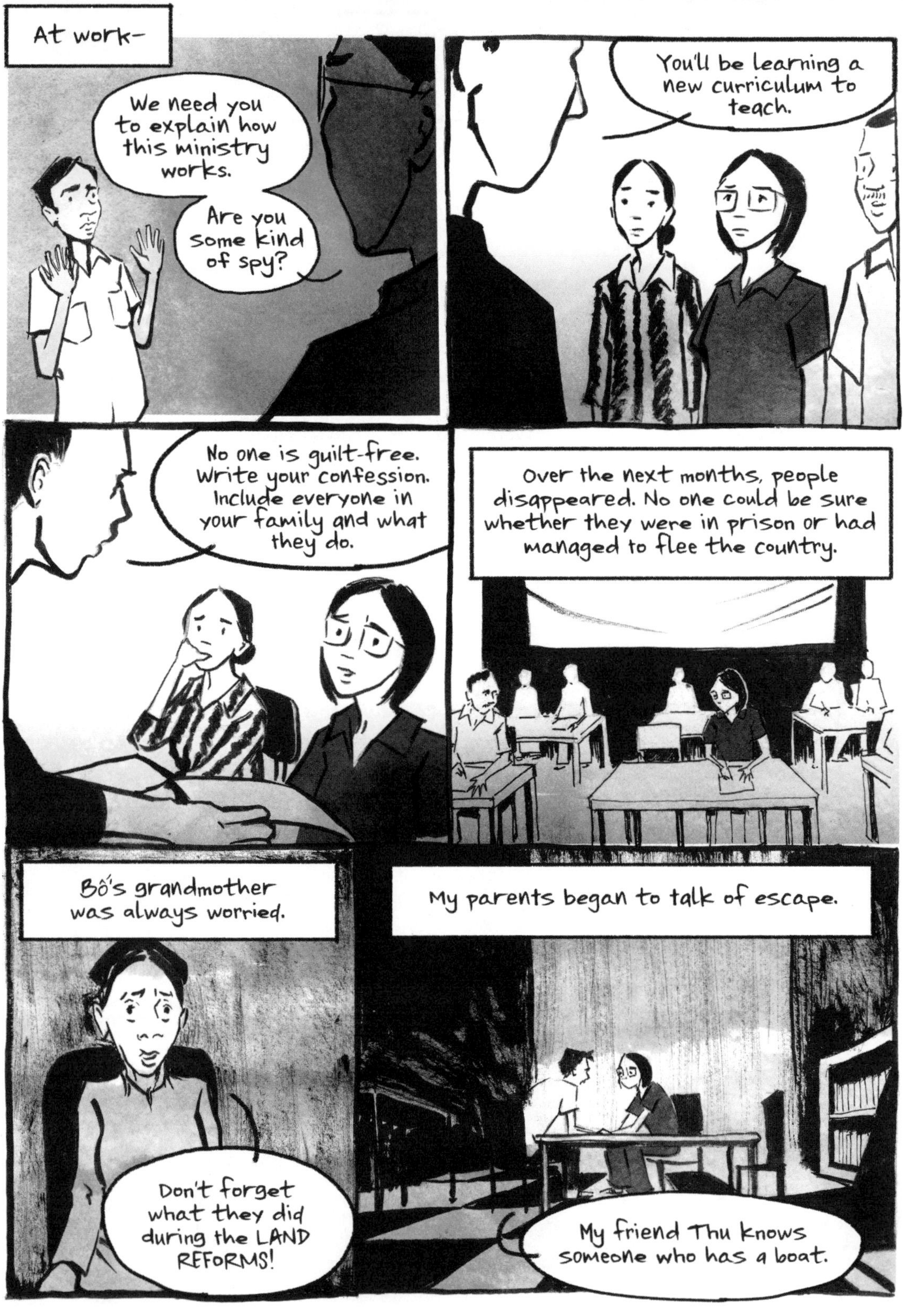
At work–
We need you to explain how this ministry works.
Are you some kind of spy?
You'll be learning a new curriculum to teach.
No one is guilt-free. Write your confession. Include everyone in your family and what they do.
Over the next months, people disappeared. No one could be sure whether they were in prison or had managed to flee the country.
Bố's grandmother was always worried.
Don't forget what they did during the LAND REFORMS!
My parents began to talk of escape.
My friend Thu knows someone who has a boat.

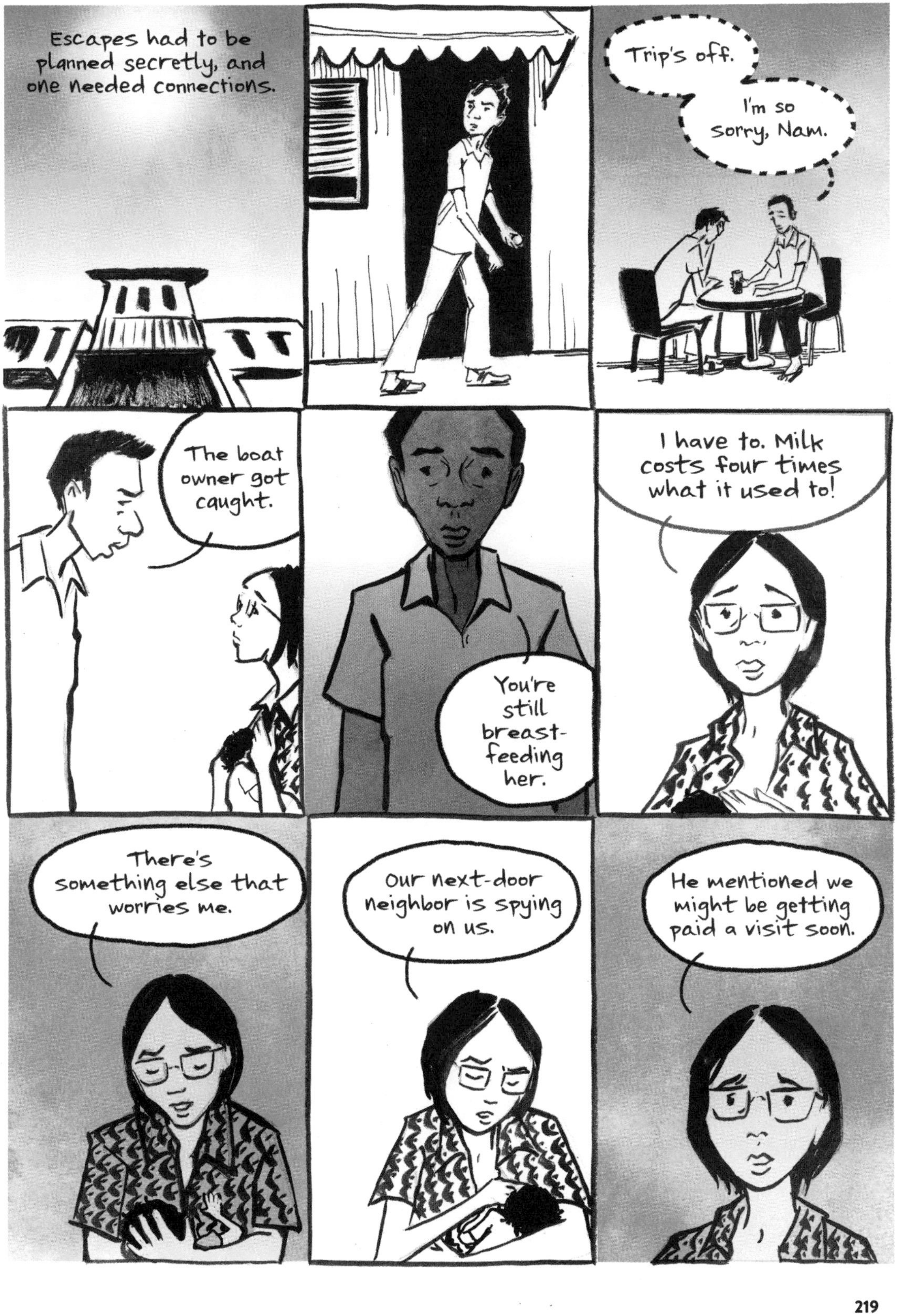
Escapes had to be planned secretly, and one needed connections.
Trip's off.
I'm so sorry, Nam.
The boat owner got caught.
You're still breast-feeding her.
I have to. Milk costs four times what it used to!
There's something else that worries me.
Our next-door neighbor is spying on us.
He mentioned we might be getting paid a visit soon.

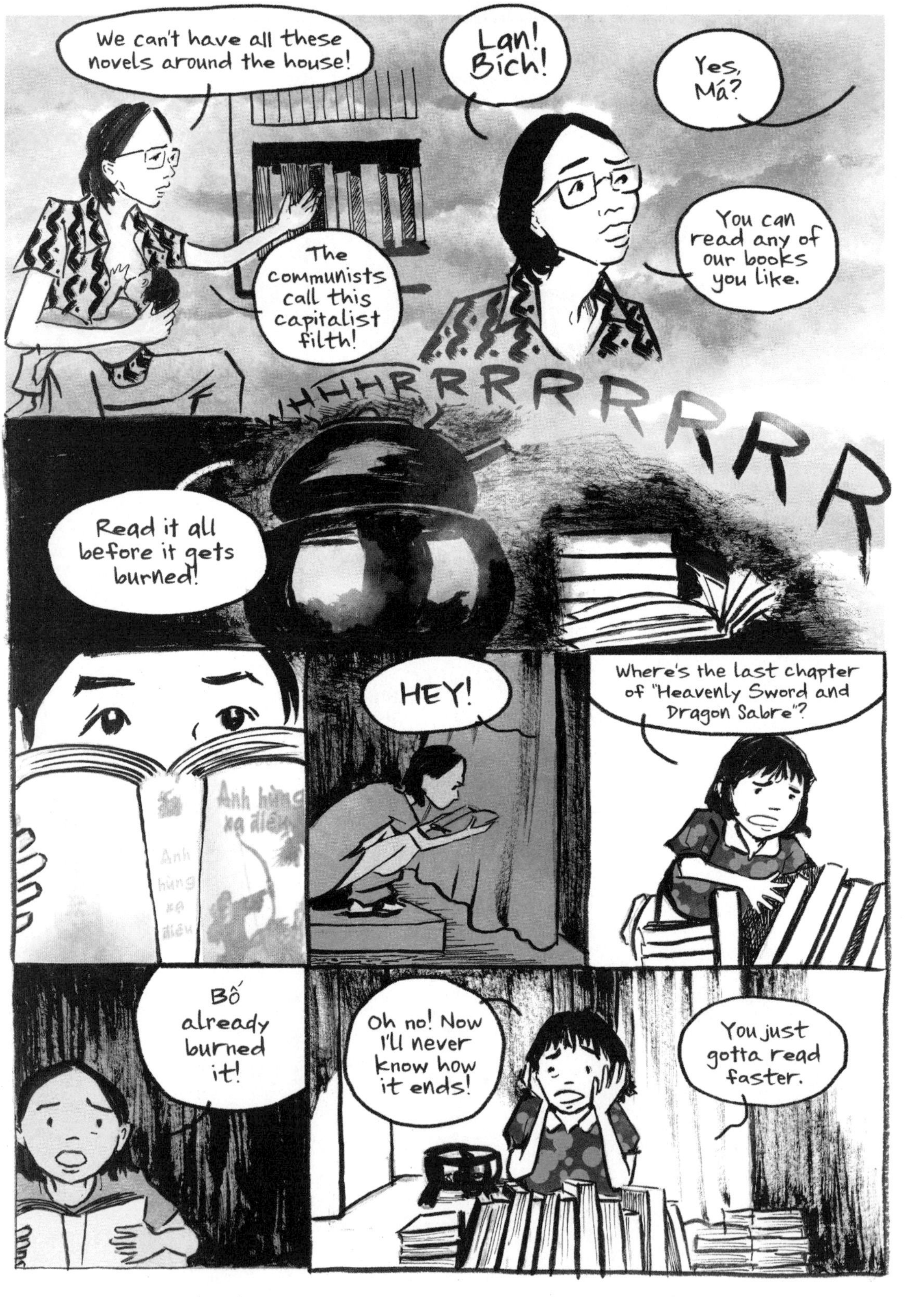
We can't have all these novels around the house!
The communists call this capitalist filth!
Lan! Bích!
Yes, Má?
You can read any of our books you like.
HHHRRRRRRRRR
Read it all before it gets burned!
Anh hùng xạ điêu
HEY!
Where's the last chapter of "Heavenly Sword and Dragon Sabre"?
Bố already burned it!
Oh no! Now I'll never know how it ends!
You just gotta read faster.

One evening, my parents got the first of many visits from our neighborhood monitor.

KNOCK KNOCK

That would be the CADRE.

Dear lord!

Smells good in here!

What are you eating?

You always eat this well?

We're eating half portions!

Wow, white rice!

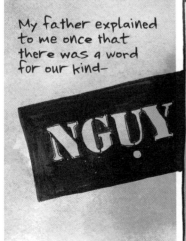

My father explained to me once that there was a word for our kind—

NGUY

It meant "false, lying, deceitful"—but it could be applied to anyone in the South.

It meant constant monitoring, distrust, and the ever-present feeling that our family could, at any moment, be separated, our safety jeopardized.

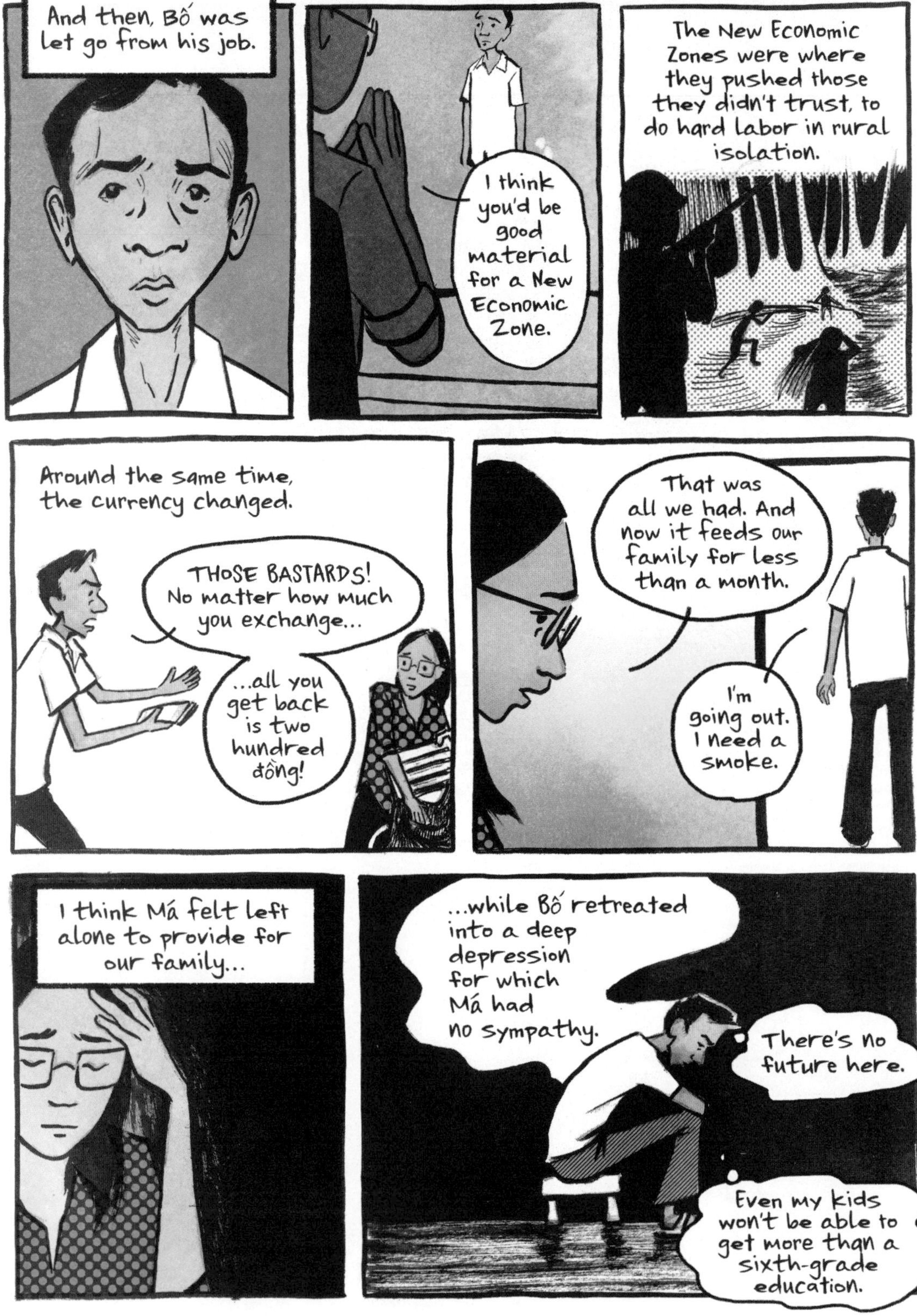
And then, Bố was let go from his job.
I think you'd be good material for a New Economic Zone.
The New Economic Zones were where they pushed those they didn't trust, to do hard labor in rural isolation.
Around the same time, the currency changed.
THOSE BASTARDS! No matter how much you exchange...
...all you get back is two hundred đồng!
That was all we had. And now it feeds our family for less than a month.
I'm going out. I need a smoke.
I think Má felt left alone to provide for our family...
...while Bố retreated into a deep depression for which Má had no sympathy.
There's no future here.
Even my kids won't be able to get more than a sixth-grade education.

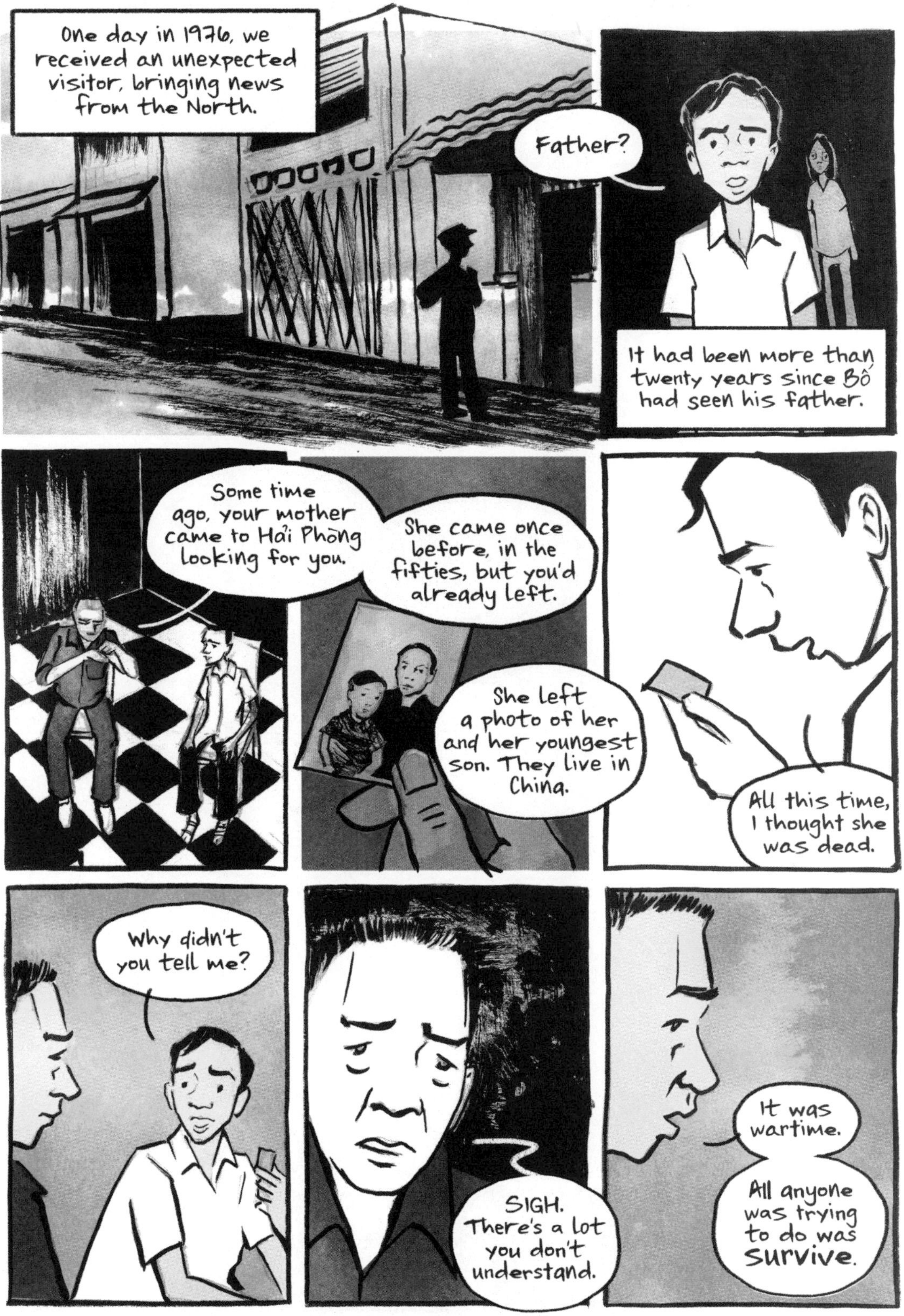
One day in 1976, we received an unexpected visitor, bringing news from the North.
Father?
It had been more than twenty years since Bố had seen his father.
Some time ago, your mother came to Hải Phòng looking for you.
She came once before, in the fifties, but you'd already left.
She left a photo of her and her youngest son. They live in China.
All this time, I thought she was dead.
Why didn't you tell me?
SIGH. There's a lot you don't understand.
It was wartime.
All anyone was trying to do was survive.

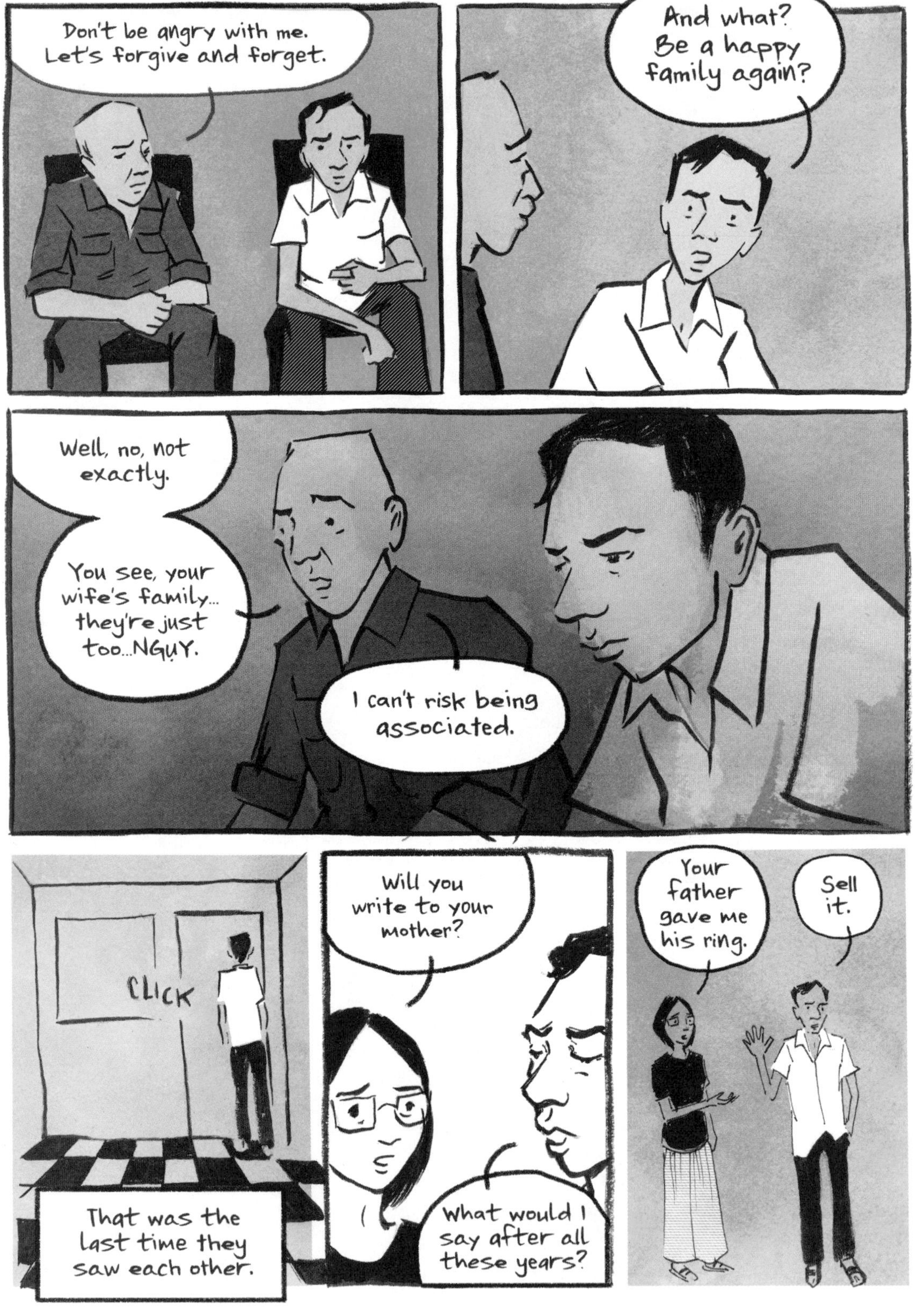
Don't be angry with me. Let's forgive and forget.
And what? Be a happy family again?
Well, no, not exactly.
You see, your wife's family... they're just too...NGỤY.
I can't risk being associated.
CLICK
That was the last time they saw each other.
Will you write to your mother?
What would I say after all these years?
Your father gave me his ring.
Sell it.

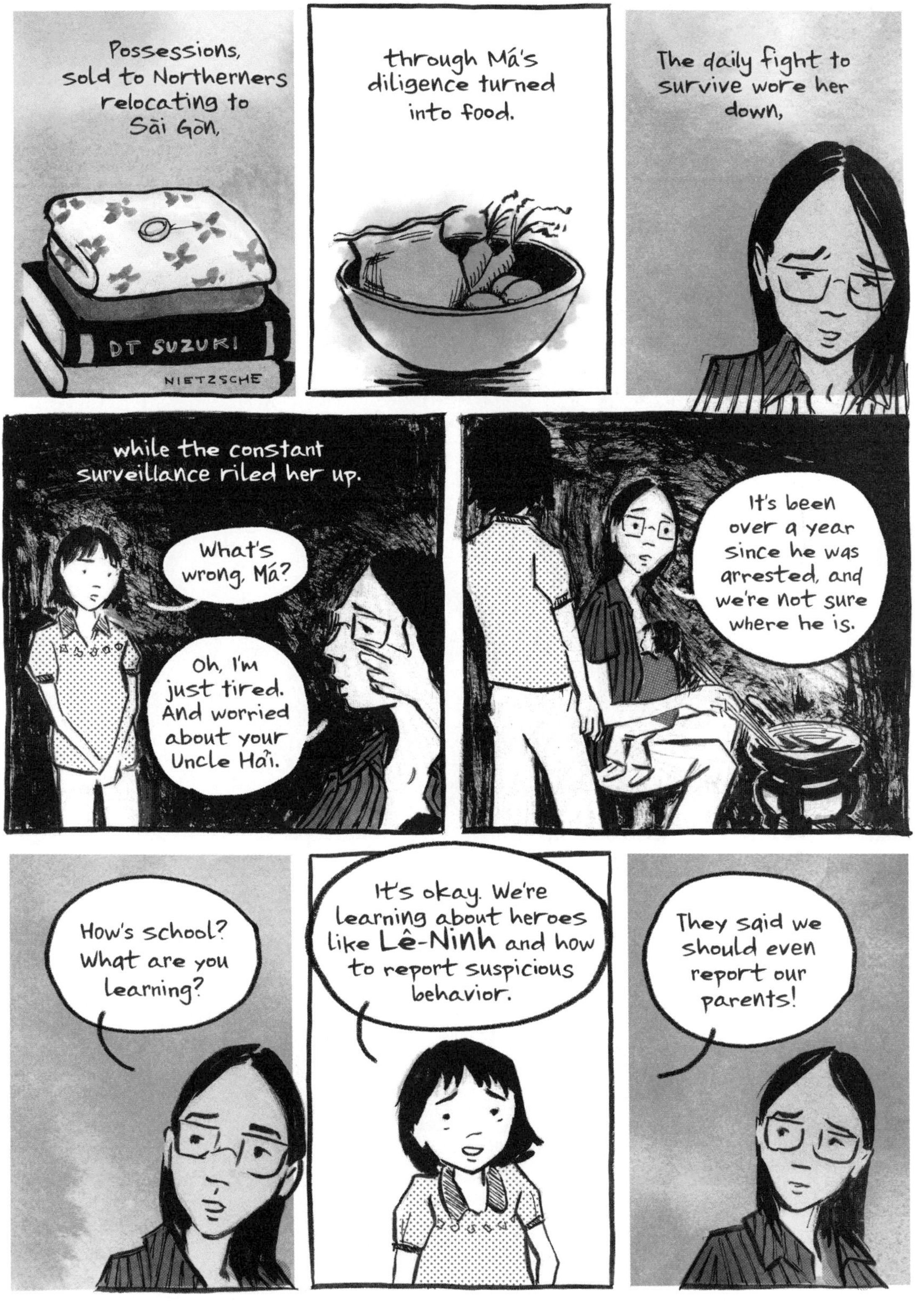

Possessions, sold to Northerners relocating to Sài Gòn,
DT SUZUKI
NIETZSCHE
through Má's diligence turned into food.
The daily fight to survive wore her down,
while the constant surveillance riled her up.
What's wrong, Má?
Oh, I'm just tired. And worried about your Uncle Hải.
It's been over a year since he was arrested, and we're not sure where he is.
How's school? What are you learning?
It's okay. We're learning about heroes like Lê-Ninh and how to report suspicious behavior.
They said we should even report our parents!

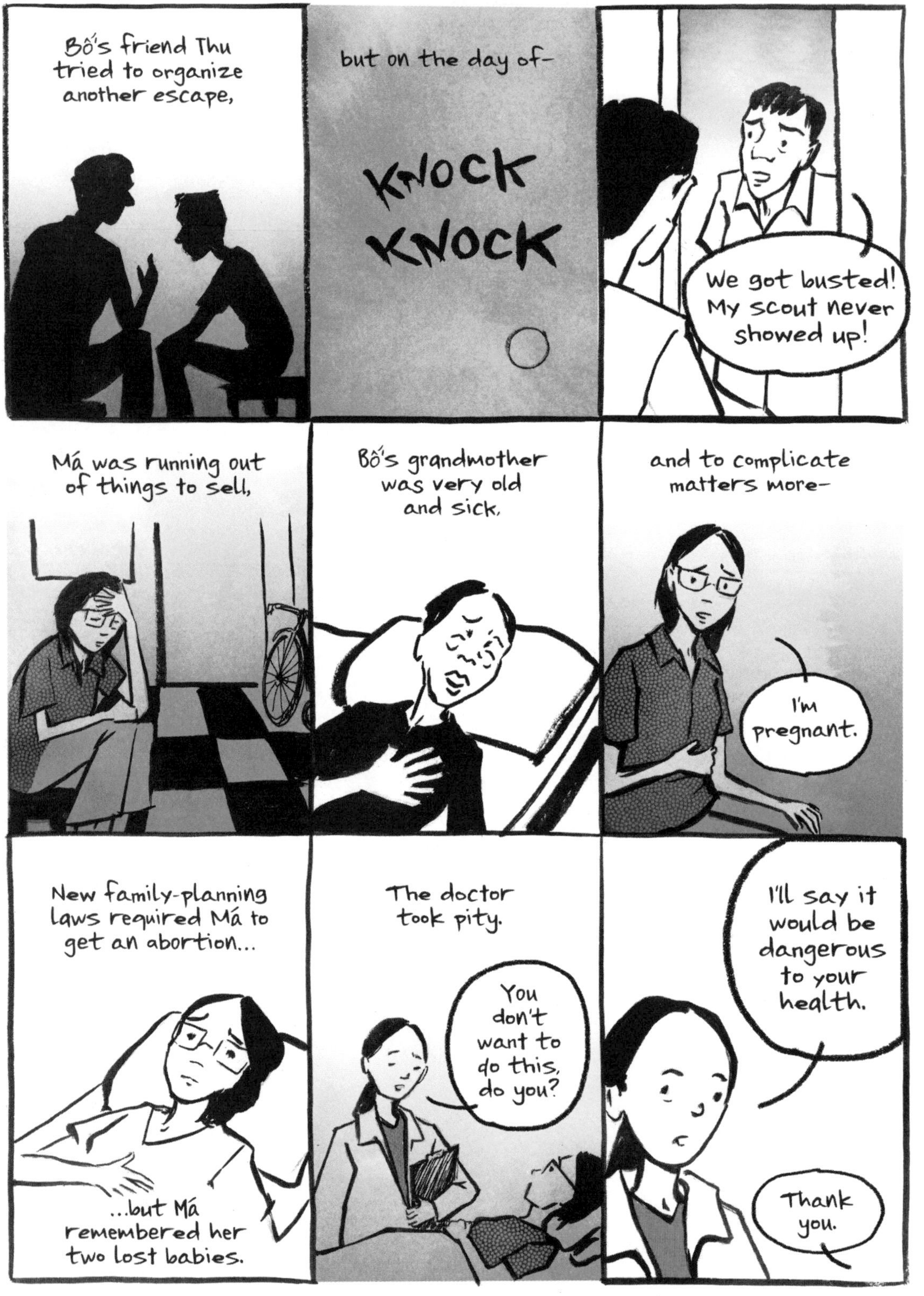
Bố's friend Thu tried to organize another escape,
but on the day of–
KNOCK KNOCK
We got busted! My scout never showed up!
Má was running out of things to sell,
Bố's grandmother was very old and sick,
and to complicate matters more–
I'm pregnant.
New family-planning laws required Má to get an abortion...
...but Má remembered her two lost babies.
The doctor took pity.
You don't want to do this, do you?
I'll say it would be dangerous to your health.
Thank you.

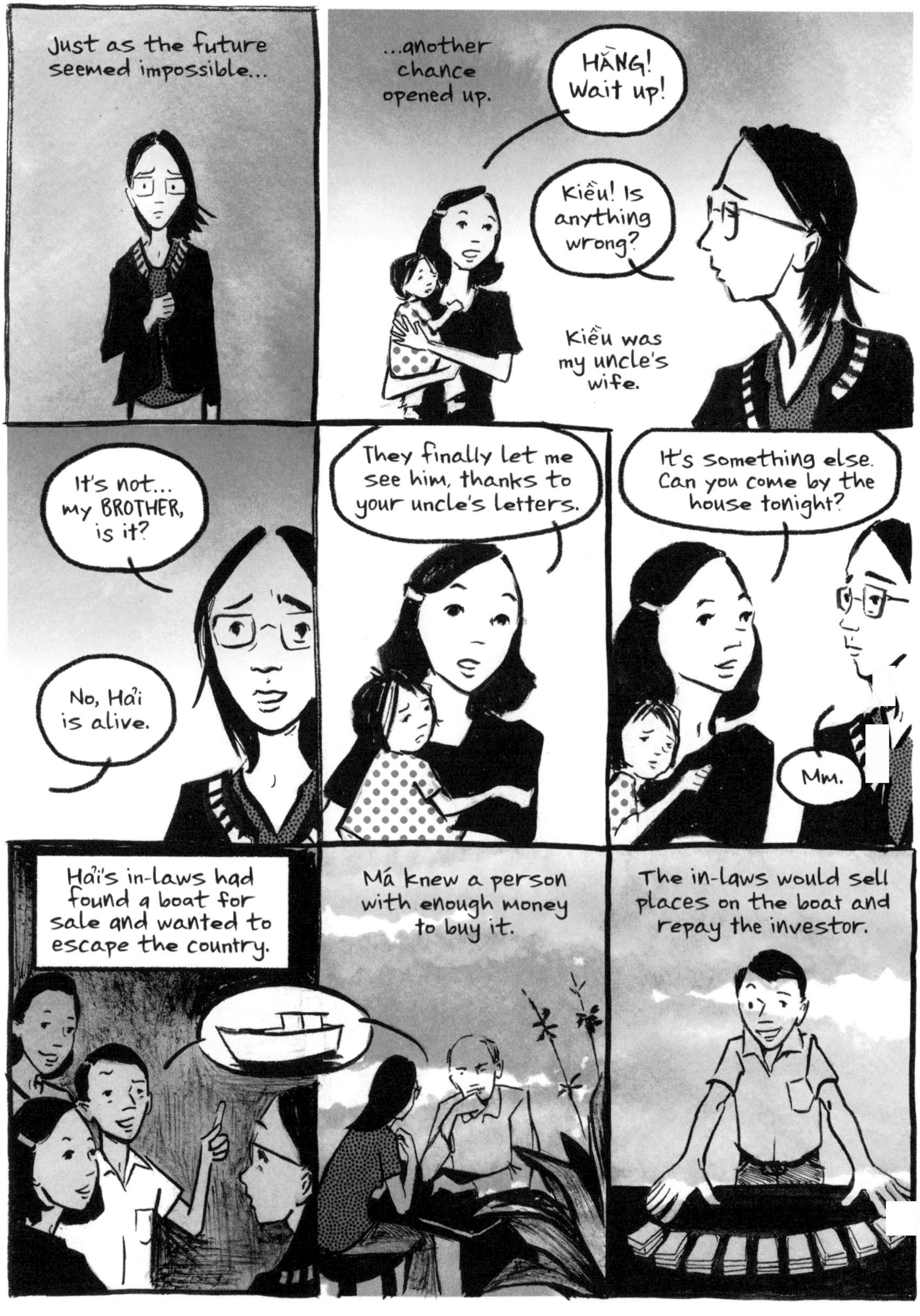

Just as the future seemed impossible...
...another chance opened up.
HẰNG! Wait up!
Kiều! Is anything wrong?
Kiều was my uncle's wife.
It's not... my BROTHER, is it?
No, Hải is alive.
They finally let me see him, thanks to your uncle's letters.
It's something else. Can you come by the house tonight?
Mm.
Hải's in-laws had found a boat for sale and wanted to escape the country.
Má knew a person with enough money to buy it.
The in-laws would sell places on the boat and repay the investor.

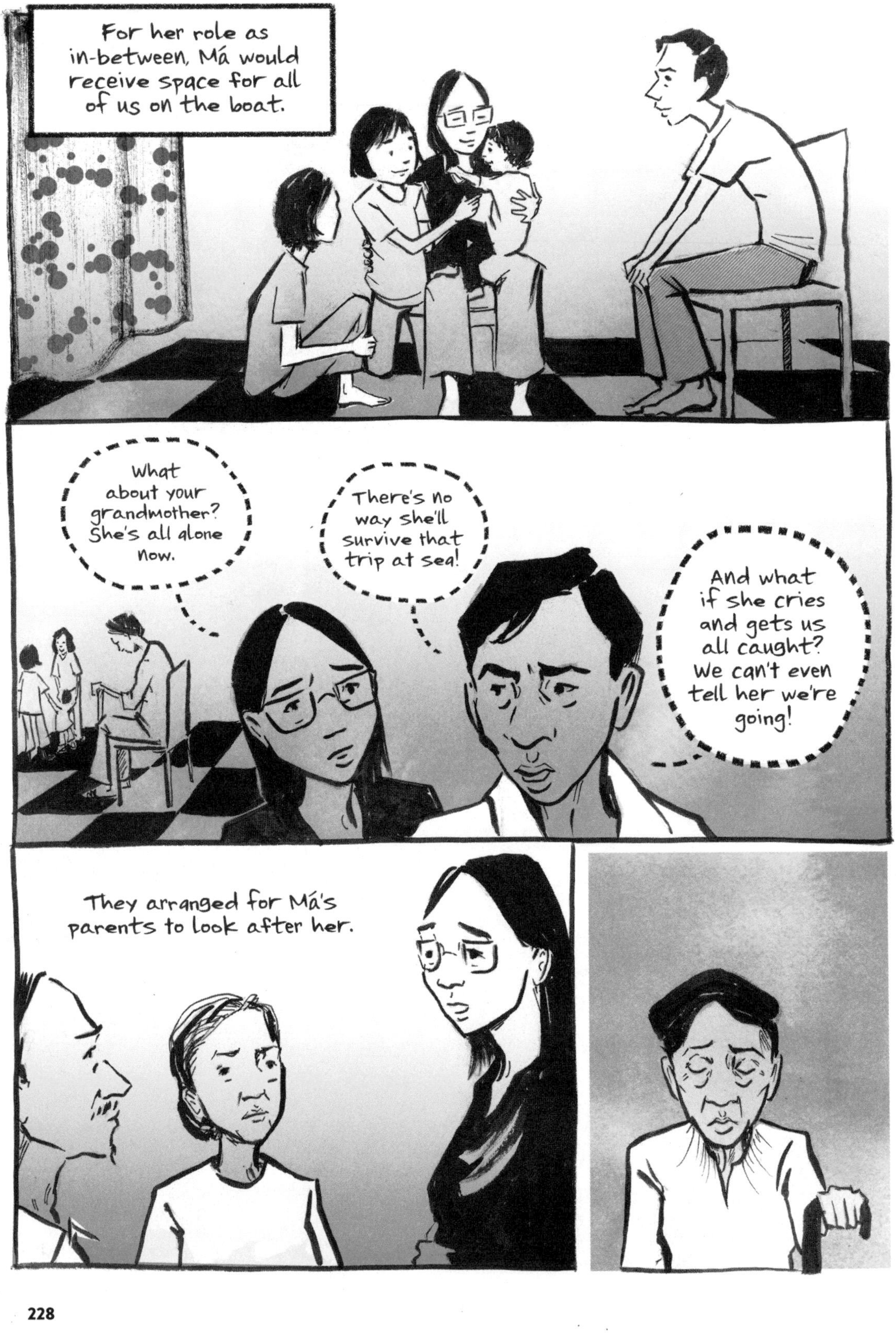
For her role as in-between, Má would receive space for all of us on the boat.
What about your grandmother? She's all alone now.
There's no way she'll survive that trip at sea!
And what if she cries and gets us all caught? We can't even tell her we're going!
They arranged for Má's parents to look after her.

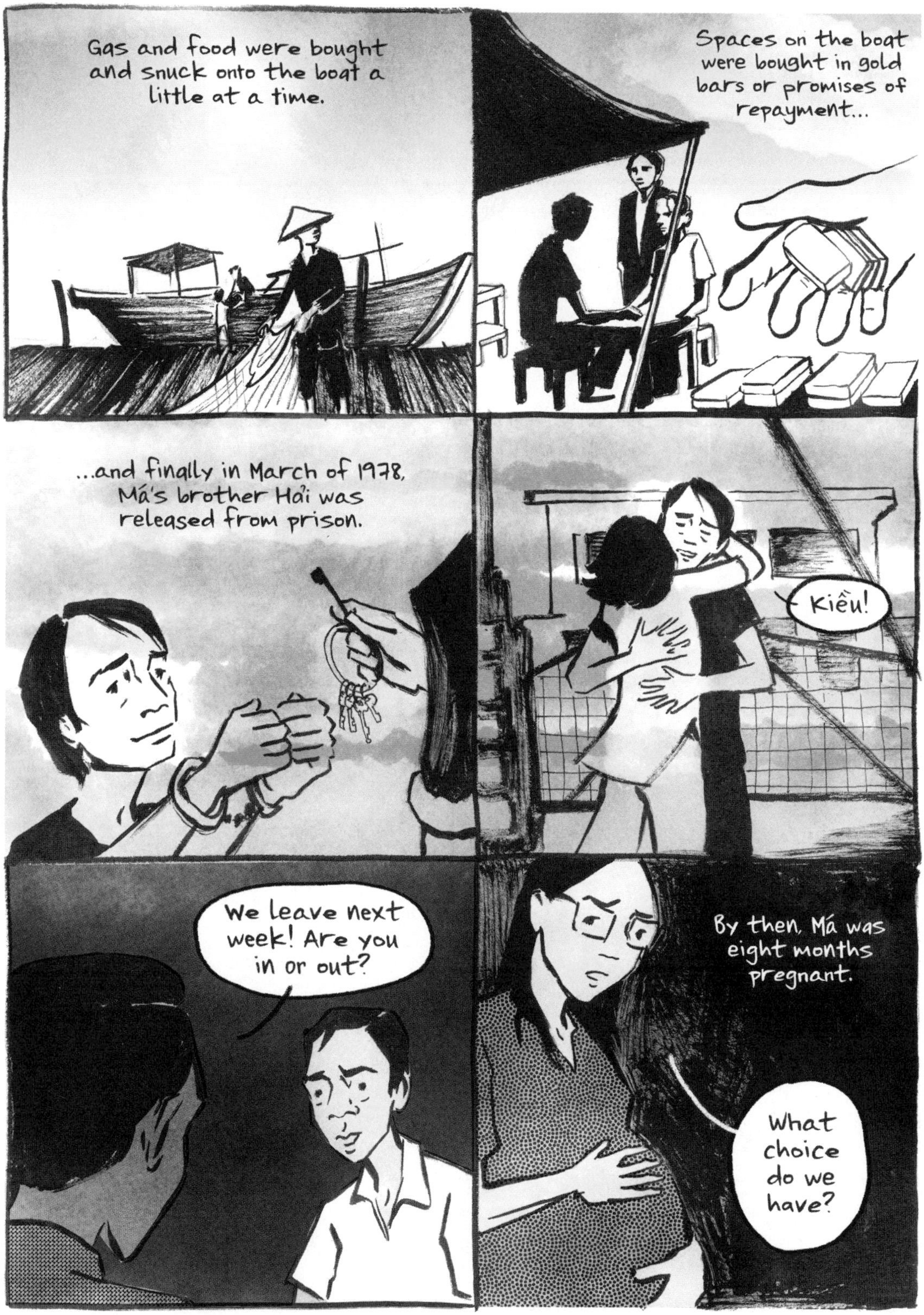
Gas and food were bought and snuck onto the boat a little at a time.
Spaces on the boat were bought in gold bars or promises of repayment...
...and finally in March of 1978, Má's brother Hải was released from prison.
Kiều!
We leave next week! Are you in or out?
By then, Má was eight months pregnant.
What choice do we have?

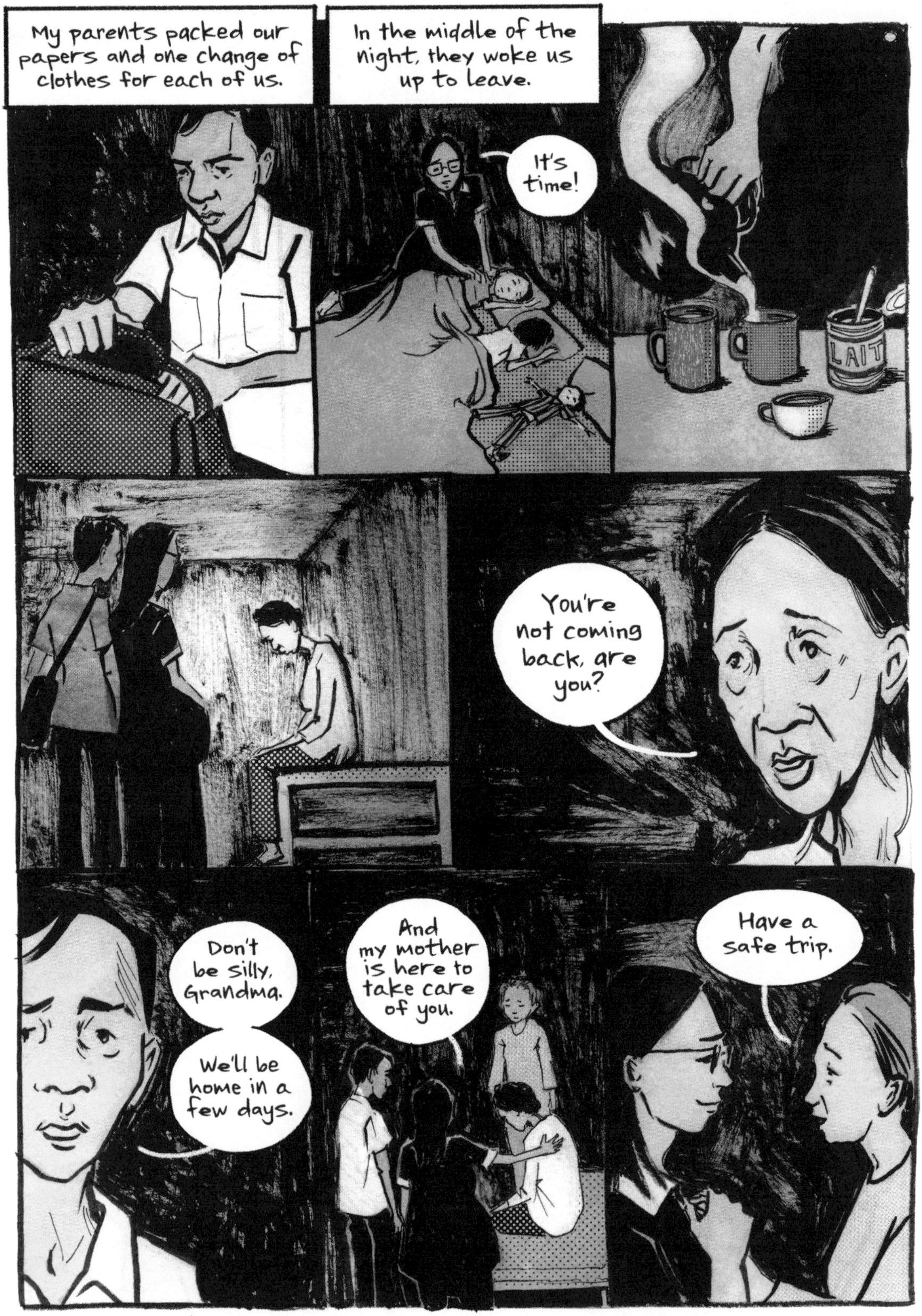
My parents packed our papers and one change of clothes for each of us.
In the middle of the night, they woke us up to leave.
It's time!
LAIT
You're not coming back, are you?
Don't be silly, Grandma.
We'll be home in a few days.
And my mother is here to take care of you.
Have a safe trip.

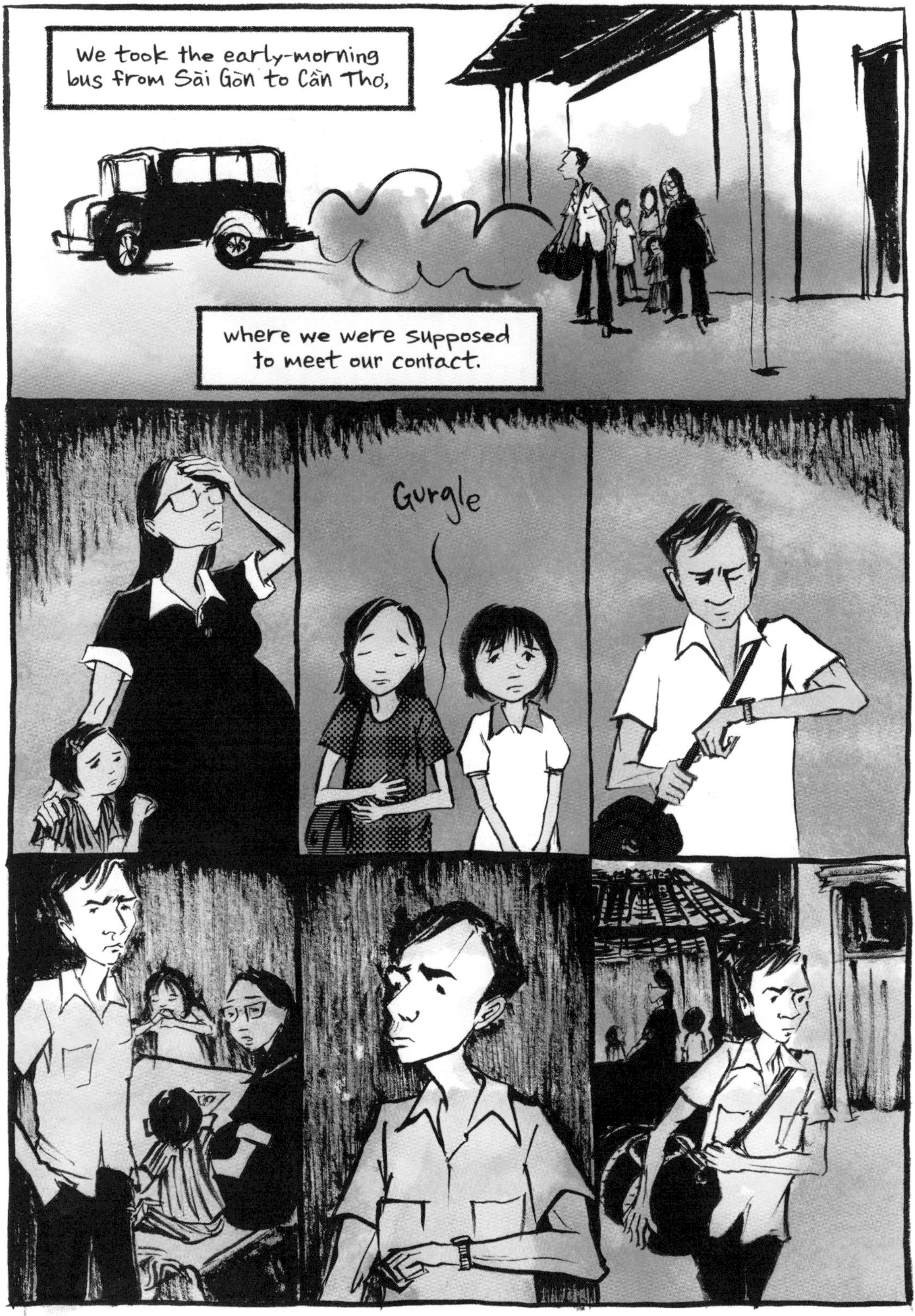
We took the early-morning bus from Sài Gòn to Cần Thơ,
where we were supposed to meet our contact.
Gurgle

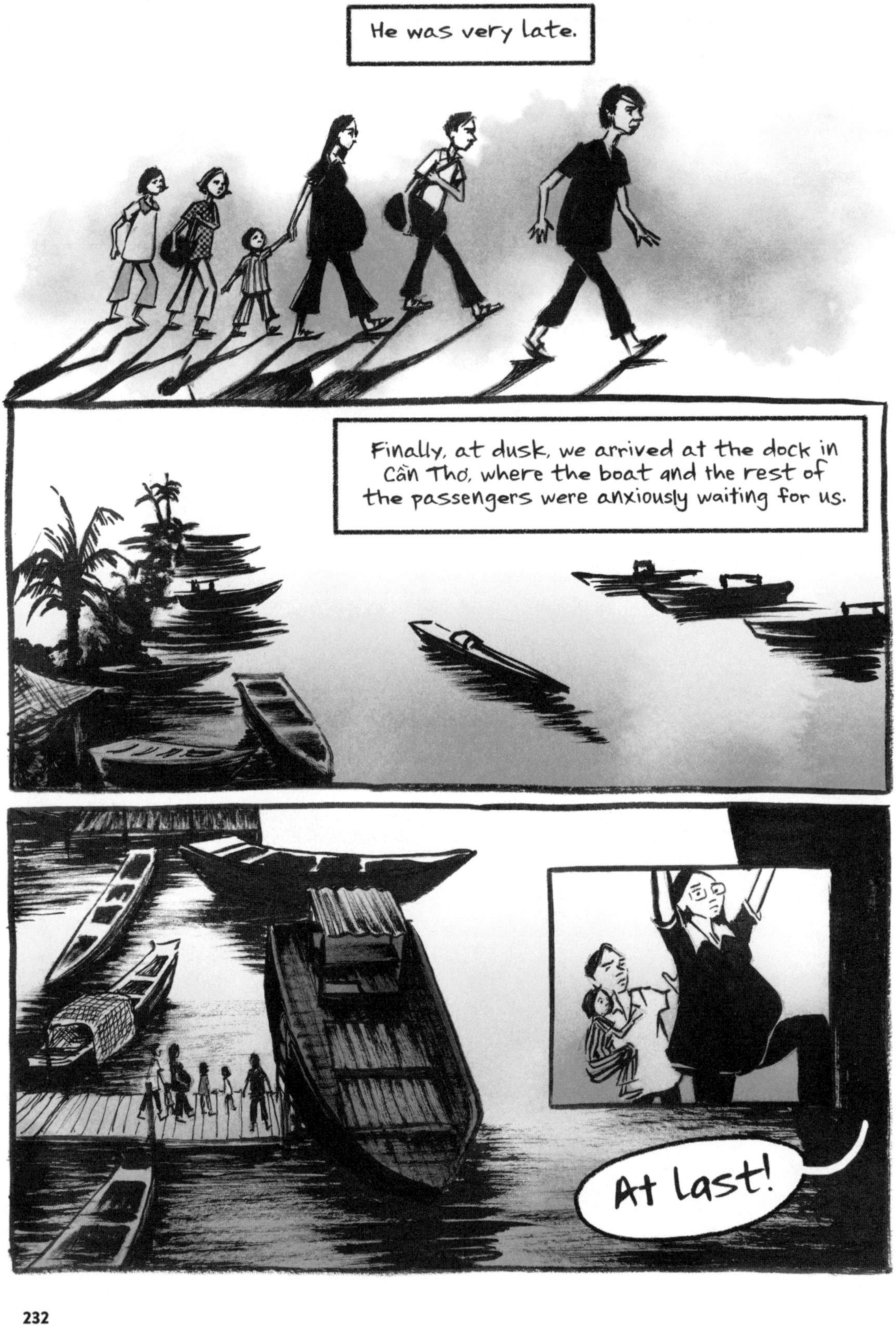
He was very late.
Finally, at dusk, we arrived at the dock in Cần Thơ, where the boat and the rest of the passengers were anxiously waiting for us.
At last!

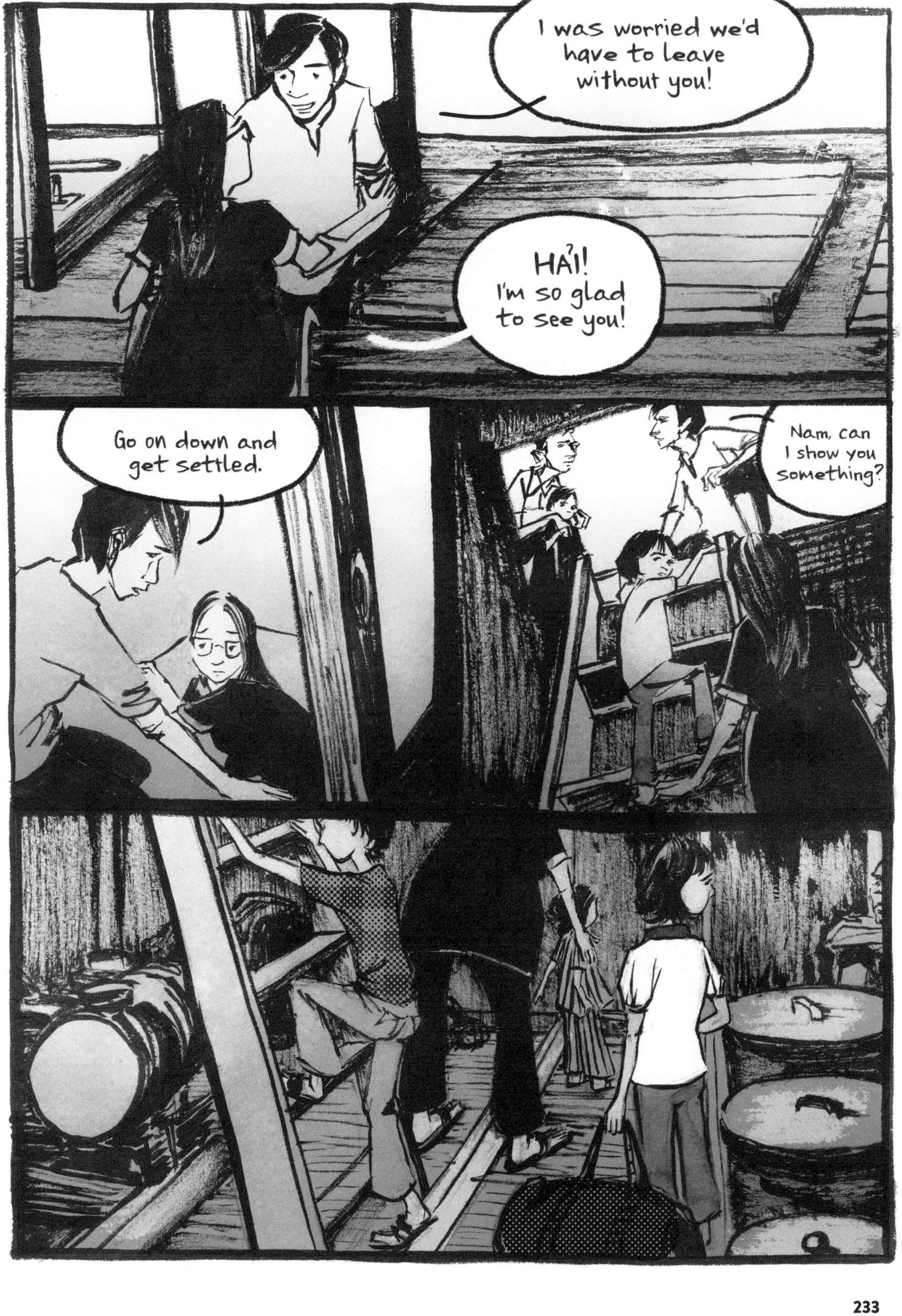
I was worried we'd have to leave without you!
HẢI! I'm so glad to see you!
Go on down and get settled.
Nam, can I show you something?

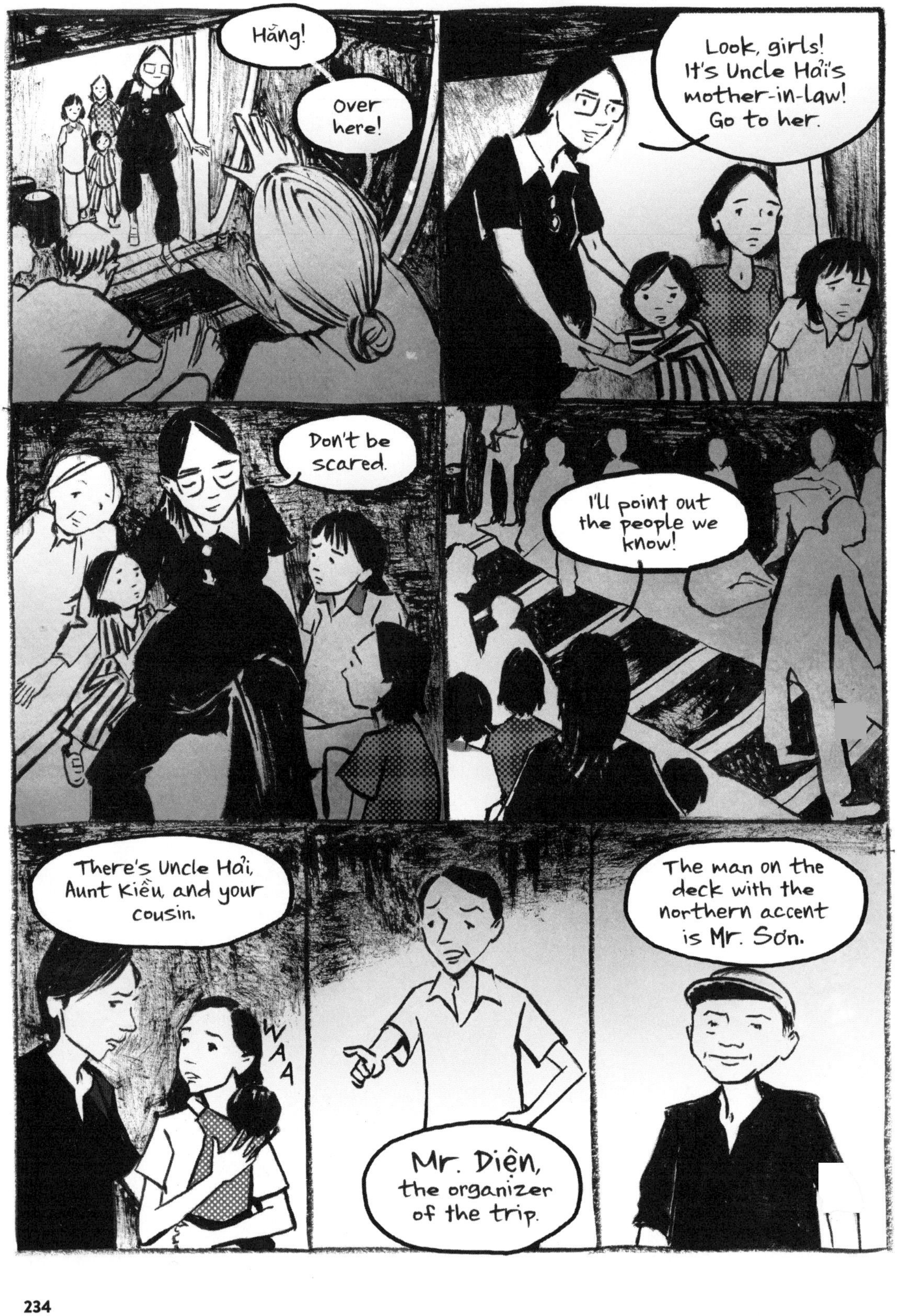
Hằng!
Over here!
Look, girls! It's Uncle Hải's mother-in-law! Go to her.
Don't be scared.
I'll point out the people we know!
There's Uncle Hải, Aunt Kiều, and your cousin.
WAA
Mr. Diện, the organizer of the trip.
The man on the deck with the northern accent is Mr. Sơn.

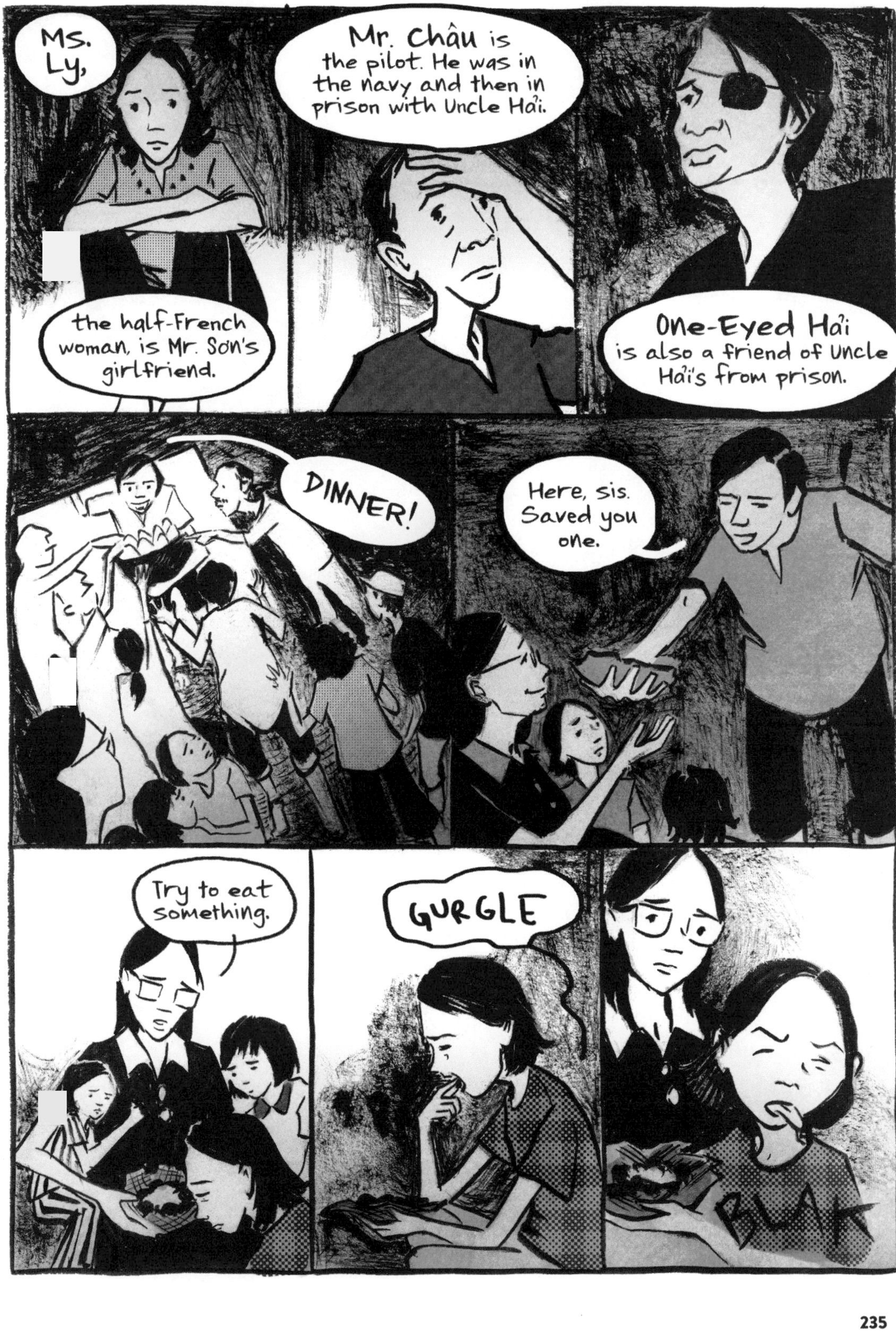
Ms. Ly,
the half-French woman, is Mr. Sơn's girlfriend.
Mr. Châu is the pilot. He was in the navy and then in prison with Uncle Hải.
One-Eyed Hải is also a friend of Uncle Hải's from prison.
DINNER!
Here, sis. Saved you one.
Try to eat something.
GURGLE
BLAK

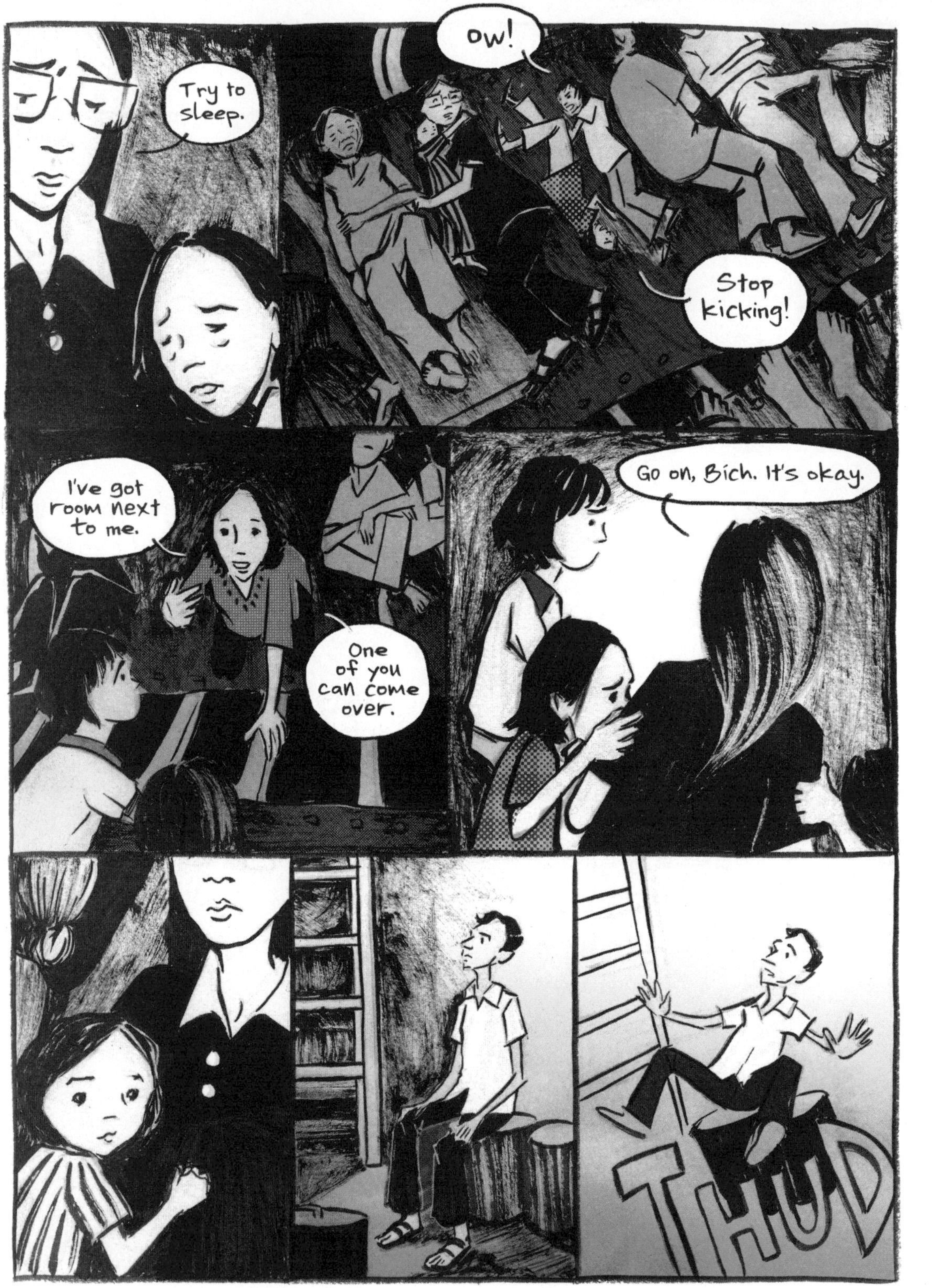
Try to sleep.
Ow!
Stop kicking!
I've got room next to me.
One of you can come over.
Go on, Bich. It's okay.
THUD

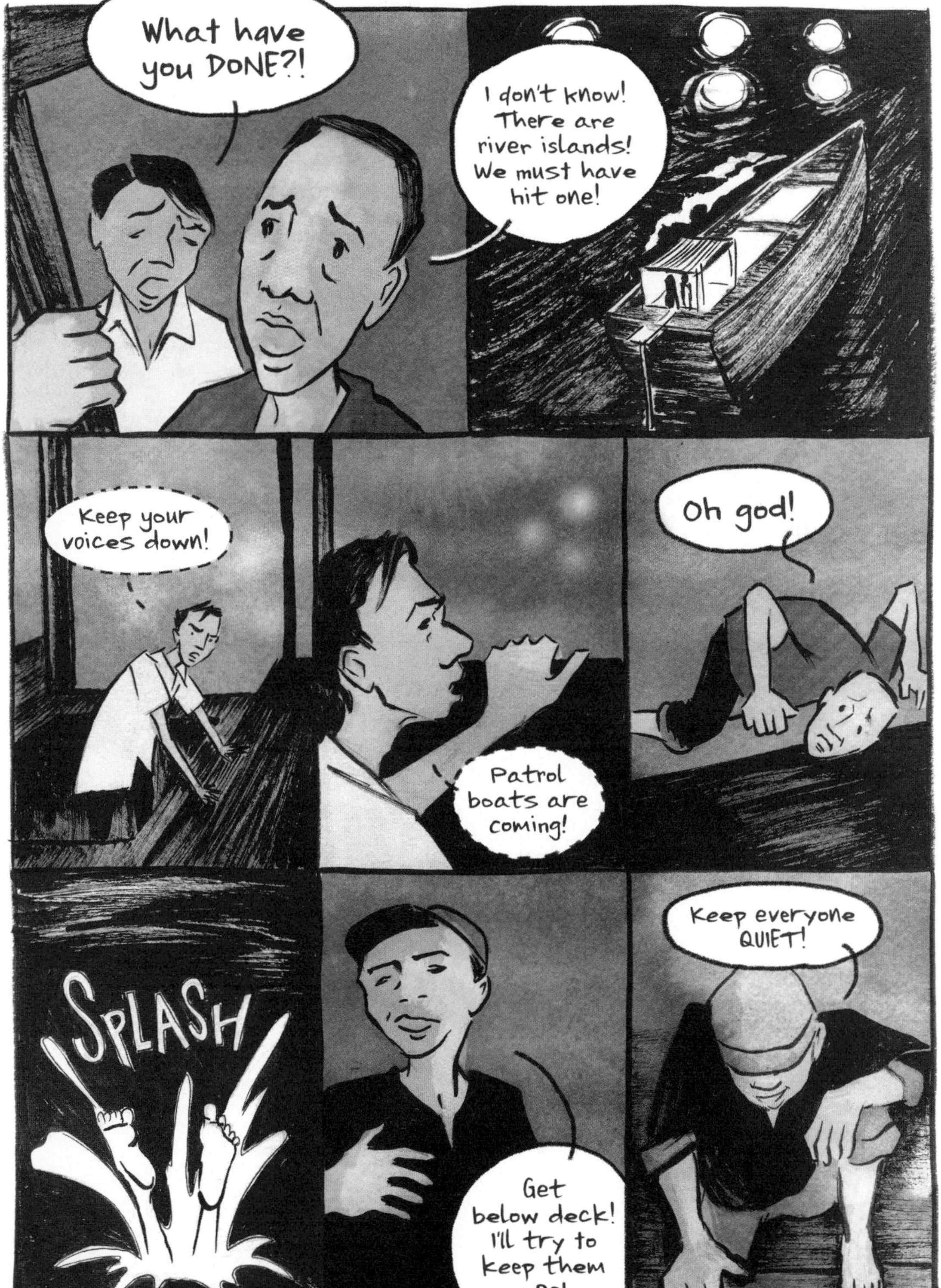
What have you DONE?!
I don't know! There are river islands! We must have hit one!
Keep your voices down!
Patrol boats are coming!
Oh god!
SPLASH
Get below deck! I'll try to keep them off!
Keep everyone QUIET!

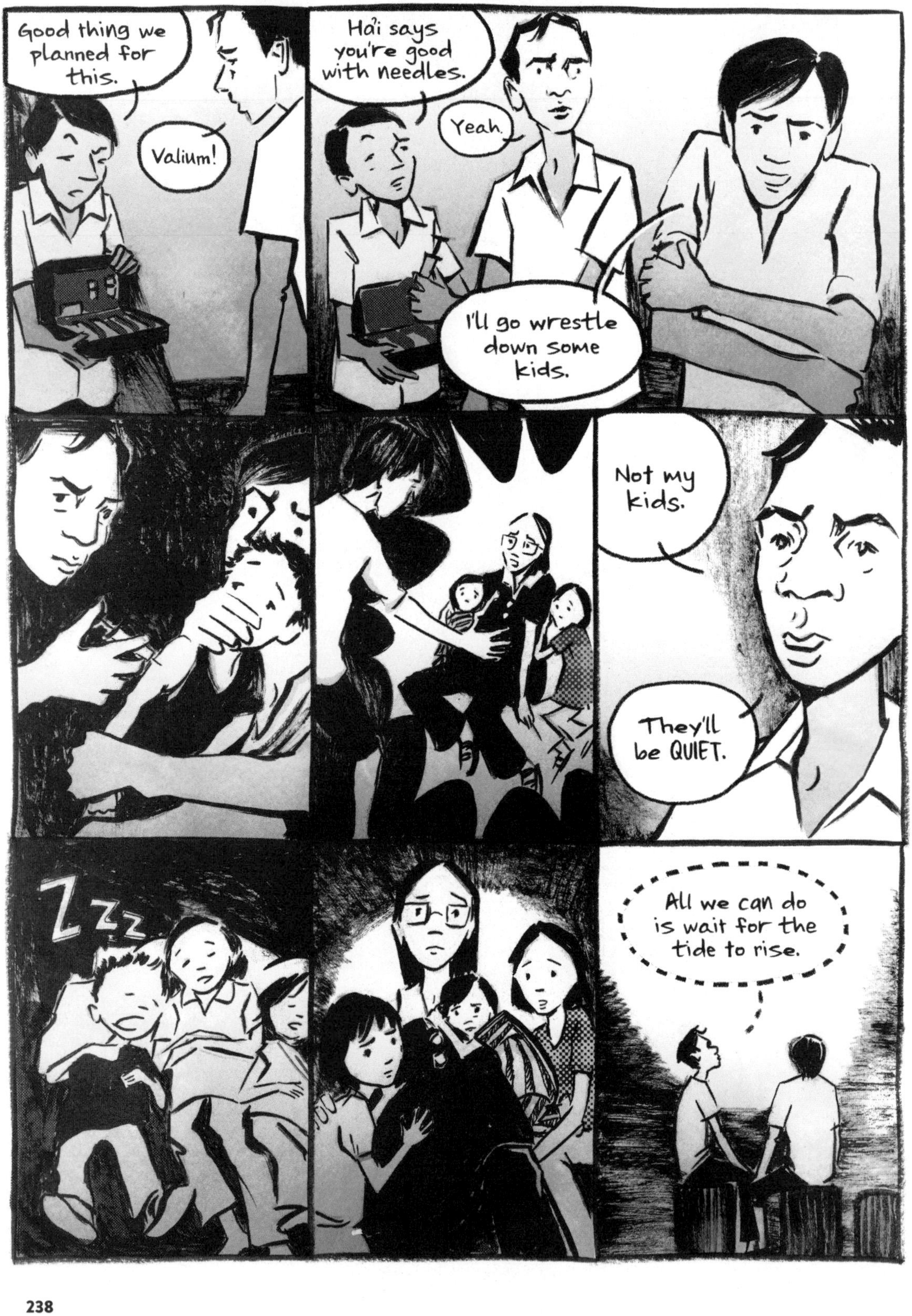
Good thing we planned for this.
Valium!
Hải says you're good with needles.
Yeah.
I'll go wrestle down some kids.
Not my kids.
They'll be QUIET.
ZZZ
All we can do is wait for the tide to rise.

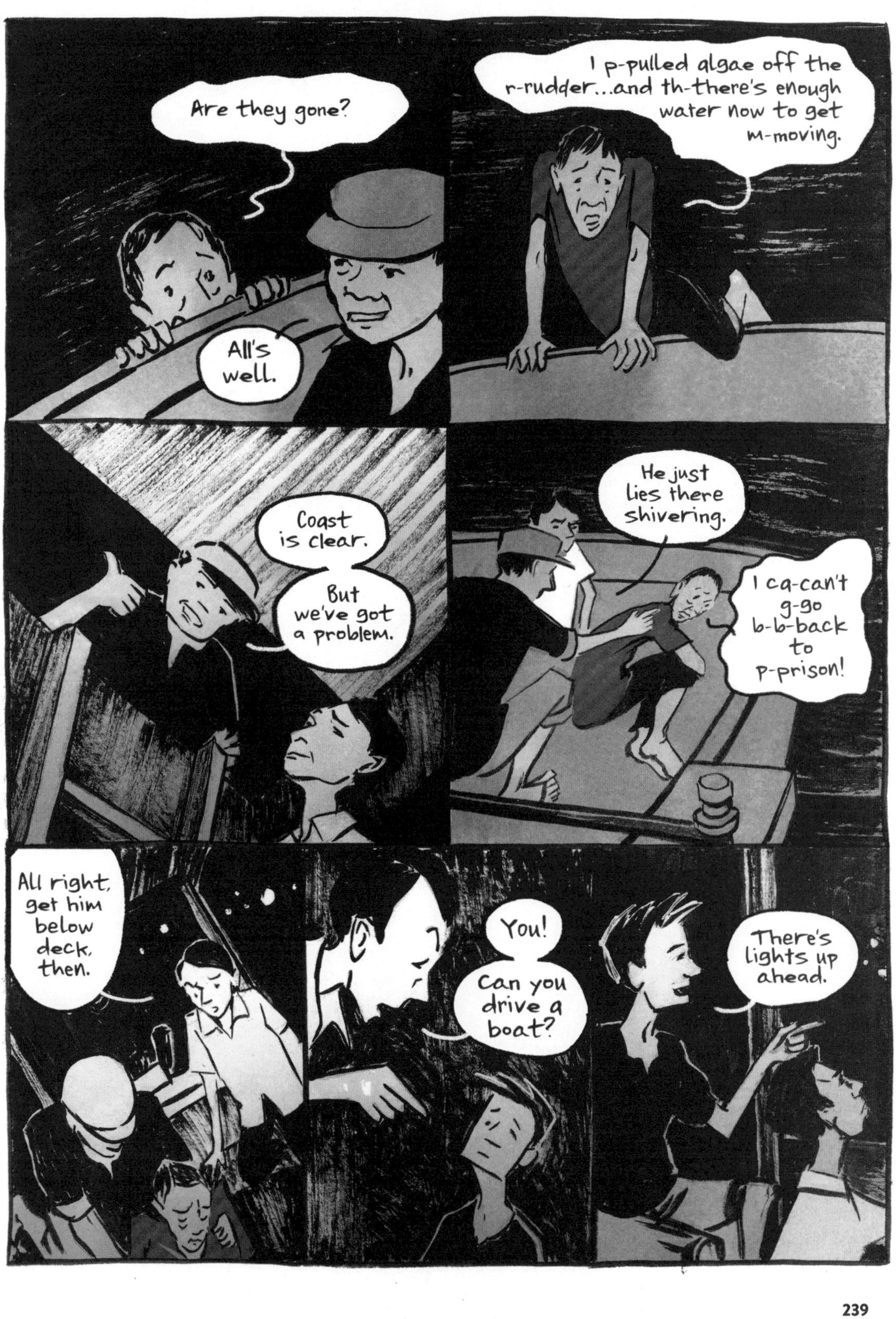
Are they gone?
All's well.
I p-pulled algae off the r-rudder...and th-there's enough water now to get m-moving.
Coast is clear.
But we've got a problem.
He just lies there shivering.
I ca-can't g-go b-b-back to p-prison!
All right, get him below deck, then.
You!
Can you drive a boat?
There's lights up ahead.

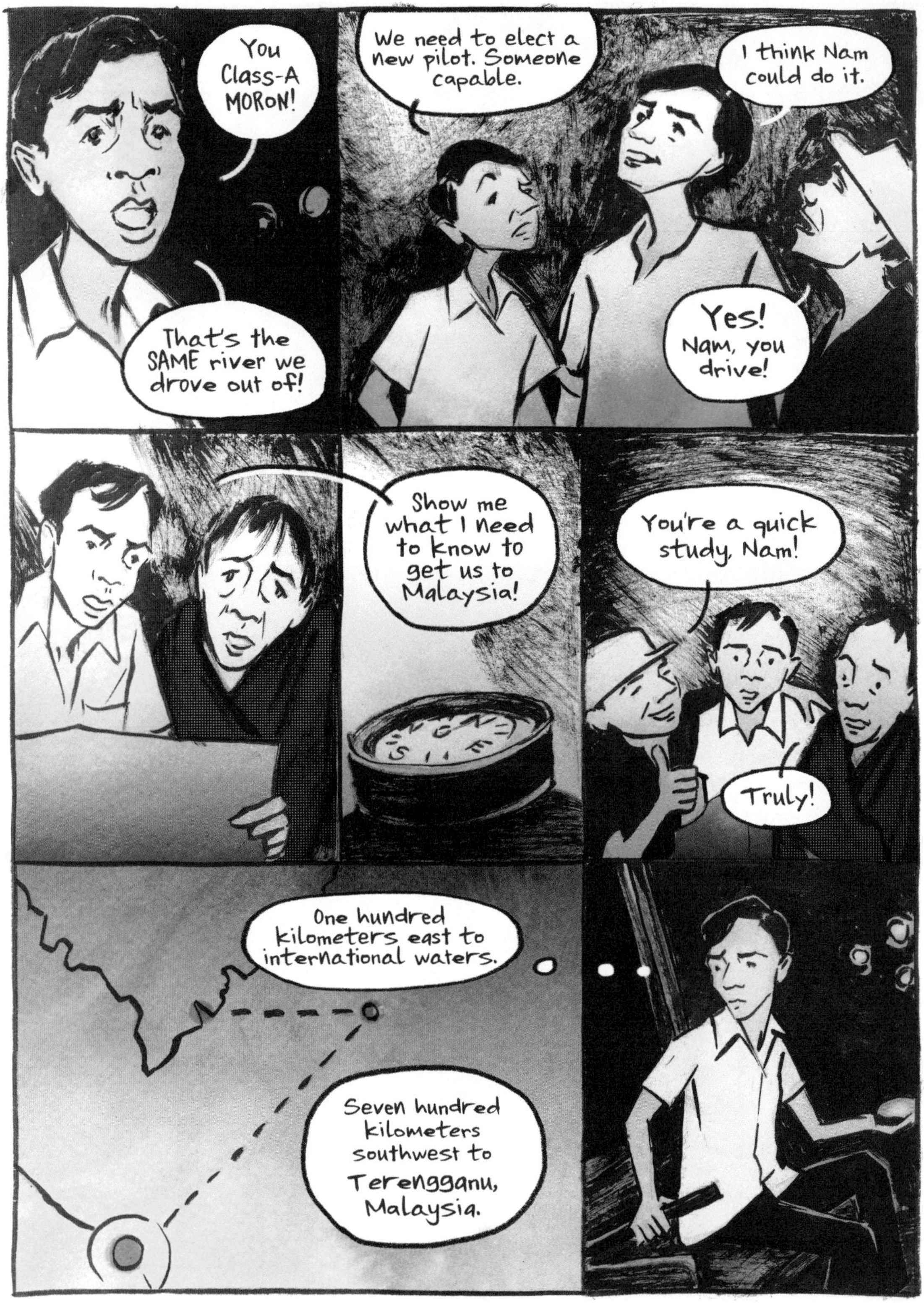
You Class-A MORON!
That's the SAME river we drove out of!
We need to elect a new pilot. Someone capable.
I think Nam could do it.
Yes! Nam, you drive!
Show me what I need to know to get us to Malaysia!
You're a quick study, Nam!
Truly!
One hundred kilometers east to international waters.
Seven hundred kilometers southwest to Terengganu, Malaysia.

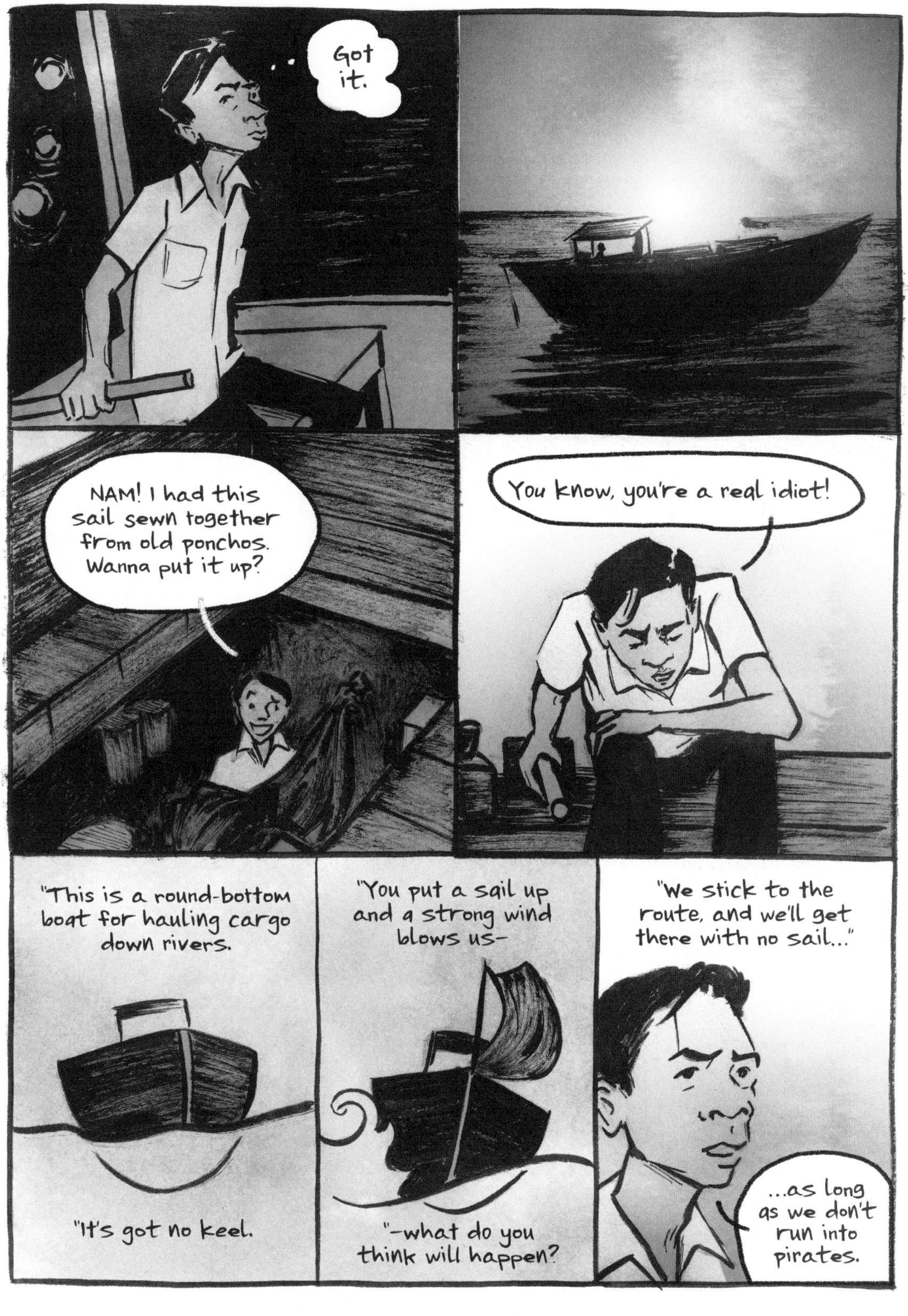
Got it.
NAM! I had this sail sewn together from old ponchos. Wanna put it up?
You know, you're a real idiot!
"This is a round-bottom boat for hauling cargo down rivers.
"It's got no keel.
"You put a sail up and a strong wind blows us-
"-what do you think will happen?
"We stick to the route, and we'll get there with no sail..."
...as long as we don't run into pirates.

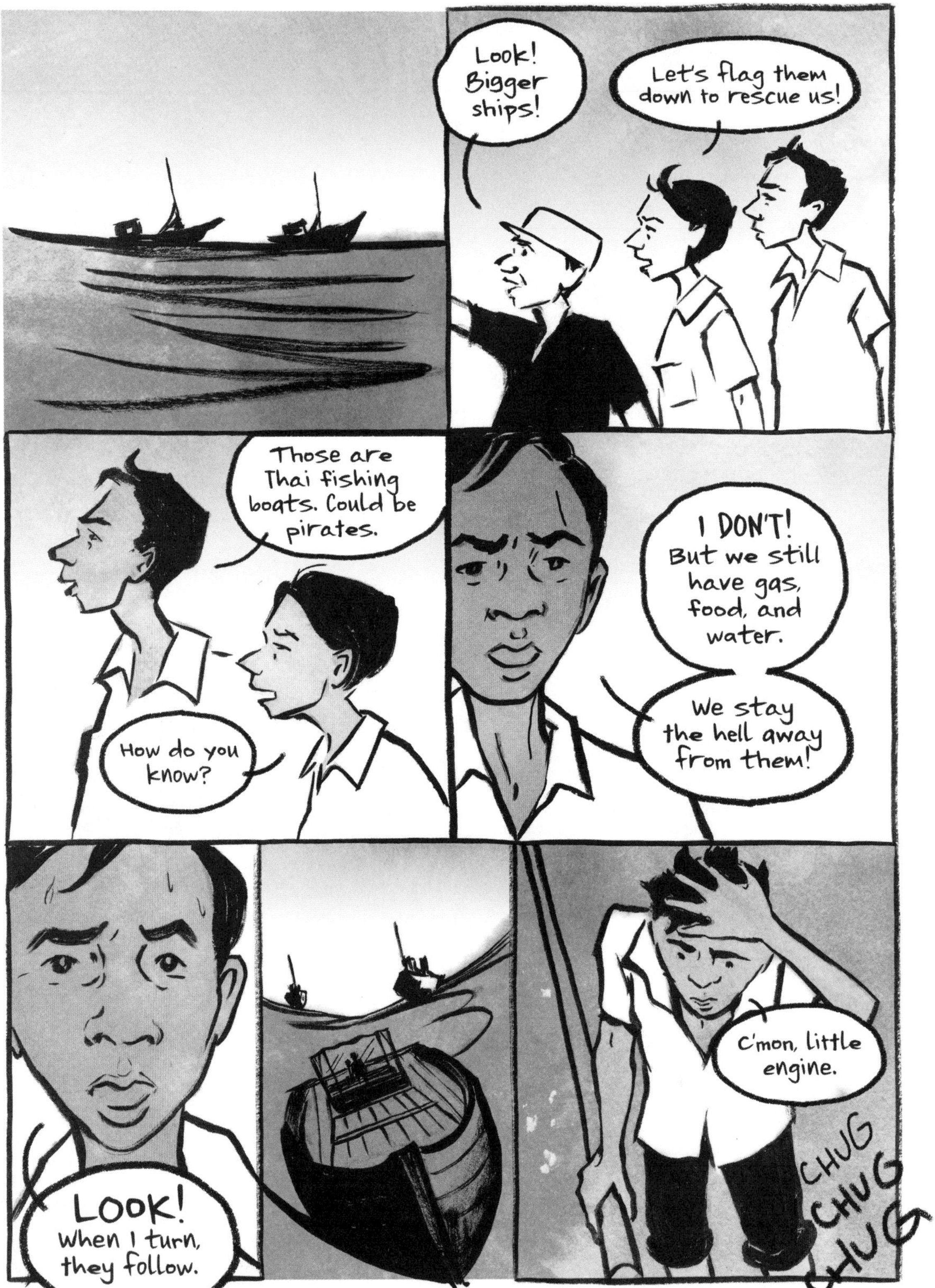
Look! Bigger ships!
Let's flag them down to rescue us!
Those are Thai fishing boats. Could be pirates.
How do you know?
I DON'T! But we still have gas, food, and water.
We stay the hell away from them!
LOOK! When I turn, they follow.
C'mon, little engine.
CHUG CHUG CHUG

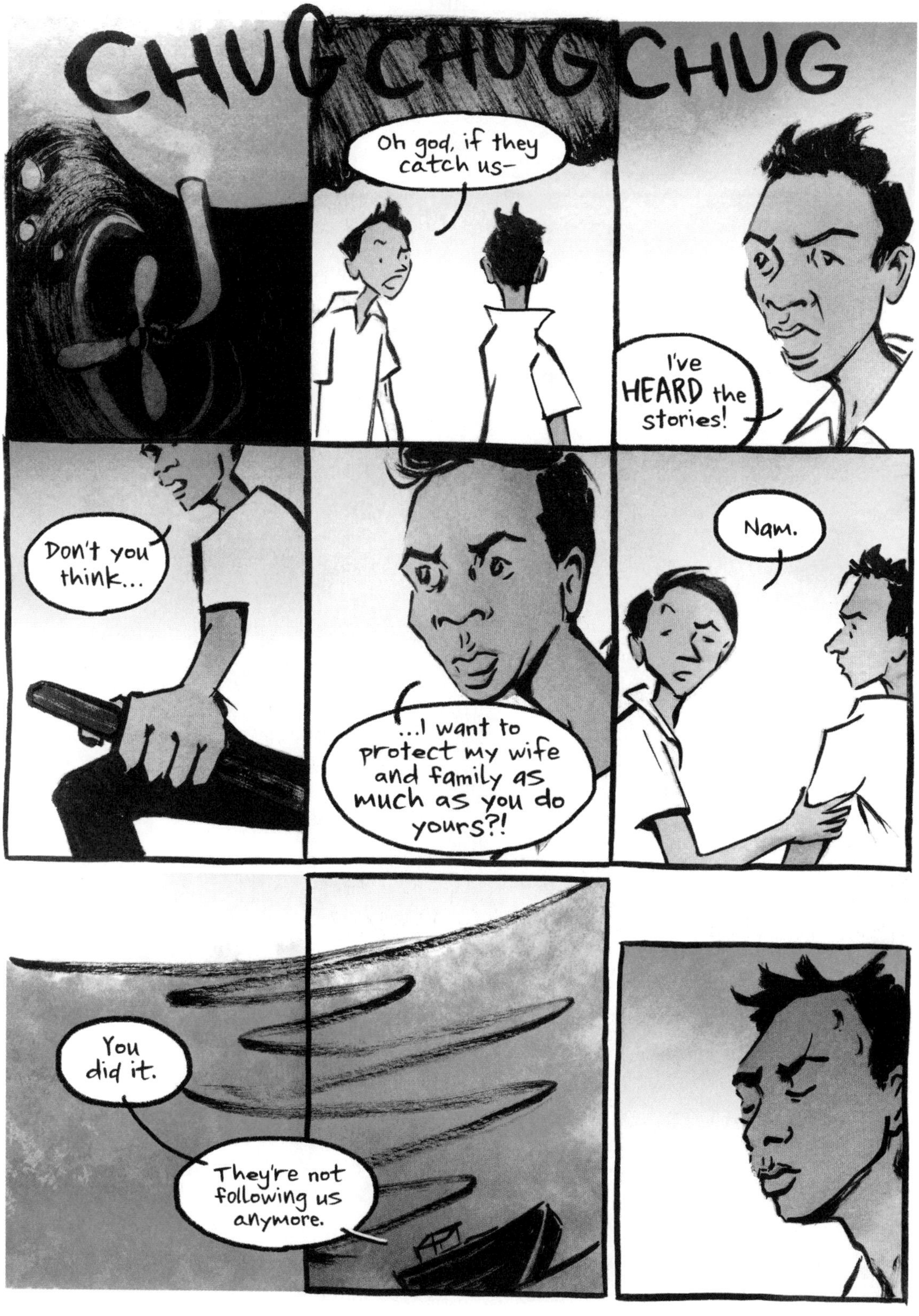

CHUG CHUG CHUG
Oh god, if they catch us–
I've HEARD the stories!
Don't you think...
...I want to protect my wife and family as much as you do yours?!
Nam.
You did it.
They're not following us anymore.

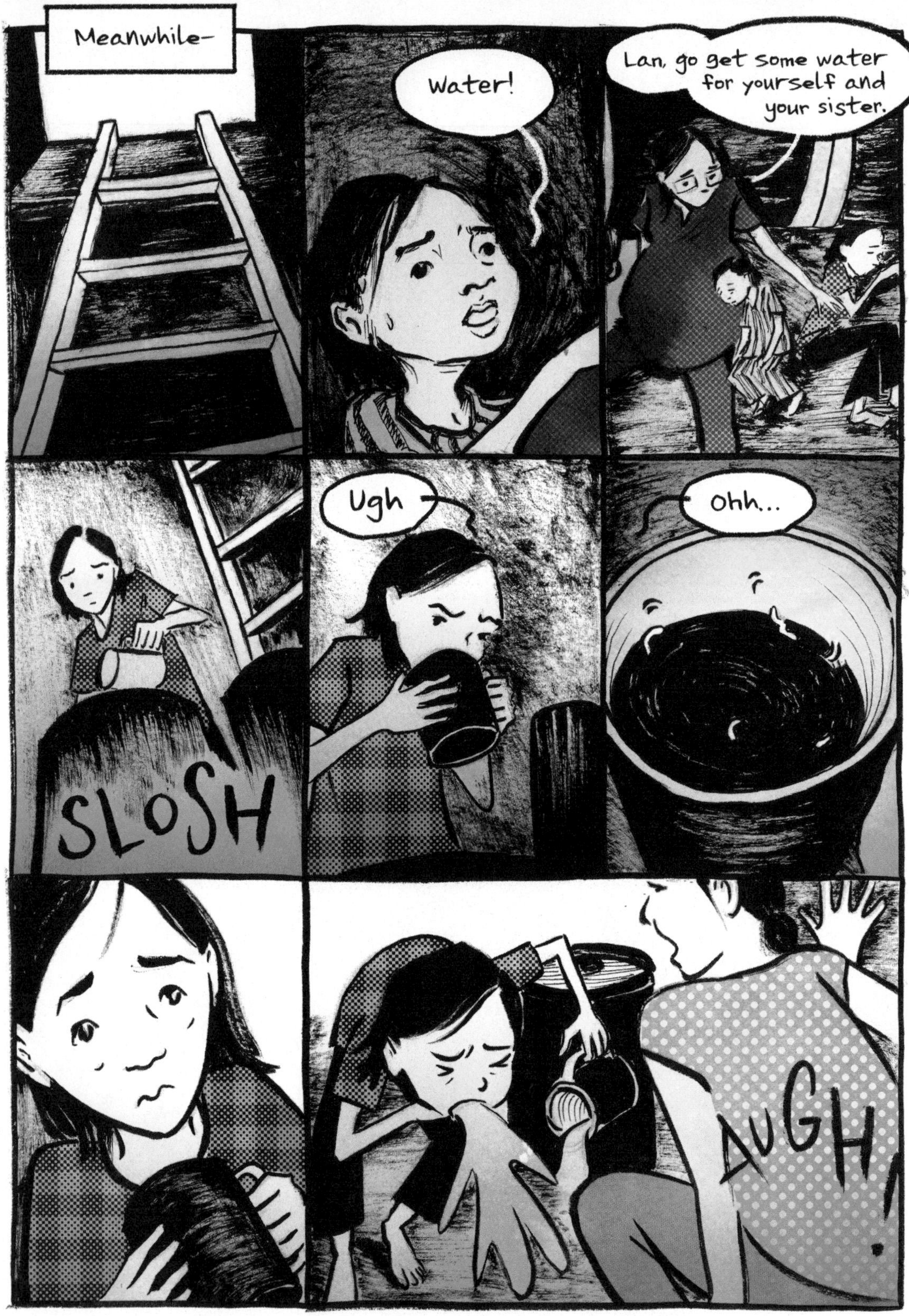
Meanwhile-
Water!
Lan, go get some water for yourself and your sister.
SLOSH
Ugh
Ohh...
AUGH!

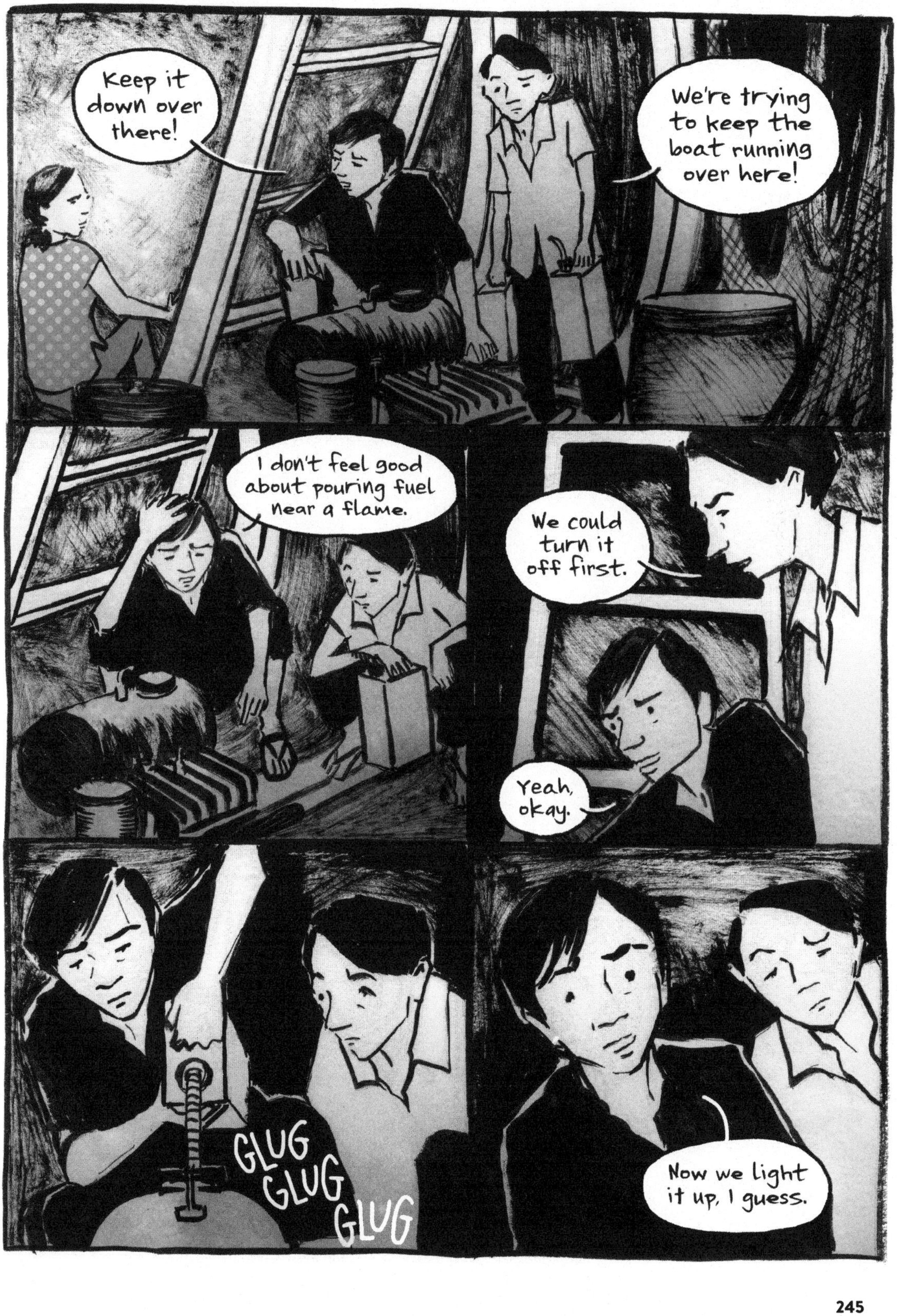
Keep it down over there!
We're trying to keep the boat running over here!
I don't feel good about pouring fuel near a flame.
We could turn it off first.
Yeah, okay.
GLUG GLUG GLUG
Now we light it up, I guess.

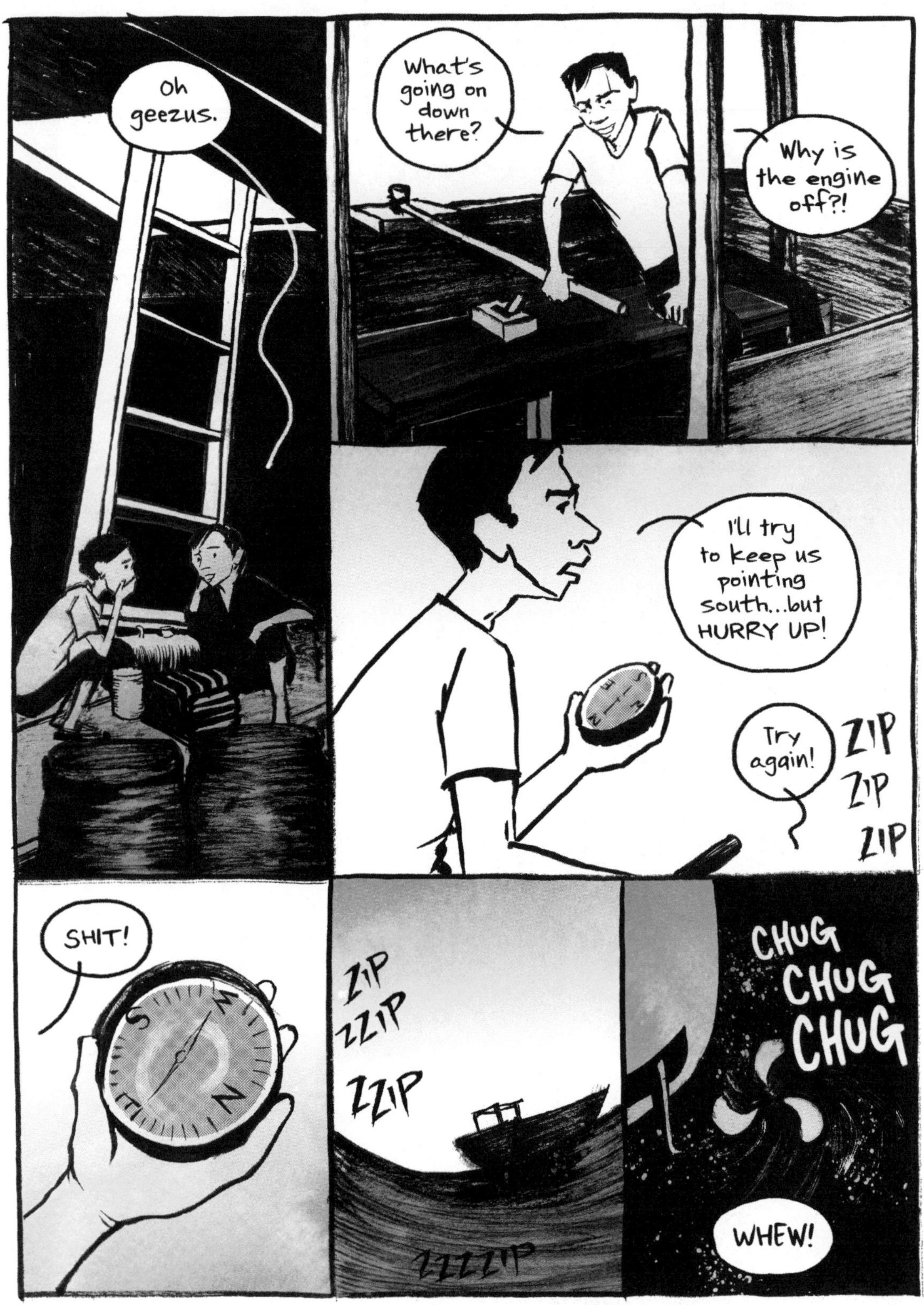
Oh geezus.
What's going on down there?
Why is the engine off?!
I'll try to keep us pointing south...but HURRY UP!
Try again!
ZIP
ZIP
ZIP
SHIT!
ZIP
ZZIP
ZZIP
ZZZZIP
CHUG
CHUG
CHUG
WHEW!

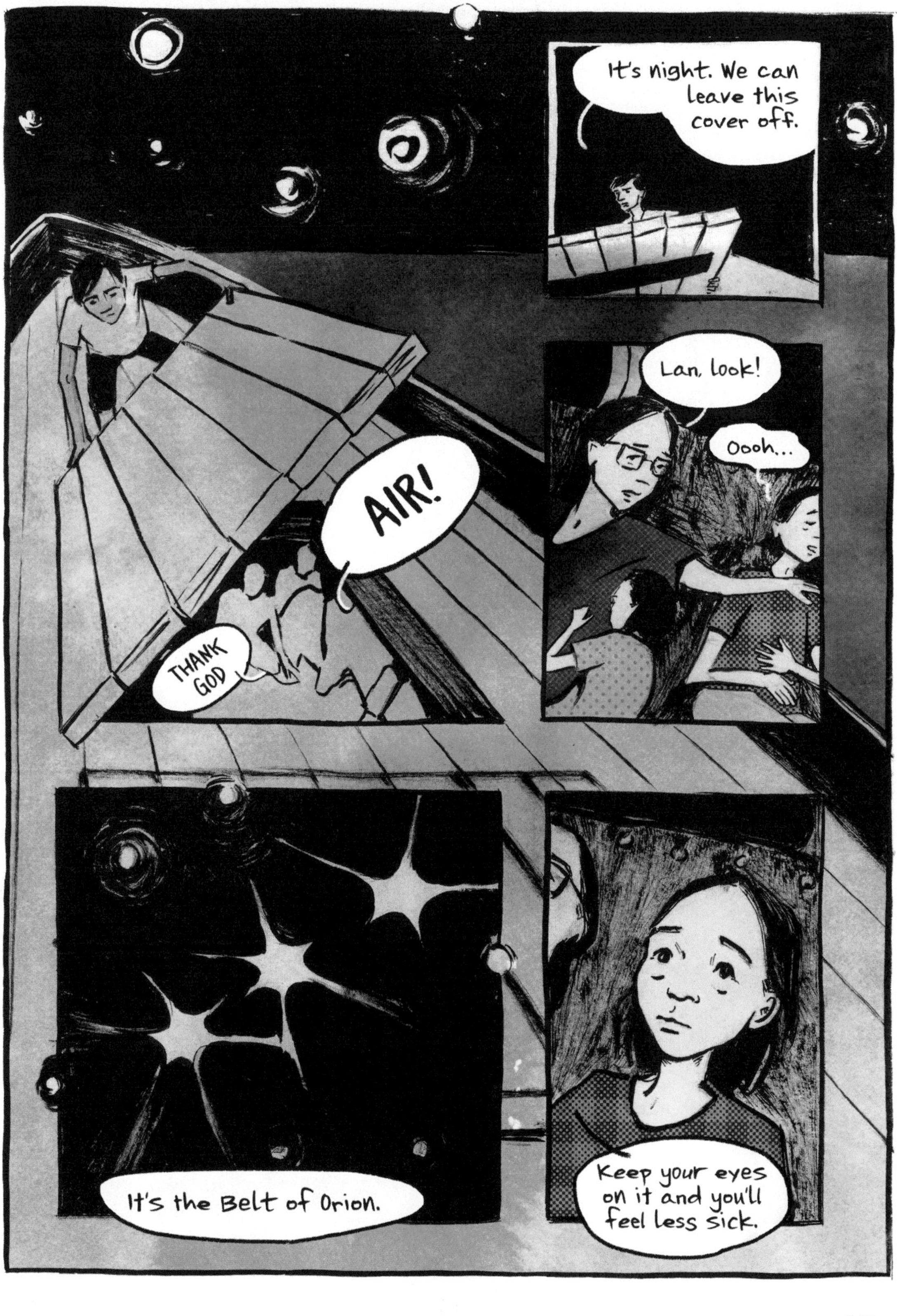
It's night. We can leave this cover off.
AIR!
THANK GOD
Lan, look!
Oooh...
It's the Belt of Orion.
Keep your eyes on it and you'll feel less sick.

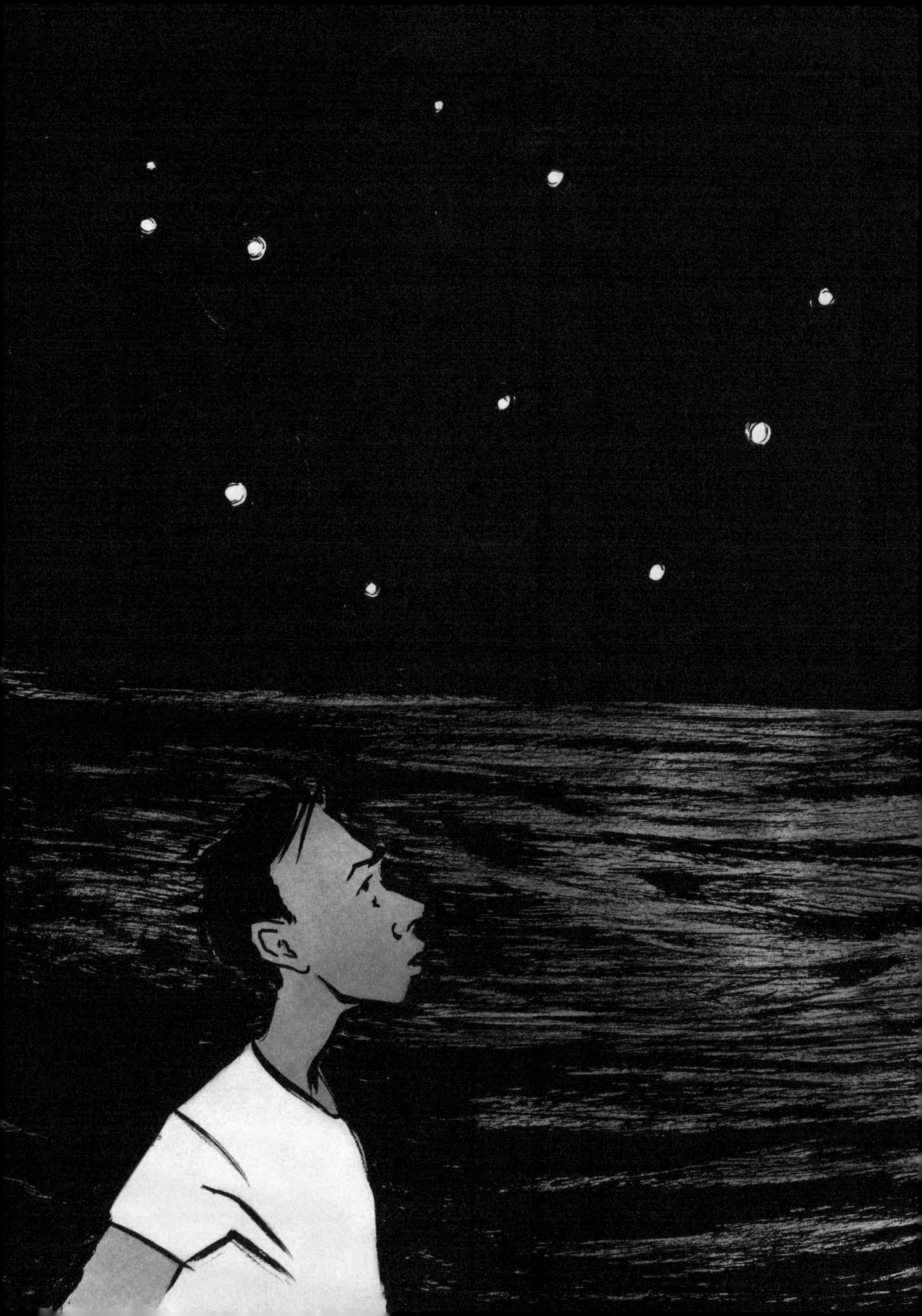

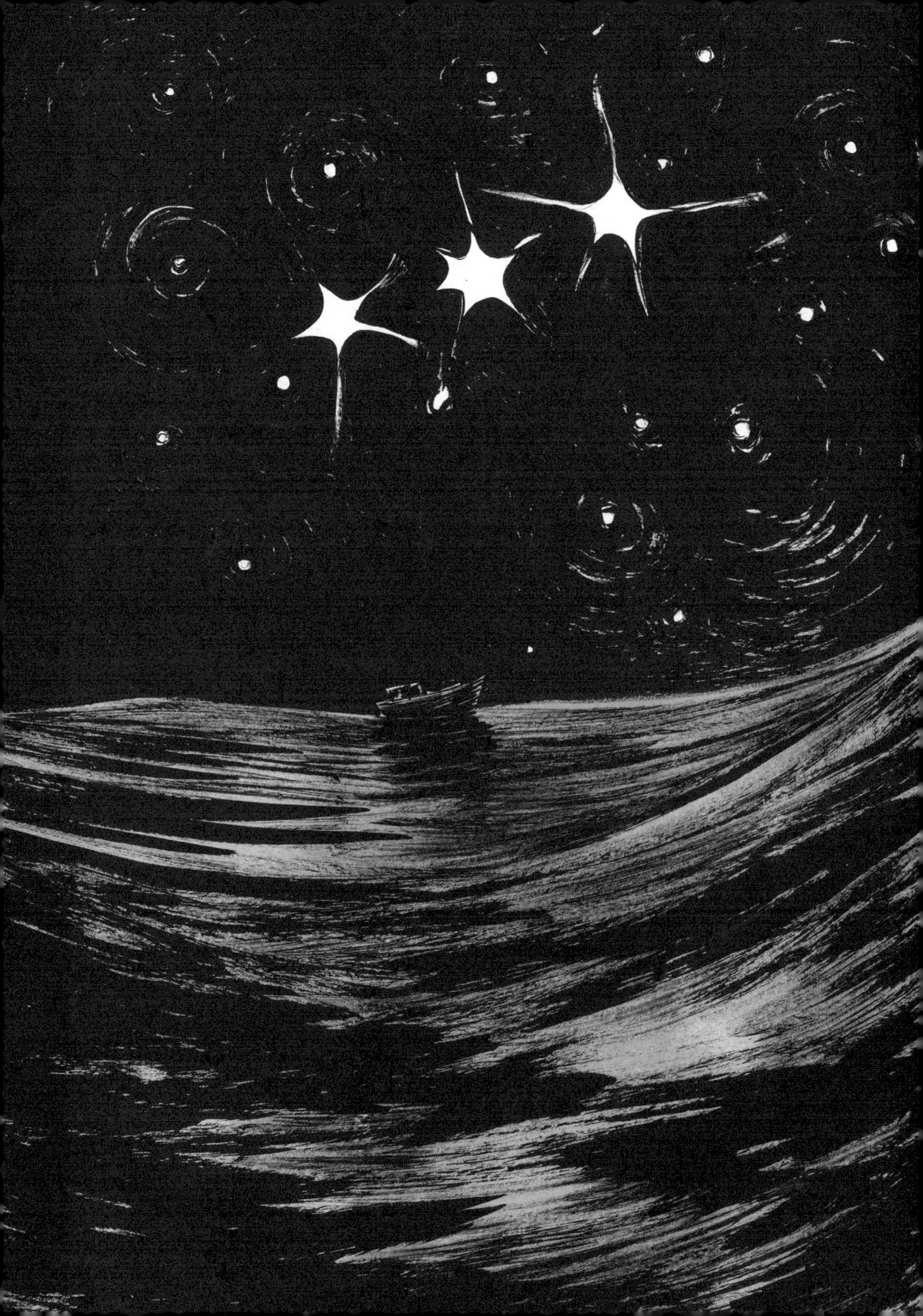

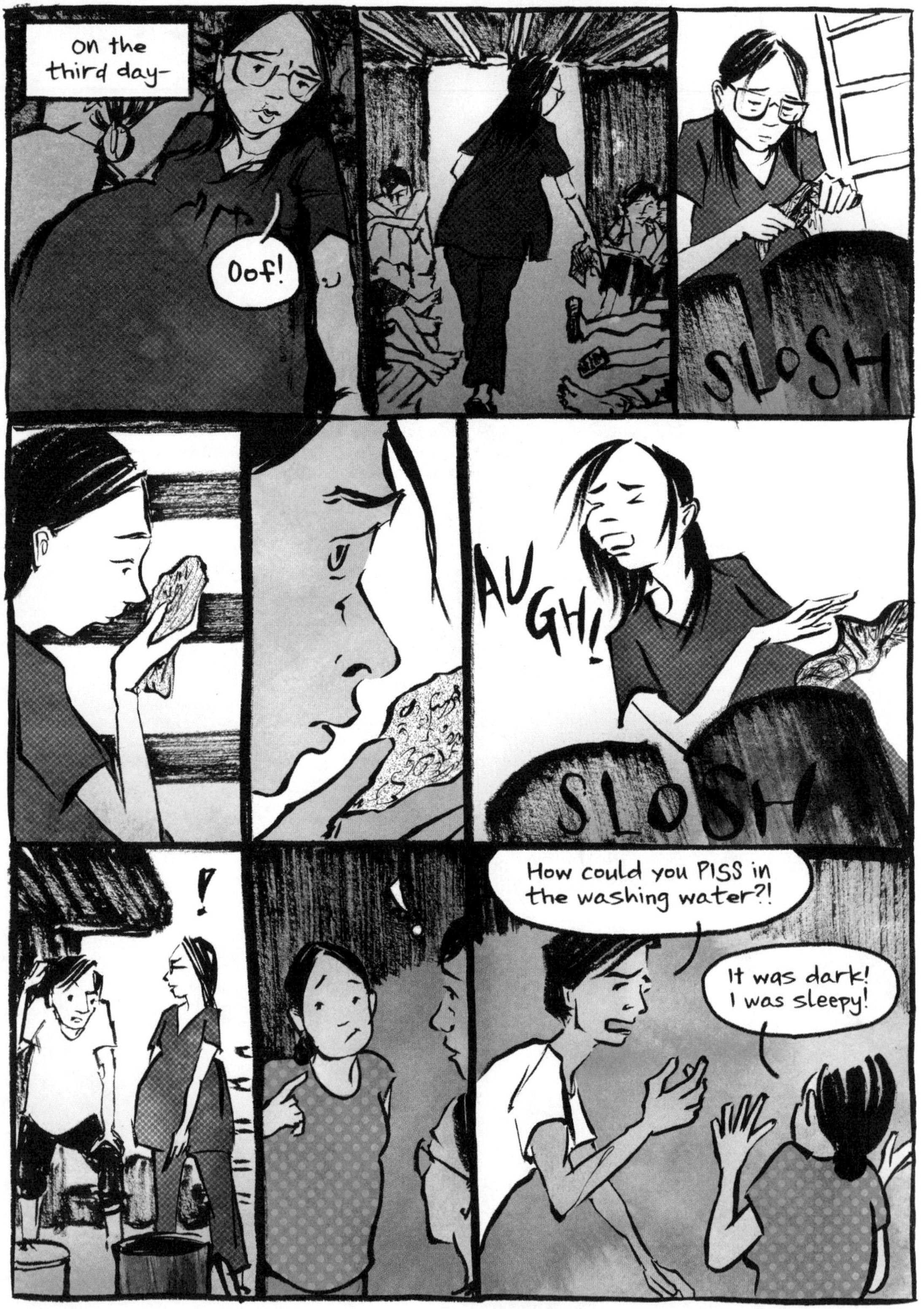
On the third day-
Oof!
SLOSH
AUGH!
SLOSH
!
How could you PISS in the washing water?!
It was dark! I was sleepy!

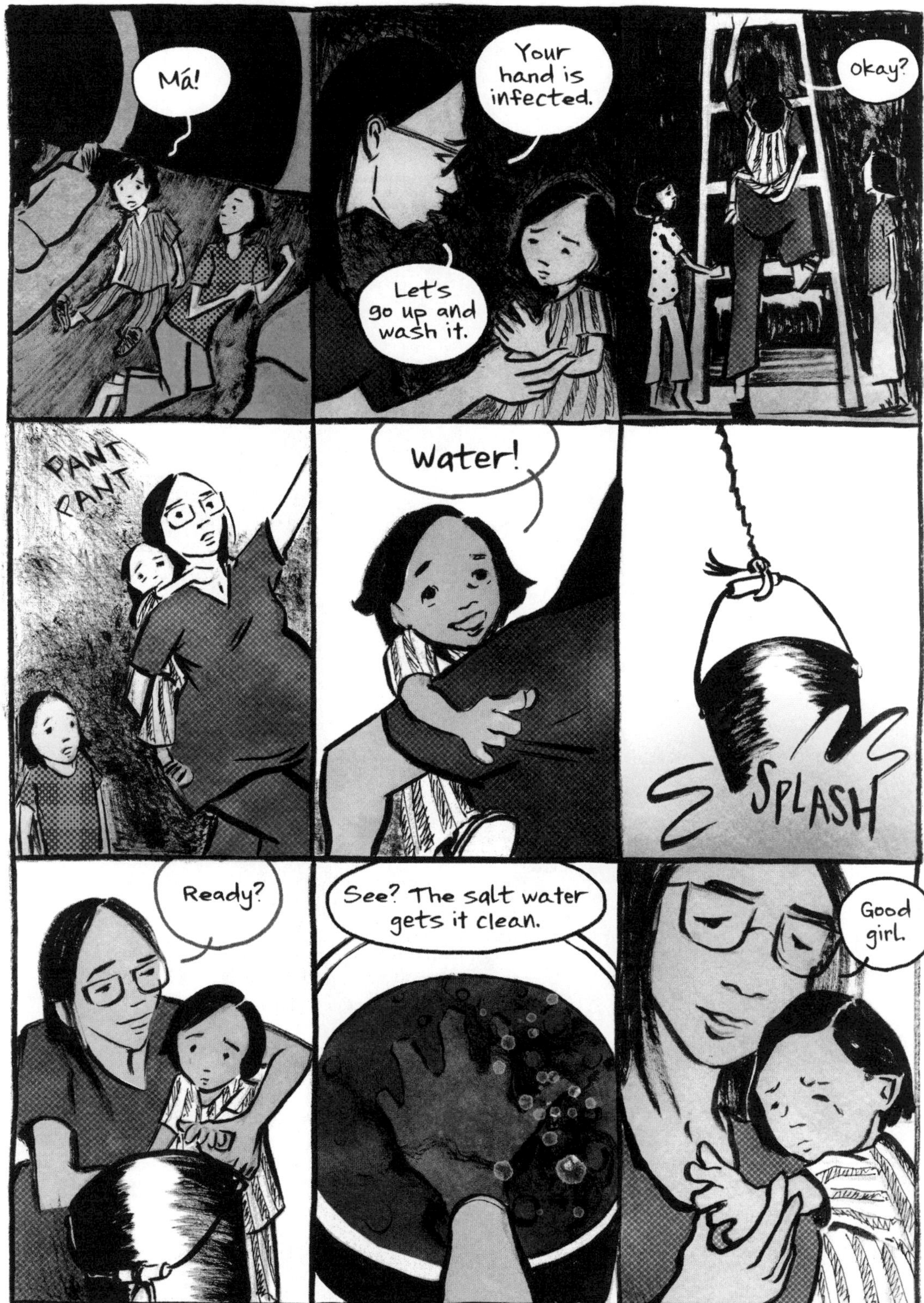

Má!
Your hand is infected.
Let's go up and wash it.
Okay?
PANT PANT
Water!
SPLASH
Ready?
See? The salt water gets it clean.
Good girl.

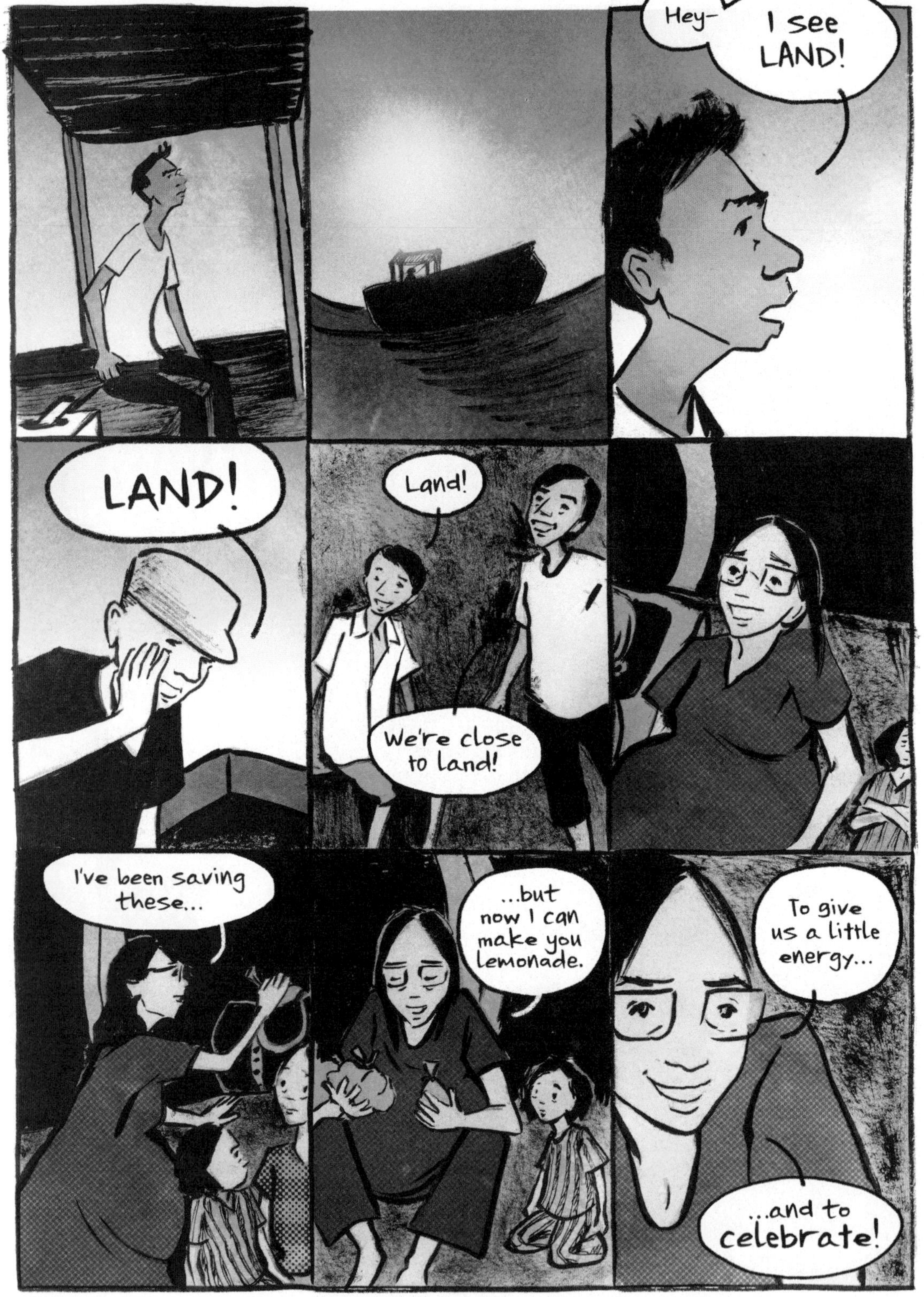
Hey-
I see LAND!
LAND!
Land!
We're close to land!
I've been saving these...
...but now I can make you lemonade.
To give us a little energy...
...and to celebrate!

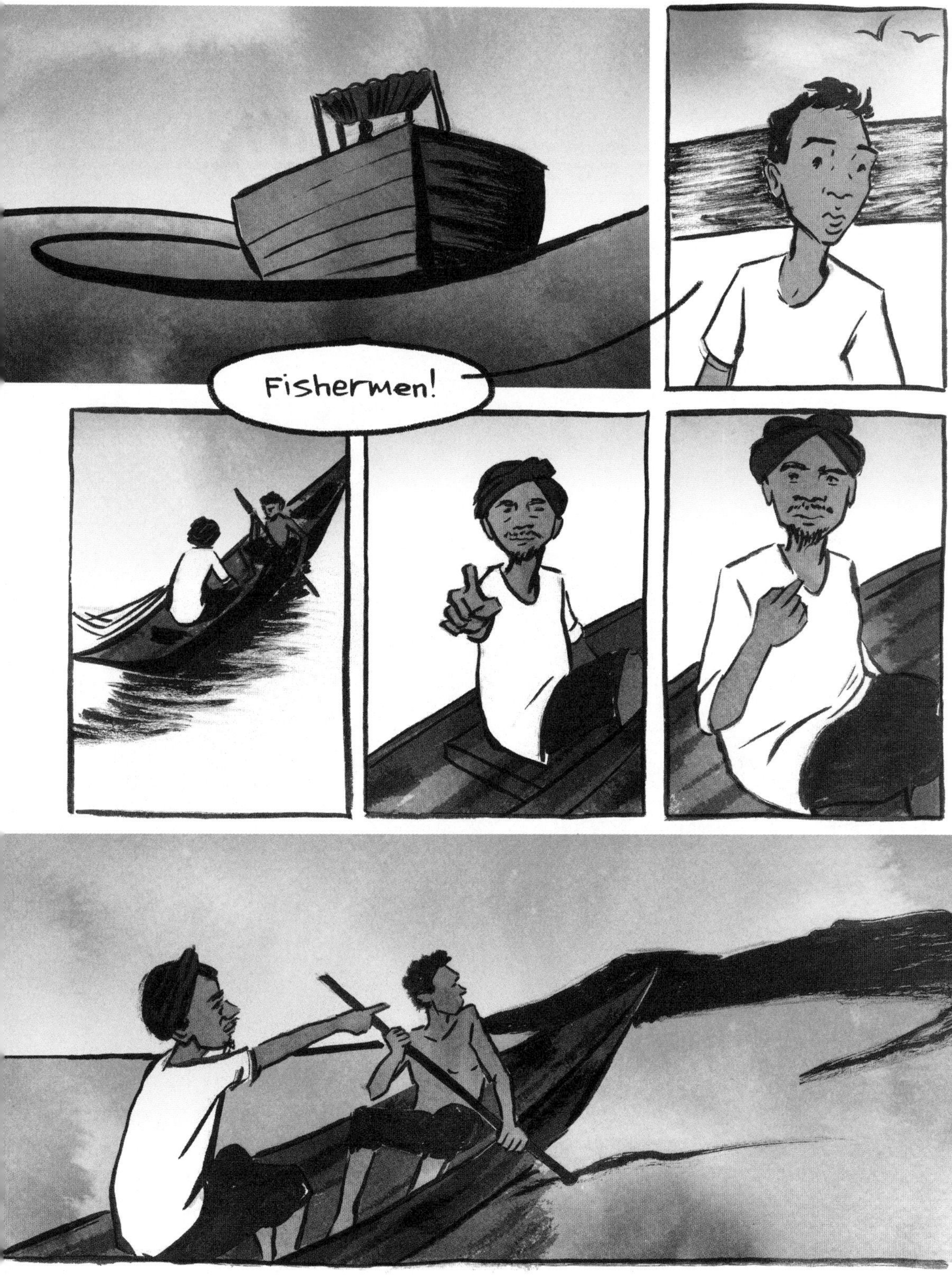
Fishermen!

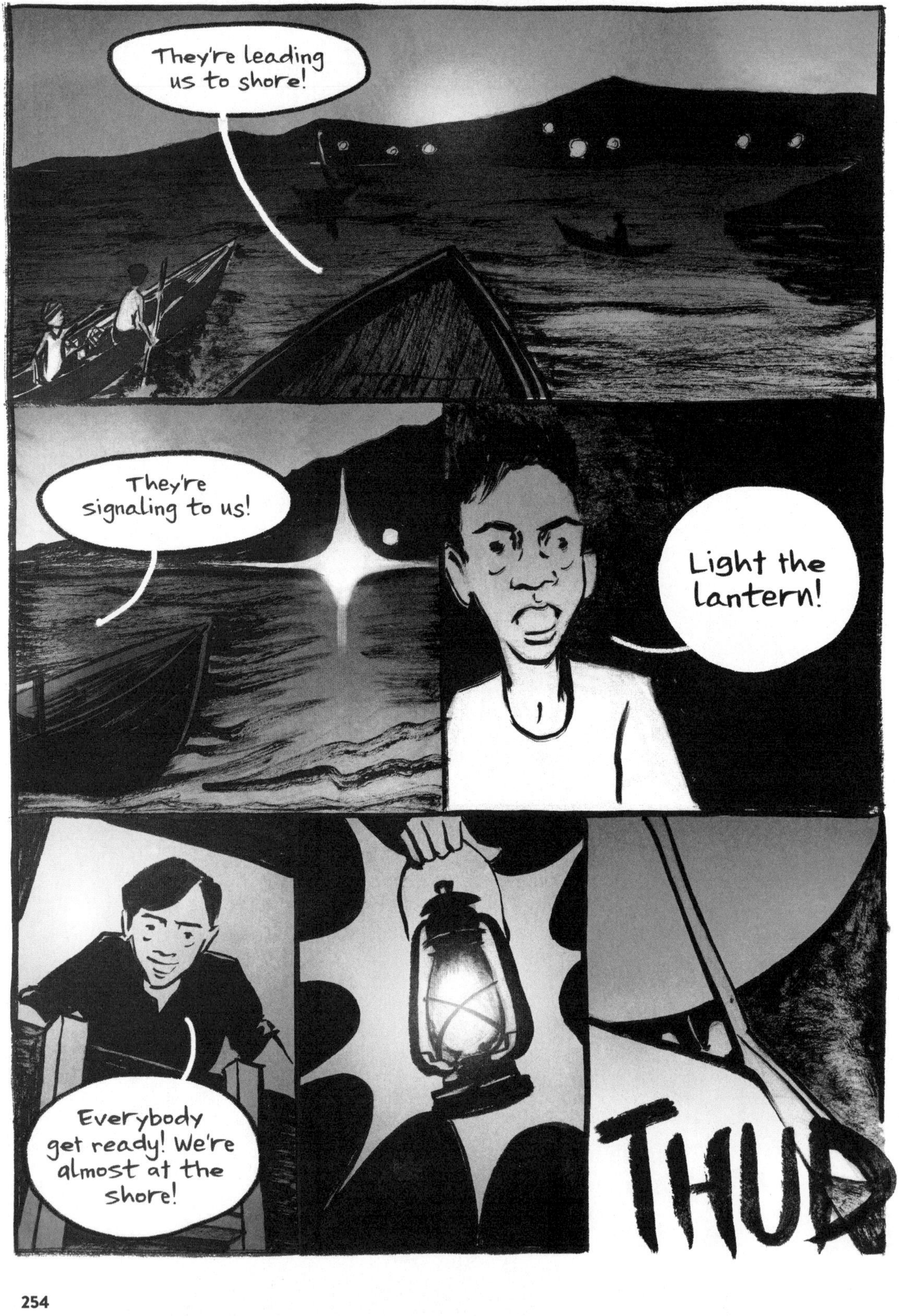
They're leading us to shore!
They're signaling to us!
Light the lantern!
Everybody get ready! We're almost at the shore!
THUD

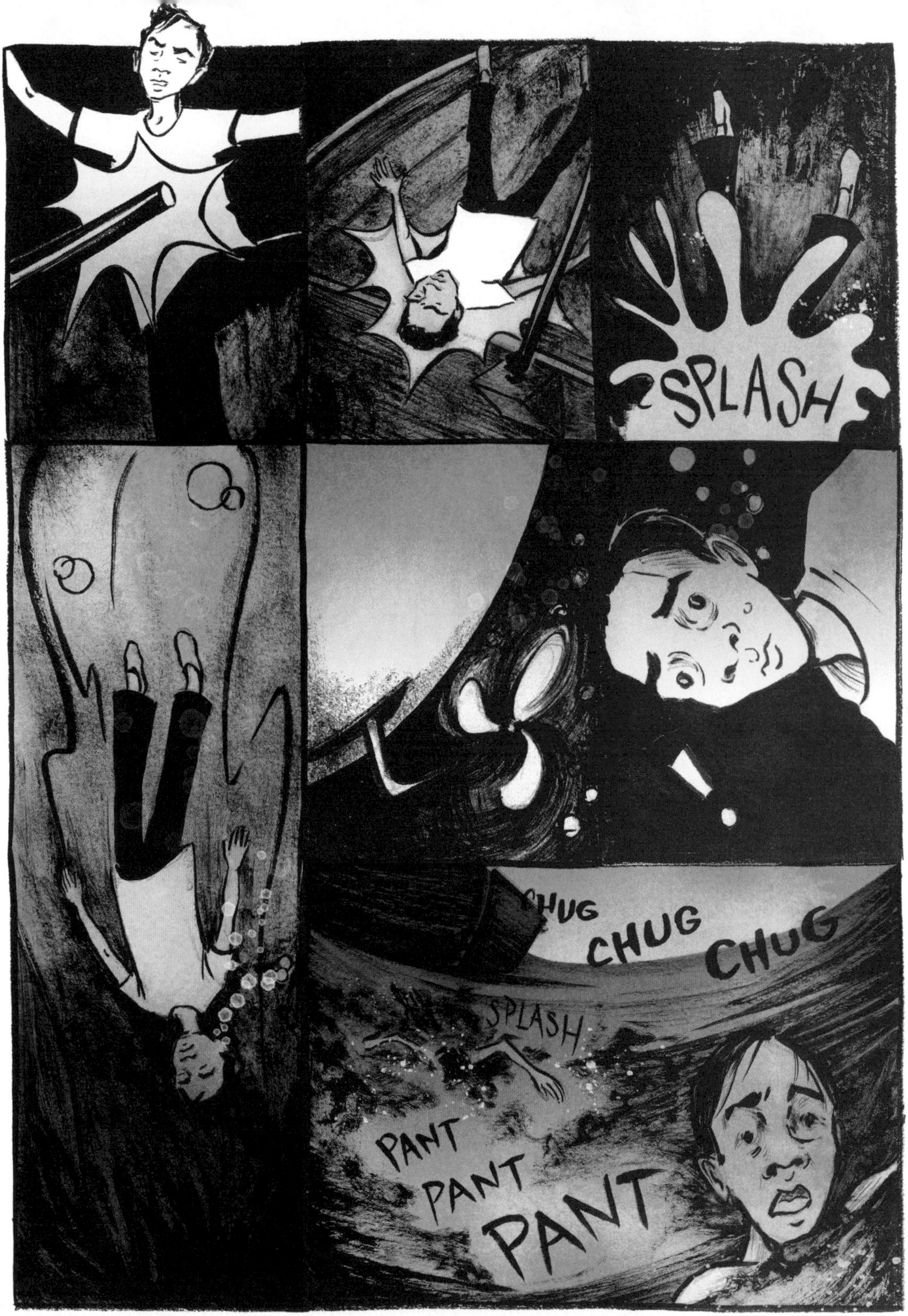
SPLASH
CHUG
CHUG
CHUG
SPLASH
PANT
PANT
PANT

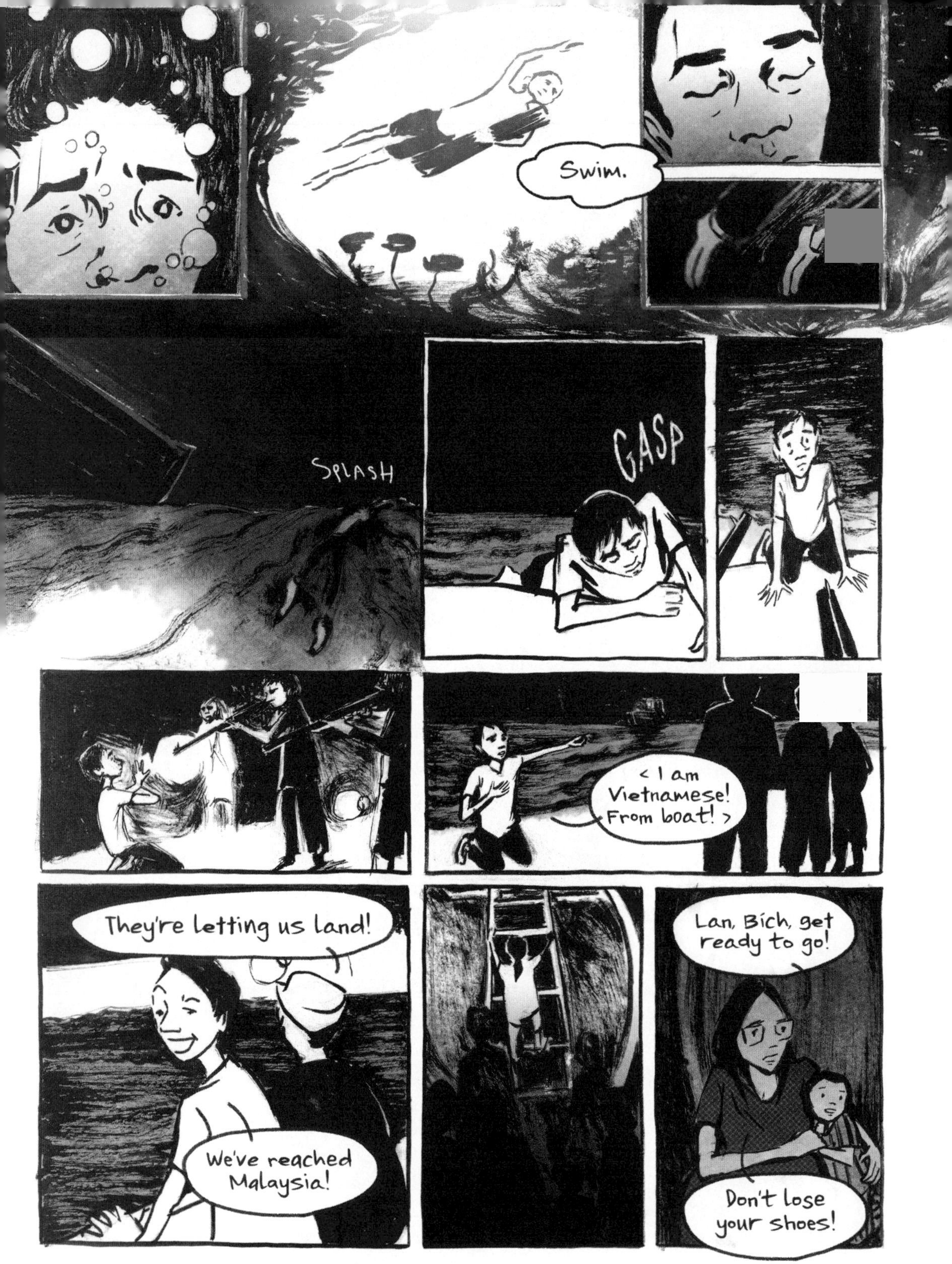
Swim.
SPLASH
GASP
< I am Vietnamese! From boat! >
They're letting us land!
We've reached Malaysia!
Lan, Bich, get ready to go!
Don't lose your shoes!

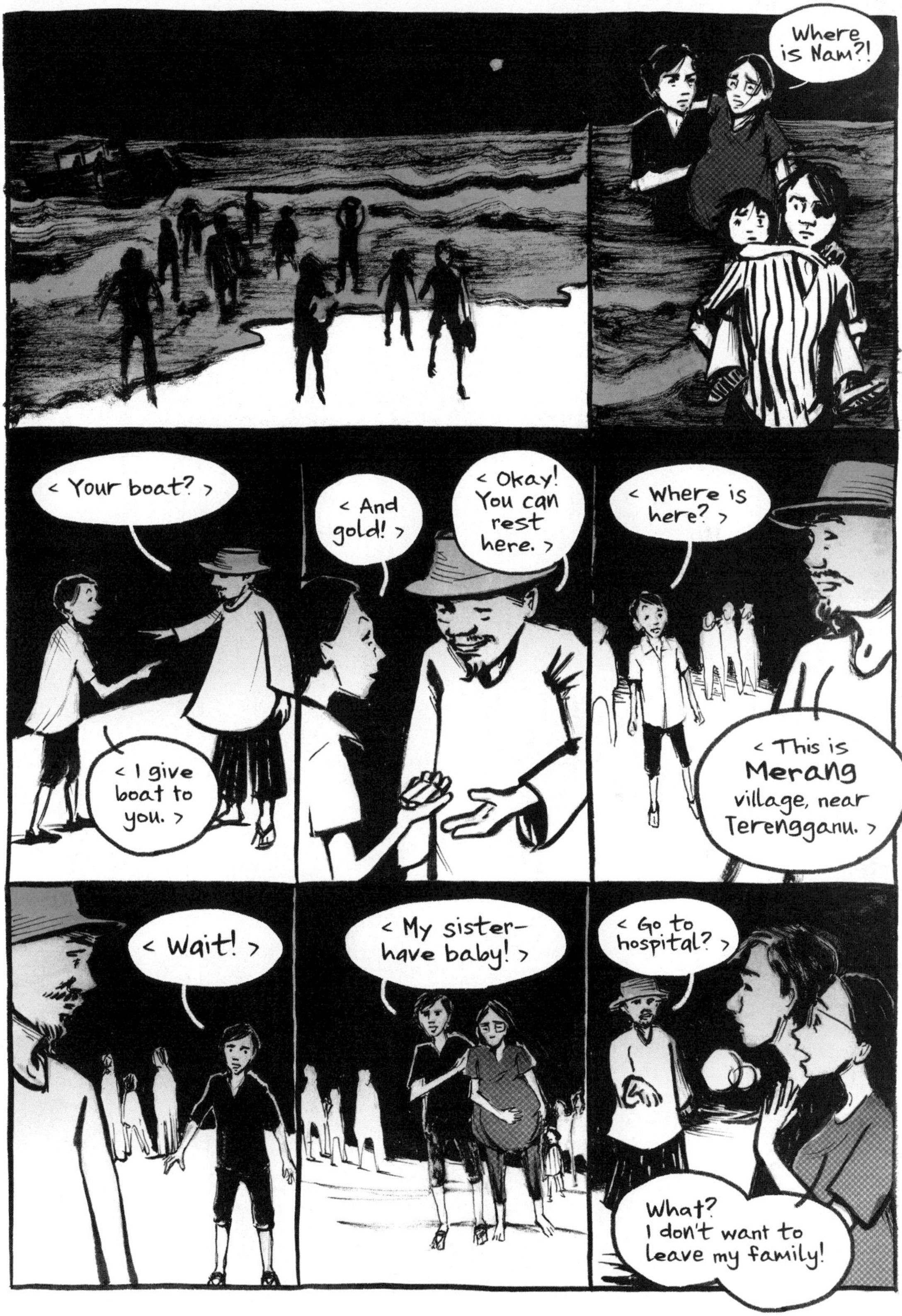
Where is Nam?!
< Your boat? >
< I give boat to you. >
< And gold! >
< Okay! You can rest here. >
< Where is here? >
< This is Merang village, near Terengganu. >
< Wait! >
< My sister- have baby! >
< Go to hospital? >
What? I don't want to leave my family!

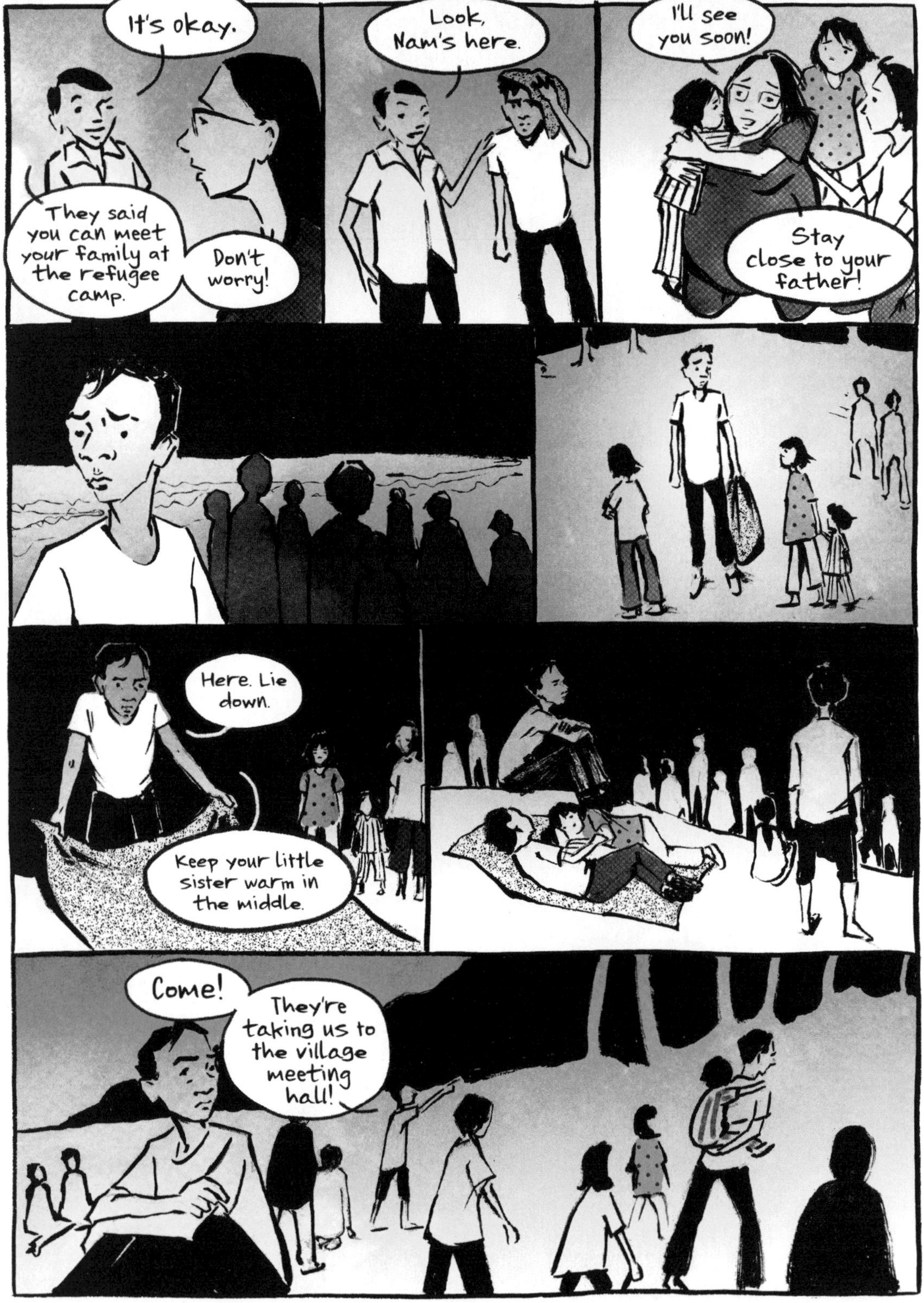
It's okay.
They said you can meet your family at the refugee camp.
Don't worry!
Look, Nam's here.
I'll see you soon!
Stay close to your father!
Here. Lie down.
Keep your little sister warm in the middle.
Come!
They're taking us to the village meeting hall!

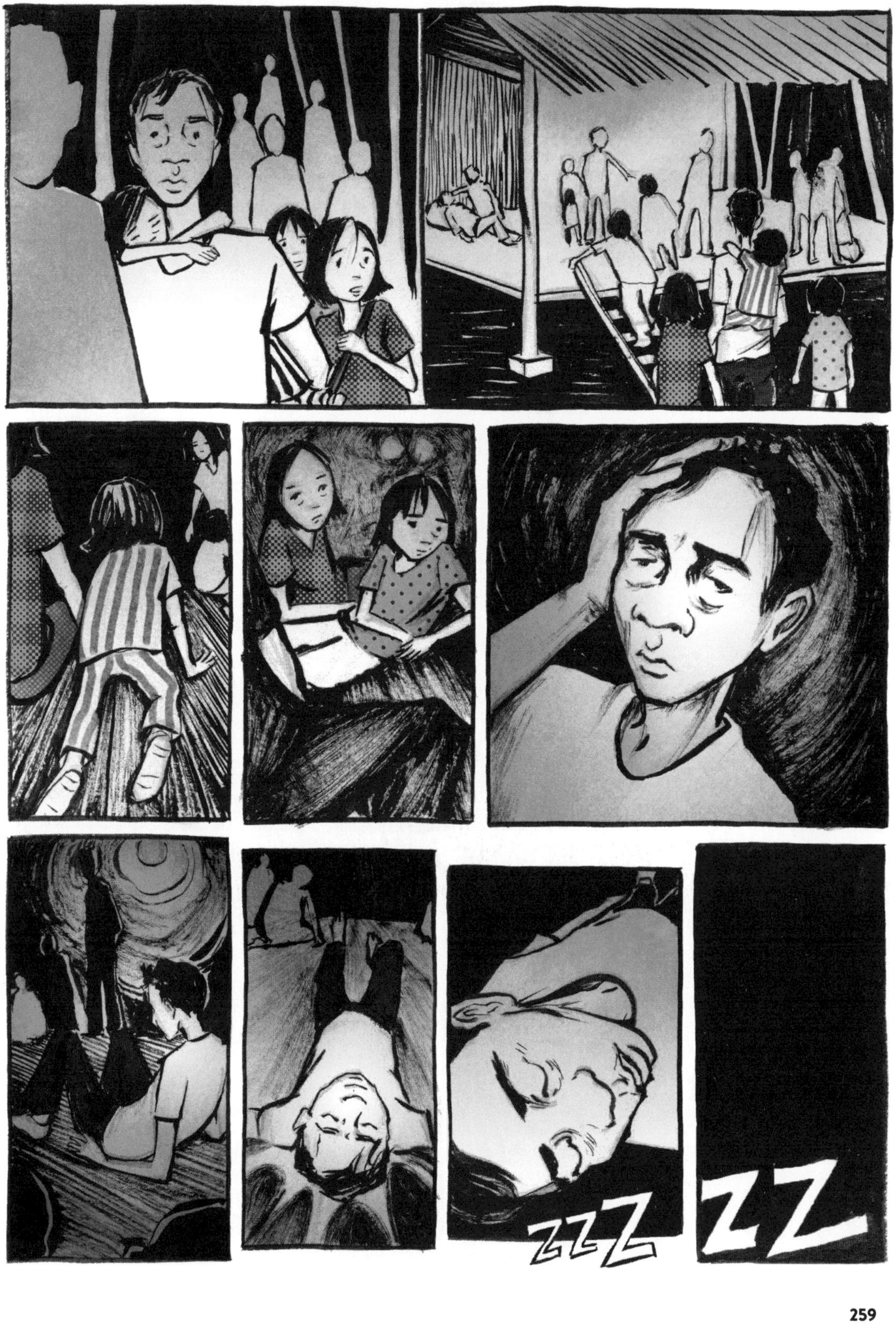
ZZZ
ZZ

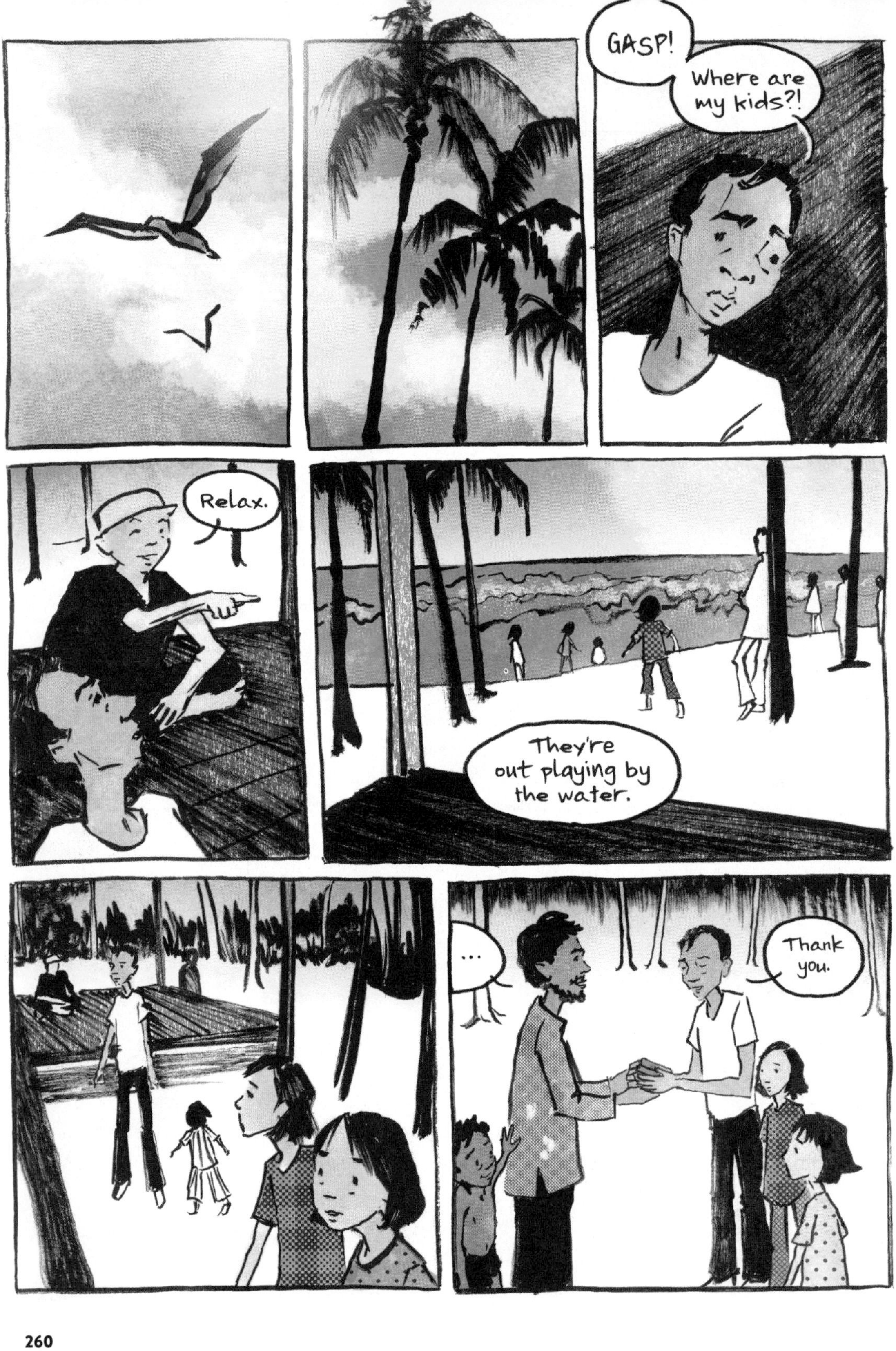
GASP!
Where are my kids?!
Relax.
They're out playing by the water.
...
Thank you.

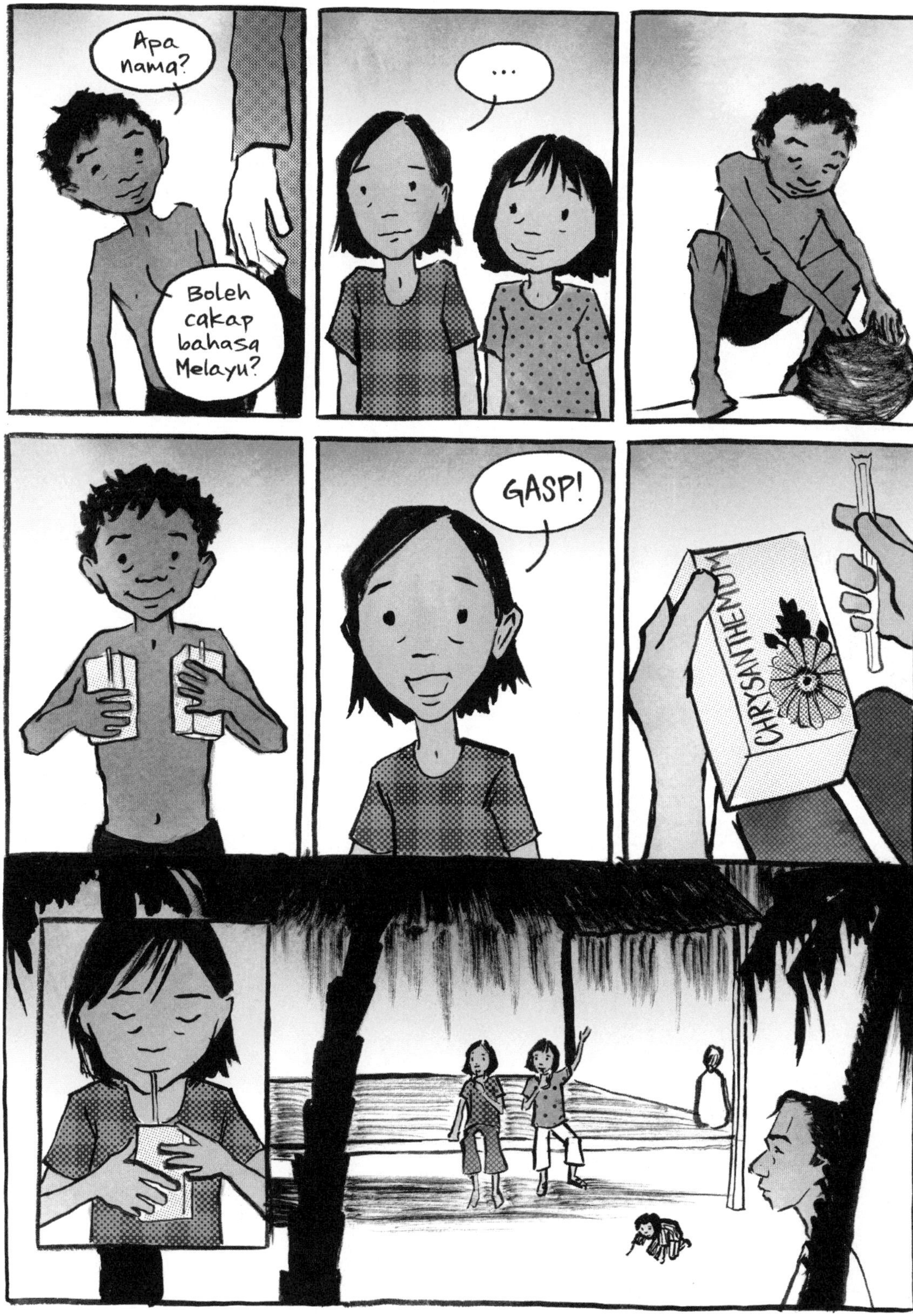
Apa nama?
Boleh cakap bahasa Melayu?
...
GASP!
CHRYSANTHEMUM

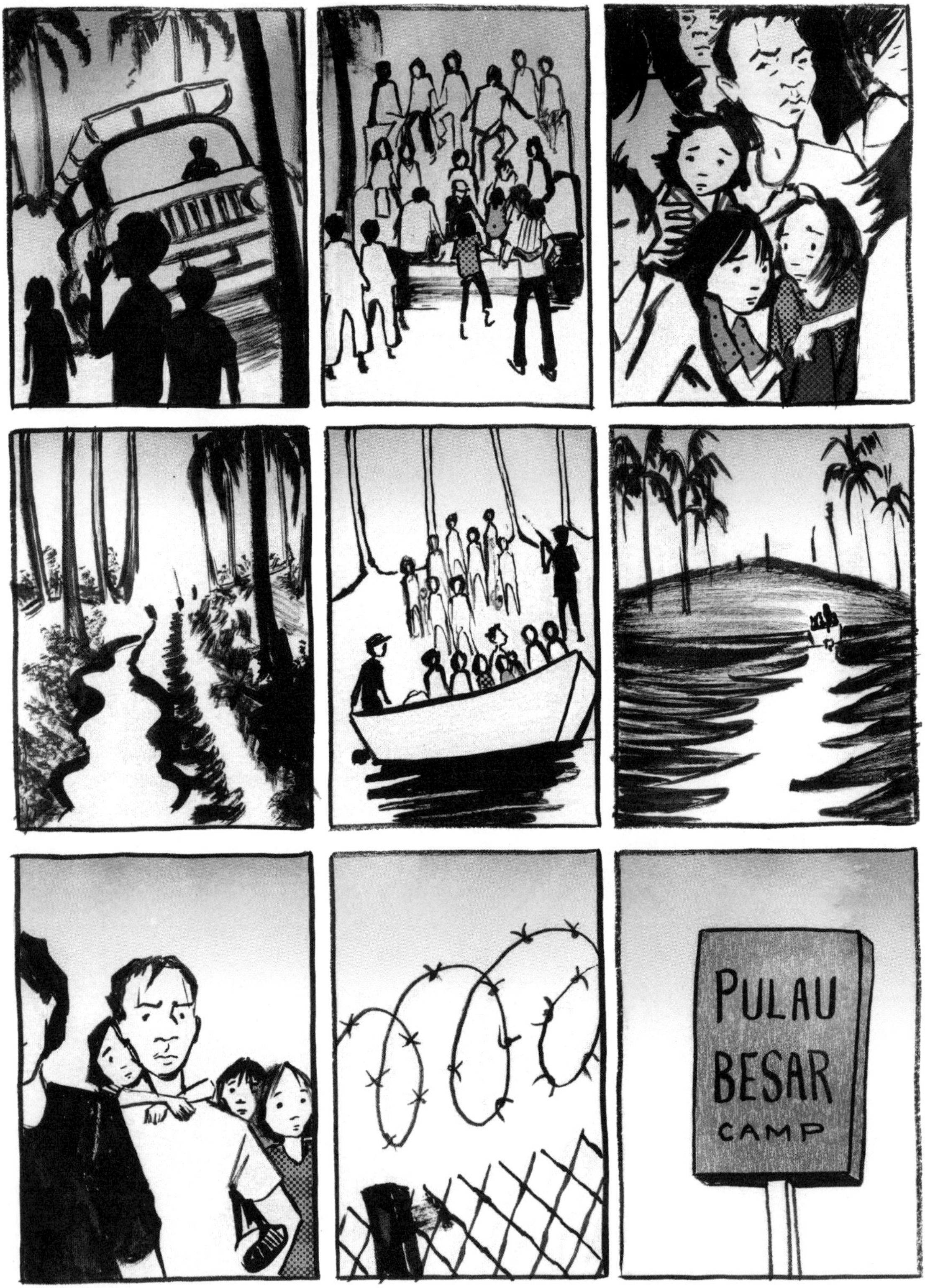
PULAU
BESAR
CAMP

CHAPTER 8
THE SHORE

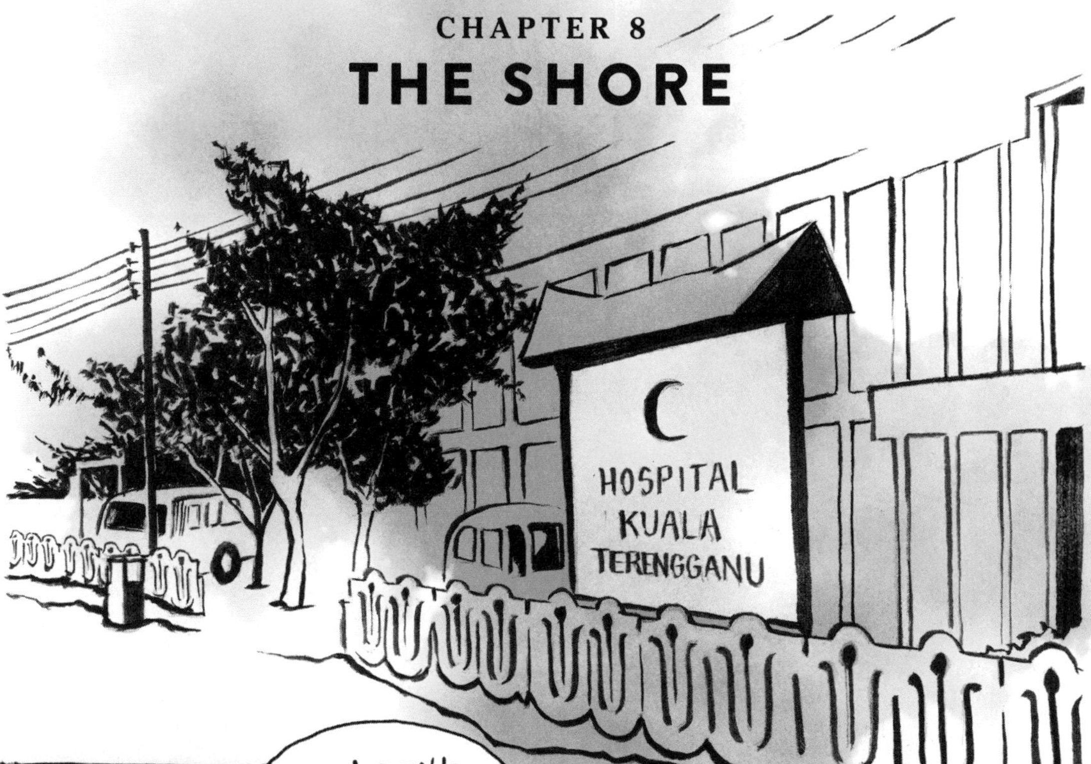
HOSPITAL
KUALA
TERENGGANU

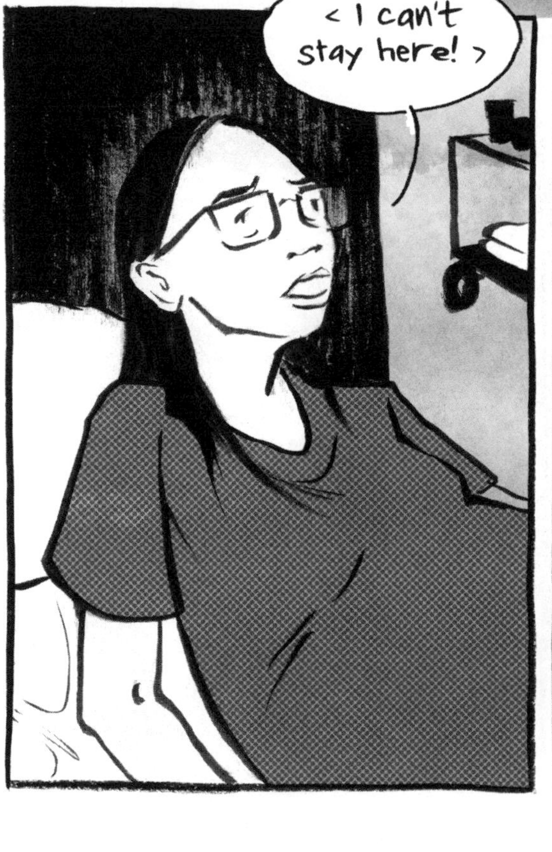
< I can't stay here! >

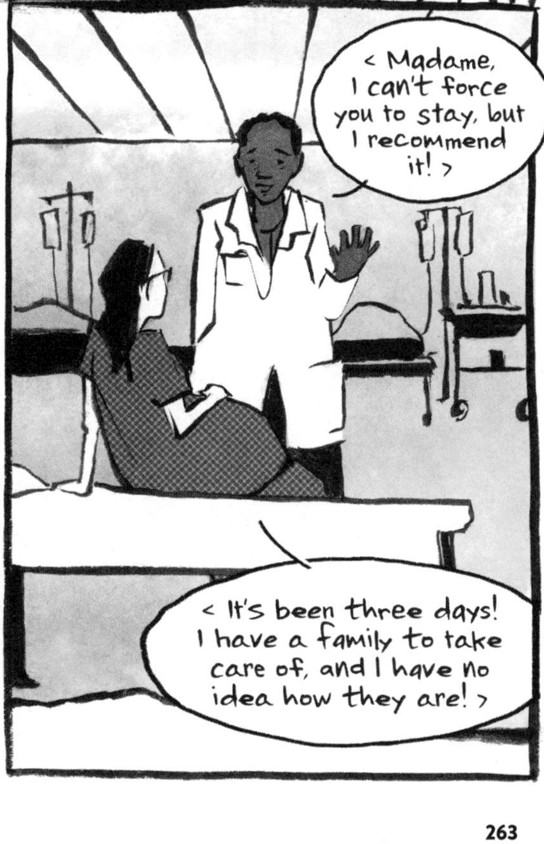
< Madame, I can't force you to stay, but I recommend it! >
< It's been three days! I have a family to take care of, and I have no idea how they are! >

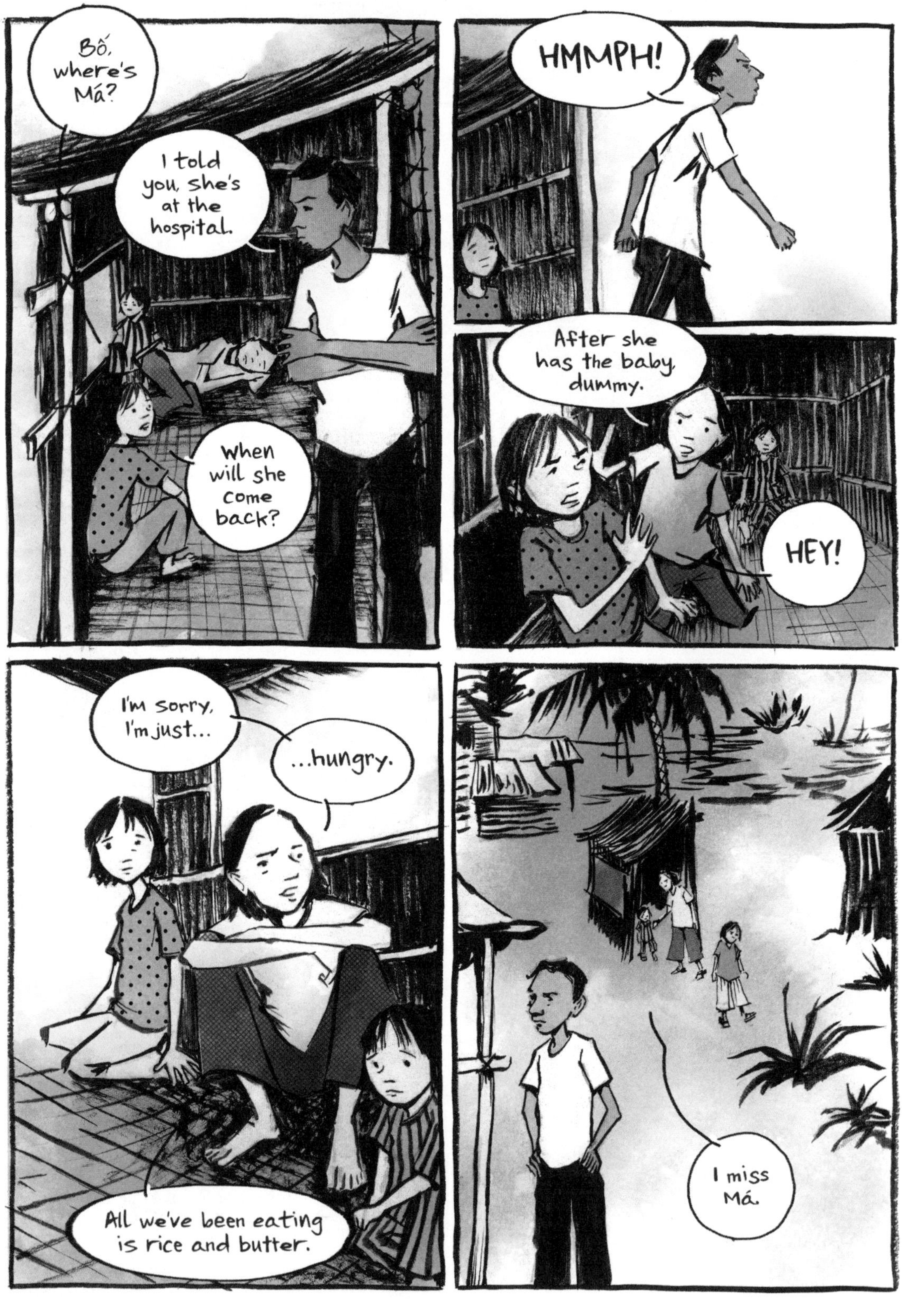

Bố, where's Má?
I told you, she's at the hospital.
When will she come back?
HMMPH!
After she has the baby, dummy.
HEY!
I'm sorry, I'm just...
...hungry.
All we've been eating is rice and butter.
I miss Má.

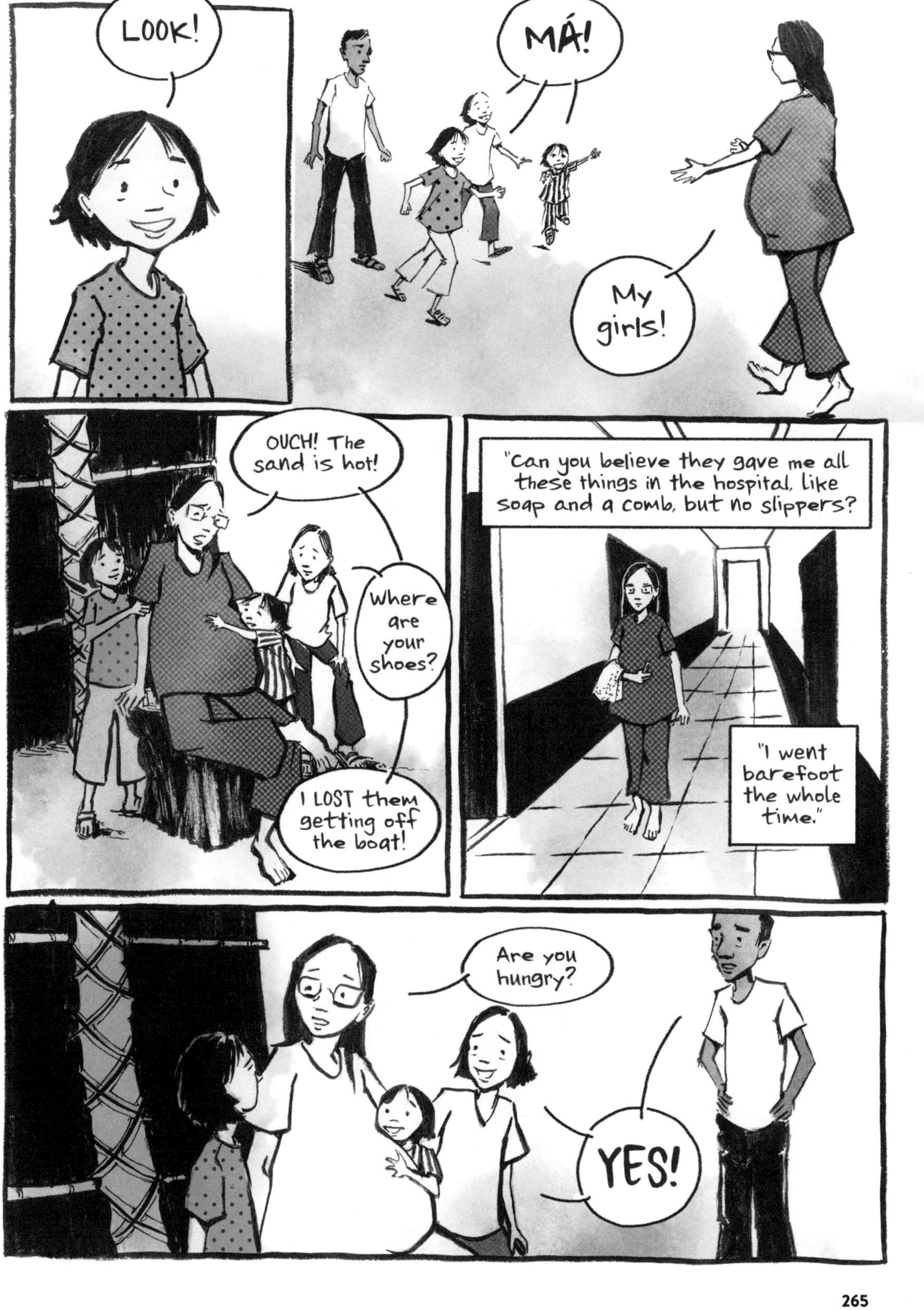
LOOK!
MÁ!
My girls!
OUCH! The sand is hot!
Where are your shoes?
I LOST them getting off the boat!
"Can you believe they gave me all these things in the hospital, like soap and a comb, but no slippers?
"I went barefoot the whole time."
Are you hungry?
YES!

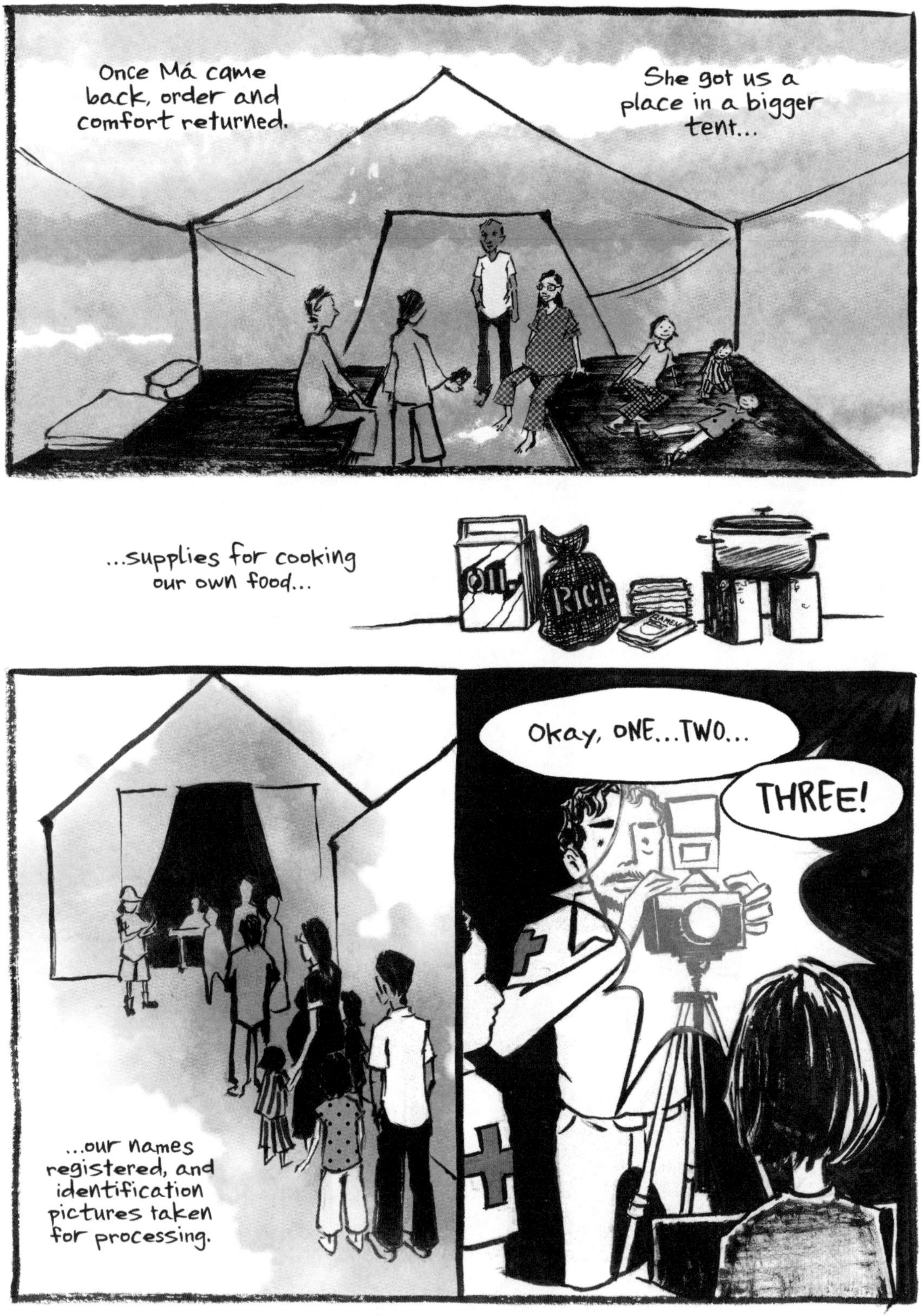
Once Má came back, order and comfort returned.
She got us a place in a bigger tent...
...supplies for cooking our own food...
OIL
RICE
RAMEN
...our names registered, and identification pictures taken for processing.
Okay, ONE...TWO...
THREE!

BUI CHI LAN
BOAT # 65/KT/5
DOA : 15-3-1978

BUI THIEN NAM
BOAT Nº 65/KT/5
DOA : 15.3.1978
DOB: 20.9.1940

We were now BOAT PEOPLE—

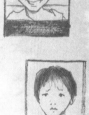

BUI NGOC BICH
BOAT # 65/KT/5
DOA: 15.3.1978
DOB: 16-1-1968

TRUONG NGOC HANG
BOAT Nº 65/KT/5
DOA : 15.3.1978
DOB : 18-8-1943

—five among
hundreds of
thousands of
refugees flooding
into neighboring
countries,
seeking asylum.

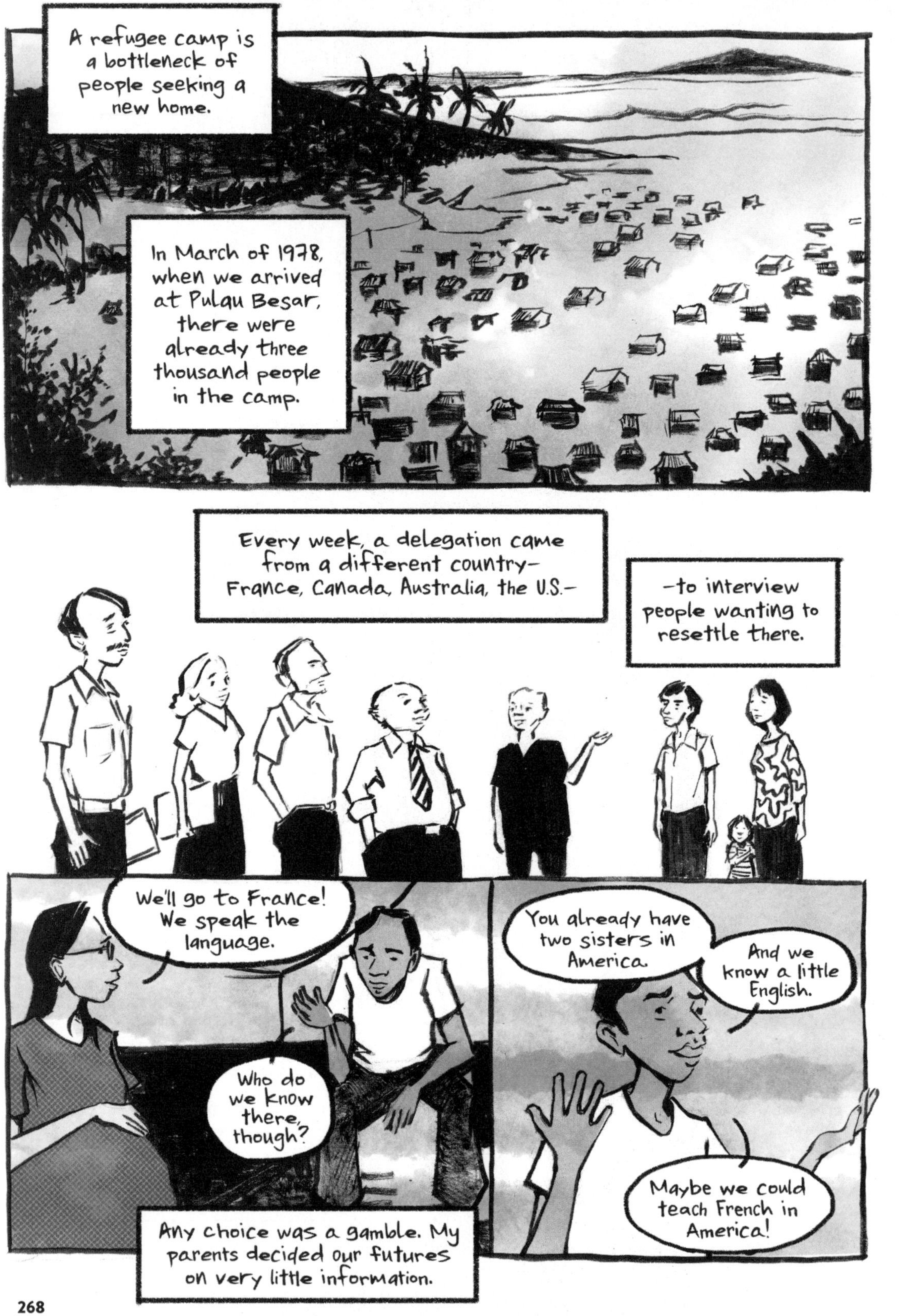
A refugee camp is a bottleneck of people seeking a new home.
In March of 1978, when we arrived at Pulau Besar, there were already three thousand people in the camp.
Every week, a delegation came from a different country— France, Canada, Australia, the U.S.—
—to interview people wanting to resettle there.
We'll go to France! We speak the language.
Who do we know there, though?
You already have two sisters in America.
And we know a little English.
Maybe we could teach French in America!
Any choice was a gamble. My parents decided our futures on very little information.

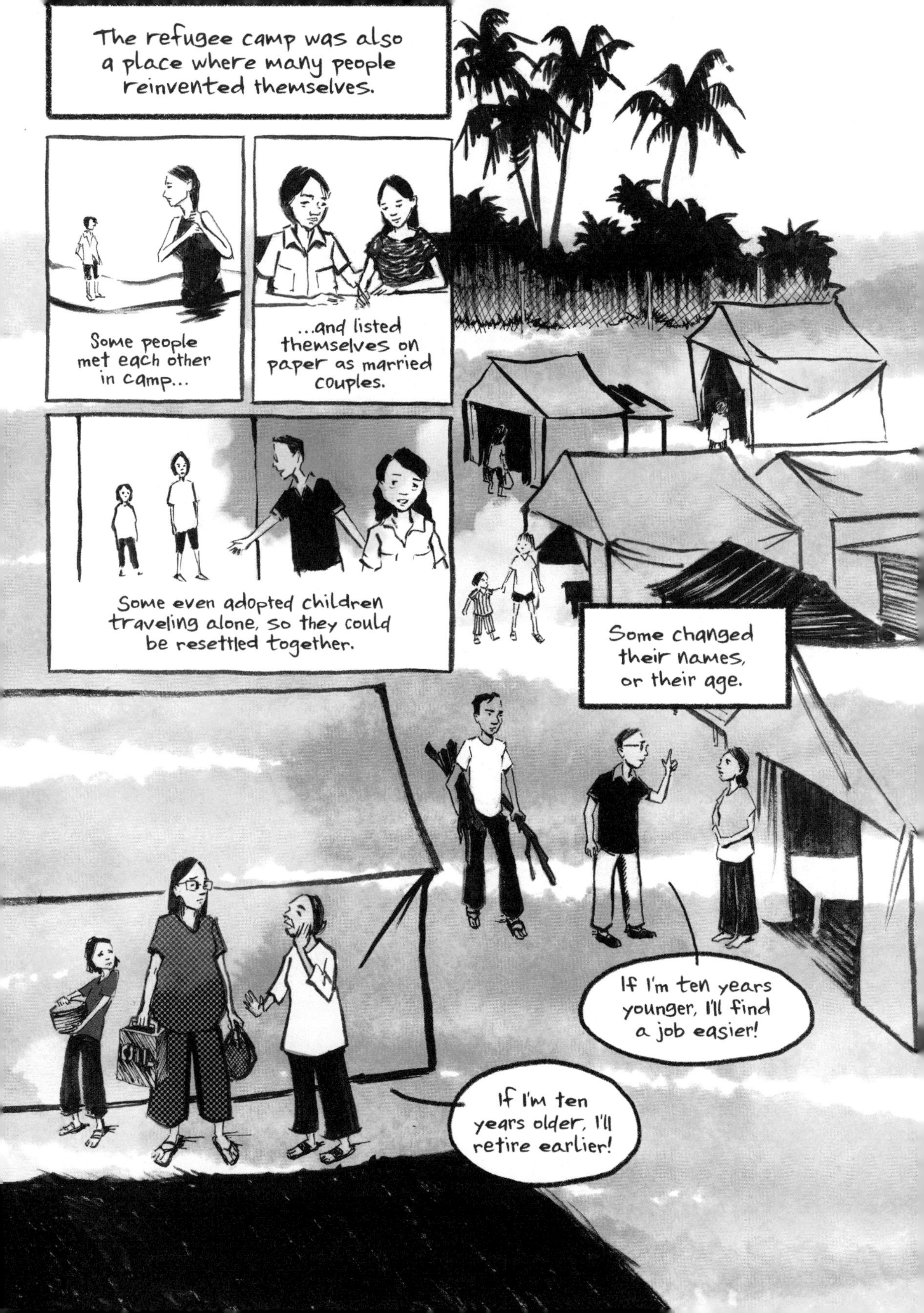
The refugee camp was also a place where many people reinvented themselves.
Some people met each other in camp...
...and listed themselves on paper as married couples.
Some even adopted children traveling alone, so they could be resettled together.
Some changed their names, or their age.
If I'm ten years younger, I'll find a job easier!
If I'm ten years older, I'll retire earlier!

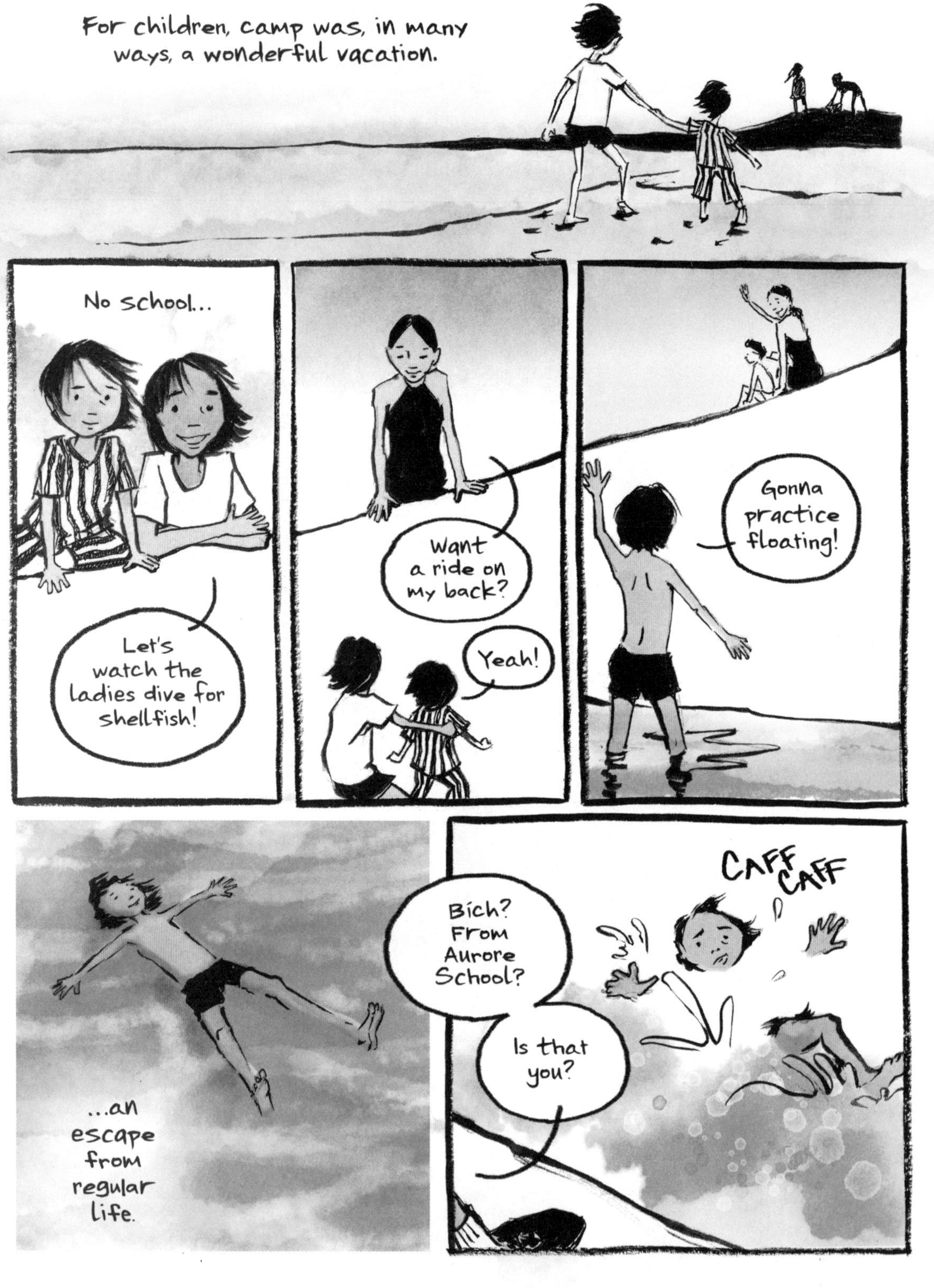
For children, camp was, in many ways, a wonderful vacation.
No school...
Let's watch the ladies dive for shellfish!
Want a ride on my back?
Yeah!
Gonna practice floating!
...an escape from regular life.
CAFF CAFF
Bich? From Aurore School?
Is that you?

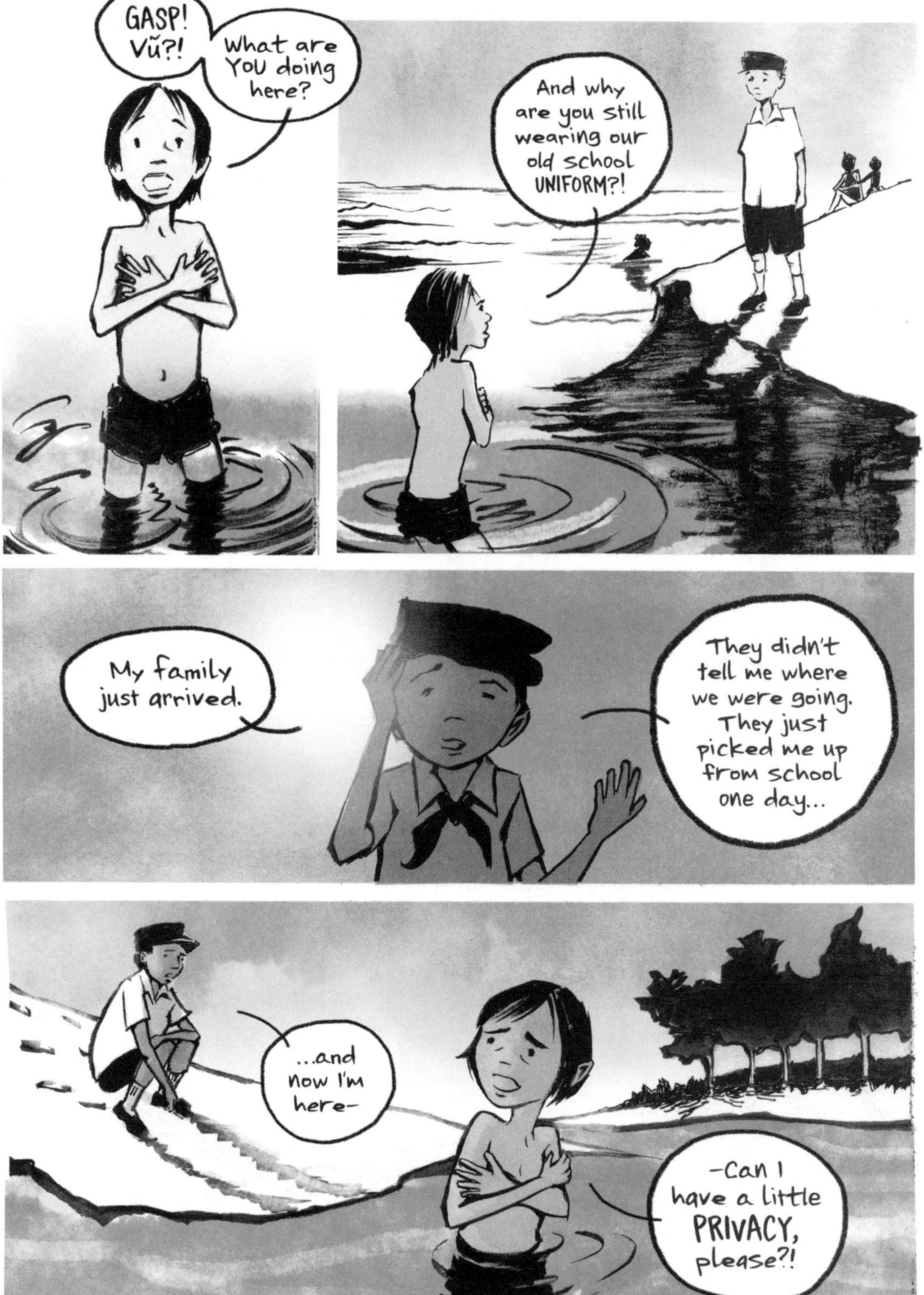
GASP! Vũ?!
What are YOU doing here?
And why are you still wearing our old school UNIFORM?!
My family just arrived.
They didn't tell me where we were going. They just picked me up from school one day...
...and now I'm here-
-Can I have a little PRIVACY, please?!

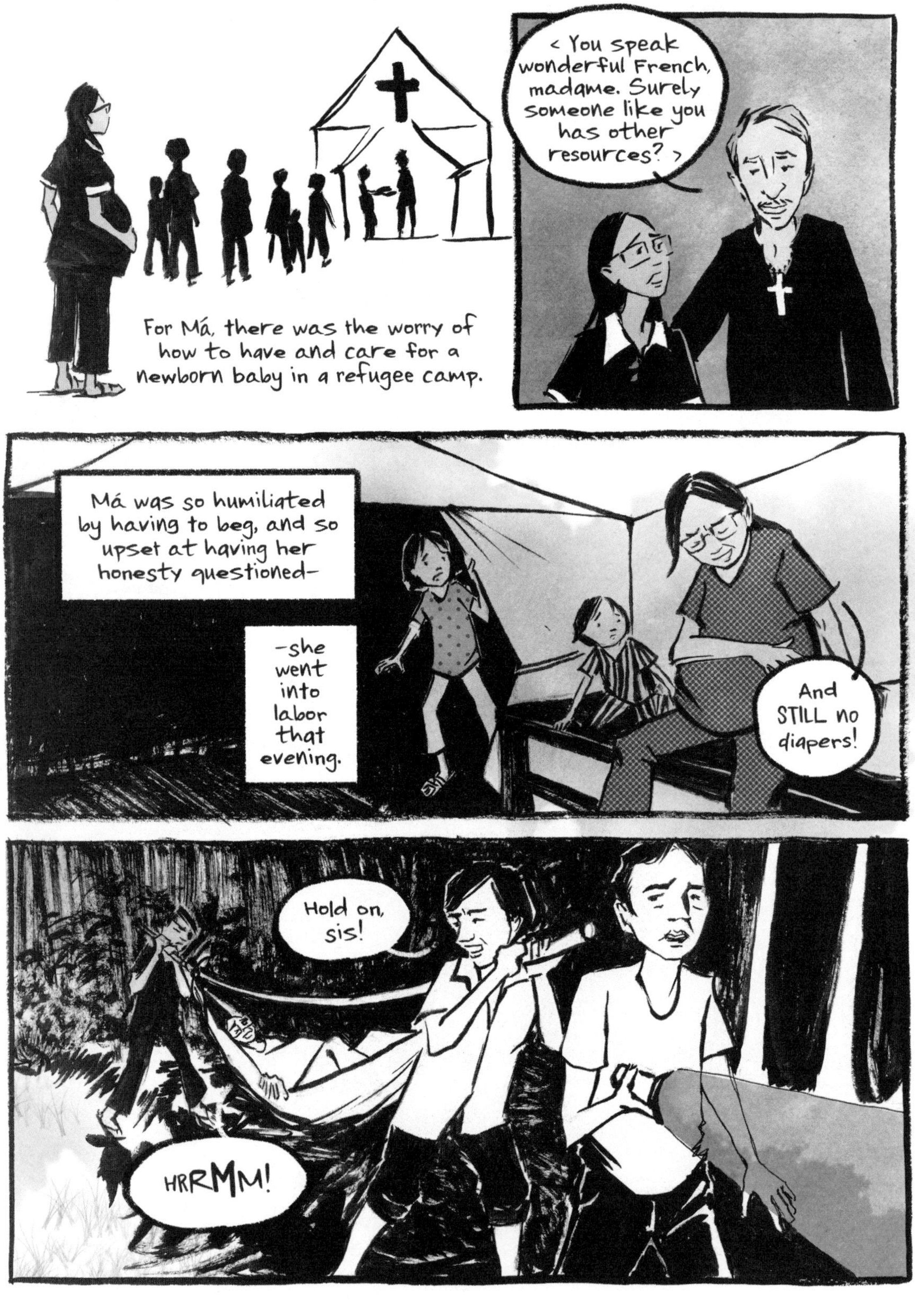
For Má, there was the worry of how to have and care for a newborn baby in a refugee camp.
< You speak wonderful French, madame. Surely someone like you has other resources? >
Má was so humiliated by having to beg, and so upset at having her honesty questioned-
-she went into labor that evening.
And STILL no diapers!
Hold on, sis!
HRRMM!

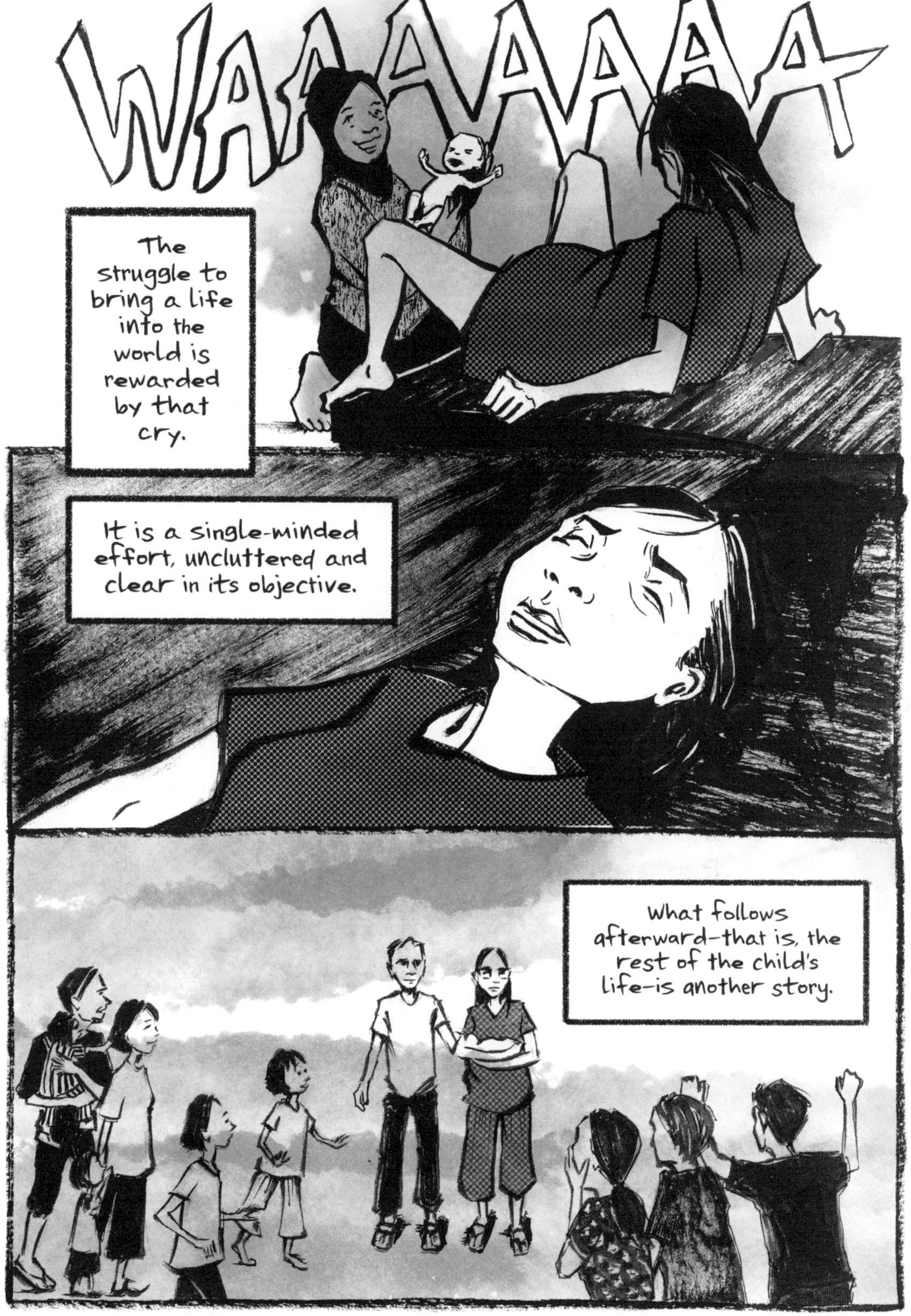
WAAAAAA
The struggle to bring a life into the world is rewarded by that cry.
It is a single-minded effort, uncluttered and clear in its objective.
What follows afterward—that is, the rest of the child's life—is another story.

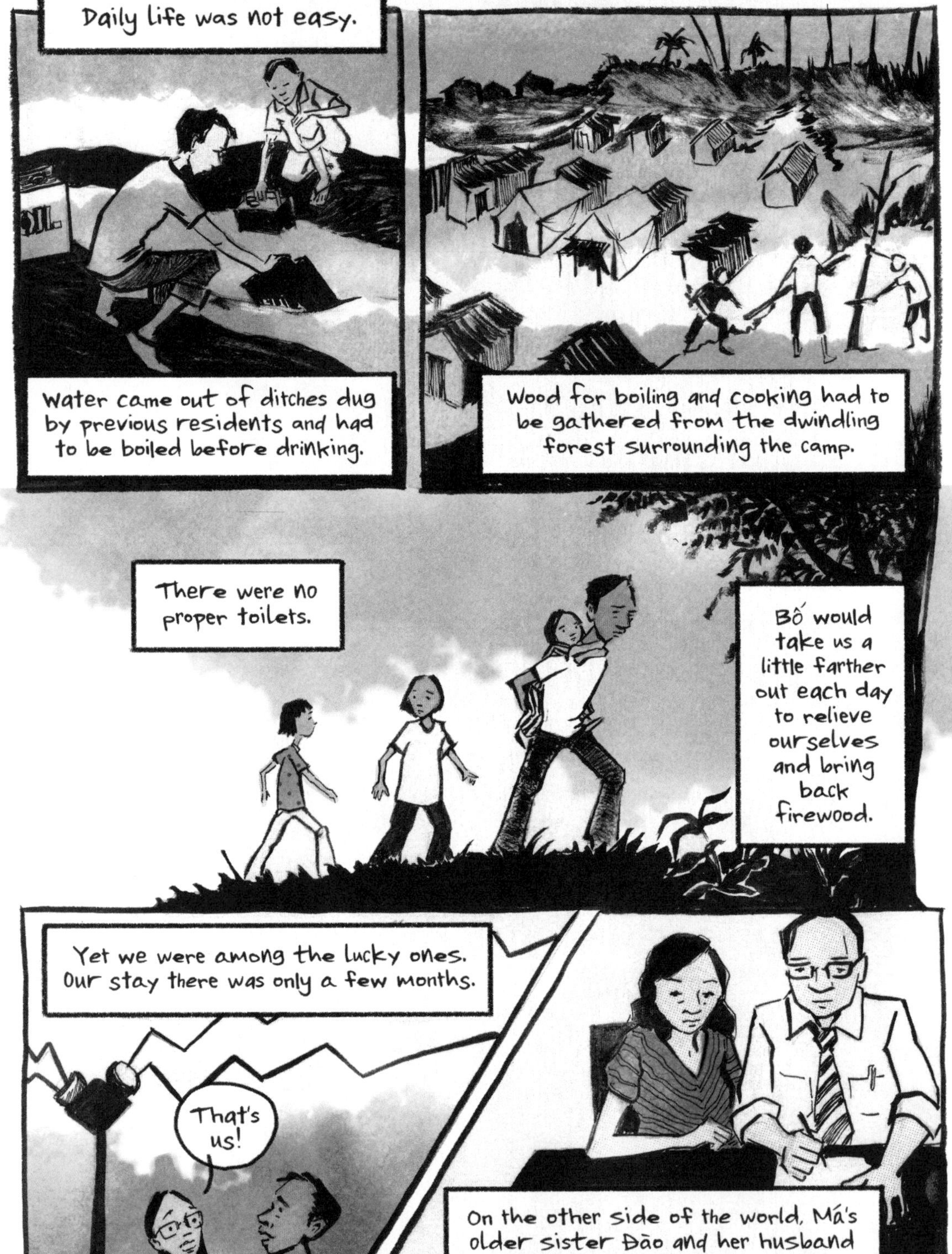
Daily life was not easy.
Water came out of ditches dug by previous residents and had to be boiled before drinking.
Wood for boiling and cooking had to be gathered from the dwindling forest surrounding the camp.
There were no proper toilets.
Bố would take us a little farther out each day to relieve ourselves and bring back firewood.
Yet we were among the lucky ones. Our stay there was only a few months.
That's us!
On the other side of the world, Má's older sister Đào and her husband acted as our U.S. sponsors and processed all our paperwork quickly.

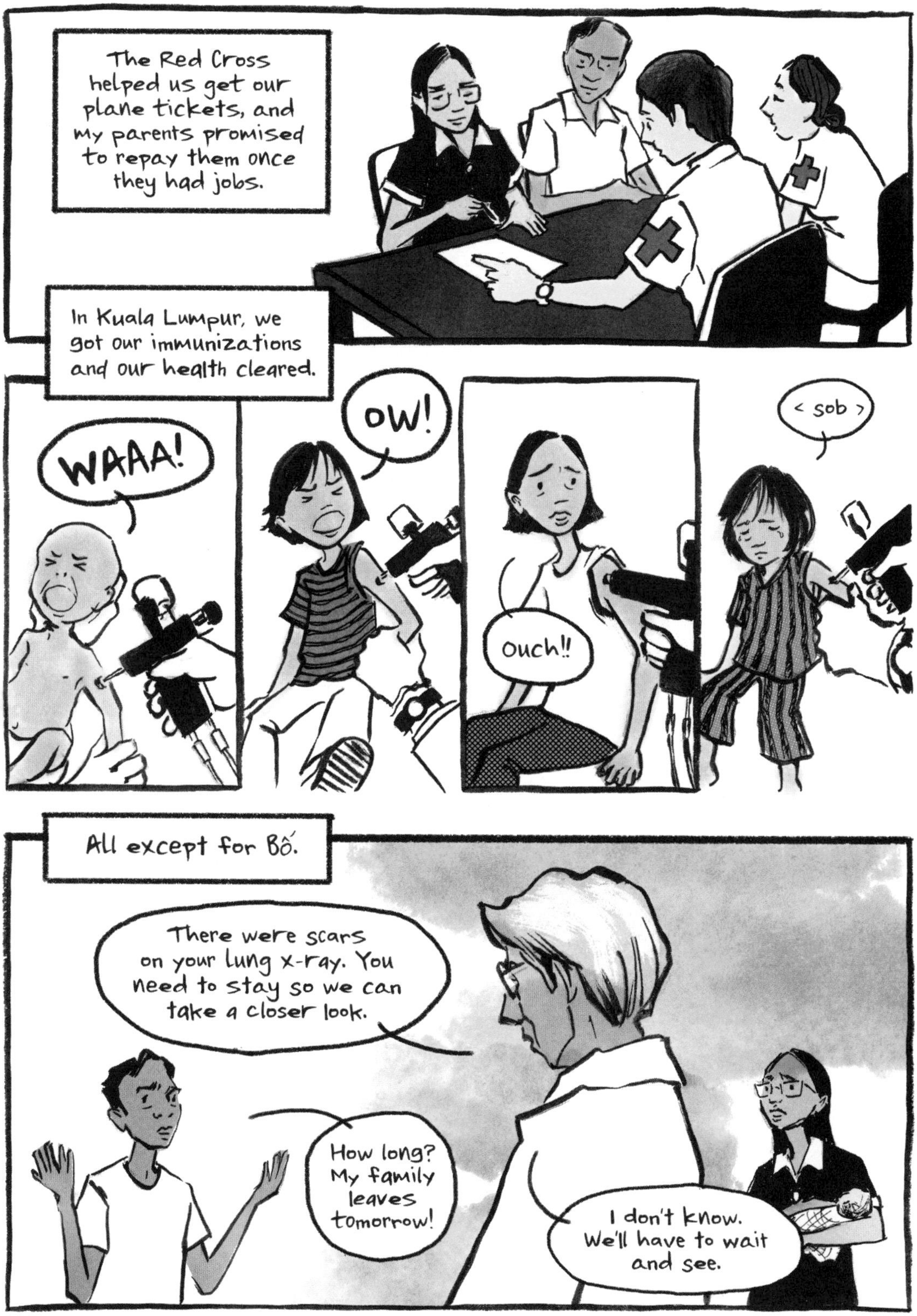
The Red Cross helped us get our plane tickets, and my parents promised to repay them once they had jobs.
In Kuala Lumpur, we got our immunizations and our health cleared.
WAAA!
OW!
Ouch!!
< sob >
All except for Bố.
There were scars on your lung x-ray. You need to stay so we can take a closer look.
How long? My family leaves tomorrow!
I don't know. We'll have to wait and see.

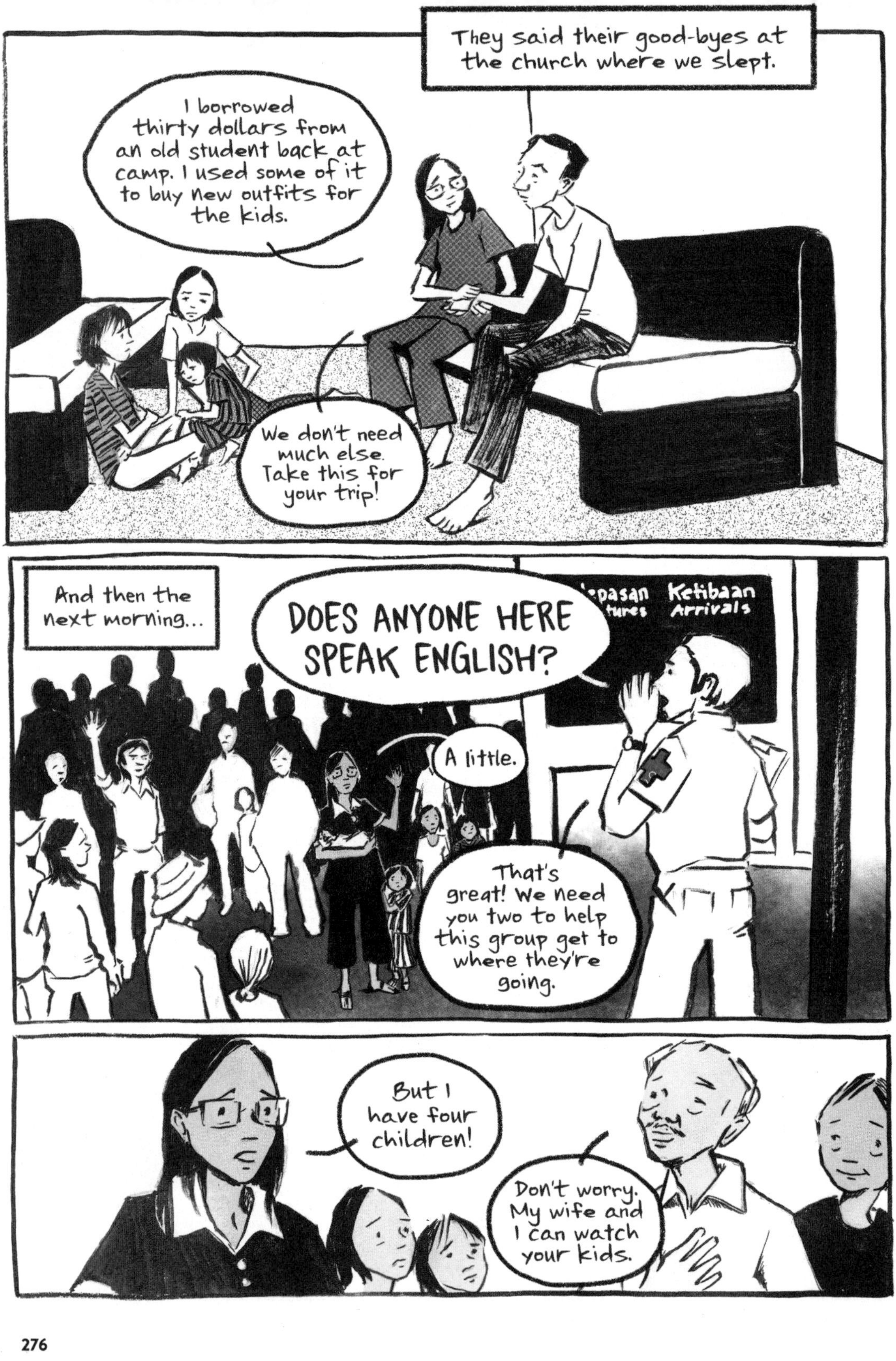
They said their good-byes at the church where we slept.
I borrowed thirty dollars from an old student back at camp. I used some of it to buy new outfits for the kids.
We don't need much else. Take this for your trip!
And then the next morning...
DOES ANYONE HERE SPEAK ENGLISH?
Ketibaan
Arrivals
A little.
That's great! We need you two to help this group get to where they're going.
But I have four children!
Don't worry. My wife and I can watch your kids.

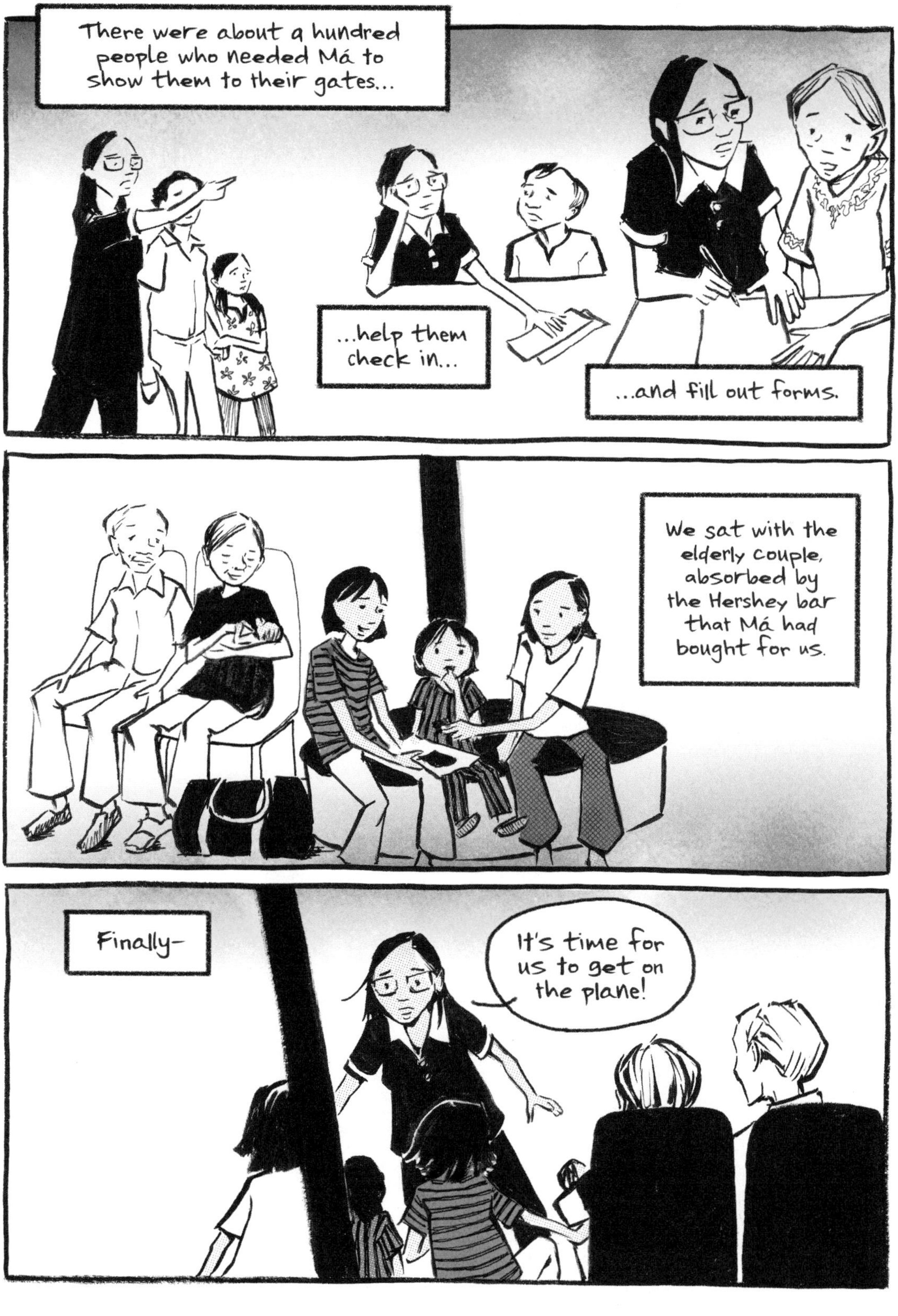
There were about a hundred people who needed Má to show them to their gates...
...help them check in...
...and fill out forms.
We sat with the elderly couple, absorbed by the Hershey bar that Má had bought for us.
Finally-
It's time for us to get on the plane!

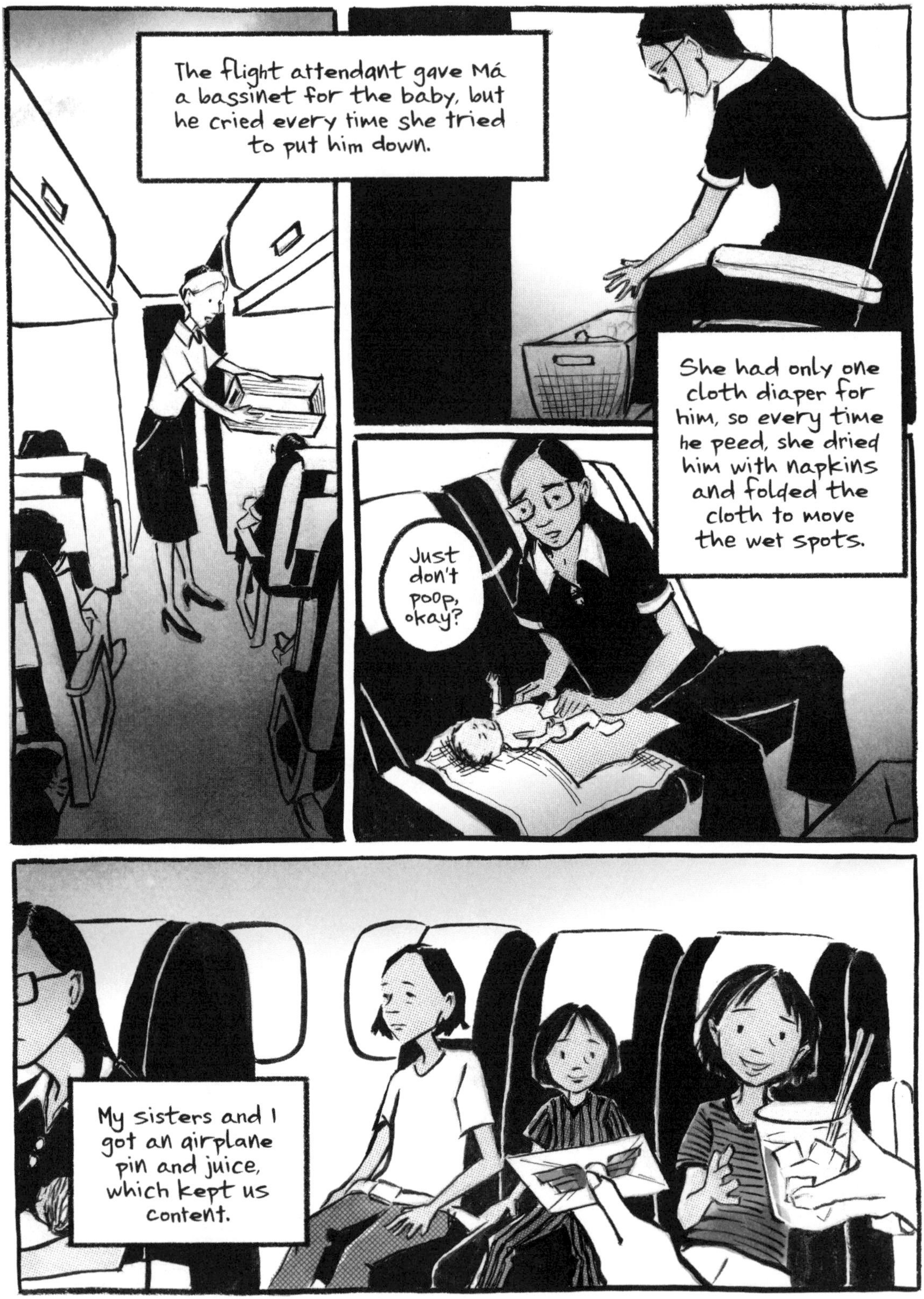

The flight attendant gave Má a bassinet for the baby, but he cried every time she tried to put him down.
She had only one cloth diaper for him, so every time he peed, she dried him with napkins and folded the cloth to move the wet spots.
Just don't poop, okay?
My sisters and I got an airplane pin and juice, which kept us content.

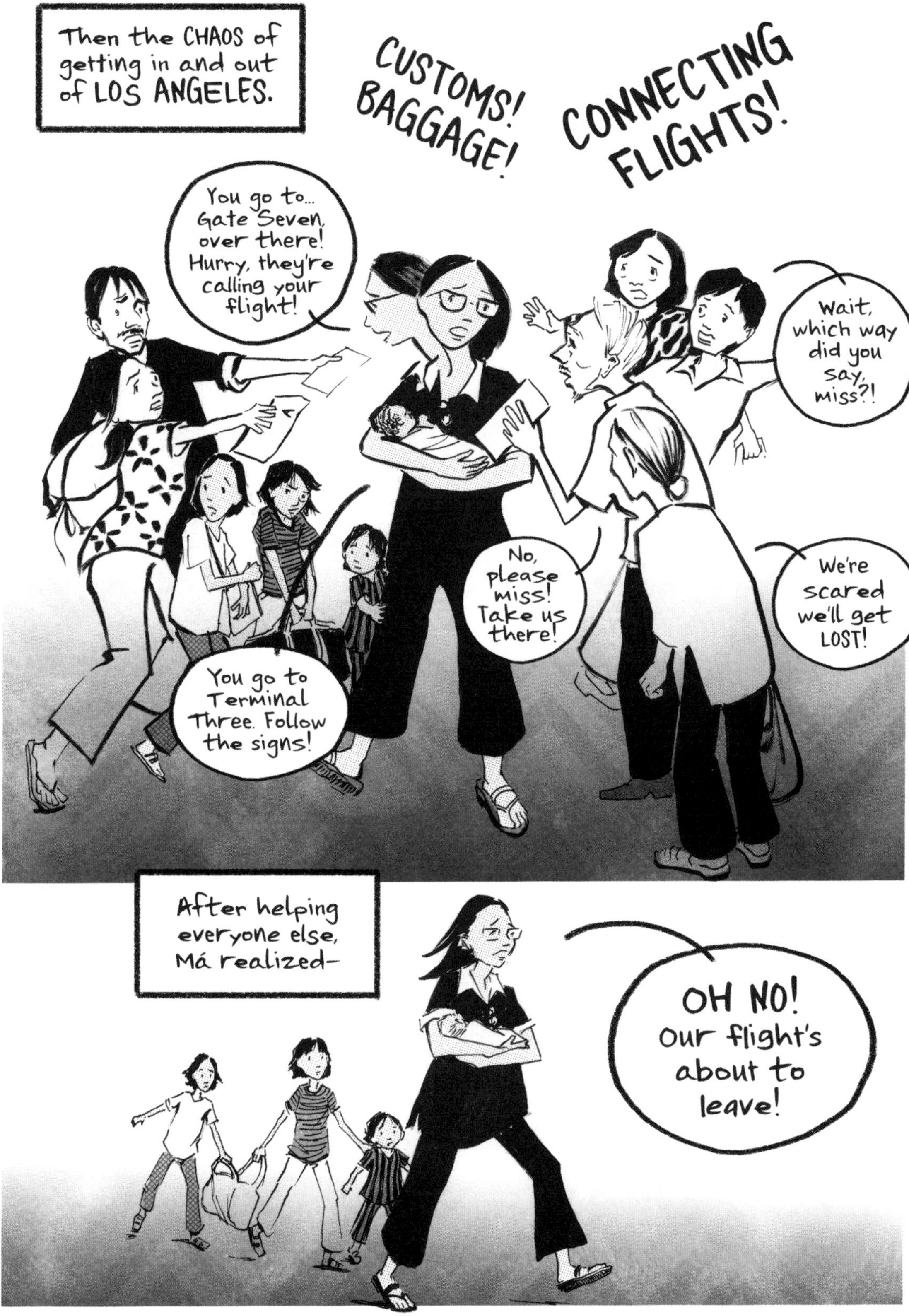
Then the CHAOS of getting in and out of LOS ANGELES.
CUSTOMS! BAGGAGE!
CONNECTING FLIGHTS!
You go to... Gate Seven, over there! Hurry, they're calling your flight!
Wait, which way did you say, miss?!
No, please miss! Take us there!
We're scared we'll get LOST!
You go to Terminal Three. Follow the signs!
After helping everyone else, Má realized—
OH NO! Our flight's about to leave!

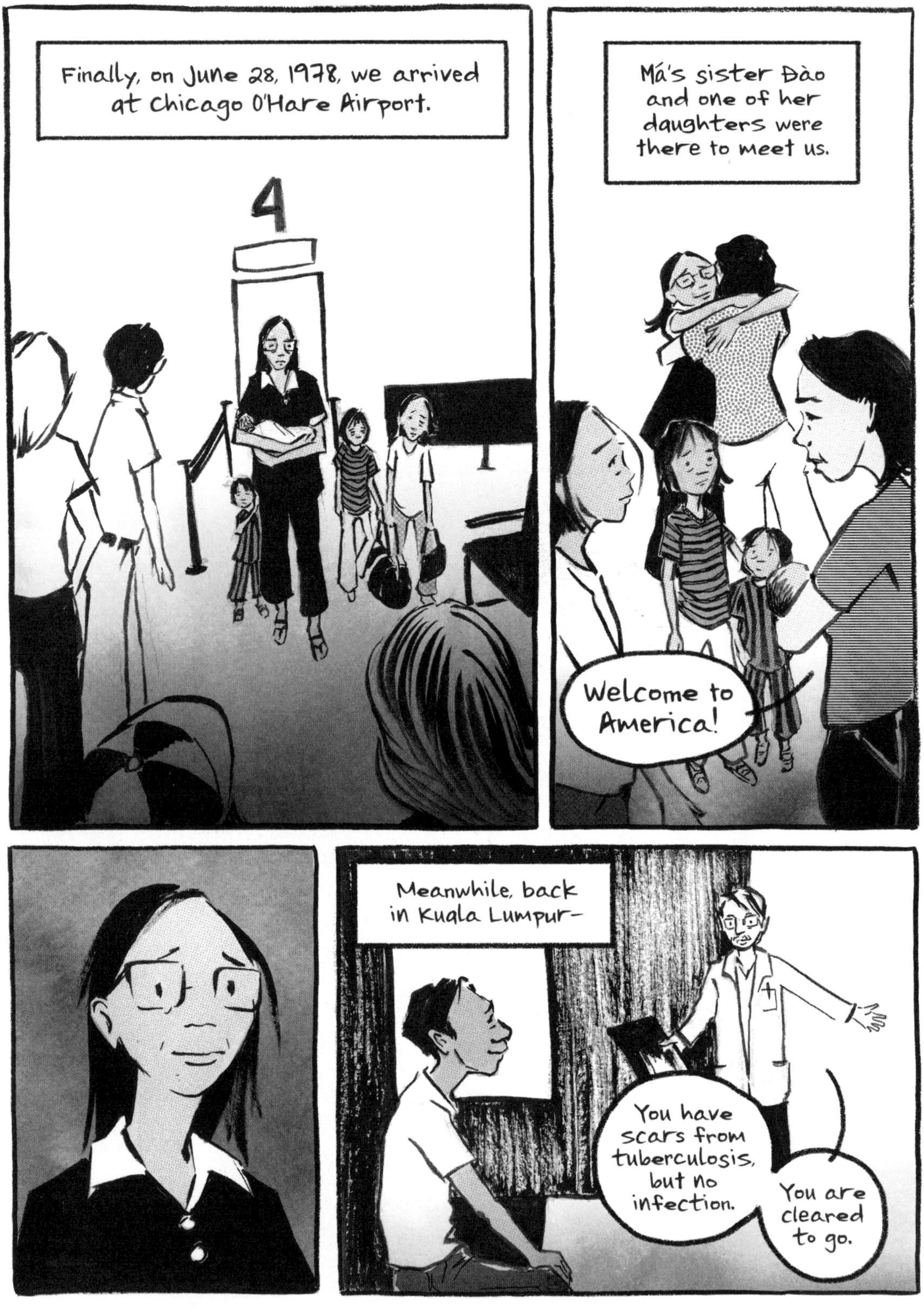
Finally, on June 28, 1978, we arrived at Chicago O'Hare Airport.
4
Má's sister Đào and one of her daughters were there to meet us.
Welcome to America!
Meanwhile, back in Kuala Lumpur–
You have scars from tuberculosis, but no infection.
You are cleared to go.

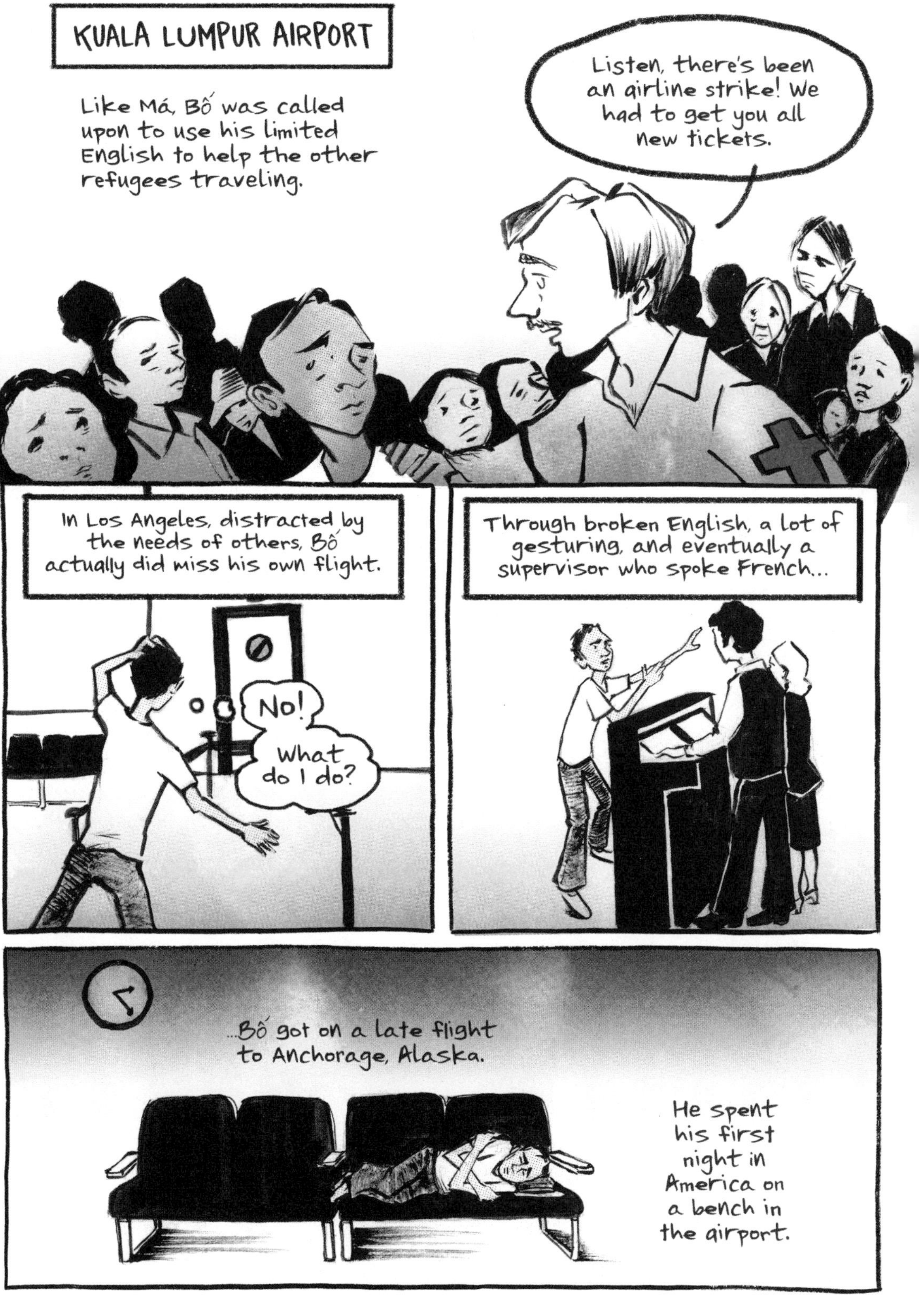
KUALA LUMPUR AIRPORT
Like Má, Bố was called upon to use his limited English to help the other refugees traveling.
Listen, there's been an airline strike! We had to get you all new tickets.
In Los Angeles, distracted by the needs of others, Bố actually did miss his own flight.
No!
What do I do?
Through broken English, a lot of gesturing, and eventually a supervisor who spoke French...
...Bố got on a late flight to Anchorage, Alaska.
He spent his first night in America on a bench in the airport.

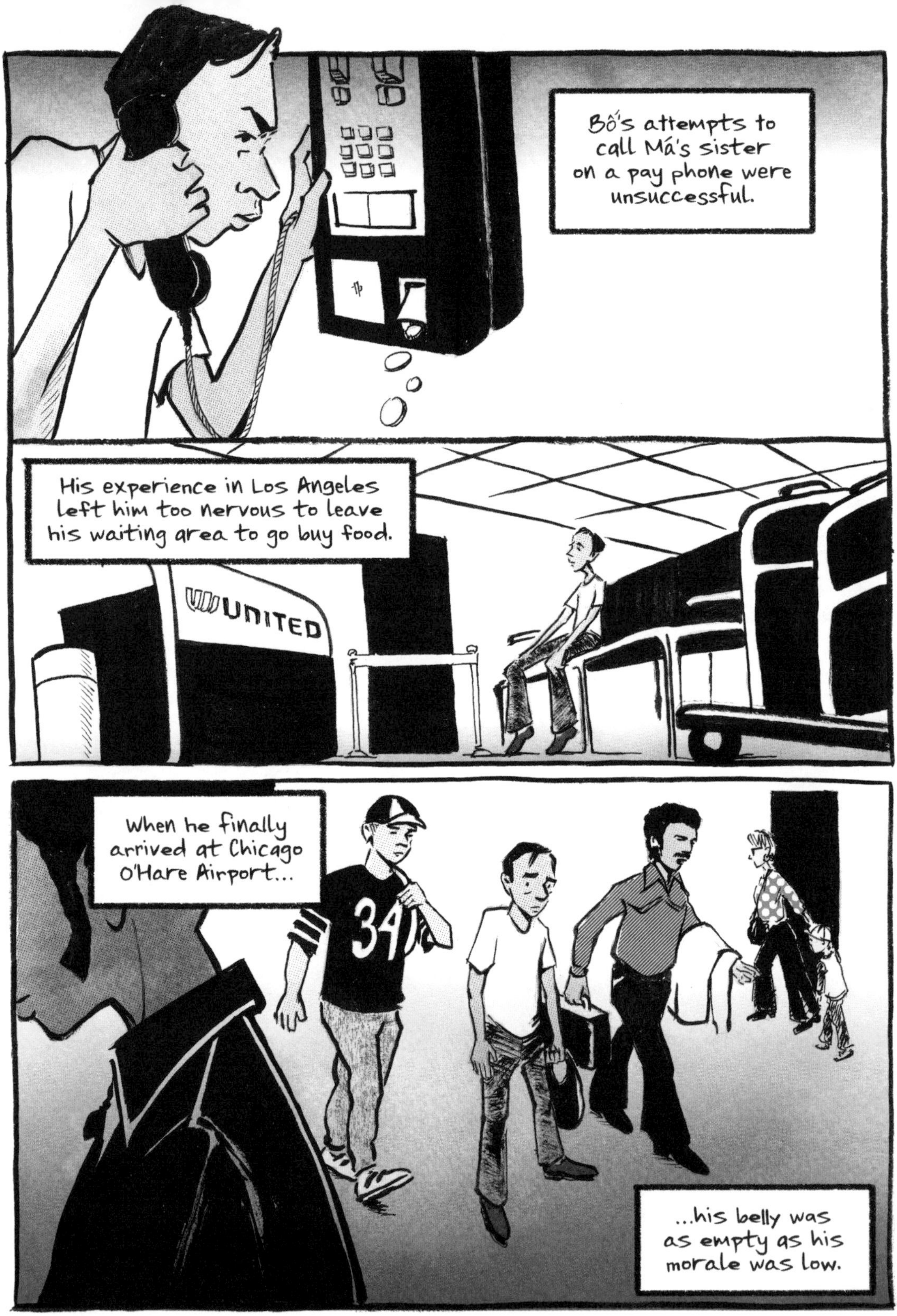
Bố's attempts to call Má's sister on a pay phone were unsuccessful.
His experience in Los Angeles left him too nervous to leave his waiting area to go buy food.
UNITED
When he finally arrived at Chicago O'Hare Airport...
34
...his belly was as empty as his morale was low.

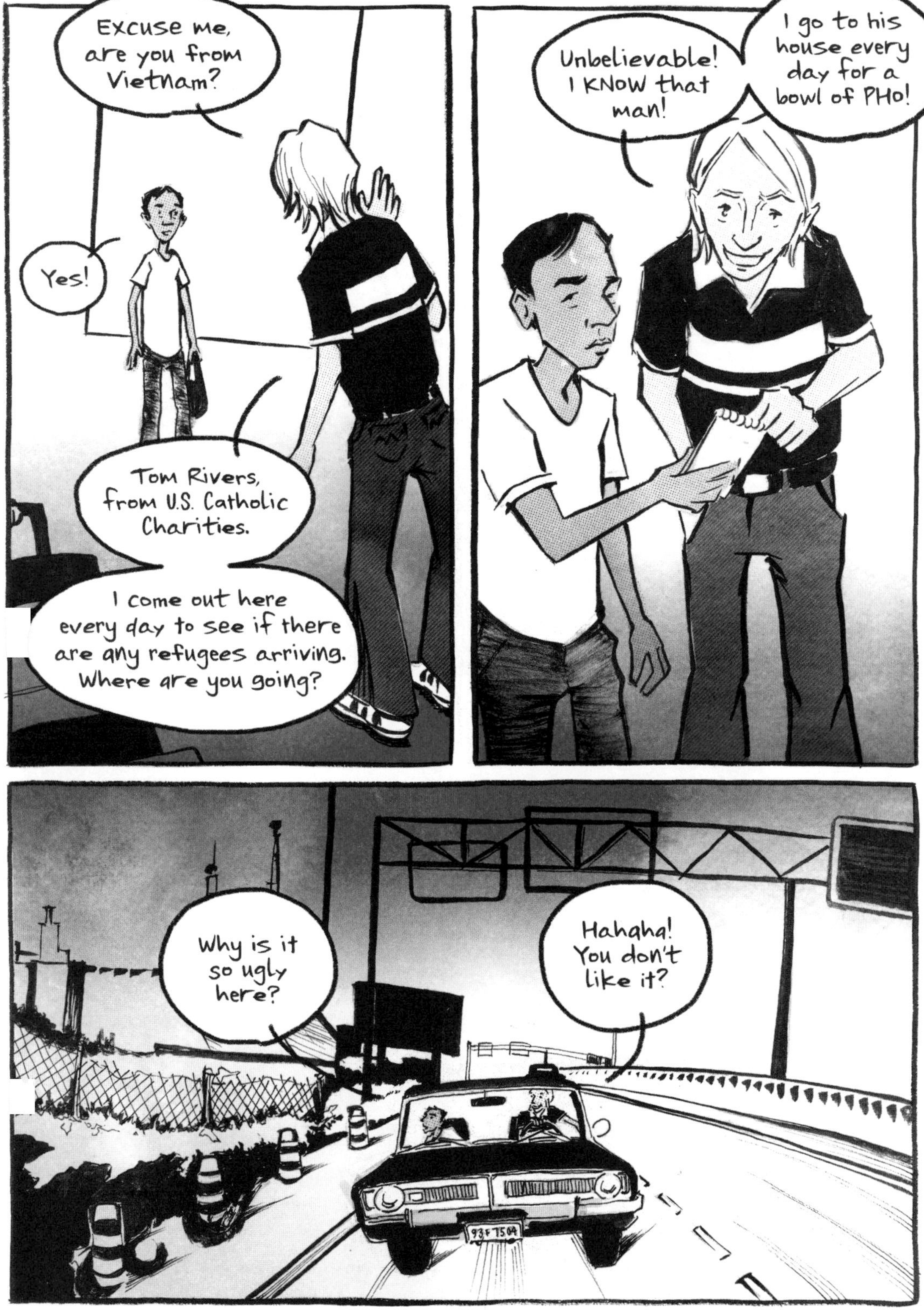
Excuse me, are you from Vietnam?
Yes!
Tom Rivers, from U.S. Catholic Charities.
I come out here every day to see if there are any refugees arriving. Where are you going?
Unbelievable! I KNOW that man!
I go to his house every day for a bowl of PHO!
Why is it so ugly here?
Hahaha! You don't like it?
93F7504

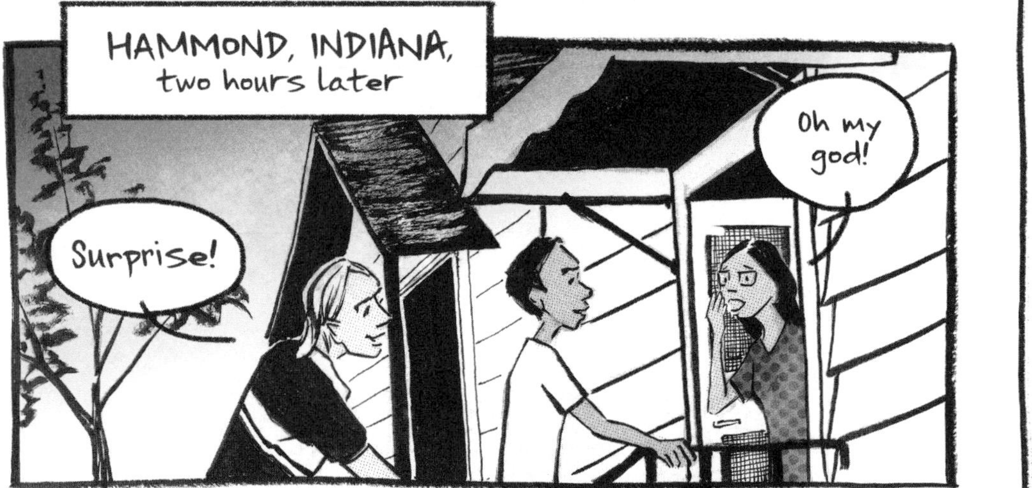
HAMMOND, INDIANA, two hours later
Surprise!
Oh my god!

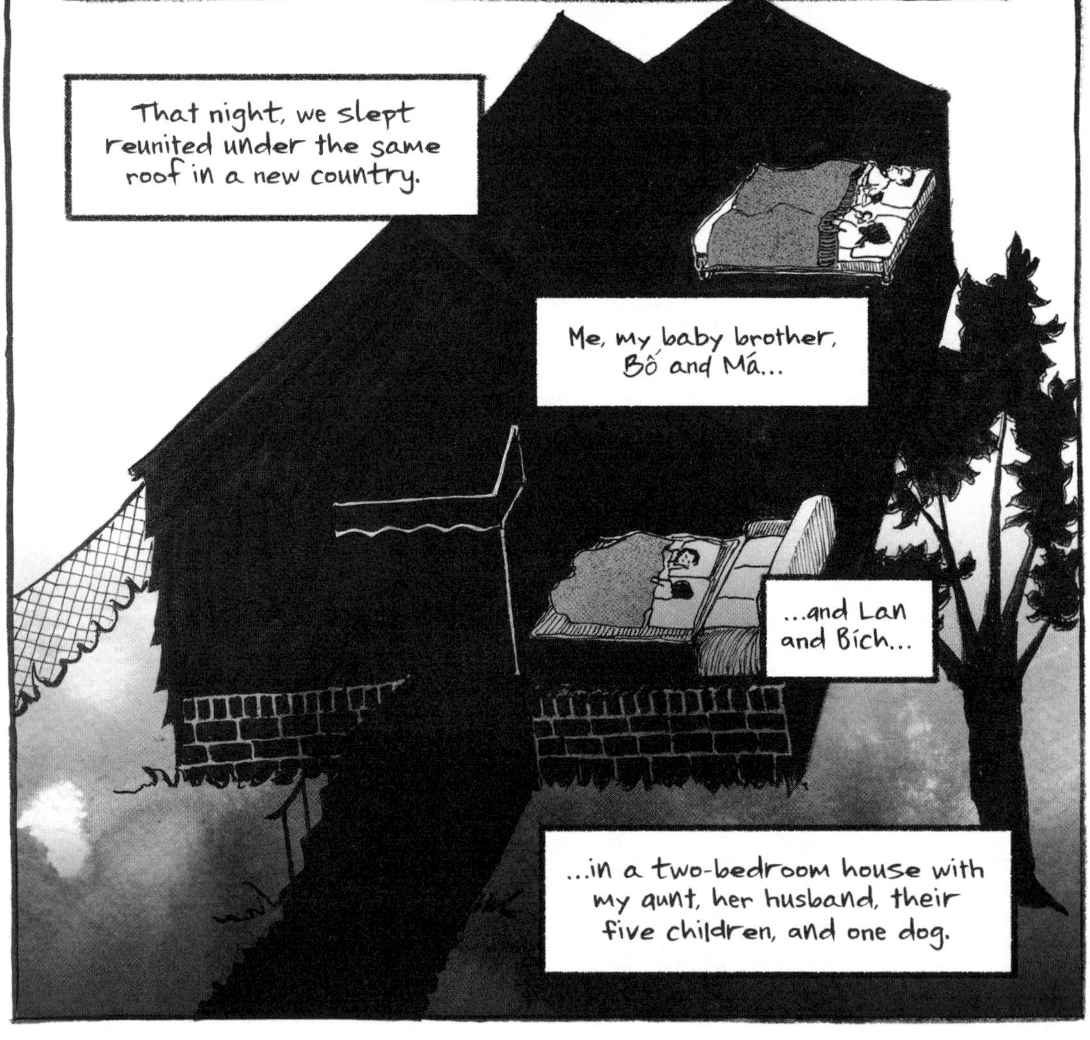
That night, we slept reunited under the same roof in a new country.
Me, my baby brother, Bố and Má...
...and Lan and Bích...
...in a two-bedroom house with my aunt, her husband, their five children, and one dog.

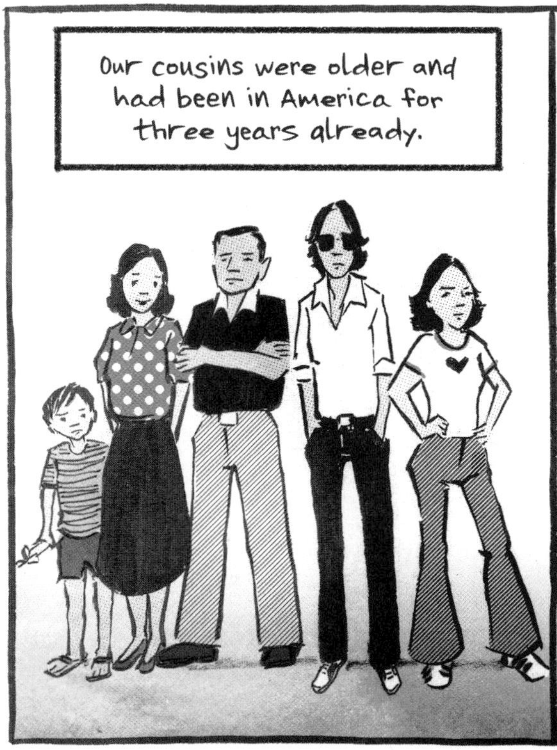
Our cousins were older and had been in America for three years already.

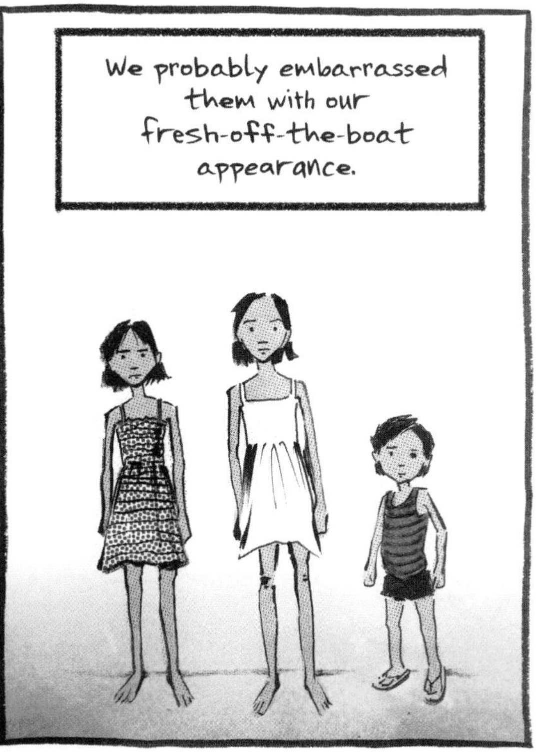
We probably embarrassed them with our fresh-off-the-boat appearance.

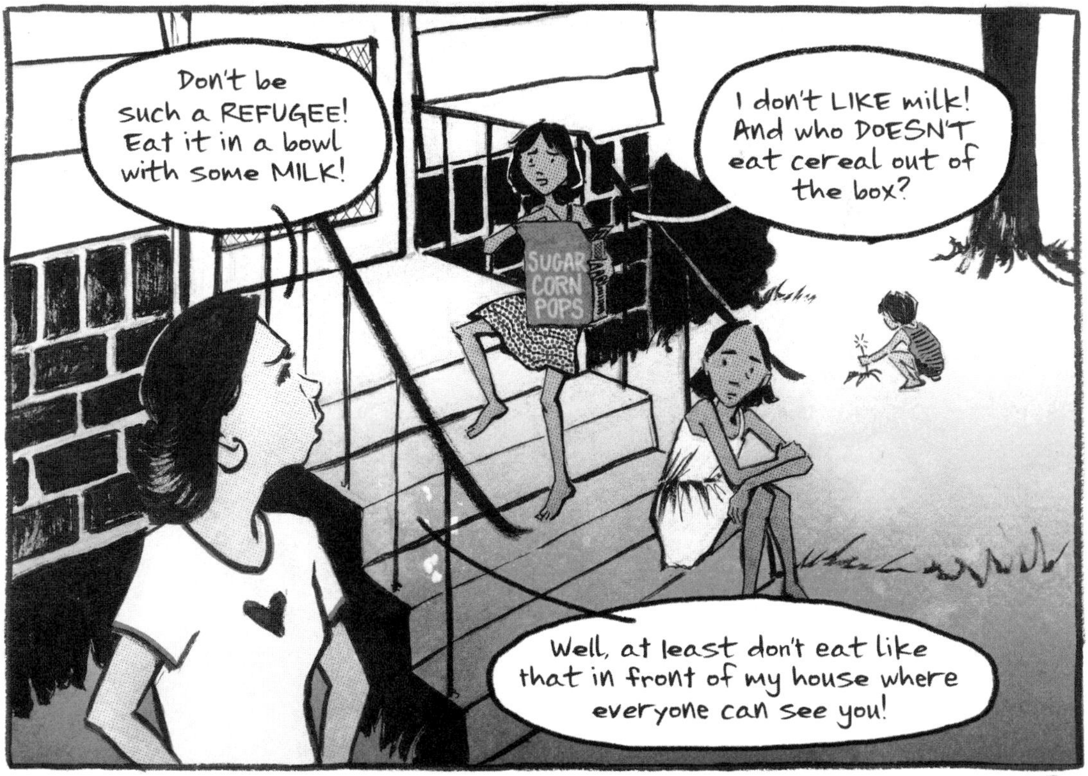
Don't be such a REFUGEE! Eat it in a bowl with some MILK!
SUGAR CORN POPS
I don't LIKE milk! And who DOESN'T eat cereal out of the box?
Well, at least don't eat like that in front of my house where everyone can see you!

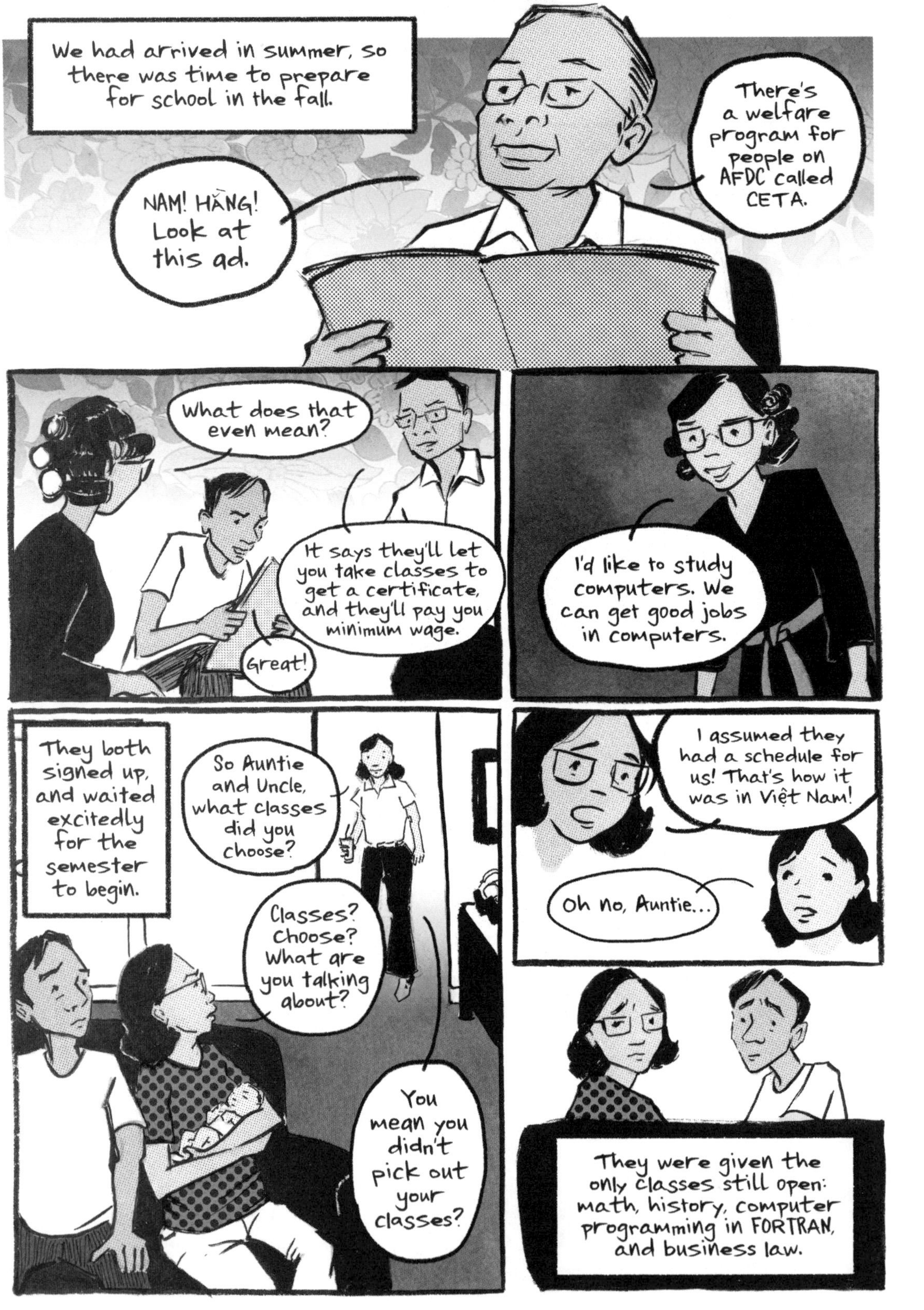
We had arrived in summer, so there was time to prepare for school in the fall.
NAM! HẰNG! Look at this ad.
There's a welfare program for people on AFDC called CETA.
What does that even mean?
It says they'll let you take classes to get a certificate, and they'll pay you minimum wage.
Great!
I'd like to study computers. We can get good jobs in computers.
They both signed up, and waited excitedly for the semester to begin.
So Auntie and Uncle, what classes did you choose?
Classes? Choose? What are you talking about?
You mean you didn't pick out your classes?
I assumed they had a schedule for us! That's how it was in Việt Nam!
Oh no, Auntie...
They were given the only classes still open: math, history, computer programming in FORTRAN, and business law.

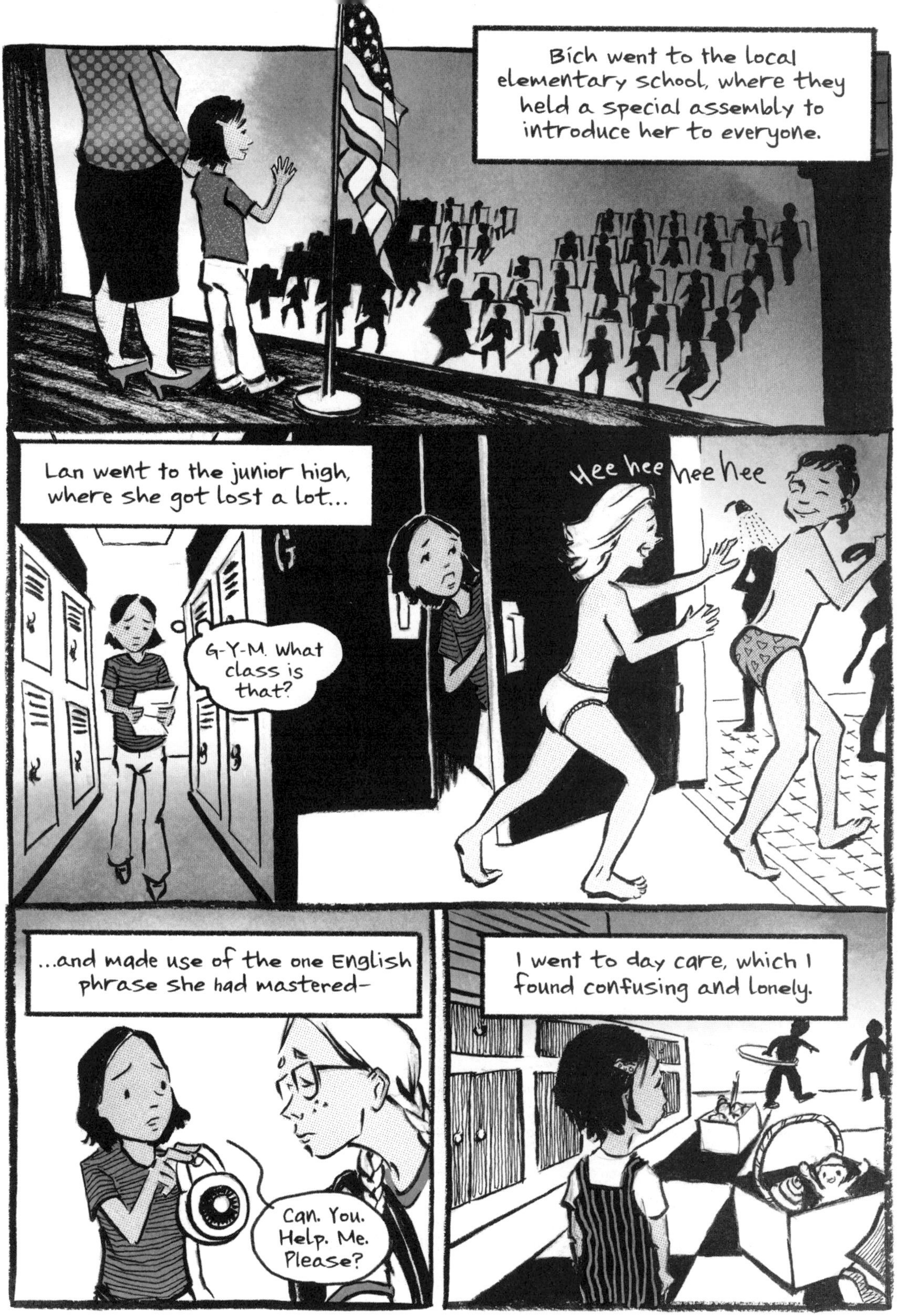
Bich went to the local elementary school, where they held a special assembly to introduce her to everyone.
Lan went to the junior high, where she got lost a lot...
G-Y-M. What class is that?
Hee hee hee hee
...and made use of the one English phrase she had mastered-
Can. You. Help. Me. Please?
I went to day care, which I found confusing and lonely.

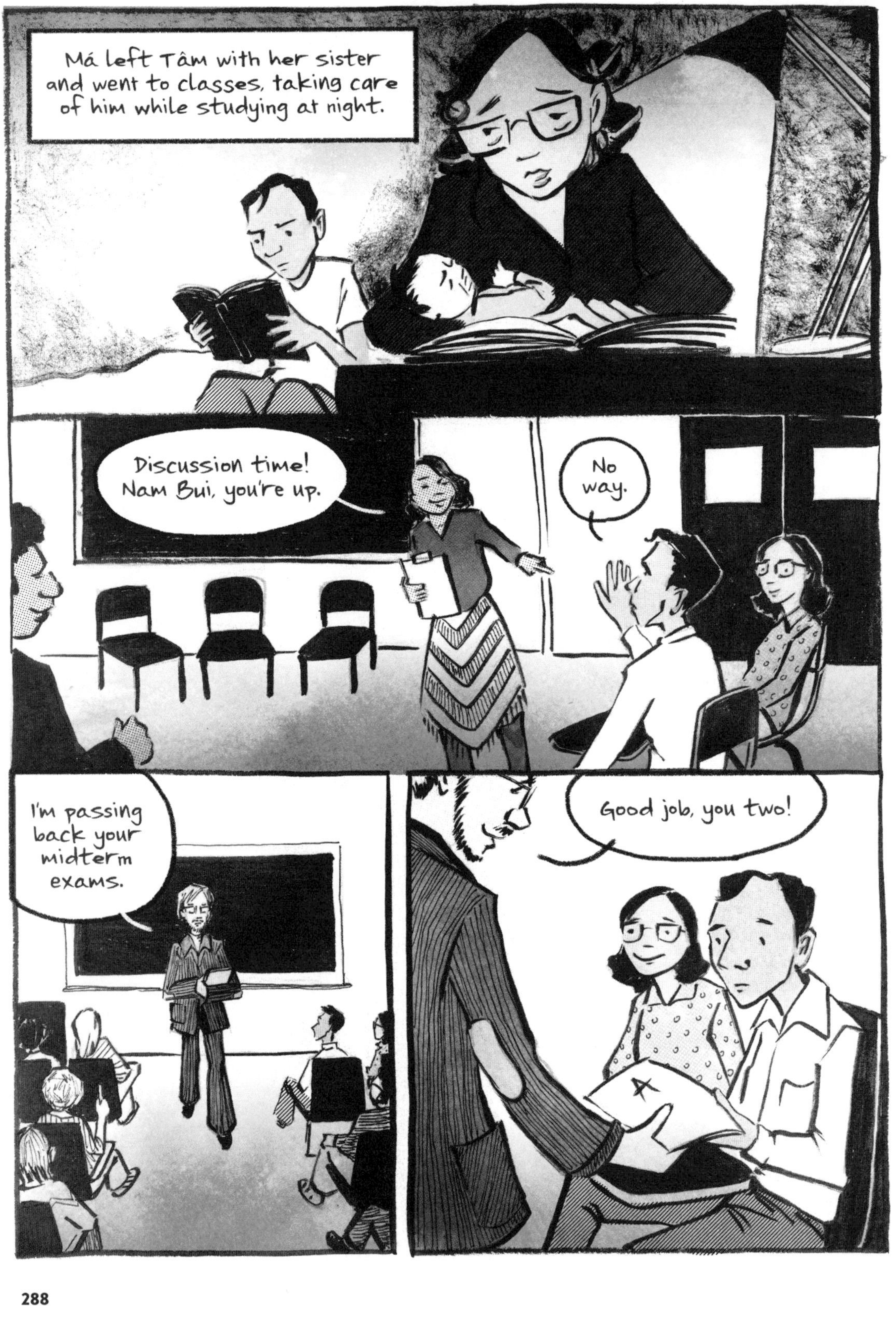
Má left Tâm with her sister and went to classes, taking care of him while studying at night.
Discussion time! Nam Bui, you're up.
No way.
I'm passing back your midterm exams.
Good job, you two!
A

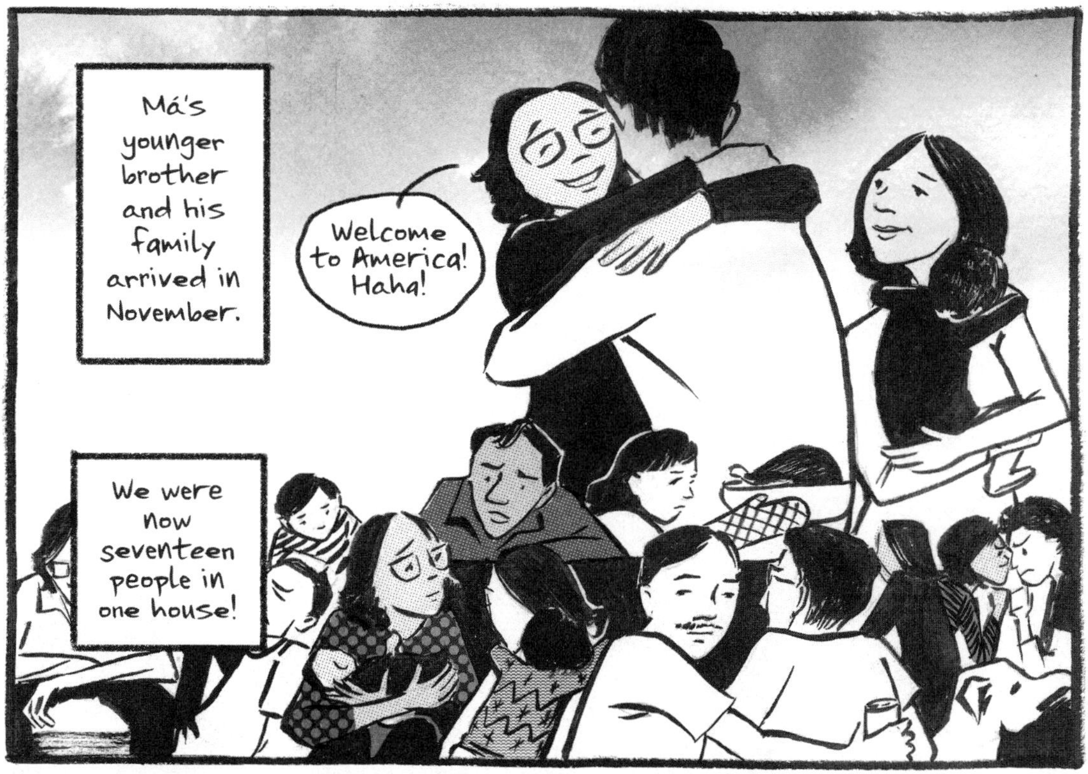
Má's younger brother and his family arrived in November.
Welcome to America! Haha!
We were now seventeen people in one house!

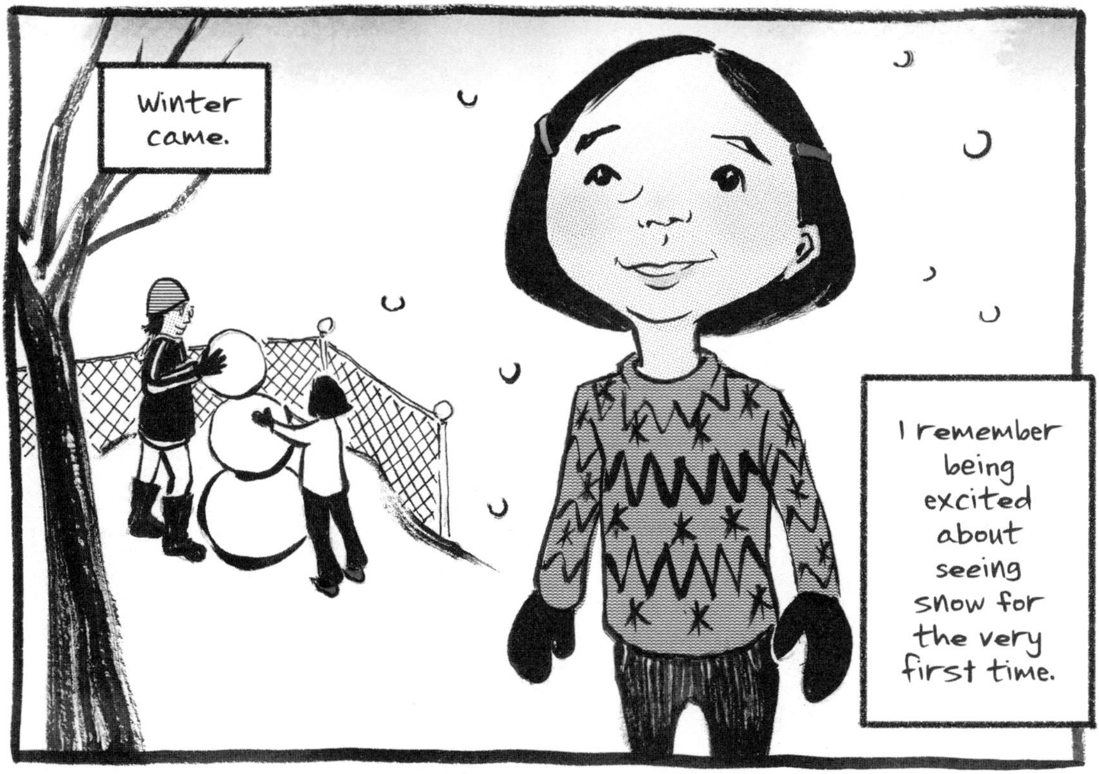
Winter came.
I remember being excited about seeing snow for the very first time.

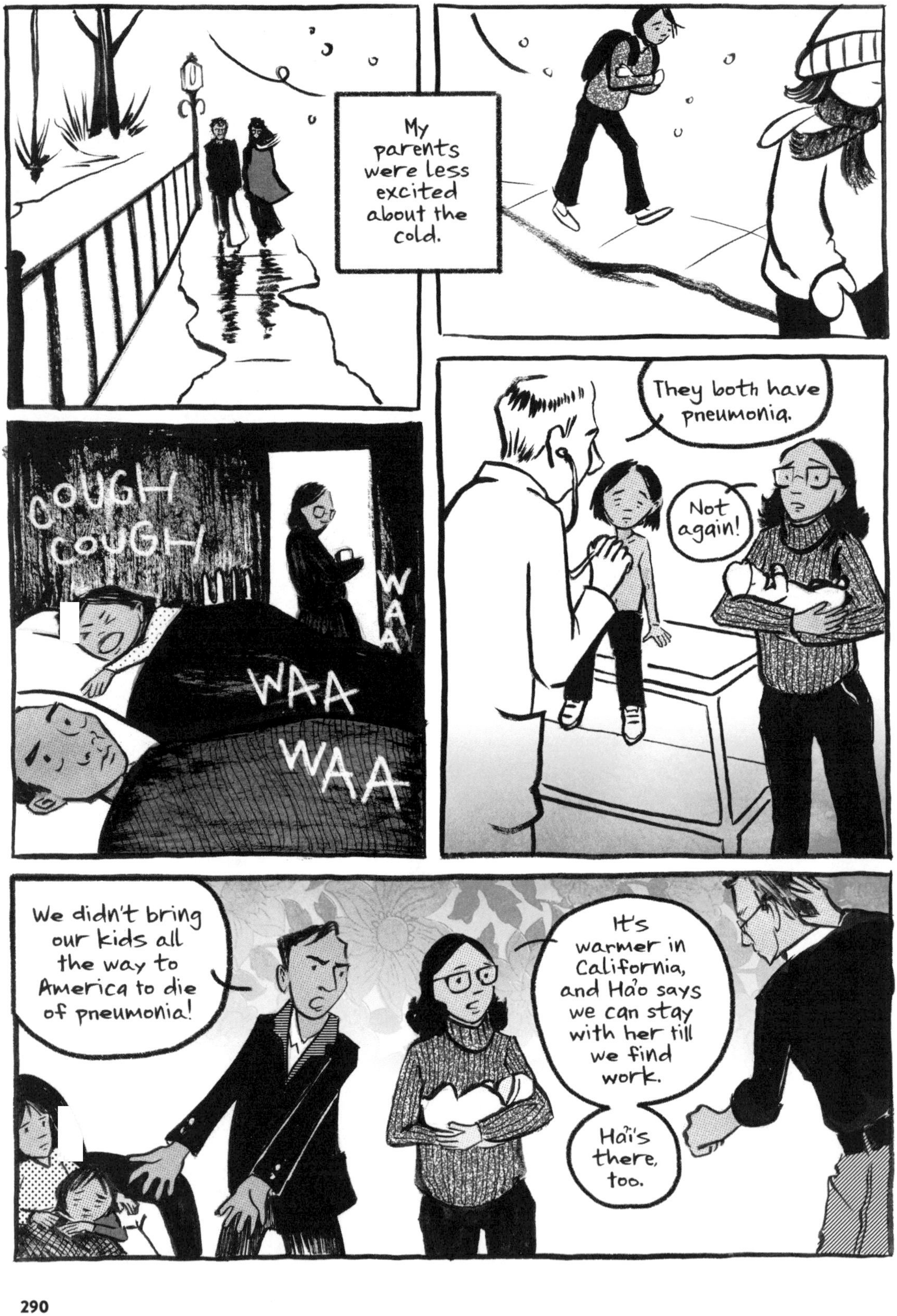

My parents were less excited about the cold.
COUGH COUGH
WAA
WAA WAA
They both have pneumonia.
Not again!
We didn't bring our kids all the way to America to die of pneumonia!
It's warmer in California, and Hảo says we can stay with her till we find work.
Hải's there, too.

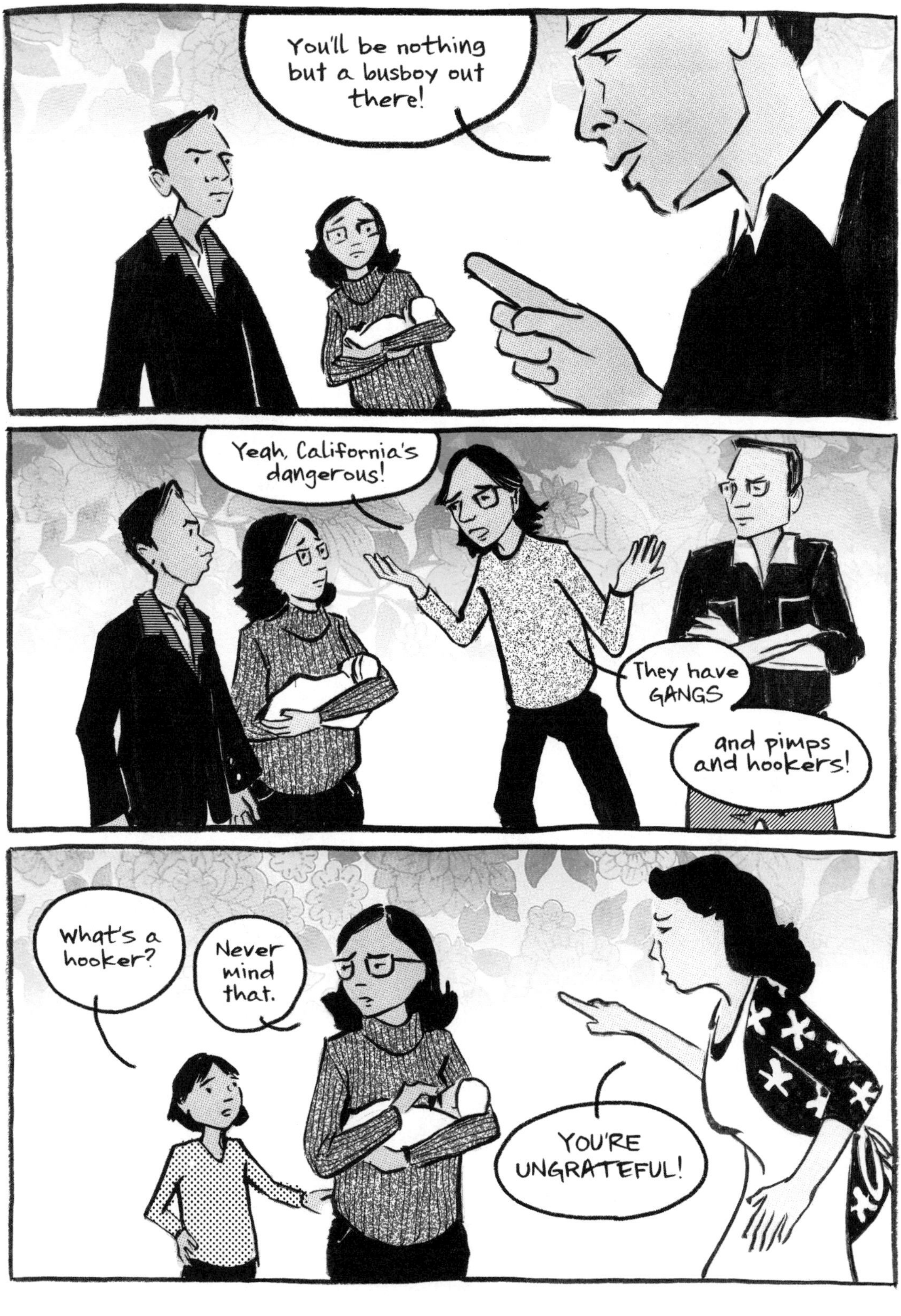
You'll be nothing but a busboy out there!
Yeah, California's dangerous!
They have GANGS
and pimps and hookers!
What's a hooker?
Never mind that.
YOU'RE UNGRATEFUL!

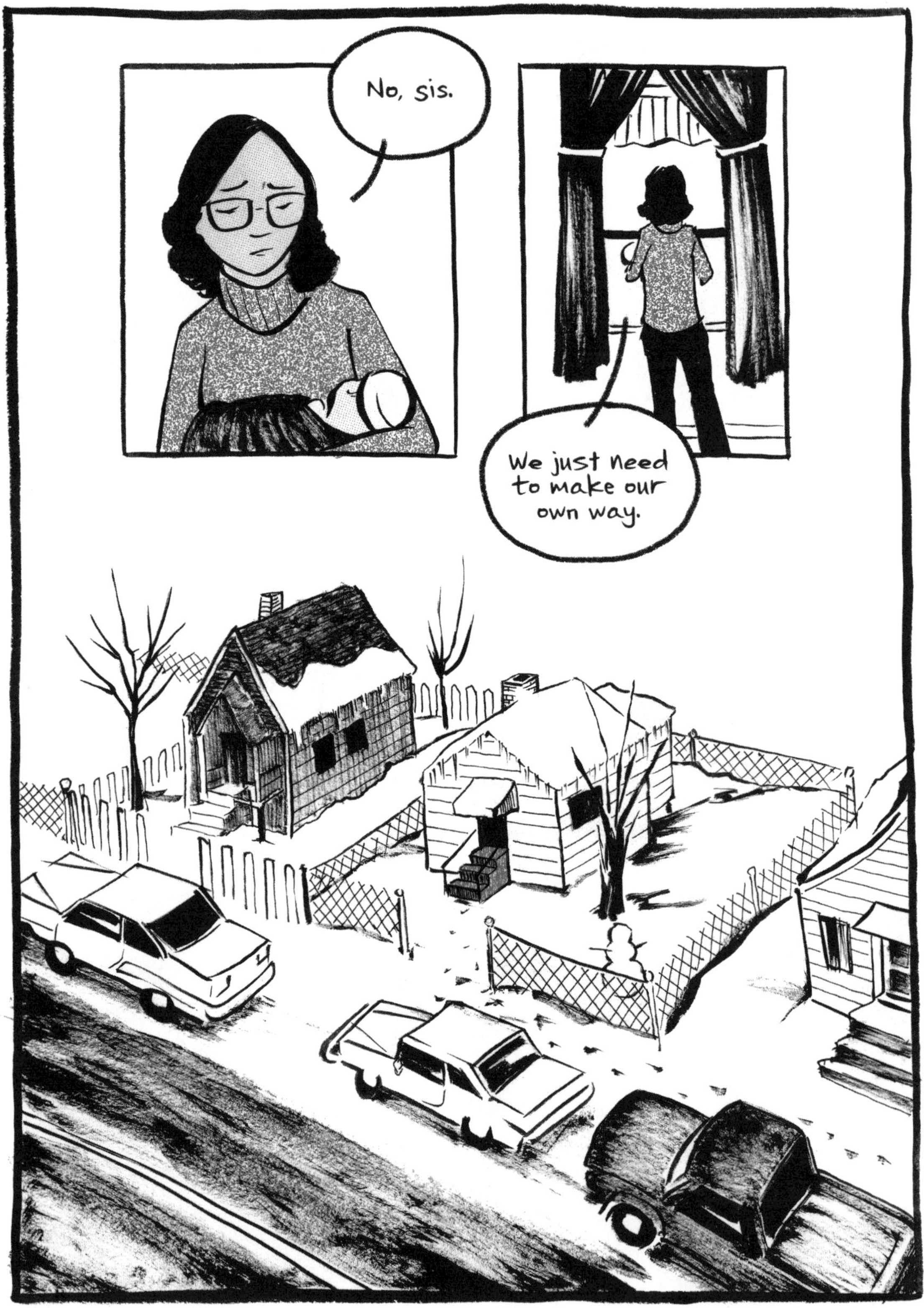
No, sis.
We just need to make our own way.

CHAPTER 9

FIRE AND ASH

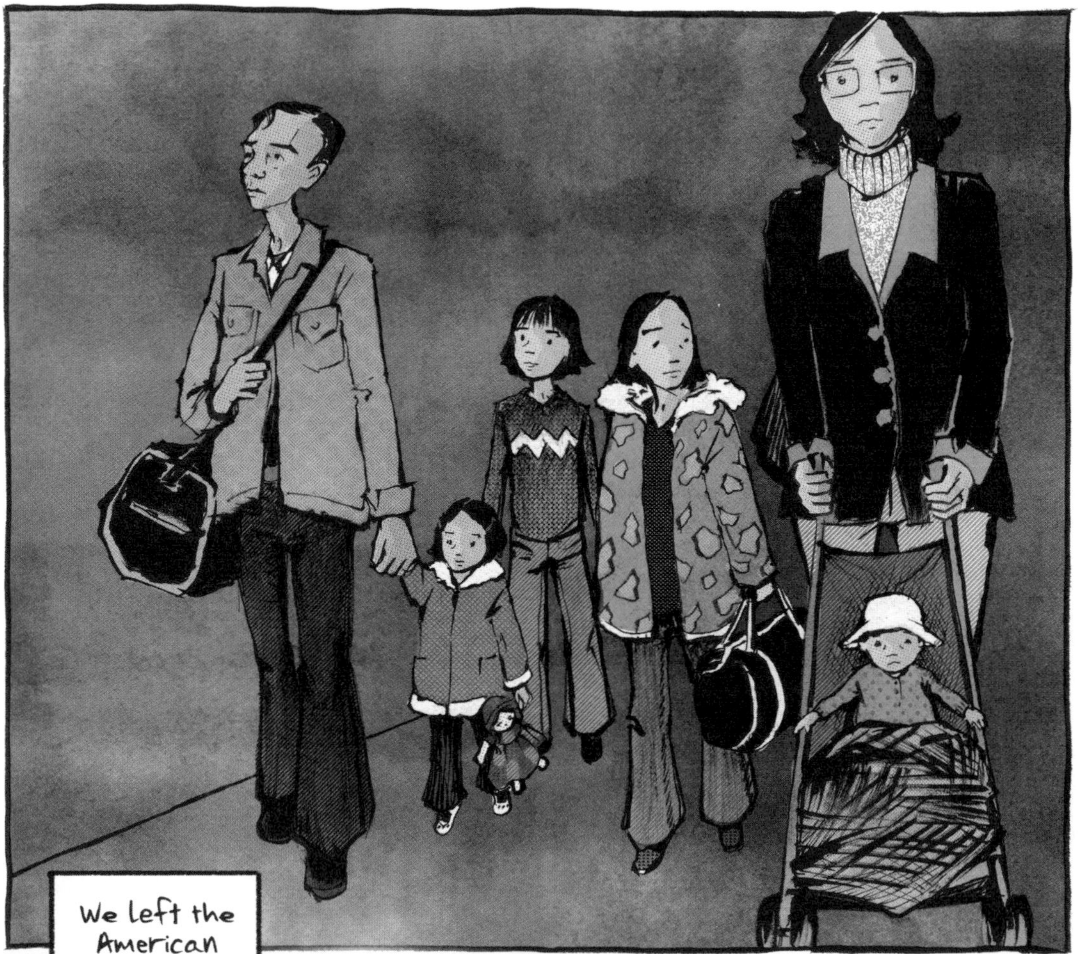
We left the American Midwest in the winter...

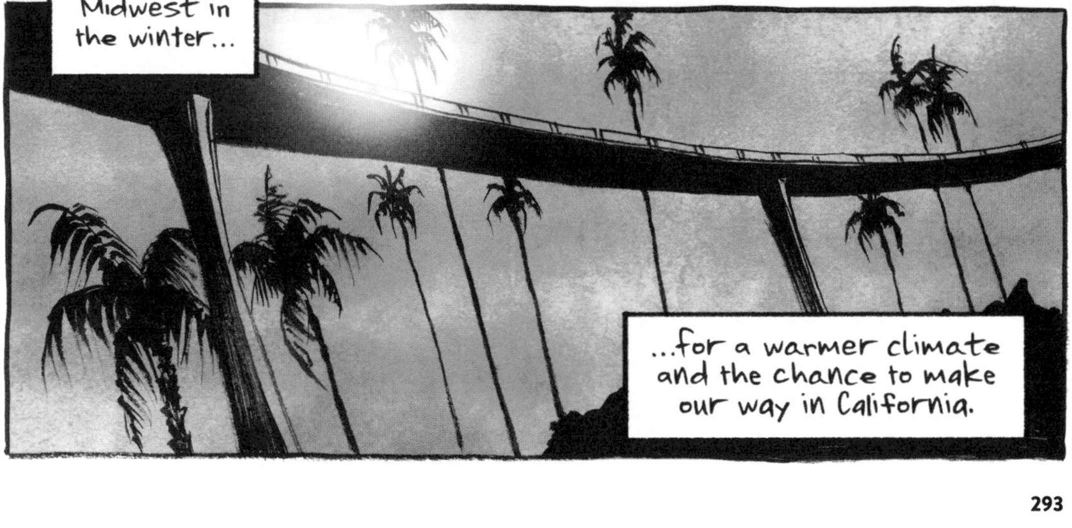
...for a warmer climate and the chance to make our way in California.

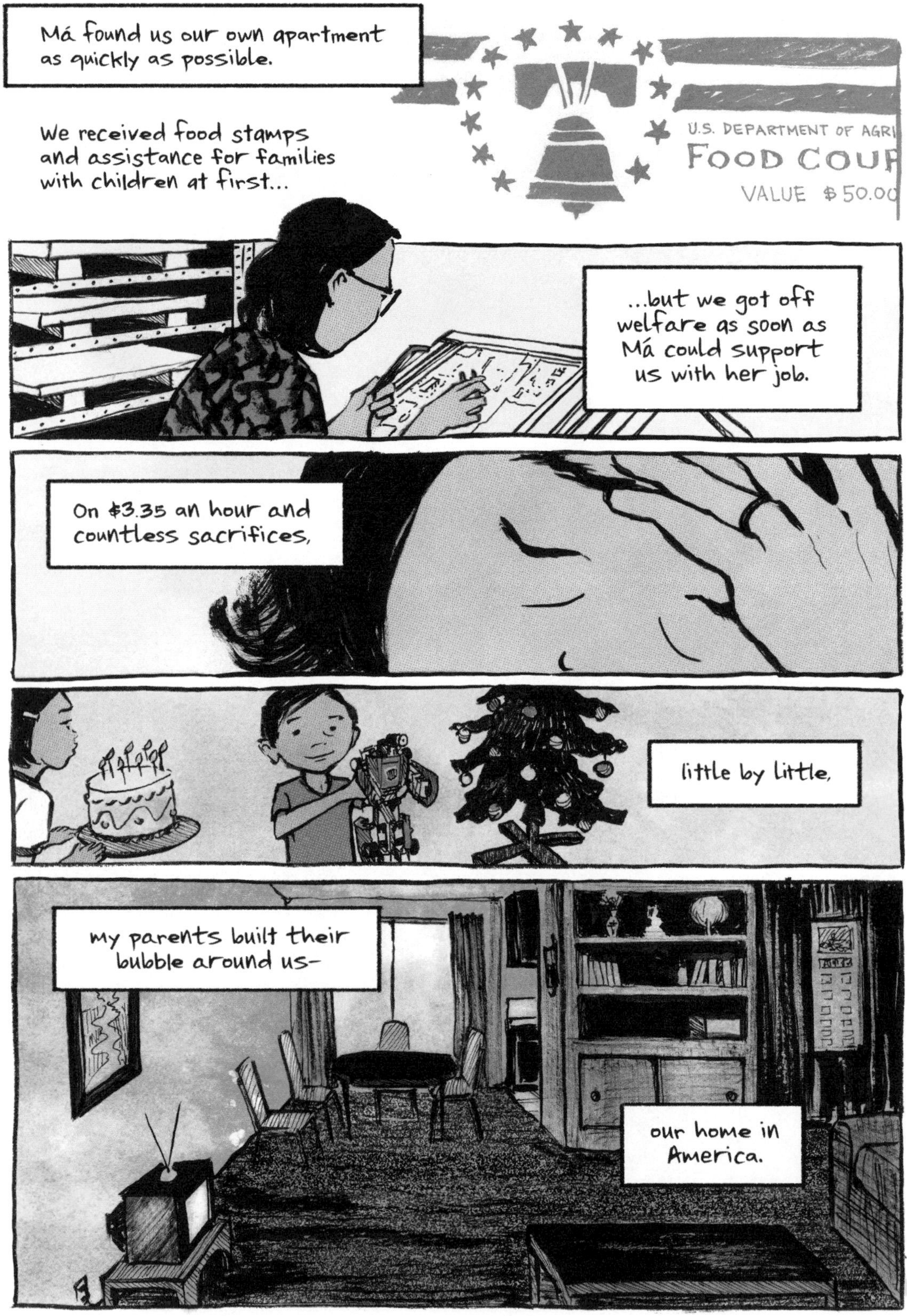
Má found us our own apartment as quickly as possible.
U.S. DEPARTMENT OF AGRI
FOOD COUP
VALUE $50.00
We received food stamps and assistance for families with children at first...
...but we got off welfare as soon as Má could support us with her job.
On $3.35 an hour and countless sacrifices,
little by little,
my parents built their bubble around us-
our home in America.

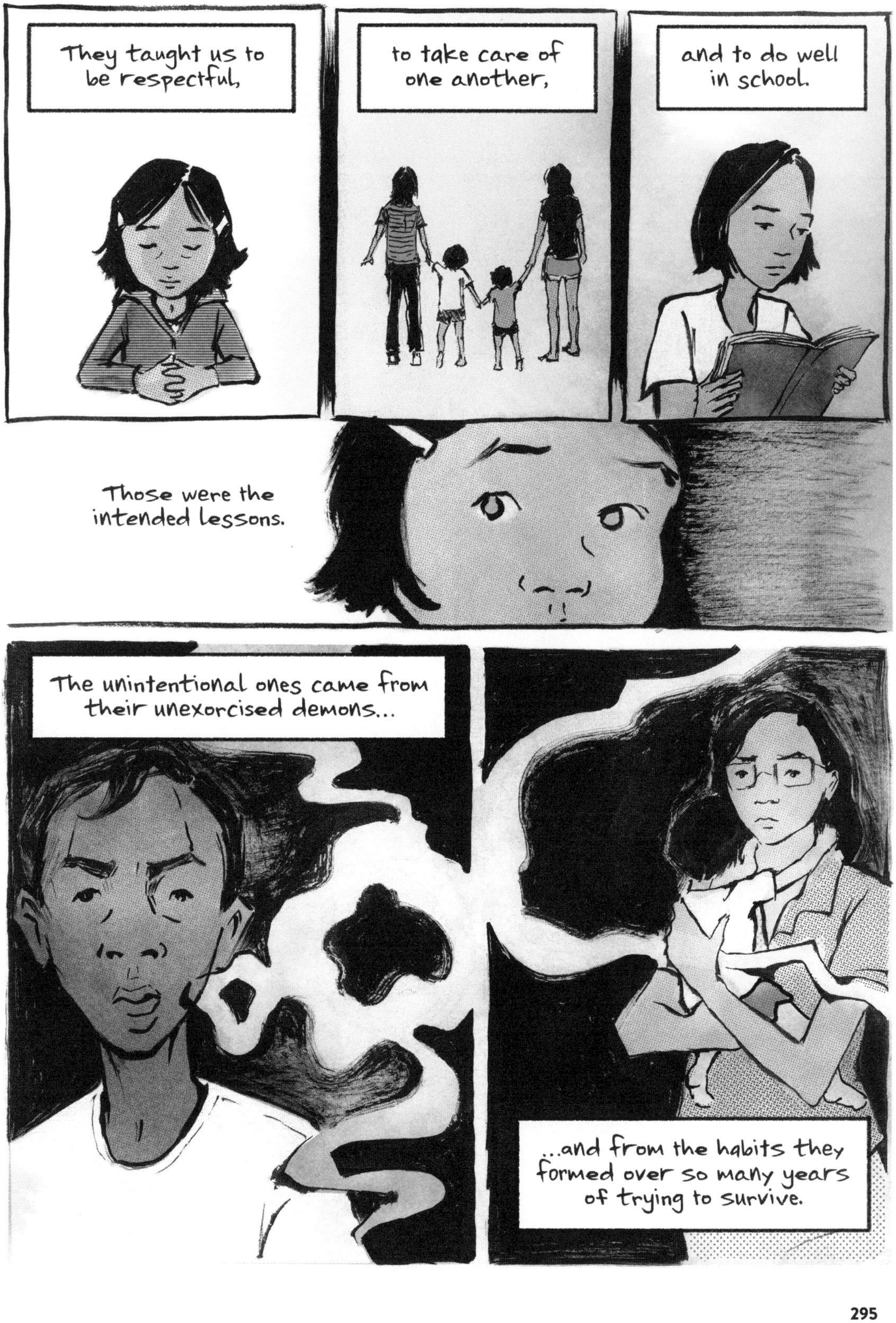
They taught us to be respectful,
to take care of one another,
and to do well in school.
Those were the intended lessons.
The unintentional ones came from their unexorcised demons...
...and from the habits they formed over so many years of trying to survive.

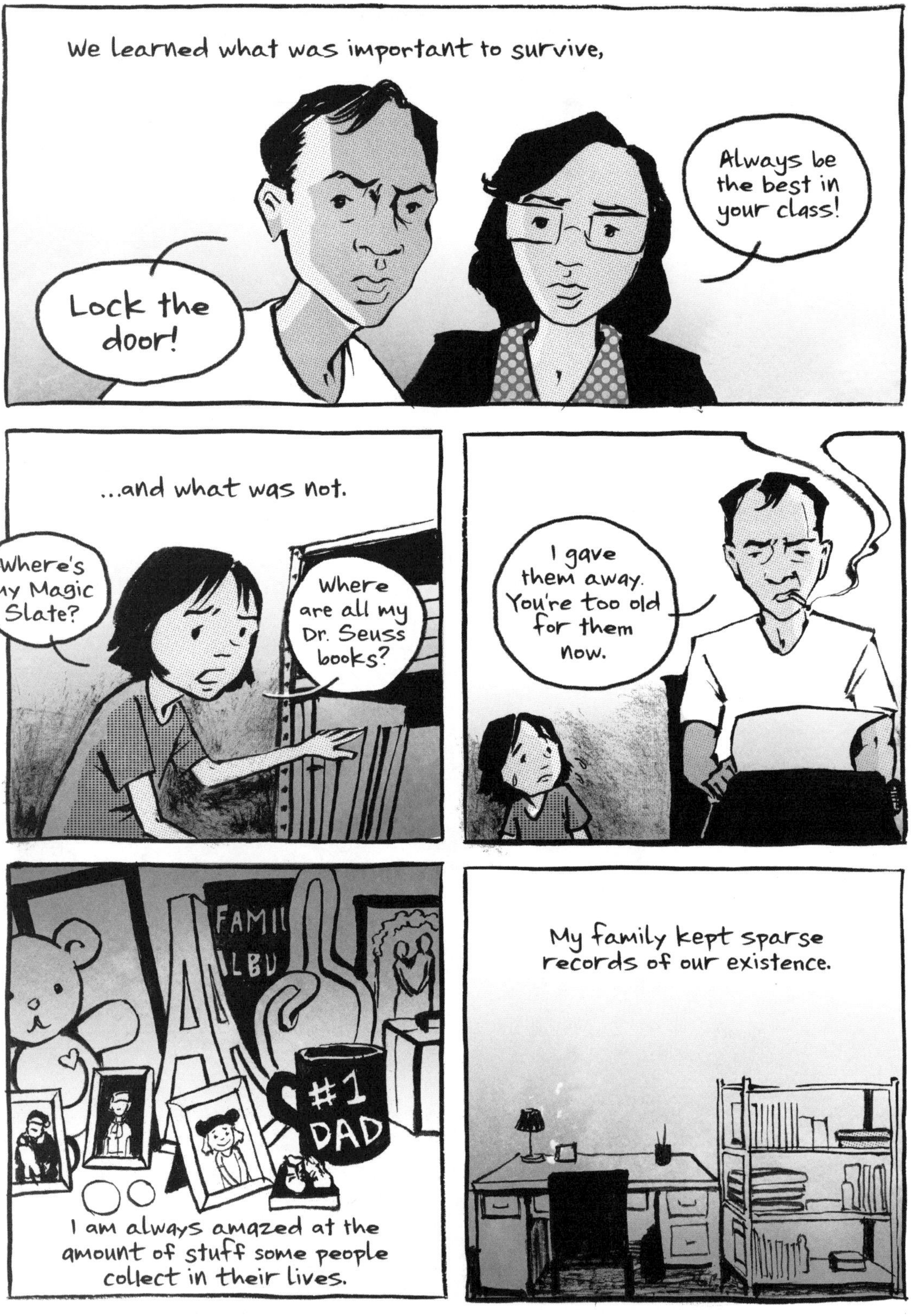
We learned what was important to survive,
Lock the door!
Always be the best in your class!
...and what was not.
Where's my Magic Slate?
Where are all my Dr. Seuss books?
I gave them away. You're too old for them now.
FAMIL
LBU
#1 DAD
I am always amazed at the amount of stuff some people collect in their lives.
My family kept sparse records of our existence.

IMPORTANT DOCUMENTS

Our most important possession was this unassuming brown file folder—

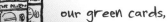

—in which my parents placed the most essential pieces of our identity.

Our birth certificates, translated and notarized,

our green cards,

and our Social Security cards.

When we began school, we were each given a brown folder of our own.

Bùi Phương Thi

Into this folder went our report cards,

Bui, Thi   E E E E E

Bui, Tam   E E E E E

certificates and awards,

CITIZEN OF THE MONTH

Thi   Bui

January 1981

1981

and the annual class picture.

No individual school pictures. Those were too expensive.

When I was nine, my parents passed the test to become American citizens, and our naturalization papers went straight into the Important Documents folder.

Eventually, Lan's and Bich's folders reached capacity,

and the awards became wooden plaques and shiny trophies that adorned their bedroom.

Má's friend from work often drove them to school functions.

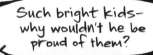

I don't understand why your husband won't go to your kids' awards nights!

Such bright kids— why wouldn't he be proud of them?

Sigh. It's just not our way to show it so much.

By the time Lan and Bich graduated high school and went to college,

CLASS OF '84
VALEDICTORIAN

CLASS OF '86
SALUTATORIAN

Má had acquired her own certificates,

piecing together lunchtime workshops and night courses to build up the career she had begun on the assembly line at three dollars an hour.

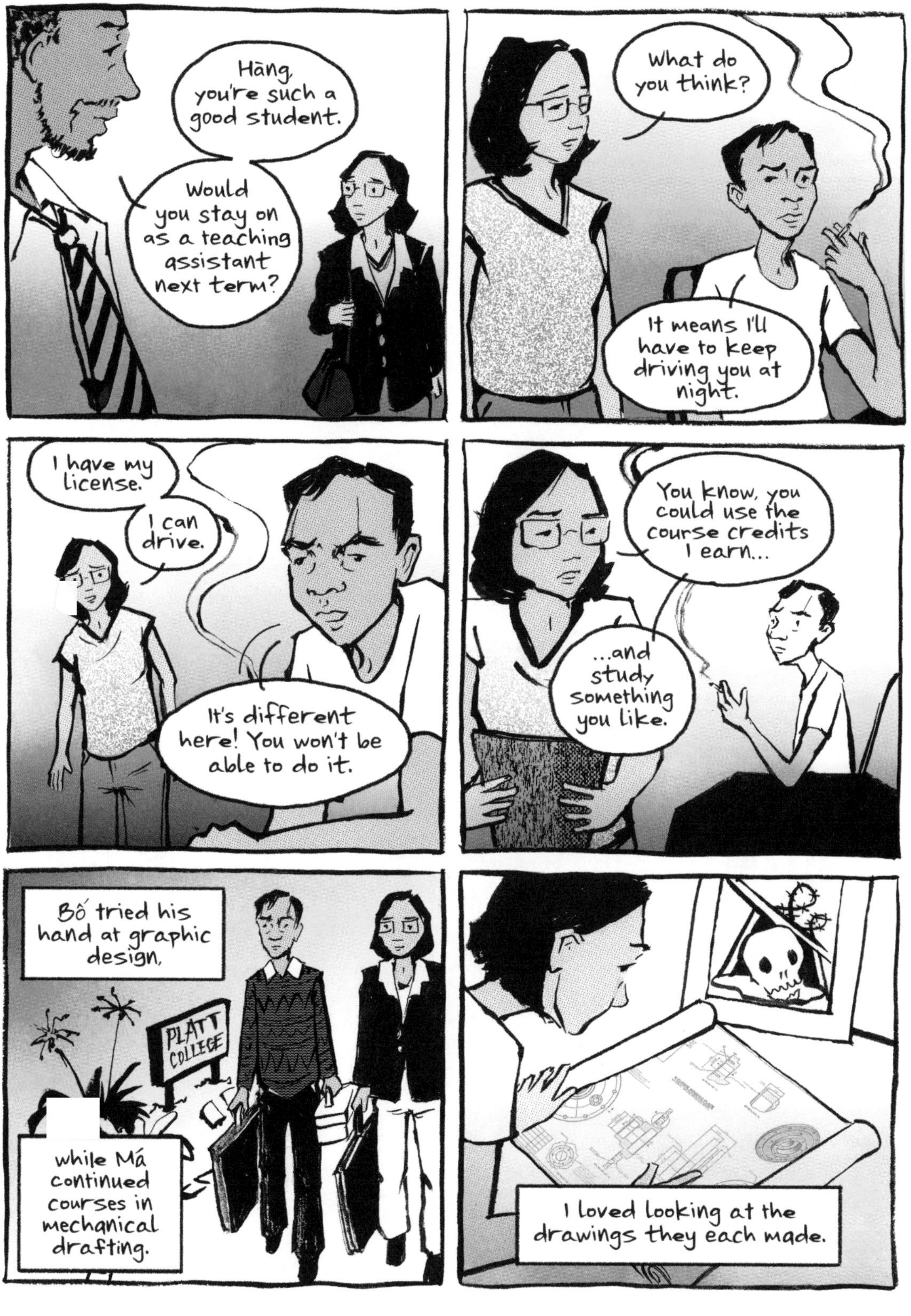
Hăng, you're such a good student.
Would you stay on as a teaching assistant next term?
What do you think?
It means I'll have to keep driving you at night.
I have my license.
I can drive.
It's different here! You won't be able to do it.
You know, you could use the course credits I earn...
...and study something you like.
Bố tried his hand at graphic design,
PLATT COLLEGE
while Má continued courses in mechanical drafting.
I loved looking at the drawings they each made.

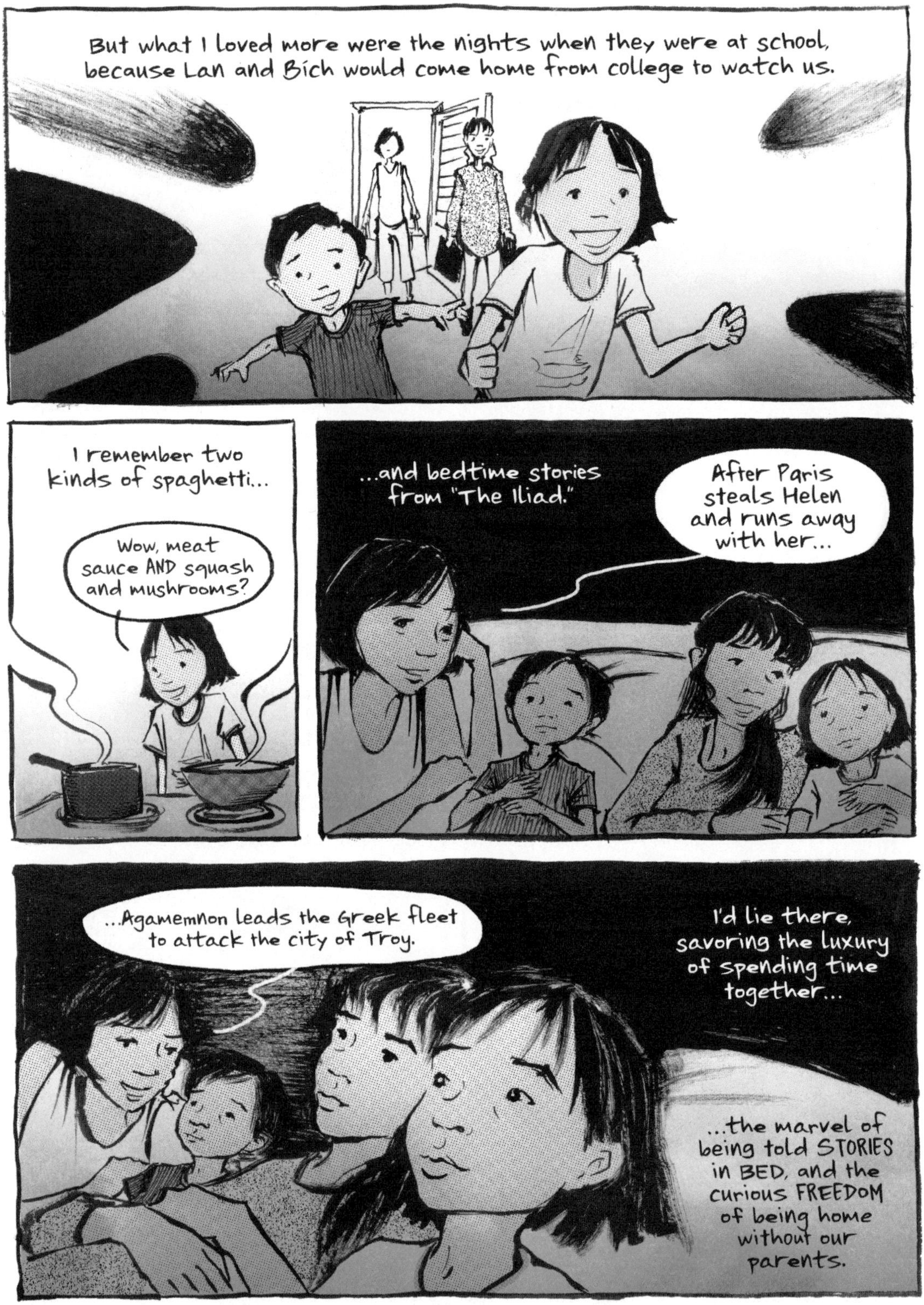

But what I loved more were the nights when they were at school, because Lan and Bích would come home from college to watch us.
I remember two kinds of spaghetti...
Wow, meat sauce AND squash and mushrooms?
...and bedtime stories from "The Iliad."
After Paris steals Helen and runs away with her...
...Agamemnon leads the Greek fleet to attack the city of Troy.
I'd lie there, savoring the luxury of spending time together...
...the marvel of being told STORIES in BED, and the curious FREEDOM of being home without our parents.

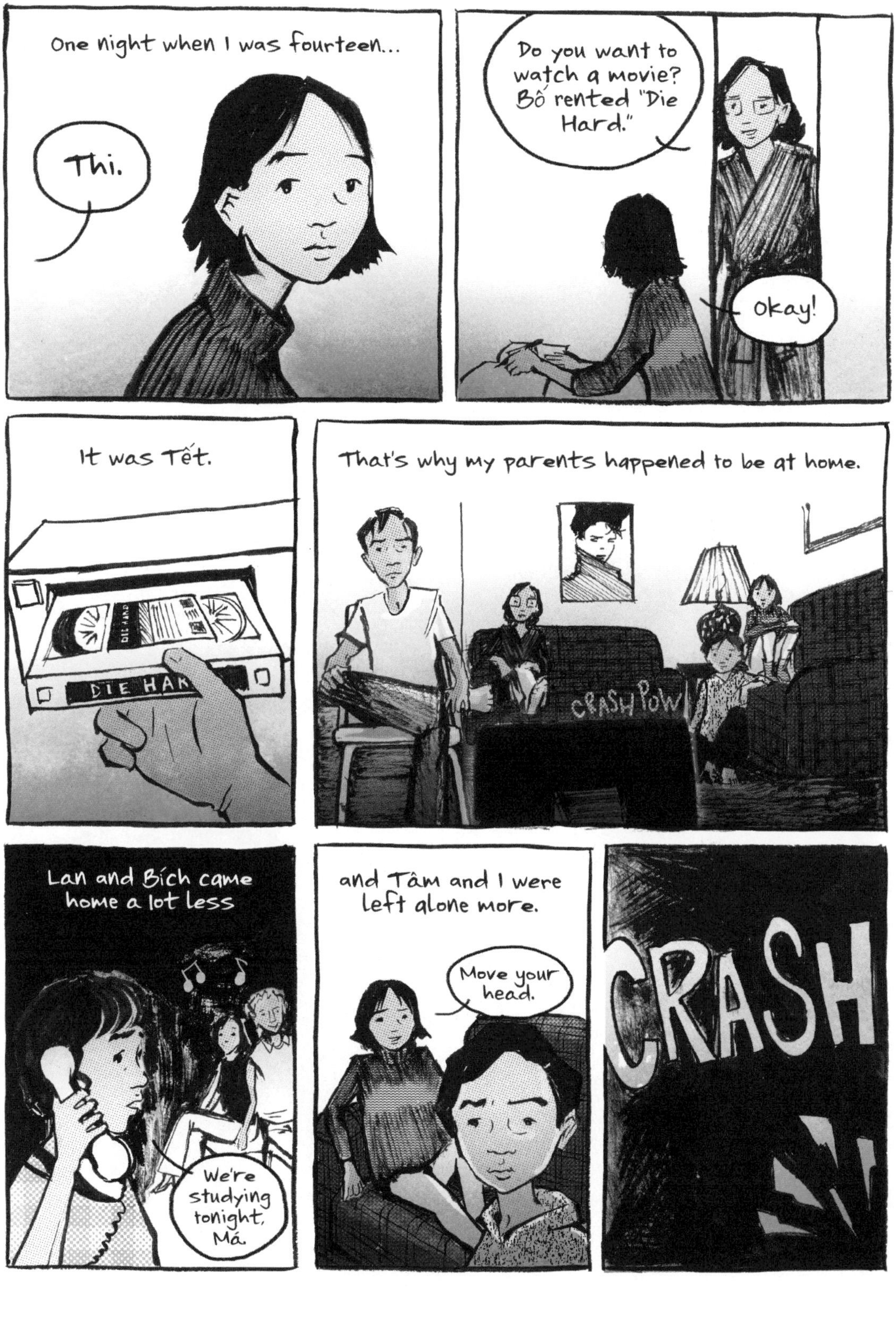
One night when I was fourteen...
Thi.
Do you want to watch a movie? Bố rented "Die Hard."
Okay!
It was Tết.
DIE HARD
That's why my parents happened to be at home.
CRASH POW
Lan and Bích came home a lot less
We're studying tonight, Má.
and Tâm and I were left alone more.
Move your head.
CRASH

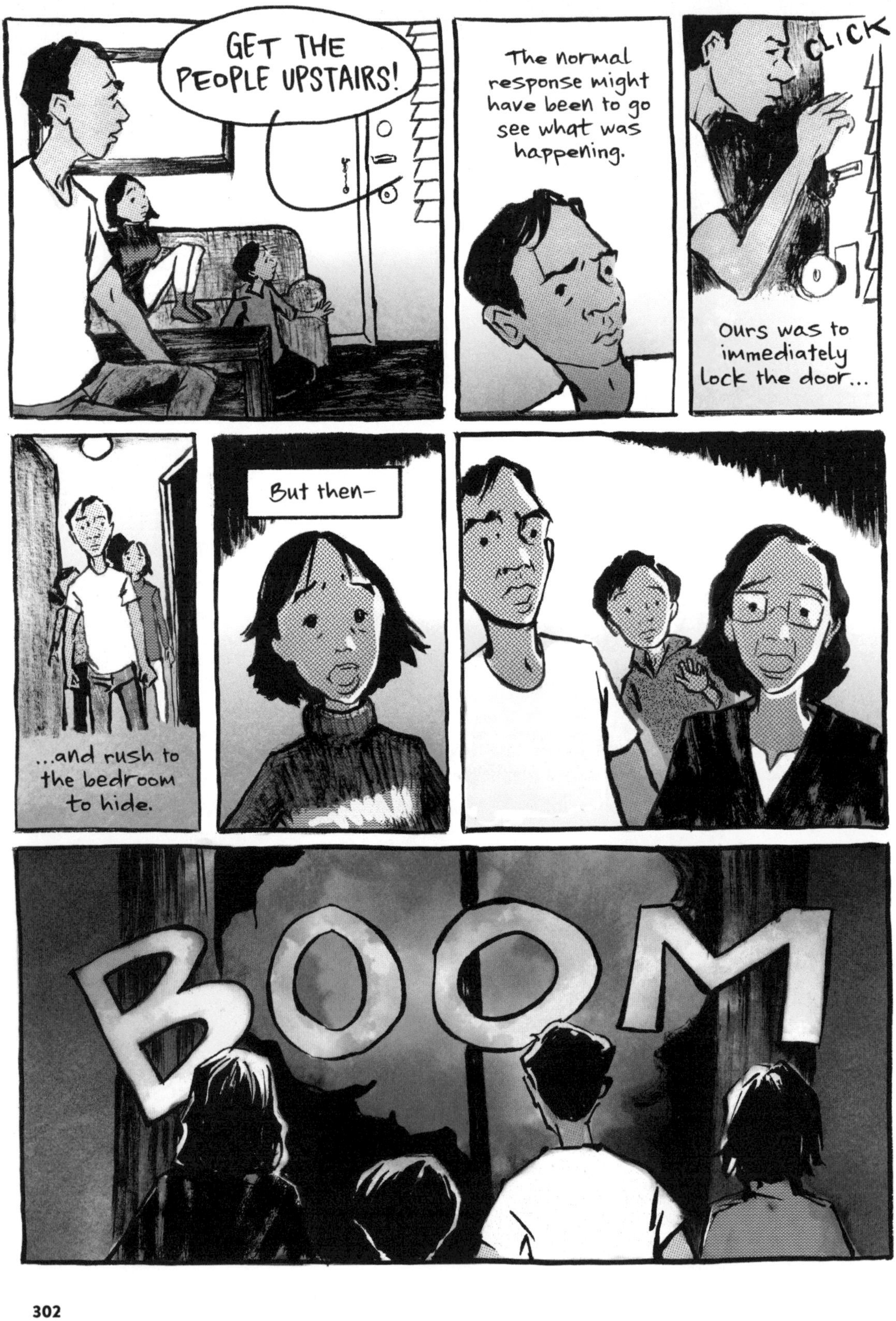
GET THE PEOPLE UPSTAIRS!
The normal response might have been to go see what was happening.
CLICK
Ours was to immediately lock the door...
...and rush to the bedroom to hide.
But then-
BOOM

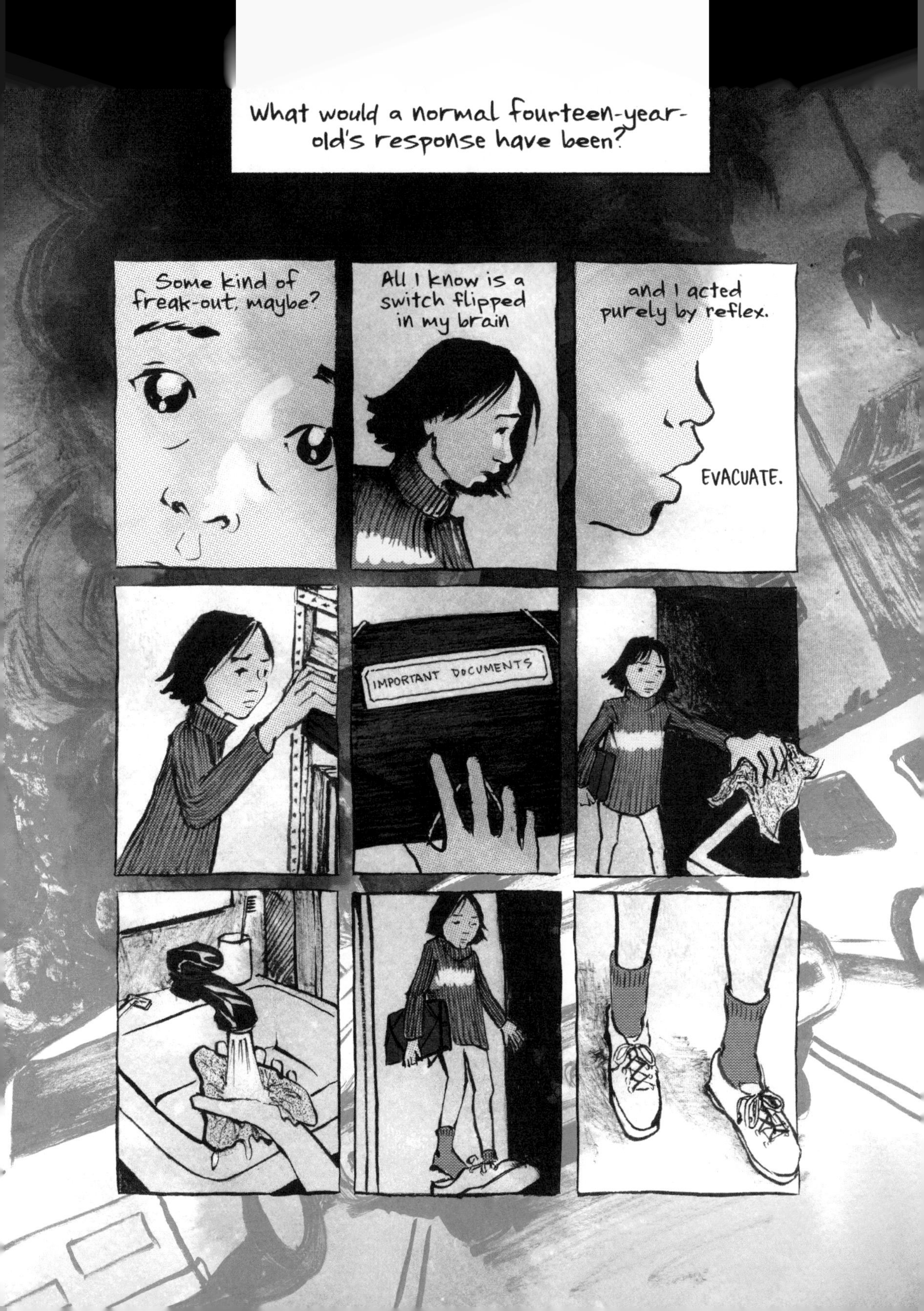
What would a normal fourteen-year-old's response have been?
Some kind of freak-out, maybe?
All I know is a switch flipped in my brain
and I acted purely by reflex.
EVACUATE.
IMPORTANT DOCUMENTS

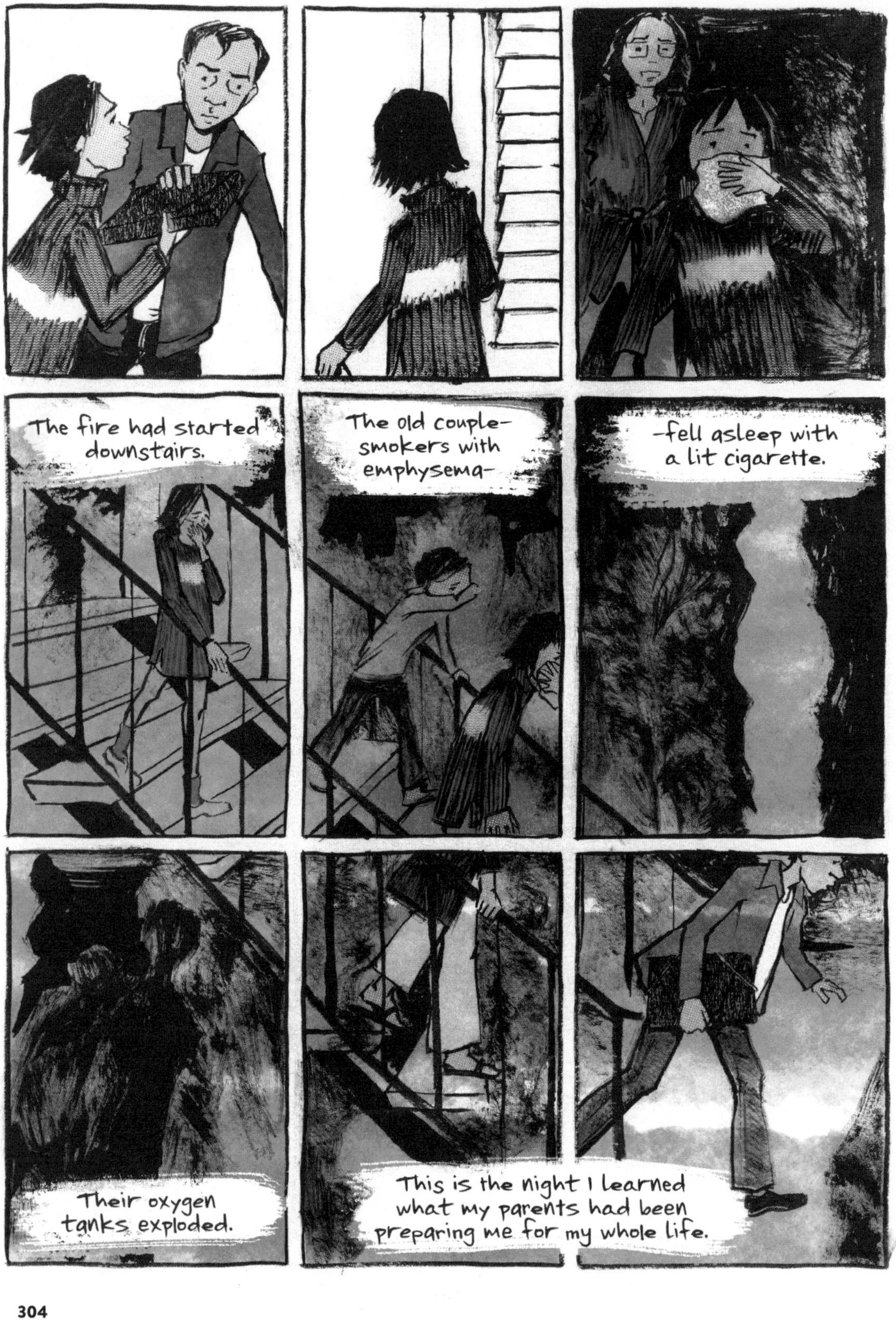

The fire had started downstairs.
The old couple-smokers with emphysema-
-fell asleep with a lit cigarette.
Their oxygen tanks exploded.
This is the night I learned what my parents had been preparing me for my whole life.

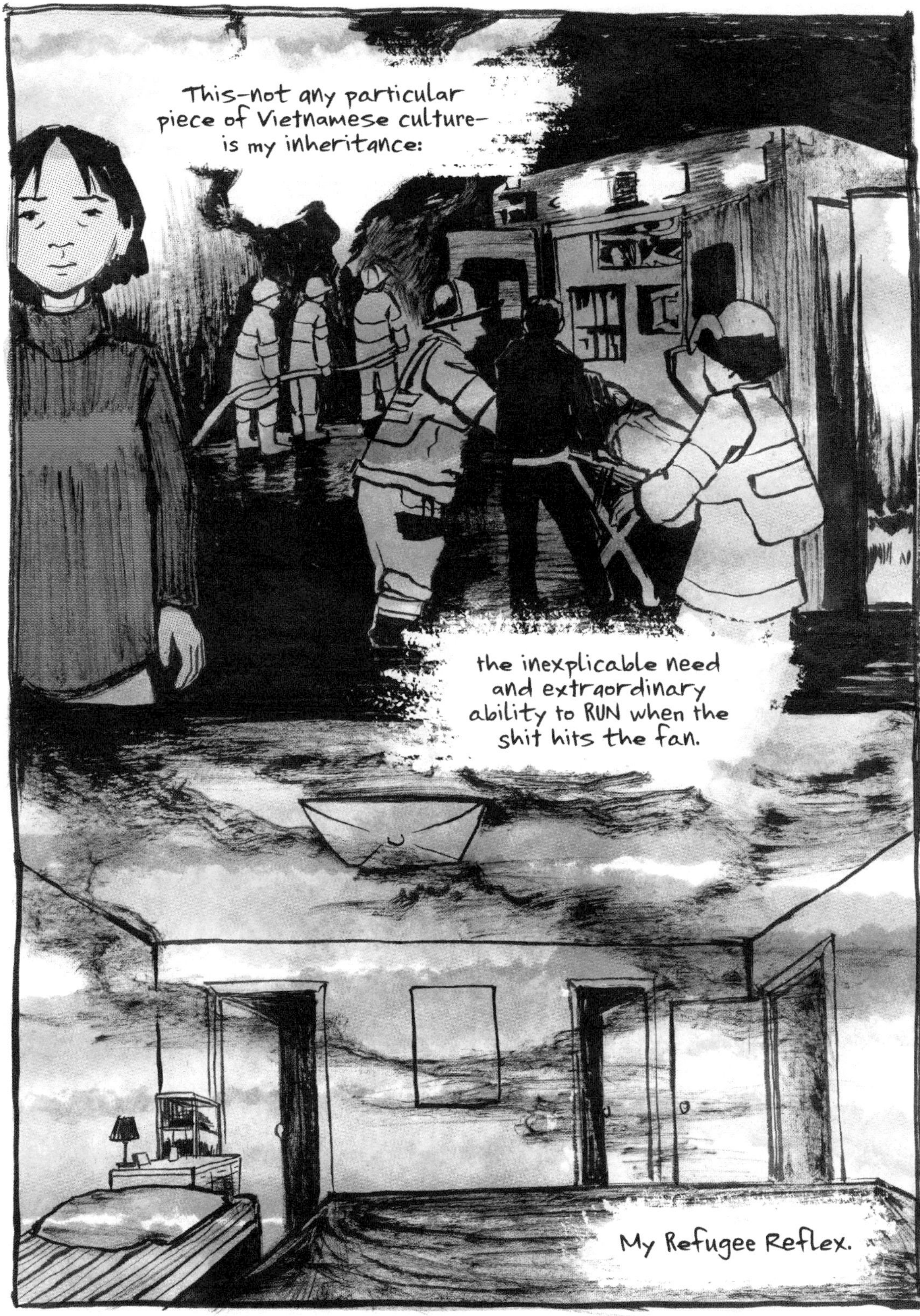
This-not any particular piece of Vietnamese culture-is my inheritance:
the inexplicable need and extraordinary ability to RUN when the shit hits the fan.
My Refugee Reflex.

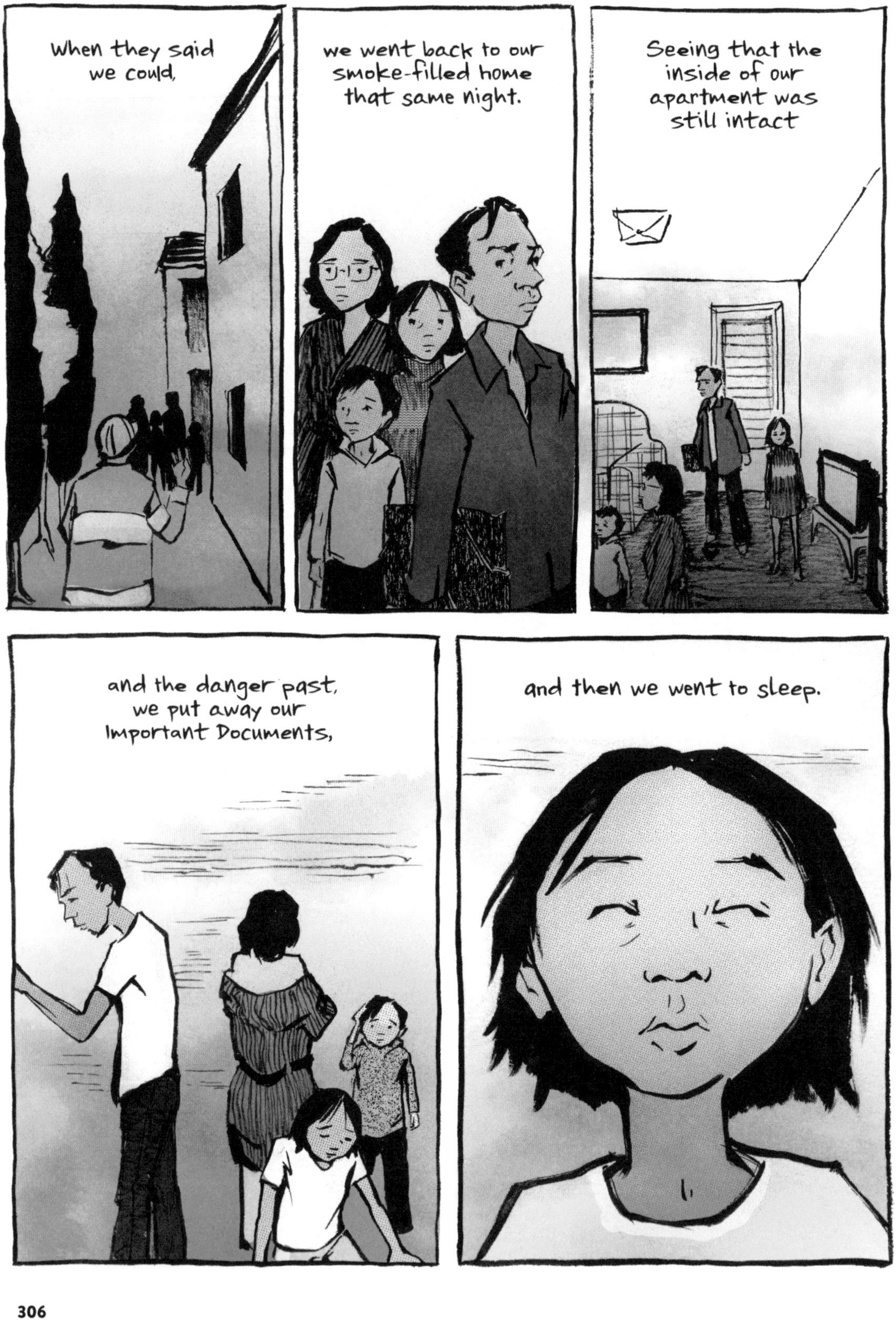
When they said we could,
we went back to our smoke-filled home that same night.
Seeing that the inside of our apartment was still intact
and the danger past, we put away our Important Documents,
and then we went to sleep.

CHAPTER 10

EBB AND FLOW

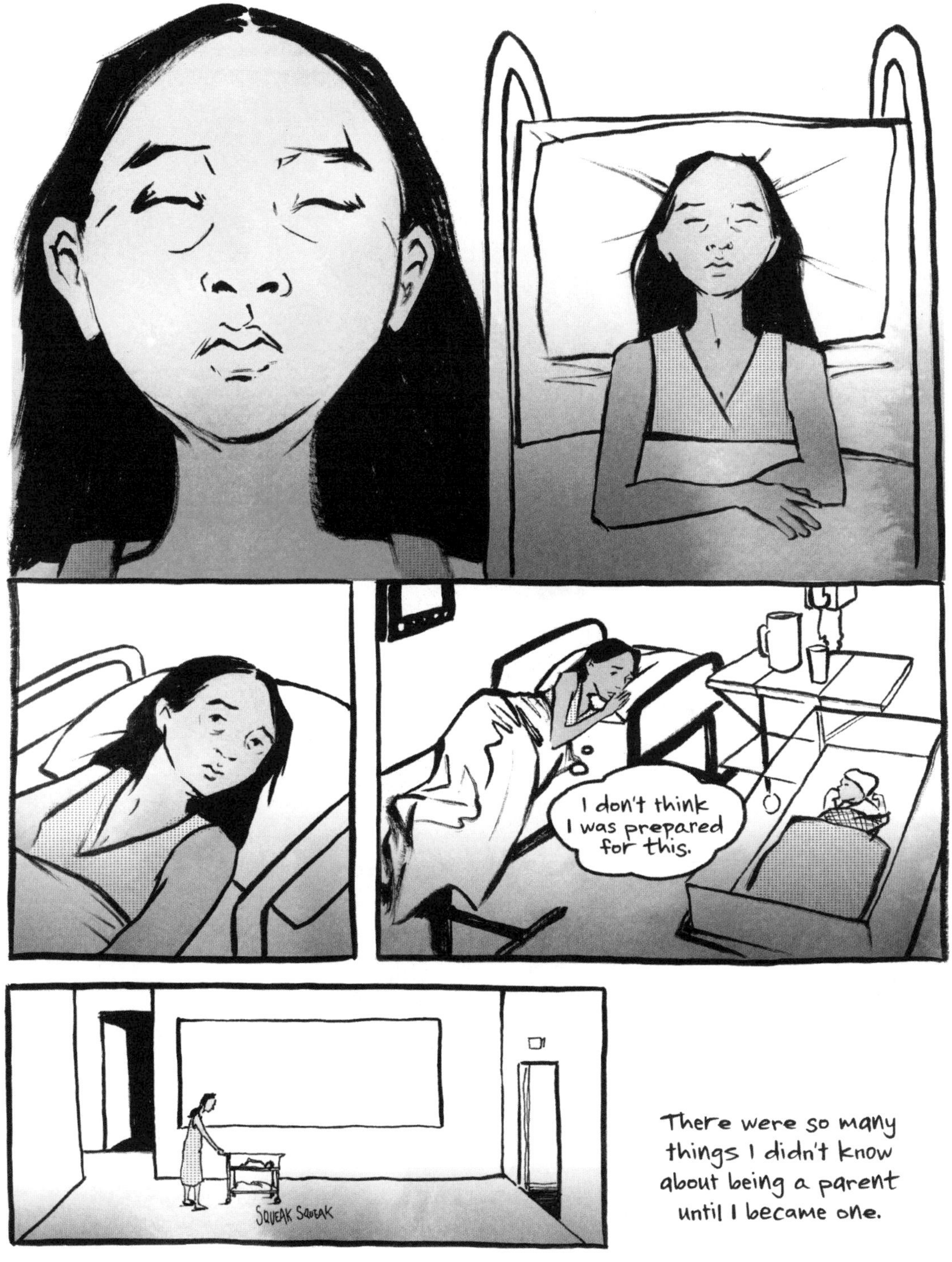
I don't think I was prepared for this.
SQUEAK SQUEAK

There were so many things I didn't know about being a parent until I became one.

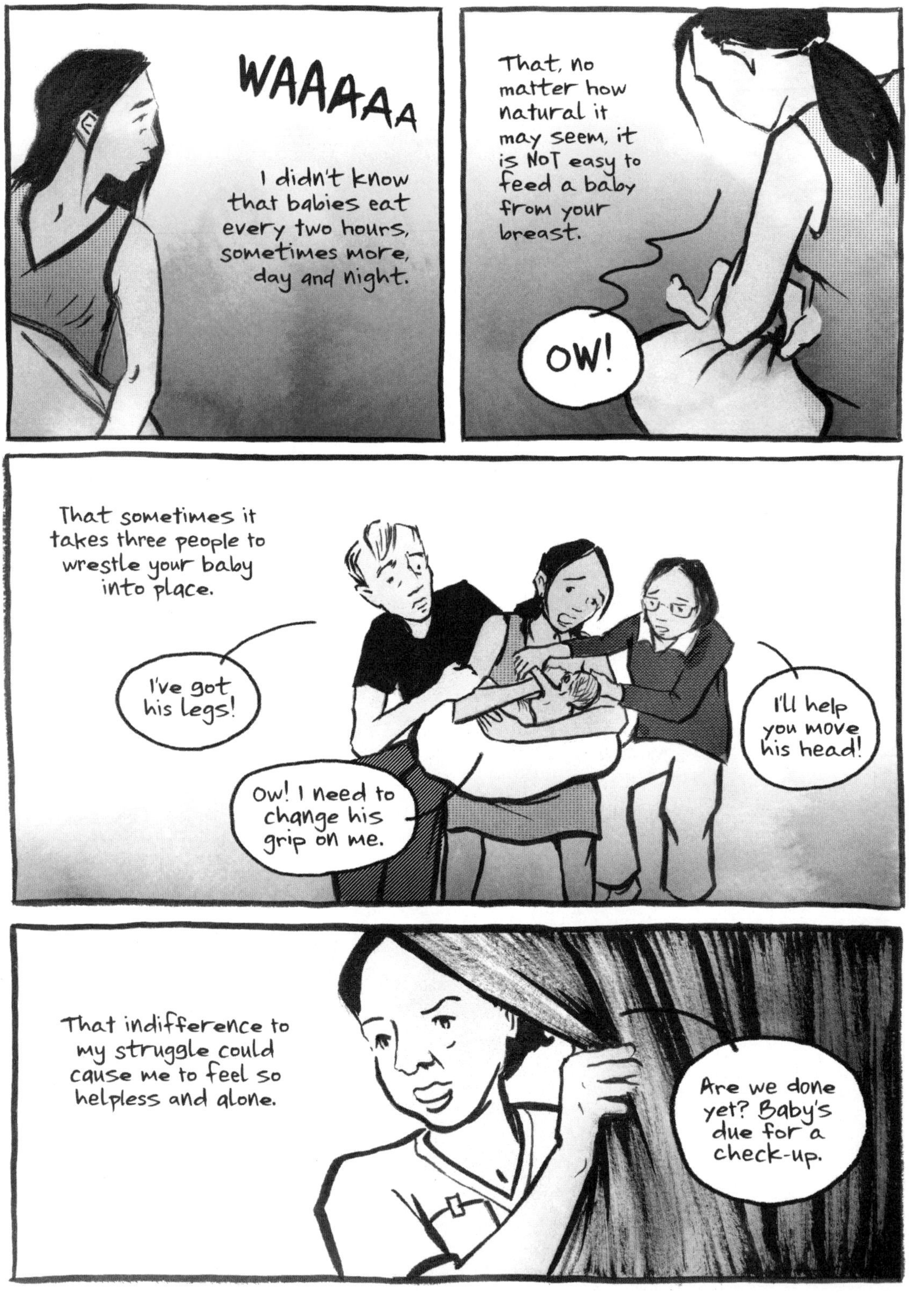
WAAAAA
I didn't know that babies eat every two hours, sometimes more, day and night.
That, no matter how natural it may seem, it is NOT easy to feed a baby from your breast.
OW!
That sometimes it takes three people to wrestle your baby into place.
I've got his legs!
Ow! I need to change his grip on me.
I'll help you move his head!
That indifference to my struggle could cause me to feel so helpless and alone.
Are we done yet? Baby's due for a check-up.

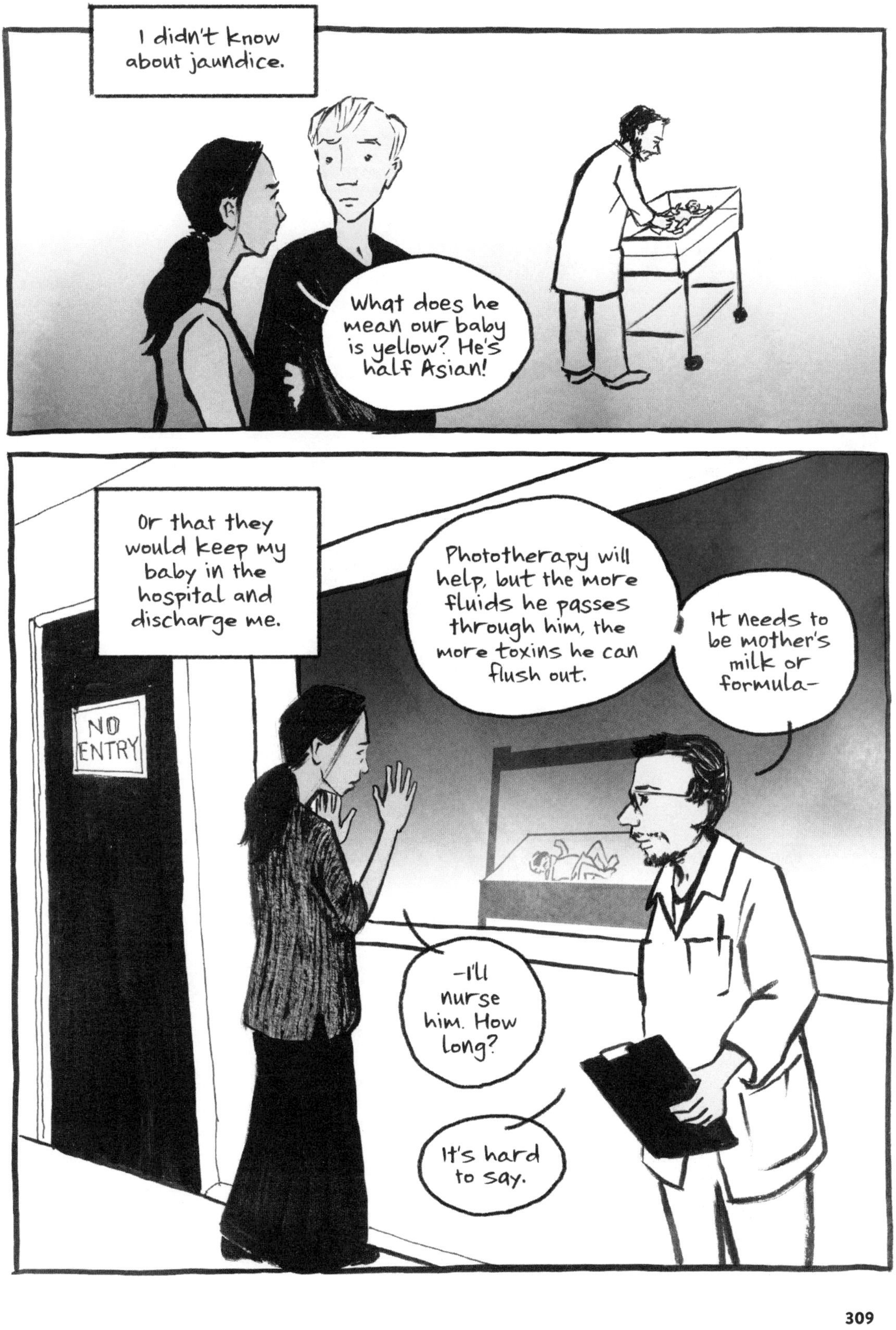
I didn't know about jaundice.
What does he mean our baby is yellow? He's half Asian!
Or that they would keep my baby in the hospital and discharge me.
Phototherapy will help, but the more fluids he passes through him, the more toxins he can flush out.
It needs to be mother's milk or formula-
NO ENTRY
-I'll nurse him. How long?
It's hard to say.

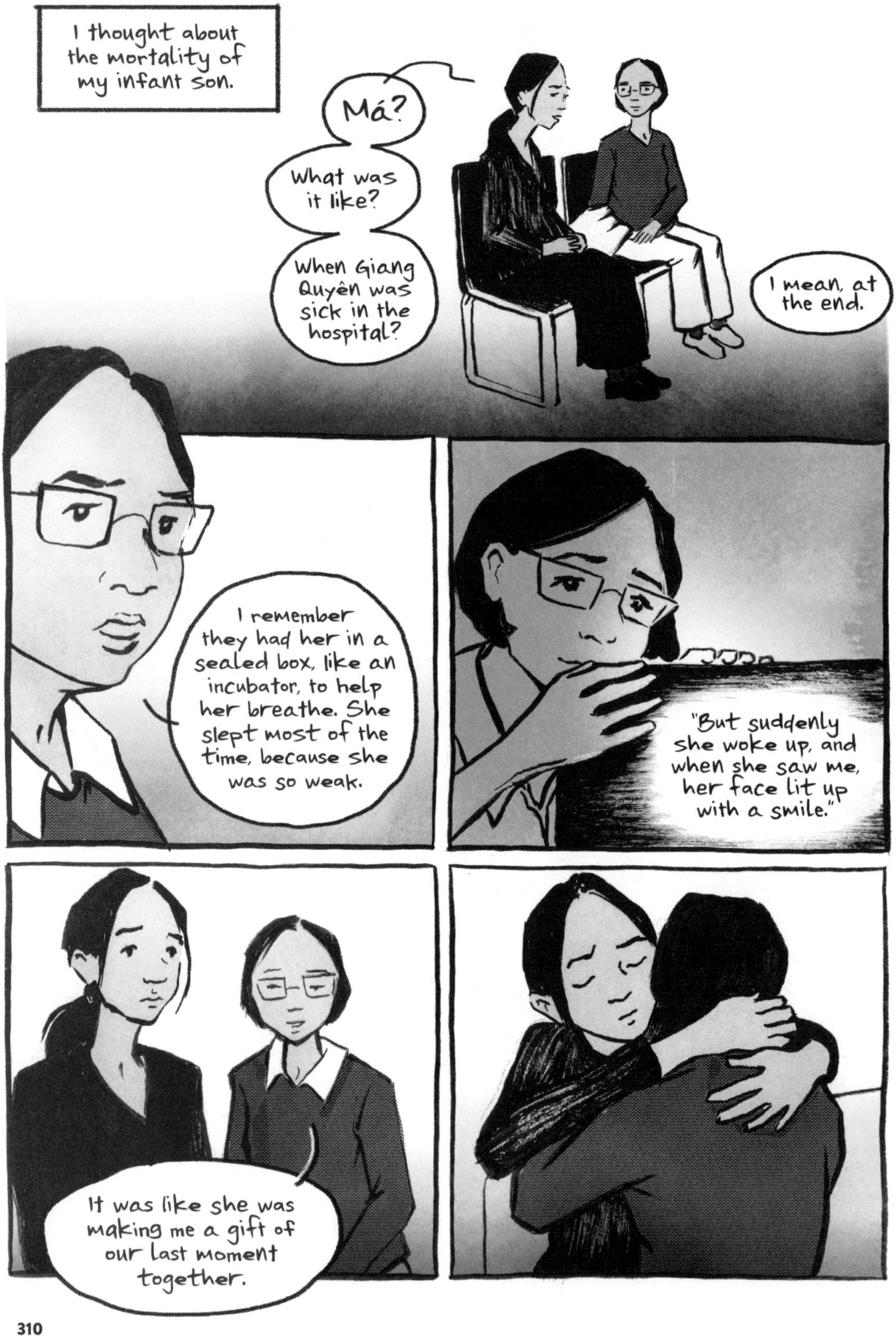
I thought about the mortality of my infant son.
Má?
What was it like?
When Giang Quyên was sick in the hospital?
I mean, at the end.
I remember they had her in a sealed box, like an incubator, to help her breathe. She slept most of the time, because she was so weak.
"But suddenly she woke up, and when she saw me, her face lit up with a smile."
It was like she was making me a gift of our last moment together.

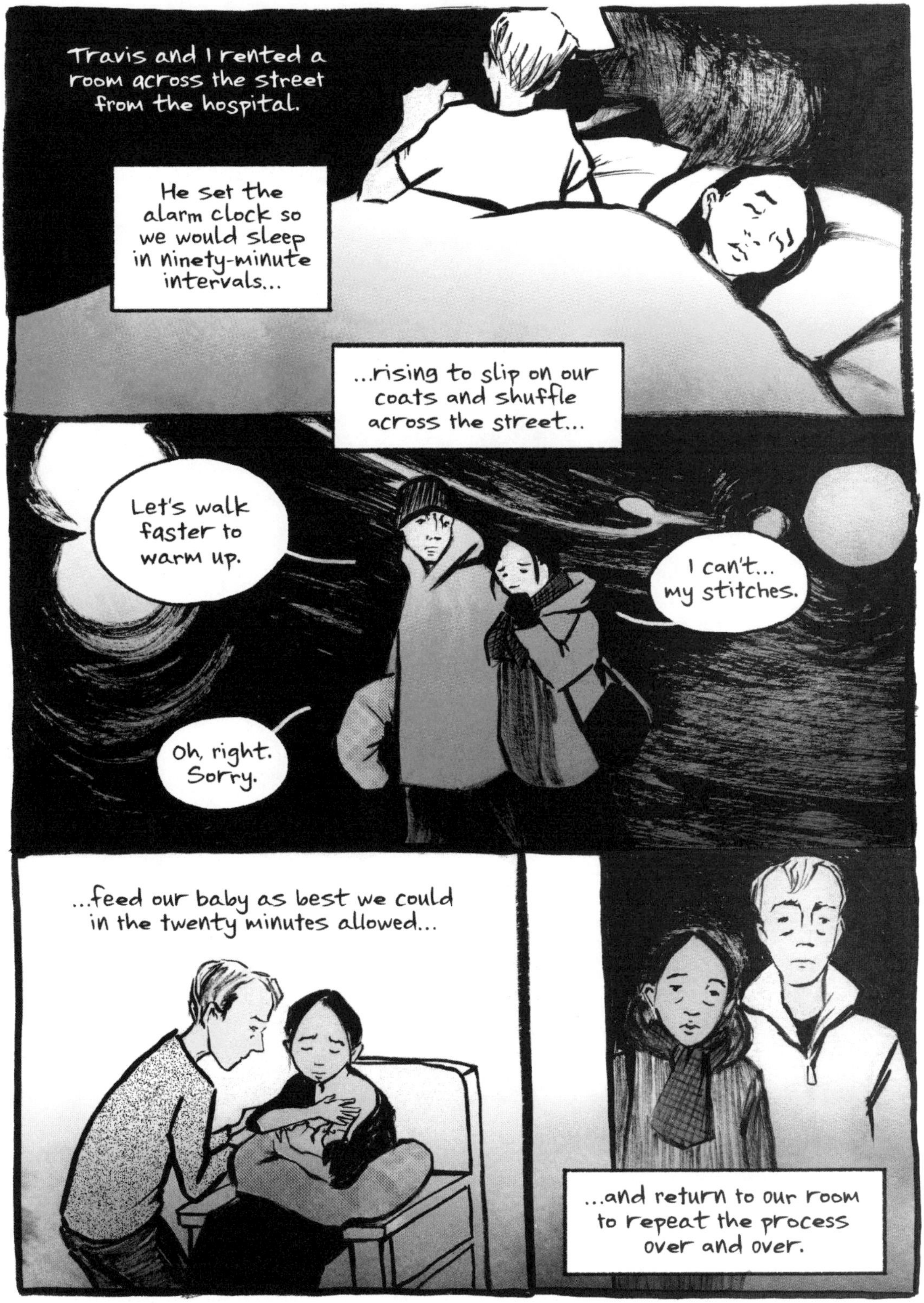

Travis and I rented a room across the street from the hospital.
He set the alarm clock so we would sleep in ninety-minute intervals...
...rising to slip on our coats and shuffle across the street...
Let's walk faster to warm up.
I can't... my stitches.
Oh, right. Sorry.
...feed our baby as best we could in the twenty minutes allowed...
...and return to our room to repeat the process over and over.

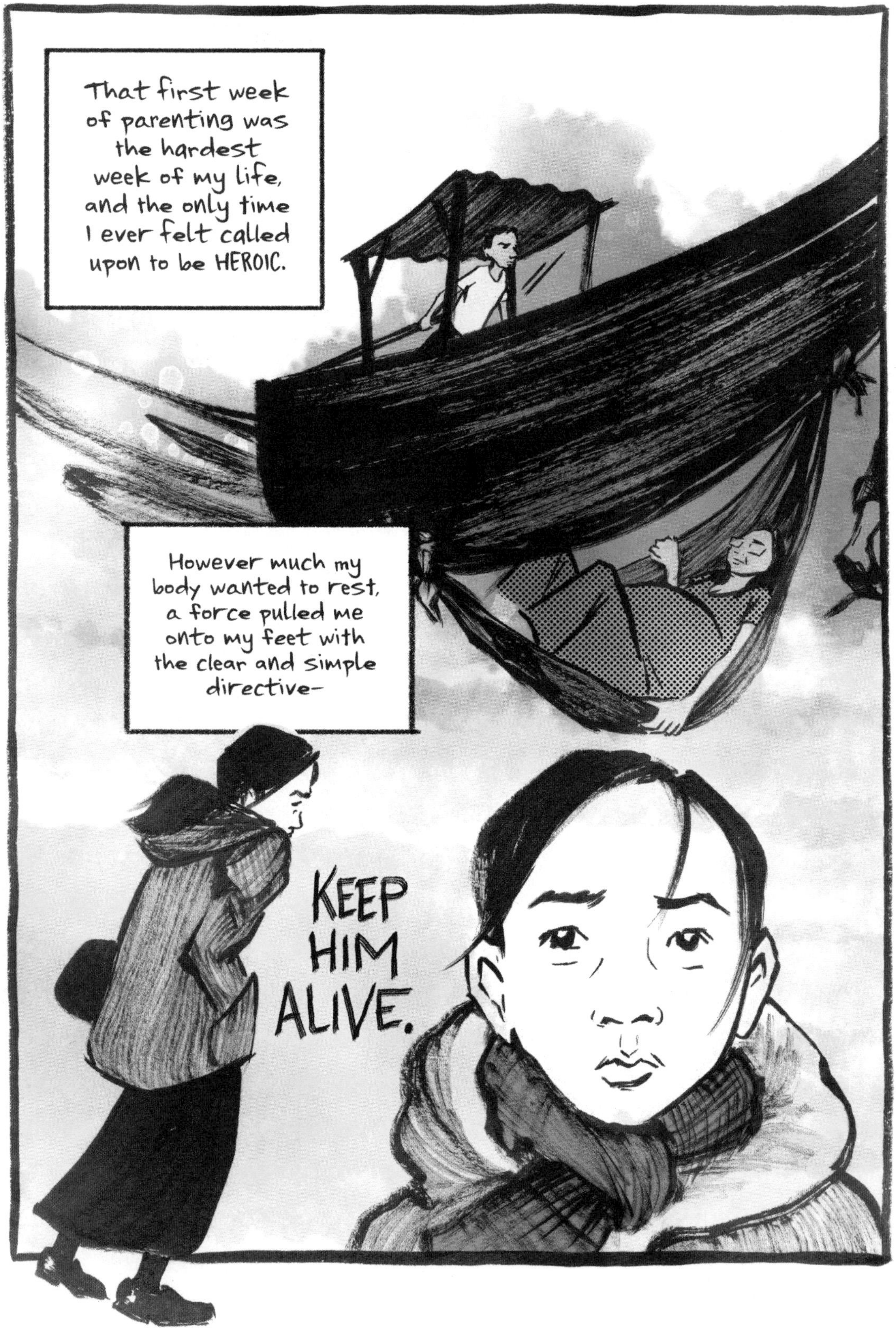
That first week of parenting was the hardest week of my life, and the only time I ever felt called upon to be HEROIC.
However much my body wanted to rest, a force pulled me onto my feet with the clear and simple directive-
KEEP HIM ALIVE.

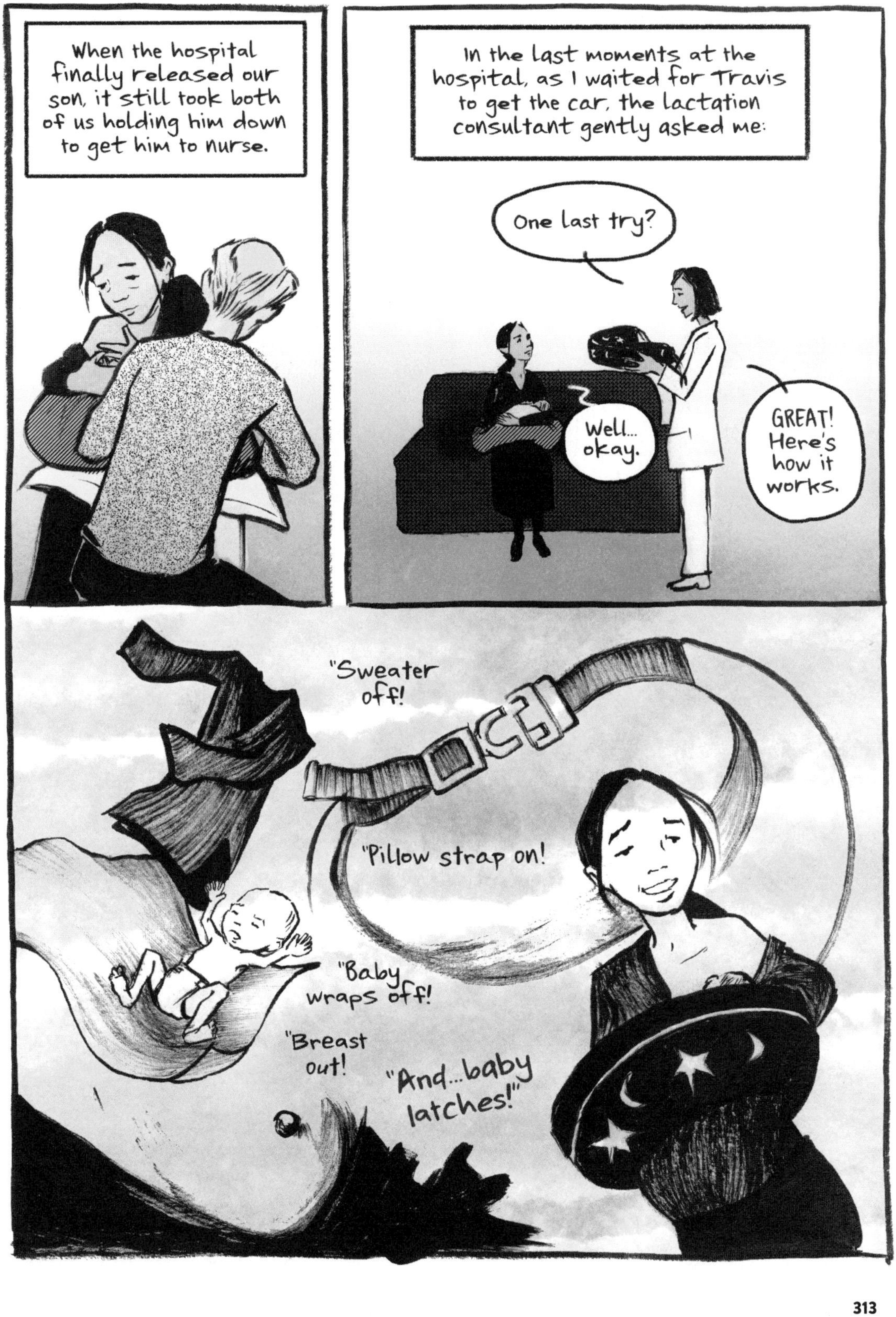
When the hospital finally released our son, it still took both of us holding him down to get him to nurse.
In the last moments at the hospital, as I waited for Travis to get the car, the lactation consultant gently asked me:
One last try?
Well... okay.
GREAT! Here's how it works.
"Sweater off!
"Pillow strap on!
"Baby wraps off!
"Breast out!
"And...baby latches!"

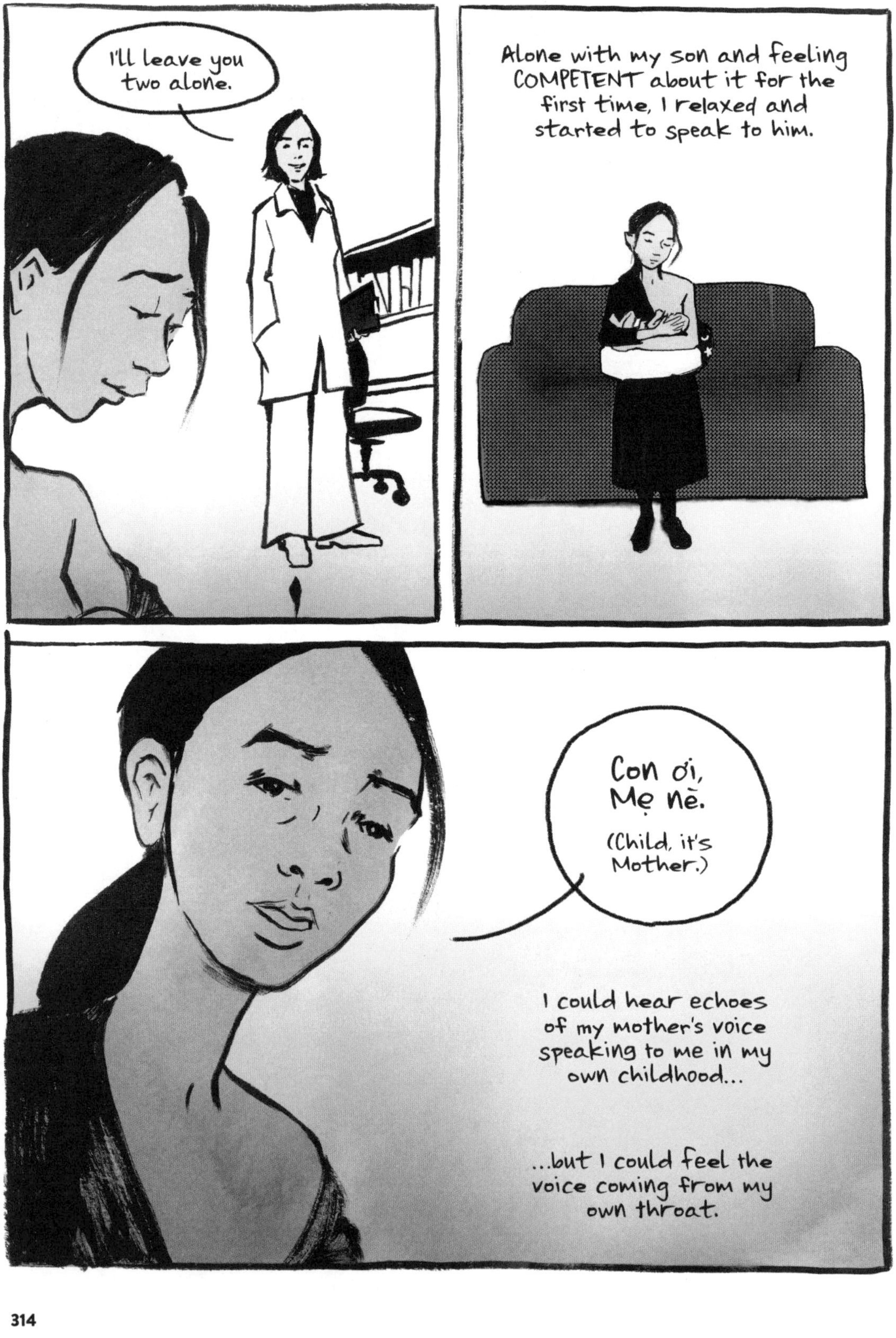
I'll leave you two alone.
Alone with my son and feeling COMPETENT about it for the first time, I relaxed and started to speak to him.
Con ơi, Mẹ nè.
(Child, it's Mother.)
I could hear echoes of my mother's voice speaking to me in my own childhood...
...but I could feel the voice coming from my own throat.

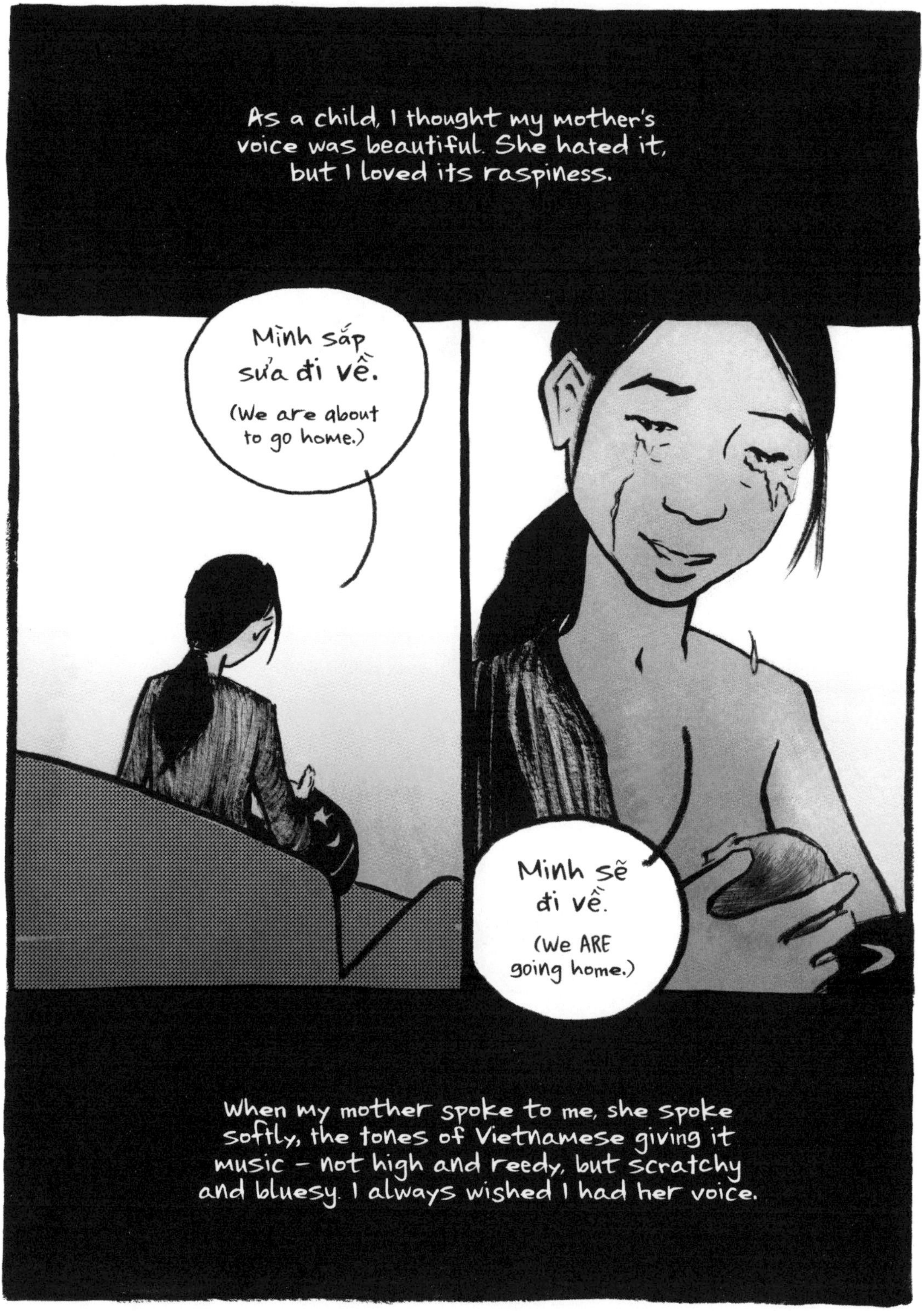
As a child, I thought my mother's voice was beautiful. She hated it, but I loved its raspiness.
Mình sắp sửa đi về.
(We are about to go home.)
Mình sẽ đi về.
(We ARE going home.)
When my mother spoke to me, she spoke softly, the tones of Vietnamese giving it music – not high and reedy, but scratchy and bluesy. I always wished I had her voice.

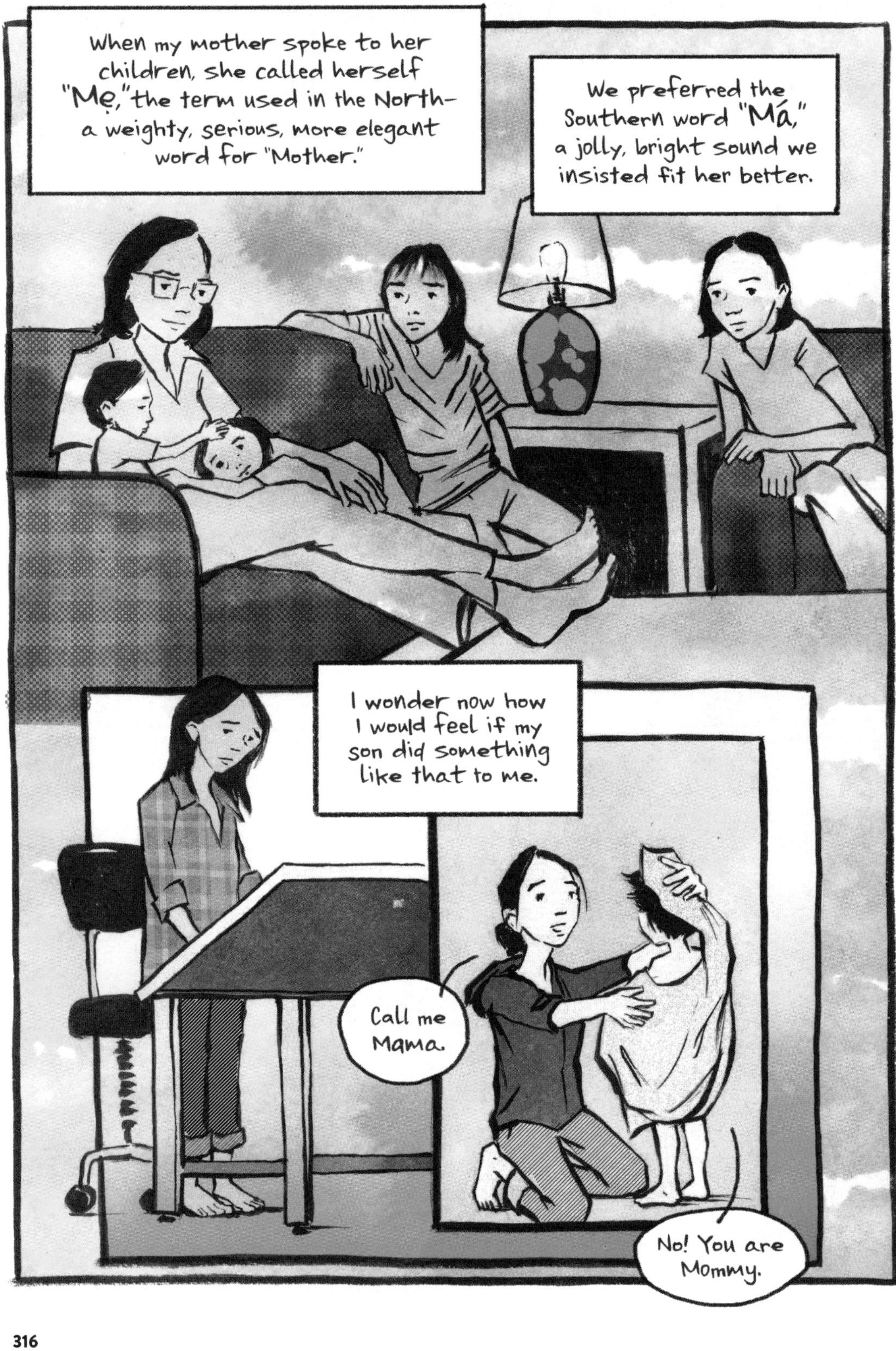
When my mother spoke to her children, she called herself "Mẹ," the term used in the North– a weighty, serious, more elegant word for "Mother."
We preferred the Southern word "Má," a jolly, bright sound we insisted fit her better.
I wonder now how I would feel if my son did something like that to me.
Call me Mama.
No! You are Mommy.

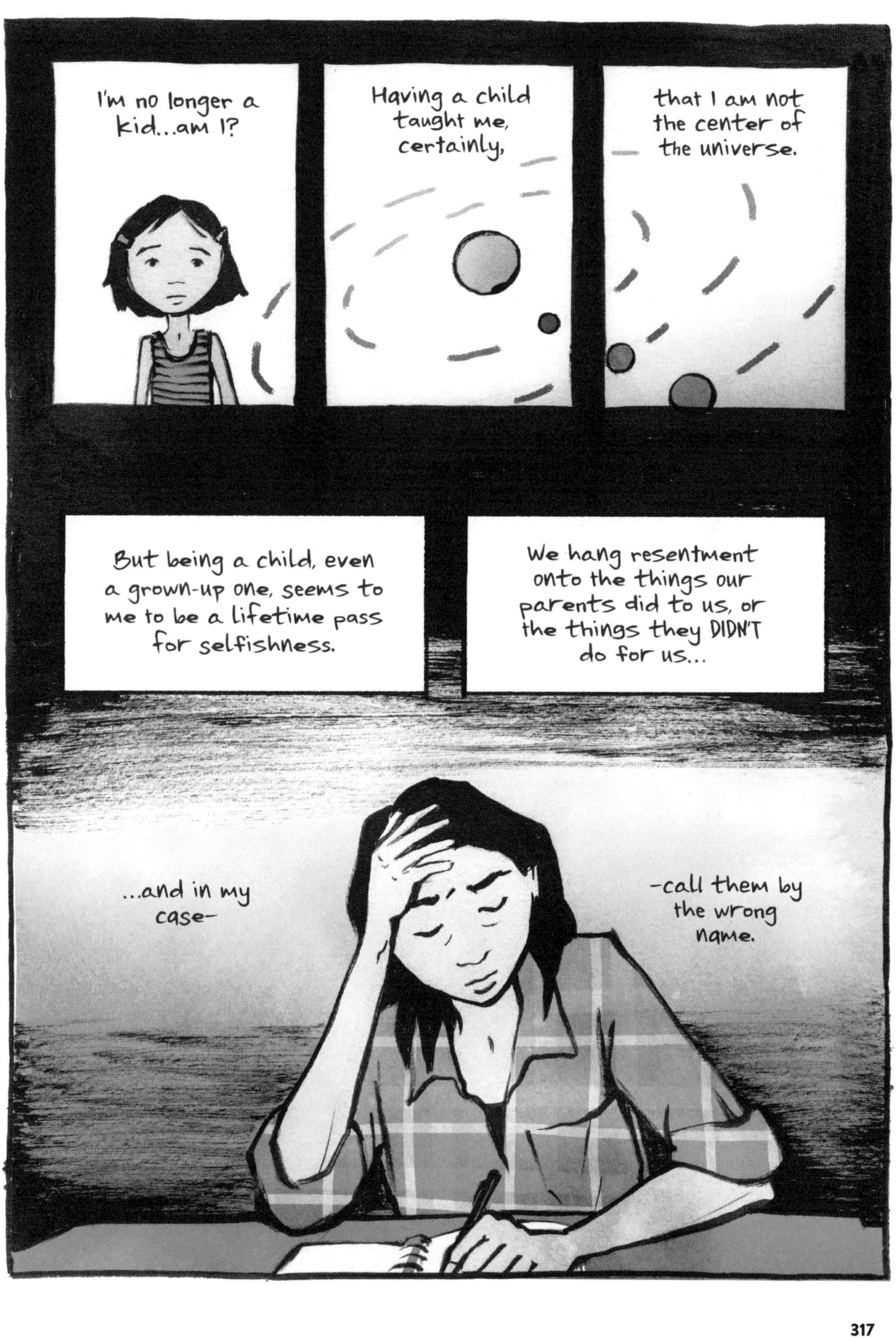
I'm no longer a kid...am I?
Having a child taught me, certainly,
that I am not the center of the universe.
But being a child, even a grown-up one, seems to me to be a lifetime pass for selfishness.
We hang resentment onto the things our parents did to us, or the things they DIDN'T do for us...
...and in my case-
-call them by the wrong name.

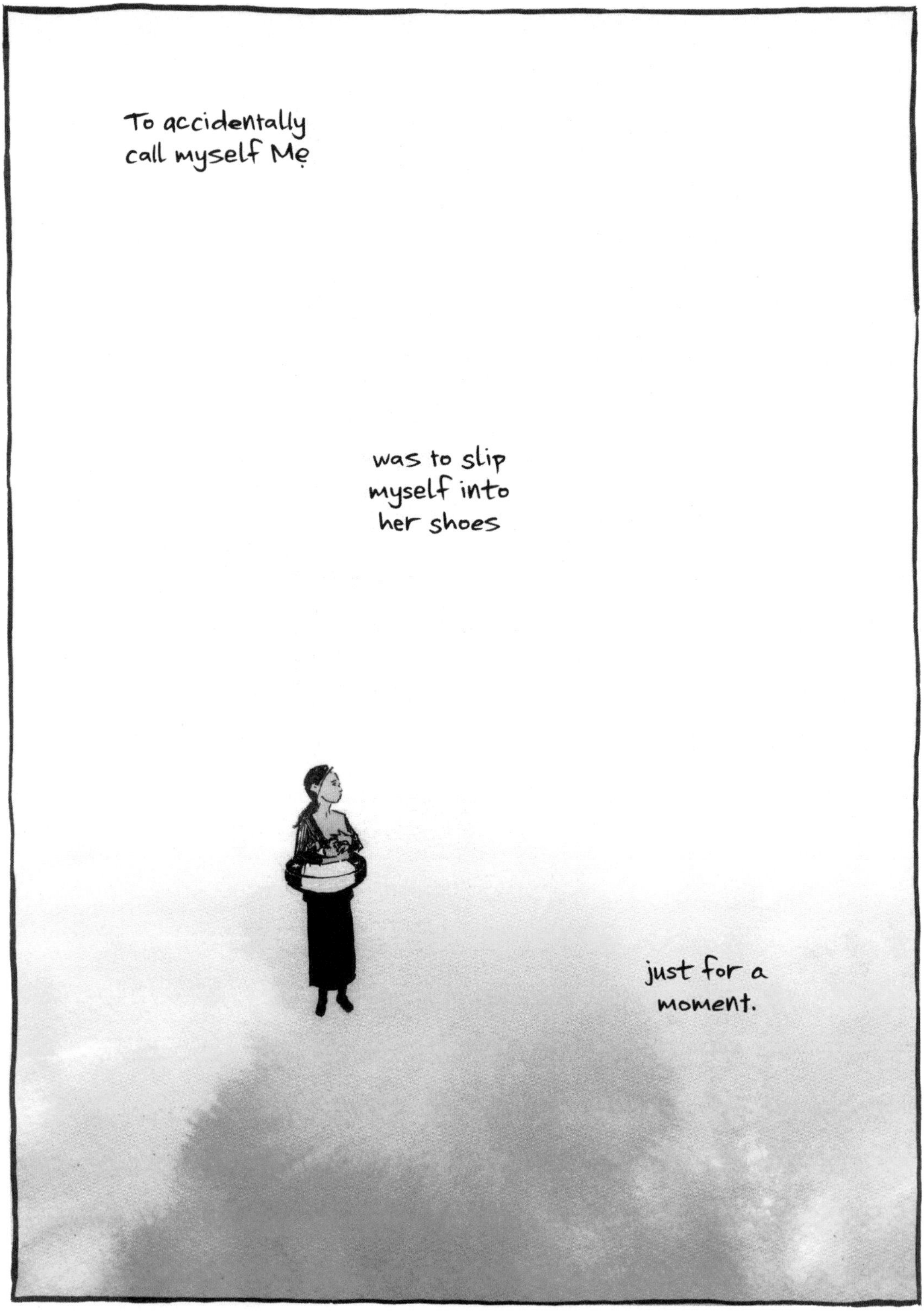
To accidentally call myself Mẹ
was to slip myself into her shoes
just for a moment.

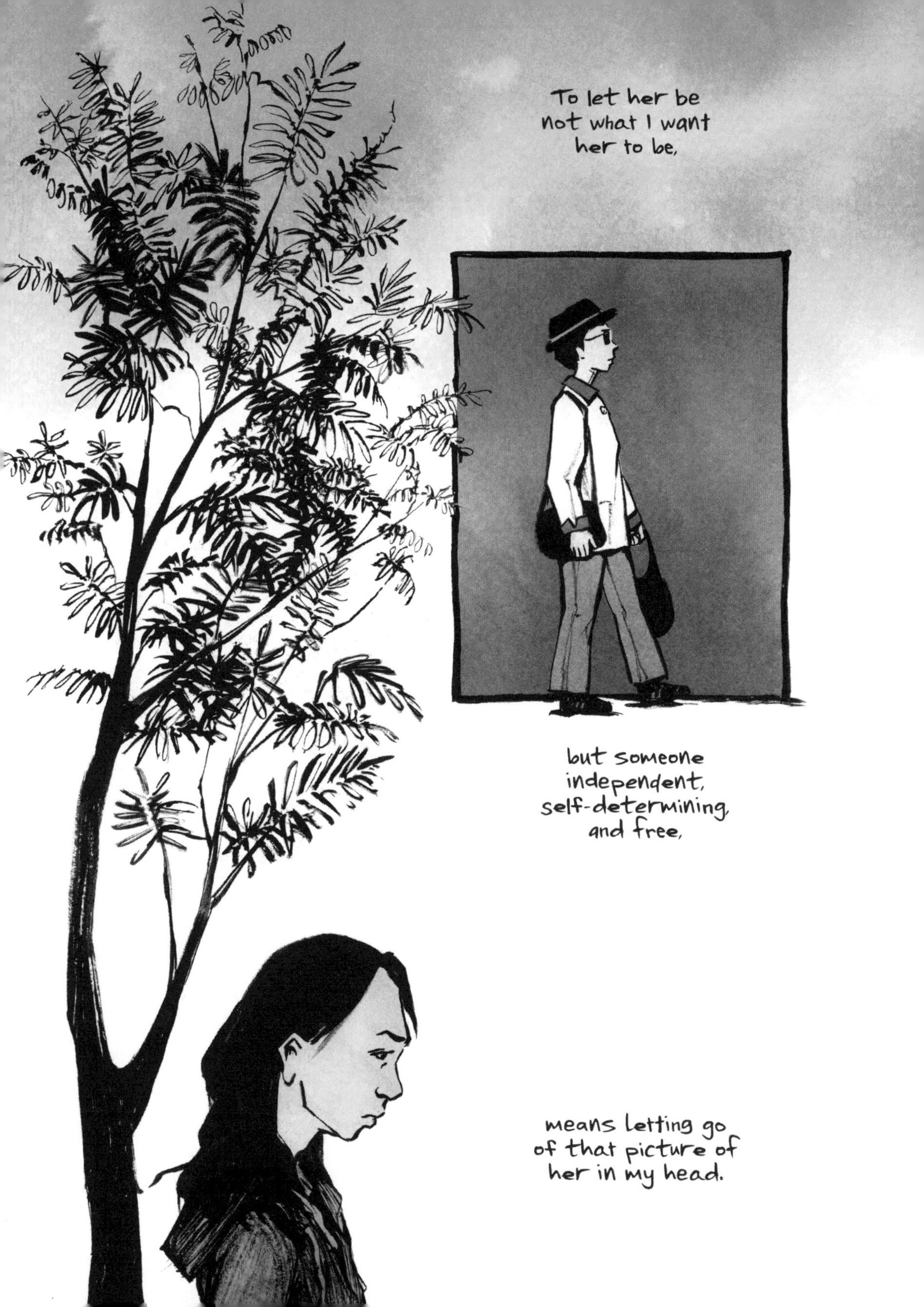

To let her be not what I want her to be,
but someone independent, self-determining, and free,
means letting go of that picture of her in my head.

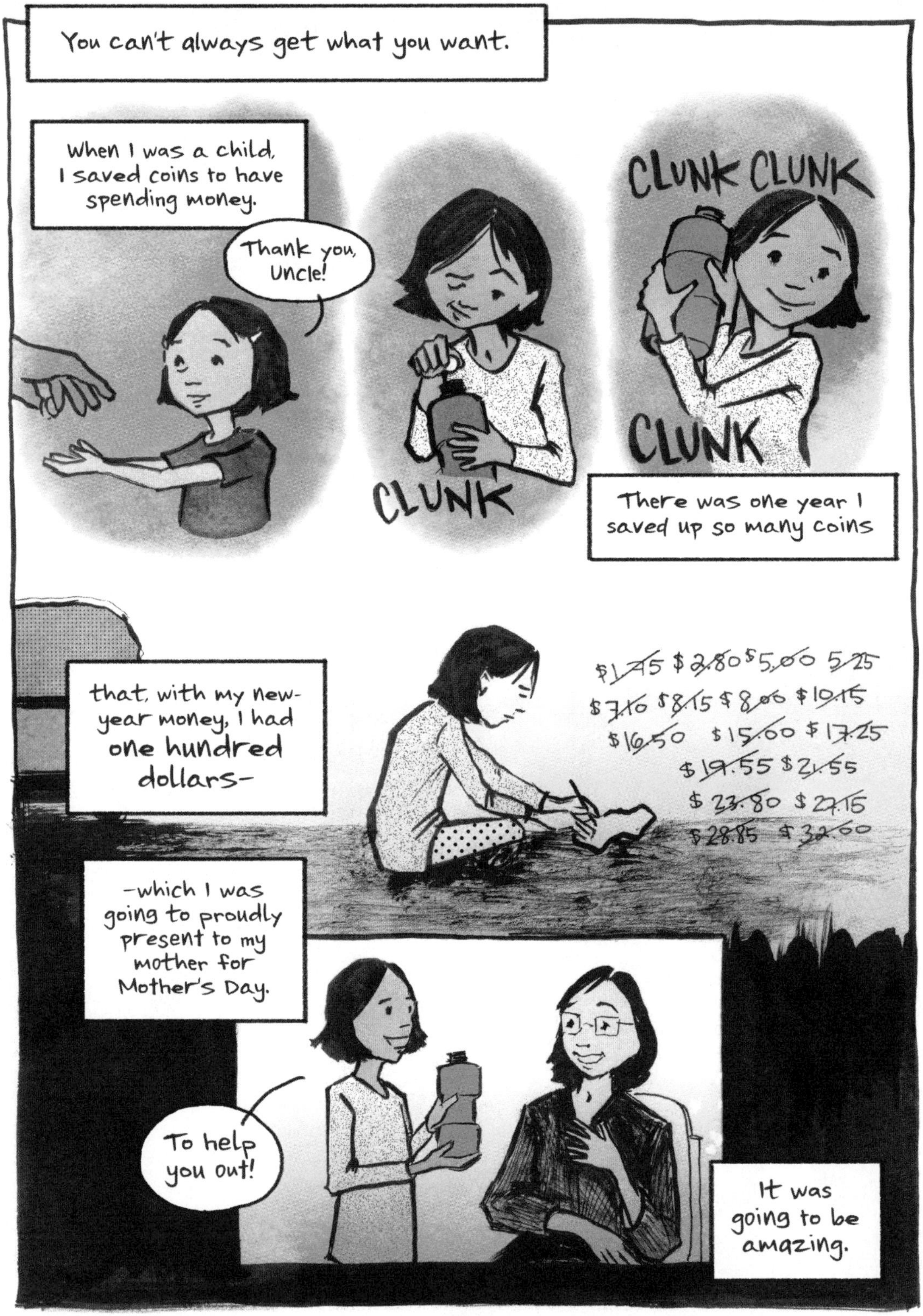
You can't always get what you want.
When I was a child, I saved coins to have spending money.
Thank you, Uncle!
CLUNK
CLUNK CLUNK
CLUNK
There was one year I saved up so many coins
that, with my new-year money, I had one hundred dollars-
$1.45 $2.80 $5.00 5.25
$7.10 $8.15 $8.00 $10.15
$16.50 $15.00 $17.25
$19.55 $21.55
$23.80 $27.15
$28.85 $32.60
-which I was going to proudly present to my mother for Mother's Day.
To help you out!
It was going to be amazing.

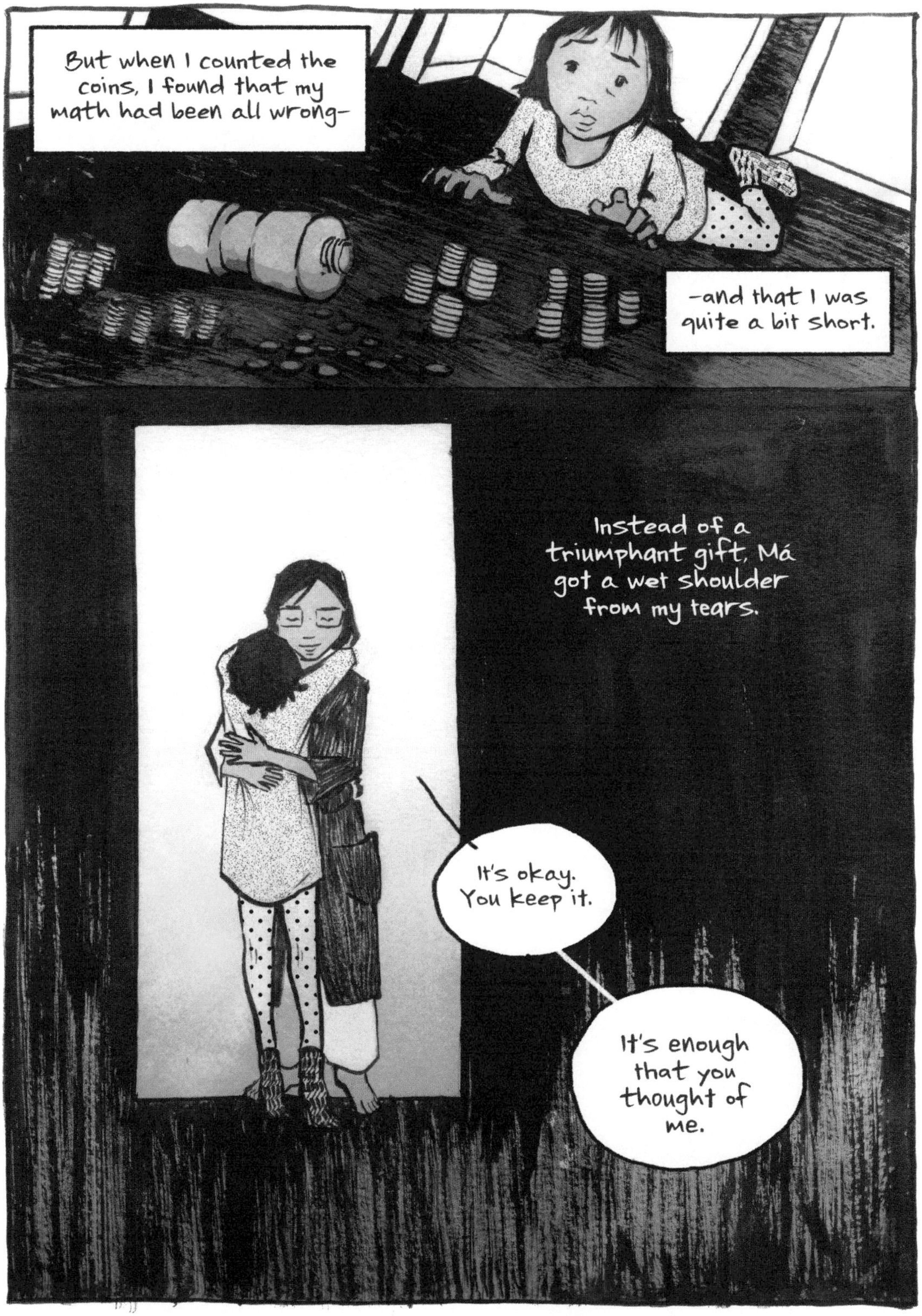
But when I counted the coins, I found that my math had been all wrong-
-and that I was quite a bit short.
Instead of a triumphant gift, Má got a wet shoulder from my tears.
It's okay. You keep it.
It's enough that you thought of me.

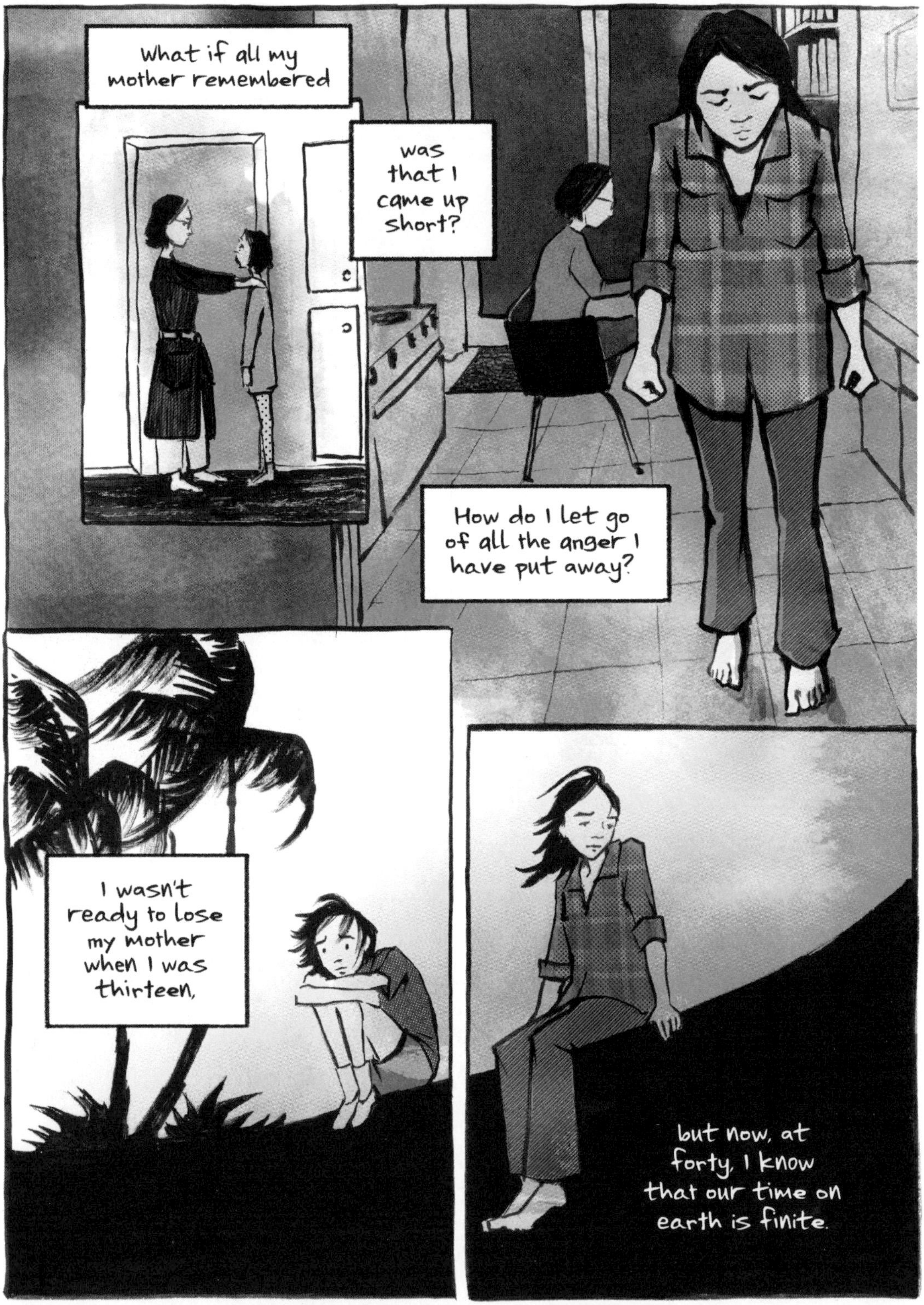
What if all my mother remembered
was that I came up short?
How do I let go of all the anger I have put away?
I wasn't ready to lose my mother when I was thirteen,
but now, at forty, I know that our time on earth is finite.

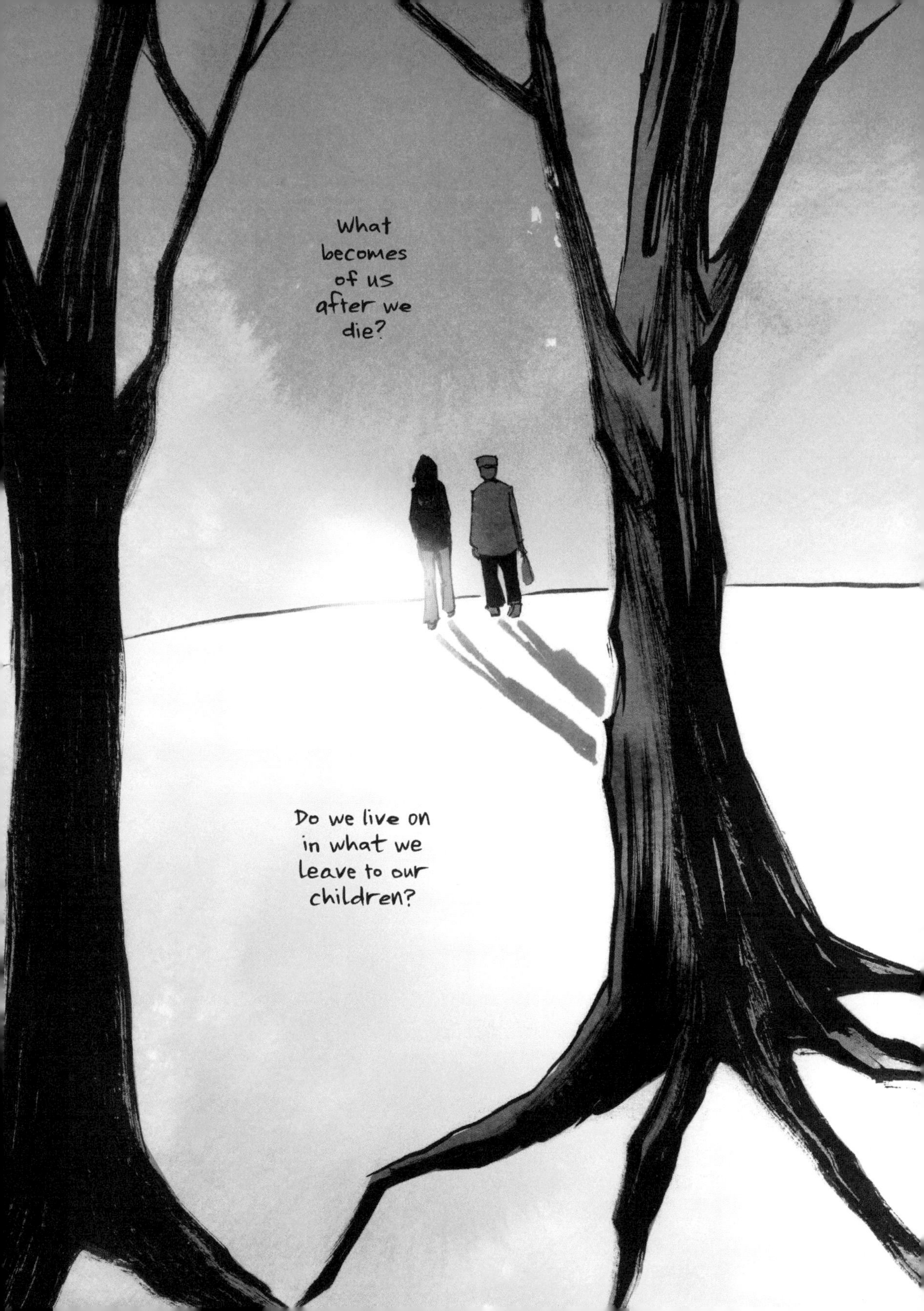
What becomes of us after we die?
Do we live on in what we leave to our children?

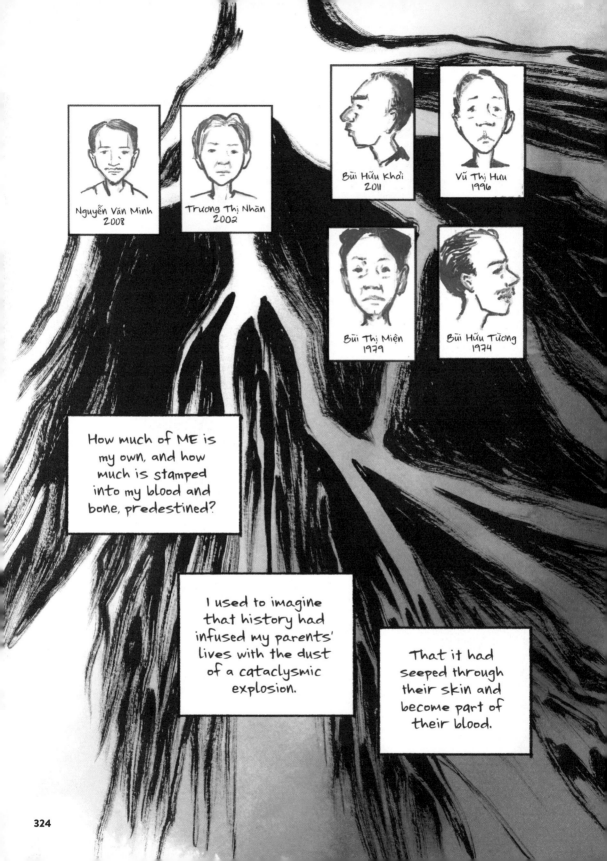

Nguyễn Văn Minh
2008

Trương Thị Nhãn
2002

Bùi Hữu Khải
2011

Vũ Thị Hưu
1996

Bùi Thị Miện
1979

Bùi Hữu Tường
1974

How much of ME is my own, and how much is stamped into my blood and bone, predestined?

I used to imagine that history had infused my parents' lives with the dust of a cataclysmic explosion.

That it had seeped through their skin and become part of their blood.

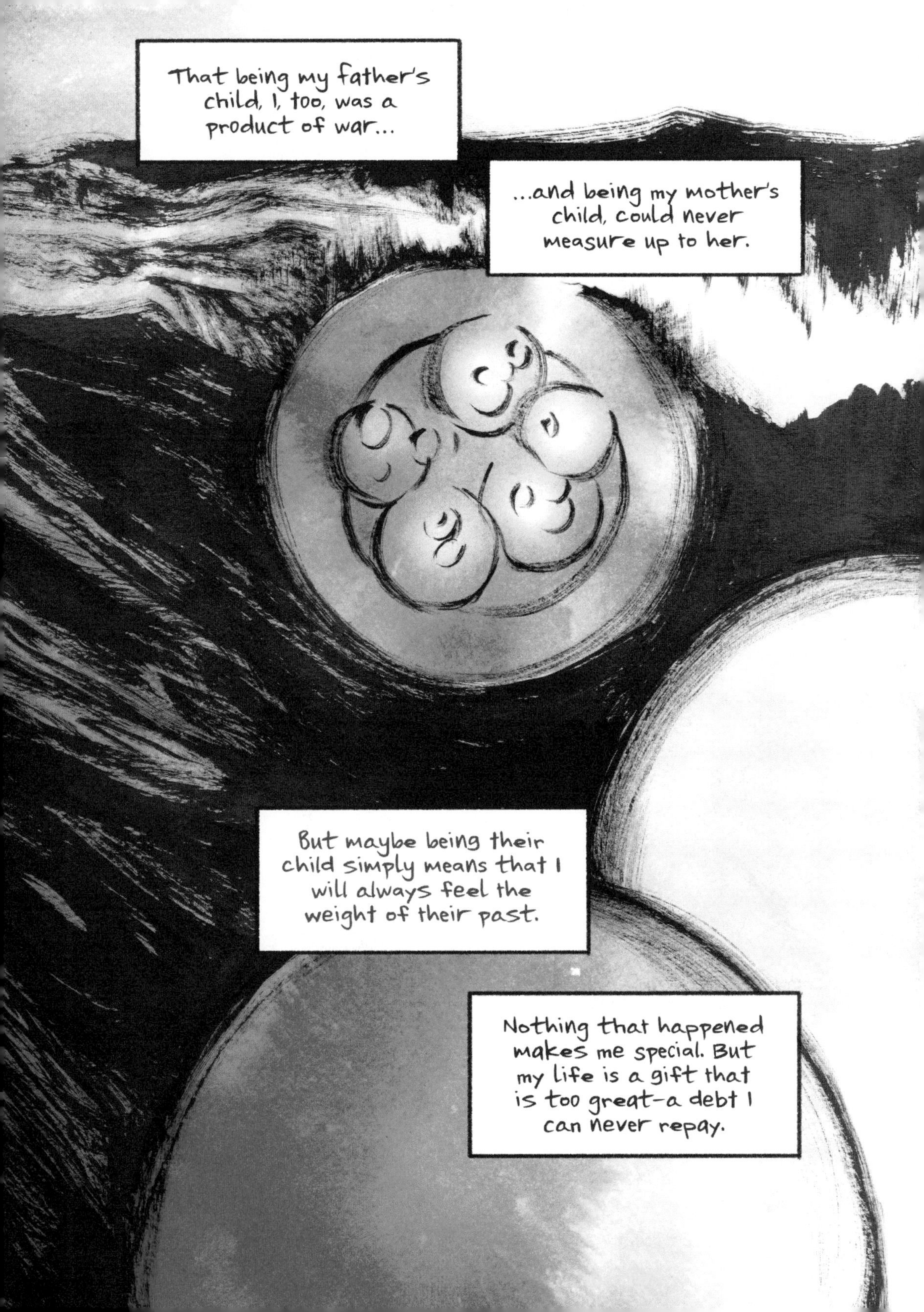
That being my father's child, I, too, was a product of war...
...and being my mother's child, could never measure up to her.
But maybe being their child simply means that I will always feel the weight of their past.
Nothing that happened makes me special. But my life is a gift that is too great—a debt I can never repay.

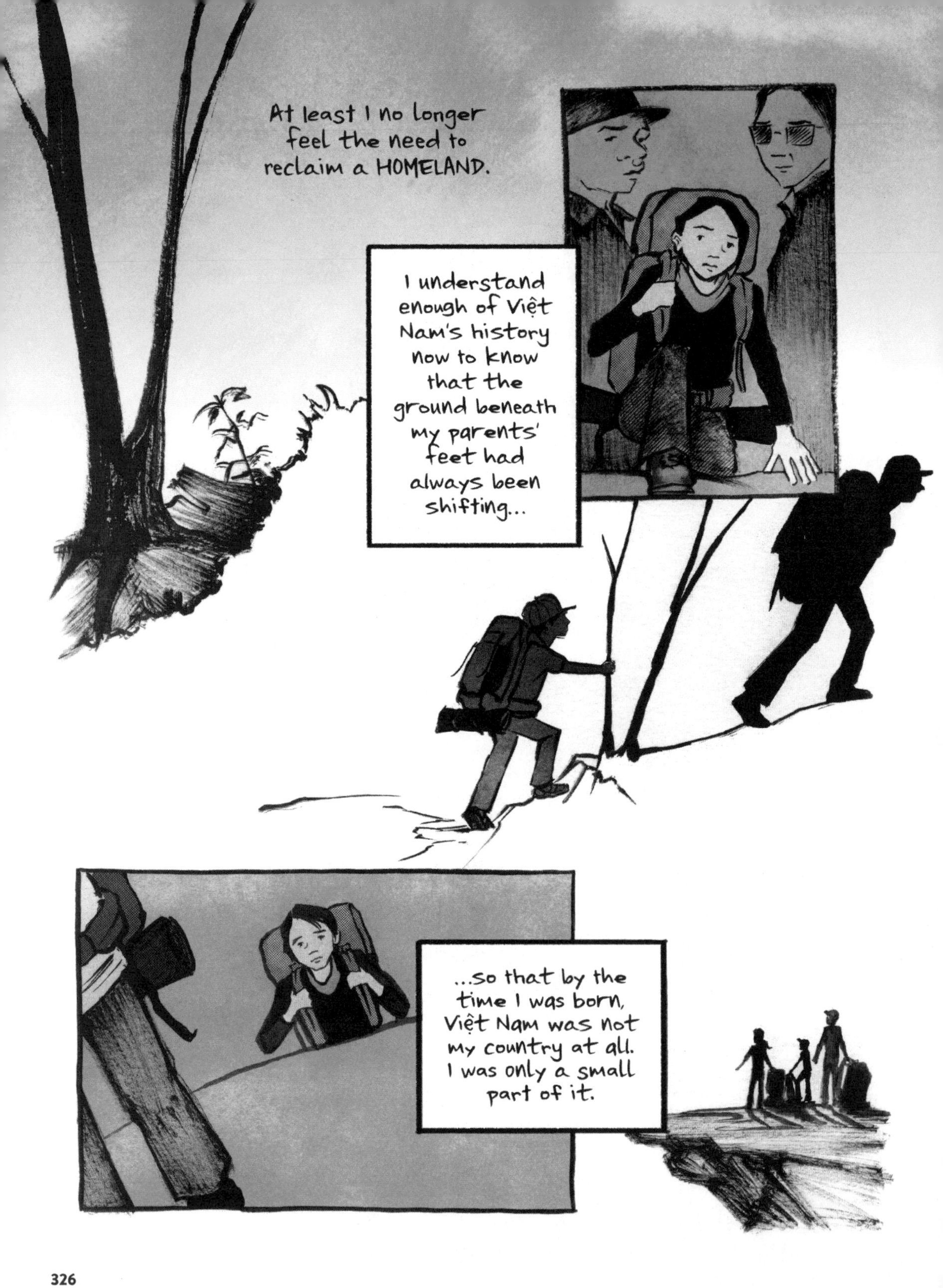
At least I no longer feel the need to reclaim a HOMELAND.
I understand enough of Việt Nam's history now to know that the ground beneath my parents' feet had always been shifting...
...so that by the time I was born, Việt Nam was not my country at all. I was only a small part of it.

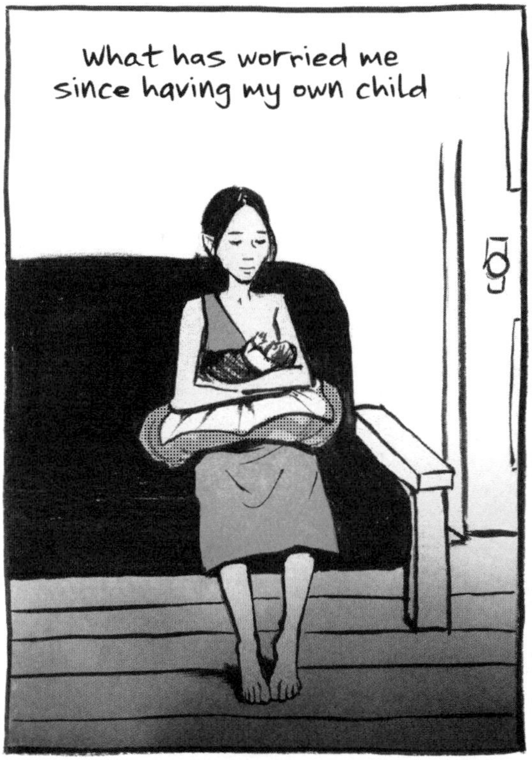
What has worried me
since having my own child

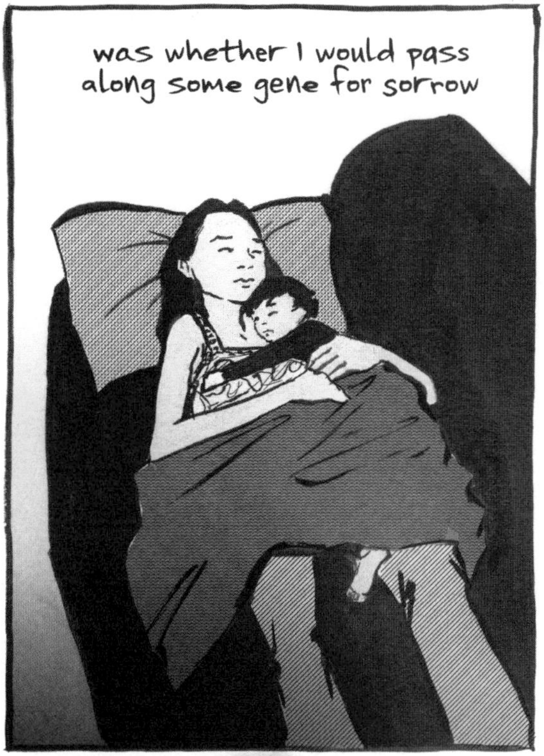
was whether I would pass
along some gene for sorrow

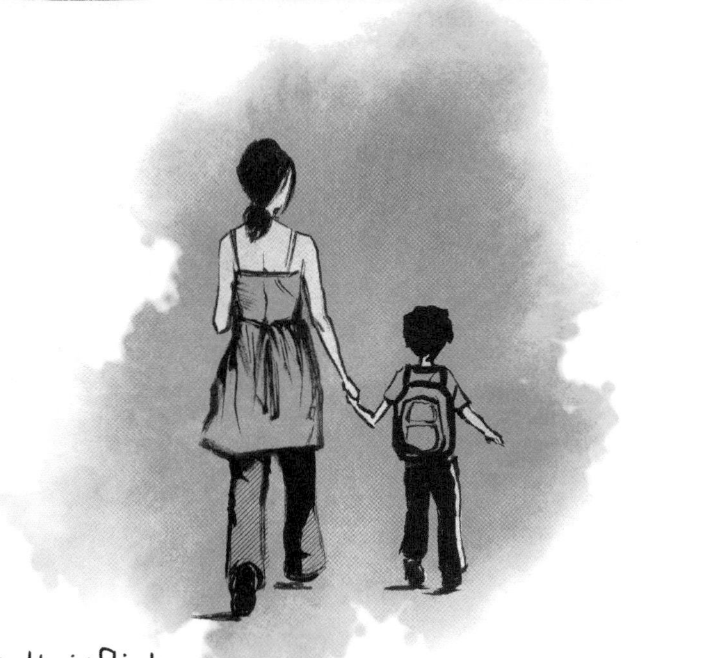

or unintentionally inflict
damage I could never undo.

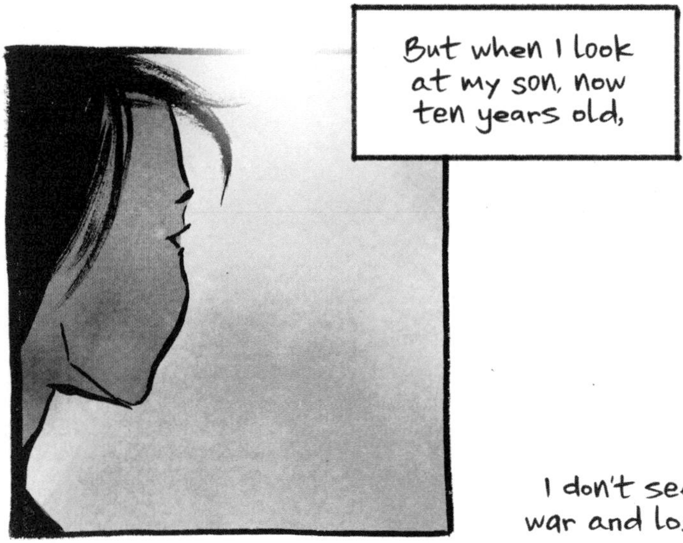
But when I look at my son, now ten years old,

I don't see war and loss

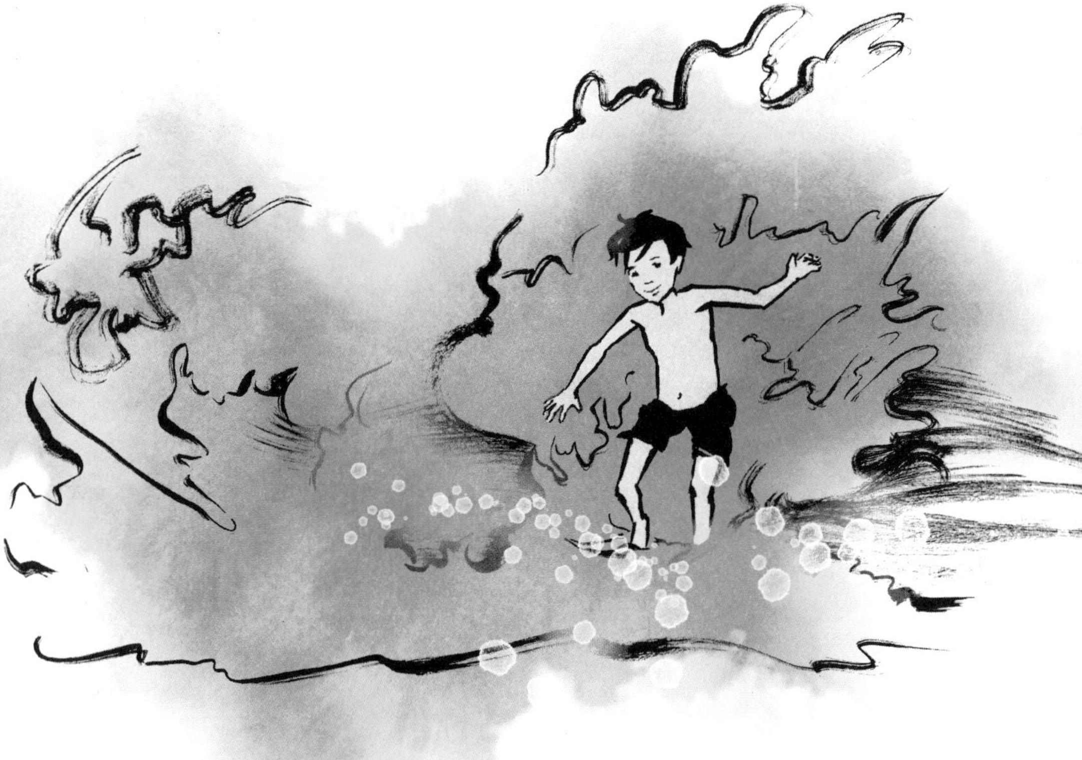

or even Travis and me.

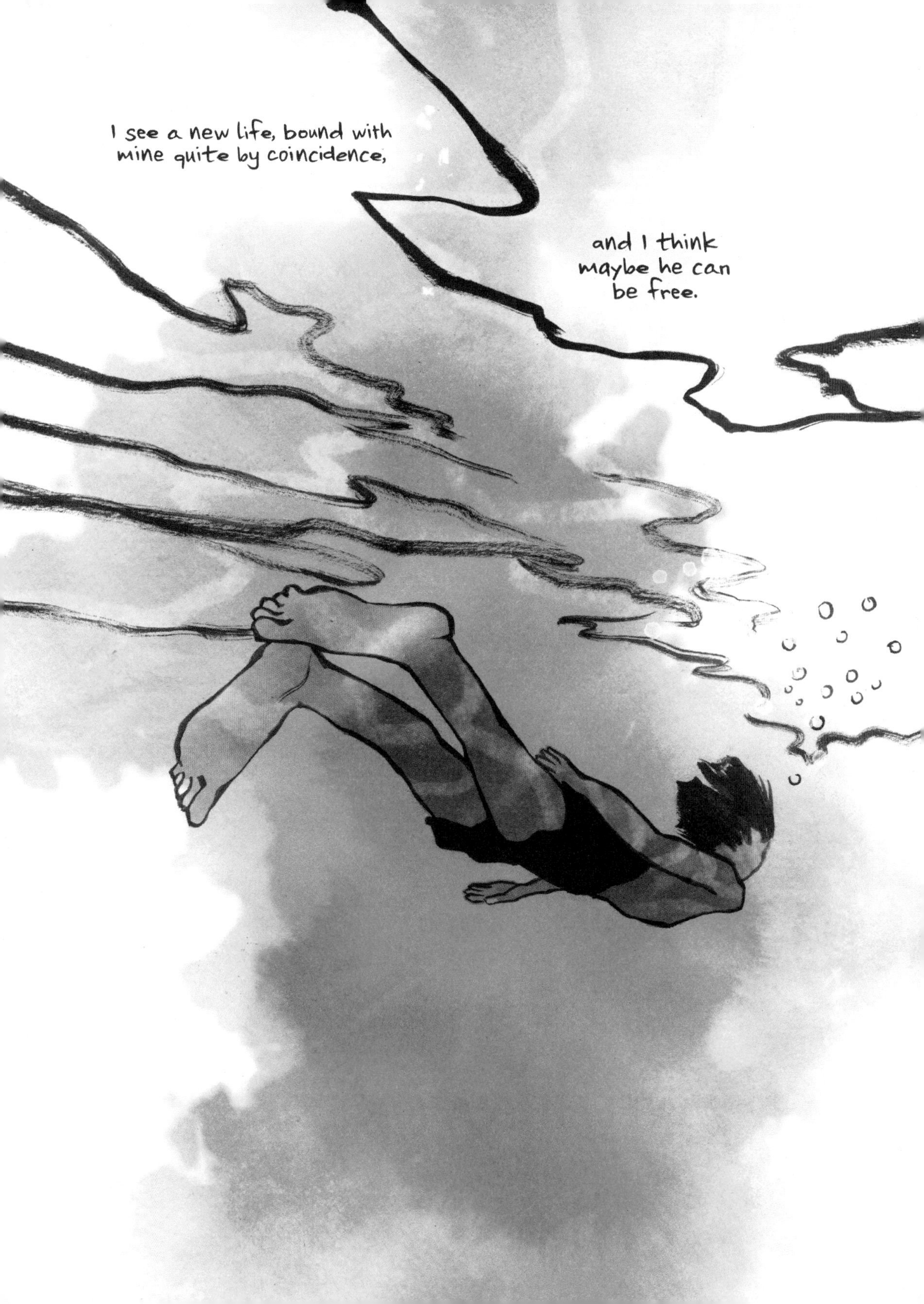
I see a new life, bound with mine quite by coincidence,
and I think maybe he can be free.

THANK YOU

Clarissa & Charlie & Pam & Jody & Nicole & Michael
Craig & Jake & my ACA family
Pat & everyone on the island
Fae & Dipti & Jane
My brother & sisters
Bố and Má
H & T